Risk Aspects of Investment-Based Social Security Reform

**A National Bureau
of Economic Research
Conference Report**

Risk Aspects of Investment-Based Social Security Reform

Edited by **John Y. Campbell and Martin Feldstein**

The University of Chicago Press

Chicago and London

JOHN Y. CAMPBELL is the Otto Eckstein Professor of Applied
Economics at Harvard University and a research associate of the
National Bureau of Economic Research. MARTIN FELDSTEIN is the
George F. Baker Professor of Economics at Harvard University and
president of the National Bureau of Economic Research.

The University of Chicago Press, Chicago 60637
The University of Chicago Press, Ltd., London
© 2001 by the National Bureau of Economic Research
All rights reserved. Published 2001
Printed in the United States of America
10 09 08 07 06 05 04 03 02 01   1 2 3 4 5
ISBN: 0-226-09255-0 (cloth)

Library of Congress Cataloging-in-Publication Data

Risk aspects of investment-based social security reform / edited by
John Y. Campbell and Martin Feldstein.
        p.   cm.—(National Bureau of Economic Research conference
report)
    Papers presented at an NBER conference held in Islamorada,
Florida, January 1999.
Includes bibliographical references and index.
    ISBN 0-226-09255-0 (cloth : alk. paper)
    1. Social security—United States—Finance—Congresses.
2. Social security—United States—Congresses.
3. Privatization—United States—Congresses. I. Campbell,
John Y. II. Feldstein, Martin S. III. Conference Report
(National Bureau of Economic Research)

HD7125 .R57 2001
368.4'3'00973—dc21

                                                      00-041798

Contents

Preface

The design of social insurance programs involves a balancing of protection and distortion. Social security pension programs protect individuals against inadequate income during retirement but also distort national saving and labor markets. Saving is distorted because traditional pay-as-you-go social security programs substitute for personal saving without a corresponding increase in public saving. Labor market behavior is distorted because the low implicit rate of return that individuals receive on their "contributions" implies that those contributions are a tax that significantly reduces compensation. Pension rules often induce early retirement because the reward for continued work is very low.

Although these issues have concerned economists for many years, it is the financing problems caused by the aging of the population that has put social security reform on the political agenda in the United States and other major industrial countries. A key idea in many of the reform proposals is to use a system of investment-based personal retirement accounts to supplement the benefits that can be financed with the existing pay-as-you-go tax rate.

The National Bureau of Economic Research has been engaged for several years in a basic study of the feasibility and potential consequences of such a reform. The first project in this study was an examination of the issues that arise in the transition from a pure pay-as-you-go system to one that involves investment-based accounts: that was Martin Feldstein's *Privatizing Social Security,* published by the University of Chicago Press in 1998. The research in that project examined the experiences of several countries that have introduced investment-based systems and studied some of the likely costs and benefits of such a transition in the United States. Although the countries that have adopted investment-based systems differed substantially in their approaches to the transition, it is clear from their experiences that investment-based systems are viable in countries with far less developed capital markets than that of the United States and with populations that are much less familiar with investing than the American public.

The social security actuaries calculate that future demographic and economic trends imply that financing the benefits projected under current law, that is, a continuation of the existing replacement rates at each point in the earnings distribution, would require raising the existing 12.4 percent tax rate (for the benefits paid to retirees, their dependents, and their surviving spouses, as well as the disabled) to more than 19 percent. NBER simulations based on the same demographic and economic projections show that combining the existing 12.4 percent pay-as-you-go payroll tax with personal retirement account deposits of no more than 2.5 percent of payroll would avoid the 19 percent payroll tax and maintain the benefits projected in current law if the accounts earn a 5.5 percent real rate of return, a figure significantly less than the actual return on a portfolio of stocks and bonds over the past fifty years.

The projections presented in the first study of this project all assumed that the rate of return is known with certainty. In contrast, the papers in this volume recognize that the future rate of return is uncertain and focus on the question: How much risk is imposed on future retirees by shifting from a pure pay-as-you-go system to a system in which a portion of benefits is investment based with funds accumulated in individual accounts that are invested in a mix of stock and bond mutual funds? As a background to this question, the volume also looks at the risk in a pay-as-you-go system caused by the uncertain future political support for benefits as the implicit rate of return declines. The introductory chapter provides a general discussion of the risk aspects of investment-based reform and summarizes the individual studies in the volume.

Three more volumes of studies will be part of this NBER project: *Administrative Aspects of Investment-Based Social Security Reform* (edited by John B. Shoven), *Distributional Aspects of Investment-Based Social Security Reform* (edited by Martin Feldstein and Jeffrey Liebman), and *Social Security Pension Reform in Europe* (edited by Martin Feldstein and Horst Siebert).

The project has benefited from the interaction of a large number of NBER and other researchers who have prepared the individual studies and participated in the five conferences at which this work was presented. The research was also helped by the extensive discussions at the NBER Summer Institute and at the meetings of the NBER Public Economics Program and the NBER Program on Aging.

The papers in this volume were presented at a conference in January

1999. Dr. Pascal Maenhout prepared the summary of the conference discussion that is included in this volume.

We are grateful to the Ford Foundation and the Starr Foundation for the financial support that has made this project possible. We also thank the individual members of the NBER staff for their help with the many aspects of the planning and execution of the research, the conference, and the volume. In addition to the researchers and research assistants who are named in the individual papers, we thank Kirsten Foss Davis, Helena Fitz-Patrick, Norma MacKenzie, and Brett Maranjian for logistic support of the meetings and assistance in the preparation of this volume.

Introduction

John Y. Campbell and Martin Feldstein

The increasing life expectancy in the United States and in other industrial countries is creating a major problem for traditional unfunded social security pension programs. In such pay-as-you-go programs, the cost of providing any level of benefits varies directly with the ratio of retirees to employees. While the tendency toward earlier and earlier retirement that is encouraged by the social security rules in many countries is exacerbating this problem (Gruber and Wise 1998), the sharp increase in the ratio of the aged to those of working age will increase the cost of pay-as-you-go programs very substantially even if age-specific retirement rates stabilize. The U.S. social security actuaries now project that the cost of providing the benefits implied by the current social security formula will rise from about 12 percent of covered payroll earnings now to more than 17 percent by 2030 and to nearly 20 percent by 2070.

The high cost to taxpayers of obtaining benefits in a pay-as-you-go system reflects the relatively low implicit rate of return that participants earn on the taxes paid in any unfunded system. As Paul Samuelson showed in his famous 1958 paper, the implicit rate of return on the tax "contributions" in an unfunded pay-as-you-go system is equal to the rate of growth of the tax base. Since the U.S. system is financed by a tax on cash wages, it is the future growth of aggregate cash wages that determines the rate of return. The social security actuaries base their calculations of the required future rise in tax rates on the assumption that future reductions in the

John Y. Campbell is the Otto Eckstein Professor of Applied Economics at Harvard University and a research associate of the National Bureau of Economic Research. Martin Feldstein is the George F. Baker Professor of Economics at Harvard University and president of the National Bureau of Economic Research.

growth rate of the population will limit this implicit real rate of return to less than 2 percent a year.

Although the U.S. social security system is essentially a pay-as-you-go program in which each year's tax receipts are used to pay the benefits of concurrent retirees, there is also a trust fund that is invested in government bonds. The rate of return on these bonds affects the amount that is available to pay annual benefits and therefore affects the overall rate of return that participants receive on the taxes that they pay. However, these interest payments are simply a transfer between government accounts. They are therefore of no aggregate economic significance, although they are capable of raising the return on payroll-tax payments at the expense of income-tax payments. But, since the trust fund is relatively small (only about two years' worth of benefits and less than 10 percent of the present value of the obligations of the social security program), the rate of return on the trust fund has very little effect on the overall implicit rate of return that participants receive on their social security taxes. As a practical matter, the implicit rate of return is determined by the rate of growth of the social security tax base, and the system effectively operates on a pay-as-you-go basis.

There are in principle three basic ways that can be used to deal with the problem of the increasing cost of a pay-as-you-go system: benefit cuts, tax increases, and prefunding. These approaches could be used either alone or in combination with each other. Some experts propose cutting future benefits so that future tax rates do not have to rise. These benefit cuts might take the form of changes within the existing structure of social security benefits (increasing the age of retirement, modifying the current post-retirement inflation adjustment, or other, more obscure alterations in rules) or of more fundamental shifts from the existing benefit structure to a uniform benefit system. A second group of proposals would maintain benefits, requiring taxes to rise substantially in the future. Finally, since neither large benefit cuts nor large tax increases are politically appealing, the forthcoming demographic shift has generated substantial interest in the idea of prefunding future benefits by setting aside resources now (through reduced benefits, increased revenue, or transfers from existing funds that would otherwise be used to finance either additional government spending or tax reductions) and investing those funds either collectively or through individual accounts. Although there are many variations of the prefunding proposal, their common feature is increasing national saving and, therefore, the nation's capital stock. The additional national income that would result from the increased capital would be earmarked to finance future retirement consumption, making it possible to maintain benefits without raising taxes.

The idea of prefunding social security benefits was rejected for a long time on the grounds that the transition generation would have to "pay twice," that is, would have to pay the pay-as-you-go taxes to finance the benefits of those who are already retired while also saving for their own retirement. With the pay-as-you-go tax now at more than 12 percent of wage income, this "double burden" suggested to some critics that employees in the transition generation might be called on to pay as much as 24 percent of their wages. Not surprisingly, such a plan was rejected as basically unfair, politically impossible, or both.

Fortunately, the extra cost to the transition generation is much smaller than the critics feared. Because the rate of return on real saving is much higher than the implicit rate of return in the pay-as-you-go system, the amount of saving required to fund any given amount of future benefits is much less than the corresponding pay-as-you-go tax rate. Moreover, since during the transition phase retirees would receive some benefits from the funded part of the system, the level of the pay-as-you-go benefits (and therefore of the pay-as-you-go tax) could be gradually reduced during the transition. Feldstein and Samwick (1997, 1998b) showed that a transition from the existing pay-as-you-go system to a pure funded defined-contribution system could be achieved without any reduction in current or future benefits and without increasing the combined amounts of the pay-as-you-go tax and the mandatory saving by more than 2 percent of wage income, that is, from the current 12.4 percent payroll tax to a maximum of 14.4 percent despite the increasing aging of the population. Moreover, after a relatively few years, the declining cost of the pay-as-you-go system that results as funded benefits begin to replace the pay-as-you-go benefits means that the combined amount that individuals would be required to pay (as payroll taxes plus retirement-account saving) would actually be less than the initial 12.4 percent payroll tax in spite of the increase in aggregate benefits as the population ages.

An alternative transition to a mixed system in which investment-based benefits substitute for the increase in the pay-as-you-go tax, that is, in which the current benefit rules are maintained permanently while the payroll tax remains unchanged at 12.4 percent of payroll as the population ages, could also be achieved with no more than an additional 2 percent of payroll (see Feldstein and Samwick 1998a; 1999). The economic studies presented at a 1996 NBER conference (Feldstein 1998) explore other aspects of the transition to a prefunded social security system and discuss how the shift to such an investment-based system was achieved in a variety of different economies around the world.

The fact that a transition to a retirement system that is wholly or partly investment based is feasible does not imply the desirability of such a policy. At a minimum, that depends on the rate of return that is earned on the investments and the effect of the shift to an investment-based system on the excess burdens of the tax system that is used to finance retirement benefits (for a discussion of these issues, see Feldstein and Samwick

[1998b, 1999]). More generally, the appropriateness of such a change depends on three key economic issues as well as on the broader questions about social norms and about the appropriate role of the state. The three issues that must be addressed are the administrative costs of a funded system, the distributional effects of shifting from a pay-as-you-go system to an investment-based system, and the market risks associated with any investment-based system.

Each of these issues is the subject of a separate part of the overall current NBER project on social security reform. John Shoven has organized a study of the administrative costs and brought together a group of experts with practical experience to discuss the issue; their analysis is presented in Shoven (2000). Feldstein and Liebman (forthcoming) have organized a project that compares the distributional effects of the current social security pension system with the distributional effects of alternative investment-based systems. The current volume presents papers dealing with the risk aspects of social security reform.

Each of the three approaches to the cost problem posed by the projected demographic change—reducing benefits, raising taxes, and shifting to some form of investment-based system—involves risks for either future taxpayers or future beneficiaries, or both. Although investment-based plans introduce a new form of risk—the risk of volatility in the market prices of investment assets—that is not present in pay-as-you-go systems, even those plans that would continue to rely exclusively on the traditional pay-as-you-go system imply important risks to future beneficiaries or retirees.

Cutting future benefits as the population ages in a way that keeps the tax rate unchanged inevitably means not only that future benefits would be lower than they would be under current rules but also that those benefits would be much more uncertain, depending on such things as the longevity of the future retirees and the level of future wages. Maintaining benefits at the same future levels as they would be under current law not only raises the expected level of future tax rates but also imposes additional risks on future taxpayers. Future tax rates must rise by more than the expected amount if retirees generally live longer or if the rate of growth of wage rates is lower than currently projected. Retirees and taxpayers are also subject to the political risk that future administrations might change the rules, either reducing benefits or increasing taxes.

Critics of investment-based plans have nevertheless emphasized that, because they involve investing in private stocks and bonds, such plans are risky, especially if individuals own the financial assets instead of investing them in a common government fund that is used to finance defined benefits. If part or all of future social security benefits are converted from an explicit defined-benefit plan provided by the government to some form of defined-contribution system based on individual investment accounts, future retirees will experience the risk of fluctuations in the market values of stocks and bonds. The extent of this risk can be reduced by using a mixture of defined-benefit and defined-contribution plans, instead of just a pure investment-based defined-contribution plan, or by providing some kind of conditional pay-as-you-go benefit that varies inversely with the performance of the market. In the limit, the government can do the investing in a government fund and provide a defined benefit, thus placing all the market risk on future taxpayers.

A primary purpose of this volume is to assess the magnitude of the risks born by retirees and taxpayers in alternative investment-based systems. The papers discuss issues of the measurement of risk and of how to model the risk that would be borne in different systems.

In thinking about the individual papers, it is important to bear in mind that the basic rationale for an investment-based system is *not* the increase in *financial* return that would be achieved by *shifting* the existing social security trust fund to a mixture of private stocks and bonds. The benefit of an investment-based system is that it involves an increase in national saving and therefore in the national capital stock. The explicit return on that increased capital stock is the source of payments for some or all of future social security benefits. The return on that increased capital is substantially higher than the implicit rate of return in the pay-as-you-go system. Although general equilibrium considerations imply that the rise in the capital stock would eventually reduce the real return to capital, calculations indicate that the decline in the return is small relative to the difference between the return on capital and the implicit return in the pay-as-you-go system. The issue, moreover, is not the uncertainty of the rate of return to the nation as a whole—that is, the uncertain pretax real marginal product of capital—but the riskiness of the return that must be borne by future retirees and taxpayers because the increased national investment is financed through private securities that are subject to substantial price fluctuations.

Each reader must judge the evidence of this trade-off for himself or herself. Our judgment is that the risks are moderate relative to the improved return and to the ability of an investment-based system to adapt to differences in individual preferences and conditions. It is possible, moreover, to modify the basic investment-based plans in ways (explored in some of the papers in this volume) that permit reducing the risk that must be borne by retirees while keeping the risk to taxpayers quite moderate.

Before turning to the individual papers, we now provide a very brief summary of their findings and how they relate to each other.

The strong recent performance of the U.S. equity market has increased interest in proposals to shift some of the social security trust funds from long-term government bonds to stocks. In chapter 1, Thomas E. MaCurdy and John B. Shoven consider two proposals that maintain a centralized social security system but reallocate its investments in this way. The two proposals, the "maintain-benefits" option of the 1994–96 Advisory Council on Social Security and the plan recently put forward by Henry Aaron and Robert Reischauer, differ in details, but both rely heavily on the equity premium—the average excess return on stocks over bonds—to reduce the seventy-five-year actuarial deficit of the social security system. MaCurdy and Shoven argue that these proposals are fatally flawed because they seek to exploit the equity premium without properly considering the investment risk associated with it. Even if social security equity investments outperform bond investments on average, there is a substantial risk that they will fail to do so over a ten- or twenty-year horizon. For example, a bootstrap analysis—drawing real stock returns randomly from realizations that actually occurred during the period 1927–97—shows that, about 25 percent of the time, equity investments underperform twenty-year inflation-indexed bonds yielding 3.5 percent.

Martin Feldstein, Elena Ranguelova, and Andrew Samwick (chap. 2) explore the effects of investment risk on a proposal for prefunding social security put forward in earlier work by Feldstein and Samwick. Feldstein and Samwick examine the effect of adding modest contributions to personal retirement accounts (PRAs)—initially set at 3 percent of earnings. Over a seventy-five-year transition period, as PRA savings accumulate, payroll taxes could decline to zero, and the PRA contribution rate could rise slightly to a steady-state 4.25 percent level. Feldstein, Ranguelova, and Samwick also consider a partial transition in which the payroll tax remains at its current level in the steady state. They assume that the PRA portfolio is invested 60 percent in equities and 40 percent in corporate bonds. They suggest that investment risk in this portfolio can be handled by a combination of a higher PRA contribution rate, to shift the distribution of retirement benefits upward, and a government guarantee that total benefits under the new system will be at least as large as those under the current system. In such a system, the probability that the government will have to make good on its guarantee is relatively small, and the expected size of the government guarantee payment, if one must be made, is also small.

Kent Smetters (chap. 3) adopts a different perspective on government minimum-benefit guarantees in investment-based social security systems. He argues that market prices should be used to evaluate the costs of such guarantees. The guarantees are equivalent to put options—social security participants are effectively granted options to put, or sell, their investments to the government at minimum prices—and option pricing theory can therefore be used to value them. Using this approach, Smetters finds significant costs even for guarantees that are extremely unlikely to be activated. The reason is that the guarantees pay off in bad states of the world with low stock prices, and the large equity premium implies that dollars payable in such states have a high market value today. Smetters also argues that increasing the PRA contribution rate is an inefficient way to address the problem because it increases benefits in good states of the world as well as in bad states. He proposes instead that higher PRA contributions should be used in effect to buy put options on behalf of social security participants. Such a policy differs from an increased PRA contribution rate in that it increases payments to participants only if stock returns turn out to be low, and it differs from a pure guarantee in that participants are asked to buy their put options rather than receiving them as a transfer from the government.

An important question is whether one can use existing market prices to value changes in the social security system. If markets are incomplete, this may not be appropriate because a nonmarginal change in the system can alter market prices. Several other papers in this volume systematically explore the effects of market incompleteness, using the overlapping-generations model as a common framework.

Antonio Rangel and Richard Zeckhauser (chap. 4) consider an overlapping-generations model with randomness in both total endowments and the distribution of endowments between generations. Their model makes the standard simplifying assumption that each generation lives only two periods and that only two generations are therefore alive at any one time. In this setting, a long-lived asset can facilitate intergenerational risk sharing by inducing young generations to pay old generations for their claims to the asset. Unfortunately, this market mechanism breaks down when efficient risk sharing requires the old to make payments to the young. In principle, this problem can be avoided by voluntary-contribution schemes sustained by self-fulfilling expectations or by government intergenerational transfers. Rangel and Zeckhauser argue, however, that voluntary-contribution schemes are unlikely to work in practice and that efficient government intergenerational transfers may be incompatible with a democratic political system since future generations cannot vote to express their interests. Thus, the authors are skeptical about the possibility of sharing risks efficiently among generations. A qualification, however, is that both market and political risk-sharing schemes are likely to work better when generations live more than two periods so that each generation overlaps and can share risks with several others.

Andrew Abel (chap. 5) takes as given the existence of a defined-benefit pension system in which a social security trust fund is accumulated as a buffer between payroll-tax receipts and pension expenses of the system. He uses the overlapping-generations framework to explore the effects of shifting the trust fund from riskless bonds to risky equities. In equilibrium, the trust fund can buy equities only if private investors are willing to sell them. Since today's private investors do not themselves bear the risks of the trust fund portfolio (their pension benefits are fixed, so the trust fund risks are borne by future generations of taxpayers), they are willing to sell only if the equity premium declines. Abel assumes that the absolute return on equities is fixed by the marginal productivity of capital, so the decline in the equity premium is accomplished by a rise in the riskless interest rate. This, in turn, induces private investors to accumulate capital more rapidly in the short run and, for plausible parameter values, in the long run as well. Abel thus builds a case that investment of the social security trust fund in equities would be good for capital accumulation and economic growth. The effect is quite small in an almost pure pay-as-you-go system of the sort the United States has today but would be larger in a prefunded system with a more substantial trust fund.

Henning Bohn (chap. 6) uses the overlapping-generations framework to consider a different type of risk, the demographic risk that a generation will be unexpectedly large or small. It is often argued that defined-benefit pay-as-you-go retirement systems handle such risks poorly because a small generation that follows a large generation (like the "baby-bust" generation following the "baby-boom" generation) faces high payroll taxes to pay for the fixed benefits of relatively numerous retirees. Bohn points out that this argument ignores a countervailing effect. In a closed economy, a large generation tends to drive down the marginal product of labor and therefore receives relatively low wages; conversely, a small generation tends to receive high wages. Bohn argues that a defined-benefit pay-as-you-go pension system helps generations share this risk more efficiently than defined-contribution or privatized systems. He also considers other types of demographic shocks, including anticipated future demographic changes and shocks to the life span of an existing generation. Results here depend more sensitively on particular assumptions, but Bohn argues that efficient risk sharing often requires the adjustment of current social security benefits in response to news about future demographic trends.

Existing retirement systems around the world are often described as defined-benefit systems since retirement benefits are defined by law. However, this ignores the fact that the systems are frequently reformed, with large effects on benefits. John McHale (chap. 7) undertakes a systematic empirical study of benefit reforms in the G7 countries during the last fifteen years. He finds that projections of rising costs under current law frequently provoke reforms that substantially reduce the benefits promised to middle-aged and younger workers. However, the benefits of citizens who are already retired or are near retirement are typically protected. This contrasts with Bohn's finding that efficient risk sharing requires adjustments of current benefits in response to demographic information. McHale conjectures that there is a large political cost to changing retirement benefits that had already been promised and are currently payable.

The remaining papers in the volume take a microeconomic perspective. They use expected-utility theory, in the context of financial investment over the life cycle, to compare alternative portfolio strategies during working life and in retirement.

Zvi Bodie (chap. 8) argues that there is considerable appeal to a system in which investors share the upside potential of risky financial assets, such as equities, but also have a guaranteed minimum level of retirement benefit. Such a system might be justified by investors' own demands for a minimum acceptable level of retirement consumption or by public policy concerns that some people are unable to save adequately or invest competently on their own behalf. Bodie points out that this pattern of benefits need not be financed through pay-as-you-go payroll taxation or through a privatized system with a government minimum-benefit guarantee. Instead, it can be provided privately through pension plans that hold a mix of inflation-indexed bonds and call options on equities or that trade dynamically in the equity market to achieve the same pattern of payoffs.

One of the important functions of a retirement system is the provision of annuities to insure retirees against the risk of unusual longevity. A natural benchmark, comparable to the current social security system, is a real annuity that provides a fixed real stream of income during an investor's lifetime. Jeffrey R. Brown, Olivia S. Mitchell, and James M. Poterba (chap. 9) ask whether real annuities can be provided within a privatized system. They argue that, despite extremely limited current availability in the United States (almost all private fixed annuities make fixed nominal payments, not fixed real payments), experience in the United Kingdom suggests that private markets can provide real annuities at reasonable cost. Brown, Mitchell, and Poterba also argue that only extremely risk-averse investors should hold pure real annuities; most investors should be willing to take on some degree of equity risk in exchange for the higher returns that have historically been available in the equity market.

Marianne Baxter and Robert G. King (chap. 10) broaden the menu of risky assets to include international equities as well as domestic equities. They show that international equities provide significant diversification benefits and should be very attractive to retired investors who are currently holding either the real annuity provided by social security or a risky portfolio of domestic assets. Baxter and King also consider the demand for international assets by younger investors who are currently working. They argue that these investors have a nontraded asset—human capital—that is more highly correlated with domestic financial assets than with international financial assets. Thus, younger investors gain even more than older investors do from the ability to invest internationally.

John Y. Campbell, João F. Cocco, Francisco J. Gomes, and Pascal J. Maenhout (chap. 11) undertake a more detailed study of the demand for financial assets by working investors. They calibrate a model of optimal portfolio choice over the life cycle, using realistic estimates of the age profile of income, its overall risk, and its correlation with financial asset returns for different demographic groups. Households are assumed to be constrained by restrictions on borrowing and short-selling risky assets. The constraints bind on young households, who would like to consume more and take on greater equity exposure. This means that changes in the retirement system that reduce the tax burden on young households and increase their equity exposure can have large welfare benefits. Heterogeneity across demographic groups appears to have important effects on optimal portfolios, suggesting the inadequacy of a "one-size-fits-all" social security system.

References

Feldstein, Martin, ed. 1998. *Privatizing social security.* Chicago: Chicago University Press.

Feldstein, Martin, and J. Liebman. Forthcoming. The distributional aspects of an investment-based social security system. In *Distributional aspects of investment-based social security reform,* ed. M. Feldstein and J. Liebman. Chicago: University of Chicago Press.

Feldstein, Martin, and A. Samwick. 1997. The economics of prefunding social security and medicare benefits. In *NBER macroeconomics annual, 1997,* ed. Ben S. Bernanke and Julio Rotemberg, 115–48. Cambridge, Mass.: MIT Press.

———. 1998a. Potential effects of two percent personal retirement accounts. *Tax Notes* 79, no. 5 (4 May): 615–20.

———. 1998b. The transition path in privatizing social security. In *Privatizing social security,* ed. Martin Feldstein. Chicago: University of Chicago Press.

———. 1999. Maintaining social security benefits and tax rates through personal retirement accounts: An update based on the 1998 Social Security Trustees report. Working Paper no. 6540. Cambridge, Mass.: National Bureau of Economic Research, March.

Gruber, Jonathan, and D. Wise, eds. 1998. *Social security and retirement around the world: Introduction and summary.* Chicago: University of Chicago Press.

Samuelson, Paul. 1958. An exact consumption-loan model of interest with or without the social contrivance of money. *Journal of Political Economy* 66:467–82.

Shoven, John, ed. 2000. *Administrative aspects of investment-based social security reform.* Chicago: University of Chicago Press.

1

Asset Allocation and Risk Allocation

Can Social Security Improve Its Future Solvency Problem by Investing in Private Securities?

Thomas E. MaCurdy and John B. Shoven

Policy makers widely accept that social security faces a long-run solvency problem. The social security trustees publish a seventy-five-year forecast of the OASDI system's finances every year. Since the 1983 amendments, the forecast has gotten consistently more ominous. Figure 1.1 shows the intermediate-assumptions forecast for the trust fund balances in 1983, 1985, and 1998.

The trustees' 1998 report has the OASDI trust fund completely depleted in 2032 (when the youngest baby boomer, born in 1964, will be sixty-eight) rather than 2063 (when the same individual will be ninety-nine years old), the forecast that immediately followed the 1983 social security amendments. The report has as the intermediate or "best-guess" forecast that the system's income (not counting net interest income on the special issue bonds held in the trust fund) will fall short of its costs beginning in 2013. In 1999, the surplus was projected to be 1.52 percent of covered payroll, but this turns negative in 2013, and, by the end of the trustees' forecasting period (2075), the annual shortfall under the intermediate set of assumptions is forecast to be 6.43 percent of covered payroll. That means that, if we operated the system strictly on a pay-as-you-go basis, the payroll tax rate would have to be increased by 6.43 percentage points to achieve balance in 2075. The 2075 OASDI deficit (with the intermediate-assumptions

Thomas E. MaCurdy is professor of economics at Stanford University, senior fellow of the Hoover Institution, and a research associate of the National Bureau of Economic Research. John B. Shoven is the Charles R. Schwab Professor of Economics at Stanford University and a research associate of the National Bureau of Economic Research.

The authors have benefited from the comments and help of John Campbell, Victor Fuchs, Jim Poterba, Sylvester Schieber, and Steve Zeldes. The authors acknowledge the fine research assistance of Stanford Ph.D. students Davide Lombardo and Clemens Sialm.

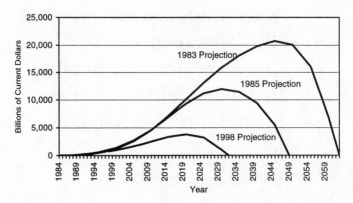

Fig. 1.1   Three forecasts of the OASDI trust fund balances

forecast) amounts to 4.26 percent of GDP. One way to look at the financial solvency problem of social security is that the intermediate forecast is for fourteen years of modest and declining surpluses, followed by ever-growing deficits as far as the eye can see. Against that we have a relatively small trust fund (currently $760 billion) that generates roughly $40 billion of interest income but that is now forecast to be completely depleted by 2032, as shown in figure 1.1. Naturally, the financial situation for OASDI is much worse under the trustees' high-cost set of assumptions. With them, the date of OASDI trust fund exhaustion is 2022. The date when payroll-tax receipts first fall short of benefit payments is 2006, and the eventual shortfall of income to costs in 2075 is 16.04 percent of taxable payroll.

The social security trustees summarize the seventy-five year outlook for OASDI by computing the long-run actuarial balance. In 1998, the seventy-five year actuarial balance was in deficit by 2.19 percent of covered payroll with the trustees' intermediate assumptions. What that means is that, had the payroll tax been immediately increased in 1998 by 2.19 percentage points and the increase maintained for the next seventy-five years, the life of the trust fund would have been extended to the seventy-five-year horizon under the intermediate set of economic and demographic assumptions. Even under this hypothetical scenario, the payroll-tax proceeds would be less than benefit payments under the currently legislated benefit structure beginning in roughly 2020. Further, the seventy-five-year actuarial balance would last for exactly one year; with every passing year, one fewer surplus year would be in the seventy-five-year window, and one more deficit year would be included. The immediate payroll-tax increase needed to fix the solvency problem of the current OASDI system permanently would be significantly greater than 2.19 percent. Steven Goss (1999), of the Office of the Actuary of the Social Security Administration, has estimated that the permanent or open-ended actuarial deficit is 4.7 percent of covered payroll under the intermediate set of assumptions.

All this illustrates the dimensions of the problem of returning the existing OASDI system to long-run solvency. Operating within the existing structure of social security, there are only two obvious paths: raise taxes or cut benefits, or both. If we take Goss's 4.7 percent of covered payroll figure for the perpetual actuarial deficit, permanently fixing the finances of the system (under the intermediate set of economic and demographic assumptions) will require immediate tax increases or benefit cuts totaling 38 percent. If the implementation of these steps is delayed, as it almost certainly will be, then the benefit cuts and tax increases will need to be larger. Neither tax increases nor benefit cuts of this magnitude are economically or politically attractive. Naturally, people are looking for a more palatable way out of the social security solvency problem.

One natural place to look is the investment returns earned on the trust fund. Currently, the trust fund is exclusively invested in special nonmarketable U.S. government bonds. When these bonds are issued, their interest rate is set at the average interest rate of marketable Treasury bonds with a maturity of four years or more. The bonds have one special feature, which offsets their nonmarketability: they are redeemable at par at any time. This feature is not generally available on publicly held bonds and notes, with the exception of U.S. government savings bonds. The special issue bonds are certainly safe, with no price risk and with the principal and interest fully backed by the U.S. government, but Treasury interest rates are somewhat less than what is offered on AAA corporate bonds and trail the average total return earned on common stocks by a wide margin.

The question that we address in this paper is whether a significant fraction of the whole solvency problem could reliably be solved by having the Social Security Administration invest the OASDI trust fund in higher-yielding private securities. The analysis in MaCurdy and Shoven (1992) suggests that such a strategy might yield an improvement in social security's finances.[1] Of course, there is a more fundamental question regarding whether society as a whole would benefit from this new asset allocation. Another question that we address is how risky such a change in the trust fund asset allocation would be and who would bear that risk. Related to this question, we discuss the feasibility of social security delivering a true defined-benefit pension program to its participants.

---

1. Our paper investigated the effects of defined-contribution accumulators consistently acquiring stocks or bonds for careers between 1926 and 1989. We showed that stock accumulators consistently ended up with more money than bond accumulators for all careers longer than twenty years in the period 1926–89. The result is weakened by the fact that we used only the actual historical pattern of financial returns and that there are only three completely independent twenty-year runs of data in the period 1926–89. We extended the data to 1876–1990 in an unpublished manuscript. There we found that the career length had to be forty years before stock accumulators always ended up ahead of bond accumulators. Once again, the data limitations do not allow one to predict with confidence the likelihood of stocks outperforming bonds for long careers. In the present paper, we try to get around the data limitations by using the bootstrap statistical procedures.

1.1 The Proposals

We focus on two of the reform proposals that rely on investing the central trust fund in higher-yielding private securities in order to maintain the general benefit structure of social security. However, our analysis is applicable to any plan that attempts to make progress on the solvency of the system by simply reallocating portfolios toward higher-yielding securities, including the plan outlined by President Clinton in his 1999 State of the Union Address. The two plans of this type that we describe in detail are the "maintain-benefits" (MB) proposal of the 1994–96 Advisory Council (often referred to as *the Bob Ball plan*) and the plan offered recently by Henry Aaron and Robert Reischauer (1998). Among the measures that both plans advocate, the asset reallocation is credited with the largest effect on reducing or eliminating the seventy-five-year actuarial deficit.

The details of the two plans are shown in table 1.1. There are many similarities between them. The numbers in the tables come directly from Aaron and Reischauer (1998, table 6-1) and from volume 1 of the *Report of the 1994–96 Advisory Council on Social Security* (SSA 1997, table 1, app. II). The figures are based on estimates of the Office of the Actuary of the Social Security Administration, assuming the intermediate alternative II economic and demographic conditions. The numbers for the same action may differ slightly for the two plans since the estimates for the Aaron-Reischauer plan were made roughly two years later than those for the MB plan. Further, the plans differ slightly in how they implement each measure. Even with that said, both proposals have the same goal—to deal with the seventy-five-year actuarial deficit within the context of the current structure of benefits. Both assume that the measurement of the CPI will be changed in ways that lower official inflation and cause the program's costs to grow more slowly.[2] Both advocate covering all newly hired state and local workers, increasing the number of years included in the AIME (average indexed monthly earnings) formula from thirty-five to thirty-eight, and taxing all social security benefits received over and above the employees' own actual contributions. Both proposals characterize their changes in the personal income taxation of social security benefits as putting them on the same basis as private pension income. However, their plans involve significantly higher taxes than the Schieber-Shoven PSA-2000 plan, which also claims to put social security and private pension benefits on the same tax footing (Schieber and Shoven 1999). The PSA-2000 plan taxes half of social security benefits on the argument that half of social security contributions were made with before-tax money (the

---

2. Many wage contracts are officially or unofficially tied to the CPI. It is not clear that the Office of the Actuary took the feedback of changing the official CPI on wages into account. If not, the gain from the restructuring of the CPI may be exaggerated.

Table 1.1   Contribution of Each Feature of the Aaron-Reischauer Plan and the
                   Maintain-Benefits Plan to the 75-Year OASDI Actuarial Deficit
                   (all numbers are % of covered payroll)

	Aaron-Reischauer Plan	Maintain-Benefits Plan
Projected long-term deficit	2.19	2.17
Effect of assumed changes by BLS in CPI measurement	−.45	−.31
Cover all newly hired state and local employees	−.21	−.22
Increase the number of years in the AIME formula from 35 to 38	−.25	−.28
Tax 85% of social security benefits	−.36	−.31
Increase the OASDI payroll tax in 2045 by a combined 1.6 percentage points	N.A.	−.22
Redirect revenue for taxation of benefits from hospital insurance to OASDI starting in 2010	N.A.	−.31
Raise the normal retirement age to 67 by 2011, and then index further increases to improvements in mortality	−.49	N.A.
Raise the age of early retirement eligibility to 64 by 2011, and then index further increases to improvements in mortality	−.23	N.A.
Gradually reduce spouse's benefit from 50 to 33.33%; raise benefits for surviving spouses to 75% of couple's combined benefit	+.15	N.A.
Gradually invest part of the trust fund assets in private stocks and bonds	−1.20	−.82
75-year deficit with plan	−.85	−.24

Note: N.A. = not applicable.

employer contribution) and half with after-tax dollars (the employee contribution). Essentially, Schieber and Shoven's plan would have half the contributions treated like a Roth IRA (after-tax contributions with tax-free withdrawals) and half like a regular IRA (before-tax contributions with taxable withdrawals). In contrast, the Aaron-Reischauer and Ball plans tax 85 percent or more of social security benefits.

The MB plan contains two features that Aaron and Reischauer did not choose to copy. One is a 1.6 percentage point payroll-tax increase in 2045, and the other is a redirection of money from Medicare to OASDI. The latter feature of the MB plan seems ill advised as the long-run finances of Medicare are in worse shape than are those of OASDI. Similarly, the Aaron-Reischauer plan contains several features not in the MB plan. These include accelerating and extending the increase in the age of normal retirement, advancing the age of early retirement, and readjusting the spousal and surviving spouse benefits. The Office of the Actuary of Social Security estimates that, both plans if enacted immediately and completely, would more than eliminate the seventy-five-year actuarial deficit of the system.

The common feature of the two plans shown in table 1.1 is that the biggest contributor to eliminating the long-run solvency problem is investing part of the OASDI trust fund in private securities. The two plans differ in the details of how they would do that. In fact, the MB plan in the 1994–96 Advisory Council report suggests that further study be given to the idea before implementation. Nonetheless, when the Advisory Council scored the plan to see whether it achieved the goal of eliminating the seventy-five-year actuarial deficit, it included the provision that the trust fund would begin investing in stocks in the year 2000 and that the proportion of trust fund assets in stocks would gradually rise until it reached 40 percent in 2015. The assumed real rate of return on the stock portion of the portfolio in the MB plan is 7.0 percent. The Aaron-Reischauer plan is to have the trust fund balances that exceed 150 percent of one year's benefits gradually invested in common stocks and corporate bonds. Since the OASDI trust fund balances currently exceed the 150 percent of annual payout criterion, the switch to private securities would begin immediately under the Aaron-Reischauer program. Remarkably, Aaron and Reischauer estimate that 55 percent of the whole actuarial deficit of 2.19 percent of payroll would be eliminated by this asset reallocation alone. They also estimate that the combination of the asset reallocation and the effect of the changes that the Bureau of Labor Statistics is making in the construction of the CPI eliminates over 75 percent of social security's projected long-term deficit. Any 75 percent cure that is this painless deserves careful scrutiny.

1.2   The Net Transaction

The net transaction involved in having the central OASDI trust fund invest a portion of its assets in common stocks is an asset swap. Social security or the federal government sells additional government bonds to the public and uses the proceeds to acquire common stock from the public. In the social security context, the system is selling one set of assets (U.S. government bonds) in order to acquire another set of assets (a diversified portfolio of common stocks) of equal value. Of course, this transaction can be examined without reference to social security's financial problems at all. The real issue is whether the government can improve the welfare of taxpayers (or social security participants) by issuing and selling bonds and using the proceeds to buy common stocks.

There are at least two reasons to be skeptical about the advantages of the net transaction being discussed. First, the total capital stock and wealth in the economy (at least to a first approximation) are unaffected by the asset swap. Therefore, the level of GDP and national income is unchanged. If social security or the government can systematically improve its financial position by making this exchange, the private sector, which presumably is on the other side of the transaction, is systematically losing. It is hard to imagine that the politicians and bureaucrats running social security are systematically getting the better of the pension fund managers and institutional investors who are buying the bonds from the government in exchange for common stocks. It is possible, of course, that the exchange could be played out on international capital markets so that Americans as a whole could conceivably end up as net winners (or losers) in the transaction. Second, there is the matter of risk. While stocks have a much higher expected return than government bonds, they also involve much higher risks (particularly given the fact that the current special issue bonds have the feature that they can be redeemed at par at any time). The two plans discussed above are very vague as to how much additional risk the system would be assuming and how that risk would be shared among taxpayers and social security participants. As we discuss in section 1.5 below, there is a real question about whether it is feasible to maintain a universal coverage defined-benefit pension plan funded with risky securities.

Having the government exchange bonds for stocks in the hope of relieving the solvency problems of social security is a form of financial engineering. The recent history of such schemes is not promising. Savings and loans sell short-term liabilities (certificates of deposit and demand deposits) and acquire higher-yielding long-term mortgages. The savings-and-loan crisis of the 1980s was brought about when short-term interest rates peaked in 1980 in the mid-teens when the savings-and-loan mortgage portfolio yielded 6–8 percentage points less. The usual yield relation did not hold, and the resulting bankruptcies and bailouts cost taxpayers massive sums of money. The Orange County debacle resulted from a similar failed attempt to exploit the shape of the yield curve. The recent massive losses of hedge funds resulted from asset swaps that failed to perform as expected. Before the U.S. government engages in exchanging bonds for stocks, careful analysis is clearly warranted.

1.3 Analyzing the Stocks-for-Bonds Swap

To gauge the riskiness of the net transaction of selling government bonds and buying corporate stocks, we use market returns from 1954 to 1997 and simulate what would have happened had the government completed the transaction. We separately look at what would have happened with the government selling ten-year and twenty-year bonds. We assume that market returns would have been unaffected by the government transaction. This almost certainly favors the exchange strategy that in reality might very well drive up interest rates and depress equity returns. The counterfactual simulations have the government selling bonds in the past, buying the S&P500 stock portfolio with the proceeds, and then paying all the bond payments (interest and principal) from the resulting stock portfolio. The strategy is deemed successful if all the payments on the bonds can be made with the stock funds with money left over. The strategy is deemed to have been a failure if the stock portfolio is unable to generate sufficient cash to make the required bond payments. In the discussion presented below, we initially explore how the strategy would have worked with the actual time series of returns generated by the stock market (and the actual historical interest rates on government bonds). The interest rates are those published in the *Economic Report of the President* (1998) and computed by the Board of Governors of the Federal Reserve System. The stock market returns are the "large company stocks" (i.e., S&P500) total return series in Ibbotson Associates (1998). The problem with this historical approach is that there are not many independent ten- or twenty-year periods in our data set (1954–97). In fact, there are only four completely independent ten-year runs of data and two of twenty years. We could add more data by examining pre-1954 information, and we do so in some of the analyses in this section. There is a serious question about whether adding data before 1954 helps or hurts when assessing the viability of a proposed strategy for the twenty-first century. The problem is that the additional data are likely to be drawn from a different regime and, therefore, may do more harm than good to the analysis. After examining the actual performance of the stock market in the period 1954–97, we report on extensive bootstrap simulations of what could have happened using the same annual return data, but now with the order of the returns randomly scrambled according to a bootstrap statistical approach.

First, we examine the case of the government borrowing money for ten years at the actual historical interest rates on U.S. government bonds and investing in the S&P500. Figure 1.2 shows the money left over at the maturity of the bonds (per dollar borrowed) after all bond payments had been made out of the stock account. The net cost of the original asset swap is zero, so any residual money is pure profit, and any residual shortfall is loss. Given our definition of success and failure, the asset-swap strategy would have failed seven times out of the thirty-four counterfactual experiments. The limitations of the actual historical record are very apparent in the results, however. Basically, the strategy of the government issuing ten-year bonds and buying the S&P500 would have worked from 1954 through 1964 and again from 1975 through 1987. However, it would have failed in seven of the ten years 1965–74. This reflects the limitations of observing only four completely independent ten-year sets of data. On an annual basis, the failure rate is seven of thirty-four, or 20.6 percent, but a more informative way of reporting it is that the failure rate is roughly one in four (from the fact that we had four non-overlapping stretches of data and the strategy worked in three of the four). It should also be noted that our criterion for success is very modest. We are not requiring that stocks

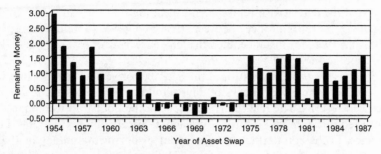

Fig. 1.2   Net money generated at the completion of a swap of ten-year U.S. government bonds for common stocks

match the 7 percent real yield assumed in scoring the MB plan. Rather, we are simply requiring that the stock returns were sufficient to pay off the bonds, which had low or even negative ex post real returns (especially in the 1970s).

While we have been focusing on the nontrivial chance of failure of the asset-swap strategy, it should also be noted that figure 1.2 indicates that it would indeed have worked twenty-seven of thirty-four times. Further, when it works, the average gain is quite substantial. The numbers in the figure represent the amount of money left in the stock account (per dollar borrowed) at the maturity of the bonds. The overall average amount left over for the thirty-four experiments is 78.5 cents per dollar borrowed; the average over the twenty-seven years with positive outcomes is almost $1.05. Of course, it is well known that, on average, stocks outperform bonds by a wide margin. What is less well known is that borrowing money for ten years to buy stocks is very risky—even with the favorable interest rates available to the government.

To acquire a better sense of how such a government asset-swap policy might work in the future, we have used the same set of 1954–97 stock returns as the basis for generating simulated sequences of returns using a moving-block bootstrap method to allow for autocorrelation. For each year 1954–97, we calculate what would have happened had the government borrowed additional money with ten-year bonds (at the actual prevailing interest rate). The stock market return in the year of the borrowing is taken as the actual return in that year. However, the succeeding real returns for the next nine years are randomly chosen in blocks of three-year sequences or "blocks" (with replacement) from the set of all realized real returns. For example, in order to calculate how this strategy would have worked in 1971, we compute the terms on the borrowed money according to the prevailing nominal interest rates in 1971. Further, we assume that the return on the stock market for the first year was the actually observed 1971 return. For the returns for the next nine years, we randomly choose three dates (with replacement, meaning that the same date could be chosen more than once) between 1954 and 1995. If we choose 1958, 1988, and 1956, for instance, then the ten-year string of real returns under this simulation would be $(R_{71}, R_{58}, R_{59}, R_{60}, R_{88}, R_{89}, R_{90}, R_{56}, R_{57}, R_{58})$, where R_t is the total real return of the S&P500 for year t. The fact that we are choosing three-year blocks of data should be apparent in this sample vector of returns. The real returns chosen via the bootstrap technique are converted into nominal returns using actual historical inflation rates. For instance, in the counterfactual experiment of borrowing money in 1971, we use the actual inflation rates for 1971–80 to generate the nominal returns resulting from the real returns chosen by the bootstrap process. For each asset-swap year, we examine one thousand such random sequences of returns.[3] The failure rate for the strategy differs by the year of the swap because of different interest rates and because of different first-year stock market returns. The results of this bootstrap simulation are shown in figure 1.3.

Implicitly, we have assumed that there is stability in the underlying probability distribution determining real stock returns during the period 1954–97 and that each observation was equally likely. Of course, it is certain that these assumptions are not entirely correct; it is also certain that many low-probability events never occurred in the observation period. Finally, we are assuming that the same underlying probability distributions that generated the 1954–97 observations will generate stock market returns in the future. In total, this is a strong set of assumptions. Nonetheless, the implied results provide important insights. According to figure 1.3, the overall failure rate is predicted to be 22.1 percent, meaning that the asset-swap policy failed 9,723 times in the 44,000 simulations we did for the combined forty-four years of analysis. The expected failure rate for the most recent ten-year period was 44.7 percent, owing to the higher real interest rates of this period. Note that these failure rates are most likely conservative since they still are based on the robust returns realized in U.S. equity markets in the period 1954–97. These failure rates may therefore form something of a lower bound on the riskiness of the asset-swap strategy going forward.[4]

The patterns of failure probabilities shown in figure 1.3 stand in sharp contrast to the success or failure patterns shown in figure 1.2 above, which uses the actual realized time series of returns. The reasons for the divergence are easily explained. The accelerating inflation of the 1970s was not fully incorporated into government interest rates until 1981 and 1982. The

3. Our preliminary analysis indicates that selecting block sizes 1, 2, 3, and 5 would not change the main findings reported here.
4. Once again, we are concentrating on the failure probability as a measure of the riskiness of the asset swap. The asset swap does work more than 50 percent of the time and often generates large profits.

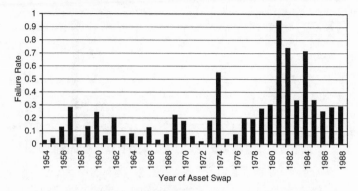

Year of Asset Swap

Fig. 1.3   Failure rate by year of asset swap for ten-year bonds, bootstrap simulations with three-year blocks, 1954–88

ex ante analysis of figure 1.3 shows that to be the period with the highest chance of failure for the ten-year bonds-for-stocks swap (particularly with the poor performance of the stock market in 1981). However, ex post the stock market has performed extraordinarily well from 1982 to the present. As a result, the asset-swap strategy would have worked in 1981 and 1982, even though our bootstrap simulations show that it had a relatively low probability of doing so. On the other hand, the ex ante failure probabilities in 1965–72 were not particularly high; nonetheless, in fact, the strategy would have failed in six of those eight years, as shown in figure 1.2. The point is that the returns that were actually experienced were just a single set of draws from an economic and financial system generating risky returns.

We perform the same analysis for twenty-year bonds. In this case, the limitations of the data are even more severe since there are only two completely independent sets of twenty-year observations in the 1954–97 data set. Therefore, it is difficult to know how to interpret the fact that the asset-swap strategy would have worked for every year 1954–77 using actual interest rates and the actual time series of stock market returns. This says very little about the underlying chance of failure with a future policy of swapping twenty-year government bonds for a diversified portfolio of common stocks. The same bootstrap approach is used in this case as with the ten-year bonds. Now, instead of a single historical set of stock market returns, we can generate thousands of simulated sequences of returns generated from a random selection of the actual annual observations. The results of doing that are shown in figure 1.4.

The pattern of failure probabilities is primarily determined by the actual pattern of nominal interest rates on government bonds and by the actual first-year return on the stock market. Therefore, it is not surprising that the general pattern of failure rates is similar in the twenty-year bond case of figure 1.4 and the ten-year bond case of figure 1.3. The high failure

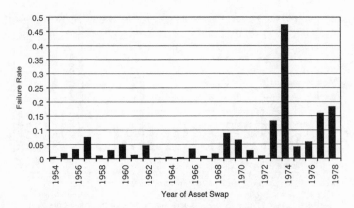

Fig. 1.4   Failure rate by year of asset swap for twenty-year bonds, bootstrap simulations with three-year blocks, 1954–78

probability (47.3 percent) for the asset-swap strategy in 1974 is due to the fact that the real return on the S&P500 in 1974 was −34.5 percent. If stocks lose more than one-third of their value immediately after bonds are sold to buy stocks, the chances of making the swap work are greatly diminished.

For twenty-year bonds, the overall predicted failure rate during 1954–78 is 6.24 percent. In the most recent ten-year period (1969–78), the failure rate is predicted to be 12.27 percent, which we view as a considerable chance of failure. This suggests that, were the government to borrow money by issuing twenty-year government bonds (assuming that it could do so without raising interest rates), and were the real returns on the stock market generated by the same process that produced the returns of 1954–97 (although with the ordering of the returns randomly scrambled), the chance that the government would have to borrow additional money when the bonds mature is about one in eight. The asset swap has a considerable chance of being counterproductive in terms of the finances of the federal government in general and social security in particular.

The historical record on interest rates also represents only a single set of realizations of what might have happened. Future real (or nominal, for that matter) interest rates may be higher or lower than what we have observed in the past. To add some robustness to our results, we examine what would have happened to the finances of the government had it issued inflation-indexed bonds and bought stocks with the proceeds. In our first experiment, we set the real interest rate on ten-year inflation-protected bonds at 3.5 percent. This is actually somewhat less than the recently observed interest rate on this type of security. Each year, the principal on the bonds is marked up to reflect realized inflation. The bonds are assumed to pay 3.5 percent interest each year on the revised (i.e., inflation-adjusted) principal amount and at maturity return the original investment marked up by cumulative inflation. The question we want to ask is how likely it is that an S&P500 stock portfolio can generate sufficient returns to pay off the claims of such inflation-indexed bonds.

Once again, we can look at how this asset swap would have fared historically could it have been accomplished without affecting the actually observed stock market returns. In this case, we have used the observed stock market returns and inflation rates for the period 1927–97 and examined counterfactual asset swaps for the sixty-one years 1927–87. Basically, we have six full and completely independent (i.e., nonoverlapping) runs of ten-year data. Figure 1.5 shows the results for this case with ten-year inflation-indexed bonds. The strategy would have failed eighteen times out of the sixty-one years examined, for a failure rate of 29.5 percent. The failures are strongly autocorrelated, however, because of the overlapping returns. If the swap strategy fails in year t, it is quite likely that it will also fail in year $t + 1$ since the two experiments involve nine common years of stock market returns. Not surprisingly, figure 1.5 shows that the asset-swap strategy would have had mixed success in the period 1927–40, followed by twenty-three years of complete success, followed by eleven years in a row of failure and, finally, by thirteen years of success. Some of the failures are quite substantial. In seven of the 1964–74 years, the government would have had to borrow a second time an amount roughly equal to its initial issuance of bonds to be able to pay the principal of the maturing bonds.

The autocorrelation in the success or failure of this strategy calls into question one aspect of the MB and Aaron-Reischauer plans that we have

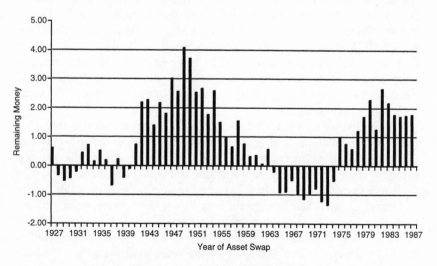

Fig. 1.5 **Net money generated at the completion of a swap of ten-year inflation-indexed U.S. government bonds for common stocks**

not yet modeled—namely, the fact that both plans advocate that the asset swaps take place continuously. Both plans would phase in the private securities investments of the OASDI trust fund only gradually. One could hope that some kind of "dollar-cost-averaging" phenomenon would make this less risky than making the asset reallocation all at once. However, the eleven failures in a row from 1964 through 1974 indicate that considerable risk remains even with such a gradual transition. Had social security engaged in this particular asset swap (ten-year inflation-indexed bonds for a portfolio of the S&P500) from 1964 through 1974, the financial crises that the system faced in 1977 and again in 1983 would have been considerably worsened.

We have also simulated how the asset swap of ten-year inflation-indexed bonds for common stocks would perform in the future if future returns and inflation rates were drawn from the 1927–97 set of realizations drawn randomly with a bootstrap technique. The predicted overall failure rate was 29 percent. That is, the stock portfolio failed to generate the necessary 3.5 percent real return required to pay off the obligations of the inflation-indexed bonds 29 percent of the time. Had we defined failure as the stock investments falling short of the 7 percent real rate of return assumed in scoring the MB plan in table 1.1, the failure rate would, of course, be much higher.

The results for twenty-year inflation-indexed bonds are similar. Figure 1.6 shows the counterfactual history for asset swaps from 1927 through 1977. The strategy would have failed eighteen times out of the fifty-one years, for a failure rate of 35.3 percent. Even more telling is the fact that it would have failed fifteen years in a row from 1959 to 1973. The strategy is very successful from 1932 through 1954 and again in 1975–77. This is not surprising since we know that the average real return on the stock market in 1927–97 has been well above 3.5 percent. The failure or limited success of the strategy for twenty years in a row (1955–74), however, is a big problem for its advocates. The overall failure rate when the 1927–97 inflation rates and stock market returns are scrambled with a bootstrap technique of choosing the observations is 25.4 percent.

Table 1.2 sums up what we have learned thus far. We have examined a total of four different cases for asset swaps based on ten-year bonds and the same four cases for twenty-year bonds. The bootstrap simulations are probably more informative regarding the future chances of success for the exchange than are the numbers based on the actual historical time series of returns. That is because the future will not be a precise replay of the past. The bootstrap simulation technique gives us a better handle on the probability of future success. If real stock market returns are generated in the future from the same distribution that generated the actual 1954–97 returns, and if real interest rates on bonds approximate 3.5 percent, then the failure rate of a strategy of swapping bonds for stocks is about 29

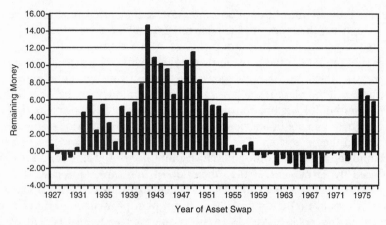

Fig. 1.6   Net money generated at the completion of a swap of twenty-year inflation-indexed U.S. government bonds for common stocks

Table 1.2   Summary of Failure Rates (%) of a Strategy of Swapping Bonds for S&P500 Stocks

Bond Maturity	Actual Interest Rates; Actual 1954–97 Time Series of Stock Market Returns	Actual Interest Rates; Bootstrap Simulations of Real Returns Chosen from 1954–97 Realizations	3.5% Inflation-Indexed Bonds; Actual 1927–97 Time Series of Inflation and Stock Market Returns	3.5% Inflation-Indexed Bonds; Bootstrap Simulations of Real Returns Chosen from 1927–97 Realizations
10 years	20.6	22.1	29.5	29.0
20 years	0	6.2	35.3	25.4

percent for ten-year bonds and 25 percent for twenty-year bonds. These figures refer to the final column of results in table 1.2. It is important to note, however, that all variations of the asset-swap simulations that we have conducted imply a considerable risk of failure.

1.4   Tax Considerations

We have ignored personal income tax issues thus far, but they deserve some consideration. The federal government collects taxes on the returns of stocks held in private hands and would recapture some of the interest payments on the bonds through tax proceeds. If the average marginal tax rate on the returns is the same for the stocks and bonds, then it is a fairly minor correction to the results presented above. For instance, assume that on the "other side" of the transaction are defined-contribution pension funds. Further, assume that, as people see that the social security trust fund is moving out of bonds and into stocks, they are willing to move in the opposite direction in their own IRA, 401(k), or other defined-contribution accounts (without a change in interest rates). If the average marginal tax rate of the pension plan holders will be 25 percent when the money is drawn out, then the government effectively owns one-fourth of the assets in the plan. If the government makes money on the swap on its own account, it loses one-fourth of its profits owing to its participation in the defined-contribution accounts (which took the other side of the asset swap) via the tax system. The failure-rate analysis of the previous section need not be modified, although the absolute size of the gains and losses is reduced by 25 percent. If the other side of the transaction consisted of corporate accounts backing defined-benefit pension promises, then the gain or loss in the funding of the pension plan presumably would be reflected in the stock of the corporation offering the defined-benefit plan. Stockholders will eventually pay capital gains taxes on their stock (sooner rather than later if the stocks are held by an actively managed mutual fund), and, once again, the government will find itself with roughly a 20 or 25 percent position on the opposite side of the swap that it thought it was engaged in. Also, once again, the failure-rate analysis of the previous section is unaffected.

We think that pensions are the most likely "other side" of the asset-swap transaction. We have also examined the case in which privately held assets are exchanged with the government. If the average marginal tax rate on the interest payments of the government exceeds the blended average marginal tax rate faced by dividends and short- and long-term capital gains from the stock returns, then the failure probabilities are slightly improved by tax considerations. The government recaptures a higher percentage of its interest payments through the tax system than it did on the return on common stocks. The effect is fairly minor, however. We were probably exploring the upper limit of the effect in assuming that the average marginal income-tax rate on interest on the bonds was 33 percent, whereas the average marginal tax rate on long-term capital gains was 20 percent. Both numbers are almost certainly on the high side, but the difference may be reasonable. With such parameters, the projected failure rate of issuing fixed-interest-rate ten-year bonds turns out to be 25.1 percent. The twenty-year-bond failure rate falls from 6.2 to 5.4 percent. The failure rate for ten-year bonds remains 21.1 percent even if somehow the stocks had paid zero taxes and the bonds faced an average marginal tax rate of 33 percent. The worst case for the government is the opposite of that, of course. If the bonds are somehow held in completely tax-free accounts and the stocks are fully taxable (33 percent on dividends and short-term capital gains and 20 percent on long-term capital gains), then the predicted failure rate with ten-year fixed-interest bonds jumps to 37.9 percent.

Our conclusion regarding taxes is that they are an important second-order consideration but that the results of the previous section—that the government issuing bonds and using the proceeds to buy stocks is very risky—is not materially altered by including the effects of taxes.

1.5   Interpretation of Failure Results

We feel that the most appropriate of our asset-swap simulations in terms of predicting the likelihood of future failure of such a policy are those that use the 3.5 percent real-interest-rate inflation-protected bonds and generate real stock returns with the bootstrap procedure. These results are relevant even if the government actually swaps nominal bonds for stocks because the real interest cost of such bonds is far more likely to approximate 3.5 percent than the negative real interest rates that prevailed in the 1970s. The result is that the asset-swap strategy has about a 25 percent chance of failure with twenty-year bonds. This means that there is a 25 percent chance that the switch into stocks will make the solvency problems of social security worse rather than better after twenty years. Of course, there is about a 50 percent chance that the strategy will not work as well as assumed by its proponents (and listed in table 1.1). That is because the 7 percent real rate of return assumed in that table is roughly the median long-run real rate of return for stocks.

Someone might take the view that, if stocks are behind after twenty years, the government can simply borrow the shortfall (or more) and buy yet more stocks. With a long enough time horizon, stocks are bound to beat out bonds, right? First, this is not quite right. It is true that the probability of a shortfall is lower the longer the time horizon. Of course, the magnitude of the shortfall in the unlikely event that stocks have a bad forty- or fifty-year run can be enormous if each intermediate shortfall is covered with more borrowed money. Second, and probably more important, the balance-sheet position of social security is economically and politically important. The social security crises of 1977 and 1983 were caused by the impending exhaustion of the OASDI trust fund. Of course, the government could have bailed out the fund by borrowing money and handing it over to social security. But that action was not seriously considered. Our point is that the trust fund would have been in even worse shape in the late 1970s and early 1980s had it been investing in stocks in the 1960s instead of in the special issue Treasury bonds. In that case, the benefit cuts and tax increases would have been even more severe than they were. One would not have been able to get through that period with the argument that we can just borrow more money and buy more stocks and sooner or later the strategy will pay off. The extra risks of stocks translate directly into riskier future benefits and taxes.

The failure probabilities that we have estimated are only as good as the modeling of the underlying process generating real stock market returns. In a number of respects, we have erred on the side of favoring the strategy. First, we have assumed that the government could engage in the swap without changing interest rates and stock market rates of return. Second, we have assumed that future stock market returns will be generated from the observed returns from 1954–97 (1927–97 in some cases). The average real rate of return on stocks from 1954–97 was 9.7 percent. The average from 1927–97 was 9.6 percent. Still, relative to either international comparisons or longer historical returns (Siegel 1994), these average returns are quite high.

For most of the results that we have presented, we have worked with three-year blocks of stock market returns. We have assumed that each of the three-year blocks observed from 1954 to 1997 is equally likely to be repeated, independent of the previous returns drawn. There is a literature on long-run mean reversion that indicates that high returns are more likely to follow low returns (and vice versa) (see, e.g., Poterba and Summers 1988; Fama and French 1988; and Campbell, Lo, and MacKinlay 1997, chap. 2). Were this true, then long-horizon investing would be safer than if returns were drawn independently from previous realizations. The statistical evidence on long-run mean reversion is not very powerful for the same reason that we have had to downplay our actual counterfactual results—there simply are not many long runs to observe in order to investigate such long-run phenomena. The empirical studies that have been conducted cannot rule out that returns are actually serially independent. With that said, all that we can say is that, if returns were generated by a process exhibiting long-run mean reversion, then the asset-swap strategy would fail less often than we have estimated. Our simulations of the asset-swap strategy using one-, two-, three-, and five-year blocks of data showed roughly the same failure probabilities. This indicates that, to the extent that it operates in under five years, mean reversion is at most a relatively weak phenomenon.

Our overall conclusion is that the simplifications in this study have not biased the results against the asset-swap policy. The relatively high mean return that we assume for equities must be at least as important an assumption as the lack of mean reversion in returns over periods greater than three years. If asked the likelihood that investing some of the central trust fund of social security in equities would worsen its finances in ten or twenty years, our best-guess answer would be that there is a 25–30 percent chance.

1.6   Is a Universal Defined-Benefit Retirement Plan Feasible?

Our conclusion thus far has the usual "no-free-lunch" ring to it. Unfortunately, one cannot eliminate the actuarial deficit of social security by swapping bonds for stocks. If it were possible, then we would also do well to eliminate the cost of the defense budget with the same maneuver. This raises the question of who bears the risks in the current social security system and who would bear the additional risks were the trust fund to invest in private securities as advocated by the MB and the Aaron-Reischauer plans. Even more fundamentally, it raises the issue of whether it is feasible for the government to offer a defined-benefit plan with universal coverage.

At one extreme, consider a defined-benefit plan offered by a financially strong company such as General Motors. The company can promise its workers a particular or "defined" benefit in retirement and fund that obligation with private stocks and bonds. The worker can accumulate a vested, safe retirement benefit (although not safe from the effects of inflation), while the firm, or, more accurately, its stockholders, bears the investment risks of the underlying portfolio. The point is that it is quite transparent how a safe benefit was created from risky investments—the risky residual claim is borne by the General Motors stockholders.

At the other extreme, consider what would happen if a self-employed person decided that he would like to provide himself a defined-benefit pension funded with stocks and bonds. Is it feasible? Can a person invest, say, $30,000 in stocks and bonds and promise himself or herself a safe retirement benefit of $3,000 per year? The answer is no since the employer bears the risk of the assets not being adequate to fund the benefits. But a self-employed person is both employee and employer. The investment risks have not been transferred at all, and, therefore, the do-it-yourself defined-benefit strategy cannot work. The only way for a self-employed person to end up with a defined-benefit-like retirement claim is to contract with an insurance company or some other third party that will provide the benefit and assume the investment risks.

Now consider a universal coverage defined-benefit social security retirement-pension system funded with risky private securities. Is it possible to provide safe retirement benefits as in the General Motors example, or is it more like the example of the self-employed person who cannot make meaningful retirement-benefit promises without the help of a third party? If everyone is in the social security system, then collectively everyone bears the investment risk, and it makes little sense to call the program a *defined-benefit* scheme. We can think of only two ways to maintain the defined-benefit nature of the system. One is to divide the population by age cohort. Conceivably, the elderly can be promised safe benefits with the young playing the role of the insurance company and bearing the investment risks of the underlying portfolio. The future payroll taxes or the future benefits of the young will be more risky if the trust fund engages in the kind of asset swap that we have been analyzing. One of the drawbacks of a defined-benefit structure is that the risks imposed on the young are not very transparent. If we maintain the defined benefits for both the old and the young, then the taxes faced by the young will be even more volatile. The point is simply that the considerable risks involved in investing in private securities, which we have documented above, have to be borne by someone. The defined-benefit nature of the system does not work very well if the investment risks are borne by those paying the personal income tax. The reason is that there is a nearly complete overlap between social security participants and those paying the personal income tax. In order to create a safe asset from a risky portfolio, the risks must be shifted to someone other than the holder of the supposedly safe claim. Shifting the risks from social security participants to taxpayers is not enough of a shift to accomplish this.

At least conceptually, the investment risks could be shifted internationally. Shiller (1998) makes this point in his theoretical paper on risks and social security. The Europeans, for instance, could play the role of the insurance company and offer Americans a safe defined-benefit pension system by assuming the investment risks themselves. There is a question of what terms they would demand to hold all the risks. Further, while it is clear that there are advantages of the young and old and the Europeans and Americans all sharing in the risks of global financial markets, it is not at all clear why one group (the young or the Europeans) should hold all the risk so that another group (the elderly Americans) can enjoy a safe, defined-benefit retirement program. The optimal risk-sharing arrangement would have everyone bearing some risk, and, thus, any optimal universal pension plan would not be strictly of a defined-benefit type.

One problem with investing the central OASDI trust fund in private securities that we have not emphasized is the danger that the investment decisions would be subject to political pressure and, therefore, would not manage risk efficiently. There would undoubtedly be pressure to invest in only American companies or only unionized companies or to allocate the investments evenly across the fifty states or not to invest in tobacco companies or those doing business in Burma. Aaron and Reischauer are confident that certain organizational structures that they propose (including the creation of a "Social Security Reserve Board") could insulate fund management from political control by elected officials. We are not so sure. It is quite possible that capital would be less efficiently allocated with government ownership of equities, meaning that the asset swap could reduce aggregate future GDP.

1.7 Conclusions

In this paper, we have examined the risk of having the central OASDI trust fund invest in private securities. We have noted that that net transaction is an asset swap with the government selling bonds to the public and using the proceeds to buy a portfolio of common stocks of equal value. The asset reallocation does not increase saving, wealth, or GDP. We examine whether it actually would improve the finances of the social security system. We adopt a convention that the asset swap is deemed successful if the stock portfolio generates sufficient cash to pay off the interest and principal of the bonds and still have money left over and a failure if the stock portfolio is insufficient to do that and the bond repayments require another round of borrowing. We have looked at several cases, including ten- and twenty-year fixed-interest-rate bonds and ten- and twenty-year inflation-indexed debt. The predicted failure rate from the bootstrap simulations of future returns ranges from 6 to 29 percent. Further, failure would be autocorrelated with long strings of possible annual failures. For instance, when we examined the counterfactual issuance of twenty-year inflation-indexed bonds, we found that the asset-swap strategy failed fifteen years in a row between 1959 and 1973. Clearly, this policy cannot reliably reduce the actuarial deficit of social security.

Individual accounts and defined-contribution pension plans certainly involve significant risks. An individual who shifts from bonds to stocks runs the same or greater risk that the move will be counterproductive after ten or twenty years. However, the defined-contribution plans have the advantage that their risks are straightforward. Further, people who want to minimize risks can invest in such safe assets as inflation-indexed bonds. The analysis of this paper has shown that an OASDI trust fund invested in private securities would generate risk for Americans, but the precise incidence of that risk would likely remain ambiguous.

References

Aaron, Henry J., and Robert D. Reischauer. 1998. *Countdown to reform: The great social security debate.* New York: Century Foundation Press.

Campbell, John Y., Andrew W. Lo, and A. Craig MacKinlay. 1997. *The econometrics of financial markets.* Princeton, N.J.: Princeton University Press.

Economic report of the president, 1998. 1998. Washington, D.C.: U.S. Government Printing Office.

Fama, Eugene F., and Kenneth R. French. 1988. Permanent and temporary components of stock prices. *Journal of Political Economy* 96, no. 2:246–73.

Goss, Stephen. 1999. Measuring solvency in the social security system. In *Prospects for social security reform,* ed. Olivia Mitchell, Robert J. Myers, and Howard Young. Philadelphia: University of Pennsylvania Press.

Ibbotson Associates. 1998. *Stocks, bonds, bills, and inflation: 1998 yearbook, market results for 1926–97.* Chicago.

MaCurdy, Thomas E., and John B. Shoven. 1992. Stocks, bonds, and pension wealth. In *Topics in the economics of aging,* ed. David A. Wise. Chicago: University of Chicago Press.

Poterba, James M., and Lawrence H. Summers. 1998. Mean reversion in stock prices. *Journal of Financial Economics* 22:27–59.

Schieber, Sylvester J., and John B. Shoven. 1999. *The real deal: The history and future of social security.* New Haven, Conn.: Yale University Press.

Shiller, Robert J. 1998. Social security and institutions for intergenerational, intragenerational, and international risk sharing. NBER Working Paper no. 6641. Cambridge, Mass.: National Bureau of Economic Research, July.

Siegel, Jeremy J. 1994. *Stocks for the long run.* Chicago: Irwin.

Social Security Administration (SSA). 1997. *Report of the 1994–96 Advisory Council on Social Security.* Vol. 1, *Findings and recommendations.* Washington, D.C.

————. Various years. *Annual report of the Board of Trustees of the Federal Old-Age and Survivors Insurance and Disability Insurance trust funds.* Washington, D.C.: U.S. Government Printing Office.

Comment   Stephen P. Zeldes

As the debate over social security reform progresses, it is becoming increasingly obvious that many of the key issues relate to uncertainty. One question that arises is in what ways the benefit payments to the elderly should be linked to the outcomes of key economic and demographic variables in the economy—such as mortality, real wages, birthrates, unemployment, interest rates, and stock returns. A second question is what techniques should be used to evaluate, on an ex ante basis, reform proposals that involve risky outcomes.

Consider first the current evaluation techniques used by the Office of the Actuary at the Social Security Administration (SSA). The actuaries estimate the most likely outcome for a set of economic and demographic variables—these are referred to as *intermediate-cost* assumptions. The *actuarial balance,* projected path of the trust fund, and *money's-worth* measures (e.g., net present value and internal rates of return to participants) are based on these assumptions. These provide a reasonable assessment of the expected outcome for the system and for individuals. They do not attempt to incorporate the riskiness of any variables. The SSA incorporates uncertainty only by describing two alternate scenarios: *high* and *low* cost. While this does provide some information about the dispersion in possible outcomes, it is an incomplete and inadequate way of dealing with uncertainty, for the following reasons. First, this technique does not assign probabilities to the different outcomes. Second, it ignores correlations between variables, both economic and demographic. Third, when examining reforms, it ignores general equilibrium effects—the effects of these reforms on the underlying demographic and economic variables.

The SSA is careful to point out that its goal is to examine expected values and that it is not attempting to account for risk. However, many

Stephen P. Zeldes is the Benjamin Rosen Professor of Economics and Finance at the Graduate School of Business, Columbia University, and a research associate of the National Bureau of Economic Research.

who use money's-worth and other SSA statistics inappropriately interpret them as corresponding to welfare or utility rankings when in fact they do not. Since most of the reform packages that have been proposed involve investment in the stock market, through either individual accounts or a central trust fund, it is particularly problematic to use non-risk-adjusted money's-worth measures to rank the attractiveness of alternative reforms, both versus the current system and versus each other (for more on this issue, see Geanakoplos, Mitchell, and Zeldes [1999]).

MaCurdy and Shoven examine the potential risks and benefits to social security of undertaking an open market operation selling Treasury bonds and using the proceeds to purchase stocks, to be held either in the trust fund or in individual accounts. This, as well as analyzing any reform plan that involves stock market investment, requires an understanding of the equity premium: the difference between the return on equities and the return on Treasury bills or bonds. How we think about the equity premium and to what we attribute it are key to understanding many of the issues raised at this conference.

Since the stock market has a higher expected return than the bond market, this change in investment policy improves both the actuarial balance of the system and the money's worth as currently measured. It also typically increases the risk. Evaluating by how much the risk increases and assessing the trade-off of whether the higher return is worth the higher risk are difficult to do and in general require using a stochastic general equilibrium model. Such an approach has been followed in many of the papers included in this volume. These models have the advantages that they remedy the three problems described above; that is, they assign probability distributions, allow for correlations between variables, and incorporate the general equilibrium effects that can be crucial to the analysis. They also, by necessity, oversimplify the world that they are modeling— sacrificing realism at the expense of tractability.

MaCurdy and Shoven have an alternative approach with a more modest goal. Rather than analyzing the entire general equilibrium model, they analyze important properties of the joint distribution of stock and bond returns.

First, consider the basic facts. Table 1C.1 shows the means and standard deviations of annual real returns on stocks and government bonds from 1926 to 1997. The average real return on the S&P500 was 9.7 percent, as compared to 2.6 and 2.3 percent on long- and intermediate-term Treasury bonds, respectively, and 0.7 percent on short-term Treasury bills. The higher historical return on stocks is seen even more dramatically in figure 1C.1. One dollar invested in December 1925 would have grown (in constant dollars) to $203.19 if invested in the S&P500, to $4.34 if invested in long-term government bonds, and to $1.58 if invested in three-month Treasury bills.

The higher average return on stocks is clear. What about the risk? Look-

Table 1C.1   **Annual Inflation-Adjusted Returns on Stocks and Government Bonds, 1926–97**

Asset	Arithmetic Average Return (%)	SD (%)
S&P500	9.7	20.5
Long-term government bond	2.6	10.5
Intermediate-term government bond	2.3	7.0
Short-term Treasury bill	.7	4.2

Source: Calculations are based on data from Ibbotson Associates.

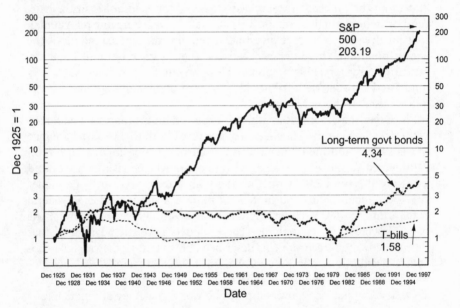

Fig. 1C.1   Stocks, long-term bonds, and Treasury bills, cumulative real returns, 1926–97

ing again at table 1C.1, we see that the standard deviations of annual real returns were 20.5 percent on stocks, 10.5 percent on long-term bonds, 7.0 percent on intermediate-term bonds, and 4.2 percent on Treasury bills. The higher standard deviation on stocks suggests that stocks are riskier than bonds, but it is not sufficient evidence, for a few reasons. First, it is possible that stocks dominate bonds in every period: for example, $r^S = r^B + \varepsilon$, where r^S is the annual return on stocks, r^B is the annual return on bonds, and ε is a random variable that has high variance but is always nonnegative (i.e., ε is ≥ 0 with probability one). In general, we need a stochastic model together with a utility function to evaluate riskiness. But, if stocks dominate bonds in this sense, then no such model is necessary. A simple glance at the data on annual returns tells us that this is not the case. There are many years when the return on stocks is negative and the return on bonds is positive. A second possibility is that risk is best measured by looking at long-horizon returns rather than annual returns. If there is sufficient mean reversion in stock returns, it is possible that, when examining long returns (e.g., twenty-year returns), stocks dominate bonds in the sense described above. An examination of twenty-year rolling annual returns indicates that there was only one twenty-year period in which stocks did not outperform both long-term bonds and Treasury bills, and even in this one period the difference was small. Some observers (e.g., Siegel 1998; and Glassman and Hassett 1998) argue that this type of evidence implies that stocks are not more risky than bonds in the long run.

There is much debate in the literature about what can be learned from the historical data about the ex ante expected return (in the past and in the future), the riskiness of stocks relative to bonds (in the past and in the future), and whether the higher expected return is/was a fair compensation for higher risk (in the past and in the future).

Table 1C.2 is my attempt to summarize the many views on this question. Where in table 1C.2 one stands is likely to be related to how attractive one finds reform proposals that involve social security investments in the stock market.

The first row of table 1C.2, the "faith-in-markets" view, argues that any equity premium that exists is fair compensation for the riskiness of stocks. Mehra and Prescott (1985) accept that expected excess returns were high in the past and that stocks were riskier but argue that they were not sufficiently risky, on the basis of a standard model of the economy, to justify the higher risk. One could interpret this result as implying either that the markets have it wrong and are providing too much compensation for stock market risk or that the standard model is wrong and is incorrectly estimating the amount of risk or expected return of the stock market. A variety of papers have attempted to explain this "equity-premium puzzle," either by arguing that ex post returns were much higher than what was expected ex ante or by arguing that with alternative utility functions risk was actually much higher than Mehra and Prescott estimated. MaCurdy and Shoven do not address the question of whether the equity premium is correctly compensating for risk, but they do challenge the view that stocks are less risky than bonds in the long run (i.e., the view represented in the rows at the bottom of the table).

MaCurdy and Shoven point out that one possible problem with simply examining long-period returns in the past is that there are not many data points, only three and a half independent twenty-year periods between 1926 and 1997—far too few to summarize the distribution of twenty-year returns adequately. They try to get around this problem of limited data by bootstrapping: they assume that the annual returns are representative of

Table 1C.2   Views about the Equity Premium

View	Very High Expected Excess Return on Stocks?		Stocks Riskier than Bonds in Long Run?		Equity Premium Correct Compensation for Risk?	
	Past	Future	Past	Future	Past	Future
"Faith-in-markets" view	Yes		Yes		Yes	Yes
Mehra-Prescott	Yes		Yes		No	
"Good-luck" theory	No (ex ante much less than ex post)		Yes		Yes	
Preference-based solutions to equity-premium puzzle	Yes		Yes		Yes	
MaCurdy-Shoven	Yes		Yes		No	
Siegel	Yes		No		No	
Glassman-Hassett	Yes (not quite as high as ex post)	No (once Dow hits 35,000)		No	No	Yes
Naive view supporting stocks for social security	Yes	Yes	No	No	No	No

the underlying probability distribution, and they draw observations randomly from the sample with replacement. They do this in two ways: first, by drawing single years of stock-return data with replacement and, second, by drawing three-year blocks of stock-return data with replacement. They then construct a thousand observations of ten- and twenty-year stock returns, match these with interest rates on ten- and twenty-year government bonds from the first year of each period, and use these constructed data to calculate a "failure rate," that is, the percentage of times for each starting year that stocks fail to outperform bonds.

I have two main criticisms of the technique used by MaCurdy and Shoven. First, they use nominal rather than real returns when performing their bootstraps. Normally, when computing excess returns on stocks relative to bonds, it makes no difference whether real or nominal returns are used as the inflation rate drops out of the differential. But with their bootstrapping method it does matter because the dates for the stock returns do not correspond to the dates covered by the interest rates. For example, the ten-year nominal interest rate in 1981 was high, reflecting high inflation expectations. MaCurdy and Shoven compare this nominal return to a series of nominal stock returns, the first year of which is 1981, but the other years of which are drawn randomly from the sample, thus likely including many years with low expected inflation. Although stock returns are unlikely to compensate for unexpected inflation, they are likely to compensate for expected inflation. Using nominal returns incorporates a mismatching that might explain why their calculated failure rate for stocks outperforming bonds is so high in the early 1980s (when expected inflation is high) and so low in the 1950s (when expected inflation is low). It would be worth reestimating their results using real returns rather than nominal ones to see whether the results are sensitive to this change.

Second, and more important, their results are unlikely to persuade those who argue that stocks are not risky over the long run. Although I do not believe this view, let me temporarily play devil's advocate. The argument that stocks are not more risky than bonds over long holding periods, even though they are over short holding periods, depends crucially on long-term mean reversion in stock returns. In other words, strings of bad returns must tend to be followed by strings of good returns. Because the bootstrap method randomly draws three-year blocks of data, it will by construction not pick up these long-term correlations. In their simulated data, a three-year period of low returns is, by construction, as likely to be followed by periods of low returns as it is by periods of high returns. Therefore, it cannot possibly capture the long-term mean reversion that is crucial to reducing the long-run riskiness of stocks.

To see this more clearly, suppose that we were looking at the riskiness, not of stocks, but of thirty-year zero-coupon bonds. For simplicity, assume that inflation was always zero. Because of real-interest-rate risk, the one-year-holding-period returns on these bonds are risky. However, high one-year returns in one part of the sample must be followed by low one-year returns later in the sample, and the thirty-year real return on these bonds is completely riskless. Were the MaCurdy-Shoven bootstrap technique applied to these bonds, it would miss the long-term mean reversion, and it would lead to the erroneous conclusion that thirty-year real returns on these bonds are very risky.

With that said, let me emphasize that the MaCurdy-Shoven conclusion that there is risk in stocks relative to bonds, even in the long run, is probably correct. Certainly, a market test would lead to this conclusion. Consider a $1 million portfolio in the S&P500. Were we to ask a large insurance company how much it would charge to guarantee that, thirty years from today, the portfolio would be worth at least as much as the amount in an initial $1 million portfolio invested in thirty-year bonds, it would probably charge a substantial amount and would certainly not provide this option for free. This is, of course, subject to the critique that insurance companies do not understand the risks of the market either.

Suppose that we accept the MaCurdy-Shoven conclusion that stocks are riskier than bonds. The next questions are whether they are sufficiently riskier to justify the high equity premium and whether social security could benefit by doing a swap of stocks for bonds. These are questions that MaCurdy and Shoven do not address. As described earlier, they require a stochastic general equilibrium model. It may very well be that there are tails of the distribution of stock returns that involve low returns and that the marginal utility of consumption is very high in those states of the world. Ignoring or downplaying those states may make the equity premium look like a giveaway.

The question of whether social security could benefit from an open market swap is not fully answered by examining the riskiness of stocks. Even if stocks completely dominated bonds over long horizons and participants in the asset markets did not realize this, we would need to balance the losses of the sellers of equity against the gains to social security participants. On the other hand, even if the equity premium is a fair compensation for the risk borne by current stock market participants, there may still be a role for social security to improve risk sharing. This could be done, for example, by providing exposure to current stock market returns to those without it: adults who are nonstockholders, children, and those not yet born (for more on this, see, e.g., Geanakoplos, Mitchell, and Zeldes [1998, 1999] and most of the papers in the present volume).

Overall, this is a helpful paper that contributes in an important way to the debate on the relative riskiness of stocks and bonds in the long run and the attractiveness of investing social security funds in the stock market. This paper and others in this volume appropriately focus the debate on the risk-return trade-offs inherent in such a change.

References

Geanakoplos, John, Olivia S. Mitchell, and Stephen P. Zeldes. 1998. Would a privatized social security system really pay a higher rate of return? In *Framing the social security debate: Values, politics, and economics,* ed. R. Douglas Arnold, Michael J. Graetz, and Alicia H. Munnell. Washington, D.C.: Brookings.
————. 1999. Social security money's worth. In *Prospects for social security reform,* ed. Olivia S. Mitchell, Robert J. Meyers, and Howard Young. Philadelphia: University of Pennsylvania Press.
Glassman, James K., and Kevin A. Hassett. 1998. Are stocks overvalued? Not a chance. *Wall Street Journal,* 30 March, A18.
Mehra, Rajnish, and Edward C. Prescott. 1985. The equity premium: A puzzle. *Journal of Monetary Economics* 15, no. 2:145–62.
Siegel, Jeremy J. 1998. *Stocks for the long run: The definitive guide to financial market returns and long-term investment strategies.* 2d ed. New York: McGraw-Hill.

Discussion Summary

Robert Shiller remarked that long-term bonds are quite risky because of the institutional feature that a single person, currently Alan Greenspan, can affect their value substantially, for instance, in response to political pressure. *Stephen Zeldes* concurred and noted that it is therefore important to consider three-asset models, with short-term bills, long-term bonds, and stocks.

James Poterba noted that dynamic hedging could be used to at least partially hedge the risk of holding equities. He also wondered whether the criticism of the discussant, Zeldes, concerning the use of nominal rather than real returns in the bootstrap simulation method would have significant implications. He noted that the correlation between equity returns and inflation is low. In response to this discussion, *John Shoven* noted that Zeldes's suggestion to repeat the simulation exercise with real returns would be incorporated in the final version of the paper.

John Campbell remarked that the Siegel view has an internal inconsistency. If stocks are less risky in the long run owing to mean reversion, then one must also accept that expected stock returns are time varying. But, in that case, one cannot logically recommend a buy-and-hold strategy, as Siegel does. Instead, mean reversion in stock returns and the associated time variation in expected equity returns imply that the optimal portfolio strategy involves some market timing. One cannot simultaneously assert that stocks are less risky in the long run owing to mean reversion and that a buy-and-hold strategy is optimal since the latter requires independently and identically distributed (i.i.d.) returns or constant expected returns. Campbell recommended that MaCurdy and Shoven be more explicit about their view on this data-generating process in the paper since it matters so much for the results.

David Cutler asked whether these experiments would not correspond more to borrowing against tax revenues than to using long-term debt since the rate of return seems to be based on wages, not on real interest rates in the economy. *Martin Feldstein* concurred but also noted that the authors are substituting stocks for bonds in the portfolio explicitly. There are two distinct policies: one in which assets are simply being swapped, without changing taxes (as suggested by Aaron and Reischauer and by Ball), and one that involves raising taxes.

When asked by *Feldstein* whether he had discussed the paper with Aaron, *Shoven* replied that Aaron was not pleased with the results. *Feldstein* responded that this was not surprising. He added that their argument would be that, although there is a small probability of a shortfall, they choose to take this risk on behalf of the taxpayer. Feldstein concluded that Shoven is well hedged, having written papers about the benefits of investing the trust fund in equities (e.g., MaCurdy and Shoven 1992) and now showing that this also involves substantial risk.

Shoven responded that one has to make the distinction between a defined-benefit and a defined-contribution plan in this respect. While a defined-contribution plan is typically perceived as risky, the defined-benefit-based plan is purported to be safe, yet is not, and becomes, moreover, significantly more risky when investing in equities.

Shoven acknowledged that any form of long-run mean reversion is not captured by the bootstrap experiment that takes an i.i.d. view. He noted that Poterba's question about the possibility of using dynamic hedging to intervene in the face of adverse conditions was worth pursuing.

Finally, Shoven emphasized that the political rhetoric appears to describe the current system as involving both defined benefits and defined taxes. This is misleading and even more incorrect when investing the trust fund in risky securities.

Reference

MaCurdy, Thomas E., and John B. Shoven. 1992. Stocks, bonds, and pension wealth. In *Topics in the economics of aging,* ed. David A. Wise. Chicago: University of Chicago Press.

2

The Transition to Investment-Based Social Security When Portfolio Returns and Capital Profitability Are Uncertain

Martin Feldstein, Elena Ranguelova, and Andrew Samwick

In this paper, we study the transition from a pay-as-you-go (PAYGO) system of social security pensions to an investment-based system in an economy in which portfolio returns and capital profitability are both uncertain. The paper extends earlier studies by Feldstein and Samwick (1997, 1998a, 1998b) that modeled the transition process in a nonstochastic environment and by Feldstein and Ranguelova (forthcoming) that examined the implication of portfolio risk after the transition to an investment-based system has been completed.

Our analysis shows that contributions to personal retirement accounts (PRAs) that are less than one-third of the projected PAYGO tax rate can eventually finance annuity payments that exceed the officially projected level of future social security pensions with very high probability. The remaining moderate level of retiree risk can be completely eliminated by a government guarantee that can be provided with very little risk to taxpayers. Although the transition to a pure investment-based system is the natural case to analyze, we also consider a more realistic policy of a transition to a mixed system that in the long run is one-third investment based and two-thirds pay as you go; this is the stochastic extension of the study by Feldstein and Samwick (1998a). It corresponds to a policy of maintaining the current payroll-tax rate and using investment-based accounts to main-

Martin Feldstein is the George F. Baker Professor of Economics at Harvard University and president of the National Bureau of Economic Research. Elena Ranguelova is a doctoral candidate at Harvard University and a research assistant at the National Bureau of Economic Research. Andrew Samwick is associate professor of economics at Dartmouth College and a research associate of the National Bureau of Economic Research.

The authors are grateful to conference and preconference participants for comments.

tain the current benefit rules instead of raising the tax rate as the population ages.

We begin the paper in section 2.1 with a summary of the social security simulation model that we use and of the statistical parameters incorporated into our simulations of alternative policy rules. Section 2.2 then sets the stage for the stochastic simulations that are the primary focus of this paper by analyzing a relatively transparent nonstochastic transition from the existing PAYGO system to a fully funded system with the same projected benefits. We consider four alternative simulations. The basic calculations assume that the funds in the PRAs earn 5.5 percent, the average postwar real portfolio rate of return on a sixty-forty stock-bond portfolio after a 0.4 percent allowance for administrative costs. An alternative simulation (presented in sec. 2.2.1) increases this return to approximately 7.5 percent by assuming that the federal government credits to the PRAs the incremental federal corporate-tax revenue that results from the PRA-induced increase in capital accumulation. Our third simulation (sec. 2.2.2) assumes a real rate of return of 3.7 percent, the riskless rate of return available now on Treasury inflation-protected securities (TIPS). The next nonstochastic simulation (sec. 2.2.3) assumes that PRA annuity payments partially offset traditional social security benefits, with the traditional PAYGO benefits reduced by ninety cents for each dollar of PRA annuity. Finally, we consider (in sec. 2.2.4) the case in which the PAYGO tax rate remains constant at 12.4 percent and calculate the path of PRA contributions that can maintain the currently projected benefits; this corresponds to a system of two-thirds PAYGO benefits and one-third investment-based benefits.

In section 2.3, we go from a world of certainty to one in which we recognize the uncertain character of the portfolio return and the volatility of the corporate profits on the incremental PRA capital. The corporate-tax collections are important because we use this revenue (in sec. 2.5) to finance conditional transfers to retirees that guarantee that retirement income will be at least as large as it would have been with the traditional PAYGO benefits implied by current law. Section 2.3 specifies the nature of the portfolio uncertainty and the capital productivity uncertainty that we take into account in the remainder of the paper and presents the historical evidence to parametize this stochastic environment.

In section 2.4, we introduce this uncertainty into the transition process and examine the implications of different PRA saving rates. For each of the PRA saving rates, we simulate ten thousand time series of benefits from the year 2000 to the year 2070. We summarize the implications of the uncertainty by presenting the distribution of these investment-based annuities (initially mixed with declining PAYGO benefits) relative to the PAYGO benefits implied by current law (to which we refer as the *benchmark* benefits) in 2010, 2020, 2030, 2050, and 2070.

The risk that retirees have an unacceptably low level of retirement income can be completely eliminated by a *conditional* PAYGO payment that fills any gap that may exist between the individual's PRA annuity and the basic benchmark benefit. Of course, this shifts the risk from retirees to concurrent taxpayers, that is, essentially to employees. Section 2.5 analyzes the extent of taxpayer risk in such an intergenerational guarantee.

Although we believe that the best way to understand the risks associated with the investment-based plans is to look at the distribution of possible outcomes, we provide explicit expected-utility-function evaluations in section 2.6 for the basic PRA plans with and without government guarantees.

Sections 2.4–2.6 focus on the transition to a system that is completely investment based, that is, that has completely eliminated any PAYGO component. Analyzing this limiting case provides a useful benchmark because it involves more risk than a mixed system that permanently combines defined benefits financed by government revenue with investment-based PRA annuities.[1] But, as a practical matter, the public policy interest in the United States (as well as in Sweden, Australia, and elsewhere) focuses on a mixed system that combines PAYGO and investment-based elements. In section 2.7, we analyze a mixed system in which the PAYGO component provides in the long run a benefit equal to about two-thirds of the projected benchmark benefit. We focus on this level of defined benefit because the PAYGO tax required to pay such a benefit is approximately equal to the current 12.4 percent payroll tax. Since preventing an increase in the payroll tax or a decrease in projected benefits is a stated goal of current U.S. public policy, this is a particularly interesting case to consider.

We begin our analysis of this mixed system in section 2.7 with the assumption that there is no additional guarantee to retirees, that is, that they are guaranteed to receive the benefits that can be financed with a 12.4 percent payroll tax but bear the risk of the uncertain return associated with the PRA annuities. We then consider the implications of adding a conditional PAYGO benefit of the type considered in section 2.5.

2.1   The Social Security Simulation Model

Our analysis is based on an extended and updated version of the simple accounting model developed in Feldstein and Samwick (1997, 1998a, 1998b). The model is now calibrated so that, with the current social security rules, it closely approximates the basic time series of benefits, revenues, and trust fund assets predicted in the 1998 social security trustees report (Board of Trustees 1998).[2]

---

1. A tax-financed defined-benefit plan is of course also subject to the political risk that benefits will be reduced by legislation (see McHale, chap. 7 in this volume).
2. The earlier papers all used the 1995 social security trustees report and assumed retirement at age sixty-five. In keeping with current law, we now assume that the "normal retire-

The unit of analysis in these simulations is the individual. Benefits for spouses and survivors, as well as disability benefits, are subsumed in the individual benefit projections in a way that satisfies the aggregate annual cost projections of the Social Security Administration. We incorporate the actual current age structure of the population, the Census Bureau projections of future births through 2050, and the projected cohort-specific life tables for individuals born through that year. To reflect the net inflow of immigrants, we scale up the projected population at every age to coincide with the aggregate population projections of the Social Security Administration.

The simulations simplify by assuming that individuals enter the labor force at age twenty-one and work until they retire at the normal retirement age (or until death if that occurs sooner). Since not everyone in the population actually works during those years, we adjust the labor force participation rate to obtain the number of covered workers in each year specified in the Social Security Administration projections.

We use the historic data for average taxable earnings in covered employment in years before 1998, as given in the *1997 Social Security Annual Statistical Supplement.* We follow the intermediate assumption in the 1998 social security trustees report (Board of Trustees 1998) that the average real wage rises at 0.9 percent per year in the future. The movements in the average real wage reflect the changing age structure of the labor force as well as the overall rate of increase in age-specific wages. More specifically, on the basis of the pattern of covered earnings by age as reported in the *1997 Social Security Annual Statistical Supplement,* we assume that annual earnings rise at $g + 3$ percent for individuals under age thirty-five, at $g + 1$ percent for individuals between thirty-five and forty-five, and at $g - 1.5$ percent for those over forty-five, where the value of g for each year is chosen to make the overall rise in wages equal to the historic record before 1998 and to the projected 0.9 percent annual rise after 1998.

Each individual employee is required to contribute a fraction of each year's earnings (up to the current ceiling on taxable earnings) to a PRA.[3] In the nonstochastic simulations with which we begin our analysis, the investments in the PRAs are assumed to earn a real logarithmic rate of return of 5.5 percent. As we describe in more detail in section 2.3, the average real log rate of return on a fund invested 60 percent in the Standard and Poor's portfolio of common stock and 40 percent in a portfolio of corporate bonds during the postwar period through 1995 was 5.9 percent.[4] We reduce this return by 0.4 percentage points for administrative

---

ment age" is sixty-five for individuals born before 1941. Those born in 1941 and later retire at age sixty-six, while those born in 1958 and later retire at age sixty-seven.

3. The deposit to the PRA could come instead from the individual's employer or from the government, a distinction that we do not pursue here.

4. Including the more recent period would increase this rate of return.

costs to produce a net real log rate of return of 5.5 percent. Although this mean log rate of return corresponds to an expected money rate of return of 6.5 percent,[5] we make the conservative assumption in this section (since we are not dealing with risk explicitly) that the real money rate of return is just 5.5 percent.

At retirement, each individual's PRA balance is used to purchase a variable annuity that invests in the same sixty-forty mix of stocks and bonds and therefore has the same 5.5 percent expected real rate of return.[6] If an individual dies before reaching retirement age, the funds in his PRA are divided among the surviving employees. As we noted above, survivor benefits are implicitly included in the benefit calculations.[7]

The 5.9 percent real log return before administrative expenses is the return earned by "untaxed" portfolio investors after the companies have paid corporate and property taxes to the federal, state, and local governments. The full rate of return earned on incremental capital before all taxes during this same period was substantially higher, approximately 8.5 percent (Poterba 1998). We return below to the implications of this for the taxes collected on incremental capital but not included in the return earned on PRA accounts.

We follow the social security trustees in assuming that the real return on the government bonds in the social security trust fund will decline gradually from the current level to a 2.8 percent real interest rate in the future. This is also a conservative assumption (although not a very important one given the relative size of the trust fund) because the Treasury inflation-protected securities now provide a real rate of return of 3.7 percent.

Because we are interested in total benefit payments and not in their distribution by income and family type, we base our calculations on average taxable earnings in each year and do not distinguish income levels or family structures. Although we therefore cannot apply the actual social security benefit rules, we can calculate average benefits under current social security law by attributing an implicit rate of return on the taxes paid by individuals in each birth cohort. The cohort-specific real rates of return of current and future retirees that we apply to these taxes are modifications of earlier estimates by Boskin et al. (1987); their estimates, which were for single-earner couples, have been adjusted to produce aggregate benefit amounts that coincide with the trustees' projections of the benefits implied by the current law for future years:

5. With the historic standard deviation of 0.125 and the assumption that the log returns are normally distributed, the corresponding "level" or "money" rate of return is 6.5 percent; i.e., if r is the log rate of return, and $E(r) = 0.055$, while the standard deviation of r is 0.125, normality implies that $E[e^r] = e^{E[r]+0.5\sigma^2} = 1.065$.

6. We describe the nature of variable annuities in detail in sec. 2.3 below.

7. An alternative assumption would be to permit preretirement bequests. Permitting such bequests reduces the funds available to survivors at retirement by about 14 percent. For more on this and related aspects of bequests, see Feldstein and Ranguelova (forthcoming).

Year of Birth	Before 1915	1915	1930	1945	1960	1975	After 1990
Real rate of return (%)	7.0	5.41	2.42	1.62	1.44	1.29	1.08

We linearly interpolate between these values to get cohort-specific rates of return for all birth years between 1915 and 1990.

Even with the lower rates of return for younger workers implied by this procedure, the projected benefits cannot be financed by the existing 12.4 percent OASDI tax rate because of the changing age structure of the population. The changing demographics cause the trust fund to be exhausted in the year 2032. Maintaining the projected benefits implied by current law (the benchmark benefits) would require raising the PAYGO tax from 12.4 to nearly 19 percent in the long run. The rapid aging of the population associated with the baby-boom generation would raise the tax rate required to fund concurrent benefits to more than 17 percent by the year 2035.

2.2 A Nonstochastic Transition from PAYGO
to Investment-Based Pensions

In this section, we begin by describing a feasible path from the existing PAYGO tax-supported system to a system that is eventually fully investment based and receives no tax support. During the transition, this requires a combination of PAYGO taxes and PRA saving deposits. We show that the transition can be achieved with an initial PRA saving deposit of 3 percent of earnings (up to the social security taxable maximum), bringing the combination of payroll taxes and PRA saving to 15.4 percent of taxable earnings. This combined amount eventually declines as the PRA annuities reduce the need for the PAYGO benefits. This decline occurs even though the aging of the population would require a rapidly rising payroll-tax rate if the pure tax-financed system continued. By the year 2070, the investment-based system can produce the "benchmark" level of benefits with a 4.25 percent PRA saving rate instead of the 18.7 percent payroll tax that would be required in a PAYGO system. This low PRA saving rate could continue for the indefinite future if the basic demographic and economic characteristics of the economy remained unchanged at the levels that they reached in 2070; improvements in mortality after that time would, however, require increases in the PRA saving rate.

There are a variety of different possible transitions that can take the system from where it is today to a fully investment-based system. The path that we analyze constrains the total retirement benefits in each year—that is, the sum of the traditional PAYGO benefit and the PRA annuity—to be at least as large as the benchmark benefits implied for future years by current law.[8] More specifically, for each cohort, as long as some PAYGO benefits are being paid, the sum of the PAYGO benefit and the PRA annuity is constrained to be exactly equal to the benchmark benefit. When the PAYGO benefit becomes zero, the PRA annuities may exceed the benchmark benefit (because the excess cannot be offset by reducing the PAYGO benefit further). The trust fund is constrained to remain positive in every year. In order to allow the PAYGO taxes to adjust smoothly, we do not impose requirements on the path of the trust fund other than that it remain positive.

The transition is assumed to begin in the year 2000. In that year, all employees from age twenty-one through age sixty-four deposit 3 percent of their wages up to the maximum taxable earnings (or have it deposited by employers or the government). The funds in the PRA account receive a 5.5 percent real rate of return. In the next year (2001), those who turn sixty-five and retire receive a very small PRA annuity.[9] Because of the small PRA annuity, the total retirement benefit of these new retirees (i.e., the sum of the regular PAYGO benefit and the PRA annuity) can be maintained at its benchmark level with a smaller PAYGO benefit. This permits the payroll tax to be reduced slightly while maintaining the initial path of the trust fund. In each successive year, the number of retirees with PRA annuities increases, and the average total value of their annuities increases because the retirees have had more years in which to accumulate PRA balances. The required PAYGO benefits and associated taxes therefore decrease over time. This reduction in the PAYGO tax permits the mandatory PRA saving rate to be increased without raising the combined burden of the two.

We can summarize the growth equation for the PRA balance as

$$(1) \qquad A(s) = 1.055 \cdot A(s - 1) + \alpha(s) \cdot W(s) - \text{ANN}(s),$$

whereas $A(s)$ is the value of the PRA balance, the 1.055 growth factor reflects the real rate of return (0.055), $\alpha(s)$ is the saving rate at time s, $W(s)$ is the wage income at time s, and $\text{ANN}(s)$ is the annuity withdrawal at time s.

Table 2.1 shows the evolution of the transition process. All the figures in rows 1–10 are expressed as percentages of taxable earnings (i.e., earn-

8. We emphasize that at this point our analysis is nonstochastic. We are really constraining the sum of the PAYGO benefit and the nonstochastic PRA annuity to be at least as large as the benchmark benefit.

9. As a practical matter, the annuity benefits after just one year of PRA contribution would be so small relative to the administrative costs that it would be more sensible to exclude everyone over some age (say fifty-five) from participating in the transition or to allow them to receive their accumulated PRA balances at retirement as a lump sum with no reduction in their regular social security benefits. To simplify the description and analysis, we do not make either modification.

Table 2.1   Transition Path of Tax Rates, PRA Contributions, and Annuities (all figures are expressed as % of taxable earnings)

	2000	2010	2020	2030	2050	2070
1. Tax rate with PAYGO system	12.40	12.40	12.40	12.40	17.29	18.70
2. Benchmark benefits	10.96	11.72	14.50	17.14	17.16	18.55
3. Trust fund with PAYGO system	25.46	40.95	39.57	6.66	0.00	0.00
4. PRA saving deposits	3.00	4.25	4.25	4.25	4.25	4.25
5. PRA annuities	0.00	0.20	1.35	4.05	13.02	19.80
6. PAYGO tax rate in transition	12.40	11.15	11.15	11.15	5.65	0.00
7. PAYGO tax rate + PRA saving rate	15.40	15.40	15.40	15.40	9.90	4.25
8. PAYGO benefits + PRA annuities	10.96	11.72	14.50	17.14	17.51	20.00
9. Trust fund	25.46	36.55	28.49	8.13	18.88	3.03
10. PRA asset balances	3.00	44.75	111.09	191.47	329.71	367.77
11. Covered earnings in billions of 1998 dollars	3,528.24	4,096.18	4,610.91	5,077.32	6,287.71	7,634.87

ings up to the maximum amount taxed by social security); aggregate taxable earnings in billions of 1998 dollars are shown in row 11.

Row 1 shows the tax rate implied by the current unfunded system. We assume that the social security payroll-tax rate would remain at its current 12.4 percent level until it becomes necessary to raise the tax rate in order to pay the benchmark level of benefits (shown in row 2 as a percentage of taxable earnings). In the early years, the tax at the current 12.4 percent is more than the amount needed to pay the benchmark benefits, and the original trust fund grows. But, after a relatively few years, the benefits exceed the revenue raised by a 12.4 percent tax. In 2020, for example, the benefits are 14.5 percent of taxable earnings, requiring a transfer from the trust fund balance to make up the 2.1 percent of taxable earnings difference between the benefits and the tax collections.[10]

The trust fund initially grows because payroll-tax receipts exceed benefit payments. It continues to grow briefly even when benefits exceed taxes because of the interest earned on its assets and the inflow of the tax on social security benefits that the Treasury transfers to the trust fund. But, even with this supplementary income, the trust fund is exhausted by 2032. This is shown in row 3. At this point, the tax rate in row 1 is raised to be equal to the benefits in row 2. By 2070, the required tax in the pure PAYGO system is 18.7 percent of taxable earnings; since these earnings are approximately 36 percent of GDP in that year, this corresponds to 7.4 percent of GDP.

Row 4 shows the PRA saving deposits, also expressed as a percentage

10. The transfer from the trust fund requires the trust fund to sell bonds to the public, increasing the unified budget deficit or reducing the unified budget surplus.

of taxable earnings (up to the maximum taxable earnings limit). These deposits start at 3.0 percent of taxable earnings for the first seven years (2000–2006) and then jump to 4.25 percent of taxable earnings in 2007, the level at which they remain. As successive birth cohorts reach retirement age, they receive PRA annuities. These annuities, shown in row 5, rise rapidly as the number of retired cohorts increases and as the PRA annuity per cohort rises in recognition of the greater number of years that each successive cohort had been contributing to the PRA accounts. The PRA annuities rise from 1.3 percent of taxable earnings in 2020 to 4.1 percent of taxable earnings in 2030, 13.0 percent of taxable earnings in 2050, and 19.8 percent of taxable earnings in 2070.

The PAYGO benefits are reduced dollar for dollar in response to the rising PRA annuities in a way that keeps the sum equal to the original benchmark benefits as long as PAYGO benefits are positive. This permits the PAYGO tax rate to be reduced. The path of the PAYGO tax during the transition is shown in row 6. The initial 12.4 percent tax rate is reduced in 2010 to 11.15 percent and remains at this level until 2039. It is then reduced by 0.5 percent of taxable earnings each year until it reaches 5.15 percent of taxable earnings in 2051. After that, it declines at 1 percent of taxable earnings per year until it is 0.15 percent of taxable earnings in 2056 and zero thereafter. After that, the income of the trust fund is sufficient to finance the remaining PAYGO obligations.

The combined PAYGO tax and the PRA deposit rate is shown in row 7. In the beginning of the transition, the combination rises from the current 12.4 percent PAYGO tax to 15.4 percent. It remains at this level in 2007, when the PAYGO tax is cut to 11.15 percent at the same time that the PRA deposit rate increases from 3.0 to 4.25 percent. Since the PRA saving rate remains permanently at 4.25 percent, the combined total begins to fall in 2040, when the PAYGO tax rate begins to decline. In 2045, the PAYGO tax is down to 8.15 percent, bringing the combined total back down to 12.40 percent of taxable earnings, the initial PAYGO tax. In contrast, the pure PAYGO system would require a 17.27 percent tax in that year to support the same level of benefits. While the pure PAYGO tax rate would rise after that year, the combined PAYGO and PRA rate falls from 12.4 percent in 2045 to 9.9 percent in 2050 and to 4.25 percent in 2057 and all subsequent years.

After the PAYGO tax rate has been reduced to zero (in 2057), further increases in the PRA annuities are reflected in a higher level of total benefits (the sum of the PAYGO benefit and the PRA annuity, shown in row 8). By 2070, the ratio of the PRA benefit to the benchmark benefit (shown in row 2) is 1.07.

The accumulated PRA assets are shown in row 9. This rises from 45 percent of taxable earnings in 2010 to 3.7 times taxable earnings in the year 2070. As a percentage of GDP, this represents a rise from about 18 percent of GDP in 2010 to about 1.5 times GDP in 2070. Since the capital stock is about three times GDP, this can also be expressed as a 6 percent rise in the capital stock after ten years and a 50 percent rise in the capital stock after seventy years.[11]

For information, we show in row 10 the level of the government social security trust fund. This could, of course, be eliminated completely once the PAYGO benefits become zero.

Finally, row 11 shows the covered taxable earnings, expressed in 1998 dollars.

2.2.1 Incremental Corporate-Tax Revenue and Supplemental Saving Deposits

The calculations summarized in table 2.1 assume that the real rate of return on PRA saving is 5.5 percent. Although this has been the historic mean log return to "nontaxable" portfolio investors on the sixty-forty portfolio investment (net of the assumed 0.40 percentage point administrative cost), it is substantially less than the real pretax marginal rate of return on additions to the corporate capital stock. The primary reason for the difference is the taxes collected by federal, state, and local governments.

The national income and product account data analyzed by Poterba (1998) imply that, during the years 1959–96, the real pretax marginal product of capital in the nonfinancial corporate sector was 8.5 percent. Of this, Poterba estimates that the federal government collected 2.2 percentage points in corporate profit taxes (an effective tax rate of 26 percent).[12] State and local governments took an additional 0.3 percentage points in profits taxes and 0.9 percentage points in property taxes. These taxes imply that the net return to portfolio investors during those years would be 5.1 percent. Although this is substantially less than the return to the sixty-forty stock-bond portfolio that we discussed above, it is the same as the mean-level return of that stock-bond portfolio for the years of the Poterba sample. This suggests that the Poterba sample of years may have had a lower than normal rate of profitability for the postwar period

11. The large long-run rise in the capital stock would have general equilibrium effects on the marginal product of capital and on real wages that we do not take into account here. A Cobb-Douglas technology, an unchanged path of human capital, the absence of international capital flows, and a 25 percent capital share imply that the marginal product of capital would decline in the very long run by about 25 percent (e.g., from 8.5 to 6.4 percent). This decline would be offset to the extent that the lower marginal tax rates induced a higher labor supply and the lower interest rate induced a greater investment in human capital. We do not pursue such general equilibrium effects here.

12. A 26 percent effective tax rate is substantially less than the statutory corporate-profits-tax rate, which is now 35 percent and which has had a higher average during the sample years. The difference reflects the deduction of state and local property and income taxes in the calculation of federal tax liability and the combination of depreciation allowances and interest deductions.

as a whole. We will nevertheless make the conservative estimate of a federal corporate-tax collection equal to 2.0 percent of the incremental capital stock.

There are three potential uses of this additional corporate-tax revenue. The most direct is to use it to finance a portion of the PRA saving deposits instead of requiring individuals and/or their employers to pay for this or using other government revenue for this purpose. A second alternative is to supplement the 5.5 percent return, raising it to 7.5 percent. Finally, in section 2.5, after the stochastic simulations have been introduced, we show how the additional corporate-tax revenue can be used to finance a benefit guarantee to retirees.

Since we take the incremental corporate-tax revenue to be 2 percent of the incremental corporate stock, we must estimate the increase in the national corporate capital stock that results from the PRAs. In principle, this requires looking beyond the PRA program itself to see how the PRA accounts might alter other private saving, something that would change over time. In the early years of the PRA program, disposable income would decline, giving individuals an incentive to reduce other saving in order to maintain a more level time path of consumption. The quantitative importance of this is, however, likely to be small since the vast majority of Americans have too little in financial assets to do any such offsetting reductions. Moreover, some individuals might be stimulated by participating in the PRA program to recognize the value of saving and therefore to increase their other saving. As the PRA system matures, the reduction in the combined total of the payroll tax and the PRA deposits (shown as the difference between row 1 and row 7 of table 2.1) would raise disposable income during working years with virtually no change in retirement incomes, inducing individuals to save more during their working years in order to smooth consumption over time. That increase in saving would make national saving rise. In our calculations, we ignore such possible changes in individual consumption and saving and assume that the nation's capital stock increases by the net inflows to the PRA accounts plus the PRA capital income (interest, dividends, and retained earnings) of those accounts.

In the current nonstochastic model, this growth of the incremental capital stock should be well measured by the market value of the PRA assets.[13] The aggregate value of the assets in the PRA accounts grows initially because the PRA deposits exceed the annuity withdrawals. But, after the early years, the primary source of the increase in the PRA asset value is the 5.5 percent return that is earned on the net assets in the PRA accounts,

---

13. In the next section, where we explicitly consider fluctuations in asset market values, we distinguish between the two and model the evolution of the incremental capital stock explicitly.

and the annuity payments eventually exceed the savings deposits. This is shown in rows 4 and 5 of table 2.1.

Using 2 percent of the incremental capital stock (i.e., the assumed additional federal corporate-tax receipts) to finance a portion of the PRA saving deposits, instead of requiring individuals and/or their employers to pay for this or using other government revenue for this purpose, has a small effect in the early years but a very substantial effect in the more distant future.[14] In 2010, the incremental corporate-tax revenue would be about $36 billion (at 1998 prices), or 0.9 percent of taxable earnings, permitting the additional PRA deposits to be reduced from 4.25 to 3.35 percent of taxable earnings.[15] But, by 2030, the incremental corporate tax revenue would be 3.83 percent of taxable earnings and would permit reducing the additional PRA deposit to 0.42 percent of taxable earnings, bringing the total from 15.5 to 11.67 percent of taxable earnings, less than the current pure PAYGO tax rate of 12.4 percent. In 2050, 2 percent of the incremental capital stock would be 6.60 percent of taxable earnings, more than enough to pay for all the 4.25 percent PRA deposit and to permit the PAYGO tax to be reduced from 5.65 to 4.30 percent. Eventually, in 2070, the incremental revenue would be 7.35 percent of taxable earnings; since there is no longer a PAYGO tax at that time and the PRA deposits are only 4.25 percent of taxable earnings, the extra corporate-tax revenue would finance the PRA program and leave 3.1 percent of taxable earnings for other uses.

We now consider the implication of an alternative use of these incremental corporate-tax funds: using this additional federal corporate-tax collection to supplement the return earned in the PRAs. More specifically, we assume that this additional corporate-tax revenue is divided among the PRA accounts in proportion to the asset value of those accounts. This raises the return on the assets in the PRA accounts from 5.5 to 7.5 percent, changing equation (1) to

$$(2) \qquad A(s) = 1.075 \cdot A(s-1) + \alpha(s) \cdot W(s) - \text{ANN}(s),$$

where $A(s)$ is the value of the PRA balance, the 1.075 growth factor reflects the real rate of return, $\alpha(s)$ is the PRA saving rate at time s, $W(s)$ is the wage income at time s, and $\text{ANN}(s)$ is the annuity withdrawal at time s.

The higher rate of return permits lower PRA saving rates to be consistent with the requirements that the benchmark benefits be financed, the trust fund remain solvent, and the PRA annuities eventually fully replace PAYGO benefits. Our calculations show that this can be satisfied with a constant 2.1 percent PRA deposit rate. The PAYGO tax drops from 12.40 to 11.40 percent in 2020 and stays at that level until 2028, when it drops

14. This is the approach used by Feldstein and Samwick (1998a).
15. These figures and others cited in this paragraph can be derived from row 10 of table 2.1.

Table 2.2   **Transition Path with Supplementary Savings Deposits (all figures are expressed as % of taxable earnings)**

	2000	2010	2020	2030	2050	2070
1. Tax rate with PAYGO system	12.40	12.40	12.40	12.40	17.29	18.70
2. Benchmark benefits	10.96	11.72	14.50	17.14	17.16	18.55
3. Trust fund with PAYGO system	25.46	40.95	39.57	6.66	0.00	0.00
4. PRA saving deposits	2.10	2.10	2.10	2.10	2.10	2.10
5. PRA annuities	0.00	0.16	1.11	3.58	13.41	20.06
6. PAYGO tax rate in transition	12.40	12.40	11.40	10.30	4.80	0.00
7. PAYGO tax rate + PRA saving rate	14.50	14.50	13.50	12.40	6.90	2.10
8. PAYGO benefits + PRA annuities	10.96	11.72	14.50	17.14	17.95	20.23
9. Trust fund	25.46	41.52	45.42	23.67	15.36	6.60
10. PRA asset balances	2.10	30.53	76.29	140.10	264.68	297.42
11. Covered earnings in billions of 1998 dollars	3,528.24	4,096.18	4,610.91	5,077.32	6,287.71	7,634.87

Note: The supplementary saving deposits are equal to 2.0 percent of the PRA asset balances and effectively raise the rate of return from 5.5 to 7.5 percent.

by 1.1 percent to 10.3 percent. In 2028, the sum of the PAYGO tax rate and the PRA deposit rate is back to 12.40 percent. The PAYGO tax rate stays at 10.3 percent until 2040, when it gets phased out at a rate of 0.5 percent per year. The PAYGO tax is therefore gone by 2060, and the only cost is the 2.1 percent PRA deposit.

These results are summarized in table 2.2, which follows the same format as table 2.1. The first three rows of table 2.2 are the same as in table 2.1. The PRA saving deposits in row 4 are substantially smaller, but the PRA annuities are larger after 2045. The combined PAYGO tax rate and PRA saving deposit is lower than 12.4 percent.

2.2.2   Implications of a Risk-Free Investment

Since we are ignoring risk at this point in our analysis, it is sensible to consider what a transition path might look like if the rate of return is reduced from the 5.5 percent mean real return on a debt-equity portfolio to the real return available on inflation-protected U.S. Treasury bonds, that is, the Treasury inflation-protected securities (TIPS). Such investments have no default risk and no risk of inflation erosion. For an investor who holds them to maturity, there is no market risk due to interest-rate fluctuations. Since the TIPS currently have a 3.7 percent real yield at a variety of maturities, we use that rate of return in these risk-free-return calculations.

Achieving a transition to a completely investment-based system with this lower real rate of return requires starting with a higher PRA saving

Table 2.3   **Transition Path with 3.7 Percent Risk-Free Rate of Return (all figures are expressed as % of taxable earnings)**

	2000	2010	2020	2030	2050	2070
1. Tax rate with PAYGO system	12.40	12.40	12.40	12.40	17.29	18.70
2. Benchmark benefits	10.96	11.72	14.50	17.14	17.16	18.55
3. Trust fund with PAYGO system	25.46	40.95	39.57	6.66	0.00	0.00
4. PRA saving deposits	5.00	6.00	6.00	7.00	8.00	8.00
5. PRA annuities	0.00	0.25	1.51	4.05	11.08	17.42
6. PAYGO tax rate in transition	12.40	11.40	11.40	10.40	9.40	0.00
7. PAYGO tax rate + PRA saving rate	17.40	17.40	17.40	17.40	17.40	8.00
8. PAYGO benefits + PRA annuities	10.96	11.72	14.50	17.14	17.16	18.61
9. Trust fund	25.46	40.87	37.49	21.87	18.79	22.43
10. PRA asset balances	5.00	61.22	136.28	215.06	366.24	440.32
11. Covered earnings in billions of 1998 dollars	3,528.24	4,096.18	4,610.91	5,077.32	6,287.71	7,634.87

Note: The 3.7 percent real rate of return implicit in these calculations is the present yield on Treasury inflation-protected securities of varying maturities.

rate than the one used in the simulations with 5.5 and 7.5 percent real rates of return. A feasible solution begins with a PRA saving rate of 5.0 percent (instead of the 3.0 percent in table 2.1) and gradually increases this to 8.0 percent while reducing the PAYGO tax rate. The specific path is summarized in table 2.3, which follows the same format as tables 2.1 and 2.2.

The PAYGO tax rate declines from the initial 12.4 percent to 11.4 percent in 2010, 10.40 percent in 2030, 9.40 percent in 2050, and zero after 2061. The combined PAYGO tax rate and PRA saving deposit (row 7) therefore remain at 17.4 percent until after 2050 but decline to 8.00 percent permanently by 2070.

Thus, even with a risk-free rate of return of only 3.7 percent, the investment-based system can support the benchmark level of benefits with a long-run saving rate of only 8.0 percent instead of the PAYGO tax rate of 18.7 percent. Even in this least-favorable case of maximum risk aversion, the investment-based approach permits using a 5 percent higher saving plus tax rate in the transition years in order to reduce the equilibrium saving plus tax rate permanently by more than 10 percent of covered earnings.

An individual who is prepared to accept some risk of lower benefits in retirement can achieve the same expected benefits with a substantially lower long-term saving rate. Before examining that possibility, we consider the implications of a partial integration of the PRA annuities and social security benefits.

2.2.3 Partial Integration of PRA Annuities and Social Security Benefits

In the transitions shown in tables 2.1–2.3, the traditional PAYGO social security benefits were effectively reduced by a dollar for every dollar of PRA annuity that individuals received. An alternative integration rule for integrating social security PAYGO benefits and the PRA annuities that might be preferred when uncertainty is recognized (and therefore when individuals have some choice about their investments) reduces regular social security benefits by less than one dollar for every dollar of annuity income.[16] When the PRA annuities are uncertain, this partial integration reduces the risk to retirees by making the PAYGO benefits more when the PRA annuities are smaller.[17]

We now study such a partial integration plan in the nonstochastic context to provide a framework for understanding the subsequent stochastic results. We use a 90 percent integration rule that provides that the regular PAYGO benefits are reduced by ninety cents for every dollar of PRA annuity.[18] We again assume a 5.5 percent rate of return and make no allowance for the possible use of the incremental corporate-tax revenue. This option provides substantially higher benefits to retirees and therefore reduces the cost of the PAYGO program by less than the analysis shown in table 2.1.

With the assumed 5.5 percent real rate of return, it is therefore necessary to have higher PRA deposits than with the dollar-for-dollar integration rule of table 2.1. There are again many possibilities. We constrain the choice by imposing the requirement that the combined PAYGO tax and PRA deposit not rise by more than 3 percent of taxable earnings, that is, that the combined amount not exceed 15.4 percent of taxable earnings. With that condition, a feasible path begins with a 3 percent PRA deposit from 2000 to 2019, rising to 4 percent from 2020 to 2032, and then to 5 percent after that. Table 2.4 presents the transition paths of the basic variables for this case.

16. Alternatively, the simulations that we have already discussed could be thought of as providing a fixed level of PAYGO benefits in each year with individuals receiving the uncertain PRA annuities as a supplement with the PAYGO benefit levels selected so that, with the expected return, the two provide the benchmark benefits.

17. Feldstein and Samwick (1998a) analyzed a plan in which the PRA contributions equal to 2 percent of taxable earnings are financed by the government (rather than by mandatory saving) and each dollar of annuity that retirees receive reduces their regular social security benefits by seventy-five cents. That analysis showed that PRA deposits equal to 2 percent of covered earnings and a 5.5 percent real rate of return would permit the projected level of benchmark benefits to be paid indefinitely with no increase in the existing 12.4 percent PAYGO taxable-earnings tax. Moreover, by the year 2030, the corporate-tax revenue generated by the incremental capital would be enough to finance fully the PRA deposits equal to 2 percent of covered earnings.

18. Alternatively, this can be interpreted as reducing the PRA annuity by 90 percent as long as that reduction does not exceed the value of the PAYGO benefits.

Table 2.4   Transition Path with 90 Percent Integration Rule (all figures are expressed as % of taxable earnings)

	2000	2010	2020	2030	2050	2070
1. Tax rate with PAYGO system	12.40	12.40	12.40	12.40	17.29	18.70
2. Benchmark benefits	10.96	11.72	14.50	17.14	17.16	18.55
3. Trust fund with PAYGO system	25.46	40.95	39.57	6.66	0.00	0.00
4. PRA saving deposits	3.00	3.00	4.00	4.00	5.00	5.00
5. PRA annuities	0.00	0.19	1.16	3.40	11.30	19.66
6. PAYGO tax rate in transition	12.40	12.40	11.40	11.40	8.90	0.00
7. PAYGO tax rate + PRA saving rate	15.40	15.40	15.40	15.40	13.90	5.00
8. PAYGO benefits + PRA annuities	10.96	11.74	14.62	17.49	18.29	20.92
9. Trust fund	25.46	41.55	45.28	24.16	12.92	12.77
10. PRA asset balances	3.00	39.48	89.85	160.56	315.31	405.71
11. Covered earnings in billions of 1998 dollars	3,528.24	4,096.18	4,610.91	5,077.32	6,287.71	7,634.87

Note: The 90 percent integration rule provides that each individual receives a PAYGO benefit equal to the benchmark level minus 90 percent of the individual's PRA annuity.

2.2.4   A Mixed System with a Permanent 12.4 Percent Earnings Tax and a 75 Percent Integration Rule

We now consider the more realistic case of a mixed system that provides retirement income through a combination of PAYGO tax-financed benefits and individual investment-based annuities. We fix the PAYGO tax rate at its current 12.4 percent level and leave it there for all future years.

We also have a constant rate of saving in the PRA accounts equal to 2.3 percent of covered earnings. We follow a 75 percent integration rule in which the traditional social security benefits in each year are reduced by 75 percent of the PRA annuity. Stated differently, 75 percent of the PRA annuity is paid to the Social Security Administration to help defray the cost of the social security annuities. The combination of the (net) PAYGO benefit and the (net) PRA annuity is therefore equal to the benchmark social security benefit plus 25 percent of the PRA annuity. The balance in the social security trust fund adjusts to reflect the difference between the benefits paid and the combination of the 12.4 percent payroll-tax revenue and the 75 percent of the PRA annuity.

These results are shown in the standard format in table 2.5. Rows 4 and 5 describe the simple combination of the 12.4 percent PAYGO tax and the 2.3 percent PRA deposit rate. Row 6 shows the gross PRA annuities (i.e., before any allowance for the 75 percent integration effect) that would result from the 2.3 percent PRA deposits. These annuities are less than 1 percent of covered earnings in 2020 but rise to 2.54 percent in 2030, 7.65 percent in 2050, and 10.75 percent in 2070.

Individuals receive the sum of their promised benchmark benefits (row

Table 2.5   **Transition Path with Mixed PAYGO and Investment-Based System: 12.4 Percent PAYGO Tax, 2.3 Percent PRA Deposits, and 75 Percent Benefit Integration (all figures are expressed as % of taxable earnings)**

	2000	2010	2020	2030	2050	2070
1. Tax rate with PAYGO system	12.40	12.40	12.40	12.40	17.29	18.70
2. Benchmark benefits	10.96	11.72	14.50	17.14	17.16	18.55
3. Trust fund with PAYGO system	25.46	40.95	39.57	6.66	0.00	0.00
4. PRA saving deposits	2.30	2.30	2.30	2.30	2.30	2.30
5. PRA annuities (Gross)	0.00	0.14	0.89	2.54	7.65	10.75
6. PAYGO tax rate in transition	12.40	12.40	12.40	12.40	12.40	12.40
7. PAYGO tax rate + PRA saving rate	14.70	14.70	14.70	14.70	14.70	14.70
8. PAYGO benefits + PRA annuities	10.96	11.76	14.72	17.78	19.07	21.24
9. Trust fund	25.45	41.33	43.85	25.31	3.13	42.74
10. PRA asset balances	2.30	30.27	63.30	112.82	183.58	199.92
11. Covered earnings in billions of 1998 dollars	3,528.24	4,096.18	4,610.91	5,077.32	6,287.71	7,634.87

2) and 25 percent of these gross PRA annuities. Equivalently, the individuals receive the entire gross PRA annuities plus the benchmark benefits reduced by 75 percent of those annuities. The combined sum is shown in row 8. In the early years of the transition, the combined total is only slightly greater than the benchmark benefits. But, by 2050, the benefits are increased by nearly 2 percent of earnings, an 11 percent rise in total benefits. By 2070, the combined benefits are equal to 21.24 percent of earnings, or 15 percent higher than they would be under the pure PAYGO system.

The partially investment-based character of this system makes the benefit increase possible despite the fact that the combination of the PAYGO tax rate and the PRA saving rate is limited to 14.7 percent instead of rising to the 18.70 percent rate required in the pure PAYGO system.

The social security trust fund (row 9) remains positive throughout the seventy-year simulation period. The value of the trust fund remains higher because the PRA benefits reduce the need for PAYGO benefits. Although the trust fund drops to a low of less than 1 percent of covered earnings in 2046, it then recovers to 3.13 percent of covered earnings in 2050 and 42.74 percent of covered earnings in 2070.

2.3 Uncertain Returns to Portfolio Investments and to the Incremental Capital Stock

A primary concern in any analysis of the desirability of shifting from a tax-financed defined-benefit plan to an investment-based defined-contribution plan is the inherent uncertainty of the returns earned on portfolio investments. This uncertainty affects the accumulation during the preretirement years as well as the return on the variable annuity that we assume is used in the postretirement years.

In addition to this portfolio uncertainty, there is also uncertainty about the amount of corporate-tax revenue that the government would collect on the incremental capital that results from the PRA saving. This is particularly relevant if that tax revenue is used to supplement or finance contributions to PRAs or to finance a government guarantee of minimum benefits.

This section describes the stochastic properties of these two sources of uncertainty that we incorporate in the analysis that follows in the rest of the paper. There are of course other sources of uncertainty that affect both tax-financed plans and investment-based plans that we do not explore here, including uncertain mortality rates,[19] birth- and immigration rates, and shifts in employment and wage rates.

2.3.1 The Uncertain Investment Return

Our analysis assumes that each individual deposits a specified fraction of each year's taxable wage income in a PRA and that the funds in that account are invested in a portfolio that is continually rebalanced to maintain 60 percent equities and 40 percent debt, approximately the debt-equity ratio of U.S. corporations.[20] At retirement, these accumulated assets are used to finance a variable annuity that we assume is invested in the same stock-bond mixture as the PRA balances were during the preretirement years.

Before looking at the stochastic specification of the portfolio returns, we describe the nature of the variable annuity. The annuity benefit that is paid in the first year of retirement, age sixty-seven (on an annuity purchased at age sixty-six), reflects the PRA assets at the beginning of the individual's sixty-sixth year, the expected mortality rates at all future ages, and the assumption that the future return will be equal to the constant expected rate of return. The annual benefits are then adjusted each year to reflect changes in the value of the annuity account that result from the difference between the realized and the expected rate of return.

More specifically, after one year, the size of the variable-annuity payment is increased or decreased from the initial value in proportion to the change in the market value of the PRA annuity assets relative to the market value that would have prevailed had the expected rate of return actually occurred. A similar revision of the annual annuity payment occurs in each subsequent year.

To derive the explicit value of the variable annuity, consider the individuals in a particular birth cohort. Let the time index coincide with the age of the cohort so that N_t is the number of individuals alive at age t. Let A_{66}

---

19. We use expected mortality rates in our calculations but do not take into account the uncertainty or instability of those rates.
20. The analysis in this section draws on Feldstein and Ranguelova (forthcoming).

be the value of the PRA assets at the beginning of the sixty-sixth year, and let R be the expected annual real rate of return on the portfolio of assets used to finance the retirement annuity. The first annuity benefit is paid at the beginning of the individual's sixty-seventh year and annually thereafter. The cost at age sixty-six of a *fixed* real annuity of $1 for life (i.e., an annuity that starts with $1 and grows in proportion to the level of consumer prices) is the actuarial present value (APV) of that dollar with discount rate R:

$$\text{(3)} \qquad \text{APV} = \sum_{t=67}^{t=100} (N_t/N_{66})(1 + r)^{-(t-66)},$$

where we assume that all individuals alive at age ninety-nine die at the end of the one hundredth year.

Since the PRA account has assets equal to A_{66} when the annuity is established, the annuity payment that the individual would receive in the sixty-seventh year is $a_{67} = A_{66}/\text{APV}$ if the expected return of R is actually realized in the sixty-sixth year. More generally, if the expected return of R is realized in every future year, the individual would continue to receive that same annuity, and the accumulated assets at age sixty-six of all members of that birth cohort would be exhausted when the last member of the cohort dies at age one hundred.

In practice, of course, the actual rate of return varies from year to year. The annuity payments are adjusted in proportion to the annual changes in the asset value in such a way that the birth cohort's accumulated fund is still exhausted over the thirty-four-year retirement period. If R_t is the actual rate of increase of the asset value during year t, the asset value at the beginning of the cohort's sixty-seventh year is $A_{67} = A_{66}(1 + R_{66})$. The annuity paid in that year is therefore $a_{67} = (A_{66}/\text{APV})(1 + R_{66})/(1 + R)$. Similarly, the annuity at age sixty-eight reflects the changes in the market value of the assets during the sixty-sixth and sixty-seventh years: $a_{68} = a_{67}(1 + R_{67})/(1 + R) = (A_{66}/\text{APV})[(1 + R_{67})/(1 + R)][(1 + R_{66})/(1 + R)]$. The last payment to those who are one hundred years old is $a_{100} = a_{99}(1 + R_{99})/(1 + R)$. Note that, if the rate of return in each period is equal to the expected rate of return, the annuity remains constant at a_{67}.

Consider now the stochastic specification of the return, R_t, on the PRA assets and on the assets used to fund the variable annuity. Recall that the portfolio is 60 percent equity and 40 percent debt. We use the S&P500 index and a Salomon Brothers corporate bond index as proxies for the stock and bond investments. Both indices are assumed to follow a geometric random walk with drift. This implies that the log returns for each type of asset are serially independent and identically distributed with given mean and variance. Thus, if $p_e(s)$ and $p_b(s)$ are the log levels of the equity and bond indices, respectively, at time s, we assume

$$\text{(4)} \qquad p_e(s) = p_e(s - 1) + \mu_e + u_e(s)$$

and

(5) $$p_b(s) = p_b(s - 1) + \mu_b + u_b(s),$$

where $u_e \sim$ i.i.d. $N(0, \sigma_e^2)$ and $u_b \sim$ i.i.d. $N(0, \sigma_b^2)$. The covariance between the stock and the bond returns is σ_{eb}.

With a continuously compounded sixty-forty equity-debt portfolio, the log level of the overall portfolio would satisfy the following random walk if there were no additions or payments:[21]

(6) $$p(s) = p(s - 1) + \mu + u(s),$$

with $u \sim$ i.i.d. $N(0, \sigma^2)$. To derive the values of μ and σ^2, we use the lognormal property of the returns.

More specifically, if μ_i^* is the mean return on asset i in level form, the mean return on the sixty-forty portfolio is the weighted average $\mu^* = 0.6$ $\mu_e^* + 0.4\mu_b^*$. Because we assume the log returns to be normally distributed, $\mu_i^* = \mu_i + 0.5 \sigma_i^2$. This implies that

(7) $$\mu + 0.5\sigma^2 = 0.6(\mu_e + 0.5\sigma_e^2) + 0.4(\mu_b + 0.5\sigma_b^2),$$

where

(8) $$\sigma^2 = 0.36\sigma_e^2 + 0.16\sigma_b^2 + 0.48\sigma_{eb}.$$

From these two equations and the mean and variance of the log returns on stocks and bonds, we can derive the log return on the portfolio and the variance of that return.

The CRSP (Center for Research in Security Prices) data for the postwar period from 1946 through 1995 imply that, for stocks and bonds, the mean real log rates of return were, respectively, 7.1 and 3.3 percent.[22] The corresponding standard deviations were 16.6 percent for stocks and 10.4 percent for bonds. The covariance of the stock and bond returns was $\sigma_{eb} = 0.0081$. Taken together, these parameters imply a log average rate of return on the sixty-forty portfolio of 5.9 percent with a standard deviation of 12.5 percent.[23] We reduce the mean log return from 5.9 to 5.5 percent to reflect potential administrative costs.[24]

In the analysis that follows, we recognize that the adjusted mean real log return of 5.5 percent for the portfolio during the period 1946–95 is only an estimate of the relevant mean for future years. Our stochastic

21. The value of the PRA portfolio during the preretirement years is also increased by the individual's annual PRA savings.

22. The bond rate of return is based on the Salomon Brothers AAA bond returns adjusted to a more typical corporate bond yield by adding 2 percentage points.

23. The portfolio return changes very little if we use the longer time period 1926–95.

24. This estimate of the administrative cost may be compared with the cost of about 0.2 percent charged now in indexed equity funds by mutual fund companies like Vanguard and Fidelity. Bond funds generally have lower administrative charges.

simulation therefore uses a two-step procedure to simulate the uncertain future annual returns. For each of ten thousand simulations, we begin by generating a mean real log return on the portfolio from a normal distribution with a mean of 0.055 and a standard deviation of 0.0175, which is equal to the standard error of the estimated mean based on the number of years in the sample. We then use this estimated realization of the mean and the standard deviation of 0.125 to generate a seventy-one-year sequence of portfolio returns from the year 2000 to the year 2070. We repeat this ten thousand times.

Although equation (6) for $p(s)$ describes the way in which the log value of the PRA account would evolve during the accumulation years were there no external additions, in practice the actual individual PRA account is also augmented by the fraction α of the individual's wage and by the distributed share of the PRA balances of those members of the cohort who die during the year. We simulate this evolution at the level of the birth cohort (rather than of the individual) by

(9) $M(s) = [1 + R(s - 1)]M(s - 1) + \alpha w(s)N(s),$

where $M(s)$ is the aggregate PRA balance for the cohort as a whole, $R(s)$ is the rate of return in period s, $N(s)$ is the number of living members of the cohort, $w(s)$ is the average wage, and α is the share of wages saved and contributed to the PRA accounts. Since this equation is in level rather than log form, the value of $1 + R(s) = \exp[r(s)]$, where $r(s)$ is the log rate of return in period s implied by

(10) $r(s) = p(s) - p(s - 1) = \mu + u(s).$

With the standard deviation of 0.125 and the assumption that the log returns are normally distributed, the "level" or "money" rate of return is 6.9 percent before subtracting the administrative costs; that is, $E[1 + R(s)] = E[\exp(r(s))] = \exp[E(r(s)) + 0.5\,\sigma^2] = 1.069.$

2.3.2   The Uncertain Return on Incremental Capital

The value of the individual's PRA annuities depends on the value of the PRA account and therefore on the market return on stocks and bonds. In contrast, the government's incremental corporate-tax revenue depends on the size of the incremental capital stock and the profitability of that capital. In our nonstochastic analysis in section 2.2, we simplified by assuming that the size of the capital stock could be represented by the market value of the PRA account and that the corporate-tax revenue could be represented by 2 percent of the PRA assets.

We now consider a more realistic evolution of the size of the capital stock and of the profitability of the capital. Let $K(s)$ be the value of the increment to the capital stock in period s as a result of the PRA saving system begun at $s = 0$. The evolution of the incremental capital stock can be written

(11) $K(s) = \{1 + [1 - \tau][\mathbf{R}(s) - r\beta - \text{sltax}] + r\beta\}K(s - 1)$

$+ \alpha(s)W(s) - \text{ANN}(s),$

where $\mathbf{R}(s)$ is the real pretax return on capital in year s, r is the real interest rate paid by firms, β is the ratio of debt to capital, sltax is the state and local tax paid per dollar of capital, τ is the effective marginal federal corporate-tax rate on profits net of interest and of state and local tax payments, $\alpha(s)$ is the PRA saving deposit as a fraction of covered earnings [$W(s)$], and $\text{ANN}(s)$ is the annuity withdrawals in that year.

In this notation, $\mathbf{R}(s)K(s - 1)$ is the pretax incremental profits before interest expenses, that is, the product of the marginal product of capital and the size of the incremental capital stock. Since β is the ratio of debt to capital, $\beta K(s - 1)$ is the corporate debt, and $r\beta K(s - 1)$ is the real interest paid on that debt.[25] Since most of the state and local taxes are property taxes, we approximate the total state and local tax as a fraction of the property tax, sltax $K(s - 1)$. Since the corporate tax at rate τ is levied on profits net of interest, the profits after taxes and interest are $[1-\tau][\mathbf{R}(s) - r\beta - \text{sltax}]K(s - 1)$. The division of these net profits between dividends and retained earnings is not relevant in the current context because, since both accrue to the PRAs, there is no difference in their tax treatment or in their contribution to PRA assets and the associated capital stock. The other sources of change in the value of the capital stock are the addition of the PRA saving deposits, $\alpha(s)W(s)$, and the subtraction of the annuity payments, $\text{ANN}(s)$.

Since $\mathbf{R}(s)$ is not a financial rate of return but the actual year-to-year profitability at the company level,[26] the $\mathbf{R}(s)$ time series will not have the serial independence property of a financial return in an efficient market. Instead, $\mathbf{R}(s)$ will exhibit the serially correlated property of a business-cycle variable. We have used the annual values of $\mathbf{R}(s)$ recently developed by Poterba (1998) to estimate the parameters of an ARIMA process. After experimenting with a variety of specifications, we estimated the following specification:

(12) $\ln \mathbf{R}(s) = 0.017 + 0.793\mathbf{R}(s - 1) + 0.562e(s - 1) + e(s),$

where the stochastic innovation $e(s)$ has mean zero and standard deviation 0.006.

Although market efficiency implies that the innovations in the portfolio-

25. We simplify by ignoring inflation and, therefore, the difference between the real interest rate and the tax-deductible nominal interest rate. We take this into account, however, in the numerical value used for the corporate-tax rate.

26. Pretax capital income of the nonfinancial corporate sector is the sum of pretax profits, net interest payments, and the property and profits taxes paid to state and local governments. The capital is the sum of reproducible equipment and structures at reproduction cost plus the estimated market value of the land. For more detail on the nature of these estimates, see Poterba (1998) and Feldstein, Dicks-Mireaux, and Poterba (1983).

return process are serially independent, they can be contemporaneously correlated with the innovations in the profitability process. To simulate the simultaneous evolution of the PRA accounts and the corporate profits, we estimate the correlation between the residual in the corporate-profitability equation (i.e., $e[s]$ in eq. [12]) and the innovation in the log rate of return that drives the PRA fluctuations (i.e., $u[s]$ in eq. [10]). Since the estimated correlation is very small, just 0.024, we do not incorporate it in our simulations.

With the process specified in equation (12) for generating values of $\mathbf{R}(s)$, it is possible to calculate the additional federal corporate-profits tax associated with the incremental capital. We begin by generating ten thousand samples of the time vector of $\mathbf{R}(s)$ values for the years 2000–2070 and for each time vector of $\mathbf{R}(s)$ values, using equation (11) to calculate a corresponding $K(s)$ series. For this calculation, we use Poterba's estimate that the state and local taxes as a fraction of the capital stock are sltax = 0.012. We take the corporate debt-capital ratio to be $\beta = 0.4$, the same share of capital that we assume in our PRA portfolio and the average share of debt on corporate balance sheets. With a real rate of interest of $r = 0.033$, we have $r\beta = 0.0132$. Finally, Poterba's estimate that federal taxes were 2.2 percent of capital during this period implies that $\tau[R(s) - r\beta - \text{sltax}] = .022$ or, with $R = .085$, $r\beta = 0.0132$, and sltax = 0.012, that the effective rate of federal tax on this measure of taxable income was $\tau = 0.37$. We then calculate the corporate tax using the same $\mathbf{R}(s)$ values in

$$(13) \qquad \text{TAX}(s) = \tau[\mathbf{R}(s) - r\beta - \text{sltax}]K(s - 1).$$

With $\tau = 0.37$, this tax equation implies that federal tax revenue at the mean value of $\mathbf{R}(s) = 0.085$ is 2.2 percent of $K(s - 1)$ and therefore approximately 2.1 percent of $K(s)$.

2.4 Individual Risk in the Transition from PAYGO Pensions to Investment-Based Pensions

We are now ready to examine the probability distribution of retirement incomes during the transition from the existing system to a completely investment-based system. Our emphasis is on assessing the risk that the incomes provided in this way will be judged to be too low and seeing the sensitivity of this risk to different PRA saving rules. The current results thus extend the analysis of individual risk in Feldstein and Ranguelova (forthcoming, sec. 3). The earlier study looked just at the risks in a fully privatized system in the year 2070, when all retirees were assumed to have contributed to PRAs throughout their working life and to have only PRA annuities and no tax-financed PAYGO benefits. In the current study, we look at individuals of different birth cohorts in different years along the transition path (2010, 2020, 2030, 2050, and 2070) and, for each cohort in

Table 2.6   PAYGO Benefits by Birth Cohort at Selected Dates (all figures are
                   expressed as % of benchmark benefits)

Age in Year 2000	2010	2020	2030	2050	2070
60	0.98	0.98	0.98	0.00	0.00
50	0.00	0.87	0.87	0.87	0.00
40	0.00	0.00	0.65	0.65	0.00
30	0.00	0.00	0.00	0.29	← 0.29
21	0.00	0.00	0.00	0.00	0.00

each year, present the probability distribution of the combined income from the PAYGO benefit and the PRA annuity.

The PAYGO benefit in each year is reduced relative to the benchmark benefits according to the schedules implied in section 2.2 above. For example, if we use the basic portfolio rate of return (with a mean real log return of 5.5 percent after administrative expenses), we reduce the PAYGO benefit of each age cohort in each year (relative to the benchmark benefit that would be paid if there were no PRA annuity) by the amount that such individuals would expect to receive from their PRA annuities if those annuities earned the expected rate of return.[27] The individual bears all the risk—both positive and negative—associated with the uncertainty of the PRA annuity. If the PRA annuity for a particular cohort in a particular year turns out to equal the annuity that would result at the expected rate of return, the combination of the PAYGO benefit and the PRA annuity would exactly equal the benchmark benefit. Table 2.6 shows the PAYGO benefits for the different age cohorts in the selected years that we examine. In the early years, the PAYGO benefits remain a substantial fraction of the benchmark level. But, by 2030, this ratio has begun to decline significantly, and, by 2070, all living cohorts are no longer receiving PAYGO benefits.

The risk that the combination of the PAYGO benefit and the PRA annuity will be unacceptably small relative to the benchmark benefit increases as we move to more distant future years. That risk can be reduced by increasing the PRA saving rate above the level that was adequate when uncertainty was ignored. A fundamentally different alternative approach is to provide a supplementary conditional PAYGO benefit; we examine this intergenerational risk-sharing approach in section 2.5.

Table 2.7 shows the distribution of "combined benefits" (i.e., the sum of the PAYGO and the PRA benefits) corresponding to the basic PRA saving rates that we used in the nonstochastic case reported in table 2.1 above: all employees save 3 percent of taxable earnings per year from the

27. Recall that the nonstochastic rate of return that we use is about 1 percent lower than the expected return based on the stochastic distribution of PRA annuities. This causes us to provide higher PAYGO annuities.

**Table 2.7   Combined Benefit Distributions by Birth Cohort at Selected Dates
(all figures are expressed as % of benchmark benefits)**

Age in Year 2000 and Percentile	2010	2020	2030	2050	2070
60:					
1	0.99	0.98	0.98	0.00	0.00
2	0.99	0.98	0.98	0.00	0.00
5	0.99	0.99	0.98	0.00	0.00
10	0.99	0.99	0.98	0.00	0.00
50	1.00	1.00	1.00	0.00	0.00
90	1.02	1.03	1.04	0.00	0.00
50:					
1	0.00	0.92	0.90	0.88	0.00
2	0.00	0.93	0.90	0.88	0.00
5	0.00	0.94	0.91	0.89	0.00
10	0.00	0.95	0.92	0.90	0.00
50	0.00	1.02	1.01	0.99	0.00
90	0.00	1.14	1.21	1.34	0.00
40:					
1	0.00	0.00	0.76	0.68	0.00
2	0.00	0.00	0.77	0.69	0.00
5	0.00	0.00	0.80	0.71	0.00
10	0.00	0.00	0.84	0.74	0.00
50	0.00	0.00	1.06	1.00	0.00
90	0.00	0.00	1.56	1.97	0.00
30:					
1	0.00	0.00	0.00	0.39	0.33
2	0.00	0.00	0.00	0.41	0.34
5	0.00	0.00	0.00	0.46	0.37
10	0.00	0.00	0.00	0.53	0.42
50	0.00	0.00	0.00	1.07	0.96
90	0.00	0.00	0.00	2.95	4.05
21:					
1	0.00	0.00	0.00	0.19	0.06
2	0.00	0.00	0.00	0.23	0.09
5	0.00	0.00	0.00	0.31	0.14
10	0.00	0.00	0.00	0.42	0.21
50	0.00	0.00	0.00	1.22	1.05
90	0.00	0.00	0.00	3.88	5.57

Note: Combined benefits are the sum of the PAYGO benefits shown in table 2.4 and the PRA annuities that result from saving 3 percent of taxable earnings from 2000 to 2006 and 4.25 percent in all future years. The PRA accounts earn a stochastic return with an expected real mean log return of 5.5 percent and a standard deviation of 12.5 percent.

year 2000 (when the transition begins) to the year 2006 and then 4.25 percent of taxable earnings in each year after that. We present results for five different birth cohorts (identified by their age in year 2000) and five different future years. We report these combined benefits as fractions of the benchmark benefit for that cohort in that year, that is, the level of benefit called for in current law. We present six points on the probability distribution corresponding to the first, second, fifth, tenth, fiftieth, and ninetieth percentiles.

Those who are sixty when the program begins have very little risk of departing from the benchmark benefits, since there are few years of PRA saving before retirement and PAYGO benefits are therefore high relative to the benchmark. The median benefit is the benchmark level, and there is less than a 1 percent chance of having less than 99 percent of the benchmark level of benefits at age seventy and 98 percent of the benchmark benefit at ages eighty and ninety. The columns for 2050 and 2070 show zeros because we assume that no individuals live beyond age one hundred.

The situation is similar for those who are fifty in the year 2000. They are not yet retired in the year 2010 (which is why zeros appear in that year). When they are seventy years old (in 2020), the distribution of combined benefits is quite tight, with only a 10 percent chance that the combined benefits are less than 95 percent of the benchmark. There is only a 1 percent chance that the benefits are less than 92 percent of the benchmark level. Although the distribution becomes wider as they age (because the variable annuity means more years of investment), even in the year 2050 (the last year for this cohort) only 5 percent of combined benefits are less than 88 percent of the benchmark.

But, when we get to the cohort that is forty years old in 2000, there is a greater risk of what might be considered unacceptably low benefits. Those who are forty years old in 2000 reach retirement age in 2027 and are seventy years old in 2030. Our analysis shows that, although the median combined benefit for this group is 106 percent of the benchmark, there is a 10 percent chance that the combined benefit will be less than 84 percent of the benchmark and a 5 percent chance that it will be 77 percent of the benchmark. These 5 and 10 percent benchmark ratios are 10 percentage points lower when the cohort reaches age one hundred.

The youngest cohort in our analysis is twenty-one years old in the year 2000 and therefore never receives any PAYGO benefits. With a 3 percent saving rate for a brief period followed by a 4.25 percent saving rate, there is a considerable chance that their PRA benefits at retirement will be unacceptably low. Table 2.7 shows that, although the median benefit for this group at age seventy-one (in 2050) is 122 percent of the benchmark, there is a 10 percent chance that it will be less than 42 percent of the benchmark and a 5 percent chance that it will be less than 31 percent of the benchmark level.

These risks can be reduced substantially by increasing the PRA saving deposits for younger cohorts. Before looking at the specific results, it should be stressed that this could be achieved either by requiring younger cohorts to make larger saving deposits into their PRA accounts or by having the government make those deposits from general revenue. This issue of the distribution of the burden during the transition is separate from the efficiency of these deposits in reducing risk and will not be considered further here.

Because the risks of low combined benefits are greatest for the employees who are aged thirty and younger at the start of the transition in the year 2000, we present results only for these younger cohorts. Table 2.8 compares three different PRA saving rules. For all employees born before 1960, that is, who were forty or older in 2000, each of the rules has a 3 percent saving rate from 2000 to 2006 followed by a 4.25 percent rate, that is, the same rule displayed in table 2.7. Rule 8A has a higher rate for those born after 1959: a 5 percent saving rate from 2000 to 2006 followed by a 6.25 percent rate. Rule 8B raises these rates to 5.00 percent followed by 6.25 percent for individuals between thirty-one and forty in 2000 and to 6.0 percent and 7.25 percent for those who were under thirty-one in 2000. Finally, rule 8C raises the rate to 8.25 for those who were under thirty-one in 2000. Each successive rule reduces the risk of a relatively low level of combined benefits but does so at an increasing cost in terms of the required PRA saving rate.

With rule 8C, the group that is thirty years old in 2000 has only a 10 percent chance of receiving combined benefits of less than 82 percent of the benchmark level when its members are eighty years old and only a 5 percent chance that those benefits will be less than 68 percent of the benchmark level. As the group reaches one hundred years old, these values decline to 57 and 47 percent, lower than most individuals would tolerate.

But, since the median payment for this birth cohort is more than twice the benchmark benefit at age eighty and 1.82 times the benchmark at one hundred, it may be possible for private markets to provide a way for individuals to trade some of the upside potential (in the top half of the probability distribution) for greater protection when there are bad market outcomes. We do not explore this further here but turn in the next section to ways in which taxpayers might provide a guarantee.

The need for some supplementation is even clearer when we look at those who are twenty-one years old in 2000. While the median benefits for this group at age seventy would be 2.78 times the benchmark benefit, there is a 5 percent chance that the benefits are less than 70 percent of the benchmark and a 1 percent chance that the benefits are less than 42 percent of the benchmark. The probability distribution implies more risk at older ages. Once again, this suggests the potential gain from private trades of upside potential for downside protection or from a government-provided protection of benefits.

A key point to be emphasized is that even the most conservative option, rule 8C, requires a tax of only 9.25 percent for the most heavily taxed younger cohorts, less than half of what they would pay after 2030 to maintain the level of benefits. Individuals may respond to this risk by saving more voluntarily or seeking market ways to reduce the risk through stock

Table 2.8   **Effects of Alternative Saving Rules on Combined Benefit Distributions by Birth Cohort at Selected Dates (all figures are expressed as % of benchmark benefits)**

Rule and Saving Rates,[a] Age in Year 2000, and Percentile	2050	2070
Rule 8a, 5 and 6.25%:		
30:		
1	0.43	0.34
2	0.47	0.36
5	0.55	0.41
10	0.64	0.48
50	1.47	1.30
21:		
1	0.28	0.09
2	0.35	0.13
5	0.47	0.21
10	0.62	0.32
50	1.85	1.58
Rule 8b, 6 and 7.25%:		
30:		
1	0.46	0.35
2	0.50	0.37
5	0.59	0.43
10	0.70	0.51
50	1.67	1.48
21:		
1	0.33	0.11
2	0.40	0.15
5	0.55	0.25
10	0.72	0.37
50	2.16	1.85
Rule 8c, 8 and 9.25%:		
30:		
1	0.50	0.37
2	0.56	0.40
5	0.68	0.47
10	0.82	0.57
50	2.07	1.82
21:		
1	0.42	0.14
2	0.52	0.19
5	0.70	0.31
10	0.93	0.48
50	2.78	2.39

Note: Combined benefits are the sum of the relative PAYGO benefits shown in table 2.6 above and the PRA annuities that result from saving 3 percent of taxable earnings from 2000 to 2006 and 4.25 percent in all future years. The PRA accounts earn a stochastic return with an expected real mean log return of 5.5 percent and a standard deviation of 12.5 percent.

[a]The saving rule is described by two numbers for each age group. The first number is the saving rate from 2000 to 2006. The second is the saving rate after that.

market options. The extent to which they do so will depend on different attitudes about risk and about the trade-off between consuming more during working years and saving more during working years in order to reduce the risk of low income during retirement.

2.5 Government Guarantees and Intergenerational Transfers

The analysis in section 2.4 shows that, although an increased saving rate can reduce the risk of relatively low combined benefits, it does so only at a cost of decreased consumption during working years and does not completely eliminate the risk. We therefore explore an alternative approach in which the government guarantees the benefits by providing a conditional benefit equal to the difference between the benchmark benefit and the combined benefit that the individual receives from the PAYGO and the PRA annuities.[28]

We recognize that this guarantee could encourage excessive risk taking by individuals to the extent that they are free to select more risky portfolios. One possible way to eliminate this incentive is to define the guarantee in terms of the *standard portfolio*. In such an approach, the government would provide a conditional benefit equal to the difference between the benchmark benefit and the combined benefit that the individual would have received from a combination of PAYGO and PRA annuities *if the PRA funds had been invested in the standard portfolio,* consisting of the 60 percent broadly based equity fund and the 40 percent bond fund. In this way, an individual is completely protected if he or she invests in the standard portfolio but bears the full benefit or cost of the risks associated with alternative portfolios. Since we focus our analysis in this paper on the risks associated with the standard portfolio, we do not discuss the issue of alternative portfolios further.

The cost of these pension guarantees depends on the rate at which individuals make PRA saving deposits during their preretirement years, with higher saving rates requiring smaller conditional guarantee payments. We therefore focus on the most expensive of the cases that we have considered, the base case in which all working individuals save 3 percent of their taxable earnings from the year 2000 to the year 2006 and then save 4.25 percent of their taxable earnings, the amounts that we analyzed in the nonstochastic case and that determine the future path of PAYGO benefits.

Table 2.9 shows the distribution of the aggregate benefit shortfall for the total of all cohorts of retirees in each year, that is, of the amount that would be necessary to supplement the combined benefits of all cohorts in

28. This is the approach analyzed in Feldstein and Ranguelova (forthcoming) for a single year rather than for the entire transition path. The tables in this section correspond to the single table 3 in that paper.

Table 2.9   Distribution of Conditional Guarantee Payments for Benchmark
                 as Minimum Total Benefit (all figures are expressed as % of
                 taxable earnings)

Percentile	2010	2020	2030	2050	2070
10	0.00	0.00	0.00	0.00	0.00
20	0.00	0.00	0.00	0.00	0.00
30	0.00	0.00	0.00	0.00	0.00
40	0.00	0.00	0.00	0.00	0.00
50	0.00	0.00	0.01	0.02	0.07
60	0.00	0.03	0.17	1.01	1.48
70	0.01	0.15	0.74	3.32	4.74
80	0.03	0.32	1.32	5.57	8.25
90	0.05	0.50	1.98	7.75	11.63
95	0.06	0.62	2.36	9.00	13.49
98	0.08	0.74	2.72	9.98	14.85
99	0.08	0.81	2.87	10.49	15.55

each year to bring each cohort's total benefit up to the benchmark level. Each entry in the table shows the probability that the total burden required to finance the conditional benefits is below the specified amount; for example, there is a 95 percent probability that the conditional benefits in the year 2030 would be less than 2.36 percent of earnings.

In 2010 and 2020, there is a 99 percent probability that the conditional transfer would be less than 1 percent of earnings. Even in 2070, when the transition to the investment-based system is virtually complete (except for retirees who are over age ninety), there is a 50 percent probability that virtually no transfer (i.e., less than one-tenth of 1 percent of covered earnings) would be needed. In the worst 10 percent of cases, the conditional transfer exceeds 11.6 percent of earnings, and, in the worst 1 percent of the cases, the conditional transfer exceeds 15.5 percent of earnings. In considering these risks to taxpayers, it should be recalled that the payroll tax of 18.7 percent that would have been required in a pure PAYGO system has been completely eliminated and replaced with the PRA saving deposits of 4.25 percent of taxable earnings. Thus, there is only about one chance in fifty that the combination of the PRA saving deposits and the tax required for the conditional benefit will exceed the 18.7 percent PAYGO tax that would be required in the pure PAYGO system. There is a 98 percent probability that the combined cost to the taxpayers of the PRA system with the conditional guarantee benefit would be less costly. Moreover, in the nearly 50 percent of simulations in which no guarantee payment is needed, the retirees receive more income from the PRA than they would have from the benchmark PAYGO benefit.

Although these conditional guarantee payments represent transfers from the working generation of taxpayers to the generation of retirees, there is a high probability that much or all of the transfer in each year can

Table 2.10   **Distribution of Net Transfers: Conditional Guarantee Payments in Excess of Available Corporate-Tax Revenue (all figures are expressed as % of taxable earnings)**

Percentile	2010	2020	2030	2050	2070
10	0.00	0.00	0.00	0.00	0.00
20	0.00	0.00	0.00	0.00	0.00
30	0.00	0.00	0.00	0.00	0.00
40	0.00	0.00	0.00	0.00	0.00
50	0.00	0.00	0.00	0.00	0.00
60	0.00	0.00	0.00	0.00	0.00
70	0.00	0.00	0.00	0.00	0.00
80	0.00	0.00	0.00	0.00	0.12
90	0.00	0.00	0.00	1.84	3.23
95	0.00	0.00	0.00	3.24	5.63
98	0.00	0.00	0.47	4.58	8.09
99	0.00	0.00	0.79	5.44	9.52

be financed by the incremental corporate income-tax payments that result from the incremental saving caused by the PRA system. We calculate for each year the distribution of the difference between the conditional transfer required to bring the combined benefit up to the benchmark level and the incremental corporate-tax revenue available for that purpose. If the incremental corporate-tax revenue is not sufficient to finance the conditional transfer, we say that a *net transfer* is required. Table 2.10 shows the distribution of net transfers.

The incremental corporate-tax revenue is sufficient to finance all the required transfers in 2010 and 2020. In 2030, the probability of any net transfer is reduced to 2 percent, and the probability of a net transfer greater than 1 percent of earnings is reduced to less than 1 percent. Even in 2050, there is only a 10 percent probability of any net transfer.

The maximum risk of transfers occurs in 2070, when the phase-in of the PRA system is complete. In the worst 5 percent of cases in 2070, the net transfer is 5.6 percent of covered earnings. Combining this with the PRA deposits of 4.25 percent of earnings gives a total net burden on taxpayers of 9.85 percent of earnings, about half the payroll tax that would be required in that year with a pure PAYGO system. There is only a 1 percent chance that the sum of the 4.25 percent PRA deposit and the net transfer 9.52 percent of earnings will exceed 13.77 percent of earnings, or about two-thirds of the payroll-tax rate, in the pure PAYGO system.

2.6   An Expected-Utility Evaluation

Although we believe that displaying the probability distributions of possible outcomes is the best way to indicate the risks of the alternative investment-based options, in this section we present explicit summary calculations based on expected values of constant-relative-risk-aversion (CRRA) utility functions.[29] We focus on the case of the individual who is twenty-one in the year 2000 and for whom the risk of the PRA option is greatest.

To evaluate the PRA options presented in section 2.4, we consider a representative individual with expected-utility function $E = E[\Sigma \, p_t \beta^{t-21} u(C_t)]$, where the summation is from $t = 21$ to $t = 100$ and $u(C_t) = (C_t^{1-\gamma} - 1)/(1 - \gamma)$. Here, E is the expectation operator, p_t is the probability of surviving to age t from age twenty-one, β is the time-discount factor at which utility is discounted, and γ is the coefficient of relative risk aversion. We do the analysis with time-discount factors of 0.98; alternative calculations with a greater discount factor ($\beta = 0.96$) and with no time-discount factor ($\beta = 1$) have very little effect on the results that we report below.

We recognize the restrictive nature of this specification. The function is additively separable, and the relative risk aversion in each period, $-u''c/u' = \gamma$, is a constant and is independent of age. Despite these limitations, these calculations may be useful to some readers as a supplement to the direct information of the outcome distributions.

The individual who is age twenty-one in 2000 earns the age-specific wage for this cohort projected by the social security actuaries and pays a proportional income tax equal to 20 percent of that wage. We consider a variety of different PRA saving rates. With a 6 percent PRA saving rate, the net income during the working years from age twenty-one to age sixty-six is 74 percent of the gross wage.[30] The individual is assumed to do no other saving, making the consumption in each preretirement year the same 74 percent of pretax wages.[31] During retirement, the individual's consumption is the variable annuity that is generated by the PRA savings since this age cohort no longer contributes to the PAYGO system.

We contrast each of the possible PRA plans with the PAYGO system in which the tax rate is 18.7 percent, making the net consumption during the preretirement years equal to 62 percent of preretirement income. This PAYGO system is assumed to provide the benchmark level of benefits prescribed in current law during each retirement year with no uncertainty.

The coefficient of relative risk aversion is the key parameter in this

29. This section draws heavily on Feldstein and Ranguelova (1998, sec. 5).
30. This represents a simplification in several ways. Although we are looking at wages for the years beginning in 2000, we are ignoring the transition problem and comparing a fully phased-in PRA system with the PAYGO system that would also exist in the more distant future. We do this to avoid the complexities of modeling the transition. We also simplify by treating the projected wages as the marginal product of capital from which all taxes and saving are subtracted.
31. The lack of other saving reduces the individual's level of retirement consumption and therefore makes the individual's utility more sensitive to fluctuations in the return to PRA saving.

expected-utility evaluation. We do not impose an explicit value of the relative risk aversion on the problem but calculate for each saving rate the coefficient of relative risk aversion that would make the representative individual prefer the "riskless" PAYGO program to the PRA program. We then repeat the analysis for the PRA system with the government guarantee.

We drew ten thousand independent histories of the eighty-year sequence (from age twenty-one in 2000 to age one hundred in 2079) of returns on the PRA savings of the representative individual and calculated the expected-utility value associated with each value of γ. Our calculations show that the PRA with a 3 percent saving rate is preferable to the PAYGO system for the relative-risk-aversion coefficient up to $\gamma = 2.6$. With a 5 percent saving rate, the critical value of γ is 3.2, while, with a 9 percent saving rate, the PRA system is preferred to PAYGO for all values of γ less than 3.85.

In considering these critical values of γ, it is useful to consider the implication of different γ values for the rate at which the marginal utility of consumption declines as income rises. A value of $\gamma = 2.6$ implies that a doubling of income causes the marginal utility of another dollar of income to fall by a factor of 6.06, that is, by $2^{2.6}$. Readers must decide for themselves whether this value of γ is "high" or "low."[32] Our judgment is that a value of γ that causes such a sharp decline in the marginal utility of income is very high. This in turn implies that individuals would prefer any of the PRA systems to the PAYGO system.

We recognize that the values of γ inferred in the finance literature from the difference between the yield on stocks and that on "risk-free" Treasury bills are substantially higher than these critical values of γ (see, e.g., Mehra and Prescott 1985; and Kocherlakota 1996). We regard those market-based values of γ as implausibly high and appropriately characterized as an equity-premium "puzzle."

2.6.1 Evaluating Government-Guarantee Plans with CRRA Expected Utility

When we turn from the pure individualistic PRA system to one with a government guarantee, we can no longer focus on a single age cohort but must consider the benefits received by all retirees aged sixty-five through one hundred and the taxes paid by employees of all ages. We therefore examine the situation during a representative year after the PRA system is fully phased in. We compare the possible outcomes of the PRA system (for alternative possible saving rates) with the PAYGO system in the long run with an 18.7 percent tax rate.

---

32. Feldstein and Ranguelova (1998, sec. 5) present a mental experiment that may help each reader decide what value of γ reflects his or her own preferences.

More specifically, we calculate the expected value of a social welfare function in the first year in which the PRA system is fully phased in. This is the year 2079, when the youngest workers in 2000 (those who are then twenty-one years old) have reached one hundred, the oldest age that we consider in our analysis. The value of the social welfare function in that year is the sum of the expected utilities of the employed taxpayers and the retirees: $\text{SWF} = E[\Sigma \; N_j u(C_j)]$, where the summation is now over the eighty cohorts identified by age (from $j = 21$ to $j = 100$), E is again the expectations operator, N_j is the number of individuals in cohort j in the year 2079, and $u(C_j)$ is the utility of the consumption of the representative individual in cohort j in that year. The form of the utility function is the same CRRA function specified above. In each of the ten thousand simulations that we do, we simulate the PRA accumulation of each cohort over the eighty-year horizon from 2000 until 2079 and then calculate the associated PRA annuity in that year for each retiree cohort. We then specify that the individuals in each retiree cohort consume the greater of the benchmark benefit and the PRA annuity of that cohort in that year.[33]

Retirees thus face no risk of consuming less than the benchmark benefit. All the adverse uncertainty is focused on the taxpayers, who must pay an uncertain tax bill. In particular, with a 6 percent PRA saving rate and a 20 percent income tax, the consumption of workers in cohort j is 74 percent of the cohort-specific wage unless they are called on to pay a supplementary tax to fill the gap between a low PRA annuity and the benchmark benefit. As we noted above, the first source of revenue to fill this gap would be the incremental corporate-tax revenue that results from the PRA capital. In our analysis, we assume that employees make annual adjustments to their consumption when needed to fill the retiree-income gap even though some form of smoothing behavior would reduce the adverse utility effects of these uncertain extra tax burdens.

We contrast this PRA system with a riskless PAYGO system with an 18.7 percent tax and with the benchmark benefits during retirement. We find that the PRA system with the government guarantee dominates the PAYGO system for each of the saving rates between 3 and 9 percent and for every CRRA parameter value up to $\gamma = 40$! These simulations tell us that a CRRA individual with any degree of risk aversion that we have considered would prefer the PRA system with government guarantees to the current PAYGO system.[34]

33. This expected social welfare function value for a single year is of course different from the expected lifetime utility that we used to evaluate the choice between PRA and PAYGO plans. It would be desirable to use a framework in which for each of the eighty cohorts we evaluated the expected present value of lifetime utility. Unfortunately, the data requirements for that calculation stretch further into the future than the projections of the social security actuaries and the Census Bureau.

34. The magnitude of the gain from shifting from a PAYGO system to a PRA system with a government guarantee depends on the value of γ. Smetters's (chap. 3 in this volume) anal-

2.7   Risk Aspects of a Mixed System of PAYGO
and Investment-Based Benefits

We return now to the type of mixed system that combines PAYGO and investment-based benefits that we discussed in the nonstochastic analysis of section 2.2.4. We fix the PAYGO tax rate at its current 12.4 percent level for all future years. We also have a constant rate of saving in the PRA accounts equal to 2.3 percent of covered earnings.

The nonstochastic simulation in section 2.4 showed that this combination of PAYGO benefits and PRA annuities would provide more than the PAYGO level of benefits if the real return in the PRA accounts is 5.5 percent. We now recognize the uncertainty of the PRA returns. We begin with the assumption that the retirees bear all the risk of this uncertain return. Thus, they receive either more or less than the benchmark benefits. We then consider an alternative arrangement in which retirees are guaranteed to receive at least the benchmark level of benefits.

Table 2.11 shows the probability distributions of the combination of PAYGO benefits[35] and PRA annuities for different birth cohorts at selected years during the transition. These combined benefits are expressed as multiples of the benchmark benefits.

For those who are sixty years old in the year 2000, the time to accumulate PRA funds is too short for the uncertainty to matter. The fifty-year-olds have fifteen years of accumulation and the uncertain returns during the annuity period. The median level of the combined payout for this cohort remains very close to the benchmark benefit, declining from 103 percent of the benchmark at age seventy to 101 percent at age one hundred. In the worst 1 percent of simulations for this group, the combined benefit remains above 94 percent of the benchmark benefit. As compensation for this downside risk, there is a 10 percent probability that the benefits will exceed 112 percent of the benchmark level at age seventy and higher multiples in subsequent years.

The forty-year-olds in 2000 are also exposed to little downside risk in this mixed system. Even in the worst 1 percent of cases, the level of combined benefits exceeds 90 percent of the benchmark at age seventy and 86 percent at age ninety. The upside potential is now greater, with a 10 percent chance of a combined benefit that exceeds the benchmark by 42 percent at age seventy and by 68 percent at age ninety.

The highest-risk cases are of course the youngest cohorts since they will

---

ysis of the cost of risk bearing in investment-based accounts relies implicitly on market-based measures of the risk premium. The high value of γ implicit in his analysis may explain his conclusion about the limited gain from adopting a PRA-type plan.

35. In this stochastic context, the PAYGO benefit for each individual in each year is calculated as the benchmark benefit minus the 75 percent of the PRA annuity that would be paid if the individual's PRA savings had earned the 5.5 percent real return.

Table 2.11   Combined Benefit Distributions by Birth Cohort at Selected Dates, Mixed PAYGO and Investment-Based System (all figures are expressed as % of benchmark benefits)

Age in Year 2000 and Percentile	2010	2020	2030	2050	2070
60:					
1	1.00	0.99	0.99	0.00	0.00
2	1.00	0.99	0.99	0.00	0.00
5	1.00	0.99	0.99	0.00	0.00
10	1.00	0.99	0.99	0.00	0.00
50	1.01	1.00	1.00	0.00	0.00
90	1.02	1.03	1.03	0.00	0.00
50:					
1	0.00	0.97	0.95	0.94	0.00
2	0.00	0.97	0.96	0.94	0.00
5	0.00	0.98	0.96	0.95	0.00
10	0.00	0.99	0.97	0.95	0.00
50	0.00	1.03	1.02	1.01	0.00
90	0.00	1.12	1.16	1.25	0.00
40:					
1	0.00	0.00	0.90	0.86	0.00
2	0.00	0.00	0.91	0.86	0.00
5	0.00	0.00	0.93	0.88	0.00
10	0.00	0.00	0.95	0.89	0.00
50	0.00	0.00	1.09	1.05	0.00
90	0.00	0.00	1.42	1.68	0.00
30:					
1	0.00	0.00	0.00	0.74	0.70
2	0.00	0.00	0.00	0.75	0.71
5	0.00	0.00	0.00	0.78	0.73
10	0.00	0.00	0.00	0.82	0.75
50	0.00	0.00	0.00	1.15	1.08
90	0.00	0.00	0.00	2.33	3.00
21:					
1	0.00	0.00	0.00	0.66	0.59
2	0.00	0.00	0.00	0.68	0.60
5	0.00	0.00	0.00	0.73	0.63
10	0.00	0.00	0.00	0.79	0.67
50	0.00	0.00	0.00	1.27	1.17
90	0.00	0.00	0.00	2.89	3.88

Note: Combined benefits are the sum of the PAYGO benefits generated by the 12.4 percent payroll tax and the PRA annuities that result from saving 2.3 percent of taxable earnings in all years. The PRA accounts earn a stochastic return with an expected real mean log return of 5.5 percent and a standard deviation of 12.5 percent.

have the greatest exposure to PRA benefits relative to PAYGO benefits when they retire. The twenty-one-year-olds in 2000 will have made PRA contributions of 2.3 percent throughout their working life and will therefore have the full risk not only in the transition but thereafter. The median combined benefit for this group is 127 percent of the benchmark PAYGO benefit. There is one chance in ten that they will face benefits of less than 79 percent of the benchmark at age seventy-one and 67 percent at age ninety-one. There is only one chance in one hundred of receiving less than 66 percent of the benchmark benefits at age seventy-one and 59 percent at age ninety-one. Another way of describing the limit to the risk faced by this cohort is to note that, for this cohort, the PAYGO benefits would represent 55 percent of the benchmark level of benefits and that any value in the PRA accounts would therefore be in excess of that. An indication of the compensating upside potential is that there is a 10 percent chance that the combined benefits will be nearly three times the benchmark benefit at age seventy-one and an even higher multiple in later years.

As we noted earlier, individuals will differ in their attitudes toward risk and toward the timing of consumption. Some individuals would save more than the required 2.3 percent in order to reduce the risk of an inadequate income in retirement. Others may seek market-based opportunities to reduce the downside risk by trading some of the upside potential.

It is again possible for the government to reduce the risk to retirees by an intergenerational guarantee, a conditional benefit that guarantees that the combination of the PRA benefit and the PAYGO benefit is at least as large as the benchmark benefit. The guarantee that we assume takes the following form: Each retiree is guaranteed that the sum of his or her payment from the government (including the basic PAYGO benefit plus any conditional benefit) plus 75 percent of PRA payment for the year will be at least equal to the benchmark benefit. Operationally, if the basic PAYGO benefit (based on the assumption of a 5.5 percent real return) plus 75 percent of the individual's PRA annuity is less than the benchmark benefit, the government supplements the PAYGO benefit by enough to bring that total up to the benchmark benefit.[36] The individual thus receives the benchmark benefit amount plus 25 percent of the PRA annuity.[37]

The cost to the taxpayers of providing this guarantee is relatively small, as shown in table 2.12. In 2050, there is essentially a 50 percent chance that no money need be given to any of the retired cohorts. By 2070, that is still essentially true; the median value of the transfer in the ten thousand simulations is equal to only 0.07 percent of earnings in that year. There is only one chance in ten that the funds needed exceed 5.32 percent of cov-

36. Recall that, if the individuals are given discretion about the investment that they make with the PRA funds, the guarantee would be defined in terms of the annuity that would have been provided by investments in the standard portfolio of a 60 percent broad stock fund and a 40 percent corporate bond fund. Thus, if the basic PAYGO benefit (based on the assumption of a 5.5 percent real return) plus 75 percent of what the individual's PRA annuity would be if the PRA deposits had always been invested in the standard fund is less than the benchmark benefit, the government supplements the PAYGO benefit by enough to bring that total up to the benchmark benefit.

37. In the unlikely event that the PRA annuity implied by the standard portfolio is so large that 75 percent of its value exceeds the benchmark benefit, the retiree gets the full PRA annuity and no government funds.

Table 2.12 **Distribution of Conditional Guarantee Payments for Mixed PAYGO-PRA System (all figures are expressed as % of taxable earnings)**

Percentile	2010	2020	2030	2050	2070
10	0.00	0.00	0.00	0.00	0.00
20	0.00	0.00	0.00	0.00	0.00
30	0.00	0.00	0.00	0.00	0.00
40	0.00	0.00	0.00	0.00	0.00
50	0.00	0.00	0.00	0.01	0.07
60	0.00	0.01	0.09	0.55	1.02
70	0.01	0.08	0.37	1.66	2.50
80	0.01	0.17	0.64	2.66	3.93
90	0.03	0.26	0.96	3.63	5.32
95	0.03	0.32	1.14	4.17	6.08
98	0.04	0.38	1.31	4.60	6.64
99	0.05	0.41	1.38	4.82	6.92

Table 2.13 **Distribution of Net Transfers: Conditional Guarantee Payments in Excess of Available Corporate-Tax Revenue in Mixed PAYGO-PRA System (all figures are expressed as % of taxable earnings)**

Percentile	2010	2020	2030	2050	2070
10	0.00	0.00	0.00	0.00	0.00
20	0.00	0.00	0.00	0.00	0.00
30	0.00	0.00	0.00	0.00	0.00
40	0.00	0.00	0.00	0.00	0.00
50	0.00	0.00	0.00	0.00	0.00
60	0.00	0.00	0.00	0.00	0.00
70	0.00	0.00	0.00	0.00	0.00
80	0.00	0.00	0.00	0.00	0.00
90	0.00	0.00	0.00	0.44	1.30
95	0.00	0.00	0.00	1.09	2.56
98	0.00	0.00	0.03	1.74	3.66
99	0.00	0.00	0.22	2.15	4.52

ered earnings and only one chance in one hundred that the required funds exceed 6.92 percent of covered earnings.

Shifting from these gross tax requirements to the revenue needed net of the incremental corporate tax reduces the needed funds substantially, as shown in table 2.13. Even in 2070, there is only one chance in ten that any net transfer will be required and only one chance in fifty that the net transfer will exceed 3.7 percent of covered earnings. Combining the 12.4 percent PAYGO tax, the 2.3 percent PRA deposits, and the 3.7 percent net transfer still gives a total of 18.4 percent of covered earnings, less than the payroll tax that would be required in a pure PAYGO system.

2.8 Conclusion

In this chapter, we examine the feasibility of a transition from the existing PAYGO system of social security to a system that is completely or partially investment based, using individual accounts invested in stock and bond mutual funds. Our analysis focuses on the uncertainty of portfolio returns and the volatility of capital stock profitability.

We begin by studying how a simple transition could work with no uncertainty. Using the 1998 social security trustees' projections and economic assumptions, we show that PRA deposits of 3 percent of taxable earnings in addition to the existing 12.4 percent payroll tax would be sufficient to start the transition and that the resulting 15.4 percent would be the maximum saving plus tax share of taxable earnings rate that would ever be necessary in the transition to a completely investment-based system. Over time, the payroll tax could be reduced (because PRA annuities reduce the need for PAYGO benefits), while the PRA saving rate rises to 4.25. By 2050, the combined saving plus tax payments are less than 10 percent, and, by 2070 (and after), the payroll tax is eliminated, and the only remaining payment is the PRA saving rate of 4.25 percent.

Our analysis then shifts to the more modest goal of a mixed system that maintains the current 12.4 percent payroll tax and uses the investment-based system to finance about one-third of benefits. We show that the social security benefits projected in current law (the benchmark benefits) can be financed by supplementing the PAYGO benefits that are possible with a 12.4 percent payroll tax with PRA annuities that result from saving 2.3 percent of taxable earnings.

We then use the postwar experience to assess the risks associated with a PRA portfolio of 60 percent stocks and 40 percent bonds. We study the risks to retirees in the transition to a completely investment-based system and in the final posttransition economy. The same mix of assets is used to finance the variable annuities after retirement. We find that the basic PRA saving path that is satisfactory in the absence of uncertainty begins to cause potential risks of low benefits to those who retire in 2050 and after. Although the median level of benefits for these cohorts is above the level of benefits projected for the pure PAYGO system under current law (the benchmark benefits), there is a 10 percent chance that the combination of PAYGO and PRA benefits will be less than 50 percent of the benchmark.

The risk of relatively low benefits can be reduced substantially by increasing the PRA saving rate for the younger cohorts of workers. For example, with a PRA saving rate that starts at 8 percent of taxable earnings and rises to 9.25 percent of taxable earnings, the cohort that is thirty years old at the time that the transition begins will have only a 10 percent chance of receiving combined benefits of less than 82 percent of the benchmark and only a 5 percent chance that those benefits will be less than 68 percent of the benchmark. Among the twenty-one-year-olds in 2000, however, the historic experience implies that there is still a small probability that retirement benefits could be substantially less than the benchmark.

We therefore explore an alternative way to reduce the risk to retirees by a system of conditional intergenerational transfers, that is, payments from the taxpayers to retirees whose combined benefits (i.e., PAYGO plus PRA) are less than the benchmark level. We assess the probability distribution of the taxes required to finance these transfers. After netting out the incremental corporate-tax receipts (i.e., the corporate-tax payments on the increased size of the corporate-sector capital that results from the PRA saving), we find that, even in 2070 (when the risk is greatest), there is only a 20 percent probability of needing any net funds to finance the transfer to retirees. Even when such additional net financing is needed in 2070, there is only a 5 percent chance that the required net transfer would exceed 6 percent of earnings. Thus, even with the PRA saving of 4.25 percent of earnings, the taxpayers would have a total burden (10.25 percent) that was only slightly more than half the payroll tax that would be required in a pure PAYGO system, while the retirees would have at least as much retirement income as they would under the pure PAYGO system.

Finally, we consider the transition to a mixed system that maintains the 12.4 percent payroll tax to finance PAYGO benefits and adds a 2.3 percent saving rate into PRAs. The high level of PAYGO benefits in this mixed system substantially reduces the risk to retirees. This risk can be completely eliminated by a government guarantee financed by a combination of additional taxes and the incremental corporate-tax revenue that results from the PRA savings. We show that the extra risk to taxpayers in providing this guarantee is very small.

References

Board of Trustees of the Social Security System. 1998. *The 1998 Annual Report of the Social Security Trustees.* Washington, D.C.
Boskin, M., et al. 1987. Social security: A financial appraisal across and within generations. *National Tax Journal* 40, no. 1:19–34.
Feldstein, M., L. Dicks-Mireaux, and J. Poterba. 1983. The effective tax rate return and the pretax rate of return. *Journal of Public Economics* 21, no. 2 (July): 129–58.
Feldstein, M., and E. Ranguelova. 1998. Individual risk and intergenerational risk sharing in an investment-based social security system. NBER Working Paper no. 6839. Cambridge, Mass.: National Bureau of Economic Research.
———. Forthcoming. The economics of bequests in pensions and social security. In *Distributional aspects of investment-based social security reform,* ed. M. Feldstein and J. Liebman. Chicago: University of Chicago Press.

Feldstein, M., and A. Samwick. 1997. The economics of prefunding social security and medicare benefits. In *NBER macroeconomics annual 1997,* ed. Ben S. Bernanke and Julio Rotemberg, 115–47. Cambridge, Mass.: MIT Press.

———. 1998a. Potential effects of two percent personal retirement accounts. *Tax Notes* 79, no. 5 (May): 615–20.

———. 1998b. The transition path in privatizing social security. In *Privatizing social security,* ed. M. Feldstein. Chicago: University of Chicago Press.

Kocherlakota, N. 1996. the equity premium puzzle: It's still a puzzle. *Journal of Economic Literature* 34:42–71

Mehra, R., and E. Prescott. 1985. The equity premium puzzle. *Journal of Monetary Economics* 15:145–61.

Poterba, J. 1998. The rate of return to corporate capital and factor shares: New estimates using revised national income accounts and capital stock data. *Carnegie-Rochester Conference Series on Public Policy* 48 (1): 211–46.

Comment   Robert J. Shiller

Feldstein, Ranguelova, and Samwick (FRS) study a number of the possible reforms of the social security system. Each reform involves the creation of personal retirement accounts (PRAs) and each the eventual elimination of the existing pay-as-you-go (PAYGO) system or reduction to a system that is only two-thirds PAYGO. The reforms appear to be feasible today, and those that do not eliminate PAYGO appear to be within the broad bounds of political acceptability.

This paper has the most concrete suggestions for reform of the social security system of any of the papers in this volume; the authors present the exact tax rates and contribution rates. Moreover, the paper takes careful account of a number of parameters of our economy and uses these to produce explicit simulations of the effects of the various reforms.

The paper centers on the transition from the current system. The transition is a topic that has often been overlooked in public discussions. FRS show policy regimes that are designed so that retirees are expected to earn at least the currently mandated social security benefit during the entire transition. In studying the reforms proposed in this paper, the focus of attention is on the risk that individuals in some cohorts will do less well than expected during the transition period if the investments used for the PRAs do badly.

The explicitness of the simulations and the attention to details concerning the current tax system and other macroeconomic parameters are important strengths of the analysis. Such strengths do not come without some inherent limitations, however. This paper does not offer a theoretical justification for the reforms suggested. While there is some welfare anal-

Robert J. Shiller is professor of economics at Yale University and a research associate of the National Bureau of Economic Research.

ysis, there is no economic argument that the proposed reforms are optimal in any welfare sense. In reading this paper, I missed seeing these and at times wondered why we were considering these particular reforms since they are not derived as optimal reforms.

Of course, we economists are not going to be able to agree completely on an optimal social security reform since we do not agree on fundamental theory. There are deep, unresolved issues for theorists, such as the equity-premium puzzle. There is no agreement on values to attach to fundamental parameters in these models, such as the risk-aversion parameters. Model builders would ideally have to consider incorporating into their models such factors as the incapability of certain elements of our population, including the mentally retarded or mentally ill, to make well-informed savings plans for their retirement and then the incentive effects, discouraging saving, of a preexisting system that bails out people who do not save. Our existing institutions in some ways discourage saving for retirement, as by means testing many benefits and services. Model builders would have to consider the anomalies in saving behavior that have been documented by some authors, anomalies that suggest human myopia or other error in savings decisions and the erratic nature of actual human saving behavior. Any practical policy discussion will also have to deal with popular notions of fairness and of interpretations of unstated past commitments, factors that are usually ignored in theoretical models.

Meanwhile, practical policy makers must move on, and, at this time of serious consideration of overhaul of the social security system, we are going to need concrete policy parameters and explicit consideration of the effects of the policy changes.

What I find most striking about the FRS simulations is that there are uneven effects on the generations, at least under certain of their assumptions. While the paper focuses on the effects across different age cohorts of social security reforms that are expected to leave the existing benefits unchanged or improved for all cohorts, the reforms do not always treat all cohorts equally, and some are made worse off. From tables 2.1 and 2.2, for example, it is clear, under the assumption that the PRA is paid by the individual, that in these nonstochastic simulations someone who is born in 1950, retires before 2020, and dies in 2030 must be made worse off since he or she makes higher payments (PAYGO tax rate plus PRA saving rate) but gets benefits no higher than the benchmark. The person is made worse off even though the increases in contributions were credited to what is called a *personal* retirement account because that person's PAYGO benefit is reduced each year by the increment to the annuity income of the PRA account. In the stochastic simulations of tables 2.7–2.13, where the PAYGO benefit is reduced each year by the expected increment to the annuity income of the PRA account, this individual is not necessarily worse off but is worse off if returns are equal to expected values. The authors also mention the possibility that the PRA is paid for by the government, so in this case it would no longer be clear that any given individual is worse off for the changes.

One wonders how the authors arrived at their decisions about the taxes in transition and afterward and whether there is any sense that the proposed transition plan is approximately optimal. This is important to know. A transition does not have to harm the young today, as some of theirs do. It might even be possible, if savings currently are artificially depressed relative to those in a competitive equilibrium by institutional incentives, to design a transition that makes the younger generation better off too. Moreover, the authors present the reforms as if they are done once and for all and no further adjustments are needed. One naturally wonders, then, whether they have any way of knowing how fast we should move to the new steady state and when we will want to change these tax rates again.

I am reminded of a capital theory literature that flourished in the 1960s about social welfare and transitions to steady states, a literature that produced the so-called turnpike theorems. It is worth remembering this literature here since it gives theories offering some guidance to social planners intending to make decisions that benefit future generations at the expense of current generations: the theory can justify taking from one generation and giving to a subsequent generation and offer some guidance on how much should be taken. I follow a version of an intergenerational optimal investment model derived by Samuelson (1972).[1] Consider a simple overlapping-generations model in which each individual who is young at time t has utility that depends on consumption when young c_{1t} (in period 1 of life) and on consumption when old c_{2t+1} (in period 2 of life):

$$(1) \qquad u = u(c_{1t}) + (1 + \theta)^{-1} u(c_{2t+1}),$$

where $u(\cdot)$ is instantaneous utility or felicity, and θ is the individual's subjective rate of time preference. The government, the social planner, has a social utility function that is defined over these individual social utility functions, taking account of the fact that, on the date of the reform, time 0, there is an existing old generation whose consumption when young can no longer be changed. The social welfare function is

$$(2) \quad U = (1 + \theta)^{-1} u(c_{20}) + \sum_{t=0}^{T-1} (1 + R)^{-t-1} [u(c_{1t}) + (1 + \theta)^{-1} u(c_{2t+1})],$$

where R is the social planner's rate of time discount, and T is the planning horizon. A plausible value of R might be $R = (1 + n)^{-1} - 1$ since this

---

1. See also Cass (1966). A concise exposition is in Blanchard and Fischer (1989, 98–102). As shown here, no account is taken of technical progress. However, under the plausible assumption of log utility, constant labor-augmenting technical progress would have no effect on the first-order conditions shown here.

would mean that the social planner treats everyone the same and takes account of the fact that there are more people in the future than in the present. This R is the Lerner (1959) discount rate. If population growth n is positive, this discount R is negative. Alternatively, it is also plausible that the government would favor the present or near future generation over generations in the more distant future, regardless of their numbers, which would mean that R is positive. Given exogenous population N_t of young people born at time t, growing at rate n per period, and given a constant returns-to-scale production function $F(K_t, N_t)$, the social planner's resource constraint is

(3) $$K_t + F(K_t, N_t) = K_{t+1} + N_t c_{1t} + N_{t-1} c_{2t}.$$

Or, redefining in terms of the capital divided by young people k_t and a function $f(k_t)$ that gives output per young person,

(4) $$k_t + f(k_t) = (1 + n)k_{t+1} + c_{1t} + (1 + n)^{-1} c_{2t}.$$

The social planner chooses capital so as to maximize the social welfare function subject to an initial capital stock k_0 and a terminal capital stock k_{T+1}. The first-order conditions for a maximum are

(5) $$(1 + \theta)^{-1} u'(c_{2t-1}) - (1 + R)^{-1}(1 + n)^{-1} u'(c_{1t}) = 0,$$

(6) $$-(1 + n)u'(c_{1t-1}) + (1 + R)^{-1}[1 + f'(k_t)]u'(c_{1t}) = 0.$$

In a steady state, with consumption, c_{1t} and c_{2t} constant through time t, and the capital-labor ratio constant through time t at k^*, we have, from (6), the modified golden rule:

(7) $$1 + f'(k^*) = (1 + R)(1 + n),$$

which implies that, if R and n are not too far from zero, the marginal product of capital is approximately equal to the social planner's time rate of discount plus the population-growth rate. There is certainly no tendency in competitive equilibria, in which individuals make their own savings decisions, for the modified golden rule to obtain, for the parameter R appears only in the social welfare function, not in equations relevant to the competitive equilibrium. There is thus a case for government intervention in the markets by creating institutions like social security, and this case does not require any such things as dynamic inefficiency to be valid. If we take $1 + R = (1 + n)^{-1}$, then the modified golden rule requires that the marginal product of capital be driven to zero (as Lerner stressed), something that certainly has not happened. Even if we do not take Lerner's extreme position, it seems likely that we have less capital than the modified golden rule would suggest. If, disregarding risk, we take the 5.5 percent per annum hypothesized by FRS as the marginal product of capital after taxes, or, say, 8.5 percent before taxes, then with a population growth rate of 1 percent a year the social discount rate would have to be 7.5 percent per annum for the modified golden rule to hold. The intergenerational discount factor $1/(1 + R)$ that we would have to apply to subsequent generations to make the modified golden rule hold would be about 0.1. Surely, we attach much more than 10 percent weight to the next generation's utility, and this is ultimately why the government interventions studied by FRS look so attractive (and why Feldstein's [1977] earlier analyses of the importance of saving looked so impressive).

Starting from a given initial capital stock that I will suppose is below the amount prescribed by the modified golden rule, the optimizing government will gradually increase the capital stock. It will not increase it too fast because the only way it can do so is to penalize the people who are alive then excessively, by making them save too much. The government weighs the relative hardship imposed on the first generation against the benefits in the future and takes a somewhat gradual transition to the modified golden rule. In fact, it can be shown that, if the initial capital-labor ratio k_0 is below the equilibrium value, the optimal policy is a gradual increase in k_t until the modified golden rule is reached, and, then, if the horizon T is far away, k_t will stay almost unchanged for a long time at its modified golden rule value, until it finally moves to the assumed terminal value k_T. It is as if the capital stock follows the path of an entry ramp onto a turnpike and then, after the transition, stays on a turnpike, the same turnpike that people starting from other initial conditions (other entry ramps) would follow.[2]

Is it possible to interpret the FRS transition path in their simulations in terms like those used by the Samuelson model? One might wonder whether it is since the FRS simulations do depict a path of increased saving at first that penalizes the young the most, at least if the PRA contribution is paid for by the individual rather than the government. The turnpike-entry-ramp shape is suggestive of the shape of the PAYGO tax rate plus PRA tax rate described in the paper. But this cannot be exactly the right interpretation of the FRS simulations since in the FRS simulations the assumption is that the marginal product of capital is exogenous and unchanged by the capital accumulation. If we altered the Samuelson model by exogenizing the marginal product of capital, then we would lose any asymmetry between generations. All generations would be treated the same, and the marginal utility of consumption would grow at a constant rate through time. Perhaps the authors would think that eventually the

---

2. Eventually, the capital stock exits from the turnpike and follows an exit path toward the terminal value of the capital stock. As we increase T to infinity, the terminal value moves off to infinity, and we stay on the modified golden rule forever; there is no exit. We must solve the problem for finite T, however, since, otherwise, the social welfare function does not converge for negative R.

PRA saving rate must be lowered if the increased capital stock brings down the marginal product of capital.

The attractiveness of the FRS plan, which guarantees expected benefits but does not guarantee the expected contributions of the young today, may lie in considerations of fairness rather than in the Samuelson considerations of optimal consumption. I think that there is a sense in which the social security system has been presented to us as promising future benefits but not future contributions. McHale (chap. 7 in this volume) has shown that, in various countries, changes in social security systems have taken the form of changes in the plan for the future, not changes in existing benefits. If this is the political environment in which we live, then the FRS simulations may be the right ones. By this interpretation, FRS are trying to move to a socially superior equilibrium without betraying any real promises.

The stochastic simulations add a critically important dimension to this analysis since investments in capital, such as stock market investments, are inherently risky. What will happen if investments are made in the PRAs and the investments do badly? The nonstochastic simulations shown in tables 2.1–2.2 could be really misleading since they assume that the 5.5 percent on the sixty-forty stock-bond portfolio is really riskless when in fact the high return merely reflects a risk premium. Perhaps it is better to look at table 2.3, which assumes a riskless 3.7 percent return.

Tables 2.7–2.13 show a picture in which the risks of a bad outcome do not look so bad, especially if we require a higher saving rate initially (to provide a better saving cushion) (table 2.8). If the government guarantees the benchmark benefit level, then the risk of a substantial tax burden caused by poor investment outcome appears to be low (table 2.9).

I think that there is some question that the risks of bad outcomes are as small as were simulated here. We are looking here at returns over many decades. The historical data on such returns are extremely sparse; we have only a few observations on the returns on the market over several decades. There is fundamental uncertainty about such issues as the extent of mean reversion in stock prices.

The extreme case considered here is one in which the government guarantees 100 percent of the benchmark benefit levels. Of course, government guarantees mean that shortfalls are met by taxing working people. The young might be doubly taxed in the transition: not only must they pay much of the transition cost to a funded system, but they must also bear the risk of underperformance, on behalf of the retired people. While the FRS simulations suggest that this risk is small, I wonder whether the considerations of past promises really require such an unequal bearing of costs.

I would have liked to have seen a stochastic version of the turnpike model above that allows us to consider the optimal risk sharing along the transition path, but I realize that that is beyond the scope of this paper.

Still, in considering the ideal reform of social security, one unconstrained by any political reality, I think that we should consider alternatives that involve better sharing of risks between generations. We should consider systems in which, as Rangel and Zeckhauser (chap. 4 in this volume) describe, there can be transfers of wealth from the old to the young (when the young are hit by bad shocks) as well as from young to old (when the old are hit by bad shocks).

If the only choices that we have to make are between the existing system with existing savings rates and one of the FRS transitions to an all-PRA or a partial PRA social security, however, I find myself attracted to one of the latter. The simulations show that the contribution rate is ultimately much smaller and, with high probability, the benefits better. Those of us who do not have very high social discount rates may find the FRS simulated reforms very attractive.

However, the timing of the adoption of these reforms may be bad. I think that the current overpricing of the stock market means that conditionally, for the foreseeable future, we cannot expect historical expected returns on the market to continue. It could be very damaging to public support of any new social security regime if its adoption is immediately followed by significant stock market losses. Alternatively, while there may be no sudden losses in the stock market, the higher valuation in the market today may mean that expected returns on the FRS sixty-forty stock-bond portfolio going forward are much less than the 5.5 percent assumed in their simulations.

References

Blanchard, Olivier, and Stanley Fischer. 1989. *Lectures in macroeconomics.* Cambridge, Mass.: MIT Press.

Cass, David. 1966. Optimum growth in an aggregation model of capital accumulation: A turnpike theorem. *Econometrica* 34:833–50.

Feldstein, Martin. 1977. Does the United States save too little? *American Economic Review* 67, no. 1:116–21.

Lerner, Abba P. 1959. Consumption-loan interest and money (Reply). *Journal of Political Economy* 67:512–18.

Samuelson, Paul A. 1972. The two-part golden rule deduced as the asymptotic turnpike of catenary motions. In *The collected scientific papers of Paul A. Samuelson* (vol. 3), ed. Robert Merton. Cambridge, Mass.: MIT Press.

Discussion Summary

Antonio Rangel asked the authors to clarify the source of the funds needed to pay off the unfunded liabilities of the current system in table 2.1. In addition, he noted that it would be useful for understanding the cost of transition to know what fraction is paid off indirectly, that is, financed by welfare gains from reductions in distortions. Second, he remarked that the analysis of the paper involves important but implicit intergenerational transfers. In combination with the risk associated with an investment-based system, the relevant benchmark to use is expected utility rather than the probability of a shortfall.

Rangel also remarked that fat tails or extreme risks could be an interesting ingredient of a study focusing on the probability of a shortfall. Finally, he noted that labor-income risk and especially the correlation of wages with equity returns could greatly affect the results. In particular, if taxes have to be increased to make up for a drop in benefits caused by a collapse in the stock market, then this tax increase will be especially painful if wages are also low.

John McHale remarked that Feldstein and Ranguelova (1998) contained very interesting utility calculations. These are missing from the current paper. Utility calculations would be very informative about the welfare of the current generation along the transition path to an investment-based system.

Stephen Ross expressed the opinion that the simulation exercise in the paper seriously underestimates the risk of equity returns. This underestimation has two sources. First, the simulation ignores the standard error for the estimate of the mean return. Taking this estimation risk into account would substantially affect the tails of the distribution. The second reason for his criticism is that normal distributions are not an appropriate modeling device for studying shortfall probabilities. Using a bootstrap technique instead would allow for fatness of the tails of the return distribution. Second, Ross noted that financial markets have elaborate ways of estimating volatilities forward. He suggested taking advantage of this technology, not only to estimate the value of the put option represented by the benefit guarantee, but also to obtain information about the volatility of returns.

Robert King made two comments. First, related to Ross's last comment, he noted that the paper describes some form of public portfolio insurance. It would be interesting to link this to other estimates of the cost of (private) portfolio insurance, perhaps on the basis of current market instruments. Second, in response to the discussion by Robert Shiller of transition dynamics, he wondered how fast the transition takes place in a Diamond-style overlapping-generations model. He added that the transition dynamics of a standard neoclassical growth model are typically believed to be quite fast.

James Poterba suggested using the utility function to value the cost of negative outcomes. He furthermore agreed with Rangel that one might want to consider labor income in this context: scenarios with low returns are typically scenarios with low wages and hence high marginal utility, making it particularly costly to pay the additional taxes necessary to provide the benefit guarantee.

Richard Zeckhauser commented on the issue of the tail probabilities. In this context, he suggested incorporating some of the insights of the paper by McHale (chap. 7 in this volume), by looking at pessimistic scenarios from the past. This should also be considered in the benchmark of a regular politically controlled pay-as-you-go social security system, possibly by allowing for downward modifications of the benefit entitlements in adverse scenarios.

Stephen Zeldes noted that the cost of transition seems low. The cost is around 3 percent of payroll for thirty-five years, followed by a period of zero cost, after which the cost becomes eventually negative. Zeldes remarked that in Geanakoplos, Mitchell, and Zeldes (1999), the transition cost was roughly computed to be 3 percent forever. These results can at least partially be reconciled by noting the difference in the assumed real equity premium earned by the investment-based system: the premium used in this work was 2.3 percent, as opposed to the 5.5 percent assumed in the Feldstein, Ranguelova, and Samwick paper. Zeldes concluded that it would be useful to know to what extent the difference in the transition cost is actually due to the rate-of-return assumption. The authors could repeat their calculations using the riskless rate instead of the historical equity premium and would thereby also conduct some useful sensitivity analysis.

John Campbell followed up on Shiller's comment about mean reversion in stock returns and noted that mean reversion cuts both ways in an interesting fashion. As mentioned by the discussant, it makes investors wary of stocks at a time when the market appears to be overvalued. However, on average, mean reversion also reduces one's estimate of the long-run risk of stocks, an idea popularized by Siegel (1998). Therefore, mean reversion may actually boost the demand for stocks, for a given equity premium.

With respect to the issue of mean reversion and the associated current wariness of stocks because of their perceived overvaluation, *Martin Feldstein* noted that this would actually make an investment-based plan more attractive. Indeed, if a severe market correction occurs in the near future, the subsequent situation is ideal for initiating such a system.

Second, Feldstein remarked that the paper does not contain a true proposal because completely eliminating the existing pay-as-you-go system is not politically feasible. Instead, the current system would most likely be complemented by a plan that corresponds to around one-third of the investment-based plan analyzed in the paper. This of course scales down all the risks correspondingly.

In response to the discussant's question of why setting up an entirely new and optimal social security system is not being considered, Feldstein noted that it was probably too complicated to redo everything and start from scratch.

Regarding the concern expressed by Rangel and Zeldes about the cost of transition, Feldstein agreed that this cost was low because of the high return to capital. He further clarified that the transition cost as computed in this paper does not reflect welfare gains in the form of smaller dead-weight losses resulting from the elimination of some distortions. He added that a full welfare analysis would incorporate these additional gains.

Feldstein noted that previous versions of the paper did report expected-utility calculations. These also contained calculations for the 1 and 2 percent tails of the distribution. The results are in line with what is obtained in this paper and will be included in the final version. Finally, the authors promised that the revised version of the paper in the volume would deal correctly with the estimation-error issue raised by Ross.

References

Feldstein, M., and E. Ranguelova. 1998. Individual risk and intergenerational risk sharing in an investment-based social security system. NBER Working Paper no. 6839. Cambridge, Mass.: National Bureau of Economic Research.

Geanakoplos, John, Olivia S. Mitchell, and Stephen P. Zeldes. 1999. Social security money's worth. In *Prospects for social security reform,* ed. Olivia S. Mitchell, Robert J. Myers, and Howard Young. Philadelphia: University of Pennsylvania Press.

Siegel, Jeremy. 1998. *Stocks for the long run.* 2d ed. New York: McGraw-Hill.

3

The Effect of Pay-When-Needed Benefit Guarantees on the Impact of Social Security Privatization

Kent Smetters

3.1 Introduction

Many plans to privatize the mostly unfunded U.S. social security defined-benefit program implicitly contain unfunded obligations of their own in the form of benefit guarantees. One example is the promise that the assets in the new private accounts will produce an annuitized retirement benefit at least equal to what the participant would have received under social security. The recent proposal by Senator Phil Gramm (1998), for example, would guarantee that workers receive an annuitized benefit equal to 100 percent of what they would have received under social security plus 20 percent of the value of the investment they build up "over their working lives." Unless the government reneges on this promise, future workers would have to be taxed on a pay-when-needed basis to make up for shortfalls. A minimum-benefit guarantee, therefore, represents an unfunded obligation that must be priced since money is not set aside ahead of time to cover the associated actuarial burden.

This paper uses a simplified version of the model presented in Smetters (1998) to report that large pay-when-needed minimum-benefit guarantees can be very costly, so costly that they can undermine and possibly reverse the salutary economic effects traditionally associated with privatization. If payroll taxes were increased over time (from 12.4 to 18.75 percent) to satisfy present-law benefits, privatization would reduce unfunded liabilities by more than a third only if the government guaranteed a benefit level

Kent Smetters is assistant professor of insurance and risk management at the Wharton School, University of Pennsylvania.

The author has benefited on numerous occasions from conversations with Zvi Bodie, Henning Bohn, Peter Diamond, and Martin Feldstein on earlier and related work. John Campbell and David Wilcox provided helpful comments.

below that currently provided by social security. This is true even though the *expected* privatized benefit is as much as five times as large as the benefit provided under social security. The reduction in unfunded liabilities is small even at a high contribution rate because the returns to all the dollars in the private account are perfectly correlated. To be sure, investing more dollars reduces the work that each dollar must do in order for the sum of dollars in the account at retirement to exceed the minimum-benefit guarantee. But the government must insure more dollars at a high contribution rate. So each dollar is being insured less, but more dollars are being insured, with only a small net effect on unfunded liabilities. The net liability decreases very little because insurance against very low equity returns is extremely valuable; the guaranteed value, therefore, decreases slowly in the total number of dollars invested. An alternative to a small pay-when-needed guarantee is to prefund it with a tax from current workers to *future* workers, which transfers resources in the opposite direction as standard pay-as-you-go financing.

3.1.1   Two Percent Accounts

To be sure, the high average historical real rate of return to equities makes replacing social security with private accounts seem almost painless. To maintain present-law benefits, social security taxes would eventually have to increase to 18.75 percent of payroll, up from 12.4 percent today. Privatizers argue that a small tax would suffice if it were invested in equities. This tax could be as low as 2 percent of payroll—the popular "2 percent accounts."[1] The only cost of this reform would be that some workers would have to pay the 2 percent tax on top of the payroll tax. But, in return, future workers will be helped by the smaller overall tax.

The *expected* small tax rate in a new privatized system is due to what Paul Samuelson once referred to as the "eighth wonder of the world": compound interest. Small differences in annual rates of return between competing saving vehicles add up to big money over many years. The intrinsic average rate of return to a mature social security system like ours equals the growth rate of the payroll-tax base. This is because payroll taxes are not invested in capital but instead mostly paid out immediately as benefits (so-called pay-as-you-go financing). This growth rate has averaged about 2 percent per year after inflation since the early 1970s and is expected to average closer to 1.1 percent per year in the future. Some analysts use an average return to stocks of about 9 percent, which includes roughly 7 percent return to equities and about 2 percent from taxes paid by corporations. Over a thirty-year saving horizon, typical for the average worker, $2 invested at 9 percent will return about the same final benefit as $18.75 invested at 1.1 percent.

1. The "2 percent" accounts were popularized by Feldstein and Samwick (1997) and have been examined as well in Shipman (1998).

But most of the tax saving that appears to come from equity investment comes from attempting to exploit the historical wedge between Treasury bonds and equities—the "equity premium." Empirically, private investors have demanded a considerable premium to accept risky investments. The return to equities above U.S. government bonds during the past century has averaged an astronomical six hundred basis points. Traditionally, this premium has been regarded as compensation for risk. Subtracting this premium from the 9 percent private market return substantially reduces the power of compound interest. At a 3 percent real annual return, the replacement-tax rate would increase from 2 to 12 percent.

To be sure, the equity premium has been a puzzle because it is higher than can be explained by compensation for risk inside the standard neo-classical infinite-horizon model with isoelastic utility.[2] The fact that the equity premium is a puzzle, however, does not mean that it represents "found money." The government can exploit the premium only if the government somehow improves market efficiency. If the government fails to improve the functioning of markets, then the equity-premium puzzle simply reflects the ignorance of economists regarding their understanding of attitudes toward risk. The puzzle does not present a costless exploitable opportunity.

3.1.2   The Risk in Stocks over Long Periods

Privatizing social security would subject a greater amount of retirement saving to market risk by moving to a system of personal accounts invested in the capital market. Equity risk is no small matter even over long horizons. Indeed, there have been fifteen years in this century alone in which the real value of the U.S. stock market fell over 40 percent in the succeeding decade.[3] Moreover, some economists believe that the market might fall another 40 percent or more during the next ten years owing to mean reversion.[4]

While it is sometimes believed that stocks have little risk over the "long run," this view is not shared by many finance economists.[5] Jagannathan and Kocherlakota (1996), for example, have shown that, even for a forty-year holding period in which stocks outperform bonds with *almost* 100 percent certainty, the optimal portfolio consists of 60 percent bonds and 40 percent stocks for a person with a reasonable aversion to risk.

---

2. Mehra and Prescott (1985). Kocherlakota (1996) provides an excellent literature review.
3. These include 1908–12, 1937, 1939, 1965–66, and 1968–73. Not all drops, however, have been sudden. The stock market declined by about 50 percent in real value between 1973 and 1975 and did not return to its pre-1973 level for almost ten years. Shiller (1996) provides an overview of market risk.
4. Campbell and Shiller (1998) argue that, contrary to the efficient market hypothesis, the price-dividend ratio is a powerful predictor of future prices. They predict a 38 percent loss in the real value of stocks over the next decade.
5. See, e.g., Bodie's (1995) extensive examination of the long-run risks associated with stocks.

The large long-run averages in the United States may be misleading for other reasons as well. First, while the U.S. market has performed well during the past century, the same has not been true for major foreign markets, which have rendered an average return of only 1.5 percent after inflation (Goetzmann and Jorion 1996). Various social security reforms might necessitate investments abroad in order to diversify across a larger capital base. Second, calculations that assume a 9 percent real return to equities also ignore the portfolio substitutions that would occur as people might reduce their other holdings of risky assets. These portfolio shifts would tend to reduce both the capital income-tax revenue received by the government and the returns that agents would receive in the rest of their portfolio. Third, using a fixed rate also ignores the fact that a larger capital stock would tend to lower interest rates.

3.1.3   Analysis of Guarantees

At least two approaches have been used to evaluate minimum-benefit guarantees in the context of social security. One method, which I will loosely call *the likelihood method,* uses Monte Carlo simulation based on the historical experience of bonds and equities to predict the likelihood that the assets in the new private accounts fail to replace the benefit provided under social security (Hieger and Shipman 1997; Feldstein, Ranguelova, and Samwick, chap. 2 in this volume). The second method uses arbitrage-pricing theory and assumes that the observable price covariances reflect underlying preferences (Smetters 1998).[6] Both approaches assume similar price moments based on similar historical data. And both approaches report marginal calculations by assuming fixed price moments; that is, they correspond to privatizing a single dollar's worth of social security benefits.

Despite their commonalities, the two approaches can paint strikingly different pictures of the cost of the benefit guarantees. Although the likelihood method does not explicitly calculate the price of a benefit guarantee, it often suggests little cost.[7] For example, Hieger and Shipman argue that, for a contribution rate at today's level, the new private accounts will fail to replace the benefit level provided under social security with only a very small probability. They do not, however, consider the transition from pay-

---

6. Bodie (chap. 8 in this volume) and Marcus (1987) have examined guarantees in related settings. Merton (1998) provides an extensive review of the use of option pricing in evaluating guarantees and numerous other policies.

7. An important exception is Bodie and Crane (1998), which considers a hypothetical worker who retires at age sixty-five, earned $50,000 in the final year of employment, and has an asset target of $446,000 at age sixty-five to provide a twenty-year stream of $30,000 on a real basis. Bodie and Crane show that, although new financial products can play an important role as investment alternatives in defined-contribution plans, a nontrivial amount of risk still remains. In particular, over 10 percent of the population fails to meet the target. For the importance of risk over long horizons, see also Bodie (1995).

as-you-go financing to funding. Feldstein, Ranguelova, and Samwick (chap. 2 in this volume) consider the transition, and their analysis recognizes that the historical data represent draws from an underlying distribution that can include shocks not yet observed. They show that using a contribution rate less than half of today's value will, with a very high probability, lead to benefits that exceed those provided under social security.

In sharp contrast, arbitrage pricing suggests that the unfunded guarantee to replace social security benefits is quite costly. Replacing one unfunded pay-as-you-go benefit with a pay-as-you-go guarantee can lead to only a small net reduction in unfunded liabilities and possibly even an increase (Smetters 1998; see below). Indeed, replacing a *fixed* defined benefit with a *minimum* benefit of the same value is in effect a benefit increase.

Both methods give correct but different information. The likelihood method stresses the modest amount of large persistent shocks in the historical data. By utility adjusting these loss probabilities, the arbitrage approach stresses the high aversion, as reflected in observable price moments, to the infrequent but large shocks, including potential shocks that have yet to be observed.

3.1.4   Limits of the Present Analysis

This paper estimates the reduction in unfunded liabilities following privatization in the presence of a benefit guarantee. In doing so, it makes several assumptions that, on being relaxed, could lead to different results. I am relaxing several of these assumptions in work in progress. The computations reported here, like those of any stylized model, should be viewed with caution.

Complete Markets

One key assumption made in this paper is that the actuarial benefit of a minimum benefit to generation t is equal to the actuarial cost imposed on generation $t + 1$. Option pricing, pioneered by Black and Scholes (1973) and Merton (1973), is used to calculate the value of the benefit guarantee. (A general formulation of arbitrage pricing is given in Ross [1976].) This allows for calculating the value of a guarantee without resorting to approximations. Option-pricing technology also takes risk into account instead of focusing on mean paths. The calculations presented here correspond to what is commonly known as the *complete markets* benchmark, which precludes any possible arbitrage possibility on the part of the government.

In reality, markets are, of course, incomplete in numerous ways. One source of market incompleteness stems from the legal prohibition of leaving negative bequests to future generations. This legal constraint prevents generation t private agents from negotiating risk-sharing deals on the behalf of future generation $t + 1$ agents. The government can overcome this limitation by precommitting future generations.[8]

The actuarial value of a benefit guarantee to one generation might, therefore, be less than or greater than the actuarial cost to the next generation once incomplete markets are taken into account.[9] The exact answer depends, in part, on the correlation of stock returns to generation t with the wages of generation $t + 1$. A tax on generation $t + 1$ is more costly to them if their wages decline at the same time. The standard assumption is that productivity is the only source of uncertainty, which, in turn, implies perfect correlation. In this case, the methodology used in this paper generally underprices the cost of the minimum-benefit guarantee to generation $t + 1$, so the already high cost of guarantees estimated here is understated. Allowing for enough imperfect correlation can shift the calculations in the other direction. Empirically, wages and stock returns appear to be highly correlated at generational frequencies. But the lack of unique long-run period averages implies that the confidence interval includes virtually all values between zero correlation and perfect correlation. The approach taken here, therefore, seems like a useful benchmark, at least until more centuries of data become available.

Marginal Analysis

All computations ignore general equilibrium effects on prices and, therefore, correspond to only a small move toward privatization. In particular, the paper reports the change in unfunded liabilities associated with privatizing a single dollar's worth of social security benefit. The property of risk aversion implies that the marginal cost of guarantee to generation $t + 1$ increases with the absolute size of the guarantee. The focus on marginal analysis, therefore, leads to an underestimate of the cost of the guarantee per dollar guaranteed.

Moral Hazard

The paper ignores two moral hazard issues that could lead to more expensive guarantees. First, it assumes that equity investment is restricted to a broad index, such as the S&P500. Allowing for more choice would tend to increase the cost of a minimum-benefit guarantee because those whose benefit is near the guarantee level would have the incentive to "go for broke." The paper also assumes that private accounts are "locked boxed" until retirement. Allowing for some early withdrawals, perhaps during a recession, could increase the cost of the guarantee.

8. This issue has been examined in the context of social security by Merton (1983) and Bohn (1998).

9. Even if the government can create wealth by completing a missing market, arbitrage pricing still gives the *opportunity cost* of using found money for a particular purpose. Found money can be spent numerous ways in a world with highly substitutable policy instruments.

Imputed Option Prices

Because options for broad stock indices are not available with generational frequency maturity dates, the analysis presented here imputes the cost of option prices using the Black-Scholes option-pricing formula. This approach might underprice the cost of a guarantee since the options on broad indices that are traded are generally more expensive than the Black-Scholes formula predicts given the variance of historical returns.

Political Uncertainty and Information

This paper ignores political uncertainty and information issues. Both these issues are likely to be considerably important. And both challenge the basic assumption inside the D.C. Beltway that contends that any viable move toward personalized accounts must incorporate a minimum benefit equal to what people would have received under social security.

Most Latin American countries, with the exception of Mexico, promise a minimum benefit that is smaller, as a fraction of average preretirement income, than the average benefit provided by the U.S. social security system. The minimum benefit in the much-touted Chilean reform, for example, equals only about 25 percent of average wages (Diamond and Valdés-Prieto 1994). Mitchell and Barreto (1997) show that these plans are quite popular and that this popularity has less to do with economics than with perception and politics. This popularity includes seeing money accumulate in one's own individual account and out of the hands of the government. Americans might be different than Chileans in both personality and history. But few Americans view their future social security benefits free from political uncertainty either. To the extent that this political uncertainty inflates people's discount rate, privatization can exploit a genuine arbitrage possibility, provided that policy makers do not, in turn, create significant uncertainty about how the new private accounts are taxed.

Privatization can also alter *perceived* net tax rates. The net social security tax rate for the main household earner is generally less than the statutory rate because the additional tax paid with an extra dollar of wages corresponds to an increase in future benefits. Social security commingles old-age insurance and redistribution, which makes calculating net tax rates difficult, thereby distorting labor supply. Reducing this complexity could result in sizable improvements to economic efficiency and welfare.

3.2 Pricing a Minimum-Benefit Guarantee

This section outlines the model used and the stylized privatization reform. Both the stylized reform and the model are similar in spirit to those analyzed in the important work of Feldstein and Samwick (1997) and of

Feldstein, Ranguelova, and Samwick (chap. 2 in this volume). The transition toward privatization is accomplished with a simple add-on tax. Following their lead, the model presented here assumes that stocks are risky but that wages and the return to social security are not.[10]

3.2.1 Model

Life-cycle agents live for two periods, and their lifetime utility is given by

$$(1) \qquad E\left\{\sum_{j=1}^{2}\lambda^{j}U(C_{j,t})|t\right\},$$

where $C_{j,t}$ is the consumption in year j by the generation t agent, and λ is the discount factor. The generation t agent earns a labor income equal to Y_1 at age 1, consumes $C_{1,t}$ at age 1, and saves the difference in either equities that pay a risky rate of return equal to e_t during period t or a risk-free bond that pays r. It is assumed that the stock process can be described by an Itō-type stochastic differential equation and, without loss in generality, has a stationary expected yield $\bar{e} \equiv E(e_t \mid t)$. The individual faces a social security payroll tax equal to τ, the proceeds of which are invested in a pay-as-you-go social security asset that pays a rate of return equal to g. The individual in period 2, therefore, has realized assets equal to

$$(2) \qquad A_{2,t} = [(1 - \tau)Y_1 - C_{1,t}] \cdot [(1 + r)\alpha + (1 + e_t)(1 - \alpha)]$$
$$+ \tau Y_1(1 + g),$$

where α $(0 \leq \alpha \leq 1)$ is the share of private assets invested in bonds, and $(1 - \alpha)$ is the share of assets invested in equities. Time subscripts for these portfolio-share variables are omitted. The first-order conditions are standard:

$$(3) \qquad U'(C_{1,t}) = \lambda(1 + r_t)E[U'(C_{2,t})|t],$$

$$(4) \qquad U'(C_{1,t}) = \lambda E[(1 + e_t)U'(C_{2,t})|t].$$

Note that, for linear utility (risk neutrality), these equations imply $r = \bar{e} \equiv E(e_t \mid t)$, that is, that the expected rate of return to equities equals the risk-free rate. Risk aversion, however, implies that $r > \bar{e}$, so it is not valid to compare these instruments on the basis of their expected payoffs.

3.2.2 Privatization Proposal

Privatization begins at time $t = 1$. Generation 0 agents, the current elderly, receive benefits under the current pay-as-you-go social security sys-

---

10. Smetters (1998) investigates the cost of guarantees in the presence of productivity shocks that affect wages, returns to capital, and returns to wage-indexed social security. Privatization tends to lead to even smaller reductions in unfunded liabilities in this context.

tem. These benefits are paid for by generation 1 agents—new workers—who, in turn, receive nothing from social security. Instead, they face an additional new payroll tax,

$$(5) \qquad \tau^N = \frac{\psi \cdot \tau(1 + g)}{(1 + \bar{e})},$$

which is used to finance the new privatized benefit. By construction, the benefit in the new private account, when invested in stocks, yields an *expected* benefit equal to ψ times the benefit provided under social security. I consider $\psi \geq 1$ here since no major privatization plan considers otherwise. The *actual* benefit can take any positive value greater than zero (owing to limited liability).

I assume that the government will wish to guarantee that a new account will replace some fraction χ of the benefit that an agent would have received under social security. A value of $\chi = 1$ means that the new account yields a benefit at least equal to what an agent would receive under social security. This is a common benchmark. Some proposals to privatize the U.S. system, however, contemplate even more generous guarantees ($\chi > 1$), so I will consider those values and smaller values.

Guarantees are financed on a pay-when-needed basis. Generation $t = 2$, therefore, bears the actuarial cost of the benefit guarantee given to generation $t = 1$. Generations $t \geq 2$ do not face the social security payroll tax but instead face only the payroll tax τ^N. Each generation receives a minimum-benefit guarantee from the next generation financed on a pay-when-needed basis. The effect of privatization on the resources of each generation is outlined in Smetters (1998).

3.2.3   Estimates of Guarantee Cost

The government finances the guaranteed minimum benefit on a pay-as-you-go basis using payroll taxes. In Smetters (1998), I show that this fiscal policy is mathematically equivalent to an intergenerational transfer of put stock options, financed on a pay-as-you-go basis, that guarantee that these accounts produce the desired minimum benefit.[11] The corresponding reduction in the ex ante value of unfunded liabilities in stochastic steady state (which incorporates changes in liabilities in the transition) for the more simple model presented in the current paper equals

$$(6) \qquad \left[1 - \psi \cdot \frac{1 + r}{1 + \bar{e}} \cdot \hat{\Omega} \right] \cdot 100\%.$$

11. In the more complicated model considered by Smetters (1998), the strike price of the relevant option is wage indexed since the minimum benefit is tied to what a person would have received under social security (which is waged indexed). That paper also considered the case in which the guarantee is not waged indexed since, in reality, most countries that have implemented privatization have not waged indexed the benefit guarantee.

The variable $\hat{\Omega}$ is the price of a one-period put option on a dollar's worth of equities with a strike price of $\$1[(\chi/\psi)(1 + \bar{e})]$ next period. This strike price has a very intuitive interpretation. A higher expected-benefit level (ψ), generated by a higher contribution rate τ^N, lowers the implicit strike price provided that the guarantee level is not also increased. This is because more dollars are being contributed to the private accounts, and therefore each dollar need not perform as well for the same minimum-benefit guarantee to be satisfied. Similarly, a higher guarantee level (χ) effectively "raises the bar" and requires each dollar to perform better, which, in turn, increases the implicit strike price. The term $(1 + r)/(1 + \bar{e})$ effectively subtracts any attempt to arbitrage between the risk-free rate and the average return to equities.

The parameters in equation (6) are directly observable or can be computed using observable prices. The value of the put option can be priced *exactly* without any additional assumptions about the preferences beyond nonsatiation using the popular Black-Scholes (1973) option-pricing theorem. This is because the underlying price moments are assumed to fully incorporate all relevant information about preferences.

Table 3.1 reports values corresponding to equation (6) for various parameter choices. Following Feldstein and Samwick (1997), the annual average risk-free rate (r) is set equal to 2 percent, and the economy's expected growth rate, g, is set equal to 1.1 percent per year. Bonds, therefore, are assumed to stochastically dominate social security. Privatization is compared against a *solvent* social security system's current-law benefits. This requires eventually increasing the payroll-tax rate to 18.75 percent. I also consider Feldstein and Samwick's choice of the average annual return to equities equal to 9 percent as one of the possible parameter values for $\bar{e}$. The standard deviation of the first differences of logged real returns on the S&P500 equals 0.20 since 1928 and 0.164 since 1949. I conservatively chose 0.16 in all calculations. Each period is assumed to represent thirty years, so the annual rates given above are converted to their thirty-year equivalents in all calculations presented here.[12]

Notice from table 3.1 that privatization with a large minimum-benefit guarantee has difficulty reducing unfunded liabilities. Consider the benchmark case $\psi = 1$, in which the contribution rate to the new accounts is chosen to produce an expected benefit equal to the current social security benefit. This case was considered by Feldstein and Samwick (1997). The model presented here closely replicates their "2 percent" contribution level, which they showed could be used to fully replace social security in the long run.[13] Without a minimum-benefit guarantee, privatization would reduce the ex ante value of unfunded liabilities by 100 percent. Modifying

12. The choice of thirty years follows the two-period illustrative calculations presented in Feldstein and Samwick (1997).
13. Feldstein and Samwick were the first to note how well the two-period framework is able to produce tax rates that are comparable to their more elaborate multiperiod model.

Table 3.1   **New Contribution Rate for Private Account, τ^N, Percentage Reduction in Unfunded Liabilities with a Minimum Benefit, Prefunding Tax Necessary to Eliminate Remaining Unfunded Liabilities, τ^F: Expected Retirement Income Equal to ψ Times Social Security Coverage, Minimum Guaranteed Benefit Equal to χ Times Social Security Coverage, and Expected Return to Equities Equal to $\bar{e}$**

Exogenous Parameters			New Payroll Tax Rate, τ^N	Percent Reduction in Unfunded Liabilities	Prefunding Tax, τ^F	Value of Put Option, $\hat{\Omega}$, per Dollar Contribution (\$)
ψ	χ	$\bar{e}$				
1	1.00	.07	.0342	21.1	.1135	3.32
1	1.00	.09	.0196	13.2	.1248	6.36
2	1.00	.07	.0684	31.6	.0983	1.44
2	1.00	.09	.0392	23.3	.1103	2.81
2	1.25	.07	.0684	10.7	.1284	1.88
2	1.25	.09	.0392	−0.4	.1442	3.68
3	1.00	.07	.1026	35.4	.0928	.90
3	1.00	.09	.0589	29.6	.1012	1.72
3	1.25	.07	.1026	17.1	.1191	1.16
3	1.25	.09	.0589	7.7	.1326	2.25
3	1.50	.07	.1026	−2.5	.1474	1.44
3	1.50	.09	.0589	−15.1	.1654	2.81
5	1.00	.07	.1710	36.4	.0914	.53
5	1.00	.09	.0981	35.1	.0933	.95
5	1.50	.07	.1710	3.9	.1381	.81
5	1.50	.09	.0981	−3.4	.1486	1.51
5	2.00	.07	.1710	−31.9	.1896	1.11
5	2.00	.09	.0981	−46.3	.2102	2.14

Note: Risk-free rate, r, equals 0.02. Growth rate of tax base, g, equals 0.011. Social security tax rate, τ, equals 0.1875. Length of each period equals 30 years.

their analysis to include a minimum-benefit guarantee, however, changes things dramatically. If the current social security benefit is guaranteed (χ = 1), unfunded liabilities are now reduced by only 13 percent. One should not be surprised by this result. Using a payroll tax of only 2 percent to replace a payroll tax of 18.75 percent places a large demand on the equity premium that is unexploitable in the model presented here. Guaranteeing that this equity premium will, in fact, materialize places a large unfunded liability on future generations. Just how accurate is this calculation? Smetters (1998) shows that, in the special case of $\psi = \chi = 1$, one can calculate the reduction in unfunded liabilities using an alternative procedure that does not rely on options pricing.[14] The estimated reduction in unfunded liabilities is almost identical for both methods.

14. The verification is technically valid only for the two-sided bet scenario in which both the downside risk and the excessive upside potential (i.e., returns in excess of expectation)

Table 3.1 shows that, even at high contribution levels, privatization has a difficult time reducing unfunded liabilities. Consider, for example, $\psi = 3$, where the expected private benefit is three times the social security benefit. The contribution level equals 6 percent of payroll, but unfunded liabilities are reduced by only 30 percent at $\chi = 1$. For $\psi = 5$, the contribution level is about 10 percent, but the reduction in unfunded liabilities is only 35 percent. Even at $\psi = 8$ (not shown), privatization reduces unfunded liabilities by only 36 percent even though the contribution rate is now almost 16 percent. A higher contribution level reduces how well *each* contributed dollar must perform in order for the sum of dollars in a private account to satisfy the minimum benefit. This is shown by the smaller value of $\hat{\Omega}$ in table 3.1 associated with higher contribution rates. A higher contribution level, however, requires insuring a *larger number* of dollars. The net effect on unfunded liabilities associated with increasing the contribution level is minimal. So, for example, at $\psi = \chi = 1$, the price of the implicit put option per dollar of contribution equals \$6.36 with a strike of \$13.27. Increasing the contribution level by five times (so that $\psi = 5$) reduces the value of the put option to only \$0.95 since the strike price is now only \$2.65 (i.e., one-fifth of \$13.27). So the sheer number of dollars being insured is now five times greater than before, but the value of the put option per invested dollar decreases by only six and a half times, resulting in only a small net decrease in the unfunded liability.

Note that the "oversaving strategy" associated with high contribution levels is not the same thing as diversification. Diversification is a powerful risk-management technique because it pools assets whose returns are not perfectly correlated. In sharp contrast, a larger contribution level simply throws in more dollars, and the return to each additional dollar is perfectly correlated with the last dollar contributed. The fundamental problem with the oversaving strategy is that it fails to make the intergenerational side payments that are necessary to significantly reduce unfunded obligations. In Smetters (1998), I show that these side payments are an automatic feature of prefunding a defined-benefit system. Since the current paper, however, is about privatization, I consider an alternative technique, which I call *a prefunding guarantee tax.*

Table 3.1 shows the value of a hypothetical prefunding tax from current to future workers that would fully eliminate all unfunded liabilities remaining after privatization:

$$(7) \qquad \tau^F = \frac{\psi \cdot \tau(1 + g)}{(1 + \bar{e})} \cdot \hat{\Omega} \bigg/ Y_1 = \hat{\Omega} \cdot \tau^N.$$

---

are passed to future generations. This would be the case if, e.g., the government were attempting to prefund the current defined-benefit system. The verification works very well in this case. Moreover, for the one-sided bet with $\psi = \chi = 1$, the ex ante value of the unfunded liabilities passed to future generations is very close to the value for the two-sided bet. The reason is that the upside potential has very little value in this case.

Table 3.2   **New Contribution Rate for Private Account, τ^N, Percentage Reduction in Unfunded Liabilities with a Minimum Benefit, Prefunding Tax Necessary to Eliminate Remaining Unfunded Liabilities, τ^f: Expected Retirement Income Equal to ψ Times Social Security Coverage, Minimum Guaranteed Benefit Equal to 0.75 Times Social Security Coverage, and Expected Return to Equities Equal to $\bar{e}$**

Exogenous Parameters			New Payroll Tax Rate, τ^N	Percent Reduction in Unfunded Liabilities	Prefunding Tax, τ^F	Value of Put Option, $\hat{\Omega}$, per Dollar Contribution ($)
ψ	χ	$\bar{e}$				
1	.75	.07	.0342	44.3	.0801	2.34
1	.75	.09	.0196	37.7	.0895	4.56
2	.75	.07	.0684	51.0	.0705	1.03
2	.75	.09	.0392	45.9	.0778	1.98
3	.75	.07	.1026	52.3	.0686	.67
3	.75	.09	.0589	49.9	.0720	1.22
5	.75	.07	.1710	52.3	.0686	.40
5	.75	.09	.0981	52.2	.0687	.70

Note: Risk-free rate, r, equals 0.02. Growth rate of tax base, g, equals 0.011. Social security tax rate, τ, equals 0.1875. Length of each period equals 30 years.

This tax would have to be used to increase public saving (i.e., instead of spending it elsewhere). In practice, this tax could be used to reduce the level of baseline debt or, for example, other pay-as-you-go liabilities associated with Medicare; a surplus would have to be invested in the capital market. Equation (7) has a straightforward interpretation: it says that full self-insurance requires current workers to purchase a put option themselves for each dollar that they invest in their new accounts via the new payroll tax, τ^N. Anything less would pass some insurance cost to future generations, who, by assumption, cannot credibly commit to provide a minimum benefit less than χ times current social security coverage. A tax equal to τ^F, therefore, eliminates all remaining unfunded liabilities after privatization.

Table 3.1 shows that, for the policy parameters $\{\psi, \chi\}$, a total tax rate $(\tau^N + \tau^F)$ of 14.5 percent is needed to fully eliminate all unfunded liabilities. The total tax rate for the policy parameters $\{\psi, \chi\} = \{5, 1\}$ is over 19 percent. The reason for the large difference is that, in the case $\{\psi, \chi\} = \{1, 1\}$, the size of the guarantee funding tax, τ^F, equals 12.5 percent, which is larger than the 9.3 percent tax for $\{\psi, \chi\} = \{5, 1\}$. Because more revenue is transferred to future generations in the case $\{\psi, \chi\} = \{1, 1\}$, it requires a smaller overall tax rate to fully eliminate all unfunded liabilities.

Table 3.2 shows the effects of reducing the guarantee level to 75 percent of the benefit provided by social security. Consider the case $\{\psi, \chi\} = \{1, 0.75\}$. Whereas privatization reduced unfunded liabilities by only 13 percent with a 100 percent guarantee, it now reduces unfunded liabilities by

38 percent with a 2 percent contribution level. Including a funding tax of 9 percent, for a total of 11 percent, fully eliminates all unfunded liabilities.

3.3 Conclusion

This paper shows that high guarantees can be quite costly. But it would be wrong to interpret these results as suggesting that a move toward personalized accounts must be a bad idea. This paper is about *pay-when-needed guarantees*. Although pay-when-needed guarantees appear to be cheap because they cost nothing up front, they can be quite costly from a risk-adjusted perspective. The balancing act facing privatizers is to select a modest guarantee level that is also *credible* over time. Alternatively, privatization could be accompanied with a generous guarantee that is prefunded with a prefunding tax from current workers to future workers.

References

Black, F., and M. J. Scholes. 1973. The pricing of options and corporate liabilities. *Journal of Political Economy* 81, no. 3:637–54.

Bodie, Z. 1995. On the risk of stocks in the long run. *Financial Analysts Journal* 55, no. 3 (May/June): 18–22.

Bodie, Z., and D. B. Crane. 1998. The design and production of new retirement savings products. Harvard Business School. Working Paper no. 98–070.

Bohn, Henning. 1998. Risk sharing in a stochastic overlapping generations economy. University of California, Santa Barbara, January. Mimeo.

Campbell, John, and Robert Shiller. 1998. Valuation ratios and the long-run stock market outlook. *Journal of Portfolio Management* 24, no. 2 (winter): 11–26.

Diamond, Peter, and Salvador Valdés-Prieto. 1994. Social security reforms. In *The Chilean economy: Policy lessons and challenges,* ed. Barry P. Bosworth, Rudiger Dornbusch, and Raúl Labán. Washington, D.C.: Brookings.

Feldstein, Martin, and Andrew Samwick. 1997. The economics of prefunding social security and medicare benefits. In *NBER macroeconomics annual 1997,* ed. Ben S. Bernanke and Julio Rotemberg, 115–48. Cambridge, Mass.: MIT Press.

Goetzmann, William, N., and Philippe Jorion. 1996. Global stock markets in the twentieth century. Yale School of Management/University of California at Irvine. Mimeo.

Gramm, Phil. 1998. Investment-based social security. U.S. Senate, Washington, D.C. Circulated mimeo.

Hieger, Melissa, and William Shipman. 1997. Common objections to a market-based social security: A response. The Cato Project on Social Security Privatization, SSP no. 10. 22 July. Available at http:/www.socialsecurity.org/pubs/ssps/sspstudies.html.

Jagannathan, Ravi, and Narayana Kocherlakota. 1996. Why should older people invest less in stocks than younger people? *Federal Reserve Bank of Minneapolis Quarterly Review* 20, no. 3 (summer): 11–23.

Kocherlakota, Narayana R. 1996. The equity premium: It's still a puzzle. *Journal of Economic Literature* 34, no. 1:42–71.

Marcus, Alan J. 1987. Corporate pension policy and the value of PBGC insurance. In *Issues in pension economics,* ed. Zvi Bodie, John B. Shoven, and David A. Wise. Chicago: University of Chicago Press.

Mehra, Rajnish, and Edward Prescott. 1985. The equity premium: A puzzle. *Journal of Monetary Economics* 15, no. 2:145–61.

Merton, Robert. 1973. Theory of rational option pricing. *Bell Journal of Economics* 4, no. 1 (spring): 141–83.

———. 1983. On the role of social security as a means for efficient risk sharing in an economy where human capital is not tradable. In *Financial aspects of the United States pension system,* ed. Zvi Bodie and John B. Shoven. Chicago: University of Chicago Press.

———. 1998. Applications of option-pricing theory: Twenty-five years later. *American Economic Review* 88, no. 3 (June): 323–49.

Mitchell, Olivia, and Flavio Ataliba Barreto. 1997. After Chile, what? Second-round pension reforms in Latin America. NBER Working Paper no. 6316. Cambridge, Mass.: National Bureau of Economic Research.

Ross, Stephen A. 1976. The arbitrage theory of capital asset pricing. *Journal of Economic Theory* 13, no. 3:341–60.

Shiller, Robert J. 1996. Price-earnings ratios as forecasters of returns: The stock market outlook in 1996. Department of Economics, Yale University. Mimeo.

Shipman, William. 1998. Facts and fantasies about transition costs. The Cato Project on Social Security Privatization, SSP no. 13. October. Available at http://www.socialsecurity.org/pubs/spss/sspstudies.html.

Smetters, Kent. 1998. Privatizing versus prefunding social security. University of Pennsylvania. Mimeo.

Comment   David W. Wilcox

A number of plans for the privatization of social security propose to guarantee that beneficiaries receive a specified minimum amount irrespective of how financial markets may perform. A guarantee of this type transfers to the government part of the risk associated with uncertain future rates of return. This fine paper by Kent Smetters notes that such a guarantee generally represents an unfunded liability of the new system and argues that this liability may be very large—indeed, possibly nearly as large as the unfunded liability associated with the current system.

The central result in Smetter's paper runs as follows: if beneficiaries are guaranteed at least their current-law benefit, and if the payroll-tax rate is set so as to generate the current-law benefit assuming that stocks yield 9 percent year in and year out, then the unfunded liability associated with the benefit guarantee is about 87 percent as large as the unfunded liability in the current system. Moreover, a strategy of "oversaving" turns out to

David W. Wilcox is assistant secretary for economic policy in the U.S. Department of the Treasury.

The views expressed in this Comment are those of the author and are not the official views of the Treasury Department.

be relatively ineffective in reducing the unfunded liability associated with the benefit guarantee: even if the payroll tax rate is set at five times the level required to generate the current-law benefit in expectation, the unfunded liability associated with the benefit guarantee is still 65 percent as large as the unfunded liability in the current system.

In chapter 2 in this volume, Feldstein, Ranguelova, and Samwick (FRS) also examine the potential cost of benefit guarantees. They estimate that the probability of the guarantee becoming binding could plausibly be designed to be quite low. And, even in the event that the guarantee is binding, they estimate that the cost in most cases would be relatively modest. Overall, FRS believe the financial burden of benefit guarantees to be manageable: "The remaining moderate level of retiree risk [of a benefit that is lower than under current law, taking into account the higher expected return on financial assets] can be completely eliminated by a government guarantee that can be provided with very little risk to taxpayers."

It could be that both papers are correct. Smetters could be correct that financial markets would place a very high price on a benefit guarantee of the type he studies, possibly because the required payment in rare cases would be very large, possibly because the circumstances in which the payment is required are precisely the circumstances in which taxpayers are especially unhappy about providing it. FRS could simultaneously be correct that the government will need to make good on a well-designed benefit guarantee with only low probability and that the required payment will in most cases be small.

Notwithstanding that both papers could be correct, they differ in two important respects. First, Smetters relies on the fundamental validity of observed securities prices as reflections of informed decisions of rational agents with sensible degrees of risk aversion, even if we economists cannot write down a simple model that explains all aspects of these data. In particular, Smetters treats the equity premium as reflecting compensation for risk and not as "a costless exploitable opportunity" for the government. By contrast, FRS question the wisdom of grounding decisions about government policy in data that we cannot fully understand or explain, save perhaps by appeal to an implausible assumption about the degree of risk aversion in financial markets. (In the context of a standard representative-agent model with isoelastic utility, the observed equity premium can be explained only by assuming an implausibly large coefficient of relative risk aversion.)

A second important dimension along which the two papers differ is the metric they use to assess the cost of a guarantee. FRS adopt a *frequentist* perspective (Smetters calls it *the likelihood approach*) and provide information about tail probabilities and the shape of distributions associated with investment outcomes. By contrast, Smetters views the issue through the prism of financial market prices that should embed all the FRS information about tail probabilities but should as well incorporate information about preferences and covariances with consumption.

In principle, there is no inherent conflict between these two approaches; they simply provide different information about the same question. Smetters evaluates the cost of a benefit guarantee at market prices. Presumably, this is a useful approach if one believes that government policies should be evaluated assuming that the price of risk is the same to the government as it is to private transactors in financial markets. By contrast, FRS provide some of the raw material that one would need to assemble in order to evaluate the cost of a benefit guarantee under the assumption that the government should be willing to transact as a risk-neutral agent.[1] All other differences between the two papers aside, one can obviously arrive at different conclusions about the desirability of a given policy depending on the price one attaches to the financial risk that may be involved in that policy.

The issue of whether risk-related aspects of government policies should be evaluated at market prices crops up in a surprising number of contexts in the practical policy-making arena. Some of these instances arise out of the budget "scorekeeping" process. By way of background, both the Congressional Budget Office and the Office of Management and Budget have important responsibilities in estimating the cost of legislative proposals moving through the Congress. The current state of the art in this area is to assign, in effect, a zero price to risk—or, to put it slightly differently, to assume that the government operates as a risk-neutral agent.

A recent instance arises in the context of the student loan program. Under current law, payments to lenders under this program are indexed to the Treasury-bill rate. On a number of occasions, Congress has considered proposals to shift the index to something more closely approximating the cost of funds to lenders in this market—perhaps the commercial paper rate or LIBOR. A move along these lines would reduce lenders' so-called basis risk (the risk associated with fluctuations in the spread between their borrowing and their lending rates). However, the government would take on a similar risk because it would still be borrowing at the Treasury-bill rate but would begin making payments indexed to some private-sector rate. Current budgetary scorekeeping practice would take account of such factors as *average* spreads between Treasury and private rates but would effectively assign a budgetary cost of zero to any basis risk assumed by the government. Swap markets, on the other hand, take quite a different view of the price of risk.

A separate set of questions pertains to the plausibility of Smetters's estimates. Of necessity, his model is of course highly stylized. Which omitted

1. I say *some* rather than *all* because FRS do not provide a complete mapping of tail probabilities and tail shapes.

features might bias his estimate of the cost of a guarantee, and in which direction? First, as Smetters notes, his model provides no discretion in the choice of a portfolio—either within the realm of equity investments (e.g., small cap vs. large cap) or in the larger design of the portfolio (e.g., whether to have any equity exposure at all). Even in the absence of moral hazard, any flexibility in portfolio choice will drive up the cost of a benefit guarantee (because the government would be left holding the downside of any available choice while beneficiaries would reap the upside), so long as the rates of return on the available alternatives are not perfectly correlated. And moral hazard would drive up the cost still further.

Second, because the agents in Smetters's model work only one period, there is no heterogeneity in the timing of earnings. In the real world, two workers who accumulate an identical entitlement to social security benefits may have quite different profiles of earnings and hence may have experienced quite different exposure to the stock market. Again, heterogeneity of this type will tend to push up the cost of a guarantee.

Third, because the agents in Smetters's model live only one period in retirement, there is no need for annuitization. In the real world, the policy process may choose to impose a requirement for annuitization in order to protect beneficiaries from outliving their social security wealth. The rate at which account balances are annuitized represents another source of financial risk, quite distinct from the pattern of equity returns, and hence another source of upward push to the actual cost of a guarantee.

The paper by Smetters touches on fundamental issues in the debate about social security reform. What makes that paper even more interesting is the productive dialogue in which it engages with the work of FRS. The social security reform process will be the beneficiary of this productive interchange.

Discussion Summary

Stephen Ross wondered why the equity-risk premium enters the analysis, given that it is being called *an arbitrage-pricing approach.* In particular, he asked why the equity-risk premium plays any role in deciding what the values of the current benefits are under any alternative plan. *Kent Smetters* responded that the experiments in this paper, as in others, are being done by choosing a payroll tax such that the expected benefit of the new system is equal to the benefit that would have been received under social security. The equity-risk premium affects the choice of the payroll tax. Put differently, one is trying to exploit the wedge between $\bar{e}$, the expected rate of return on equities, and g, the return that social security would have given.

Effectively, the results suggest that this wedge cannot be exploited in the case of risk adjustment.

Ross concluded that using the term *arbitrage* in the context of the paper might be misleading as the analysis does use a utility-based model. *Deborah Lucas* concurred.

Robert King raised the issue that option prices generated by the Black-Scholes formula are independent of the equity premium. *Smetters* replied that, although the equity premium does not explicitly appear in the formula, it does matter through the strike price chosen.

Martin Feldstein emphasized that this entire discussion is a very fundamental issue and encouraged subsequent discussions about the role of the equity premium in the social security reform debate.

James Poterba inquired why Smetters did not consider looking at the market price of long-term options on a broad index of stocks in order to gauge the cost of obtaining a truncated distribution of returns, similar to the one implicit in a benefit guarantee. Depending on one's view of the Arrow-Lind theorem, an interesting alternative for using the tax system to redistribute the risk of a shortfall is to have financial market participants bear it. The issue at the core of the debate is which arrangement bears this risk in the most efficient way.

Zvi Bodie remarked that such options are traded only for maturities up to three years. Longer-maturity instruments are available only over the counter.

John Shoven noted that it could be argued that both Smetters and Feldstein, Ranguelova, and Samwick probably set themselves too high a goal in their papers as the current social security system does not provide a benefit guarantee either. He wondered whether it was not too ambitious to try to replace the current system with one that is far superior in terms of benefit guarantees.

In a similar vein, *Feldstein* asked Smetters to point out what reduction in unfunded liabilities would correspond to a scenario where the guarantee (χ) equals 75 percent rather than 100 percent. He noted that the results across the rows in table 3.1 looked roughly linear and symmetrical and wondered whether it was therefore correct to infer from rows 3 and 5 that the reduction in unfunded liabilities would be in the 50 percent range for χ equal to 75 percent. *Smetters* confirmed this.

With reference to Poterba's question, *Antonio Rangel* remarked that, even if the market were cheaper than the tax system in bearing the risk of a shortfall, it would not yield full efficiency in an intergenerational context.

Henning Bohn noted that the pricing approach in this paper assumes complete markets. This standard assumption might not be valid in the context of the paper because future unborn generations, currently not exposed to equity risk, might not assess the same price for the bailout of a cohort in the event of a shortfall as the generation currently alive would.

This issue relates to the potential imperfection in risk sharing from an ex ante perspective in overlapping-generations models. The shadow value of receiving a certain guarantee might be different across different cohorts.

Andrew Samwick asked Smetters to clarify the difference between his setup and the one in the Feldstein, Ranguelova, and Samwick paper. In particular, row 2 of table 3.1 shows a payroll tax τ^N of around 2 percent and a reverse pay-as-you-go tax τ^R of 12.4 percent. Although these numbers are quite similar to some of the exercises reported in Feldstein, Ranguelova, and Samwick, the results are not. The discussant, *David Wilcox,* pointed out that there is a third tax, not reported in the table, which is the tax on the current generation to bear the unfunded liability of the current system.

John Campbell stated that he wanted to follow up on Bohn's remark. Some models of the equity premium emphasize constraints faced by the young. For instance, Constantinides, Donaldson, and Mehra (1998) explain the equity premium by imposing borrowing constraints on the young. They have a substantial amount of human capital and would like to borrow to invest in equities, but they cannot. This rationalizes a high equity premium. In that context, a government system that in effect relaxes the constraint by using the taxing power of the government would affect asset prices. This possibility is excluded by Smetters's assumption of fixed market prices.

Smetters stated that the portfolio choice is restricted and that this ignores potential sources of moral hazard. Not doing so would increase the unfunded liabilities. Also, the focus of the paper is on a two-period model, which eliminates some sources of risk, as Wilcox noted. Enriching the model with either of these features would be an interesting extension.

With respect to Poterba's remark, Smetters stated that he initially examined market data for two-year options on a broad stock index. He found that these are overpriced by the market, according to the Black-Scholes formula. Moreover, the Arrow-Lind theorem assumes orthogonality, which is not the case in the model of the paper.

Smetters agreed with Shoven's comment that the current system does not completely commit to paying out the promised benefits.

Regarding incomplete markets, Smetters made two points. First, it is not obvious to tell from current models whether hedging is cheaper for the government than for private agents in the case of incomplete markets. Second, even if it were cheaper for the government so that there would be some arbitrage surpluses, the costs in the paper are to be interpreted as opportunity-cost calculations. In other words, if these surpluses did exist, they could be used for other purposes as well.

Finally, Smetters agreed with Campbell that the introduction of frictions, for instance, borrowing constraints, would have important implications for this line of research.

Reference

Constantinides, George, John Donaldson, and Rajnish Mehra. 1998. Junior can't borrow: A new perspective on the equity premium puzzle. NBER Working Paper no. 6617. Cambridge, Mass.: National Bureau of Economic Research.

4

Can Market and Voting Institutions Generate Optimal Intergenerational Risk Sharing?

Antonio Rangel and Richard Zeckhauser

We study economies confronted with generational risks. Such risks are shocks that affect all the members of a generation but have a smaller effect on other generations. They include the risk of having a bear market during the years one saves for retirement, being the age cohort that goes off to an extended war, or having one's prime employment years during a recession. With significant shocks of this sort, there are substantial benefits to intergenerational risk sharing. For example, young generations could insure the elderly against inadequate stock market performance. Indeed, precisely this risk-sharing measure has been discussed in the current debate on social security reform.

The central question of this paper is, Can market institutions or government actions generate efficient intergenerational risk sharing? Both markets and governments have the potential to promote risk sharing, markets through the trade of financial instruments, governments through social insurance programs. Each has potential on the intergenerational front since there are financial instruments that last for many generations and some social insurance programs, such as social security or subsidized education, transfer resources across generations. However, our analysis dashes hopes. We show that markets have problems generating optimal

Antonio Rangel is assistant professor of economics at Stanford University. Richard Zeckhauser is professor of political economy at the John F. Kennedy School of Government, Harvard University, and a research associate of the National Bureau of Economic Research.

The authors thank Peter Boasserts, John Campbell, David Cutler, Peter Diamond, Martin Feldstein, Peter Hammond, Matthew Jackson, Chad Jones, John Ledyard, Jeffrey Liebman, Marcos Lisboa, Greg Mankiw, Stephen Morris, Giussepe Moscarini, Thomas Nechyba, Ben Polack, Thomas Sargent, Chris Sims, Steve Tadelis, and participants in the Macro seminar at Harvard and Yale, the Public Economics seminar at Harvard, and the NBER preconference for their helpful comments.

insurance and that self-interested voters may defeat government efforts to overcome market failures.

We use a simple endowment economy with uncertainty and overlapping generations to study the problem of intergenerational risk sharing. Each period there is uncertainty about the size of the aggregate endowment and its distribution between young and old. To see the role for intergenerational risk sharing, consider an extreme example in which the entire endowment goes either to the young or to the old. Absent a risk-sharing arrangement, agents consume nothing half the time, a woefully bad outcome. By contrast, a contingent claim or government program that transfers resources from young to old when the old get nothing, and vice versa, increases the welfare of every generation.

Optimality is a straightforward concept in deterministic economies but not in stochastic economies with overlapping generations. In the latter, at least two notions of optimality are frequently used: ex ante and interim efficiency. Both define Pareto improvements in the standard way—"a policy is Pareto improving if, and only if, it improves someone's welfare without hurting anyone else"—but differ on what the word *anyone* means. For the proponents of ex ante efficiency, identity is given solely by time of birth. Thus, an individual born in a given period but in two different states of the world is the same person. The advocates of interim efficiency disagree. For them, identity is given by time of birth and state of the world at birth. In the interim view, every generation has many different incarnations, and a policy can be Pareto improving only if it does not decrease the welfare of any of them. Many results in the literature on intergenerational risk sharing hold for one notion of optimality but not the other. Not surprisingly, there is spirited intellectual debate about which criterion is appropriate. We sidestep this debate and, like the rabbi in many a story, declare both sides correct. In particular, we show that both markets and voting institutions have difficulties generating desirable outcomes whether judged by ex ante or interim efficiency.

We start the analysis by establishing, as a benchmark, the intergenerational transfers that yield efficient outcomes. Clearly, efficient risk sharing would be achieved if a disinterested social planner orchestrated the transfers. But such a figure, however often invoked in economics, is chimerical. Efficient risk sharing will emerge only if it is generated endogenously by the institutions in our society. In other words, to determine what risk spreading will take place, we need to examine the intergenerational transfers that will be generated by markets and governments.

Among the market's finer achievements is its ability to spread risks in static economies. Financial assets, derivatives, and contingent claims are among the instruments that markets deploy as they reallocate risks to those who can bear them most cheaply. Should not such instruments, at least if the asset structure is rich enough, be able to spread risks optimally across generations? Alas not. First, since agents cannot trade before they are born, they cannot buy ex ante insurance. The aspiration level for markets is at best interim efficiency. Unfortunately, even this far lower hurdle presents problems. To understand why, it is useful to study markets with varying asset structures.

First, consider an economy with contingent commodities. Within it, agents facing the risk of a stock market collapse could insure themselves by purchasing contingent claims that pay off only given that eventuality. They could finance these purchases by selling contingent claims that pay off when the stock market booms. These trades provide valuable insurance because they shift consumption from high- to low-consumption states. However, with overlapping generations, trade takes place sequentially, and agents can trade only with coexisting generations, who face similar risks. As a result, these valuable trades do not take place.

Next, add an infinitely lived asset to this economy. The asset, call it *money,* pays no dividends and offers no consumption value. Infinitely lived assets are important because they generate intergenerational transfers when traded at positive prices. If prices fluctuate in the right way, these transfers even have the potential to generate efficient risk sharing. In fact, money generates interim efficient insurance in some, although not all, economies. Positively priced money generates backward transfers, those from young to old. Forward transfers can arise only if money trades at a negative price. But, in equilibrium, the price of money can never be negative since the older generation could simply destroy it rather than sell it. Thus, money can provide efficient risk sharing only when backward transfers are what is required. Unfortunately, many interesting generational risks, such as stock market risk, sometimes require transfers from old to young. Here, efficient risk sharing has the young help the old when the market drops but lets the young participate in the gains when the market booms.

Finally, consider an economy with a market mechanism that can generate forward transfers. This mechanism is a voluntary scheme in which each generation makes voluntary contributions during its youth and receives, as payoffs in old age, the contributions of the next young generation.[1] Such an asset could be run by any infinitely lived institution and is in spirit an intergenerational Ponzi scheme. Here, unlike the case of money, nothing "real" is exchanged. Yet the two assets are extremely similar. Agents are willing to provide (invest in) them only if they believe that future generations will do the same. Since money pays no dividends and has no consumption value, agents will buy it only when they believe that their successors will do the same. Thus, there is always an equilibrium in which money

1. As far as we know, Demange and Laroque (1999) is the first publication describing this mechanism.

has no value. Similarly, in the voluntary scheme, there is an equilibrium with zero contributions. In both cases, the value of the asset depends on self-fulfilling expectations. The only difference between them is that the voluntary system can generate negative contributions and thus forward transfers. As a result, with a voluntary pay-as-you-go mechanism, there is always an equilibrium that yields interim efficient risk sharing. However, as we argue later in the paper, this equilibrium is unlikely to arise.

These three institutions—contingent commodities, infinitely lived assets, and voluntary transfer mechanisms—represent the archetypal market structures that might generate efficient risk sharing. Since none of them works in all cases, it is natural to ask whether government policy can ride to the rescue. Obviously, a government acting as social planner could help by carrying out the transfers required for optimality. The government, after all, does have the power to transfer income across generations and thereby share risks efficiently. But the government's objectives are determined by political pressure, not by an innate desire to correct inefficiencies. Thus, the only interventions that are feasible are those that are desired by a majority of the voters.

A government with the power to carry out transfers between generations could use this power to implement optimal generational risk sharing. But it could also use it to carry out a selfish, purely redistributional policy. Voters, young and old, might choose to stick with the efficient risk-sharing rule, but they might vote to expropriate the other generation instead. Since old citizens die at the end of the period, they always favor imposing a big redistributive tax on the young. For example, even if the stock market boomed, they might favor taxing the young and, if in the majority, might vote that policy.

The young have different incentives, which may lead them to behavior that at least has a nobler cast. There are equilibria in which, even though they are in political control, the young implement an optimal risk-sharing rule that requires transfers to the elderly. They ascribe to what we label *the golden transfer policy:* transfer unto your predecessors as you would have your successors transfer unto you. Not only do the young refrain from expropriating the elderly, but they give actual transfers because they want to get equivalent transfers from the next generation of young voters. Thus, if the median voter is always young, as such a voter might be with consistent population growth, equilibria can readily emerge that offer efficient ex ante risk sharing, even when the immediate interest of the median voter would be to defect, indeed, to impose transfers in precisely the opposite direction.

Our applause should be restrained, however, since there is always another equilibrium at which the generations ignore risk-sharing considerations and expropriate each other to the extent that voting power and the Constitution allow. In this case, every generation is worse off than it would be with generational autarky, where the initial allocation prevailed and no transfers were possible.

The formal conclusions of this paper are dreary. The real world offers a somewhat brighter picture since the story of intergenerational overlap on which we rely is extreme, with lives lasting but two periods. If agents were to live for, say, seventy-five or more periods, both market and voting institutions would accomplish considerably more risk sharing. With just three-period lives, the young and the middle-aged generations can insure each other against the next period's risk since they will then be alive together. For example, the young might sell contingent claims against a stock market plunge, receiving in return some claims in case of boom. As overlaps expand, the market's performance improves, although full efficiency remains out of reach. Longer life spans will also tend to lure voters more toward cooperative behavior and less toward expropriation. Other features of the political landscape, for example, nongenerational concerns or risk sharing within generations, also have the ability to temper generational ruthlessness.

We conclude this introduction by relating our work to the existing literature. The main contribution of this paper is to take both market and political institutions seriously. There is a series of papers (see Bohn 1998; Enders and Lapan 1982; Fisher 1983; Gale 1994; Green 1977; Gordon and Varian 1988; and Smith 1982) that describe a range of circumstances under which market institutions produce insufficient risk sharing and thus leave open a role for Pareto-improving government interventions. Some of these papers use more realistic models of the economy, but, unlike ours, they do not study whether institutions that might overcome the inefficiency are feasible.

Obviously, our approach is also related to the literature on monetary equilibria in stochastic economies (see, e.g., Demange and Laroque 1998, 1999; Lucas 1972; Manuelli 1990; Muench 1977; and Peled 1982, 1984). However, there are important differences between the two approaches. We are interested in money as one of several mechanisms that might generate an optimal sequence of intergenerational transfers. In some sense, we follow a top-to-bottom approach. We first characterize the optimal transfers and then concentrate on specific institutions that might be able to generate them. By contrast, this literature follows a bottom-to-top approach. It considers the specific case of markets with money and shows that, whenever monetary equilibrium in which money trades at positive prices exists, it yields interim but not ex ante efficient risk sharing. Using our different approach, we show that money can fail to produce sufficient risk sharing, even when interim efficiency is the measuring rod.

Section 4.1 presents a model of the economy. Section 4.2 explores what might be meant by efficient risk sharing between generations. Section 4.3 introduces retirement risk as a specific form of generational risk, setting the stage to examine the risk-spreading performance of alternative institutions. Section 4.4 spotlights the strengths and vulnerabilities of market institutions as risk-sharing instruments. Section 4.5 gives parallel treatment to voting institutions. Section 4.6 concludes.

4.1 A Model of the Economy

Consider a simple overlapping-generations economy in which every period $t = 0, \pm 1, \pm 2, \ldots$, a new generation t is born and lives for two periods, t and $t + 1$. To focus on intergenerational risk sharing, suppose that there is only one agent per generation. Every period agents receive an endowment that depends on the state of the world θ. This is a pure exchange economy, and the endowments cannot be stored. Thus, every period aggregate consumption equals the aggregate endowment. Let $e^y(\theta_t)$ denote the endowment of the young in period t, $e^o(\theta_t)$ the endowment of the old, and $E(\theta_t)$ the aggregate endowment. The set of states is finite, and the endowment process is independently and identically distributed (i.i.d.), with the probability of θ given by $\pi(\theta)$.

Each generation is born after that period's uncertainty is resolved. This assumption is important because it implies that young and old cannot enter into mutually beneficial risk-sharing agreements. After its birth, a generation faces uncertainty only in old age, and, since only future generations can insure them against this risk, there are no gains from trading with the elderly alive at the time.

The preferences of generation t are given by

$$u(c_t^y, c_{t+1}^o) = f(c_t^y) + f(c_{t+1}^o),$$

where c_t^y and c_{t+1}^o denote, respectively, its consumption when young and in old age. We assume that f is continuously differentiable, strictly concave, and increasing and satisfies $\lim_{x \to 0} f'(x) = \infty$ and $\lim_{x \to 0} f(x) = -\infty$. These standard properties guarantee interior solutions to the maximization problems described below. The last two properties indicate a very strong desire for consumption smoothing since they imply that any amount of positive consumption in both periods is preferred to an allocation with zero consumption in either youth or old age.

An allocation is a function that specifies the consumption of young and old for any possible history of shocks. Given the purpose of our analysis and the nature of the model, we focus on stationary allocations in which consumption depends only on the current state of the world. In addition, feasibility requires that

$$c^y(\theta) + c^o(\theta) \leq E(\theta) \quad \text{for all } \theta.$$

As we will see below, optimal intergenerational risk sharing requires carrying out intergenerational transfers between young and old that might

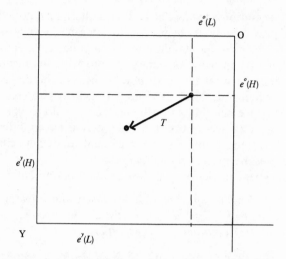

Fig. 4.1   Endowments of old and young in high and low states

depend on the state of the world. A risk-sharing rule is a function $T(\theta)$ that specifies the transfer from young to old in state θ; negative values indicate transfers in the opposite direction. Clearly, a sharing rule generates allocations equal to

$$c^y(\theta) = e^y(\theta) - T(\theta) \quad \text{and} \quad c^o(\theta) = e^o(\theta) + T(\theta).$$

Figure 4.1 gives a graphic representation of the economy that will be useful later on. The diagram is a variation of the well-known Edgeworth box. Consider an economy with only two states, high and low. The dimensions of the box are given by the size of the aggregate endowment, the low state on the horizontal axis, the high state on the vertical axis. A point in the box denotes how the endowment is distributed between young and old in each state. (The endowments of the old are measured from the upper-right-hand corner.) For example, the central point represents a sharing rule in which young and old always consume the same amounts. Endowments and final allocations are denoted by points, risk-sharing rules by vectors.

4.2   What Is Efficient Risk Sharing?

The goal of this paper is to understand whether market and political institutions can generate optimal risk sharing. Hence, the analysis starts with a discussion of optimality. This notion is so widely used in economics that the reader might find it surprising that a discussion is needed at all. The problem is that, while the concept of optimality is straightforward in deterministic economies, the same is not true in stochastic models with overlapping generations. In fact, at least two alternative notions are frequently (and passionately) used: ex ante and interim efficiency. Both define Pareto improvements in the standard way—"a policy is Pareto improving if, and only if, it improves someone's welfare without hurting anyone else"—but differ on what the word *anyone* means. The disagreement is based on a different conception of identity. Is identity given solely by time of birth, or is it given by time of birth and the state of the world at birth? In other words, is an agent born in a given period but in different states of the world the same agent? For the proponents of ex ante efficiency, he is. The advocates of interim optimality disagree.

The disagreement carries over to the definition of optimality:

DEFINITION 1. *Ex ante optimality: A stationary allocation $c(\,\cdot\,)$ is ex ante Pareto optimal if there does not exist another feasible stationary allocation $\bar{c}(\,\cdot\,)$ such that for every generation t*

$$\sum_{\theta}\sum_{\hat{\theta}} \pi(\theta)\pi(\hat{\theta})u(\bar{c}_t^{\,y}(\theta),\bar{c}_t^{\,o}(\hat{\theta})) \geq \sum_{\theta}\sum_{\hat{\theta}} \pi(\theta)\pi(\hat{\theta})u(c_t^{y}(\theta),c_t^{o}(\hat{\theta})),$$

with strict inequality for at least one generation.

DEFINITION 2. *Interim optimality: A stationary allocation $c(\,\cdot\,)$ is interim Pareto optimal if there does not exist another feasible stationary allocation $\bar{c}(\,\cdot\,)$ such that for every generation t and every state θ*

$$\sum_{\hat{\theta}} \pi(\hat{\theta})u(\bar{c}_t^{\,y}(\theta),\bar{c}_t^{\,o}(\hat{\theta})) \geq \sum_{\hat{\theta}} \pi(\hat{\theta})u(c_t^{y}(\theta),c_t^{o}(\hat{\theta})),$$

with strict inequality for at least one pair (t, θ).

In the ex ante view, since agents are able to compute expected utility before their birth, well-being is determined by the average welfare of their different incarnations. These averages have no meaning for the proponents of interim optimality. For them, consciousness and identity cannot precede birth, and, thus, when an agent is able to evaluate utility for the first time, he incorporates in his calculations all the information that he has at birth. As a result, he dislikes a policy that may have increased his welfare ex ante but decreases it in the particular state in which he is born.

An interim Pareto improvement is less likely to exist than an ex ante one. In the ex ante view, a Pareto improvement can occur when a generation wins in some incarnations, loses in others, but is better off on average. This is not interim Pareto improving, however, because it hurts some incarnations. As a result, every ex ante efficient allocation is also interim efficient, but not vice versa.

Which notion is the correct one?[2] Clearly, the answer to this question

2. This question has been the subject of a long debate that started, at least, with the publication of Lucas (1972). Lucas proposed an ex post notion of optimality in which agents

must be based on the merits of the notion, not on whether market or political institutions are able to generate that type of optimality. One must first select the optimality criteria and only then study which institutions are able to generate it.

Peled (1982) argues for interim efficiency because it mirrors the informational structure of the economy. In particular, it assumes that agents evaluate policy with the same information that they have when they trade in the market or when they vote: the young generation t knows θ_t but not θ_{t+1}. By contrast, the informational structure in the ex ante view has the flavor of a Rawlsian veil of ignorance in which agents evaluate policy before their birth.

This is a sound argument, but it is not sufficient to rule in favor of interim efficiency. If agents could travel out of time and trade before their birth, with knowledge about when they will be born but not about how uncertainty will be resolved, they would buy ex ante insurance. Thus, agents do not insure ex ante because they are technologically constrained (time travel not having been invented yet). But they would remove the constraint if they could find a way. In this view, the ex ante transfers can be seen as a way of removing the technological constraint. Agents would experience the technology as an improvement, and, as a result, they also view the ex ante transfers as Pareto improving.

Since both efficiency notions have significant standing and the goal of this paper is not to advocate for one or the other, we sidestep the debate by analyzing the risk-sharing properties of institutions under both points of view. As an added benefit, the reader might find that the analysis sheds light on the differences between them.

In the rest of this section, we characterize the set of optimal risk-sharing rules. Let us look first at ex ante optimality. The set of ex ante efficient stationary allocations is given as

$$\max \sum_{\theta} \sum_{\hat{\theta}} \pi(\theta)\pi(\hat{\theta})u(c^y(\theta), c^o(\hat{\theta})),$$

subject to

$$c^y(\theta) + c^o(\theta) \leq E(\theta) \quad \text{for all } \theta.$$

The properties of $f(\,\cdot\,)$ imply that the optimal allocation is uniquely determined by the first-order conditions

---

know how uncertainty is resolved throughout their lives. This notion is unsatisfactory because it rules out, by assumption, any gains from insurance. Muench (1977) pointed out these problems—which Lucas acknowledged in a reply (see Lucas 1977)—and proposed the ex ante and interim notions as an alternative. In a classic paper, Peled (1982) responded to Muench by forcefully defending interim optimality. The literature has used ex ante and interim notions ever since.

(1) $$f'(c_{EA}^y(\theta)) = f'(E(\theta) - c_{EA}^y(\theta)),$$

which imply the simple risk-sharing rule

$$c_{EA}^y(\theta) = c_{EA}^o(\theta) = \frac{1}{2}E(\theta).$$

Thus, the ex ante optimal allocation is independent of how the endowment is distributed between young and old. As we will see in a moment, the same is true for interim efficient allocations.

Now look at interim optimality. Let $\gamma(\theta_1), \ldots, \gamma(\theta_n)$ be strictly positive weights satisfying $\Sigma \, \gamma(\theta) = 1$. The set of interim efficient stationary allocations is given by the solution, for all possible weights, to[3]

(2) $$\max \sum_\theta \sum_{\hat\theta} \gamma(\theta)\pi(\hat\theta)u(c^y(\theta), c^o(\hat\theta)),$$

subject to

$$c^y(\theta) + c^o(\theta) \le E(\theta) \quad \text{for all } \theta.$$

Once more, we get that, for each vector of weights $\gamma(\,\cdot\,)$, the solution is fully and uniquely characterized by the first-order conditions

(3) $$\gamma(\theta)f'(c_{IN}^y(\theta)) = \pi(\theta)f'(E(\theta) - c_{IN}^y(\theta)).$$

The difference between the two sharing rules can be seen in figure 4.2. The dotted curve denotes the locus of interim efficient allocations. By contrast, the unique ex ante allocation is the point EA lying at the center of the box. Thus, for every endowment point, there is a unique ex ante efficient risk-sharing rule but many interim efficient ones.

We will see below that institutions have a harder time generating forward transfers, which go from old to young, than backward transfers, which go from young to old. Thus, it is important to identify the cases in which forward transfers are needed to restore efficiency. Figures 4.3 and 4.4 provide an answer to this question. The diagram in figure 4.3 can be used to describe both the economy with endowment e and, by moving the endowment point around, the class of economies with that aggregate endowment. As figure 4.3 illustrates, the optimal ex ante risk-sharing rule requires a transfer toward EA, regardless of the endowment's location. Southwest movements indicate transfers from young to old, whereas northeast movements indicate forward transfers. We can see that the only economies in which ex ante efficiency can be restored using backward transfers are those to the northeast of EA. In other words, for a large class

---

3. This program yields an ex ante optimal allocation if, and only if, $\gamma(\theta) = \pi(\theta)$. This is another way of seeing that ex ante efficiency implies interim efficiency, but the opposite is not true.

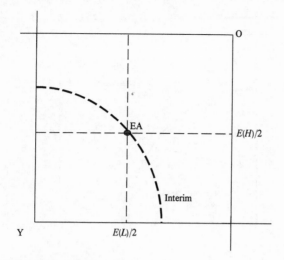

Fig. 4.2   Efficient risk-sharing rules

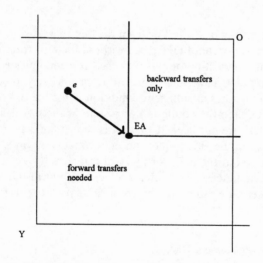

Fig. 4.3   Transfers that restore ex ante efficiency

of economies, optimal ex ante risk sharing requires the use of transfers from old to young in at least one state of the world.

In figure 4.4, we repeat the analysis for the case of interim efficiency. Since the set of efficient allocations has now increased, the problem is less severe. However, it is still the case that any economy to the southwest of the optimal locus must employ forward transfers to achieve an efficient outcome. Thus, as the diagram shows, forward transfers are needed under either criterion.

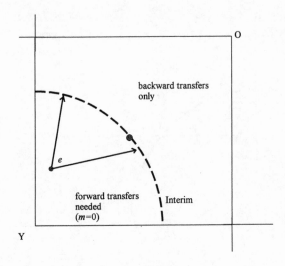

Fig. 4.4   Transfers that restore interim efficiency

Some of the results below follow from the fact that, in some economies, optimal risk sharing cannot take place without forward transfers. Clearly, these results are interesting only if this class of economies is empirically relevant. So, in practice, when are forward transfers likely to be necessary? As figure 4.4 illustrates, a sufficient condition is for the old to be significantly wealthier than the young in every state of the world. By contrast, forward transfers are not needed when it is the young who are wealthier, for example, when the elderly have no endowments in any state. In fact, some papers rule out the need for forward transfers by concentrating exclusively on the later case. The difference between our results and those in the previous literature can be attributed, in large part, to this restrictive assumption.

4.3   Example: Retirement Risk

The possibility of a stock market collapse and its effects on the welfare of retirees is an important issue in this volume and a prominent example of generational risks. For this reason, it is useful to look at an example that focuses precisely on this issue. Suppose that agents have a constant endowment when young but face uncertainty about their retirement income, which depends on stock market performance over their earning years. For concreteness, the stock market either collapses (L) or booms (H), with equal probability. This is represented by the endowment process $e^y(L) = e^y(H) = 2$, $e^o(L) = 1$, and $e^o(H) = 4$. Agents' preferences are logarithmic.

Aggregate output fluctuates widely; it is 3 in the low state and 6 in the high state. Furthermore, all the gains during booms accrue to the elderly, who also take all the losses during downturns. The efficient ex ante risk-sharing rule,

$$T^{EA}(L) = \frac{1}{2} \quad \text{and} \quad T^{EA}(H) = -1,$$

is an intuitive arrangement in which the young insure the elderly against the downturn, for example, if the stock market collapses and, in return, the elderly share the windfall from bull markets.

It is worth emphasizing that this insurance arrangement differs significantly from the minimum-pension guarantees that are often discussed in the social security literature. First, this risk-sharing rule is two sided, as would be expected given that both generations bear risk. Retirees are protected against retirement risk, but they have to share the gains during booms. Second, the size of transfers depends on the entire state of the economy, not just on the performance of the stock market. This is an important feature because the cost of insuring the elderly depends on the income of the young. The young can insure the elderly only to the extent that their income remains relatively high during stock market collapses. In our example, this condition is satisfied; it is reflected in the relative size of the transfers.

This example also illustrates the differences between ex ante and interim efficiency. In the absence of any insurance arrangements, the expected utility at birth is 1.38 regardless of the state of the economy. The ex ante risk-sharing rule yields an average expected utility at birth, calculated of course before the agent is born, equal to 1.50. But agents born in the low state have only 1.15 units of expected utility. Thus, they are happy to renege on the insurance arrangement.

4.4 Market Institutions

We have shown that efficient risk sharing requires intergenerational transfers and characterized the transfers that restore efficiency. But a social planner who could carry them out exists only in the scribblings of economists. Thus, efficient risk sharing can occur only if the transfers are generated endogenously by the institutions in the economy. This leads to the central question of this paper: Are there institutions capable of generating efficient intergenerational risk sharing? Two types of institutions are often suggested as possible solutions: markets and government. We study market institutions in this section and government intervention in the next and show that both have shortcomings as mechanisms for sharing risks between generations.

Intuitively, one would expect the market to provide optimal insurance given a sufficiently rich asset structure in the economy. Although this intuition holds for static economies and even for dynamic economies with infinitely lived agents, it fails if there is limited overlap among generations. There are two reasons for this failure, the first straightforward, the second more subtle. The first problem is that agents cannot buy ex ante insurance since they can trade only after they are born. Thus, the market can provide at best interim insurance. The second problem presents a challenge even for this weaker notion of insurance. In an overlapping-generations economy, trade takes place sequentially. Each period, only the generations alive at the time can trade with each other. As we will see below, this restricts dramatically the amount of intergenerational risk sharing that takes place, even in economies with a rich asset structure.

To understand better the restrictions imposed by sequential trading and the role that different assets play in intergenerational risk sharing, this section studies three markets with different asset structures. First, we study markets with contingent claims. Next, we add an infinitely lived asset, like money, that pays no dividends but is sold from one generation to the next. Finally, we consider a new type of mechanism that resembles a voluntary pay-as-you-go social security system.

4.4.1   Contingent Claims

Consider an economy in which two types of commodities are exchanged every period: (1) that period's consumption good and (2) contingent claims for next period. Since trading takes place after the uncertainty has been resolved, prices might depend on the state of the world. Let $p(\cdot \mid \theta)$ denote the price of contingent commodities in state θ, where $p(\hat{\theta} \mid \theta)$ buys one unit of next period's consumption if the state of the world turns out to be $\hat{\theta}$. We normalize the price of this period's commodity to 1 so that all contingent prices are real prices.

The equilibrium in this market is easily characterized. At any positive price, the elderly demand zero contingent commodities. If they could, they would sell short since they die at the end of the period and thus can default on their obligations. But we assume that short selling is not allowed.[4] As a result, there are no intergenerational transfers in equilibrium. The price of the contingent claims adjusts so that the young demand exactly their endowment, no claims are exchanged, and no risk sharing takes place.

A young agent born in state θ faces the following market problem:

$$\max f(c^y(\theta)) + \sum_{\hat{\theta}} \pi(\hat{\theta}) f(c^o(\hat{\theta})),$$

---

4. This assumption is necessary, not only to get results that make sense, but also to get the existence of equilibrium.

subject to

$$c^y(\theta) + \sum_{\hat{\theta}} p(\hat{\theta}|\theta)c^o(\hat{\theta}) \leq e^y(\theta) + \sum_{\hat{\theta}} p(\hat{\theta}|\theta)e^o(\hat{\theta}).$$

Thus, the equilibrium vector of prices is given by

$$p(\hat{\theta}|\theta) = \frac{\pi(\hat{\theta})f'(e^o(\hat{\theta}))}{f'(e^y(\theta))} \quad \text{for all } \hat{\theta}.$$

As we would expect, the price of contingent commodities is high for states in which the agent gets a poor outcome and low when he does well. For example, in the case of retirement risk, we get $p(L \mid H) = p(L \mid L) = 1$ and $p(H \mid H) = p(H \mid L) = 0.25$. At a price of four to one, agents facing the possibility of a stock market crash would choose no insurance. Thus, we have obtained the following result:[5]

PROPOSITION. *The market with contingent claims has a unique equilibrium in which no intergenerational transfers, and thus no risk sharing, take place.*

One could think that the problem is due to market incompleteness, not the structure of sequential trading. After all, in our discussion, we included only one contingent commodity, whereas Arrow-Debreu markets have one contingent claim for every possible state and period. That would be incorrect. The result remains unchanged even if we introduce the entire set of contingent commodities.

The no-trade result, however, depends crucially on two other assumptions of the model. First is the assumption of one (representative) agent per generation. In a more realistic model with many agents and heterogeneity within generations, some trade would occur. However, all the trades would be between the members of the same generation. No intergenerational trade, and thus no intergenerational risk sharing, would take place. For this reason, and given the objectives of this paper, studying the one-agent case imposes no conceptual loss.

A more problematic assumption is that lives last for two periods. In a more realistic model in which agents live for seventy-five periods and with almost an equal number of overlaps, the trading of contingent commodities generates intergenerational transfers and thus risk sharing. To see why, consider the natural extension to three-period lives. Here, young and middle-aged agents face risks during the next period of their lives and can insure each other using contingent claims. It is natural to conjecture that the market efficiency increases with the number of overlaps and that it

5. Cass and Shell (1983) obtained a similar result, and Baxter (1989) contains an identical result.

reaches 100 percent in the limit case of infinitely lived agents. As far as we know, however, this problem has not been solved.

4.4.2 Contingent Claims and Infinitely Lived Assets

Can an infinitely lived asset help overcome the problems that come from limited generational overlap? Consider an economy that, in addition to the contingent claims described above, has an infinitely lived asset that has neither productivity nor consumption value. Following Samuelson's (1958) classic paper, we refer to this asset as *money*. The introduction of money is valuable in this context because it generates intergenerational transfers when traded at a positive price and, as long as the prices fluctuate in appropriate fashion, it even has the potential to provide some intergenerational risk sharing.

Let M be the amount of money in the economy and $m(\theta)$ its price in state θ. Consider the market problem of an agent born in state θ:

$$\max_{z(\cdot),\mu} f(c^y(\theta)) + \sum_{\hat\theta} \pi(\hat\theta) f(c^o(\hat\theta)),$$

subject to

$$c^y(\theta) \le e^y(\theta) - m(\theta)\mu - \sum_{\hat\theta} p(\hat\theta|\theta) z(\hat\theta)$$

and, for all $\hat\theta$,

$$c^o(\hat\theta) \le e^o(\hat\theta) + m(\theta)\mu + z(\hat\theta).$$

These budget constraints can be rewritten as

$$(4) \qquad c^y(\theta) + \sum_{\hat\theta} p(\hat\theta|\theta) c^o(\hat\theta) \le \left[e^y(\theta) + \sum_{\hat\theta} p(\hat\theta|\theta) e^o(\hat\theta) \right]$$
$$+ \left[\sum_{\hat\theta} p(\hat\theta|\theta) m(\hat\theta) - m(\theta) \right] \mu.$$

In equilibrium, the following no-arbitrage condition holds in every state θ:

$$\sum_{\hat\theta} p(\hat\theta|\theta) m(\hat\theta) \le m(\theta).$$

Otherwise, agents could make a "profit" by selling $m(\hat\theta)$ units of contingent claims in each market, using the proceeds to buy money that is used to service the claims, and keeping the difference. Thus, in equilibrium, the budget constraint reduces to

$$(5) \qquad c^y(\theta) + \sum_{\hat\theta} p(\hat\theta|\theta) c^o(\hat\theta) \le \left[e^y(\theta) + \sum_{\hat\theta} p(\hat\theta|\theta) e^o(\hat\theta) \right],$$

and agents do not have a strict incentive to buy money. Agents can achieve the same amount of risk sharing buying contingent commodities. We will return to this issue later in the section.

Can money generate optimal risk sharing between generations? It has long been recognized that, since agents can trade only after they are born, money cannot generate ex ante risk sharing. However, there exists a large literature in macroeconomics (see, among others, Peled 1982, 1984; Manuelli 1990; and Demange and Laroque 1998, 1999) that studies the interim efficiency of monetary economies. These papers study conditions under which an interim weak first welfare theorem (WFWT) can be established. The first welfare theorem (FWT) states that every market equilibrium is efficient. By contrast, the WFWT holds if there is always a market equilibrium that is efficient, even when there are other inefficient equilibria.

It is easily seen that this market institution cannot satisfy the FWT because there is always an equilibrium with $m(\theta) = 0$ for all θ. In this case, money might change hands, but no real resources are transferred, and thus no risk sharing takes place. The problem is that monetary equilibria depend on expectations. Since money pays no dividends and has no consumption value, agents are willing to buy it only if they believe that they will subsequently be able to sell it for a positive and profitable price.

However, the problem is even worse.

THEOREM. *Both the ex ante and the interim WFWT fail for a market with contingent claims and money as its risk-sharing instruments.*

This result derives from a very simple fact. In equilibrium, the price of money can never be negative. In a state with negative prices, the old would burn their money rather than sell it. Also, an equilibrium in which $m(\theta) = 0$ for some states and $m(\hat{\theta}) > 0$ for some other states cannot exist; that is because the young would have an infinite demand for money in the first class of states and markets would not clear. We can thus conclude that money trades at positive prices in any equilibrium that generates intergenerational transfers. But this implies that, although money can generate either no transfers or backward transfers, it can never produce transfers from old to young. As a result, as figure 4.4 shows, the interim WFWT fails because all the economies in the southwest part of the box need forward transfers to restore efficiency. In fact, these economies have a unique equilibrium in which money has no value. Since ex ante efficiency implies interim efficiency, this argument also establishes the failure of the ex ante WFWT.

At face value, this theorem seems to contradict results in the previous literature that prove that any equilibrium in which money trades at nonzero prices is interim efficient. But there is no contradiction. As figure 4.4 shows, the problem is that equilibria with positive money prices might not exist. In those economies, the market cannot generate even efficient interim risk sharing.[6] As we discussed before, forward transfers are not necessary if one assumes that the endowment process is to the northeast of the interim efficient frontier. This assumption is made in several papers in the literature.

The failure of the WFWT depends crucially on forward transfers being necessary for interim efficient risk sharing. Thus, it is important to ask whether any of our assumptions are essential for this effect. In particular, one might be suspicious of the lack of an initial period in our economy. Recall that $t = 0, \pm1, \pm2. \ldots$. After all, if the economy is truncated at $t = 0$, the risk-sharing policy depicted in figure 4.4 is not interim Pareto improving. Here, the elderly at time 0 make transfers without receiving anything in exchange.

To explore this issue, consider a variation of our model in which there is an initial generation born at time 0, and suppose, as before, that the endowment process is characterized by a point in figure 4.4. If the endowment lies to the northeast of the interim frontier, then backward transfers are enough to restore interim efficiency, and the interim WFWT holds. Thus, suppose that the endowment lies to the southwest of the frontier, the case that causes problems in our model. The existence of a first generation changes the set of interim efficient allocations. To see why, consider the lower-left-hand corner of the box, an endowment process in which the elderly always get everything. The endowment allocation is interim efficient in the truncated economy because it gives the maximum feasible consumption to generation 0. Thus, the interim WFWT trivially holds for this economy. Similarly, we conjecture that the interim WFWT holds for all the other truncated economies in this region.

It is important to emphasize, however, that interim efficiency holds because the existence of an initial generation makes Pareto improvements difficult, not because the market is generating the "right" intergenerational transfers. As before, there are risk-sharing rules that use forward transfers and make every generation, except the first one, better off. Therefore, the main insight generalizes to the case of economies with an initial generation: the interim efficient risk-sharing arrangements that everyone but the first generation favors cannot, in general, be generated by the market.

To understand better the differences between ex ante and interim insurance, it is useful to revisit the example of retirement risk. Figure 4.5 depicts the nontrivial monetary equilibrium that arises in this case. Money prices are $m(L) = m(H) = m = 0.4435$. Thus, the trading of money restores interim efficiency, but it generates constant backward intergenerational transfers. From the ex ante point of view, this arrangement is quite coun-

6. Demange and Laroque (1999) allow money to take negative prices, and thus they are able to obtain a WFWT. The explanation is that their "negative money" resembles more the voluntary pay-as-you-go system studied in the next subsection than standard fiat money.

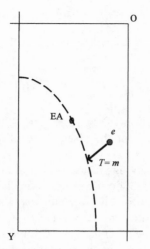

Fig. 4.5   Equilibrium with money

terintuitive. With money, the young always make a transfer to the old, which insures the old against the possibility of a stock market collapse. But, in contrast to ex ante risk sharing, the old do not share any of the gains from a stock market boom. In fact, since

$$c^o(L) = \frac{1}{2} + m \quad \text{and} \quad c^o(H) = 4 + m,$$

the old end up consuming more in both states of the world.

4.4.3   Voluntary Pay-as-You-Go Mechanisms

The key problem with money as a risk-sharing mechanism is that it cannot generate forward transfers. In this section, we study a market mechanism that can. A voluntary pay-as-you-go system is basically an intergenerational Ponzi scheme in which each generation makes voluntary contributions during its youth and receives, as payoffs in old age, the voluntary contributions of the next generation. Such a mechanism could be run by an infinitely lived institution, for example, the government.

The return from investing in this asset is proportional to the aggregate contributions of the next generation and inversely proportional to the aggregate contributions of the present generation. Consider the market problem of an agent born in state θ. If we let $\tau(\theta)$ denote aggregate contributions, the return on investing one unit is $\tau(\hat{\theta})/\tau(\theta)$ when tomorrow's state is $\hat{\theta}$. Thus, the agent solves

$$\max_{z(\cdot),\,\alpha} f(c^y(\theta)) + \sum_{\hat{\theta}} \pi(\hat{\theta})g(c^o(\hat{\theta})),$$

subject to

$$(6) \qquad c^y(\theta) + \sum_{\hat{\theta}} p(\hat{\theta}|\theta)c^o(\hat{\theta}) \le [e^y(\theta) + \sum_{\hat{\theta}} p(\hat{\theta}|\theta)e^o(\hat{\theta})]$$

$$+ [\sum_{\hat{\theta}} p(\hat{\theta}|\theta)\tau(\hat{\theta}) - \tau(\theta)]\frac{\alpha}{\tau(\theta)},$$

where α is his contribution to the asset. The agent is a price taker, and thus he takes the "price" of the asset, or, more precisely, the aggregate contributions, as given.

As in the case of money, agents are willing to invest only if they believe that future generations will do the same. Thus, there is always an equilibrium in which $\tau(\theta) = 0$ for all θ and no risk sharing takes place. This suggests that money and voluntary pay-as-you-go systems are very similar assets, even though in the latter case no "commodity" or piece of paper is exchanged. This is not surprising because the value of both assets depends on self-fulfilling expectations.

A careful examination of the budget constraints (6) and (4) shows that the two assets are almost identical. To see why, suppose that $M = 1$ so that there is only one unit of money in the economy. In this case, μ denotes the share of the money supply that the agent is willing to hold, and, in equilibrium, we must have $\mu = 1$. Similarly, in (6), $\alpha/\tau(\theta)$ denotes the share of contributions that the agent is willing to make, and, in equilibrium, $\alpha = \tau(\theta)$. But this implies that, as long as $m(\theta) = \tau(\theta)$ for all θ, the two assets are identical, and we have the following result:

PROPOSITION. *If contributions cannot be negative, then there is a one-to-one correspondence between the equilibria in the market with money and the equilibria in the market with a voluntary pay-as-you-go mechanism.*

In common parlance, a market economy with money and a voluntary pay-as-you-go social security scheme can achieve precisely the same outcomes. But what if we allow the young generation to extract resources from the social security scheme rather than pay into it? This enables the pay-as-you-go scheme to generate the forward transfers that are needed to restore interim efficiency, a capability not available to the market economy with money:

THEOREM. *If negative contributions are possible, an economy with a voluntary pay-as-you-go mechanism can satisfy the interim WFWT but not the ex ante one.*[7]

How should we interpret a negative contribution? Strictly speaking, it is a loan in which the cost of borrowing is determined by the actions of

---

7. The proof of this result follows from the analysis of Demange and Laroque (1999).

the next generation. Suppose that today's young generation contributes $-T$ to the system and that the next generation also contributes $-T$. Then the asset amounts to a loan with an interest rate equal to 1. On the other hand, the loan is free if the next generation decides to contribute 0.

It is important to emphasize that, with unrestricted contributions, a generation that buys the asset could find itself with an arbitrarily large liability. In a voluntary pay-as-you-go system, the "dividend" that the asset pays is determined by the actions of the next generation, which could decide to borrow an arbitrarily large amount. Of course, such behavior does not take place in equilibrium because the next generation would do the same, but such an action is a possibility. This is particularly problematic since, as we saw in (5), in equilibrium the price of the contingent commodities is such that agents do not have a strict incentive to buy the asset. So why should they take the risk? Thus, the equilibrium with $\tau(\theta) = 0$, and no risk sharing, is more plausible than the equilibrium with negative prices.

We can conclude that these archetypal market institutions cannot generate ex ante efficient risk sharing and are unlikely to generate interim efficiency, at least for a large class of economies. Can government policy come to the rescue?

4.5 Voting Institutions

The government has the power to transfer income across generations and thus to provide risk sharing. However, its objectives are determined by political pressure, not by an innate desire to correct inefficiencies. Thus, the problem with government, unlike the market, is not what it has the power to do but what it is likely to do given its power. In this section, we characterize the risk-sharing rules that arise as the result of the electoral process that guides government.

Each period there is an election in which all the agents alive at the time vote. Although many issues are decided in a typical election, here we model only the choice of intergenerational redistribution. The policy space in state θ is given by

$$P(\theta) = \{T : - e^o(\theta) \leq -\underline{R}(\theta) \leq T \leq \overline{R}(\theta) \leq e^y(\theta)\},$$

where T is the transfer from young to old that is implemented in the period and $[-\underline{R}(\theta), \overline{R}(\theta)]$ are exogenously given constitutional constraints on intergenerational expropriation. We assume that $-\underline{R}(\theta) < 0 < \overline{R}(\theta)$ so that both forward and backward transfers are possible. Clearly, efficient risk sharing arises only if voters always choose the optimal transfer $T^*(\theta)$ that we characterized in section 4.2 above.

Every period the young choose policy with probability λ and the old with probability $1 - \lambda$. We refer to the generation choosing policy as *the median voter.* If $\lambda = 1$, the young always choose policy, for example, in an economy with a rapidly growing population, whereas, if $\lambda = 0$, the old always determine policy, for example, when the old are well organized politically (e.g., through AARP). The model implicitly assumes that voters' preferences are determined by age. Although this assumption is not a good description of voting behavior for a wide range of issues (e.g., abortion or school prayer), it seems justified for intergenerational redistribution, where the effect that the policy has on an agent depends only on his age (for evidence in this regard, see Poterba [1997]).

Given these assumptions, the voting institution can be modeled as the following infinitely repeated game:

- Every period t, nature selects θ_t and chooses the identity of the median voter.
- After observing these outcomes, the median voter chooses a policy $p_t \in P(\theta_t)$.
- There is complete information about the history of previous policies and states. History at time t is denoted by

$$h_t = (\dots, \theta_{t-2}, \theta_{t-1}; \dots, p_{t-2}, p_{t-1}).$$

- The set of political equilibria is given by the set of sequential equilibria of this game.

Let $p^o(\theta, h)$ denote the policy that an old median voter selects in state θ, given history h. Define $p^y(\theta, h)$ similarly. Strictly speaking, voters have only one decision to make: how much to transfer between young and old. However, in order to understand better the politics of intergenerational risk sharing, it is useful to think of the policy space as having two dimensions:

$$P(\theta) \subseteq \{I : I = T^*(\theta), 0\} \times \{R : -\underline{R}(\theta) \leq R \leq \overline{R}(\theta)\},$$

that is

$$p(\theta) = \{T^*(\theta), 0\} + R(\theta).$$

The first dimension, $I \in T^*(\theta)$, 0, measures whether the efficient risk-sharing transfer is taking place. The second dimension, $R \in [-\underline{R}(\theta), \overline{R}(\theta)]$, measures the amount of pure intergenerational redistribution. This representation emphasizes an important feature of the political process: once the door is open to carry out transfers between the generations, voters can choose optimal risk sharing, but they can also choose expropriation. Take, as an example, the case of retirement risk, and suppose that the median voter is always old. When the stock market collapses, these voters can tax the young and vote a minimum pension to themselves, as efficiency considerations demand. But they can also raise the taxes of the young in the case of a boom where, following the dictates of ex ante risk sharing, they are supposed to tax themselves.

The first step in analyzing the model is to note that an old median voter always chooses no risk sharing and maximum redistribution:

(7) $$p^o(\theta, h_t) = \overline{R}(\theta).$$

Since the elderly are not affected by future policy, their best option is to maximize current consumption, and, given the opportunity, they expropriate the young. From their point of view, the choice of taxes is purely about redistribution, not about risk sharing; after all, they do not face any more risks. Thus, we can interpret the vote of the elderly as a decision not to carry out any risk sharing and to expropriate the young as much as possible. In the expanded version of the game, this can be written as

$$\tilde{p}^o(\theta, h_t) = (0, \overline{R}(\theta)).$$

What about young voters? As was the case with the market, the equilibrium of this model depends on the beliefs that present generations have about the behavior of future generations. There are, thus, two types of outcomes: Markovian equilibrium, in which no risk sharing takes place, and non-Markovian equilibrium, with optimal risk sharing.

In a Markovian equilibrium, agents maximize their payoff for the period because they believe that their actions do not affect the behavior of future voters. In this case, the young also expropriate as much as possible:

$$p^y(\theta, h_t) = -\underline{R}(\theta).$$

As before, we can interpret their vote as a decision to focus purely on redistributive politics, without any concern for risk sharing ($\tilde{p}^y(\theta, h_t) = (0, -\underline{R}(\theta))$).

We can conclude that, in a Markovian equilibrium, every generation expropriates the others as much as possible and that the direction of expropriation depends on who ends up as the median voter. It is important to emphasize that, when there are few constraints on expropriation, for example, if $\underline{R}(\theta) = e^o(\theta)$ and $\overline{R}(\theta) = e^y(\theta)$, agents are worse off here than with generational autarky, where no risk sharing takes place.

There are also non-Markovian equilibria in which the young voters implement the optimal risk-sharing policy and resist the temptation of expropriating the elderly. Consider, for example, the following strategy:

(8) $p^y(\theta, h) =$

$$\begin{cases} T^*(\theta) & \text{if, at } h, \text{ all the previous young median voters chose } T^*(\theta); \\ -\underline{R}(\theta) & \text{otherwise.} \end{cases}$$

Here, optimal risk sharing takes place as long as every previous young generation has done the same. But, if there is any deviation from this behavior, they revert to the short-sighted expropriation strategy $(0, -\underline{R}(\theta))$. Cooperation does not depend on the behavior of the old since everyone knows that they always vote for expropriation. Using strategies of this type, we can establish the following result:

THEOREM. (1) *If there are no limits to intergenerational expropriation* $(\underline{R}(\theta) = e^o$ *and* $\underline{R}(\theta) = e^y(\theta))$, *then there are political equilibria in which the optimal (ex ante or interim) risk-sharing rule is implemented whenever the median voter is young.* (2) *Thus, if the median voter is always young* $(\lambda = 1)$, *there are equilibria that generate both interim and ex ante efficient risk sharing.* (3) *However, regardless of who is the median voter, there is always an equilibrium in which there is no risk sharing, and full expropriation takes place.*

The proof of this theorem reveals the essence of the problem. As we discussed above, the elderly always expropriate as much as possible. Thus, to check that the strategies (7) and (8) are a political equilibrium, we only need to verify the incentives of the young, who make decisions in two types of situations: (1) histories in which every previous young generation followed the efficient risk-sharing policy and (2) histories in which there was a deviation from this code of behavior.

Consider the first case, and suppose that the state of the world is θ. The young median voter knows that, if the next median voter is old, he will choose $\overline{R}(\theta)$. On the other hand, if the next median voter is young, he will copy the behavior that the young voter chooses today; that is, expropriation will trigger expropriation, whereas optimal risk sharing will maintain optimal risk sharing. Thus, if the agent chooses $T^*(\theta)$, his lifetime payoff becomes

$$f(e^y(\theta) - T^*(\theta)) + \lambda \left\{ \sum_{\hat{\theta}} \pi(\hat{\theta}) f(e^o(\hat{\theta}) + T^*(\hat{\theta})) \right\}$$

$$+ (1 - \lambda) \left\{ \sum_{\hat{\theta}} \pi(\hat{\theta}) f(e^o(\hat{\theta}) + \overline{R}(\hat{\theta})) \right\}.$$

On the other hand, if he decides not to cooperate with the risk-sharing rule, he is better off expropriating the elderly as much as possible $(T = -\underline{R}(\theta))$, reaping a payoff equal to

$$f(e^y(\theta) + \underline{R}(\theta)) + \lambda \left\{ \sum_{\hat{\theta}} \pi(\hat{\theta}) f(e^o(\hat{\theta}) - \underline{R}(\hat{\theta})) \right\}$$

$$+ (1 - \lambda) \left\{ \sum_{\hat{\theta}} \pi(\hat{\theta}) f(e^o(\hat{\theta}) + \overline{R}(\hat{\theta})) \right\}.$$

Thus, he cooperates as long as

$$f(e^y(\theta) - T^*(\theta)) + \lambda\left\{\sum_{\hat{\theta}} \pi(\hat{\theta})f(e^o(\hat{\theta}) + T^*(\hat{\theta}))\right\}$$

is greater than

$$f(e^y(\theta) + \underline{R}(\theta)) + \lambda\left\{\sum_{\hat{\theta}} \pi(\hat{\theta})f(e^o(\hat{\theta}) - \underline{R}(\hat{\theta}))\right\}.$$

For λ sufficiently large, the left-hand side is approximately equal to the interim expected utility[8] generated by the risk-sharing policy $T^*(\theta)$. By contrast, the right-hand side gives the payoff, in expected-utility terms, of the Markovian equilibrium in which every generation expropriates as much as it can. Without bounds of expropriation, $\underline{R}(\theta) = e^o(\theta)$ and $\overline{R}(\theta) = e^y(\theta)$, this payoff becomes

$$f(E(\theta)) + \lambda\left[\sum_{\hat{\theta}} \pi(\hat{\theta})f(0)\right].$$

So we finally conclude that the young choose optimal risk sharing over expropriation since they have a strong desire for consumption smoothing ($\lim_{x\to 0} f(x) = -\infty$).

Now consider the second type of history. According to (7) and (8), future voters will ignore the risk-sharing rule and expropriate a coexisting generation as much as possible. As a result, present voters have no incentive to refrain from expropriation, and they also choose $T = -\underline{R}(\theta)$.

An interesting property of the previous equilibrium is that young agents are willing to implement the optimal ex ante transfer even though they constitute a majority and vote only after they are born. Since part of the uncertainty has been revealed, agents might have an incentive to default from the risk-sharing rule. For example, in the case of retirement risk, agents born in the low state get a payoff of 1.15 with insurance and 1.38 without insurance. Yet the previous analysis shows that they are willing to give a transfer to the elderly when the stock market collapses.

In this example, the only reason why young voters are willing to help the elderly is that failure to do so would trigger an expropriation precedent that could hurt them in old age. A risk-sharing rule is interim individually rational if, regardless of the state in which the agent is born, it is better than the initial endowment. Since the ex ante insurance arrangement is not interim individually rational, the promise of future insurance is not enough incentive to go along with it. The required additional incentive is provided by the possibility of expropriation.

---

8. That is, the expected utility conditional on knowing that the state of the world at birth is θ.

Consider the problem of designing a constitution that specifies the rules of the political process. Can we modify the rules in a way that makes optimal risk sharing more likely and rules out the possibility of intergenerational expropriation? One important lesson from the previous analysis is that risk sharing is more likely if the young always choose policy. However, youth dominance is not enough. Given that the Markovian equilibria always exist, we are faced with a perverse trade-off. In order to avoid short-sighted expropriation, restricting the policy space to something like

$$P(\theta) = \{T^*(\theta), 0\},$$

where expropriation might be prohibited through, say, a constitutional amendment, seems desirable. In this case, each generation can choose only to implement the optimal transfer or to do nothing; it cannot expropriate. However, ruling out expropriation could prove detrimental:

PROPOSITION. *The voting institution with a restricted policy space $\{T^*(\theta), 0\}$ and in which the median voter is always young can support only risk-sharing rules that are interim individually rational. Thus, in general, it can generate interim but not ex ante efficient risk sharing.*

The problem with restricting the policy space is that it supports only risk-sharing rules that are interim individually rational. A risk-sharing policy is interim individually rational if it does not decrease the expected utility of an agent, conditional on knowing the state of the world at birth. As the case of retirement risk illustrates, in most cases of interest this condition is not satisfied. Thus, we are left with a Hobson's choice: we can either go with a restricted policy space, which rules out extreme expropriation but also sacrifices ex ante insurance, or go with the unrestricted policy space, which generates optimal risk sharing and no expropriation in the good equilibrium but produces disastrous outcomes in the bad one.[9]

Can government intervention generate efficient intergenerational risk sharing? The government certainly has on paper the power to carry out the efficient policy. For example, in the case of retirement risk, it could help retirees by taxing the young when the stock market crashes and similarly tax the elderly when the market booms. However, our analysis suggests that, as long as government policy is determined by self-interested citizens' votes, intergenerational transfers will be driven more by redistributive politics than by risk-sharing considerations.

---

9. The political economy of ex ante insurance is very similar to the political economy of public investment in future generations. The necessary and sufficient conditions to get optimal investment in future generations are explored in detail in Rangel (1998).

4.6   Conclusions

Our conclusions are not happy: neither market nor political institutions can be counted on to generate efficient intergenerational risk sharing. Reality may be less dreary since our stark results follow from the assumption of two-period lives. As lives extend, overlaps increase, and trade in contingent commodities generates useful risk sharing. Similarly, the incentives to expropriate diminish with longer lives. Thus, market and voting institutions may do better than in our models, but our main conclusion holds: neither can be relied on to restore full efficiency.

Our analysis here is positive. The goal is to understand whether and when existing institutional arrangements generate efficient risk sharing. Although our analysis applies to all generational risks, including wars and economic declines, in the context of this volume it is important to consider the implications of our analysis for the current debate on social security reform.

The first implication is that, since markets cannot generate optimal risk sharing, a system of individual accounts cannot produce an efficient allocation. In a market with a rich-enough asset structure, agents can buy a lot of insurance against events like a stock market crash, but not perfect insurance. The size of the efficiency loss is an open empirical question.

This inefficiency can be corrected only by a government policy that carries out transfers between young and old, with the size and direction of the transfers depending on the state of the world. Thus, a combination of private accounts and a contingent pay-as-you-go system, which is able to transfer income in both directions, in principle dominates the pure private system.

But the second major lesson of this paper casts doubt on turning that potential into reality. The political economy of intergenerational transfers—that is, the fact that generations have to vote for the transfers that are made—may prevent a politically responsive government from intervening successfully. In some extreme cases, it may impose expropriating transfers that reduce the welfare of every generation.

It is important to emphasize, however, that the possibility of market failure does not rule in favor of a purely private approach to social security. There are many government policies, besides risk sharing, that redistribute income between generations. Government debt and the choice of the tax base are two prominent examples. Medicare most directly transfers to the elderly.[10] These dimensions are subject to the same redistributive

10. Arguably, Medicare should be considered in conjunction with social security as a significant transfer program from young to old. Medicare's trustees project that its expenditures will compose 6.5 percent of GNP by the middle of the next century.

politics that we study in this paper. Thus, intergenerational expropriation can take place even if the government turns social security over to the private sector. The same elderly who would use risk sharing to expropriate the young during a stock market boom can use debt to achieve an identical goal. This paper shows that government policy may not be able to provide optimal insurance. It does not show, however, that intergenerational redistribution is higher when the government is involved in social security.

The lessons of our overlapping-generations model for efficiency can be distilled briefly. The risk sharing brought by market institutions is always welcomed but never sufficient. The government has the power to generate efficient risk sharing, but sometimes that power is deployed insufficiently or perversely.

References

Baxter, M. 1989. Money and market incompleteness in overlapping generations models. *Journal of Monetary Economics* 24:69–91.

Bohn, H. 1988. Risk sharing in a stochastic overlapping generations economy. University of California, Santa Barbara. Mimeo.

Cass, D., and K. Shell. 1983. Do sunspots matter? *Journal of Political Economy* 91, no. 2:193–227.

Demange, G., and G. Laroque. 1998. Optimal intergenerational risk sharing and capital accumulation. Département et Laboratoire d'Economie Théorique et Appliquée, Ecole Normale Superieure, Paris. Typescript.

———. 1999. Social security and demographic shocks. *Econometrica* 67, no. 3 (May): 527–42.

Enders, W., and H. Lapan. 1982. Social security taxation and intergenerational risk sharing. *International Economic Review* 23:647–58.

Fisher, S. 1983. Welfare aspects of government issue of indexed bonds. In *Inflation, debt, and indexation,* ed. Rudiger Dornbusch and Mario Henrique Simonsen. Cambridge, Mass.: MIT Press.

Gale, D. 1994. The efficient design of public debt. In *Financial innovation and risk sharing,* ed. Franklin Allen and Douglas Gale. Cambridge, Mass.: MIT Press.

Gordon, R., and H. Varian. 1988. Intergenerational risk sharing. *Journal of Public Economics* 37:180–202.

Green, J. 1977. Mitigating demographic risk through social insurance. NBER Working Paper no. 215. Cambridge, Mass.: National Bureau of Economic Research.

Lucas, R. 1972. Expectations and the neutrality of money. *Journal of Economic Theory* 4:103–24.

———. 1977. Reply to Muench, Polemarchakis, and Weiss. *Journal of Economic Theory* 15:351–52.

Manuelli, R. 1990. Existence and optimality of currency equilibrium in stochastic overlapping generations models: The pure endowment case. *Journal of Economic Theory* 51:268–94.

Muench, T. 1977. Efficiency in a monetary economy. *Journal of Economic Theory* 15:325–44.

Peled, D. 1982. Informational diversity over time and the optimality of monetary equilibria. *Journal of Economic Theory* 28:255–74.

———. 1984. Stationary Pareto optimality of stochastic asset equilibria with overlapping generations. *Journal of Economic Theory* 34:396–403.

Poterba, J. 1997. Demographic structure and the political economy of public education. *Journal of Policy Analysis and Management* 16:48–66.

Rangel, A. 1998. Forward and backward intergenerational goods. Stanford University. Mimeo.

Samuelson, P. 1958. An exact consumption-loan model of interest with or without the social contrivance of money. *Journal of Political Economy* 66, no. 6:467–82.

Smith, A. 1982. Intergenerational transfers as social insurance. *Journal of Public Economics* 19:97–106.

Comment   Thomas J. Sargent

The Questions

The paper under discussion takes up an important issue from an interchange among Muench (1977), Lucas (1977), and Peled (1982): how to compare consumption allocations in an overlapping-generations economy. Rangel and Zeckhauser adopt Muench's proposed ex ante utility measure for comparing stationary allocations in overlapping-generations economies. Muench called it ET-PO (equal treatment-Pareto optimality). *Equal treatment* means stationarity (people experiencing the same random state at different times receive the same consumption allocation). Muench computed utility "prior to birth" by averaging utilities across all the states into which a person had a chance of being born.

The alternative to ET-PO is promoted by followers of Lucas (1977) and Peled (1982), who argued that the nonoptimality often detected by the ET-PO test has an obvious source in an information advantage of a planner over the decision makers and that it is too easily used to criticize good equilibria from a superior vantage point. Lucas (1977, 351) noted that, "in *any* general equilibrium model with differently endowed risk averse agents, many allocations which are Pareto optimal will not be if pre-endowment insurance markets are admitted." Joining the spirit of Lucas's remark, Peled formulated the concept of conditional Pareto optimality, which is based on expected utilities conditioned on the same information that the agents have when they make decisions. Peled advocated conditional Pareto optimality because it uses an information structure that mirrors that possessed by decision makers. Peled went on to show that there always exists a conditionally Pareto-optimal competitive equilibrium,

Thomas J. Sargent is the Donald Lucas Professor of Economics at Stanford University, a senior fellow of the Hoover Institution, and a research associate of the National Bureau of Economic Research.

sometimes with and sometimes without valued fiat money (depending on the parameters). Peled's model has a stochastic version of Samuelson's (1958) result for nonstochastic overlapping-generations models that it is possible for a single asset (government debt or fiat currency) to cure a failure of a (nonmonetary) competitive equilibrium to be Pareto optimal.

Which welfare criterion should we prefer, Muench's or Peled's? Rangel and Zeckhauser are more enthusiastic proponents of Muench's criterion than Muench himself. Muench embraced his measure halfheartedly: "I am not asserting that the ET-PO criterion for optimality is the appropriate one. It seems to imply that all future generations agree before history begins. How can this be democratically achieved?" (1977, 325). An accomplishment of Rangel and Zeckhauser's is to investigate Muench's question. They describe a voting system (a description of a list of voters, a sequence of voting dates, and a protocol for the objects to be voted on) that can attain the ET-PO criterion "democratically." But they seem not to like their voting system, partly because it has an implementation problem (in addition to the ET-PO equilibrium, another very bad allocation is also an equilibrium), partly because the choice set must be specified to allow bad out-of-equilibrium outcomes to support good equilibrium outcomes, and perhaps also partly because it is not democratic from the viewpoint of old people.

Plan of This Comment

I shall devote most of my Comment to empathizing with Rangel and Zeckhauser's sympathy for Muench's prebirth utility criterion. I would like to add some empirical ammunition to their case by departing from the details of their setup while embracing its spirit. I want to reinterpret and broaden the risks. My reinterpretation of those risks is designed to amplify the claim that the welfare issue that Rangel and Zeckhauser raise is quantitatively important.

Rangel and Zeckhauser's Setup

Rangel and Zeckhauser study market and political arrangements in a pure endowment, doubly infinite (t "starts" at $-\infty$ and "ends" at $+\infty$) horizon model with overlapping generations of two-period-lived people. People within a generation have identical endowments and preferences. Preferences are stationary in the sense that a person born at $t + j$ values time $t + j + k$ consumption in the same way that a person born at time t values time $t + k$ consumption. Agents are endowed only with time-dated goods bearing the same dates that they are alive, and they care only about those same goods. At each date t, endowments of both young and old depend on the realization of a single random variable θ that takes discrete values $[\theta_1, \ldots, \theta_n]$ where $\mathrm{prob}(\theta = \theta_i) = \pi_i$.

Rangel and Zeckhauser restrict themselves to studying stationary allocations; that is, they depend only on θ, not on calendar time. They propose to compare the Pareto efficiency of various allocations in terms of two different ideas of what identifies a person. Let $v(\theta)$ be the optimum value function for a young agent born in state θ. Rangel and Zeckhauser study welfare measures based on utility comparisons with two possible datings: (1) the conditional on θ or "interim" optimum value $v(\theta)$ and (2) the prebirth or ex ante optimum value $Ev = \Sigma_i\, \pi_i v(\theta_i)$.

By excluding heterogeneity within a generation, Rangel and Zeckhauser focus on intergenerational risk sharing. To emphasize the potential quantitative significance of the substantive issue that they are raising, I prefer to recast their discussion of the ex ante versus the interim welfare criteria in another setting, one that highlights intragenerational risk sharing. In Rangel and Zeckhauser's model, there are different types and risks to be shared only because people are born at different phases of the "business cycle" indexed by θ. In longer-lived overlapping-generations models, Rangel and Zeckhauser point out that much, if not most, of such risk could probably be insured by trading a small number of assets. So it seems likely that the ex ante versus the conditional on type welfare distinction acquires more quantitative importance if we introduce within-generation heterogeneity across types.

Coincident but Heterogeneous Agents

Thus, consider instead the kind of environment to which Lucas alluded in the quotation reproduced above. Let there be a stable distribution of types of people, where a type is a permanent attribute that cannot be controlled and that affects earnings from labor. Even in a standard general equilibrium model with coincident life spans, the ex ante versus the conditional on type welfare issue arises: welfare comparisons depend on whether utilities are evaluated before or after types are determined. A standard (Arrow-Debreu) way to set things up would be to take types as realized and to permit trading of a complete set of history-dependent claims to consumption bundles. The coincident lifetime complete markets model satisfies the two fundamental welfare theorems for a welfare criterion based on conditional on type utilities. But, from the prebirth viewpoint of "persons" whose types are uncertain, a competitive equilibrium allocation would be dominated by allocations that get more sharing across types. Only if agents could trade "before birth" would the welfare theorems hold for this economy.

Insurance for Types with Very Low Labor Income

Thinking about private arrangements for trading "before birth" requires a model with parents and children. Children cannot trade before their births, but their parents can and would often want to. Thus, consider any of a number of conditions that dramatically reduce earnings potential and that are realized at birth. I believe that private insurance for these conditions is not sold now. This is curious because many of these conditions are easy to verify and involve no moral hazard. I offer the following calculations as rough estimates of what such insurance would cost. The four conditions—autism, cerebral palsy, Down syndrome, and spina bifida—have the following incidences per ten thousand live births in the United States: 4.5, 20, 12.5, and 5. So take the probability of having one of them to be .0042. With a stationary population, to purchase an annuity paying $50,000 per year conditional on a child having one of these disorders would then cost a one-time payment of $4,200 per child.[1]

My reaction to these figures is that such insurance seems cheap to provide. Why does private insurance not exist? Why is it not provided by the government or at least by the U.S. government?

Prebirth Risk for Workers

In terms of their earnings ability, the low or zero-earnings types of people just mentioned are extreme values from a distribution of types. Applied economists have adduced ample quantitative evidence for the importance of types characterized by unobserved abilities that are valued in the labor market. I shall mention a couple of sources for estimates that might help give quantitative content to the theoretical welfare distinction. Of course, because variations of ability in the range that we are now considering are much harder to disentangle from effort, they are more difficult to insure through private arrangements. I will return to this point below. But first let me give some numbers.

Evidence from Twins Studies

Behrman, Rosenzweig, and Taubman (1994) present evidence for substantial labor market-relevant endowment heterogeneity. They use observations on identical twins to identify the effect of individual-specific endowments on log earnings. They estimate that 27 percent of the variance of log earnings from labor is due to variance in individual-specific endowments. Behrman, Rosenzweig, and Taubman also discuss how some of these individual effects might be insured through sharing within families

---

1. I am capitalizing the per person cost of $210.00 per year at an interest rate of 5 percent per year.

or creating new family links through marriage. In particular, they discuss whether schooling and marriage serve to attenuate or reinforce the individual-specific effects on earnings. They estimate that schooling is allocated to reinforce, and marriage matches made to attenuate, the individual-specific effects.

Fixed Effects in Income Dynamics

Another kind of evidence for heterogeneity comes from the literature on quantitative long-lived overlapping-generations models. Storresletten, Telmer, and Yaron (STY) (1998) have constructed a numerical long-lived overlapping-generations model for analyzing some proposed social security reforms.[2] In their model, agents receive an exogenous stochastic endowment sequence, which STY choose to match to labor income. (Like Rangel and Zeckhauser, STY abstract from labor-supply decisions.) Agents can save in the form of a small number of assets, including physical capital. Because their model is basically a life-cycle version of a precautionary savings model, STY want a realistic specification of the labor-income dynamics. To calibrate their model to the contemporary United States, they use (Panel Study on Income Dynamics (PSID) data on labor earnings to create a specification that captures both (a) the personal labor-income dynamics and (b) the dispersion of the cross-sectional labor-income distribution by age of workers. To capture both of these, STY use a model with fixed effects, that is, different types. We can use their estimates to calibrate the importance of "type" in determining labor-income variance.

Thus, STY use the following transitory-permanent fixed-effects statistical model for the substantial part of the log of labor earnings u_{it} of the ith person at age t that cannot be explained by education and various other control variables:

(1a) $$u_{it} = \alpha_i + z_{it} + \varepsilon_{it},$$

(1b) $$z_{it} = \rho z_{it-1} + \eta_{it}.$$

Here, $\varepsilon_{it}, \alpha_i,$ and η_{it} are each normally and independently distributed and with mean zero and variances $\sigma_\varepsilon^2, \sigma_\alpha^2,$ and σ_η^2, respectively, and $|\rho| < 1$. The model (1) makes u_{it} a mixture of a transitory piece ε_{it}, a persistent piece z_{it}, and a person-specific fixed effect α_i. Through precautionary savings, an individual can self-insure much of the transitory and persistent components (at least if ρ is sufficiently smaller than unity); the fixed effect cannot be self-insured after birth. Model (1) implies the following covariances:

2. I thank Amir Yaron for discussing with me aspects of the rough calculations reported below on the basis of the STY paper.

(2a)
$$\text{var}(z_{it}) = \rho^2 \text{var}(z_{it-1}) + \sigma_\eta^2,$$

(2b)
$$\text{var}(u_{it}) = \sigma_\alpha^2 + \text{var}(z_{it}) + \sigma_\varepsilon^2,$$

(2c)
$$\text{cov}(u_{it}, u_{it-j}) = \sigma_\alpha^2 + \text{cov}(z_{it}, z_{it-j}),$$

(2d)
$$\text{cov}(z_{it}, z_{it-j}) = \rho^j \text{var}(z_{i,t-j}).$$

To initialize (2b), STY assume that $\text{var}(z_{i,-1}) = 0$.

STY use samples drawn from the PSID to fit the parameters of this model. First, they use pooled time series to estimate ρ, σ_ε^2, and σ_η^2. Setting $\sigma_\alpha^2 = 0$, they use these parameters to compute the cross-sectional distribution of income by age: the theoretically computed cross-sectional dispersion (without the fixed effects) increases with age, but for all ages it is below the actual cross-sectional dispersion of adjusted income u_{it} calculated directly from the PSID data. This observation impels STY to add the fixed effect through σ_α^2 and to adjust ρ to match the cross-sectional distribution of u_{it}. They attain the parameter values $\sigma_\alpha^2 = .326$, $\sigma_\varepsilon^2 = .005$, $\sigma_\eta^2 = .019$, $\rho = .98$. With these parameter values, the model roughly reproduces the level, upward slope, and curvature of the empirical cross-sectional income variance-age relation. These estimates of the variances imply a cross-sectional standard deviation of the log of income for the youngest workers of $\sqrt{.35}$; this implies that the variance of the *level* of income is approximately $\exp(.35)[\exp(.35) - 1] = .5947$. The observed initial cross-sectional standard deviation of the level of income was \$2,100 (in 1968 dollars). (The mean level of income [per adult-equivalent members of household] was \$3,300.) Thus, to get comparable units for the STY study, it is appropriate to multiply their standard deviation by $2,100/\sqrt{.5947}$ to convert it into 1968 dollars.

To assess the implication of these parameters for Rangel and Zeckhauser's issue of ex ante versus conditional evaluation of utility, we can use STY's specification to compute the variance of the expected present discounted value of $\exp u_{it}$ defined as

(3)
$$\text{PV} = E \sum_{t=0}^{T} R^{-t} \exp u_{it}.$$

Here, E is the mathematical expectation with respect to the distribution generated by process (2). The variance of (3) measures the lifetime labor income risk faced by an agent before he or she is born. Part of the variance of (3) comes from the fixed effect α_i, with the remaining part coming from chance income variations realized during the lifetime. For STY's specification with $R = 1.04$ and a working life of $T = 45$ years, I compute that the standard deviation of (3) is \$40,500 (in 1968 dollars) and that 69 percent of the variance is due to the fixed effect α. A standard deviation of \$40,500 is substantial compared to an estimate of the average present

Table 4C.1   **90-10 Quantile Ratio, After-Tax and -Transfer Personal Income**

Country and Year	P_{90}-P_{10}
Finland, 1991	2.75
Sweden, 1992	2.78
Belgium, 1992	2.79
Netherlands, 1991	3.05
Germany, 1989	3.21
France, 1984	3.48
Canada, 1991	3.90
United Kingdom, 1991	4.67
United States, 1991	5.78

value of income of $83,000 (in 1968 dollars) that can be coaxed from STY's figures. Thus, the income variance is substantial, as is the fraction of it due to the fixed effect. The 69 percent portion of the variance due to the fixed effect would be weighed by Rangel and Zeckhauser's ex ante welfare criterion, not by the conditional criterion.

Insurability of Working Types

The diverse individual-specific effects of "abilities" described in the previous two sections are not observable and can be inferred only by sophisticated statistical procedures. It is therefore not surprising that the private market does not offer to insure them. However, at least implicitly, societies provide social insurance for them through tax and transfer schemes. If we assume that abilities are equally distributed across countries, after-tax and -transfer income distributions across countries provide hints about the variation of the magnitude of the social insurance against realization of ability. For various countries, table 4C.1 shows 90-10 percentile ratios for measures of after-tax, after-transfer income. The data are from Smeeding (1998), who reports that the income data include rents and interest but exclude capital gains and various in-kind transfers. Smeeding conjectures that including in-kind transfers would make less equal countries still less equal. The figures in table 4C.1 confirm what is widely known: that there is substantially more sharing across types in Northern European countries than in the United States.

Efficiency and Equality

Rangel and Zeckhauser's model and my use of STY's statistics probably overstate the case for using the ex ante criterion. It is probably not a good idea to interpret the figures presented in table 4C.1 with a model with exogenous labor income. Work in the tradition of Shavell and Weiss (1979) points to worthwhile incentives that are sustained by unequal consumption distributions. Shavell and Weiss assume that labor market outcomes are partly the result of a worker's hidden actions. In making consumption outcomes depend on the history of observed labor market outcomes, Shavell and Weiss's planner spreads the consumption distribution over time to reward workers who probably are partly lucky and probably also taking more productive private actions. Thus, the Shavell-Weiss unemployment-compensation designer uses risk and the worker's aversion to it to manage incentive problems. Wealth distributions that spread out during time as a way optimally to trade off risk and efficiency have emerged in a variety of models in this tradition (e.g., Green 1987; Phelan and Townsend 1991; and Thomas and Worrall 1990). The pure endowment economies under discussion here do not allow us to think about this issue.

Welfare Criteria and Transition Issues

Welfare criteria based on conditional versus ex ante expected utility answer different questions and so cannot be evaluated without regard to the question at issue. Similarly, welfare criteria like Muench's ET-PO that compare only stationary allocations address questions like, What kind of society operating forever according to stationary allocation rules would you like to be born into? The criteria must be adjusted to answer questions that by their nature compare nonstationary allocations. Thus, Storesletten, Telmer, and Yaron (1998) and others in the Auerbach and Kotlikoff (1987) tradition who seek quantitatively to compare alternative proposals to reform social security arrangements struggle to adopt a welfare criterion that appropriately weighs conflicting interests. For evaluating proposals to change preexisting arrangements, at a minimum we need an initial stationary equilibrium, a new terminal one, and a transition path between them. For analyzing transition issues, the most popular framework within the Auerbach-Kotlikoff tradition is the one-sided infinite-horizon economy studied by Samuelson and Peled, in which there is an initial old generation most of whose uncertainties have been resolved and who have entitlements that have to be respected in evaluating welfare. I recommend reading the paper by Storesletten, Telmer, and Yaron (1998) alongside Rangel and Zeckhauser's paper because of how they struggle to get as far as possible using an ex ante welfare criterion and stationary equilibria to analyze alternative reform proposals.

References

Auerbach, Alan J., and Laurence J. Kotlikoff. 1987. *Dynamic fiscal policy.* Cambridge: Cambridge University Press.
Behrman, Jere R., Mark R. Rosenzweig, and Paul Taubman. 1994. Endowments and the allocation of schooling in the family and in the marriage market: The twins experiment. *Journal of Political Economy* 102, no. 6:1131–74.

Green, Edward J. 1987. Lending and the smoothing of uninsurable income. In *Contractual arrangements for intertemporal trade (Minnesota Studies in Macroeconomics, vol. 1)*, ed. Edward C. Prescott and Neil Wallace. Minneapolis: University of Minnesota Press.

Lucas, Robert E., Jr. 1977. Reply to Muench and Polemarchakis and Weiss (1977). *Journal of Economic Theory* 15:351–52.

Muench, Thomas J. 1977. Efficiency in a monetary economy. *Journal of Economic Theory* 15:325–44.

Peled, Dan. 1982. Informational diversity over time and the optimality of monetary equilibria. *Journal of Economic Theory* 28:255–74.

Phelan, Christopher, and Robert M. Townsend. 1991. Computing multi-period, information-constrained optima. *Review of Economic Studies* 58, no. 5:853–81.

Samuelson, Paul. 1958. An exact consumption-loan model of interest with or without the social contrivance of money. *Journal of Political Economy* 66:467–82.

Shavell, Steven, and Laurence Weiss. 1979. The optimal payment of unemployment insurance benefits over time. *Journal of Political Economy* 87 (December): 1347–62.

Smeeding, Timothy M. 1998. U.S. income inequality in a cross-national perspective: Why are we so different? In *The inequality paradox: Growth of income disparity,* ed. James A. Auerbach and Richard S. Bebous. Washington, D.C.: National Policy Association.

Storesletten, Kjetil, Chris Telmer, and Amir Yaron. 1998. The risk sharing implications of alternative social security arrangements. Carnegie-Mellon University. Mimeo.

Thomas, Jonathan, and Tim Worrall. 1990. Income fluctuation and asymmetric information: An example of a repeated principal-agent problem. *Journal of Economic Theory* 51, no. 2:367–90.

Discussion Summary

Henning Bohn made two remarks. First, he stated that the assumption of stationarity seems very critical in the context of interim efficiency: interim efficiency imposes no constraints whatsoever unless one operates in stationary environments. It seems, therefore, that the sharpness of the results of the paper hinges crucially on the stationarity assumption rather than on the efficiency concept used. Second, with respect to social security and policy issues, Bohn noted that, if one looks for some benchmark to judge different policies, then only ex ante efficiency would be a useful concept, especially if the government might affect the allocation (as opposed to exercises where the only uncertainty concerns the endowment).

Robert King remarked that some discussion of the public finance literature on the income tax might be useful: ultimately, a zero marginal tax rate is optimal, yet very few social institutions implement a marginal tax rate close to zero. The social security system is apparently one that does. Second, the fixed-effects coefficient α_i of Storesletten, Telmer, and Yaron to which the discussant, Thomas Sargent, refers could be the result of parental investments. Therefore, if one thinks about redistribution mechanisms in this context across individuals, one could be influencing the incentives that parents would have to make such investments.

Following up on King's remark, *Amir Yaron* commented on the variance decomposition of the present value of lifetime income reported in the Storesletten, Telmer, and Yaron paper and referred to by Sargent. Yaron noted that the fraction of the standard error of lifetime income due to the fixed-effects term (α_i) ranges from 0.4 to 0.75, depending on the empirical procedure. Of course, even the lower bound of these estimates reveals the importance of individual fixed effects for someone's lifetime earnings potential. He agreed with King's remark about the relevance of education and therefore of parental investments.

Stephen Ross noted that there is a relation between the choice of efficiency and the choice of a model, going either backward or forward. If one considers, for example, a model that starts at a particular point, interim efficiency should not be achieved because, while it is possible to tax backward through a sufficiently high interest rate, one cannot tax forward. Ross further remarked that he found the concept of ex ante optimality or equal treatment Pareto efficiency disturbing as it treats cohorts to be born in the remote future in the same way as the generation currently alive. He stated that he strongly favored attaching a smaller weight to those remote generations than to the current one. He added that the concept is moreover politically infeasible.

Zvi Bodie inquired whether the discussant knew why the insurance contracts he mentioned, insuring the risk of being born with illnesses that adversely affect the lifetime ability to earn income, are not being offered. He added that moral hazard was presumably not the reason. He concluded that it might be in the interest of insurance companies to offer these contracts.

Thomas Sargent elaborated on his discussion of the results of Behrman, Rosenzweig, and Taubman, documenting the importance of substantial labor market-relevant permanent-endowment heterogeneity. He noted that these authors also study the covariation of this innate ability with two other variables, education and marriage. They find that education acts to reinforce innate differences while marriage dampens them.

In response to the discussions and comments, *Antonio Rangel* made the following points. First, he noted that, although he often has strong opinions, this is not the case in the debate on the choice of the efficiency concept. The paper studies the performance of institutions under both efficiency criteria without in any way advocating the concept of ex ante efficiency. Second, with respect to Bohn's comment about the importance of the stationarity assumption, Rangel clarified that, while the stationarity assumption is innocuous, modeling time as doubly infinite is crucial for the results of the paper. In particular, the absence of any first generation is what drives many of the results, including the disagreement with the findings of Peled, as remarked by Sargent.

Finally, Rangel pointed out that the choice between the ex ante and the interim efficiency concept is often trivial, especially in static models. He gave examples of idiosyncratic or intragenerational risks where taking an ex post perspective is obviously meaningless. On the contrary, in the model presented in the paper, considering intergenerational risks instead, the choice is nontrivial, and both concepts are interesting alternatives.

Richard Zeckhauser noted that no forward or backward altruism is assumed in the model. Agents care only about themselves, except perhaps for strategic, game-theoretic reasons.

5

The Social Security Trust Fund, the Riskless Interest Rate, and Capital Accumulation

Andrew B. Abel

The social security trust fund in the United States currently has about $0.75 trillion in assets. Its assets are projected to grow to almost $2 trillion (1998 dollars) in the year 2016. As the baby-boom generation begins to retire and collect social security benefits in the second decade of the twenty-first century, the social security trust fund will shrink, and it is projected to run out of assets in the year 2032.[1] The prospect that the social security system will run large deficits and exhaust the social security trust fund has given rise to a variety of proposals to "save social security." Some proposals are designed to exploit the equity premium, which is the excess of the rate of return on equity over the riskless interest rate. Since the equity premium has historically averaged several hundred basis points per year, it may be tempting to shift some of the assets of the social security trust fund (which currently holds only bonds) from bonds to equity. In this paper, I analyze the effects on the equilibrium equity premium and the equilibrium growth rate of the capital stock of such a portfolio change.

I have three goals in this paper. First, I want to develop a tractable stochastic dynamic general equilibrium model of social security and national capital accumulation with an endogenous equity premium. Second, although tractability dictates that the model be relatively simple, I want to calibrate the model numerically and would like the calibrated model to be

Andrew B. Abel is the Robert Morris Professor of Banking and professor of economics at the Wharton School of the University of Pennsylvania.

The author thanks Henning Bohn, John Campbell, Bill Dupor, Robert King, Deborah Lucas, Amir Yaron, and participants in the NBER preconference and conference for helpful comments. The author also thanks Farshad Mashayekhi for excellent research assistance.

1. Table III.B2 of Board of Trustees (1998) reports projections for the assets of the combined OASI and DI trust funds. The year-end projections based on intermediate cost assumptions in constant (1998) dollars are $756.9 billion for 1998 and $1,960.4 billion for 2016.

quantitatively plausible in some dimensions. In particular, I would like the model to be able to match the historical average equity premium and the historical average growth rate of capital. Third, I want to apply the model to analyze the effects on the equity premium and the growth rate of capital of investing some of the social security trust fund in risky capital.

A natural starting point for a model of social security and capital accumulation is Diamond's (1965) classic model of government debt in a neoclassical economy, which has been applied to analyze the effects of social security on national capital accumulation in a deterministic context.[2] In order to achieve the goals of this paper, I modify the Diamond model in two important ways. First, because the Diamond model is a deterministic one, the equity premium is identically zero in that model. Since I want to model the equilibrium equity premium, I introduce risk so that a positive average equity premium is a feature of equilibrium. Second, to help keep the analysis tractable, I replace the neoclassical production function with an AK model that is consistent with endogenous growth. I introduce risk in the model by assuming that productivity is stochastic.

I model four sets of economic actors—firms, individuals, the Treasury, and the social security system—and I describe the behavior of each of these sets of economic actors in the first four analytic sections of the paper. The behavior of firms is presented in section 5.1, where I present the stochastic AK technology and then derive the equilibrium wage and risky return on capital. With a stochastic AK technology, the rate of return on capital is stochastic but exogenous. The stochastic nature of the rate of return on capital allows for a positive equity premium in equilibrium. The exogenous nature of this risky rate of return keeps the model tractable. Although the risky rate of return is exogenous in this model, the riskless interest rate is endogenous, so the equity premium is also endogenous. Any change in the riskless interest rate is matched by a change in the equity premium of the same magnitude but in the opposite direction. Thus, I will focus attention on the behavior of the equilibrium riskless interest rate, recognizing that the results directly translate into results about the equity premium.

The consumption/saving and portfolio decisions of individuals are analyzed in section 5.2. My choice of a specification of the utility function reflects the tension between analytic tractability and quantitative realism. To achieve analytic tractability, I assume that the utility function is characterized by an intertemporal elasticity of substitution equal to one, as is the case, for example, with logarithmic utility. However, with logarithmic utility, the coefficient of relative risk aversion also equals one, and quantitative realism dictates a coefficient of relative risk aversion greater than one. Thus, I use a special case of the preferences introduced by Epstein and

---

2. For a textbook example, see Blanchard and Fischer (1989, 110–13).

Zin (1989) and Weil (1990) to allow for a coefficient of relative risk aversion greater than one and an intertemporal elasticity of substitution equal to one.

Although the behavior of firms and individuals is based on explicit maximization, I do not attempt to specify the objective functions of the Treasury and the social security system and then derive optimal policy. Instead, I specify policy functions for each of these fiscal institutions in sections 5.3 and 5.4. To prevent the amount of Treasury debt from becoming too large or too small in the face of stochastic shocks, I assume that the Treasury adjusts taxes and government purchases in response to deviations of the debt-GDP ratio from a target value. As for the social security system, I examine a pay-as-you-go defined-benefit system and allow social security taxes to adjust when the ratio of the social security trust fund to the aggregate capital stock deviates from its target value. In addition, I assume that the social security trust fund can choose how to allocate its portfolio to riskless bonds and risky capital.

Firms, individuals, the Treasury, and the social security system interact in capital markets to determine the riskless interest rate (and hence the equity premium) and the growth rate of the aggregate capital stock. This model has a convenient recursive structure. The riskless interest rate is determined by portfolio-allocation decisions of individuals and does not depend on the aggregate level of the capital stock. Then, given the value of the riskless interest rate, the saving decisions of individuals determine the growth rate of the capital stock. The presentation of results in section 5.5 reflects this recursive structure.

I examine the riskless interest rate in subsection 5.5.1. An increase in the amount of riskless bonds relative to the amount of capital causes the riskless interest rate to increase (equivalently, the equity premium to fall) because individuals must be induced to hold a higher share of riskless assets in their portfolios. In particular, if the social security trust fund sells some bonds to the public in exchange for risky capital, then, in the context of a pay-as-you-go defined-benefit system, the real interest rate must increase to induce individuals to increase the share of riskless assets in their portfolios.

After analyzing the equilibrium riskless interest rate in subsection 5.5.1, I analyze the equilibrium value of the growth rate of the capital stock in subsection 5.5.2. The growth rate of the capital stock is determined by the amount of saving in the economy. I show that, if the social security trust fund sells some bonds in exchange for risky capital, the capital stock in the following period will be higher than if the social security trust fund held only bonds. This effect arises because the change in the portfolio of the social security trust fund causes the riskless interest rate to increase, which reduces the present value of the social security benefits that current workers expect when they retire. In response to this reduction in the present value of lifetime income, current workers reduce their consumption and increase their saving. The effect on the saving of future generations involves additional effects operating through the adjustment of taxes to satisfy the budget constraints and policy functions of the Treasury and the social security system. I focus my analysis of saving by future generations by considering *constant growth paths,* which I define and analyze in subsection 5.5.2. Proposition 6 in this subsection presents a sufficient condition for the growth rate of the capital stock along a constant growth path to increase when the share of the social security trust fund invested in risky capital increases.

I explore the quantitative plausibility of the model in section 5.6, where I show that the endogenous riskless interest rate and growth rate of capital along a constant growth path can match the historical average values of these variables for reasonable values of the preference parameters. I also explore the sensitivity of these endogenous variables to various parameters and calibrated values of variables. In addition, I show that an increase in the share of the social security trust fund that is invested in risky capital will increase the growth rate of capital along a constant growth path because the sufficient condition in proposition 6 is satisfied in the baseline calibration and in the sensitivity analysis. Quantitatively, the model suggests that investing a modest fraction of the social security trust fund in risky capital will have only small effects on the riskless interest rate and the growth rate of the capital stock.

I present concluding remarks in section 5.7. Various technical derivations are relegated to appendixes A–E.

5.1   Factor Prices in General Equilibrium

The economy consists of overlapping generations of people who live for two periods. At the beginning of period t, a continuum of people with measure N_t is born. Each of these people inelastically supplies one unit of labor when young in period t and does not supply any labor when old in period $t + 1$.

Output in period t is produced using labor and capital. In period t, firm i uses labor, $N_{i,t}$, and capital, $K_{i,t}$, to produce output, $Y_{i,t}$, according to the production function

$$(1) \qquad Y_{i,t} = A_t K_{i,t}^{\alpha}(N_{i,t} K_t)^{1-\alpha},$$

where $A_t \geq A_L > 0$ is an independently and identically distributed (i.i.d.) productivity shock with mean $\overline{A}$,[3] K_t is the aggregate capital stock at the beginning of period t, and $0 < \alpha < 1$. The production function in equation

---

3. A_L is the greatest lower bound for A_t. In addition, I assume that there is a positive probability that A_t is within a small neighborhood of A_L. Specifically, $\mathrm{pr}\{A_t \geq A_L\} = 1$, and, for all $\varepsilon > 0$, $\mathrm{pr}\{A_L \leq A_t \leq A_L + \varepsilon\} > 0$.

(1) is consistent with endogenous growth (see, e.g., Barro and Sala-i-Martin 1995, 150).

Factor prices are determined in competitive markets, and the rental price of each factor equals its marginal product. Thus, the wage rate in period t, w_t, is

$$(2) \qquad w_t = (1 - \alpha)A_t\left(\frac{K_{i,t}}{N_{i,t}}\right)^{\alpha} K_t^{1-\alpha},$$

and the gross rate of return to capital in period t, R_t, is

$$(3) \qquad R_t = \alpha A_t\left(\frac{N_{i,t}K_t}{K_{i,t}}\right)^{1-\alpha}.$$

In equilibrium, each firm will choose the same capital-labor ratio so that $K_{i,t}/N_{i,t} = K_t/N_t$ for all i. Now assume that the population is constant over time, adopt the normalization $N_t \equiv 1$, and substitute $K_{i,t}/N_{i,t} = K_t$ in equations (2) and (3) to obtain

$$(4) \qquad w_t = (1 - \alpha)A_t K_t$$

and

$$(5) \qquad R_t = \alpha A_t.$$

The gross rate of return on capital is random and has mean $\overline{R} = \alpha\overline{A}$.

5.2 Individual Optimization

Each person faces an optimization problem that includes a saving/consumption decision and a portfolio decision. I will solve the optimization problem of a person born in period t after first specifying the person's budget constraint and then specifying the person's utility function.

A representative person born at the beginning of period t supplies one unit of labor in period t and receives wage income equal to w_t. Also in period t, the person pays taxes T_t^T to the Treasury and pays social security taxes T_t^S. Both types of taxes are lump sum. I have distinguished taxes paid to the Treasury from taxes paid to the social security system so that I can keep track of the Treasury's outstanding debt and the amount of Treasury bonds held by the social security trust fund.

A young person in period t has disposable income of $w_t - T_t^S - T_t^T$, which can be used for consumption and the purchase of riskless bonds and risky capital. Riskless bonds purchased in period t pay a gross rate of return r_{t+1} in period $t + 1$. Let B_{t+1}^P be the value of riskless bonds purchased by a young person in period t (the superscript P denotes that the bonds are privately held, in contrast to bonds held by the social security trust fund). The person also purchases risky capital K_{t+1}^P, which pays a gross rate of return R_{t+1} in period $t + 1$. Since consumption when young, C_t, plus the purchases of bonds and risky capital equals disposable income,

$$(6) \qquad C_t = w_t - T_t^S - T_t^T - B_{t+1}^P - K_{t+1}^P.$$

Let X_{t+1} be the consumption of an old person in period $t + 1$. This consumption is financed by the riskless bonds and risky capital purchased in period t and by social security benefits. Riskless bonds are worth $r_{t+1} B_{t+1}^P$, and risky capital is worth $R_{t+1} K_{t+1}^P$. Social security benefits consist of two components. One component is $\theta_1 w_{t+1} = \theta_1(1 - \alpha)A_{t+1}K_{t+1}$, which is proportional to the actual wage in period $t + 1$. The other component is $\theta_0 \overline{w}_{t+1}$, where $\overline{w}_{t+1}$ is the expected value of w_{t+1} conditional on information available at the end of period t. Since the capital stock K_{t+1} is known at the end of period t, $\overline{w}_{t+1} = (1 - \alpha) \overline{A}K_{t+1}$. Taking account of both components of the social security benefits, the total amount of social security benefits, Q_{t+1}, received by an old person in period $t + 1$ is

$$(7) \qquad Q_{t+1} = \theta_0(1 - \alpha)\overline{A} K_{t+1} + \theta_1(1 - \alpha)A_{t+1}K_{t+1}.$$

I assume that $\theta_0 \geq 0$ and $\theta_1 \geq 0$. It is convenient, although not strictly accurate, to refer to the parameters θ_0 and θ_1 as *replacement rates* for social security. Because the social security benefits received by an old person do not depend on the amount of social security taxes paid by that person or on any decision made by that person, I describe the system in this model as *a defined-benefit system.*

The solution of the person's optimization problem is facilitated by using equation (5) to rewrite the social security benefits in equation (7) as

$$(8) \qquad Q_{t+1} = \theta_0(1 - \alpha)\overline{A} K_{t+1} + \theta_1 \frac{1 - \alpha}{\alpha} R_{t+1} K_{t+1}.$$

Because w_{t+1} is perfectly correlated with R_{t+1} in this model, the claim on future social security benefits can be viewed as consisting of a riskless asset plus a risky asset with a payoff that is perfectly correlated with the rate of return on risky capital, as illustrated in equation (8).

I assume that individuals do not have a bequest motive and thus that they consume all available resources when they are old. Taking account of privately held bonds and risky capital as well as social security benefits, Q_{t+1}, yields

$$(9) \qquad X_{t+1} = \left[B_{t+1}^P + \frac{\theta_0(1 - \alpha)\overline{A} K_{t+1}}{r_{t+1}} \right] r_{t+1}$$

$$+ \left(K_{t+1}^P + \theta_1 \frac{1 - \alpha}{\alpha} K_{t+1} \right) R_{t+1}.$$

Suppose that each person born at the beginning of period t has the following utility function, which is a special case of the parametric class of preferences developed by Epstein and Zin (1989) and Weil (1990) and used by Bohn (1998a) to study intergenerational risk sharing:[4]

(10) $U_t = \ln C_t + \dfrac{\delta}{1 - \phi} \ln E_t\{X_{t+1}^{1-\phi}\}$ where $0 < \phi \neq 1$ and $\delta > 0$.

For the utility function in equation (10), the intertemporal elasticity of substitution equals one, and the coefficient of relative risk aversion over second-period consumption is ϕ. I have chosen to specify a unitary intertemporal elasticity of substitution to simplify the consumption/saving decision and to help keep the general equilibrium analysis tractable. A standard time-separable utility function with a constant coefficient of relative risk aversion constrains the coefficient of relative risk aversion to equal the inverse of intertemporal elasticity of substitution, which equals one in this case. However, I do not constrain the coefficient of relative risk aversion to equal one because various studies of the equity-premium puzzle have shown that it is difficult, or perhaps impossible, to account for the large historical average value of the equity premium, $R_{t+1} - r_{t+1}$, with a coefficient of relative risk aversion as low as one.

The optimization problem of a young person in period t is to choose C_t, B_{t+1}^P, and K_{t+1}^P to maximize the utility function in equation (10) subject to the constraints in equations (6) and (9). The solution to this problem is easily expressed in term of Ω_t, the present value of lifetime resources, which is

(11) $\Omega_t \equiv w_t - T_t^T - T_t^S + \dfrac{\theta_0(1 - \alpha)\overline{A}\,K_{t+1}}{r_{t+1}} + \theta_1\dfrac{1 - \alpha}{\alpha}K_{t+1}.$

The present value of lifetime resources consists of disposable income, $w_t - T_t^T - T_t^S$, plus the present value of the social security benefits[5] to be received in period $t + 1$,

$$\dfrac{\theta_0(1 - \alpha)\overline{A}\,K_{t+1}}{r_{t+1}} + \theta_1\dfrac{1-\alpha}{\alpha}K_{t+1}.$$

4. If $\phi = 1$, the utility function is $U_t = \ln C_t + \delta E_t\{\ln X_{t+1}\}$.
Individuals may also obtain utility from government purchases. I assume that any utility from government purchases is additively separable from utility of the consumer's own consumption.
5. In computing the present value of future social security benefits, the riskless component, $\theta_0(1 - \alpha)\overline{A}K_{t+1}$, is discounted by the riskless rate, r_{t+1}, and the risky component,

$$\theta_1\dfrac{1 - \alpha}{\alpha}R_{t+1}K_{t+1},$$

is discounted by the risky rate, R_{t+1}.

Let a_{t+1} be the value of a young person's total assets at the end of period t. These assets consist of direct holdings of riskless bonds, B^P_{t+1}, and risky capital, K^P_{t+1}, plus the present value of future social security benefits,

$$\frac{\theta_0(1 - \alpha)\overline{A} K_{t+1}}{r_{t+1}} + \theta_1 \frac{1-\alpha}{\alpha} K_{t+1}.$$

Thus,

$$(12) \qquad a_{t+1} \equiv B^P_{t+1} + K^P_{t+1} + \frac{\theta_0(1 - \alpha)\overline{A} K_{t+1}}{r_{t+1}} + \theta_1 \frac{1 - \alpha}{\alpha} K_{t+1}.$$

As shown in equation (A5) in appendix A, the optimal value of a_{t+1} is

$$(13) \qquad a_{t+1} = \frac{\delta}{1 + \delta} \Omega_t.$$

To describe the optimal allocation of a young person's portfolio, let γ_{t+1} be the share of the total portfolio a_{t+1} devoted to risky assets, consisting of risky capital, K^P_{t+1}, and the present value of risky future social security benefits

$$\theta_1 \frac{1 - \alpha}{\alpha} K_{t+1}.$$

More precisely,

$$(14) \qquad \gamma_{t+1} \equiv \frac{K^P_{t+1} + \theta_1 \frac{1 - \alpha}{\alpha} K_{t+1}}{a_{t+1}}.$$

The definitions in equations (12) and (14) imply that $1 - \gamma_{t+1}$ is the share of a young consumer's total portfolio devoted to riskless assets, consisting of riskless bonds, B^P_{t+1}, and the present value of riskless future social security benefits

$$\frac{\theta_0(1 - \alpha)\overline{A} K_{t+1}}{r_{t+1}}.$$

Let $\gamma(r_{t+1})$ denote the optimal value of γ_{t+1}. This notation emphasizes that the optimal portfolio allocation depends on the riskless interest rate, r_{t+1}, which is an endogenous variable in this model. The optimal portfolio allocation also depends on the distribution of the risky rate of return, R_{t+1}, but this distribution is exogenous in this model, so the notation does not reflect this dependence. The optimal value of γ_{t+1} is characterized in appendix B, where it is shown that, if $\phi \leq 1$, then $\gamma'(r_{t+1}) < 0$. If $\phi > 1$, then $\gamma'(r_{t+1})$ may be negative, zero, or positive. Henceforth, I restrict attention to the case with $\gamma'(r_{t+1}) < 0$.[6]

The definition of γ_{t+1} in equation (14) and the optimal value of a_{t+1} in equation (13) imply the following expressions for optimal holdings of assets by a young person at the end of period t:

$$(15) \qquad B_{t+1}^P + \frac{\theta_0(1 - \alpha)\overline{A}\,K_{t+1}}{r_{t+1}} = [1 - \gamma(r_{t+1})]\frac{\delta}{1 + \delta}\Omega_t,$$

and

$$(16) \qquad K_{t+1}^P + \theta_1\frac{1 - \alpha}{\alpha}K_{t+1} = \gamma(r_{t+1})\frac{\delta}{1 + \delta}\Omega_t.$$

The riskless interest rate r_{t+1} affects the private demand for capital in two ways. Since I am restricting attention to the case in which $\gamma'(r_{t+1}) < 0$, an increase in the riskless interest r_{t+1} causes consumers to shift their portfolios toward the riskless asset and away from risky assets, thereby reducing the private demand for capital, for a given present value of lifetime resources Ω_t. In addition, if $\theta_0 > 0$, an increase in r_{t+1} reduces the present value of riskless social security benefits and thus reduces Ω_t, as shown in equation (11). This reduction in Ω_t reduces the private demand for capital. Thus, an increase in r_{t+1} reduces the private demand for capital both by changing the composition and (if $\theta_0 > 0$) by reducing the size of private portfolios.

5.3 The Treasury's Revenues, Expenditures, and Debt

The social security trust fund in the United States holds several hundred billion dollars of bonds issued by the Treasury. Because these bonds are liabilities of the Treasury and assets of the social security trust fund, it is important to treat the Treasury and the social security system separately. In this section, I specify the Treasury's behavior.

The budget constraint of the Treasury is

$$(17) \qquad B_{t+1} = r_t B_t + G_t - T_t^T,$$

where B_t is the amount of Treasury debt outstanding at the end of period $t - 1$ (equivalently, the beginning of period t), r_t is the gross rate of return

---

6. In the calibration in sec. 5.6, the value of ϕ exceeds one so that, in principle, $\gamma'(r_{t+1})$ can be positive, negative, or zero. For all the cases examined in tables 5.1–5.3 below, $\gamma'(r_{t+1}) < 0$.

on these bonds, G_t is the Treasury's expenditure on purchases of consumption goods[7] during period t, and, as in section 5.2, T_t^T is the tax revenue collected from young consumers by the Treasury during period t.

A simple approach to modeling fiscal policy is to assume that government purchases, G_t, and Treasury taxes, T_t^T, are each proportional to aggregate output, $A_t K_t$, and then to let the stock of Treasury debt evolve according to equation (17). However, in the face of stochastic shocks to A_t, the stock of debt could become arbitrarily large or arbitrarily small (indeed, negative and large in absolute value). Therefore, I will modify the simple assumptions of proportional government purchases and taxes so that purchases are reduced and/or taxes increased if the stock of debt is above some target level. Similarly, if the stock of debt is below the target, then purchases are increased and/or taxes cut.

To measure the size of the Treasury's debt relative to the size of the economy, define $b_{t+1} \equiv B_{t+1}/K_{t+1}$ as the ratio of Treasury debt to the aggregate capital stock.[8] Let β be the "target" value of b_{t+1}. I have put the word *target* in quotation marks because the Treasury does not literally aim to set b_{t+1} equal to β. The Treasury moves the value of b_{t+1} toward β according to the following policy function:

$$(18) \qquad b_{t+1} - \beta = \rho_B(b_t - \beta) + \rho_A(g - \tau)(A_t - \overline{A}),$$

where $\rho_B \geq 0$ and $\rho_A \geq 0$ are parameters governing the evolution of the debt-capital ratio b_t, and τ and g are parameters related to Treasury taxes and purchases, as described below.

If Treasury taxes were $T_t^T = \tau A_t K_t$, and if government purchases were $G_t = g A_t K_t$, then $(g - \tau)(A_t - \overline{A})K_t$ would be the amount by which net government expenditures (i.e., government purchases less taxes) in period t exceed the amount that was expected at the end of the previous period (when K_t was known). The Treasury can respond to unexpected net expenditures by increasing taxes, reducing government purchases, or increasing its outstanding debt. If the Treasury completely insulates the size of its debt from unexpected shocks by changing taxes and government purchases appropriately, then $\rho_A = 0$ in equation (18). Alternatively, if $\rho_A > 0$, then the Treasury finances at least part of unexpected net expenditures by increasing its debt.

Let D_t be the primary deficit in period t. Since the primary deficit is the amount by which government purchases (which do not include interest

7. I assume that all capital formation in the economy is done by the private sector so that all the Treasury's expenditure on goods is for consumption goods.

8. The size of a country's debt is often expressed as a debt-GDP ratio, B_t/Y_t, which is $B_t/A_t K_t$ in this model. The measure that I use in this paper is proportional to $B_t/\overline{A}K_t$, which is the ratio of debt to "trend" GDP, $\overline{A}K_t$.

payments on government debt) exceed taxes, the Treasury's budget constraint in equation (17) implies

(19) $$D_t = G_t - T_t^T = B_{t+1} - r_t B_t.$$

The Treasury policy function in equation (18) implies a value for the primary deficit. Multiplying both sides of equation (18) by K_{t+1}, substituting the resulting expression for B_{t+1} in equation (19), and recalling that $B_t = b_t K_t$ yield

(20) $$D_t = [\beta + \rho_B(b_t - \beta) + \rho_A(g - \tau)(A_t - \overline{A})]K_{t+1} - r_t b_t K_t.$$

Given the value of the primary deficit in equation (20), the values of G_t and T_t^T still need to be determined. To the extent that D_t in equation (20) differs from $(g - \tau)A_t K_t$, government purchases and/or taxes need to be adjusted. I introduce a "tax responsiveness" parameter λ to determine how much of the required adjustment in $G_t - T_t^T$ is achieved by adjusting taxes. Whenever there is a gap between D_t and $(g - \tau)A_t K_t$, a fraction $\lambda(0 \leq \lambda \leq 1)$ of this gap is closed by changing taxes, and a fraction $1 - \lambda$ is closed by changing government purchases. Specifically,

(21) $$T_t^T = \tau A_t K_t - \lambda[D_t - (g - \tau)A_t K_t],$$

and

(22) $$G_t = gA_t K_t + (1 - \lambda)[D_t - (g - \tau)A_t K_t].$$

The amount of taxes collected by the Treasury can be rewritten by substituting equation (20) into equation (21) to obtain[9]

(23) $$T_t^T = [(1 - \lambda)\tau + \lambda g]A_t K_t + \lambda r_t b_t K_t$$
$$- \lambda[\beta + \rho_B(b_t - \beta) + \rho_A(g - \tau)(A_t - \overline{A})]K_{t+1}.$$

The expression for Treasury tax revenue in equation (23) can be simplified in special cases. For instance, if the tax-responsive parameter λ equals zero, the Treasury's tax revenue is simply $T_t^T = \tau A_t K_t$.[10] In this case, any gap between the primary deficit and $(g - \tau)A_t K_t$ is closed completely by adjusting government purchases.

9. Government purchases can be rewritten as

$$G_t = [\lambda g + (1 - \lambda)\tau]A_t K_t - (1 - \lambda)r_t b_t K_t$$
$$+ (1 - \lambda)[\beta + \rho_B(b_t - \beta) + \rho_A(g - \tau)(A_t - \overline{A})]K_{t+1}.$$

10. One might think of this case as being one of complete tax smoothing by the Treasury, although it must be noted that, since all taxes are lump sum, the usual argument for tax smoothing does not apply here.

5.4 The Social Security System

The social security system collects taxes from young people and pays benefits to old people. Any excess of taxes over benefits is added to the social security trust fund, and any excess of benefits over taxes is paid from the social security trust fund.

Let $S_t \geq 0$ be the value of the social security trust fund at the beginning of period t. Currently in the United States, the social security trust fund is invested entirely in Treasury bonds, which pay a rate of return r_t. However, there are proposals to invest part of the social security trust fund in equities, which are modeled as risky capital in this paper. To account for this possible change, let K_t^S be the amount of risky capital held by the social security trust fund at the beginning of period t, and define $\gamma_{S,t} \equiv K_t^S/S_t \geq 0$ as the fraction of the social security trust fund invested in risky capital with a rate of return R_t. The condition $\gamma_{S,t} \geq 0$ rules out the possibility that the social security trust fund takes a short position in risky physical capital.

Let B_t^S be the value of riskless bonds held by the social security trust fund at the beginning of period t, and note that $1 - \gamma_{S,t} = B_t^S/S_t$ is the fraction of the social security trust fund invested in riskless bonds. The rate of return on the social security trust fund, R_t^S, is

$$(24) \qquad R_t^S \equiv (1 - \gamma_{S,t})r_t + \gamma_{S,t}R_t.$$

The budget constraint of the social security trust fund is

$$(25) \qquad S_{t+1} = R_t^S S_t + T_t^S - Q_t.$$

I have described the behavior of social security benefits, Q_t, and the rate of return, R_t^S. To complete the description of the behavior of the social security system, I must specify either the behavior of social security taxes, T_t^S, or the evolution of the size of the trust fund, S_t. I will specify the evolution of S_t, and thus T_t^S will be determined as a residual from equation (25).[11]

---

11. I have specified the social security system as a pay-as-you-go defined-benefit system, but the framework is flexible enough to model a fully funded defined-contribution system in which the social security taxes collected from workers are placed in the social security trust fund. A fully funded defined-contribution system can be modeled by specifying the amount of taxes collected from workers, T_t^S, and the fraction of the social security trust fund invested in risky capital, $\gamma_{S,t+1}$. The size of the social security trust fund at the beginning of period $t + 1$ is $S_{t+1} = T_t^S$, and the social security benefits in period $t + 1$ are

$$Q_{t+1} = R_{t+1}^S S_{t+1} = (1 - \gamma_{S,t+1})r_{t+1}S_{t+1} + \gamma_{S,t+1}R_{t+1}S_{t+1}.$$

Comparing this expression for social security benefits to the expression in eq. (8) and recalling that $\underline{S}_{t+1} = s_{t+1}K_{t+1}$ imply the following values for θ_0 and θ_1: $\theta_0 = (1 - \gamma_{S,t+1})r_{t+1}s_{t+1}/((1 - \alpha)A)$, and $\theta_1 = \alpha\gamma_{S,t+1}s_{t+1}/(1 - \alpha)$. A fully funded defined-contribution social security

Define $s_t \equiv S_t/K_t$ as the ratio of the social security trust fund to the aggregate capital stock, and let σ be the "target" value of s_t. The social security system does not aim to set s_t equal to σ in every period, but it tries to prevent s_t from wandering too far from σ by adhering to the following policy function:

$$(26) \qquad s_{t+1} - \sigma = \rho_S(s_t - \sigma) + \rho_R(R_t^S - \overline{R}_t^S)s_t,$$

where $\overline{R}_t^S \equiv (1 - \gamma_{S,t})r_t + \gamma_{S,t}\overline{R}$ is the expected value of R_t^S conditional on information available at the end of period $t - 1$, and $\rho_S \geq 0$ and $\rho_R \geq 0$ are constants that parametrize the evolution of the social security trust fund relative to the capital stock. If $\rho_R = 0$, the size of the social security trust fund is completely insulated from shocks to the rate of return, R_t^S. In this case, the ratio of the social security trust fund to the capital stock, s_{t+1}, is always equal to the target value, σ. If $\rho_R > 0$, then, when the return on the social security trust fund, R_t^S, is higher than expected, at least part of the unexpected return is used to increase the size of the social security trust fund. The parameter ρ_S measures the persistence of changes in the ratio s_t.

The amount of social security taxes, T_t^S, is determined as a residual from equation (25). Substituting equation (26) into equation (25), using equation (24), and solving for T_t^S yield

$$(27) \qquad T_t^S = Q_t - R_t^S s_t K_t + [\sigma + \rho_S(s_t - \sigma)$$
$$+ \rho_R\gamma_{S,t}(R_t - \overline{R})s_t]K_{t+1}.$$

5.5 General Equilibrium

Now that I have specified the behavior of firms, individuals, the Treasury, and the social security system, I will analyze the general equilibrium that arises when these economic actors interact in capital markets. The dynamic general equilibrium describes the equilibrium evolution of four endogenous variables: the riskless interest rate r_t, the aggregate capital stock K_t, the debt-capital ratio b_t, and the social security trust fund-capital ratio s_t. The dynamic behavior of these four variables is governed by a nonlinear difference equation system that is recursive. Given the values of r_t, K_t, b_t, s_t, and the exogenous variable A_t (and the implied value of R_t), the value of b_{t+1} is determined by the Treasury policy function in equation (18), and the value of s_{t+1} is determined by the social security policy function in equation (26). As I will show below, the equilibrium value of r_{t+1} is determined by the optimal portfolio shares using the values of b_{t+1} and

---

system has no effect on the equilibrium riskless interest rate (see n. 12 below) or on the growth rate of capital (see n. 17 below).

s_{t+1}. Finally, the value of K_{t+1} is determined using optimal saving behavior and the values of r_{t+1}, b_{t+1}, and s_{t+1}.

I consider a closed economy so that all the bonds issued by the Treasury, B_{t+1}, are held either by the domestic private sector, which holds the amount B^P_{t+1}, or by the social security trust fund, which holds the amount $(1 - \gamma_{S,t+1})S_{t+1}$. Therefore,

$$(28) \qquad B^P_{t+1} = B_{t+1} - (1 - \gamma_{S,t+1})S_{t+1}.$$

Similarly, all the capital in the economy, K_{t+1}, is held either by the domestic private sector, which holds the amount K^P_{t+1}, or by the social security trust fund, which holds $\gamma_{S,t+1}S_{t+1}$. Therefore,

$$(29) \qquad K^P_{t+1} = K_{t+1} - \gamma_{S,t+1}S_{t+1}.$$

I will restrict attention to equilibria in which the amount of Treasury debt outstanding, B_t, is positive, the social security trust fund, S_t, is non-negative, and young consumers hold positive amounts of both bonds and capital in their portfolios. Since $\gamma_{S,t+1} \geq 0$, equation (28) implies that a sufficient condition for young consumers to have positive holdings of bonds is

$$(30) \qquad b_{t+1} > s_{t+1}.$$

Equation (29) implies that young consumers will have positive holdings of risky capital in equilibrium if

$$(31) \qquad \gamma_{S,t+1}s_{t+1} < 1.$$

Henceforth, I will assume that the conditions in equations (30) and (31) hold for all t.

5.5.1 The Equilibrium Riskless Interest Rate

The equilibrium riskless interest rate is determined by the optimal portfolio shares. It follows from equations (15) and (16) that

$$(32) \quad \gamma(r_{t+1})\left[B^P_{t+1} + \frac{\theta_0(1 - \alpha)\overline{A}K_{t+1}}{r_{t+1}} \right]$$

$$= [1 - \gamma(r_{t+1})]\left(K^P_{t+1} + \theta_1 \frac{1 - \alpha}{\alpha}K_{t+1} \right).$$

Using equations (28) and (29) and the definitions $b_{t+1} \equiv B_{t+1}/K_{t+1}$ and $s_{t+1} \equiv S_{t+1}/K_{t+1}$, equation (32) can be rewritten as

$$(33) \quad 0 = \gamma(r_{t+1})\left[1 + b_{t+1} - s_{t+1} + \frac{\theta_0(1 - \alpha)\overline{A}}{r_{t+1}} + \theta_1\frac{1 - \alpha}{\alpha}\right]$$

$$- 1 + \gamma_{S,t+1}\, s_{t+1} - \theta_1\frac{1 - \alpha}{\alpha}.$$

Equation (33) determines the equilibrium riskless interest rate r_{t+1}.[12] Alternatively, it can be solved to obtain the equilibrium value of $\gamma(r_{t+1})$, which is

$$(34) \quad \gamma(r_{t+1}) = \frac{1 + \theta_1\dfrac{1 - \alpha}{\alpha} - \gamma_{S,t+1}\, s_{t+1}}{1 + \theta_1\dfrac{1 - \alpha}{\alpha} + b_{t+1} - s_{t+1} + \dfrac{\theta_0(1 - \alpha)\overline{A}}{r_{t+1}}}.$$

Equation (34), along with the conditions in equations (30) and (31), implies the following:

PROPOSITION 1. *In equilibrium, $0 < \gamma(r_{t+1}) < 1$.*

Proposition 1 states that, in equilibrium, young consumers hold positive amounts of risky assets in their portfolios. It is well known that an optimal portfolio will include positive holdings of risky assets only if the expected rate of return on risky assets is greater than the riskless rate of return.[13] Thus, proposition 1 implies the following corollary:

COROLLARY 1. *In equilibrium, $r_{t+1} < \overline{R}$.*

The following proposition, which is proved in appendix C, describes the properties of the equilibrium riskless rate of return defined implicitly in equation (33):

12. In a fully funded defined-contribution system

$$\frac{\theta_0(1 - \alpha)\overline{A}}{r_{t+1}} + \theta_1\frac{1 - \alpha}{\alpha} = s_{t+1},$$

and

$$\theta_1\frac{1 - \alpha}{\alpha} = \gamma_{S,t+1} s_{t+1},$$

as may be verified using the expressions for θ_0 and θ_1 in n. 11 above. In this case, the equilibrium condition for the riskless interest rate in eq. (33) becomes $0 = \gamma(r_{t+1})(1 + b_{t+1}) - 1$, which implies that the equilibrium riskless interest rate is independent of changes in the size or portfolio allocation of a fully funded defined-contribution social security system.

13. For any strictly increasing, strictly concave function $u(\ )$, $u'[r + \gamma(R - r)]\,(R - r) < u'(r)(R - r)$ if $R - r \neq 0$ and $\gamma > 0$. Thus, for nondegenerate distributions of R, $E\{u'[r + \gamma(R - r)](R - r)\} < u'(r)E\{R - r\}$. Therefore, if $E\{R\} \leq r$, then $E\{u'[r + \gamma(R - r)](R - r)\} < 0$, and the condition for the optimal value of γ, $E\{u'[r + \gamma(R - r)](R - r)\} = 0$, cannot hold. Thus, in order for the optimal value of γ to be positive, $E\{R\}$ must exceed r.

PROPOSITION 2. *Suppose that* $\gamma'(r_{t+1}) < 0$.[14] *Let* $r(b_{t+1}, s_{t+1}, \gamma_{S,t+1}, \theta_0, \theta_1)$ *be the unique value of* r_{t+1} *that satisfies equation (33). Then*

$$\frac{\partial r}{\partial b_{t+1}} > 0,$$

$$\text{sign}\left(\frac{\partial r}{\partial s_{t+1}}\right) = \text{sign}[\gamma_{S,t+1} - \gamma(r_{t+1})],$$

$$\text{sign}\left(\frac{\partial r}{\partial \gamma_{S,t+1}}\right) = \text{sign}(s_{t+1}),$$

$$\frac{\partial r}{\partial \theta_0} > 0,$$

$$\frac{\partial r}{\partial \theta_1} < 0.$$

Before interpreting the various effects in proposition 2, it is worth recalling that, since the risky rate of return R_{t+1} is invariant to policy in this model, any change in the riskless interest rate is equivalent to a change in the equity premium of the same magnitude but in the opposite direction.

An increase in b_{t+1}, the ratio of Treasury bonds to the capital stock, increases the equilibrium interest rate in order to induce private investors to devote a larger share of their portfolios to riskless bonds. Similarly, if the social security trust fund has a positive balance ($s_{t+1} > 0$) and sells some riskless bonds in exchange for stock, thereby increasing $\gamma_{S,t+1}$, the equilibrium interest rate on bonds must increase in order for private investors to be willing to hold a higher ratio of bonds to stocks directly in their own portfolios.[15]

The effect of an increase in the size of the social security trust fund, represented as an increase in s_{t+1}, depends on the sign of $\gamma_{S,t+1} - \gamma(r_{t+1})$. If the share of the social security trust fund held in risky capital ($\gamma_{S,t+1}$) is smaller than the share of private portfolios held in risky capital, as is the case in the United States, where $\gamma_{S,t+1} = 0$, then an increase in the size of the social security trust fund, s_{t+1}, effectively reduces the ratio of riskless bonds to risky capital available to private investors. In order for these

---

14. As shown in app. B, the condition $\gamma'(r_{t+1}) < 0$ holds if $\phi \leq 1$. If $\phi > 1$, then $\gamma'(r_{t+1})$ may not be negative for some values of r_{t+1}, so the proof of uniqueness does not hold. Nevertheless, the effects on r_{t+1} of changes in b_{t+1}, s_{t+1}, $\gamma_{S,t+1}$, θ_0, and θ_1 in this proposition hold for any solution to eq. (33) for which $\gamma'(r_{t+1}) < 0$. As mentioned in n. 6 above, this condition holds for all cases in tables 5.1–5.3 below.

15. Recall that the social security system analyzed here is a defined-benefit system, so the change in the portfolio allocation of the social security trust fund does not affect the claims on future social security benefits held by workers.

investors to willingly reduce the ratio of riskless bonds to risky capital in their portfolios, the riskless interest rate must fall.

The "replacement rates" θ_0 and θ_1 have opposite effects on the equilibrium riskless interest rate. An increase in θ_0 increases the riskless component of the social security benefit that young people anticipate and effectively increases the holding of riskless assets by young people. In order for these people to be willing to increase their riskless holdings, the riskless interest rate must increase. However, an increase in θ_1 increases the risky component of the social security benefit that young consumers anticipate and effectively increases the holding of risky assets in private portfolios. The riskless interest rate must fall in order to induce consumers to be willing to hold an increased share of risky assets in their portfolios.

The equilibrium condition in equation (33) illustrates the extent to which the separate balance sheets of the Treasury and the social security trust fund can be consolidated for the purpose of determining the equilibrium riskless interest rate. Inspection of equation (33) implies the following proposition:

PROPOSITION 3. *For the purpose of determining the equilibrium riskless interest rate, all the information on the balance sheets of the Treasury and the social security trust fund is captured by*

$$v_{t+1} \equiv b_{t+1} - s_{t+1} + \frac{\gamma_{S,t+1}}{\gamma(r_{t+1})} s_{t+1}.$$

COROLLARY 2. *If* $\gamma_{S,t+1} = 0$, *then the effects of* b_{t+1} *and* s_{t+1} *on the riskless interest rate are captured entirely by* $b_{t+1} - s_{t+1}$.

If $\gamma_{S,t+1} = 0$, as is currently the case in the United States, the social security trust fund is held entirely in riskless bonds. In this case, for the purpose of determining the equilibrium riskless interest rate, the balance sheets of the Treasury and the social security trust fund can be consolidated. The only information needed from the separate balance sheets of these entities is the net amount of bonds, normalized by the aggregate capital stock, $b_{t+1} - s_{t+1}$, issued by the consolidated entity. However, even in this case, the balance sheets of the Treasury and the social security trust fund cannot, in general, be consolidated for the purpose of determining the growth rate of the capital stock. (For the more stringent conditions under which these balance sheets can be consolidated for the purpose of determining the growth rate of the capital stock, see proposition 4 below.)

COROLLARY 3. *If* $\gamma_{S,t+1} = \gamma(r_{t+1})$, *then the effects of* b_{t+1} *and* s_{t+1} *on the riskless interest rate are captured entirely by* b_{t+1}.

According to this corollary, if the social security trust fund maintains a risky portfolio share $\gamma_{S,t+1}$ equal to the share of risky assets in private portfolios,[16] $\gamma(r_{t+1})$, the equilibrium interest rate is independent of the size of the social security trust fund. In this case, changes in the size of the social security trust fund have no effect on the ratio of riskless assets to risky assets available to the private sector, and hence the equilibrium riskless interest rate is unaffected by such changes.

5.5.2   The Growth Rate of the Capital Stock

In this subsection, I use the optimal saving behavior of individuals, along with the saving behavior of the Treasury and the social security system, to determine how much capital is accumulated in the economy. Then I will analyze how the growth rate of the aggregate capital stock is affected by a change in the portfolio of the social security trust fund.

In a closed economy, the bonds and capital held by the private sector, $B_{t+1}^P + K_{t+1}^P$, plus the value of the social security trust fund, S_{t+1}, equal the aggregate capital stock, K_{t+1}, plus the value of bonds issued by the Treasury, B_{t+1}. This relation can be derived by adding equations (28) and (29) to obtain

$$(35) \qquad B_{t+1} + K_{t+1} = B_{t+1}^P + K_{t+1}^P + S_{t+1}.$$

The size of the portfolio of the private sector, $B_{t+1}^P + K_{t+1}^P$, can be calculated from equations (11), (15), and (16) to obtain

$$(36) \qquad B_{t+1}^P + K_{t+1}^P = \frac{\delta}{1 + \delta}(w_t - T_t^T - T_t^S)$$

$$- \frac{1}{1 + \delta}\left[\frac{\theta_0(1 - \alpha)\overline{A}}{r_{t+1}} + \theta_1 \frac{1 - \alpha}{\alpha}\right]K_{t+1}.$$

The growth rate of the capital stock can be determined by substituting equation (36) into (35) and performing a tedious set of substitutions. To streamline the notation, define

$$(37) \qquad \omega_t \equiv (s_t, b_t, A_t, \theta_0, \theta_1).$$

Appendix D shows that[17]

---

16. Recall that $\gamma(r_{t+1})$ is the share of risky assets—which include risky capital and the claim on risky future social security benefits—in the portfolios of young consumers, which consist of bonds, risky capital, and the riskless and risky components of future social security benefits.

17. In a fully funded defined-contribution social security system, $-(1 - \alpha)(\theta_0\overline{A} + \theta_1 A_t) + [(1 - \gamma_{S,t})r_t + \gamma_{S,t}R_t]s_t = (-\alpha A_t + R_t)\gamma_{S,t}s_t = 0$, where the first equality follows from the expressions for θ_0 and θ_1 in n. 11 above and the second equality follows from eq. (5). Therefore, $H_0(r_t, \gamma_{S,t}, \omega_t) = \delta\{[1 - \alpha - (1 - \lambda)\tau - \lambda g]A_t - \lambda r_t b_t\}$. Using the fact that

$$\frac{\theta_0(1 - \alpha)\overline{A}}{r_{t+1}} + \theta_1 \frac{1 - \alpha}{\alpha} = s_{t+1}$$

$$(38) \qquad \frac{K_{t+1}}{K_t} = \frac{H_0(r_t, \gamma_{S,t}, \omega_t)}{H_1(r_{t+1}, \gamma_{S,t}, \omega_t)},$$

where

$$(39) \qquad H_0(r_t, \gamma_{S,t}, \omega_t) \equiv \delta\{[1 - \alpha - (1 - \lambda)\tau - \lambda g]A_t$$
$$- (1 - \alpha)(\theta_0 \overline{A} + \theta_1 A_t)$$
$$+ [(1 - \gamma_{S,t})r_t + \gamma_{S,t}R_t]s_t - \lambda r_t b_t\}$$

and

$$(40) \qquad H_1(r_{t+1}, \gamma_{S,t}, \omega_t) \equiv 1 + \delta + \frac{\theta_0(1 - \alpha)\overline{A}}{r_{t+1}} + \theta_1 \frac{1 - \alpha}{\alpha}$$
$$+ (1 + \delta - \delta\lambda)[\beta + \rho_B(b_t - \beta) + \rho_A(g - \tau)(A_t - \overline{A})]$$
$$- [\sigma + \rho_S(s_t - \sigma) + \rho_R(R_t - \overline{R})\gamma_{S,t}s_t].$$

I will restrict attention to cases in which $H_0 > 0$ and $H_1 > 0$. Although H_0 and H_1 defy simple interpretations that are literally correct, for the sake of exposition I will offer loose interpretations. The term H_0 can be loosely interpreted as the disposable income of the young consumers,[18] and factors that increase the disposable income of the young consumers tend to increase capital accumulation. The term H_1 can be loosely interpreted as the ratio of noncapital wealth held by young consumers to the aggregate capital stock, where the noncapital wealth consists of Treasury bonds and claims on social security benefits.[19] Factors that increase this ratio tend to reduce capital accumulation.

(see n. 12 above) along with the social security policy function in eq. (26), $H_1(r_{t+1}, \gamma_{S,t}, \omega_t)$ $= 1 + \delta + (1 + \delta - \delta\lambda)[\beta + \rho_B(b_t - \beta) + \rho_A(g - \tau)(A_t - \overline{A})]$. Since both H_0 and H_1 are independent of the parameters of a fully funded defined-contribution social security system, the growth rate of the capital stock, $K_{t+1}/K_t = H_0/H_1$, is independent of the parameters of such a system.

18. More precisely, if $s_t = \sigma$, $A_t = \overline{A}$, and $b_t = \beta$, then $H_0 K_t = \delta(w_t - T_t^T - T_t^S - \lambda\beta K_{t+1}$ $+ \sigma K_{t+1})$. If $\beta = \sigma = 0$, then $H_0 K_t$ is strictly proportional to the disposable income of young consumers, $w_t - T_t^T - T_t^S$.

19. More precisely, if $\lambda = 1$,

$$H_1 = 1 + \delta + \frac{\theta_0(1 - \alpha)\overline{A}}{r_{t+1}} + \theta_1 \frac{1 - \alpha}{\alpha} + b_{t+1} - s_{t+1},$$

where

$$\frac{\theta_0(1 - \alpha)\overline{A}}{r_{t+1}} + \theta_1 \frac{1 - \alpha}{\alpha}$$

is the present value of the claim on future social security benefits relative to the aggregate capital stock K_{t+1}, and if $\gamma_{S,t+1} = 0$, $b_{t+1} - s_{t+1}$ is the amount of Treasury bonds held by young consumers relative to the aggregate capital stock.

Inspection of equations (39) and (40) implies the following proposition about the consolidation of the balance sheets of the Treasury and the social security trust fund:

PROPOSITION 4. *If* $\gamma_{S,t} = 0$, $\lambda = 1$, *and* $\rho_S = \rho_B$, *then, for the purpose of determining the growth rate of the capital stock, all the information on the balance sheets of the Treasury and the social security trust fund is captured by* $b_t - s_t$, *and the information contained in the targets* β *and* σ *is captured by* $\beta - \sigma$.

Recall from corollary 2 that, if the social security trust fund holds only riskless bonds, then, for the purpose of determining the riskless interest rate, the balance sheets of the Treasury and the social security trust fund can be consolidated. For the purpose of determining r_t, the net indebtedness of the consolidated entity, $b_t - s_t$, is a sufficient statistic for b_t and s_t. However, for the purpose of determining the growth rate of the capital stock, a more stringent set of conditions is required to be able to consolidate the balance sheets of the Treasury and the social security trust fund. In addition to $\gamma_{S,t} = 0$, the parameter λ must equal one, and the persistence parameters ρ_B and ρ_S must be equal. The parameter λ must equal one because all adjustment in the net income of the social security system takes place through adjusting the taxes on the young. With $\lambda = 1$, all adjustment in the net income of the Treasury will also take place through adjusting taxes on the young.

The following two lemmas help prove and interpret the effects of changes in the portfolio of the social security system on the growth rate of the capital stock:

LEMMA 1. $$\frac{\partial H_0(r_t, \gamma_{S,t}, \omega_t)}{\partial r_t} = \delta[(1 - \gamma_{S,t})s_t - \lambda b_t].$$

Consider an increase in r_t that increases the amount of interest paid by the Treasury during period t by b_t dollars. This increase in r_t will increase the amount of interest received by the social security trust fund by $(1 - \gamma_{S,t})s_t$ dollars.[20] According to the social security policy function in equation (26), the social security system will not change the size of the trust fund in period $t + 1$ and thus will use the additional interest earnings to reduce social security taxes in period t by $(1 - \gamma_{S,t})s_t$ dollars. According to the Treasury policy function in equation (18), the Treasury will not change the size of its debt and thus will respond to the increased cost of debt service by increasing taxes by λb_t dollars. Taking account of both

20. The increase in interest payments by the Treasury is $B_t \Delta r_t = b_t$, which implies that $\Delta r_t = b_t/B_t = 1/K_t$. The increase in the interest earned by the social security trust fund is

$$(1 - \gamma_{S,t})S_t \Delta r_t = (1 - \gamma_{S,t})S_t \frac{1}{K_t} = (1 - \gamma_{S,t})s_t.$$

social security taxes and Treasury taxes, the total taxes paid by young consumers in period t fall by $(1 - \gamma_{S,t})s_t - \lambda b_t$ dollars, and the disposable income of young consumers increases by this amount. If $(1 - \gamma_{S,t})s_t - \lambda b_t > 0$, the increase in disposable income of young consumers increases H_0 and increases the size of portfolios held by young consumers.

A change in the riskless interest rate r_{t+1} affects H_1 as described in the following lemma:

LEMMA 2. $\dfrac{\partial H_1(r_{t+1}, \gamma_{S,t}, \omega_t)}{\partial r_{t+1}} = -\dfrac{\theta_0(1 - \alpha)\overline{A}}{r_{t+1}^2} \leq 0.$

If $\theta_0 > 0$, an increase in r_{t+1} reduces the present value of the claim on future riskless social security benefits held by young consumers, thereby reducing H_1, the ratio of noncapital wealth to capital in the portfolios of young consumers.

Now consider a change in $\gamma_{S,t+1}$, the share of the social security trust fund that is held in risky capital. The following proposition applies to a change in the portfolio of the social security trust fund at the end of period t after b_t, s_t, r_t, and K_t have been determined:

PROPOSITION 5. If $\theta_0 > 0$ and $s_{t+1} > 0$, then

$$\left.\frac{dK_{t+1}}{d\gamma_{S,t+1}}\right|_{K_t, r_t, \omega_t} > 0.$$

Proof.

$$\left.\frac{dK_{t+1}}{d\gamma_{S,t+1}}\right|_{K_t, r_t, \omega_t} = -\frac{H_0}{H_1^2}\frac{\partial H_1}{\partial r_{t+1}}\frac{\partial r_{t+1}}{\partial \gamma_{S,t+1}} \cdot K_t > 0$$

because

$$\frac{\partial H_1}{\partial r_{t+1}} = -\frac{\theta_0(1 - \alpha)\overline{A}}{r_{t+1}^2} < 0$$

(from lemma 2) and

$$\text{sign}\left(\frac{\partial r_{t+1}}{\partial \gamma_{S,t+1}}\right) = \text{sign}(s_{t+1})$$

(from proposition 2).

An increase in $\gamma_{S,t+1}$ has no direct effect on either $H_0(r_t, \gamma_{S,t}, \omega_t)$ or $H_1(r_{t+1}, \gamma_{S,t}, \omega_t)$. However, an increase in $\gamma_{S,t+1}$ increases the riskless interest rate r_{t+1}, provided that $s_{t+1} > 0$. The resulting increase in r_{t+1} reduces the present value of riskless social security benefits, which implies that the present value of lifetime resources, Ω_t, falls. In response to the fall in Ω_t, consumers reduce their consumption and increase their saving so that national capital accumulation increases.

COROLLARY 4. *If* $\theta_0 = 0$ *or* $s_{t+1} = 0$, *then*

$$\frac{dK_{t+1}}{d\gamma_{S,t+1}}\bigg|_{K_t, r_t, \omega_t} = 0.$$

This corollary implies, for instance, that, if all social security benefits are risky so that $\theta_0 = 0$, then a change in the portfolio of the social security trust fund at the end of period t will have no effect on K_{t+1}.

Constant Growth Paths

I have shown that, given the capital stock K_t and the riskless interest rate r_t, an increase in the risky share of the social security trust fund, $\gamma_{S,t+1}$, at the end of period t increases the riskless interest rate r_{t+1} and the aggregate capital stock K_{t+1} in the following period. In this section, I focus on the long-run effects of a change in the portfolio allocation of the social security trust fund. I will focus on *constant growth paths,* which I define to be paths along which $\gamma_{S,t} = \gamma_S$ and $A_t = \overline{A}$ for all t so that $R_t = \overline{R}$, $b_t = \beta$, and $s_t = \sigma$ for all t.[21] Along such paths, the riskless interest rate and the growth rate of capital will be constant. Let r denote the constant value of the riskless interest rate along a constant growth path, and let η be the constant value of K_{t+1}/K_t along a constant growth path.

The equilibrium condition for the interest rate along a constant growth path is derived by substituting $b_{t+1} = \beta$ and $s_{t+1} = \sigma$ into equation (33) to obtain

$$(41) \quad \gamma(r)\left[1 + \beta - \sigma + \frac{\theta_0(1-\alpha)\overline{A}}{r} + \theta_1\frac{1-\alpha}{\alpha}\right]$$
$$- 1 + \gamma_S\sigma - \theta_1\frac{1-\alpha}{\alpha} = 0.$$

Similarly, the values of H_0 and H_1 along a constant growth path are derived by setting $\gamma_{S,t} = \gamma_S$, $A_t = \overline{A}$, $R_t = \overline{R}$, $b_t = \beta$, and $s_t = \sigma$ in equations (39) and (40), to obtain

$$(42) \quad H_0^*(r, \gamma_S, \sigma, \beta, \overline{A}, \theta_0, \theta_1) \equiv \delta\{[(1-\alpha)(1-\theta_0-\theta_1)$$
$$- (1-\lambda)\tau - \lambda g]\overline{A}$$
$$+ [(1-\gamma_S)r + \gamma_S\overline{R}]\sigma - \lambda r\beta\}$$

21. Of course, consumers do not know in advance that the realizations of A_t and R_t will always be equal to their respective expectations, so they take account of risk in making portfolio-allocation decisions.

and

(43) $\quad H_1^*(r, \gamma_S, \sigma, \beta, \overline{A}, \theta_0, \theta_1) \equiv 1 + \delta + \dfrac{\theta_0(1 - \alpha)\overline{A}}{r}$

$$+ \; \theta_1 \dfrac{1 - \alpha}{\alpha} + (1 + \delta - \delta\lambda)\beta - \sigma,$$

where the asterisks on H_0^* and H_1^* indicate that these terms are evaluated along a constant growth path.

The equilibrium condition in equation (41) for the riskless interest rate r along a constant growth path is identical (with appropriate relabeling of variables) to the equilibrium condition for the riskless interest rate in equation (33). Thus, the following corollary to proposition 2 describes the response of the riskless interest rate to various changes along a constant growth path:

COROLLARY 5. *Suppose that* $\gamma'(r) < 0$. *Let* $\tilde{r}(\beta, \sigma, \gamma_S, \theta_0, \theta_1)$ *be the unique value of r that satisfies equation (41). Then*

$$\frac{\partial \tilde{r}}{\partial \beta} > 0,$$

$$\text{sign}\left(\frac{\partial \tilde{r}}{\partial \sigma}\right) = \text{sign}[\gamma_S - \gamma(\tilde{r})],$$

$$\text{sign}\left(\frac{\partial \tilde{r}}{\partial \gamma_S}\right) = \text{sign}(\sigma),$$

$$\frac{\partial \tilde{r}}{\partial \theta_0} > 0,$$

$$\frac{\partial \tilde{r}}{\partial \theta_1} < 0.$$

Again, recall that any change in the riskless interest rate is matched by a change in the equity premium of equal size but in the opposite direction.

Now consider the effect on η, the growth rate of the capital stock along a constant growth path, of a permanent change in γ_S:

PROPOSITION 6. *If*

$$\delta[(1 - \gamma_S)\sigma - \lambda\beta] + \eta\frac{\theta_0(1 - \alpha)\overline{A}}{r^2} \geq 0$$

along a constant growth path with $\sigma > 0$, *then* $d\eta/d\gamma_S > 0$.

Proof.

$$
\frac{d\eta}{d\gamma_S} = \frac{1}{H_1^*}\left(\frac{\partial H_0^*}{\partial \gamma_S} + \frac{\partial H_0^*}{\partial r}\frac{\partial r}{\partial \gamma_S}\right) - \frac{\eta}{H_1^*}\left(\frac{\partial H_1^*}{\partial \gamma_S} + \frac{\partial H_1^*}{\partial r}\frac{\partial r}{\partial \gamma_S}\right)
$$

$$
= \frac{1}{H_1^*}\delta\left\{(\overline{R} - r)\sigma + [(1 - \gamma_S)\sigma - \lambda\beta]\frac{\partial r}{\partial \gamma_S}\right\}
$$

$$
+ \frac{\eta}{H_1^*}\left(\frac{\theta_0(1 - \alpha)\overline{A}}{r^2}\frac{\partial r}{\partial \gamma_S}\right)
$$

$$
= \frac{\delta}{H_1^*}(\overline{R} - r)\sigma
$$

$$
+ \frac{1}{H_1^*}\left\{\delta[(1 - \gamma_S)\sigma - \lambda\beta] + \eta\frac{\theta_0(1 - \alpha)\overline{A}}{r^2}\right\}
$$

$$
\times \frac{\partial r}{\partial \gamma_S} > 0.
$$

since $\overline{R} > r$ (corollary 1) and $\partial r/\partial \gamma_S > 0$ (corollary 5).

A permanent increase in γ_S has a direct effect on H_0^* and indirect effects on both H_0^* and H_1^* operating through the riskless interest rate. The direct effect on H_0^* arises because an increase in γ_S increases the average earnings of the social security trust fund as it shifts its portfolio toward assets with a higher expected rate of return. The increase in the average portfolio earnings of the social security trust fund allows the social security tax on young consumers to be reduced, thereby increasing their disposable income. The increase in the disposable income of young consumers increases the amount of capital that they hold in their portfolios.

The indirect effects on H_0^* and H_1^* arise because an increase in γ_S increases the riskless interest rate (corollary 5). An increase in the riskless interest rate increases the interest earnings of the social security trust fund and increases the interest payments made by the Treasury. These changes in interest flows induce the social security system and the Treasury to change the amount of taxes collected from young consumers. As explained in the interpretation of lemma 1, these changes in taxes increase the disposable income of young consumers by an amount proportional to $(1 - \gamma_S)\sigma - \lambda\beta$, which is captured by the change in H_0^*. In addition, the increase in the riskless interest rate reduces H_1^* by reducing the present value of the future riskless social security benefits to be received by young consumers. This reduction in H_1^* increases the growth rate of the capital stock.

The direct effect on H_0^* and the indirect effect on H_1^* both increase the growth rate of the capital stock. However, the indirect effect on H_0^* can increase or decrease the growth rate of the capital stock depending on whether $(1 - \gamma_S)\sigma - \lambda\beta$ is positive or negative. Proposition 6 states a sufficient condition for the indirect effect on H_1^* to dominate the indirect effect on H_0^* so that an increase in γ_S unambiguously increases η. Corollary 6 below presents a condition for the indirect effect on H_0^* to increase η so that there is no conflict between the indirect effect on H_0^* and the indirect effect on H_1^*. In this case, of course, an increase in γ_S increases η. Corollary 7 presents an even stronger condition that guarantees that an increase in γ_S increases η. This condition, $\lambda = 0$, can be interpreted as complete tax smoothing. Thus, in the presence of complete tax smoothing, an increase in γ_S unambiguously increases the growth rate of the capital stock η.

COROLLARY 6. *If* $(1 - \gamma_S)\sigma - \lambda\beta \geq 0$ *along a constant growth path with* $\sigma > 0$, *then* $d\eta/d\gamma_S > 0$.

COROLLARY 7. *If* $\lambda = 0$ *along a constant growth path with* $\sigma > 0$, *then* $d\eta/d\gamma_S > 0$.

5.6   Calibration of the Model

In this section, I calibrate the model for a constant growth path. This calibration will serve two purposes. First, the calibration will shed light on the quantitative plausibility of the model. Second, the calibration will provide a quantitative measure of the effect of a change in γ_S on the growth rate of the capital stock. In particular, the calibration can be used to determine whether the condition in proposition 6 is satisfied so that an increase in γ_S increases the capital stock growth rate η along a constant growth path.

One approach to calibrating the model would be to specify values for the parameters of preferences and technology, the parameters of the social security policy function, the parameters of the Treasury policy function, and the distribution of the stochastic productivity variable A_t and then to compute the implied values of the riskless interest rate r and the growth rate of the capital stock η. I will make two modifications to this approach. The first modification, which is a trivial change, is to specify the distribution of the risky rate of return $R_t = \alpha A_t$ instead of specifying the distribution of A_t. The second modification is more fundamental. Instead of specifying the values of the preference parameters ϕ and δ and then computing the implied values of r and η, I will find the values of the preference parameters ϕ and δ for which the values of r and η implied by the model match the corresponding empirical values, which I denote as $\hat{r}$ and $\hat{\eta}$, respectively.

Because the coefficient of relative risk aversion ϕ affects only the portfolio-allocation decision while the time-preference discount factor δ affects only the saving/consumption decision, the values of these parameters that match $\hat{r}$ and $\hat{\eta}$ can be determined separately. Specifically, the coefficient of relative risk aversion ϕ is determined by the riskless-interest-rate equilibrium condition in equation (41) with $\hat{r}$ substituted for r. The empirical value $\hat{r}$, along with the values of the other parameters in this equation, implies a value for $\gamma(\hat{r})$. There is a unique value of the coefficient of relative risk aversion ϕ for which the optimal value of the portfolio share γ equals the value of $\gamma(\hat{r})$ implied by the equilibrium condition in equation (41).[22]

The value of the time-preference discount factor δ is chosen so that the growth rate of capital implied by the model, H_0^*/H_1^*, equals the empirical value of the growth rate, $\hat{\eta}$. Matching the implied and the empirical values of the growth rate of capital yields

(44) $$H_0^* = \hat{\eta} H_1^*.$$

Since H_0^* and H_1^* are both linear functions of the time-preference discount factor δ, equation (44) is a linear function of δ that can be easily solved for the value of δ that allows the model to match the empirical growth rate of capital.

Because individuals are assumed to live for only two periods, each period in the model is half an adult lifetime. The length of a period is important for variables, such as rates of return, and parameters, such as the rate of time preference, that are expressed per unit of time. I will report annual values of these variables and parameters, and I will make adjustments to take account of the fact that a period is many years. Specifically, I will assume that a period in the model lasts N years. I will calculate the time-preference discount factor δ as $\delta = (1 + v)^{-N}$, where v is the annual rate of time preference. Similarly, I will calculate the (gross) riskless interest rate per period r as $r = (1 + r_{ann})^N$, where r_{ann} is the (net) riskless interest rate per year. It will be convenient to define the following empirical values on a (net) annual basis: $\hat{r}_{ann} \equiv \hat{r}^{-N} - 1$ and $\hat{\eta}_{ann} \equiv \hat{\eta}^{-N} - 1$.

Converting the distribution of the (net) annual risky rate $R_{ann,t}$ to a distribution of the risky rate per period R_t involves an additional consideration. Suppose that the distribution of the annual risky rate is a two-point distribution with $1 + R_{ann,t} \in \{\mu + \chi, \mu - \chi\}$. If the annual risky rate were perfectly serially correlated over the N years of the period, then the (gross) risky rate per period would be a two-point distribution with $R_t \in \{(\mu + \chi)^N, (\mu - \chi)^N\}$. However, if the annual risky rate is not perfectly serially correlated, this two-point distribution would overstate the variance per N-year period. In fact, the presence of mean reversion in stock

22. $\lim_{\phi \to \infty} \gamma^* = 0$ and $\lim_{\phi \to 0} \gamma^* = \infty$, so there is at least one value of ϕ for which the optimal value γ^* equals the value implied by the equilibrium condition for the riskless interest rate. As shown in eq. (B11) in app. B, $d\gamma^*/d\phi < 0$ so that such a value of ϕ is unique.

prices—equivalently, negative serial correlation in stock returns—suggests that even assuming that the annual risky rate is i.i.d. over time would overstate the variance per N-year period. To allow for negative serial correlation in stock returns, I assume that (gross) annual risky returns follow a first-order two-point Markov process with

(45) $1 + R_{\text{ann},t} \in \{\mu + \chi, \mu - \chi\}$ and $\text{pr}\{R_{\text{ann},t+1} = R_{\text{ann},t}\} = 1 - \varphi$.

Under the Markov process in equation (45), the (gross) annual risky return $1 + R_{\text{ann},t}$ has a mean equal to μ, a standard deviation equal to χ, and a first-order serial correlation equal to $1 - 2\varphi$.

The accumulation of annual returns over an N-year period is used in the portfolio-allocation decision of young consumers. As shown in equation (A4) in appendix A, the portfolio-allocation decision involves the choice of γ_{t+1} to maximize an expression containing

(46) $$E_t\left\{[(1 - \gamma_{t+1})r_{t+1} + \gamma_{t+1}R_{t+1}]^{1-\phi}\right\},$$

where the (gross) returns, r_{t+1} and R_{t+1}, are measured over an N-year period. Defining

(47) $$z_{\text{ann},t+j} \equiv [(1 - \gamma)(1 + r_{\text{ann}}) + \gamma(1 + R_{\text{ann},t+j})]^{1-\phi},$$

the expression in equation (46) can be written as $E_t\{\Pi_{j=1}^N z_{\text{ann},t+j}\}$. If the annual risky return $R_{\text{ann},t}$ follows a two-point Markov process, then $z_{\text{ann},t}$ will also follow a two-point Markov process. Lemma 3 in appendix E presents a simple method for computing $E_t\{\Pi_{j=1}^N z_{\text{ann},t+j}\}$.[23]

Table 5.1 contains the baseline values of the parameters used to calibrate the constant growth path. I use the moments of the annual risky rate of return reported by Mehra and Prescott (1985) for the period 1889–1978. Specifically, I set μ equal to 1.0698, which implies a 6.98 percent annual mean (net) risky return, and I set the standard deviation, χ, equal to 0.1654 per year. Fama and French (1988) report that, for return horizons of one year, the serial correlation of stock returns is negative but not significantly different from zero. The serial correlation of stock returns becomes significantly negative as the horizon is lengthened to two years and declines until the horizon is about three to five years. In order to capture this mean reversion in stock prices over longer periods, I specify an annual serial correlation of -0.1, which implies $\varphi = 0.55$.

Each period in the model represents half an adult lifetime. More specifically, the first period of a person's life corresponds to time in the labor force and the second period to retirement. I have chosen to set N, the

---

23. An alternative approach to calibrating N-period returns would be to calculate the empirical moments of N-period returns. The approach that I use in this paper is more flexible in that it allows N to be changed easily. In the baseline calibration, $N = 30$, and the sensitivity analysis reports results for $N = 25$ and $N = 35$.

Table 5.1   Baseline Calibration

Risky Rate (annual)			
Mean, μ (gross return per year)	1.0698	φ (serial correlation $= 1 - 2\varphi$)	0.55
Std. dev., χ (per year)	0.1654	Number of years per period, N	30

Treasury Policy Function			
Government purchases parameter, g	0.2	Tax responsiveness, λ	0.1
Tax parameter, τ	0.2	Target bond ratio, β	0.25

Social Security Policy Function			
Riskless replacement rate, θ_0	0.15	Target trust fund ratio, σ	0.035
Risky replacement rate, θ_1	0.0	Risky trust fund share, γ_S	0.0
Share of capital in production function, α			0.375

Empirical Moments to Fit			
Riskless rate, $\hat{r}_{ann}$ (% per year)	0.80	Growth rate, $\hat{\eta}_{ann}$ (% per year)	1.3

Preference Parameter Values that Fit Empirical Moments			
Coefficient of relative risk aversion, ϕ	7.7577	Time preference, ν (% per year)	0.6874

number of years per period, equal to thirty, which is a compromise between the larger numbers of years in the workforce and the smaller number of years in retirement.

For the tax-policy function, I have set the government-purchases parameter g and the tax parameter τ both equal to 0.2, which is the approximate share of government purchases in GDP in the United States. It is difficult to pin down the value of the tax-responsiveness parameter λ, which is the fraction of the adjustment in the primary deficit that is achieved by changing taxes. Complete tax smoothing is represented by $\lambda = 0$. I set $\lambda = 0.1$ in the baseline simulation, and I explore the quantitative effect of λ in tables 5.2 and 5.3 below. I set the baseline value of the target bond-capital ratio, β, equal to 0.25. In 1997, the ratio of Treasury debt held by the public and by the social security trust fund to the stock of fixed private capital was 0.254.

In the baseline calibration, I treat the benefits in the pay-as-you-go social security system in the United States as riskless. Thus, I set the risky replacement rate θ_1 equal to zero. I set the riskless replacement rate θ_0 equal to 0.15. This value may seem low, but it is higher than the 12.4 percent social security tax rate, and it is almost twice as high as the ratio of social security benefits to compensation of employees in 1996 (which was 0.0787).[24] In 1997, the social security trust fund was 3.6 percent as large as the fixed private capital stock in the United States. I set the target value of the trust fund-capital ratio, σ, equal to 0.035 in the baseline. Since the social security trust fund is currently invested entirely in bonds, I set $\gamma_S = 0$ in the baseline calibration.

Over the past half century in the United States, the share of labor income in GDP has averaged 0.625, with a standard deviation of only 0.009.[25] Since the labor share is $1 - \alpha$, I set $\alpha = 0.375$ in the baseline calibration.

I calibrate the model to match two empirical moments: the average riskless interest rate, $\hat{r}_{ann}$, and the average growth rate of the capital stock, $\hat{\eta}_{ann}$. For $\hat{r}_{ann}$, I use 0.8 percent per year, which is the average value of the riskless interest rate reported by Mehra and Prescott (1985) for the period 1889–1978. As for the growth rate of the capital, it is important to note that the population and the labor force are constant across generations in the model. Thus, the appropriate empirical counterpart of the growth rate of capital in the model is the empirical growth rate of the capital-labor ratio. Over the period 1947–97, the fixed private capital stock in the United States grew by 3.17 percent per year, and employment grew by 1.65 percent per year, implying that the capital-labor ratio grew by approximately 1.52 percent per year. However, over the shorter period 1967–97, the annual growth of capital slowed to 2.90 percent per year, and the growth rate of employment increased to 1.87 percent per year, so the growth rate of the capital-labor ratio declined (relative to the longer time period) to 1.03 percent per year. I will use an intermediate value of 1.3 percent per year for $\hat{\eta}_{ann}$.

The last row of table 5.1 reports the values of the preference parameters for which the riskless interest rate r and the growth rate of the capital stock η calculated by the model match their empirical counterparts. Specifically, with a coefficient of relative risk aversion, ϕ, of 7.7577 and a rate of time preference, v, of 0.6874 percent per year, the model matches the riskless interest rate and the growth rate of the capital stock. The values of these preference parameters are quite plausible.[26]

Table 5.2 reports the results of a sensitivity analysis that varies one pa-

---

24. Of course, this ratio in 1996 significantly understates the replacement ratio because the large population of baby-boom workers means that the ratio of workers to retirees is temporarily (for a few decades) high.

25. The labor share Λ is computed as the solution of the following equation:

$$\frac{\text{compensation of employees} + \Lambda(\text{proprietors' income})}{\text{GDP}} = \Lambda.$$

26. The literature on the equity-premium puzzle typically requires a coefficient of relative risk aversion ϕ well above ten to match moments of asset returns. However, one should not regard the relatively low and reasonable value of 7.7577 for ϕ as a resolution of the equity-premium puzzle because the model in the paper has not been calibrated to the variability of consumption.

Table 5.2   **Sensitivity Analysis: Changing One Parameter at a Time**

Parameter	Parameter Value	r_{ann}^{a}	η_{ann}^{a}	Parameter	Parameter Value	r_{ann}^{a}	η_{ann}^{a}
μ	1.05	−1.18	−0.62	μ	1.09	2.82	3.26
χ	0.12	2.75	1.96	χ	0.22	−1.01	0.44
φ	0.5	0.32	1.10	φ	0.6	1.28	1.48
N	25	0.27	0.55	N	35	1.25	1.84
θ_0	0.10	0.14	1.87	θ_0	0.20	1.27	0.76
θ_1	0.05	0.65	0.83	θ_1	0.10	0.51	0.34
σ	0.01	0.83	1.27	σ	0.06	0.77	1.33
γ_S	0.15	0.82	1.32	γ_S	0.30	0.83	1.35
g	0.15	0.80	1.35	g	0.25	0.80	1.25
τ	0.15	0.80	1.73	τ	0.25	0.80	0.81
λ	0.0	0.80	1.30	λ	0.2	0.80	1.30
β	0.20	0.75	1.36	β	0.30	0.85	1.24
α	0.32	1.20	2.11	α	0.43	0.43	0.48
ϕ	4.00	2.68	1.94	ϕ	10.00	0.05	0.97
ν^a	0.0	0.80	1.79	ν^a	1.40	0.80	0.77

[a]% per year.

rameter at a time. Each row of the table reports two values of a parameter that differ from the baseline value and also reports the implied (net) annual values of the riskless interest rate, r, and the growth rate of capital, η, along a constant growth path. For parameters that are not equal to zero in the baseline, table 5.2 reports results for one value larger than in the baseline and one value smaller than in the baseline. For parameters that equal zero in the baseline, table 5.2 reports results using two values larger than zero.

The most glaring result in table 5.2 arises when μ, the (gross) mean annual risky rate of return, is reduced to 1.05, which is a 5 percent average annual (net) rate of return. In this case, the model produces a riskless interest rate of −1.18 percent per year and a growth rate of capital of −0.62 percent per year. These results are far from their empirical counterparts. However, in judging the implications of these results for the empirical plausibility of the model, it is important to remember that the preference parameters ϕ and ν used in this calculation were calibrated under the assumption that the mean return μ is 1.0698. When $\mu = 1.05$, the model can match the empirical values of r and η by using the following values for the preference parameters: $\phi = 3.8186$, and $\nu = -1.35$ percent per year. Although a coefficient of relative risk aversion of 3.8 is very reasonable, the negative rate of time preference is a bit curious.[27]

27. Setting the rate of time preference equal to zero and using a coefficient of relative risk aversion ϕ equal to 3.8186 imply $r_{ann} = 0.80$ percent per year and $\eta_{ann} = 0.51$ percent per year when $\mu = 1.05$.

Table 5.3		Risky Trust Fund When $\sigma = 0.14$		
		$\gamma_S = 0.0$	$\gamma_S = 0.15$	$\gamma_S = 0.30$
			$\lambda = 0.1$	
r_{ann} [a]		0.69	0.75	0.81
η_{ann} [a]		1.41	1.51	1.60
			$\lambda = 0.9$	
r_{ann} [a]		0.69	0.75	0.81
η_{ann} [a]		1.44	1.54	1.63

[a]% per year.

A primary issue motivating this paper is the effect of investing part of the social security trust fund in risky capital. The social security trust fund in the United States is currently invested entirely in riskless bonds, so I set $\gamma_S = 0$ in the baseline calibration. The sensitivity analysis in table 5.2 reports the results of increasing γ_S to 0.15 and to 0.3. The value of γ_S that is considered in current policy discussions is about 0.15. Increasing γ_S to 0.15 in the model increases the riskless interest rate to 0.82 percent per year (from 0.80 percent per year in the baseline) and increases the rate of growth of the capital stock to 1.32 percent per year (from 1.30 percent per year in the baseline). These effects are small because the social security trust fund is small relative to the capital stock.[28]

Along a constant growth path, the ratio of the social security trust fund to the capital stock equals its target value σ. The small value of σ used in the calculations reported above was chosen to match the current value of the ratio of the social security trust fund to the capital stock in the United States. However, the trust fund is projected to grow substantially over the next several years, reaching a peak value in the year 2016 that is 2.6 times as large as its current value.[29] Indeed, it is the prospect of a large trust fund that has fueled interest in investing part of the trust fund in equities. Table 5.3 presents the effects of investing part of the trust fund in risky capital along a constant growth path with $\sigma = 0.14$, which is four times

---

28. Formally, applying the implicit function theorem to equations (C3) and (C5) in app. C along a constant growth path implies

$$\frac{\partial r}{\partial \gamma_s} = -\frac{\sigma}{\gamma'(r)\left[1 + \beta - \sigma + \frac{\theta_0(1-\alpha)\overline{A}}{r} + \theta_1\frac{1-\alpha}{\alpha}\right] - \gamma(r)\frac{\theta_0(1-\alpha)\overline{A}}{r^2}},$$

so that $\lim_{\sigma \to 0} \partial r/\partial \gamma_S = 0$. Thus, when the trust fund-capital ratio σ is small, the effect of γ_S on the interest rate is small. The proof of proposition 6 indicates that $\partial\eta/\partial\gamma_S$ is the sum of a term that is proportional to σ and a term that is proportional to $\partial r/\partial\gamma_S$. Thus, $\partial\eta/\partial\gamma_S$ will be small if σ is small.

29. This projection, which is taken from the Board of Trustees (1998), is based on the assumption that the trust fund is invested entirely in bonds. If the trust fund earns a higher rate of return by investing in risky capital, then it would reach an even larger value.

as high as in the baseline calculations. Even with this much larger trust fund, investing 15 percent of the trust fund in risky capital has only modest effects on the riskless interest rate and the growth rate of capital. The riskless interest rate increases by only six basis points, and the growth rate of the capital stock increases by 0.1 percent per year.

The baseline calibration in table 5.1 above is based on a value of $\lambda = 0.1$. However, the value of λ, which measures the responsiveness of taxes to changes in the primary deficit needed to satisfy the Treasury policy function, is not well determined. In principle, it could be anywhere between zero and one. Recall that the sufficient condition in proposition 6 for an increase in γ_S to increase η depends on the value of λ. A higher value of λ makes this condition less likely to hold. To see whether a higher value of λ can violate this condition, suppose that $\lambda = 1$, which is its maximum admissible value. In this case, the sufficient condition in proposition 6 is

$$\delta[(1 - \gamma_S)\sigma - \beta] + \eta\frac{\theta_0(1 - \alpha)\overline{A}}{r^2} \geq 0.$$

In the baseline calculation,

$$\delta[(1 - \gamma_S)\sigma - \beta] = -0.175,$$

and

$$\eta\frac{\theta_0(1 - \alpha)\overline{A}}{r^2} = 1.729,$$

so the sufficient condition in proposition 6 is satisfied by a wide margin even when $\lambda = 1$. Thus, for any allowable value of λ, an increase in γ_S increases η, the growth rate of the capital stock along a constant growth path.

In addition, λ has a very small effect on the calculated responses of the interest rate and the growth rate of capital to a change in γ_S. The top panel of table 5.3 reports the values of the riskless interest rate and the growth rate of capital when $\lambda = 0.1$, and the bottom panel reports the results for $\lambda = 0.9$. The values of the riskless interest rate are identical in the top and bottom panels because the equilibrium condition for the riskless interest rate in equation (41) is independent of λ. Although the growth rate of capital is not independent of λ, the growth rates differ by only three basis points when λ increases from 0.1 to 0.9.[30]

---

30. Since

$$\delta[(1 - \gamma_S)\sigma - \beta] + \eta\frac{\theta_0(1 - \alpha)\overline{A}}{r^2}$$

is an increasing function of σ (provided that the trust fund is not entirely invested in risky capital), the sufficient condition holds for higher values of σ, such as $\sigma = 0.14$, as in table 5.3.

5.7 Concluding Remarks

I have shown that shifting some of the assets of the social security trust fund from bonds to risky capital increases the growth rate of the capital stock in the following period and along a constant growth path. This finding is virtually the opposite of the result in Abel (in press), where I show that such a portfolio shift of the social security trust fund reduces the amount of capital accumulation in the following period. Although there are various modeling differences between the two papers, the fundamental reason for the apparent difference in results is that the earlier paper analyzes a defined-contribution social security system and the current paper analyzes a defined-benefit social security system.[31] In both papers, when the social security trust fund moves into risky capital, the expected income of the trust fund increases, and this increase in expected income is passed along to individuals. In a defined-contribution system, a natural policy experiment is to hold the contribution fixed, and thus the gains from increased trust fund earnings accrue to individuals as increased retirement benefits when they are old. In response to increased retirement benefits, young consumers increase their current consumption and thus reduce capital accumulation. In a defined-benefit system, a natural policy experiment is to hold the benefit fixed, and thus the gains from increased trust fund earnings accrue to individuals in the form of lower taxes when they are young. In response to increased disposable income when young, consumers increase their saving when they are young, and thus capital accumulation increases.

Confining attention to defined-benefit social security systems, and holding social security benefits fixed as analyzed in the current paper, it might appear that the social security trust fund should invest in risky capital because this change in its portfolio allocation will increase the growth rate of the capital stock. However, there are still several questions that future research must address, even in the context of this model, to reach a strong policy recommendation about the allocation of the assets in the social security trust fund. First, the results about the effect on the growth rate of the capital stock are confined to constant growth paths along which all shocks take on their mean values. Of course, one of the concerns about

31. There is also a major modeling difference between the two papers. In the current paper, which examines a defined-benefit social security system, all individuals in a given cohort are identical, and they all hold portfolios with both bonds and risky capital. As shown analytically in nn. 12 and 17 above, a change in the portfolio of a defined-contribution social security system would have no effect on the riskless interest rate or the growth rate of capital in this sort of model because individuals would offset the effects of changes in the social security trust fund's portfolio by changing their own portfolios. The previous paper, which analyzes a defined-contribution system, introduces intracohort heterogeneity of earnings and fixed costs of investing in risky capital so that low-income individuals will not hold any risky capital directly in their portfolios. With this modification, changes in the portfolio of the social security trust fund are no longer neutral, even in a defined-contribution system.

investing some of the social security trust fund in risky capital is the risk that the rate of return may turn out to be very low. A normative welfare analysis would have to take into account the entire distribution of outcomes. In addition, a normative analysis would have to recognize that government purchases in this model are endogenous. To the extent that individuals obtain utility from government purchases, I have assumed that any utility from government purchases is additively separable from the utility of private consumption. Although this assumption is sufficient to analyze optimal private behavior and competitive equilibria, it does not address the welfare consequences of endogenous changes in the level of government purchases.

Intergenerational risk sharing is another important aspect of the welfare analysis of various social security policies. Bohn (1998b) analyzes the intergenerational sharing of various risks in considering the effects of including equities in the social security trust fund. While the framework that I have developed in this paper focuses on a narrower set of risks, it suggests the possibility of additional channels to share risks intergenerationally by allowing the Treasury's debt-capital ratio and the social security trust fund-capital ratio to vary across time and across generations in response to shocks. The various ρ_i parameters ($i = A, B, R, S$) reflect opportunities to share risks across time and across generations. Exploration of these opportunities is left for future research.

Appendix A

The Consumption and Portfolio Decision of an Individual

Using the definitions of Ω_t, a_{t+1}, and γ_{t+1} in equations (11), (12), and (14), respectively, it is convenient to rewrite the expression for consumption when young in equation (6) as

(A1) $$C_t = \Omega_t - a_{t+1}$$

and consumption when old in equation (9) as

(A2) $$X_{t+1} = [(1 - \gamma_{t+1})r_{t+1} + \gamma_{t+1}R_{t+1}]a_{t+1}.$$

The consumer's optimization problem can be rewritten by substituting equations (A1) and (A2) into equation (10) to obtain

(A3) $$\max_{a_{t+1}, \gamma_{t+1}} \ln(\Omega_t - a_{t+1}) + \delta \ln a_{t+1} + \delta\psi(\gamma_{t+1}, r_{t+1}),$$

where[32]

32. If $\phi = 1$, $\psi(\gamma_{t+1}, r_{t+1}) \equiv E_t\{\ln[(1 - \gamma_{t+1})r_{t+1} + \gamma_{t+1}R_{t+1}]\}$.

(A4) $\psi(\gamma_{t+1}, r_{t+1}) \equiv \dfrac{1}{1 - \phi} \ln E_t \big\{ [(1 - \gamma_{t+1}) r_{t+1} + \gamma_{t+1} R_{t+1}]^{1-\phi} \big\}$

$$\text{if } 0 < \phi \neq 1.$$

The optimal level of saving and consumption is determined by differentiating the maximand in equation (A3) with respect to a_{t+1} and setting the derivative equal to zero to obtain

(A5) $$a_{t+1} = \frac{\delta}{1 + \delta} \Omega_t.$$

The portfolio-allocation problem is solved by differentiating $\psi(\gamma_{t+1}, r_{t+1})$ with respect to γ_{t+1} and setting the derivative equal to zero to obtain

(A6) $$E_t \{ [(1 - \gamma_{t+1}) r_{t+1} + \gamma_{t+1} R_{t+1}]^{-\phi} (R_{t+1} - r_{t+1}) \} = 0.$$

Equation (A6) implicitly defines the optimal value of γ_{t+1}, which is the share of an individual's total portfolio devoted to risky assets. This equation holds for any $\phi > 0$, including the case of logarithmic utility, $\phi = 1$.

Let $\gamma(r_{t+1})$ be the value of γ_{t+1} that solves equation (A6). Appendix B derives the properties of $\gamma(r_{t+1})$.

Appendix B

Properties of $\gamma(r)$

If $E_t\{R_{t+1}\} - r_{t+1} = 0$, then $E_t\{r_{t+1}^{-\phi}(R_{t+1} - r_{t+1})\} = 0$, which implies that $\gamma_{t+1} = 0$ satisfies equation (A6). Therefore, if $E_t\{R_{t+1}\} - r_{t+1} = 0$, the optimal value of γ_{t+1} is zero, so

(B1) $$\gamma(E_t\{R_{t+1}\}) = 0.$$

As the gross riskless interest rate, r_{t+1}, approaches $R_L \equiv \alpha A_L$ from above, the optimal value of γ_{t+1} becomes arbitrarily large. That is,

(B2) $$\lim_{r_{t+1} \downarrow R_L} \gamma(r_{t+1}) = \infty.$$

To analyze the derivative of $\gamma(r_{t+1})$ with respect to r_{t+1}, define

(B3) $$F(\gamma, r, \phi) \equiv E\{x^{-\phi}(R - r)\},$$

where[33] $x \equiv r + \gamma(R - r) > 0$ and $r \geq R_L$. Observe from equation (A6) that the optimal value of γ, γ^*, solves

---

33. Both r and R are assumed to be positive. I restrict attention to values of γ for which $x > 0$ because optimality requires that $\operatorname{pr}\{x > 0\} = 1$.

(B4) $$F(\gamma*,r,\phi) = 0.$$

Differentiating equation (B3) with respect to γ yields

(B5) $$F_\gamma(\gamma,r,\phi) = -\phi E\{x^{-\phi-1}(R - r)^2\} < 0.$$

Since $F_\gamma(\gamma, r, \phi) < 0$, there is a unique value of γ that solves $F(\gamma, r, \phi) = 0$ for given values of r and ϕ.

The response of $\gamma*$ to a change in r is given by $\gamma'(r) = d\gamma*/dr = -[F_r(\gamma*, r, \phi)]/F_\gamma(\gamma*, r, \phi)]$. Since $F_\gamma(\gamma*, r, \phi) < 0$, the sign of $\gamma'(r)$ is the same as the sign of $F_r(\gamma*, r, \phi)$. Differentiating equation (B3) with respect to r yields

(B6) $$F_r(\gamma,r,\phi) = E\{-\phi x^{-\phi-1}(1 - \gamma)(R - r) - x^{-\phi}\}.$$

Use the fact that $R - x = (1 - \gamma)(R - r)$ to rewrite equation (B6) as

(B7) $$F_r(\gamma,r,\phi) = E\{-\phi x^{-\phi-1}R + (\phi - 1)x^{-\phi}\}.$$

Inspection of equation (B7) reveals that, if $\phi \le 1$, then $F_r(\gamma, r, \phi) < 0$ and hence $\gamma'(r) < 0$. In the case with $\phi > 1$, there is no general result for the sign of $\gamma'(r)$. Even when the distribution of R is a symmetrical two-point distribution, the sign of $\gamma'(r)$ is not determinate.

To determine the effect of a change in the coefficient of relative risk aversion, ϕ, differentiate $F(\gamma, r, \phi)$ with respect to ϕ to obtain

(B8) $$F_\phi(\gamma,r,\phi) = -E\{x^{-\phi}(R - r)\ln x\}.$$

If $R - r < 0$, then $\ln x < \ln r$, provided that $\gamma > 0$. Therefore, if $R - r < 0$, then $x^{-\phi}(R - r)\ln x > x^{-\phi}(R - r)\ln r$. Similarly, if $R - r > 0$, then $\ln x > \ln r$, provided that $\gamma > 0$. Therefore, if $R - r > 0$, then $x^{-\phi}(R - r)\ln x > x^{-\phi}(R - r)\ln r$. Thus, if the optimal value $\gamma*$ is positive, then, when $\gamma = \gamma*$,[34]

(B9) $$E\{x^{-\phi}(R - r)\ln x\} > E\{x^{-\phi}(R - r)\ln r\} = 0.$$

Substituting equation (B9) into equation (B8) yields

(B10) $$F_\phi(\gamma, r, \phi) < 0.$$

Therefore, since $F_\gamma(\gamma, r, \phi) < 0$,

(B11) $$\frac{d\gamma*}{d\phi} < 0,$$

which means that an increase in the coefficient of relative risk aversion, ϕ, leads to a reduction in γ, the share of the portfolio devoted to the risky asset.

---

34. I am assuming that the distribution of R is nondegenerate so that $\text{pr}\{R \ne r\} > 0$.

Appendix C

Proof of Proposition 2

Define the function $f(r_{t+1}, b_{t+1}, s_{t+1}, \gamma_{S,t+1}, \theta_0, \theta_1)$ as the right-hand side of equation (33). This function is continuous in r_{t+1} for $\alpha A_L \equiv R_L < r_{t+1} \leq \bar{R} \equiv E_t\{R_{t+1}\}$. Equation (B1) and the condition in equation (31) imply

(C1) $$f(E_t\{R_{t+1}\}, b_{t+1}, s_{t+1}, \gamma_{S,t+1}, \theta_0, \theta_1) < 0.$$

Equation (B2) and the condition in equation (30) imply

(C2) $$\lim_{r_{t+1} \downarrow R_L} f(r_{t+1}, b_{t+1}, s_{t+1}, \gamma_{S,t+1}, \theta_0, \theta_1) = \infty.$$

Equations (C1) and (C2) and the fact that $f(r_{t+1}, b_{t+1}, s_{t+1}, \gamma_{S,t+1}, \theta_0, \theta_1)$ is continuous in r_{t+1} for $r_{t+1} \in (R_L, \bar{R}]$ imply that there is at least one value of $r_{t+1} \in (R_L, \bar{R}]$ for which $f(r_{t+1}, b_{t+1}, s_{t+1}, \gamma_{S,t+1}, \theta_0, \theta_1) = 0$.

To prove that the equilibrium value of r_{t+1} is unique, differentiate $f(r_{t+1}, b_{t+1}, s_{t+1}, \gamma_{S,t+1}, \theta_0, \theta_1)$ with respect to r_{t+1}, and use the assumption in proposition 2 that $\gamma'(r_{t+1}) < 0$ to obtain

(C3) $$\frac{\partial f}{\partial r_{t+1}} = \gamma'(r_{t+1}) \left[1 + b_{t+1} - s_{t+1} + \frac{\theta_0(1 - \alpha)\bar{A}}{r_{t+1}} + \theta_1 \frac{1 - \alpha}{\alpha} \right]$$
$$- \gamma(r_{t+1}) \frac{\theta_0(1 - \alpha)\bar{A}}{r_{t+1}^2} < 0.$$

Since $\partial f / \partial r_{t+1} < 0$, the value of r_{t+1} for which $f(r_{t+1}, b_{t+1}, s_{t+1}, \gamma_{S,t+1}, \theta_0, \theta_1) = 0$ is unique.

To analyze the effects of various variables on the riskless interest rate, compute the following partial derivatives:

(C4) $$\frac{\partial f}{\partial b_{t+1}} = \gamma(r_{t+1}) > 0,$$

(C5) $$\frac{\partial f}{\partial \gamma_{S,t+1}} = s_{t+1}$$

(C6) $$\frac{\partial f}{\partial s_{t+1}} = \gamma_{S,t+1} - \gamma(r_{t+1}),$$

(C7) $$\frac{\partial f}{\partial \theta_0} = \gamma(r_{t+1}) \frac{(1 - \alpha)\bar{A}}{r_{t+1}} > 0,$$

(C8) $$\frac{\partial f}{\partial \theta_1} = -\frac{1 - \alpha}{\alpha}[1 - \gamma(r_{t+1})] < 0,$$

where the inequalities in equations (C4), (C7), and (C8) follow from proposition 1.

The implicit-function theorem implies that

$$\frac{\partial r(b_{t+1}, s_{t+1}, \gamma_{S,t+1}, \theta_0, \theta_1)}{\partial z} = -\frac{\partial f/\partial z}{\partial f/\partial r_{t+1}}$$

where $z \in \{b_{t+1}, s_{t+1}, \gamma_{S,t+1}, \theta_0, \theta_1\}$.

Therefore, sign $\{[\partial r(b_{t+1}, s_{t+1}, \gamma_{S,t+1}, \theta_0, \theta_1)]/\partial z\} = $ sign $(\partial f/\partial z)$.

Appendix D
Derivation of the Growth Rate of the Capital Stock

Substitute equation (36) into equation (35), use the definitions $b_{t+1} \equiv B_{t+1}/K_{t+1}$ and $s_{t+1} \equiv S_{t+1}/K_{t+1}$, and multiply both sides of the resulting equation by $1 + \delta$ to obtain

(D1) $(1 + \delta)(b_{t+1} + 1 - s_{t+1})K_{t+1}$

$$= \delta(w_t - T_t^T - T_t^S) - \left[\frac{\theta_0(1 - \alpha)\overline{A}}{r_{t+1}} + \theta_1\frac{1 - \alpha}{\alpha}\right]K_{t+1}.$$

The amount of social security taxes can be rewritten by substituting equation (24) into equation (27) to obtain

(D2) $T_t^S = [\sigma + \rho_S(s_t - \sigma) + \rho_R(R_t - \overline{R})\gamma_{S,t} s_t]K_{t+1}$

$$+ Q_t - [(1 - \gamma_{S,t})r_t + \gamma_{S,t}R_t]s_t K_t.$$

Use equation (7) to substitute for Q_t in equation (D2) to obtain

(D3) $T_t^S = \Phi(T_t^S, K_{t+1})K_{t+1} + \Phi(T_t^S, K_t)K_t,$

where

(D4) $\Phi(T_t^S, K_{t+1}) \equiv \sigma + \rho_S(s_t - \sigma) + \rho_R(R_t - \overline{R})\gamma_{S,t} s_t$

and

(D5) $\Phi(T_t^S, K_t) \equiv (\theta_0\overline{A} + \theta_1 A_t)(1 - \alpha)$

$$- [(1 - \gamma_{S,t})r_t + \gamma_{S,t}R_t]s_t.$$

Now rewrite the Treasury's tax revenue in equation (23) as

(D6) $$T_t^T = \Phi(T_t^T, K_{t+1})K_{t+1} + \Phi(T_t^T, K_t)K_t,$$

where

(D7) $$\Phi(T_t^T, K_{t+1}) \equiv -\lambda[\beta + \rho_B(b_t - \beta) + \rho_A(g - \tau)(A_t - \overline{A})]$$

and

(D8) $$\Phi(T_t^T, K_t) \equiv [(1 - \lambda)\tau + \lambda g]A_t + \lambda r_t b_t.$$

Substitute equations (D3) and (D6) into equation (D1) and use equation (4) to obtain

(D9) $$\left[(1 + \delta)(b_{t+1} + 1 - s_{t+1}) + \frac{\theta_0(1 - \alpha)\overline{A}}{r_{t+1}} + \theta_1\frac{1 - \alpha}{\alpha}\right]K_{t+1}$$

$$= \delta[(1 - \alpha)A_t K_t - \Phi(T_t^S, K_{t+1})K_{t+1} - \Phi(T_t^S, K_t)K_t$$

$$- \Phi(T_t^T, K_{t+1})K_{t+1} - \Phi(T_t^T, K_t)K_t].$$

Now use the definitions in equations (D4), (D5), (D7), and (D8) to rewrite equation (D9) as

(D10) $$H_1 K_{t+1} = H_0 K_t,$$

where

(D11) $$H_1 \equiv (1 + \delta)(1 + b_{t+1} - s_{t+1}) + \frac{\theta_0(1 - \alpha)\overline{A}}{r_{t+1}}$$

$$+ \theta_1\frac{1 - \alpha}{\alpha} + \delta[\sigma + \rho_S(s_t - \sigma) + \rho_R(R_t - \overline{R})\gamma_{S,t}s_t]$$

$$- \delta\lambda[\beta + \rho_B(b_t - \beta) + \rho_A(g - \tau)(A_t - \overline{A})]$$

and

(D12) $$H_0 \equiv \delta\{[1 - \alpha - (1 - \lambda)\tau - \lambda g]A_t$$

$$- (1 - \alpha)(\theta_0\overline{A} + \theta_1 A_t)$$

$$+ [(1 - \gamma_{S,t})r_t + \gamma_{S,t}R_t]s_t - \lambda r_t b_t\}.$$

Rewrite the expression for H_1 by substituting the Treasury policy function from equation (18) and the social security policy function from equation (26) into equation (D11) to obtain

(D13) $H_t \equiv 1 + \delta + (1 + \delta - \delta\lambda)[\beta + \rho_B(b_t - \beta)$

$\qquad + \rho_A(g - \tau)(A_t - \overline{A})] - [\sigma + \rho_S(s_t - \sigma)$

$\qquad + \rho_R(R_t - \overline{R})\gamma_{S,t} s_t] + \dfrac{\theta_0(1 - \alpha)\overline{A}}{r_{t+1}} + \theta_1 \dfrac{1 - \alpha}{\alpha}.$

Appendix E
The Expectation of Multiyear Returns

LEMMA 3. *Let $z_t \in \{Z(1), \ldots, Z(J)\}$, and define the transition probabilities $p(i,j) \equiv \mathrm{pr}\{z_{t+1} = Z(j) \mid z_t = Z(i)\}$ and unconditional probabilities $\pi(j) \equiv \mathrm{pr}\{z_t = Z(j)\}$. If $\Pi' \equiv [\pi(1), \ldots, \pi(J)]$, M is the $J \times J$ matrix with (i, j) element $m(i, j) \equiv p(i, j) Z(j)$ and $\mathbf{i}$ is a $J \times 1$ vector of ones, then $E\{z_{t+1} \cdots z_{t+N}\} = \Pi'(M^N)\mathbf{i}$.*

Proof.

(E1) $E\{z_{t+1} \cdots z_{t+N} \mid z_t = Z(i)\}$

$\qquad = \displaystyle\sum_{j_1, \ldots, j_N} [p(i, j_1)p(j_1, j_2) \cdots p(j_{N-1}, j_N)][Z(j_1)Z(j_2) \cdots Z(j_N)].$

Use the definition $m(i, j) \equiv p(i, j) Z(j)$ to rewrite the conditional expectation as

(E2) $E\{z_{t+1} \cdots z_{t+N} \mid z_t = Z(i)\} = \displaystyle\sum_{j_1, \ldots, j_N} m(i, j_1)m(j_1, j_2) \cdots m(j_{N-1}, j_N).$

Define

(E3) $\qquad y(N, i, j) \equiv \displaystyle\sum_{j_1, \ldots, j_{N-1}} m(i, j_1)m(j_1, j_2) \cdots m(j_{N-1}, j).$

Equations (E2) and (E3) imply

(E4) $\qquad E\{z_{t+1} \cdots z_{t+N} \mid z_t = Z(i)\} = \displaystyle\sum_j y(N, i, j).$

The unconditional expectation is

(E5) $\qquad E\{z_{t+1} \cdots z_{t+N}\} = \displaystyle\sum_{i,j} \pi(i) y(N, i, j).$

Observe from equation (E3) that

(E6) $y(N + 1, i, k) = \displaystyle\sum_j \sum_{j_1, \ldots, j_{N-1}} m(i, j_1)m(j_1, j_2) \cdots m(j_{N-1}, j)m(j, k).$

Equations (E3) and (E6) imply

(E7) $$y(N + 1, i, k) = \sum_j y(N, i, j) m(j, k).$$

Rewrite equation (E7) in matrix form as

(E8) $$Y_{N+1} = Y_N M,$$

where the (i, j) element of Y_{N+1} is $y(N + 1, i, j)$ and the (i, j) element of Y_N is $y(N, i, j)$.

The solution of the matrix difference equation in (E8) is

(E9) $$Y_N = M^N.$$

Therefore, the definition of Y_N and equations (E5) and (E9) imply

(E10) $$E\{z_{t+1} \cdots z_{t+N}\} = \sum_{i,j} \pi(i) y(N, i, j) = \Pi'(M^N) \mathbf{i}.$$

References

Abel, Andrew B. In press. The effects of investing social security funds in the stock market when fixed costs prevent some households from holding stocks. *American Economic Review.*

Barro, Robert J., and Xavier Sala-i-Martin. 1995. *Economic growth.* New York: McGraw-Hill.

Blanchard, Olivier J., and Stanley Fischer. 1989. *Lectures on macroeconomics.* Cambridge, Mass.: MIT Press.

Board of Trustees of the Federal Old-Age and Survivors Insurance and Disability Insurance Trust Funds. 1998. *1998 annual report.* Washington, D.C.: U.S. Government Printing Office.

Bohn, Henning. 1998a. Risk sharing in a stochastic overlapping generations economy. Department of Economics, University of California, Santa Barbara. Mimeo.

———. 1998b. Should the social security trust fund hold equities? An intergenerational welfare analysis. Department of Economics, University of California, Santa Barbara. Mimeo.

Diamond, Peter A. 1965. National debt in a neoclassical growth model. *American Economic Review* 55, no. 5:1126–50.

Epstein, Larry G., and Stanley E. Zin. 1989. Substitution, risk aversion, and the temporal behavior of consumption and asset returns: A theoretical framework. *Econometrica* 57, no. 4:937–70.

Fama, Eugene F., and Kenneth R. French. 1988. Permanent and temporary components of stock prices. *Journal of Political Economy* 96, no. 2:246–73.

Mehra, Rajnish, and Edward C. Prescott. 1985. The equity premium: A puzzle. *Journal of Monetary Economics* 15, no. 2:145–61.

Weil, Philippe. 1990. Nonexpected utility in macroeconomics. *Quarterly Journal of Economics* 105, no. 1:29–42.

Comment   Deborah Lucas

Faced with a large projected social security deficit, a number of economists and policy makers have suggested moving a portion of the social
security trust fund out of government securities and into the stock market.
These proposals raise myriad questions. Would real gains be achieved, or
would the government's actions be largely undone by private actions? How
would such a change affect the relative return on safe and risky assets?
How would it affect private savings and investment behavior? How would
it affect risk sharing and income distribution within and across generations? Although progress can be made on some of these questions using
partial equilibrium models, a complete analysis clearly requires a general
equilibrium approach. This paper makes an important contribution to the
policy debate by providing a general equilibrium framework that is ame-
nable to a variety of interesting policy experiments.

Although essential for a complete analysis, one cost of the general equilibrium approach is a loss of transparency. My main goal in this discussion
is to offer additional intuition for the main results and some thoughts on
which results are likely to be robust. I will also discuss why some of the
simplifying assumptions, although useful for analytic purposes, might
hide some potentially large costs and benefits and might reduce the predicted general equilibrium effect. The rest of this Comment is organized
as follows: First, I recap the main results and the intuition behind them.
These issues are discussed in the context of a simple model that is useful
for laying out the key sensitivities. Then I address some more specific aspects of the theoretical model and its calibration that bear on the robustness of the results. I conclude that, although the model is a useful tool
for examining the qualitative effects of policy changes, the quantitative
implications are less compelling.

General Equilibrium Revisited

Two main results emerge from the overlapping-generations production
economy considered in this paper. The first is that, for most parameterizations, increasing the share of the trust fund invested in risky assets tends
to increase the risk-free rate and thereby lower the equity premium (since
the return on risky capital is fixed by the technology). The second is that,
with some further restrictions on parameters, this policy change also increases capital accumulation. Calibration of the model suggests that, although these effects are present, they are small in economic terms. For

Deborah Lucas is the Donald C. Clark/Household International Distinguished Professor
of Finance at the Kellogg Graduate School of Management, Northwestern University, and
a research associate of the National Bureau of Economic Research.

instance, all else equal, changing the share of the trust fund in risky assets from 0 to 15 percent increases the risk-free rate from 0.8 percent per year to 0.82 percent per year. It also increases the average annual per capita growth rate of the capital stock from 1.3 to 1.32 percent.

Quantitatively, then, the model suggests that such a policy change will have a relatively small effect on equilibrium rates of return and aggregate output growth. It is natural to ask why this is the case in this model and whether it is likely to hold more generally. To think about this, consider the following simplified version of the model that abstracts from the details of the production technology, tax policy, and the evolution of the trust fund.

People live for two periods and have lifetime utility

$$U(c_0) + \beta E[V(c_1)].$$

In the first period of life, they receive income I_0 (e.g., from wages and any inheritance), pay taxes, τ, and save B^p in bonds and S^p in stocks. In the second half of life, consumption is financed out of any additional income I_1, the gross returns on stocks and bonds, R^s and R^b, and social security payments that have a present value of X. A fraction γ of social security payments is contingent on the realized return on stocks, and a fraction $(1 - \gamma)$ is risk free. In the first period of life, there is uncertainty about R^s and I_1. Then consumption each period can be written as

$$c_0 = I_0 - \tau - B^p - S^p,$$

$$c_1 = I_1 + B^p R^b + S^p R^s + \gamma X R^s + (1 - \gamma) X R^b.$$

Assuming no borrowing or short-sales restrictions, asset prices and investment policy are determined by combining market-clearing conditions with individual Euler equations. This results in two standard equations that characterize the equilibrium return on bonds and stocks, given the investment policy of individuals. Conversely, given returns, these equations characterize investment policy:

$$\frac{\beta E[V'(I_0 + B^p R^b + S^p R^s + \gamma X R^s + (1 - \gamma) X R^b) R^b]}{U'(I_0 - \tau - B^p - S^p)} = 1,$$

$$\frac{\beta E[V'(I_0 + B^p R^b + S^p R^s + \gamma X R^s + (1 - \gamma) X R^b) R^s]}{U'(I_0 - \tau - B^p - S^p)} = 1.$$

The reason to write down these equations is as a reminder of the factors that can potentially influence asset returns and investment policy in any standard model. These include changes in tax policy, changes in the incentive to work if I_j is endogenous, and borrowing or short-sales constraints that may prevent young people from offsetting changes in social security investment policy. This latter effect would turn the equalities given above into inequalities for constrained agents and result in market prices reflecting the marginal rate of substitution of unconstrained agents.

It is quite possible for a policy change to be neutral in this setting. Consider, for instance, a small increase in γ, $\Delta\gamma$, financed by a corresponding increase in stockholdings by the trust fund and a decrease in bondholdings. If there are no restrictions on B^p and S^p, then, holding all other policy variables constant, the following would be an equilibrium. People increase their bond holdings by $\Delta\gamma X$, buying what the trust fund sells, and conserving the portion of second-period income that is risk free. Similarly, they decrease their stockholdings by $\Delta\gamma X$, selling what the trust fund buys and conserving the portion of second-period income exposed to stock market risk. Asset returns remain unchanged since the first-order condition continues to hold. Investment in the first period, and hence growth, would also be unaffected because the aggregate investment in stocks is constant.

What breaks this neutrality in Abel's model? Since taxes are lump sum, they do not directly influence the incentive to work or invest. Borrowing or short-sales constraints are also not the answer because parameters are chosen such that, in the absence of the trust fund holding stocks, people choose to hold positive amounts of both assets. Furthermore, the policy experiments do not cause people to hit corners. This leaves the government's tax and expenditure policy, broadly defined, as the reason for nonneutrality. The way policy shows up is through adjustments in social security tax rates, federal tax rates, government expenditures, and government bonds outstanding. In Abel's model, these quantities move according to fixed reaction functions. The reaction functions are structured so that government policy partly offsets productivity shocks, effectively using the trust fund and fiscal policy to spread risks across generations in a way that would be impossible in an overlapping-generations model with only private-sector transactions.

If the government policy function is the cause of the nonneutrality, it remains to understand the precise direction of the nonneutrality. That is, why does the equity premium tend to fall, and why does investment tend to grow?

On the question of why the equity premium falls, the suggested intuition is that, if the government sells bonds, there must be an incentive for individuals to buy the bonds, and this tends to put upward pressure on the risk-free rate. Although broadly speaking this must be correct, we have seen that, if government policy is otherwise neutral, the change in government investments can occur with no change in equilibrium returns. An alternative way to interpret the drop in the predicted equity premium is that it is due to the reduced consumption risk in the second period that results from increased risk sharing via the government's reaction function.

More generally, if the net effect of any policy change is to decrease second-period consumption risk and particularly correlated risk, the equity premium will tend to fall. Conversely, the premium will rise if the policy results in riskier outcomes for stock market participants.

On the question of why investment increases, as suggested in the paper, a primary driver is that the policy experiment assumes that taxes on the young tend to fall. That is, rather than any gains from the higher average stock market returns being used to increase average benefits in the second period, it is assumed that expected gains to the government are used to reduce taxes. The wealth effect of this reduction in taxes tends to increase private savings, along with first-period consumption. As shown in his earlier analysis (Abel 1998), if instead the policy experiment were to use the higher average returns to increase the expected benefits for the old, the effect on saving would be the opposite since social security would partially crowd out private saving. The effect of a policy change on risk is also a major consideration for the level of savings. We know from other models that, for utility specifications exhibiting high risk aversion, a small increase in second-period consumption risk can result in a large increase in precautionary savings, and conversely for a risk reduction. For the parameterization considered, the effect of reduced risk was more than offset by the wealth effect, but, in general, the response of savings will be very sensitive to the details of the policy implementation and the utility specification.

Finally, it should be noted that the model is structured so that it is possible to consider two distinct aspects of social security interaction with the equity markets. It is possible to vary the portion of the trust fund invested in the market and independently vary the degree to which benefits are tied to market outcomes. Although this distinction is not emphasized, it is implicit in the parameterizations considered. Both aspects are important for evaluating the likely effect of the various proposals now being considered. For instance, the model implies that, if, as under one leading proposal, benefits continue to be guaranteed by the government but part of the trust fund is invested in stocks, the young will bear greater tax risk. It would be interesting to use the model to look more closely at the welfare implications of such proposals.

Modeling Assumptions and Alternatives

The comments presented above suggest that this model is indeed useful for thinking qualitatively about the general equilibrium effects of investing part of the social security trust fund in the market. It is more difficult, however, to have confidence in its quantitative implications. In this section, I focus on the assumptions in the theoretical model and calibration that might affect the quantitative results.

Market Structure

In general, a two-period overlapping-generations structure is convenient for computing analytic results because it makes each individual's decision problem relatively simple. For interpreting calibration results, however, it creates some complications. The most significant of these is the extremely limited private risk sharing that this structure allows owing to the minimal overlap between generations. This creates a large role for a benevolent government because that is the only entity that can enforce contracts across disconnected generations. Other analyses have shown that, as the assumed number of periods of life increases, this dichotomy between the effectiveness of government and private arrangements declines. Although not necessarily the case, the severe market incompleteness may magnify the effect of policy changes on savings and asset prices because it reduces the opportunities for offsetting private-sector contracts. If one were to look at welfare implications, the insurance gains from the existence of a larger trust fund would likely be overstated for the same reason.

The two-period overlapping-generations model has the further drawback that, if one must interpret each period as thirty years, it is not possible to capture the nuances of transition effects on intergenerational transfers that are likely to be critical. A related problem is the assumption of a constant population since many of the stresses in the current system arise from the changes in the relative size of different generations. In particular, this has implications for the incidence of tax liability.

Homogeneous Agents

The assumption of homogeneous agents, none of whom face binding borrowing constraints, seems likely to create a downward bias on the extent to which the policy change affects asset returns. Previous work (e.g., Geanakoplos, Mitchell, and Zeldes 1998) has pointed to the evidence that many young people are up against a borrowing constraint and that social security taxes are likely to crowd out private savings for this group. This suggests that investing more of the trust fund in the market on behalf of these constrained agents may be welfare improving. To the extent that stockholdings are highly concentrated owing to market frictions rather than to risk preferences, the improved risk sharing resulting from shifting stock market risk to nonstockholders would tend to result in a lower equity premium. On the other hand, if many people avoid risky investments simply because they are risk averse, exposing them to market risk via the trust fund may reduce welfare. Whether these effects are quantitatively important is unclear but worthy of consideration.

Heterogeneity in tax effects across generations and wealth classes may also be important in practice. Investment behavior and expected returns will be most sensitive to the effect of policies on the rich, while labor income is likely to be most sensitive to the tax and benefit implications for the middle class. The assumption of lump-sum taxes, combined with the assumption of homogeneity, abstracts from these effects.

Government Policy

As shown above, government fiscal policy is the main driver of general equilibrium effects. One might argue that, in the scenarios considered, the assumed government policy is in some respects overly benign and in others insufficiently benevolent. The assumption of lump-sum taxes is benign relative to the current tax structure, where social security taxes create a disincentive to work. At the same time, the proposed government-policy function is not optimal. The trust fund size and Treasury debt levels are targeted to be stationary relative to output, with gradual adjustments toward these goals over time. Although risk sharing could presumably be improved if benefits were designed to increase spanning, it is assumed throughout the analysis that they do not. As discussed earlier, some risk-sharing benefits are achieved by virtue of the government's tax and expenditure policies, but to what extent risk sharing is improved is unclear. A useful extension of the analysis would be to consider a variety of other policy functions.

Implications of the Equity-Premium Puzzle

The discussion in this section thus far has been largely cautionary, and it would be reasonable to take the calibration results as telling despite these potential biases or omissions. More problematic is the fact that the quantitative results are based on a model that cannot explain observed asset returns. As is noted in the paper, the only way to make the base case consistent with the historical equity premium is to assume an unrealistically volatile consumption process. The way in which this is accomplished is by choosing a technology in which wages and market returns have a correlation of one and in which the productivity shocks are chosen to match the observed volatility of stock market returns rather than the observed volatility of output. This is in contrast to the data, in which the volatility of output is a small fraction of the volatility of the stock market. The high correlation between wages and stock returns is also problematic on an annual basis, but perhaps less so over the thirty-year periods represented by the model.

The inflated volatility of consumption risk is important because the background level of this risk influences the elasticity of demand for risky assets. Hence, it influences the predictions about the effect of policy changes on asset returns and on the precautionary demand for savings. If neither this model nor any of its close relatives can explain the relation between asset returns and physical quantities, it is hard to be confident that it can reliably predict the change in asset returns resulting from a change in physical quantities.

Of course, the equity-premium puzzle is a problem, not only for the analysis in this paper, but for the entire debate over whether welfare would be improved by investing social security funds in the stock market. Until we can agree on whether the observed equity premium is really a puzzle or whether our theoretical models are misspecified, the economically right course of action will remain elusive.

References

Abel, Andrew B. 1998. The aggregate effects of including equities in the social security trust fund. Wharton School, University of Pennsylvania. Typescript.

Geanakoplos, John, Olivia Mitchell, and Steve Zeldes. 1998. Would a privatized social security system really pay a higher rate of return? Yale University. Typescript.

Discussion Summary

James Poterba noted that, although the model presented is already very involved, the next generation of models may call for some synthesis of the insights of this paper with features of John McHale's paper. In particular, it seems crucially important to understand what benefit and tax policies would result from a change in the portfolio allocation of the social security trust fund. We do not currently have empirical evidence to analyze this question, but the type of cross-country data that McHale uses in his work would be helpful in this regard. Ultimately, the goal should be to enrich the government sector or the social security sector of the model to shed light on the question of which generation would benefit from tax reductions or benefit increases when the portfolio composition of the social security trust fund is shifted toward equities. Poterba also followed up on a remark made by the discussant, Deborah Lucas, and noted that everyone in the model holds risky assets. This prediction is counterfactual. Limited stock market participation seems important to consider when thinking about investing the social security trust fund in equities, especially in the light of such potential market frictions as transaction costs.

Robert King wondered whether there was any empirical evidence supporting the prediction of the model that, probably even absent any social security system, the ratio of government debt to GDP or of government debt to capital affects rates of return. He also commented that, although he appreciated the model for its tractability, it probably features an inefficiently low rate of growth. Reasoning from the perspective of the endogenous-growth literature, the growth rate is too low because the market interest rate is below the social marginal product of capital owing to the presence of external effects of capital accumulation.

John McHale remarked that the paper yielded interesting results in terms of who gains from the shift in the portfolio allocation of the social security trust fund toward equities. From the paper's conceptualization of a defined-benefit system, it appears that the current generation stands to gain. Investing the social security trust fund in stocks allows them either to enjoy lower tax rates when young (as less prefunding is required), keeping the benefits unchanged, or to have higher benefits when old, keeping tax rates constant. This is not always what is envisioned in debates: the benefits are often expected to accrue mainly to future generations, not to the currently young.

Antonio Rangel noted that the conclusions of this paper contradict the ones obtained in a previous paper by the author (Abel 1998), owing to differences in the modeling assumptions concerning the government sector. He suggested adding political economy considerations to the analysis in order to resolve this issue.

David Cutler remarked that it is hard to think about a social security trust fund in the model as there seems to be no reason for having one. One justification for a social security system might be that people are myopic when saving for retirement in the sense that they discount the future more than the government does. This should have important implications for the effects and welfare gains of the experiments considered in the paper. He concluded that adding a discussion of why we have a social security trust fund would be useful.

In response to these remarks and suggestions, *Andrew Abel* made the following comments. First, with respect to the fact that the experiments are only ceteris paribus interventions, he agreed but added that all variables adjust endogenously. *Deborah Lucas* clarified that she was interested in an experiment in which taxes were changed simultaneously with the change in γ_s, the portfolio allocation of the social security trust fund.

With respect to Ricardian equivalence, *Abel* responded that it would obtain only for a defined-contribution social security system, not for a defined-benefit plan. He further acknowledged that analyzing the issues considered in the paper in a multiperiod overlapping-generations model was important, as are borrowing constraints, labor supply decisions, and distortionary taxation. Regarding the correlation between wages and interest rates, he pointed out that, although low at an annual frequency, the correlation coefficient grows to 0.8 or 0.9 over a thirty-year period, as documented in Jermann (1999).

Concerning the target σ for the social security trust fund, Abel replied that it could be zero or even negative. Relating to Cutler's comment, he noted that a utility-maximizing theory of the government was missing from the analysis.

Finally, in response to McHale's question, Abel emphasized the difference between the question of which generation benefits and at what stage in the life cycle a generation receives the benefit.

References

Abel, Andrew B. 1998. The aggregate effects of including equities in the social security trust fund. Wharton School, University of Pennsylvania. Typescript.

Jermann, Urban. 1999. Comment on Robert J. Shiller, "Social security and institutions for intergenerational, intragenerational, and international risk sharing." *Carnegie-Rochester Conference Series on Public Policy* 50 (June): 205–12.

6

Social Security and Demographic Uncertainty
The Risk-Sharing Properties of Alternative Policies

Henning Bohn

All over the world, declining population growth rates and rising life expectancy are creating problems for public retirement systems. With a constant population structure, a pay-as-you-go (PAYGO) social security system could operate at constant tax and replacement rates. But, when the ratio of retirees to workers rises, either tax rates must be raised, or the replacement rate must be reduced. These demographic changes are the driving force behind the current social security reform debate.

This paper considers the design of social security from an ex ante perspective. Once a demographic shock is realized, a debate on how to adjust taxes and benefits is necessarily a distributional debate. A lighter burden on one generation implies a heavier burden on other generations. From an ex ante perspective, in contrast, demographics is a stochastic process, and the design questions are about risk sharing. Different realizations of birthrates and survival rates have an effect on the financial status of government programs and, more broadly, on the set of feasible allocations of national resources. Policy questions are then questions of efficiency: How can the financial risks created by demographic uncertainty be shared by different generations? What are the risk-sharing implications of alternative policy rules? Moreover, we can evaluate specific policy actions ("reforms") taken in response to demographic changes in terms of whether they represent efficient responses to the underlying shocks.

I examine demographic changes in a Diamond (1965)-style neoclassical growth model with overlapping generations, building on Bohn (1998). Government policy is potentially welfare improving because future generations are naturally excluded from financial markets. They cannot insure

Henning Bohn is professor of economics at the University of California, Santa Barbara.

themselves against macroeconomic or demographic risks.[1] In this setting, I characterize the general properties of alternative social security systems, with a focus on four specific alternatives: a PAYGO social security system with defined benefits (DB); a PAYGO system with defined contributions (DC); a private/privatized system; and a "conditionally prefunded" system.

The two PAYGO systems are relevant because existing social security systems in many developed countries, including the United States until 1983, are pure PAYGO systems. If the worker-retiree ratio is constant, DB and DC are observationally equivalent. But, when the retiree-worker ratio rises, the key issue for PAYGO social security is whether taxes are held constant and benefits reduced or whether benefits are held constant and taxes increased. This choice is at the heart of the current U.S. policy debate.

The analysis of a privatized system is motivated by the current discussion about systems in which individuals fund their own retirement, at least in part. A fully privatized system represents this policy option in pure form.[2]

Finally, the "conditionally prefunded" social security system is intended to capture key features of the post-1983 U.S. system. The U.S. social security debate is heavily influenced by the Social Security Administration's seventy-five-year extrapolations of current policy. Whenever the seventy-five-year forecast shows a significant revenue gap, public pressure seems to arise to reform the system.[3] If one takes this linkage seriously and assumes that projected funding gaps systematically trigger tax and benefit changes, one obtains a well-defined pattern of intergenerational transfers, namely, a system in which trust funds are accumulated or drawn down in response to demographic shocks. For the stylized representation of such a system, I assume that net benefits are fixed one generational period in advance, at a level that depends negatively on anticipated changes in the retiree-worker ratio.[4]

The paper derives four main sets of results, namely, about the implications of variable birthrates, about variations in longevity, about the different positive effects of alternative policies, and about their efficiency properties.

1. To simplify, I abstract from private risk sharing and from Ricardian bequests.
2. Some of the privatization literature distinguishes between private savings without government intervention and "privatized" social security, meaning a funded system that is mandatory and government regulated. For the intergenerational issues discussed in this paper, this distinction is irrelevant.
3. For example, the 1983 reform was supposed to cover the then-existing revenue gap through tax increases that would accumulate a trust fund sufficient to carry social security through the years of baby-boom retirement. Much of the current debate is also about closing the projected funding gap.
4. There is an apparent consensus that benefit changes ought to be phased in slowly and that the benefits of current retirees cannot be touched. The reform debate is about varying *future* benefit levels in response to anticipated demographic pressures, not about moving to a true PAYGO-DC system with variable benefits to current retirees. McHale (chap. 7 this volume) suggests that social security reforms in other countries follow a similar pattern.

First, members of a small cohort generally benefit from being in a small cohort even if the government operates a DB social security system. This finding deserves emphasis because the main concern in the current reform debate has been about the plight of the baby-bust generation, about the fact that DB imposes relatively high taxes on small cohorts that support preceding larger cohorts. Large cohorts are, however, worse off than small ones if there is no DB social security: their high labor supply drives down the wage rate when the cohort is young; their desire to save reduces the return on capital as they age. Conversely, small cohorts enjoy favorable factor-price movements. They are better off than large cohorts even with a DB social security system unless taxes are so high that the fiscal burden dominates the factor-price effects.

In the model, the magnitude of the factor-price effects relative to the fiscal burden depends on the elasticity of factor substitution and on the level of social security taxes. With Cobb-Douglas technology (as the benchmark), the factor-price effects dominate if the ratio of tax rate (θ) to one minus the tax rate, $\theta/(1 - \theta)$, is below the capital share in output. For the United States, this condition is satisfied by a wide margin, suggesting that the factor-price effects of birthrate changes should dominate the fiscal effects. The current debate about social security reform, in contrast, focuses on fiscal pressures and virtually ignores factor-price effects.[5]

One may wonder, of course, to what extent the results from the two-period model are empirically realistic. The empirical evidence is unfortunately very limited, largely because it takes decades of data to obtain a single generation-length observation. Empirical evidence in related areas—cross-country growth and studies of relative wages—suggests, however, that demographic changes have wage effects broadly consistent with the overlapping-generations model (see sec. 6.5 below).

The second set of results is about unexpected changes in old-age mortality. The implications for the allocation of risk depend significantly on the individual predictability of death, on the availability of fair annuities, and on who might receive any accidental bequests. Under a variety of assumptions, lower old-age mortality increases the need for retirement consumption. The efficient response to a longer retirement period is then to increase social security benefits. This argument applies if deaths are individually foreseeable, or if savings are annuitized so that accidental bequests are small, or if accidental bequests are distributed within a cohort.

5. The Social Security Administration's long-run projections of the social security system's financial status are, e.g., based on extrapolating historical trends. Neither the linkage between cohort size and factor prices nor the insurance role of DB social security is a new idea. Easterlin (1987) provides much broader arguments about the advantages of being in a small cohort. Smith (1982) provides a numerical example illustrating the insurance role of DB social security. The point here is that the factor-price effects are large relative to the fiscal effects under empirically plausible assumptions and therefore important for social security reform.

Reduced benefits might be efficient, however, if lower old-age mortality reduces the accidental bequests received by workers.[6]

Third, a comparison of alternative policies shows that a fully privatized system has essentially the same risk-sharing properties as a DC PAYGO system. This is because neither a DC PAYGO nor a privatized system imposes higher taxes on the young when the retiree-worker ratio rises, whereas a DB system does. For risk-sharing purposes, a partially privatized system (say, combining a smaller DC plan with individual accounts) is therefore equivalent to a mixture of DB and DC systems. A conditionally funded DB system mimics a partially privatized system with regard to anticipated demographic changes, but it behaves like a pure DB system when unexpected changes occur.

Fourth, none of the above systems is fully efficient. Efficient policy responses (if any) should take place as soon as a demographic shock is revealed. Moreover, efficiency requires that all risks are shared by all generations, making no exception for current retirees. This requirement is violated by DB and DC systems because both fail to vary current retiree benefits in anticipation of future changes in the retiree-worker ratio, for example, when the current birthrate changes. I have argued elsewhere (Bohn 1999b) that the *political* viability of social security requires at least a one-period-ahead commitment to retiree benefits (see also McHale, chap. 7 in this volume). This may explain why the political debate takes for granted that current retirees are exempt from reforms. From a risk-sharing perspective, such an exemption is nonetheless a glaring inefficiency.

Although this paper focuses on demographic risks, I should briefly comment on other sources of uncertainty, notably on productivity risk and stock market risk.[7] Productivity shocks are arguably the most important source of long-run uncertainty about wages and capital income (Bohn 1999a). In an overlapping-generations setting, productivity risk is not necessarily allocated efficiently across cohorts. Policy tools such as government debt and social security implicitly shift risk across cohorts (Bohn 1998). Social security, especially a wage-indexed system, has an important role in this context because it provides a means of intergenerational redistribution that is more "neutral" with regard to risk shifting than government debt.

6. In the current reform debate, increased longevity is often cited to justify an increased "normal" retirement age, i.e., reduced benefits for a given retirement age. Some proposals even call for an indexing of the retirement age to life expectancy. The efficiency considerations of this paper provide support for such proposals only if the accidental bequest channel is empirically important. This is an open question.

7. There is also a huge literature on how social security helps share individual-level risks such as disability, mortality, and cross-sectional income uncertainty (see, e.g., Storesletten, Telmer, and Yaron 1999). Such risks may well be responsible for the existence and popularity of social security, but they are beyond the scope of this paper.

Stock market risk has recently received considerable attention in the social security literature. Here, one should distinguish work on "privatized" retirement (investment options in "individual accounts") from work on intergenerational risk sharing through the social security trust fund. Individual accounts are essentially irrelevant from a generational perspective because the returns accrue to the contributors (Bohn 1997). Trust fund investments, on the other hand, reallocate risk across generations because future taxpayers are the residual claimants in any DB system. Bohn (1997, 1999a), Smetters (1997, chap. 3 in this volume), Shiller (1999), and Abel (1998, chap. 5 in this volume) discuss some of the positive and normative implications of alternative trust fund investments. This paper abstracts from most financial market issues to focus on demographics. But I include a simple productivity shock to demonstrate that shocks to the labor force have very different welfare implications than productivity shocks even though both have the same effect on the effective capital-labor ratio. The productivity shock also illustrates how easily other shocks could be added.

The paper is organized as follows. Section 6.1 describes the model. Section 6.2 examines the risk-sharing implications of alternative social security policies. Section 6.3 studies the implications of missing annuities markets and of accidental bequests. Section 6.4 derives necessary conditions for efficient risk sharing and their implications for social security policy. Section 6.5 comments on extensions of the model and on empirical issues. Section 6.6 concludes.

6.1 A Model with Stochastic Population Growth

This section examines risk sharing in a modified Diamond (1965)-style overlapping-generations model with stochastic population growth and stochastic total factor productivity.

6.1.1 Population Dynamics and Preferences

In the Diamond model, generation t enters as working-age adults in period t and retires in period $t + 1$. For modeling demographic uncertainty, it is important, however, that individuals are born long before they enter the labor force. In terms of generational time units, society has about one period advance notice about changes in the retiree-worker ratio. Hence, I will assume that generation t is born in period $t - 1$, works in period t, and retires in period $t + 1$. At time t, N_t^C is the number of generation $t + 1$ children, N_t^W the number of generation t workers, and N_t^R the number of generation $t - 1$ retirees.

To limit the scope of the paper, I assume throughout that childbearing is exogenous. Each of the N_t^W workers of generation t has b_t children so that $N_t^C = N_t^W \cdot b_t$. To make the future workforce somewhat unpredictable,

I assume that only a fraction μ_{1t+1} of children survives into adulthood.[8] Then the growth rate of the workforce, $N_{t+1}^W/N_t^W = \mu_{1t+1} \cdot N_t^C/N_t^W = \mu_{1t+1} \cdot b_t = 1 + n_{t+1}^W$, is partially predictable, but not perfectly. The variables μ_{1t} (survival rate) and b_t (birthrate) are assumed independently and identically distributed (i.i.d.). Throughout, individuals in a cohort are identical, individual survival probabilities equal the aggregate survival rate, and all variables are treated as continuous, including b_t.

Parents care about their children's consumption when the children live in their household. Their preferences do not include an altruistic bequest motive, however. This assumption is important because fiscal policy would be irrelevant if all generations were linked through Ricardian bequests. Since Altonji, Hayashi, and Kotlikoff (1996) find that private intergenerational risk sharing is highly imperfect empirically, it is a reasonable assumption in this context. Bequests may nonetheless occur "accidentally" if mortality is stochastic and annuity markets are imperfect, as I will explain below.

Parents make decisions about their own consumption c_t^W and about their childrens' consumption c_t^0 (per child). Throughout, I assume homothetic (constant relative risk aversion [CRRA]) preferences to obtain balanced growth. Let

$$u_t^1 = \frac{1}{1 - \eta} \cdot [\rho^W \cdot (c_t^W)^{1-\eta} + b_t \cdot \rho_0(b_t) \cdot (c_t^0)^{1-\eta}]$$

be the parent's period t utility, where $\eta > 0$ is the inverse elasticity of intertemporal substitution. The per child weight $\rho_0(b_t)$ may depend on the number of children: it seems reasonable to assume that $0 < \rho_0(b_t) \leq \rho^W$ and that $b_t \cdot \rho_0(b_t)$ is nondecreasing in the number of children. For any level of household consumption $c_t^1 = c_t^W + b_t \cdot c_t^0$, the parent's optimality condition

$$b_t \cdot \rho^W \cdot (c_t^W)^{-\eta} = \rho_0(b_t) \cdot (c_t^0)^{-\eta}$$

then implies that u_t^1 can be written as an indirect utility over household consumption,

$$u_t^1(c_t^1) = \rho_1(b_t) \cdot (c_t^1)^{1-\eta}/(1 - \eta),$$

where

$$\rho_1(b_t) = \rho^W \cdot \{1 + b_t \cdot [\rho_0(b_t)/b_t/\rho^W]^{1/\eta}\}^\eta$$

---

8. Otherwise, $N_{t+1}^W = N_t^C$ would be known at time t. One may also interpret μ_{1t+1} as reflecting uncertainty about immigration. But, since immigration would raise subtle welfare questions (how to include immigrants in the welfare function), I will not address immigration explicitly, and I interpret all uncertainty about N_{t+1}^W as survival uncertainty.

depends on the number of children. Under the assumptions outlined above, the elasticity of the weight ρ_1 with respect to the birthrate, $\gamma_\rho = \rho_1 / b_t \cdot (b_t/\rho_1)$, is in the interval $0 \le \gamma_\rho \le \eta$.

Overall, children matter for the analysis for two reasons. Their birth provides advance notice about the size of future adult cohorts, and they affect their parents' spending needs. Thus, the model accounts not only for old-age dependency but also for variations in youth dependency. Otherwise, the model with children works just like Diamond's two-period overlapping-generations model.

Now consider retirement. As old-age survival improves, more workers survive into the retirement period, and those who survive live longer. For social security, these changes matter only through their combined effect on the ratio of retirees to workers.[9] For individual behavior, however, an anticipated longer life span may have different implications than a reduced probability of a sudden death. For a known life span, retiree consumption needs are presumably proportional to the length of the retirement period. Retiree consumption needs will also increase if the rate of unanticipated deaths declines in a setting with fair annuities. This is because individuals without a bequest motive will place all their assets into annuities. The return on fair annuities is inversely related to the average survival rate. A rising survival rate will therefore require more savings to support a given consumption level, as in the case of a longer life span. If annuities are unavailable, however, or too expensive to be commonly used, a rising survival rate increases the probability that retirees consume their assets and do not leave accidental bequests. The cases with and without annuities have different policy implications and therefore deserve to be modeled carefully.

To capture a variable life expectancy in the overlapping-generations setting, I model the retirement period as a fractional period. At the start of period t, a fraction $1 - \mu_{2t}$ of all generation $t - 1$ workers dies. The remainder, μ_{2t}, learn that they will live for a period of length $\phi_t \in (0, 1]$. Both the survival probability and the conditional length of life have predictable and unanticipated components: $\mu_{2t} = \mu_{2t-1}^e \cdot \mu_{2t}^u$ and $\phi_t = \phi_{t-1}^e \cdot \phi_t^u$, where μ_{2t}^u and ϕ_t^u are i.i.d. shocks revealed at the start of period t, and μ_{2t-1}^e and ϕ_{t-1}^e are i.i.d. shocks revealed in period $t - 1$.[10] The product

---

9. The two changes may have different effects if the social security replacement rate varies with age or if one accounts for Medicare. In the United States, social security is fixed in real terms at retirement so that the replacement rate tends to fall with age, but the value of Medicare is rising with age. In the model, the replacement rate is assumed constant within each generational period.

10. For simplicity, I treat ϕ_t and μ_{2t} as level-stationary even though technical progress in medical technology suggests an upward drift. Drift terms would require an analysis of "unbalanced" growth paths. This could be done (for a deterministic analysis, see Bohn 1999b), but it would be cumbersome and would not provide new insights about risk sharing. Autocorrelation could also be accommodated, but it would not affect the main results and is therefore omitted.

$\mu_{2t-1}^e \cdot \phi_{t-1}^e$ may be interpreted as the life expectancy at retirement. Conditional on survival, the period t utility of the old is assumed proportional to the length of life, $u_{t+1}^2 = \phi_t \cdot (c_{t+1}^2)^{1-\eta}/(1-\eta)$.[11]

Finally, generation t's overall preferences combine the utility over working-age consumption $u_t^1(c_t^1)$ and retirement consumption $u_{t+1}^2(c_{t+1}^2)$:

$$(1) \quad U_t = I_{1t} \cdot \left[u_t^1(c_t^1) + I_{2t+1} \cdot \rho_2 \cdot u_{t+1}^2(c_{t+1}^2) \right]$$

$$= \frac{1}{1-\eta} \cdot I_{1t} \cdot \left[\rho_1(b_t) \cdot (c_t^1)^{1-\eta} + \rho_2 \cdot \phi_{t+1} \cdot I_{2t+1} \cdot (c_{t+1}^2)^{1-\eta} \right],$$

where the random variables I_{1t} and I_{2t+1} are 0-1 indicators for individual survival into adulthood and retirement, and ρ_2 captures time preference. In expectation, $E[I_{1t}] = E[\mu_{1t}] = \mu_1$ and $E_t[\phi_{t+1} \cdot I_{2t+1}] = \phi_t^e \cdot \mu_{2t}^e$ are equal to the respective aggregate values.

Overall, the population dynamics are such that the future labor force and the future worker-retiree ratio are quite predictable one period ahead, but not perfectly. This limited predictability is important for modeling social security because it motivates why policy reforms are debated with some lead time before demographic changes actually take place.

6.1.2   The Macroeconomic Setting

The macroeconomic setting is intentionally kept simple to focus on the demographics. Each working-age person inelastically supplies one unit of labor. Output is produced with capital K_t and labor N_t^W:

$$(2) \qquad\qquad Y_t = K_t^\alpha \cdot (A_t \cdot N_t^W)^{1-\alpha},$$

where α is the capital share, and A_t is the economy's total factor productivity. Productivity follows a stochastic trend $A_t = (1 + a_t) \cdot A_{t-1}$ with i.i.d. growth rate a_t. Capital depreciates at the rate δ, implying a national resource constraint

$$(3) \qquad Y_t + (1 - \delta) \cdot K_t = c_t^1 \cdot N_t^W + c_t^2 \cdot \phi_t \cdot \mu_{2t} \cdot N_{t-1}^W + K_{t+1}.$$

Some extensions are examined in section 6.5.[12]

The wage rate $w_t = (1 - \alpha) \cdot A_t \cdot [K_t/(A_t \cdot N_t^W)]^\alpha$ and the return on capital $R_t^k = \alpha \cdot [K_t/(A_t \cdot N_t^W)]^{\alpha-1} + (1 - \delta)$ both depend on the capital-labor ratio. Since K_t is known in period $t - 1$, it is convenient to define

---

11. One may interpret u_t^2 as an indirect utility obtained by maximizing $\int_0^{\phi t} [c(s)]^{1-\eta}/(1-\eta)ds$ over a continuous consumption stream $c(s)$, subject to a resource constraint limiting $\int_0^{\phi t} c(s)ds$. Implicitly, this abstracts from within-period interest and discounting.

12. Bohn (1998) has shown how this setting can be generalized, e.g., to include a variable labor supply, temporary productivity, government spending, and a production function with an elasticity of substitution different from one, but such complicating features would be distracting here.

the state variable $k_{t-1} = K_t/(A_{t-1} \cdot N_{t-1}^W)$ that scales the capital stock by lagged productivity and the lagged labor force. Wages and interest rates then depend on k_{t-1}, on current productivity growth, and on the current workforce growth.

To model policy, I abstract from all government activity but social security.[13] The government collects payroll taxes on wages w_t at a rate θ_t from all workers and pays benefits to retirees at a replacement rate β_t. The cost of social security is the product of the number of surviving retirees $N_t^R = \mu_{2t} \cdot N_{t-1}^W$, their length of life ϕ_t, and the level of benefit $\beta_t \cdot w_t$. The system's revenues are $\theta_t \cdot w_t \cdot N_t^W$. For given replacement rate β_t, the PAYGO budget constraint therefore implies a payroll-tax rate of

$$(4) \qquad \theta_t = \beta_t \cdot \phi_t \cdot \mu_{2t} \cdot \frac{N_{t-1}^W}{N_t^W} = \beta_t \cdot \frac{\phi_t \cdot \mu_{2t}}{b_{t-1} \cdot \mu_{1t}}.$$

The ratio $(\phi_t \cdot \mu_{2t})/(b_{t-1} \cdot \mu_{1t})$ can be interpreted as the "average" retiree-worker ratio (after smoothing over ϕ_t).

Interesting special cases of the PAYGO system are the defined-benefit (DB) system with $\beta_t = \beta^*$ and the defined-contribution (DC) system with $\theta_t = \theta^*$ and $\beta_t = (1 + n_t^W)/(\phi_t \cdot \mu_{2t}) \cdot \theta^*$. Since individuals are not liquidity constrained, government-mandated savings (sometimes called *privatized* or *individual accounts* systems) would simply reduce private savings (Bohn 1997). A privatized social security system is therefore equivalent to $\theta^* = 0$. In a mixed system consisting of individual accounts plus a PAYGO component, one should interpret θ_t and β_t as the taxes and benefits of the PAYGO component.

A system with government-run trust funds is somewhat more complicated if the system promises benefits that do not depend on the performance of the trust fund (as in the United States). Generational accounting implies that each cohort's net benefits are equal to the system's PAYGO component, that is, to the statutory benefits minus the proceeds from the trust fund built up by the same cohort's payroll taxes (see Bohn 1997). In the United States, the buildup of the current trust fund started in 1983 in response to a funding gap in the Social Security Administration's long-run projections. Projected funding gaps are similarly influencing the current debate. Such gaps arise from two principal sources, rising life expectancy and reduced birthrates. Hence, one may interpret the current U.S. system as a defined-benefits system that accumulates trust funds in response to either a rise in life expectancy, $\mu_{2t}^e \cdot \phi_t^e$, or a fall in the birthrate, b_t. Since a trust fund buildup is equivalent to a reduction in net benefits, such a

---

13. This approach is nonetheless quite general because government transfers matter only through different cohorts' generational accounts. Hence, social security can be interpreted broadly as a stand-in for other intergenerational transfers.

"conditionally prefunded" system can be represented parsimoniously by a benefit function $\beta_t = \beta(\mu_{2t}^e, \phi_t^e, b_t)$ with $\partial\beta/\partial\mu_2^e < 0$, $\partial\beta/\partial\phi^e < 0$, and $\partial\beta/\partial b > 0$.

McHale's (chap. 7 in this volume) analysis of recent pension reforms around the world suggests that a variable-benefit function of this type is empirically realistic for other countries, too. In the countries studied by McHale, reforms were generally triggered by anticipated funding gaps. Benefits to current retirees remained virtually unchanged, but benefits to future generations were reduced. This implies a benefit function with the same features as in the conditionally prefunded system.

More generally, a variety of social security systems with and without prefunding can be reinterpreted as PAYGO systems with an appropriately state-contingent benefit function. Hence, I will use the PAYGO notation throughout the paper.

6.1.3   Individual Behavior

Individuals maximize their expected utility (1) subject to their budget constraints. The main complications are potential imperfections in the market for private annuities.

When working, individuals earn an after-tax wage income $w_t \cdot (1 - \theta_t)$ and possibly receive accidental bequests Q_t^1 (defined below). Denoting savings by s_t, the first-period budget equation is

$$(5) \qquad c_t^1 = w_t \cdot (1 - \theta_t) + Q_t^1 - s_t.$$

If fair annuities exist, they offer a return R_{t+1}^k/μ_{2t+1} that is above the return on nonannuitized savings.[14] Hence, all savings should be annuitized. Empirically, however, private annuities are so costly that the bulk of private savings is not annuitized (Congressional Budget Office 1998).

To gauge the significance of this apparent market imperfection, first consider the case with fair annuities.[15] If all assets are annuitized, surviving retirees will spend their private resources $R_{t+1}^k/\mu_{2t+1} \cdot s_t$ at the rate $1/\phi_{t+1}$, and there are no bequests. Retirement consumption (including receipts from social security) is then

---

14. Either one may assume that individual annuity payoffs are indexed to the ex post survival rate μ_{2t+1}; or, if annuity contracts promise a payoff R_{t+1}^k/μ_{2t}^e linked to the expected survival rate, one may note that annuity firms, like all other firms, are owned by the old so that the annuity firms' aggregate profit $R_{t+1}^k - \mu_{2t} \cdot R_{t+1}^k/\mu_{2t}^e$ accrues to the old. In either case, the old bear the risk of unexpected mortality changes.

15. Ideally, one might want to include a model of why private annuities are so costly (e.g., a model of adverse selection), but this would excessively complicate the analysis. Hence, I focus on two simple polar cases, fair annuities and prohibitively costly private annuities. In the latter case, I implicitly assume that social security has a cost advantage. This is perhaps plausible because a mandatory system avoids adverse selection.

(6a)
$$c_{t+1}^2 = \frac{R_{t+1}^s}{\mu_{2t+1} \cdot \phi_{t+1}} \cdot s_t + \beta_t \cdot w_{t+1},$$

and savings are determined by the individual optimality condition

(7a)
$$\rho_1(b_t) \cdot (c_t^1)^{-\eta} = \rho_2 \cdot E_t[\phi_{t+1} \cdot I_{2t+1}] \cdot E_t\left[\frac{R_{t+1}^s}{\mu_{2t+1} \cdot \phi_{t+1}} \cdot (c_{t+1}^2)^{-\eta}\right]$$
$$= \rho_2 \cdot E_t[R_{t+1}^k \cdot (c_{t+1}^2)^{-\eta}].$$

Note that mortality cancels out in (7a). Also, all individual and policy constraints depend on the length of life and on the survival rate only through their product $\phi_t \cdot \mu_{2t}$. Hence, under the assumption of perfect annuities, survival uncertainty μ_{2t} can be subsumed into ϕ_t and does not have to be examined separately.

Second, suppose that annuities do not exist (or are prohibitively costly). Then those who die at the start of their retirement period must leave accidental bequests. On aggregate, bequests of

(8)
$$R_{t+1}^k \cdot s_t \cdot (1 - \mu_{2t+1}) \cdot N_t^W = Q_{t+1}^1 \cdot N_{t+1}^W + Q_{t+1}^2 \cdot N_{t+1}^R$$

accrue either to workers (the next generation, Q_{t+1}^1) or to other retirees (the same generation, Q_{t+1}^2).

The surviving retirees will spend their private resources $R_{t+1}^k \cdot s_t$ at the rate $1/\phi_{t+1}$. Including bequests and social security, retirement consumption is

(6b)
$$c_{t+1}^2 = \frac{R_{t+1}^k}{\phi_{t+1}} \cdot s_t + \frac{Q_{t+1}^2}{\phi_{t+1}} + \beta_t \cdot w_{t+1}.$$

Savings are determined by the first-order condition

(7b)
$$\rho_1(b_t) \cdot (c_t^1)^{-\eta} = \rho_2 \cdot E_t[\phi_{t+1} \cdot I_{2t+1}] \cdot E_t\left[\frac{R_{t+1}^s}{\phi_{t+1}} \cdot (c_{t+1}^2)^{-\eta}\right]$$
$$= \rho_2 \cdot \mu_{2t}^e \cdot E_t[R_{t+1}^k \cdot (c_{t+1}^2)^{-\eta}].$$

Savings decisions now involve the probability of survival, μ_{2t}^e, and they are distorted because individuals do not value bequests. Moreover, accidental bequests affect the distribution of resources across cohorts to the extent that they go to the young (if $Q_t^1 > 0$).[16]

Despite this multitude of effects, annuities turn out to be relatively un-

16. If all bequests go to the old, missing annuities have only an incentive effect but no redistributional effect because (6b) would then imply that the retirement income $R_{t+1}^k/\phi_{t+1} \cdot s_t + Q_{t+1}^2/\phi_{t+1} = [R_{t+1}^s/(\mu_{2t+1} \cdot \phi_{t+1})] \cdot s_t$ is the same as with annuities.

important except for studying time-varying survival probabilities per se (see sec. 6.3 below). Intuitively, savings distortions ($\mu_{2t}^e < 1$) affect the level of economic activity, but they leave the propagation of other shocks and their effect on the different cohorts largely unchanged. And bequests ($Q_1 > 0$) give the young some exposure to shocks affecting capital income, but the effect is proportional to the size of such bequests relative to wage income, which is likely small.

Because of these complications and the fact that annuitized survival risk is economically equivalent to length-of-life risk, I abstract from old-age survival risk for much of the analysis and focus instead on length-of-life uncertainty (setting $\mu_{2t} \equiv \mu_{2t}^e \equiv 1$). Since shocks to survival uncertainty *with* fair annuities can be subsumed into ϕ_t, the ϕ_t shocks in this analysis can be interpreted as reflecting both shocks to the length of life and "diversifiable" (through annuitization) survival uncertainty. When I explicitly add survival uncertainty later (sec. 6.3), it will be sufficient to model the case *without* annuities because annuitized survival uncertainty is already covered under ϕ_t.

With either assumption about annuities, the basic dynamics are similar to the Diamond (1965) model. Each period, the young divide their wage income (and bequests, if any) between consumption and savings. Savings determine the next period's capital stock, $K_{t+1} = N_t^W \cdot s_t$, which determines the wage rate for the next young generation. Since I am not interested in issues of dynamic inefficiency, I assume that $\rho_2 \cdot \mu_{2t}^e / \rho_1(b_t)$ is low enough (for all μ_{2t}^e, b_t) that the economy is dynamically efficient.

With all the shocks and flexibly parametrized preferences, the model does not generally have a closed-form solution. As in Bohn (1998), I therefore follow the real business cycle and finance literature and examine log-linearized solutions—analytically derived ones, however, not numerically simulated ones. To ensure balanced growth, I assume a stationary policy rule for the replacement rate β_t. Without government, the model would have a Markov structure with K_{t-1} and the shocks $Z = \{b_t, b_{t-1}, \mu_{1t}, \phi_t^u,$ $\phi_t^e, \phi_{t-1}^e, \mu_{2t}^u, \mu_{2t}^e, \mu_{2t-1}^e, a_t\}$ as state variables. Adding more state variables would be uninteresting. I assume, therefore, that the policy rule is a function of at most these variables so that the model with government has the same structure.[17]

Given the Markov structure, the log deviation of any variable (y) from the perfect foresight path is an approximately linear function of the log deviations of the state variables. Unless otherwise noted, let symbols without the time subscript refer to steady states and hats (^) denote log devia-

17. Without government, one could treat n_t^W and ϕ_t as state variables instead of their components. The components will have different effects, however, if policy treats expected and unexpected changes differently, e.g., in the conditionally prefunded system. Hence, I treat the components of n_t^W and ϕ_t as distinct state variables throughout.

tions.[18] The log-linearized law of motions for any variable y can be written as[19]

$$
(9) \qquad \hat{y}_t = \pi_{yk} \cdot \hat{k}_{t-1} + \sum_{z \in Z} \pi_{yz} \cdot \hat{z}_t,
$$

where π_{yz} denotes the coefficient for state variable z. The π_{yz} coefficients can be interpreted as elasticities of y with respect to z.

The main variables of interest are the consumption of workers and retirees and the level of capital investment. Since the young divide their labor income between consumption and savings, c_t^1 and k_t depend on all shocks affecting the wage rate, on the incentives to save (R_{t+1}^k), and on the payroll tax. The consumption of the old depends on all shocks affecting capital income and social security benefits (see eqq. [6a] and [6b]). The resulting elasticity coefficients for various specifications of the model are listed in several tables discussed in the following sections.

To illustrate the practical implications of the model, I also provide the elasticity coefficients implied by a simple numerical example. For example, assume a capital share of $\alpha = 1/3$, full depreciation ($\delta = 1$), payroll taxes of $\theta = 0.15$, zero population growth ($n = 0$), a steady-state productivity growth factor of $1 + a = 1.35$ (1 percent annual growth for a thirty-year generational period), and an elasticity of substitution of $1/\eta = 1/3$. The effective retirement period—length times probability—is $\phi \cdot \mu_2 = 1/2$ (where $\phi = 1/2$ and $\mu_2 = 1$, except in sec. 6.3 below), and the time preference ρ_2 is set such that, in steady state, workers save 25 percent of their disposable income.[20]

6.2   The Risk-Sharing Properties of Alternative Systems

This section examines the positive effects of demographic shocks on the fortunes of different cohorts. The main sources of demographic uncertainty are shocks to the workforce and shocks to the number of retirees. For this section, I abstract from shocks that would trigger accidental be-

18. For example, $\hat{c}_t^1 = \ln(c_t^1) - \ln(c^1)$. When growth rates are involved, the "1+" is suppressed for notational convenience, as in $\hat{n}_t^w = \ln(1 + n_t^w) - \ln(1 + n^w)$.

19. An intercept term could be added to reflect average "displacements" from the deterministic paths caused, e.g., by risk aversion and precautionary savings (see Bohn 1998). But, since the focus here is on fluctuations, not level variables, intercept terms are omitted.

20. The example is motivated by the calibrated overlapping-generations model in Bohn (1999a), which can be consulted for a discussion of calibration issues. The assumed full depreciation is a convenient simplification, but it implies a caveat: setting $\delta = 1$ reduces the autocorrelation of capital (π_{kk}) and therefore understates the propagation of shocks. This is acceptable here because the analysis focuses on the impact effects. Setting $\delta = 1$ also reduces the level of R^k, which I offset by raising ρ_2 enough that the savings rate roughly matches the empirical investment share in GDP. This is why I calibrate savings, not the time preference.

quests (setting $\mu_{2t} \equiv \mu_{2t}^e \equiv 1$) and assume that all variations in old-age mortality are either changes in the known length of life or annuitized.

6.2.1   Defined Benefits

To start, consider an economy with constant social security benefits (DB). It will provide a benchmark for studying variable benefits below. Table 6.1 summarizes the log-linearized equilibrium responses of workers and retirees to various shocks.

First, consider an unanticipated shock to the number of workers ($\hat{n}_t^W = \hat{\mu}_{1t}$; panel A). A large number of workers has a clear positive effect on the old ($\pi_{c2\mu1} > 0$) because the reduced capital-labor ratio increases the old generation's capital income. The effect on the young is in principle ambiguous. With a defined-benefit system, members of a large cohort pay less social security tax (θ). But a large workforce also reduces the wage rate, as captured by negative α terms. The negative effects dominate whenever $\alpha > \theta/(1 - \theta)$. For plausible capital shares (0.3–0.4), this inequality holds unless the tax rate is well over 20 percent. If $\alpha > \theta/(1 - \theta)$, workers' income, consumption, and savings decline in response to a positive shock to the workforce, whereas retiree consumption rises. This is also true in the numerical example: $\alpha = 1/3 > \theta/(1 - \theta) = 0.176$; $\pi_{c1\mu1} = -0.131$ and $\pi_{k\mu1} = -0.235$ are negative; and $\pi_{c2\mu1} = 0.436$ is positive.

The main conclusion, to be reexamined below, is that, for plausible parameters, *large cohorts tend to be demographically disadvantaged.* Conversely, being in a small cohort is beneficial. Even though small cohorts face relatively high taxes under a defined-benefit system, they also enjoy high wages and high returns on savings.

Second, consider shocks to the current birthrate b_t (table 6.1, panel B). If one ignores children's expenses (setting $\gamma_\rho = 0$ for this argument), shocks to the birthrate are like shocks to the labor force that become known one period in advance. With defined benefits, such shocks have no effect on the old ($\pi_{c2b} = 0$). News about next period's labor force is relevant for the young, however, because they expect to be alive when the shock actually hits the retiree-worker ratio. Looking forward, they know that changes in b_t have the same effect in period $t + 1$ as the μ_{1t+1} shocks discussed above. A high birthrate b_t has a positive effect on retired generation t workers. But, provided $\alpha > \theta/(1 - \theta)$, it has a negative effect on generation $t + 1$ workers.

The response of period t workers is most likely an increase in current consumption and a reduction in savings. Specifically, table 6.1 shows that the elasticities π_{c1b} and π_{kb} depend on the interaction of three effects. First, expected retirement income rises because a high future workforce reduces next period's capital-labor ratio and raises the return on current savings. This income effect is captured by the positive γ_{c2nw} term in π_{c1b} and π_{kb}. Second, the increased return triggers a substitution effect in the opposite

Table 6.1   **Macroeconomic Dynamics with Defined Benefits**

Effect on:	Elasticity Coefficients	Numerical Example
	A. Shocks to the Current Workforce, μ_{1t} and b_{t-1}	
Retirees	$\pi_{c2\mu1} = \pi_{c2b1} = \gamma_{c2nw} > 0$	.436
Workers	$\pi_{c1\mu1} = \pi_{c1b1} = -\Delta_c \cdot \left[\alpha - \dfrac{\theta}{1-\theta}\right]$ is negative, provided $\alpha > \dfrac{\theta}{1-\theta}$	$-.131$
Investment	$\pi_{k\mu1} = \pi_{kb1} = -\Delta_k \cdot \left[\alpha - \dfrac{\theta}{1-\theta}\right] < 0$	$-.235$
	B. Shocks to the Current Birthrate, b_t	
Retirees	$\pi_{c2b} = 0$	0
Workers	$\pi_{c1b} = [1 - \Delta_c \cdot (c^1/A)y^1] \cdot (\gamma_{c2nw} - \pi_{Rk}/\eta + \gamma/\eta)$	.080
Investment	$\pi_{kb} = -\Delta_k \cdot (c^1/A)/y^1 \cdot (\gamma_{c2nw} - \pi_{Rk}/\eta + \gamma_p/\eta)$	$-.240$
	C. Shocks to the Current Length of Life, ϕ_t^u and ϕ_{t-1}^e	
Retirees	$\pi_{c2\phi u} = \pi_{c2\phi e1} < 0$	$-.769$
Workers	$\pi_{c1\phi u} = \pi_{c1\phi e1} = -\Delta_c \cdot \dfrac{\theta}{1-\theta} < 0$	$-.147$
Investment	$\pi_{k\phi u} = \pi_{k\phi e1} = -\Delta_k \cdot \dfrac{\theta}{1-\theta} < 0$	$-.265$
	D. Shocks to Life Expectancy (future length of life), ϕ_t^e	
Retirees	$\pi_{c2\phi e} = 0$	0
Workers	$\pi_{c1\phi e} = -[1 - \Delta_c \cdot (c^1/A)/y^1] \cdot \gamma_{c2\phi} < 0$	$-.288$
Investment	$\pi_{k\phi e} = \Delta_k \cdot (c^1/A)/y^1 \cdot \gamma_{c2\phi} > 0$	.865
	E. Changes in Lagged Capital and Productivity, k_{t-1} and a_t	
Retirees	$\pi_{c2k} = -\pi_{c2a} = \gamma_{c2k} > 0$	.333
Workers	$\pi_{c1k} = -\pi_{c1a} = \Delta_c \cdot \alpha > 0$	.278
Investment	$\pi_{kk} = -\pi_{ka} = \Delta_k \cdot \alpha > 0$	.500

Notes: The effect on retirees, on workers, and on investment refers to the effect of the shock(s) named in the panel head on the variables $(c^1/A)_t$, $(c^2/A)_t$, and $\hat{k}_t$. Since these variables are scaled by the productivity trend A_t, the coefficients for productivity shocks at a_t are negative. The effects of productivity shocks on consumption and investment levels, $1 + \pi_{c2a} > 0$, $1 + \pi_{c1a} > 0$, and $1 + \pi_{ka} > 0$, are nonetheless positive.

The column "Numerical Example" refers to the elasticity values in the numerical example described in the text.

Variables without time subscripts refer to the steady state. The symbols not already defined in the text are as follows:

$\delta^* = \dfrac{\delta \cdot k/an}{(c^2/A) \cdot \phi/(1+n^w)} \in (0, 1)$, share of old capital in retiree income; $an = (1 + a) \cdot (1 + n^w)$;

$\gamma_{c2k} = (1 - \delta^*) \cdot \alpha + \delta^* \in (0, 1)$, effect of a higher capital-labor ratio on the old;

$\gamma_{c2nw} = 1 - \gamma_{c2k} - (1 - \delta^*) \cdot \dfrac{\theta \cdot (1 - \alpha)}{\alpha + \theta \cdot (1 - \alpha)} = \dfrac{(1 - \delta^*) \cdot (1 - \sigma) \cdot \alpha \cdot (1 - \theta)}{\alpha + \theta \cdot (1 - \alpha)} \in (0, 1)$, effect of a higher current labor force on the old;

$\gamma_{c2\phi} = 1 - (1 - \delta^*) \cdot \dfrac{\theta \cdot (1 - \alpha)}{\alpha + \theta \cdot (1 - \alpha)} \in (0, 1)$, effect (absolute value) of a longer life span on the old;

$\pi_{Rk} = (1 - (1 - \delta)/R^k) \cdot (1 - \alpha) \in (0, 1)$, effect (absolute value) of a higher capital-labor ratio on the return to capital;

$y^1 = w/A \cdot (1 - \theta)$, income of the young scaled by productivity;

$\Delta_c = \dfrac{[\gamma_{c2k} + \pi_{Rk}/\eta]}{(c^1/A)/y^1 \cdot (\gamma_{c2k} + \pi_{Rk}/\eta + \gamma_{c2\beta} \cdot \pi_{Bk}) + k/y^1} > 0$, marginal effect on consumption when the income of the young rises; and

$\Delta_k = \dfrac{1}{(c^1/A)/y^1 \cdot (\gamma_{c2k} + \pi_{Rk}/\eta + \gamma_{c2\beta} \cdot \pi_{Bk}) + k/y^1} > 0$, marginal effect on capital investment when the income of the young rises.

direction (the $-\pi_{Rk}/\eta$ term). Finally, expenses for children increase the consumption needs of working-age families (the γ_ρ term with $\gamma_\rho > 0$). Unless the elasticity of intertemporal substitution is high enough to offset both other effects, the net effects are higher consumption ($\pi_{c1b} > 0$) and lower investment ($\pi_{kb} < 0$). In the numerical example, these signs apply even for $\gamma_\rho = 0$; $\pi_{c1b} = 0.08$, and $\pi_{kb} = -0.24$.[21]

Overall, a change in the birthrate triggers changes in consumption and capital investment before it actually affects the labor supply. The effect over time is traced out in figures 6.1 and 6.2. For the figures, I consider a one-time 20 percent *reduction* in the birthrate b_t applied to the elasticities of the numerical example.[22] In period t, retirees (generation $t - 1$) are unaffected. Workers (generation t) realize that the next working-age cohort will be small, which will reduce the return on savings. Assuming that the negative income effect dominates the substitution effect, generation t will reduce their consumption c_t^1 and raise savings k_t. In period $t + 1$, the lower return reduces generation t's consumption despite the increased savings (see fig. 6.1). Generation $t + 1$'s consumption rises, in contrast, because of higher wages. Wages are higher because of the low labor supply and because of the higher capital stock (see fig. 6.2). The increased wage outweighs the increase in tax rates. Since the capital stock rises, subsequent generations are better off, too.

Note that the increased period t savings merely magnify the change in period $t + 1$ wages. A reduction in b_t would make the baby-bust generation better off *even if* the preceding generation did not save more (say, if $1/\eta$ were large enough that $\pi_{kb} = 0$). Increased savings further improve the consumption opportunities of the baby-bust generation and its successors, but this savings response is not crucial.[23]

In terms of the current policy debate, the analysis here suggests that we are perhaps too worried about the baby-bust generation and its ability to pay defined benefits to the baby boomers. Instead, the baby-bust generation can look forward to a substantial growth in wages, whereas the baby-

---

21. Recall that $\gamma_\rho \in [0, \eta]$. For the upper bound $\gamma_\rho = \eta = 3$, one obtains $\pi_{c1b} = 0.455$ and $\pi_{kb} = -1.365$. Unless otherwise noted, I use $\gamma_\rho = 0$ for the example numbers—for simplicity and to avoid exaggerating the birthrate effects.

22. The 20 percent is somewhat less than both the projected increase in the retiree-worker ratio from 1990 to 2020 (the baby-boom retirement) and the decline in the ratio of the age zero to age twenty-nine population to the age thirty to age fifty-nine population between 1960 and 1990 (the baby bust). The example is indicative of the shape of the impulse-response functions in general, provided $\alpha > \theta/(1 - \theta)$ and $\gamma_{c2nw} + \gamma_\rho/\eta > \pi_{Rk}/\eta$. One exception: for large γ_ρ, the sign of $\hat{c}_{t+1}^2$ and the relative magnitude of $\hat{c}_t^1$ and $\hat{c}_{t+1}^2$ could be reversed, namely, if reduced expenses for children dominate the baby boomers' behavior; but this seems unrealistic.

23. For proof, recall the analysis of μ_{1t} shocks, where anticipation effects did not arise. This point is worth noting because the prediction of higher savings is specific to the overlapping-generations approach. If one assumed Ricardian bequests instead, a fertility decline would likely trigger a slight decline in savings (see Cutler et al. 1990).

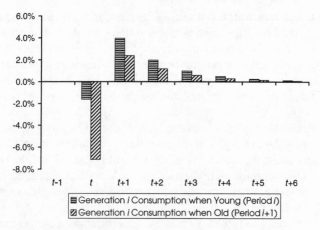

Fig. 6.1   Consumption responses to a birthrate shock

Note: The bars show the percentage deviations of consumption from the steady state in response to a one-time, 20 percent reduction in the birthrate in period t, applied to the parameter values of the numerical example with a defined-benefit social security system. The responses are collected by generation, not by period. The responses under generation $i = t + 2$ refer, e.g., to the changes in c_{t+2}^1 (generation $t + 2$ when young) and c_{t+3}^2 (generation $t + 2$ when old).

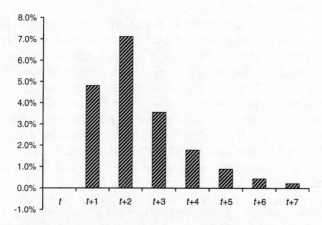

Fig. 6.2   Response of the capital-labor ratio to a birthrate shock

Note: The bars show the percentage deviations of the capital-labor ratio k_t from its steady state in response to a one-time, 20 percent reduction in the birthrate in period t, applied to the parameter values of the numerical example with a defined-benefit social security system.

boom generation may suffer because the small succeeding cohort reduces the return on capital.

The overlapping-generations model produces strikingly different results than one would obtain in a partial equilibrium analysis (say, a trend extrapolation of the type used by the Social Security Administration). This is due to the endogenous factor prices. If one took wages and interest rates as given, a small workforce would leave retirees unaffected, it would make workers worse off because of higher taxes, and, since workers would save less, it would make future generations worse off. If one accounts for factor-price effects, however, the partial equilibrium results are reversed. The effect of factor-price movements dominates the fiscal effect of labor force changes.

The latter finding relies, of course, on the general equilibrium properties of this particular two-period overlapping-generations model. Perhaps most significantly, the factor-price effects would be smaller if the elasticity of factor substitution were higher, for example, with constant elasticity of substitution technology. This and other robustness issues are examined in section 6.5 below.[24]

Third, returning to table 6.1 (panel C), consider a shock to the number of retirees, $\hat{\phi}_t = \phi_t^u$. A large number of retirees directly reduces retiree consumption because the old have to spread their capital income over a longer period (or, in case of annuitized savings, over more people). Capital investment and worker consumption are also reduced to the extent that an increased retiree-worker ratio triggers higher payroll taxes. Thus, defined-benefit social security helps share the risk of shocks to the length of life across cohorts.

Fourth, consider a current shock to ϕ_t^e, the expected length of life ("life expectancy") in period $t + 1$. Table 6.1, panel D, shows that current life expectancy has an effect on the young, who will experience a longer life, but no effect on the old ($\pi_{c2\phi e} = 0$, as in the case of b_t shocks). Looking forward, a lagged length-of-life shock matters through its effect on the actual number of retirees (ϕ_{t+1}), like the unexpected shock ϕ_{t+1}^u. The young have an incentive to increase their savings and to reduce their current consumption ($\pi_{k\phi e} > 0$, $\pi_{c1\phi e} < 0$).[25] This risk is not shared with the old.

Finally, consider the capital and productivity coefficients in table 6.1, panel E. Not surprisingly, a high capital-labor ratio raises capital and labor incomes, hence consumption and savings. This makes k_t autocorrelated and propagates shocks. Productivity shocks have a negative effect on consumption and capital when scaled by productivity (c_t^1/A_t, c_t^2/A_t, and k_t) because a rise in A_t raises output less than one for one. In level terms, however, a positive shock to a_t raises consumption (c_t^1, c_t^2) and per capita savings $k_t \cdot A_t$.

Since a shock to productivity affects the capital-labor ratio like an unexpected shock to the workforce, one may wonder to what extent the μ_{1t} and

---

24. To avoid clutter, I proceed with the basic model and defer all extensions and empirical issues.

25. The overall effects of increased life expectancy over time could be traced out as in fig. 6.1 above, but the results would just confirm the increase in savings and the reduction in per capita consumption.

a_t shocks have similar effects. If social security is small ($\theta = 0$), positive shocks to a_t and μ_{1t} will indeed increase retiree consumption by the same amount ($1 + \pi_{c2a} = \pi_{c2\mu1}$ for $\theta = 0$). They have very different effects on current workers, however, since an increase in A_t raises the wage while a rise in N_t^W reduces the wage rate. For $\theta > 0$, a_t and μ_{1t} shocks also have different effects on retirees because they have different distributional effects through social security.

6.2.2   Variable Benefits

The analysis so far has shown that most shocks affect different generations differently or even in opposite directions. This suggests some scope for improved risk sharing. The section examines how the allocation of risk is modified by policies with variable social security benefits.

Alternative policies are defined by their elasticity coefficients $\pi_{\beta z}$, that is, by how the replacement rate β responds to different shocks. Table 6.2 shows how the equilibrium dynamics of consumption and capital investment are affected in general by alternative $\pi_{\beta z}$ values. To help interpret the general results, table 6.3 displays the elasticity coefficients corresponding to the four main policy alternatives—the DB, DC, privatized, and conditionally prefunded social security systems—in the numerical example.[26]

In general, the elasticity formulas in table 6.2 include the same elements as the corresponding formulas in table 6.1 above, but there are additional terms that capture the effects of a changing replacement rate. The policy coefficients are generally weighted by the size of government transfers relative to the cohort's income, which is $\gamma_{c2\beta}$ for retirees and $-\theta/(1 - \theta)$ for workers. For workers, the effect is then divided between consumption and savings in proportions $\Delta_c : \Delta_k$.

Any policy that reduces prospective benefits when the birthrate declines and/or life expectancy rises is characterized by policy coefficients $\pi_{\beta b1} > 0$ and/or $\pi_{\beta \phi e1} < 0$. A pure defined-contribution system would have $\pi_{\beta \mu1} = \pi_{b1} = 1$ and $\pi_{\beta \phi u} = \pi_{\beta \phi e1} = -1$. Since U.S. retirees have generally been protected against unexpected shocks, the U.S. system seems to maintain defined benefits with respect to unexpected changes ($\pi_{\beta \phi u} = \pi_{\beta \mu1} = 0$) but allow benefits to change after a phase-in, suggesting $\pi_{\beta b1} \neq 0$ and $\pi_{\beta \phi e1} \neq 0$. The tax increases and the trust fund buildup since 1983 suggest that the U.S. system is somewhere between a DC and a DB system with respect to anticipated changes, that is, $0 < \pi_{\beta b1} < 1$ and $0 > \pi_{\beta \phi e1} > -1$. These stylized facts are captured by the conditionally prefunded system ("prefunded" in table 6.3). For the numerical illustration of this system, I assume that $\pi_{\beta b1} = 0.5$ and that $\pi_{\beta \phi e1} = -0.5$.

In the case of shocks to the workforce, table 6.3 (panel A) shows that defined contributions and privatized systems magnify the *negative* expo-

26. The numerical example is broadly indicative of how the elasticities compare in general.

Table 6.2   Dynamics with Variable Social Security Benefits

Effect on:	Elasticity Coefficients

A. Shocks to the Current Workforce, μ_t and b_{t-1}

Retirees:
$$\pi_{c2\mu1} = \gamma_{c2nw} + \gamma_{c2\beta} \cdot \pi_{\beta\mu1}, \qquad \pi_{c2b1} = \gamma_{c2nw} + \gamma_{c2\beta} \cdot \pi_{\beta b1}$$

Workers:
$$\pi_{c1\mu1} = -\Delta_c \cdot \left(\alpha - \frac{\theta}{1-\theta}\right) - \Delta_c \cdot \frac{\theta}{1-\theta} \cdot \pi_{\beta\mu1}, \qquad \pi_{c1b1} = -\Delta_c \cdot \left(\alpha - \frac{\theta}{1-\theta}\right) - \Delta_c \cdot \frac{\theta}{1-\theta} \cdot \pi_{\beta b1}$$

Investment:
$$\pi_{k\mu1} = -\Delta_k \cdot \left(\alpha - \frac{\theta}{1-\theta}\right) - \Delta_k \cdot \frac{\theta}{1-\theta} \cdot \pi_{\beta\mu1}, \qquad \pi_{kb1} = -\Delta_k \cdot \left(\alpha - \frac{\theta}{1-\theta}\right) - \Delta_k \cdot \frac{\theta}{1-\theta} \cdot \pi_{\beta b1}$$

B. Shocks to the Current Birthrate, b_t

Retirees:
$$\pi_{c2b} = \gamma_{c2\beta} \cdot \pi_{\beta b}$$

Workers:
$$\pi_{c1b} = [1 - \Delta_c \cdot (c^1/A)/y^1] \cdot [\gamma_{c2nw} - \pi_{Rk}/\eta + \gamma_p'/\eta] - \Delta_c \cdot \frac{\theta}{1-\theta} \cdot \pi_{\beta b} + (1 - \Delta_c \cdot (c^1/A)/y^1) \cdot \gamma_{c2\beta} \cdot \pi_{\beta b1}$$

Investment:
$$\pi_{kb} = -\Delta_k \cdot (c^1/A)/y^1 \cdot [\gamma_{c2nw} - \pi_{Rk}/\eta + \gamma_p/\eta] - \Delta_k \cdot \frac{\theta}{1-\theta} \cdot \pi_{\beta b} - \Delta_k \cdot (c^1/A)/y^1 \cdot \gamma_{c2\beta} \cdot \pi_{\beta b1}$$

C. Shocks to the Current Length of Life, ϕ_t^u and ϕ_{t-1}^e

Retirees:
$$\pi_{c2\theta u} = -\gamma_{c2b} + \gamma_{c2\beta} \cdot \pi_{\beta\theta u}, \qquad \pi_{c2\theta e1} = -\gamma_{c2b} + \gamma_{c2\beta} \cdot \pi_{\beta\theta e1}$$

Workers:
$$\pi_{c1\theta u} = -\Delta_c \cdot \frac{\theta}{1-\theta} - \Delta_c \cdot \frac{\theta}{1-\theta} \cdot \pi_{\beta\theta u}, \qquad \pi_{c1\theta e1} = -\Delta_c \cdot \frac{\theta}{1-\theta} - \Delta_c \cdot \frac{\theta}{1-\theta} \cdot \pi_{\beta\theta e1}$$

Investment:
$$\pi_{k\theta u} = -\Delta_k \cdot \frac{\theta}{1-\theta} - \Delta_k \cdot \frac{\theta}{1-\theta} \cdot \pi_{\beta\theta u}, \qquad \pi_{k\theta e1} = -\Delta_k \cdot \frac{\theta}{1-\theta} - \Delta_k \cdot \frac{\theta}{1-\theta} \cdot \pi_{\beta\theta e1}$$

D. Shocks to Current Life Expectancy, ϕ_t^e

Retirees $\qquad \pi_{c2\phi e} = \gamma_{c2\beta} \cdot \pi_{\beta\phi e}$

Workers $\qquad \pi_{c1\phi e} = -[1 - \Delta_c \cdot (c^1/A)/y^1] \cdot (\gamma_{c2\phi} - \gamma_{c2\beta} \cdot \pi_{\beta\phi e1}) - \Delta_c \cdot \dfrac{\theta}{1-\theta} \cdot \pi_{\beta\phi e}$

Investment $\qquad \pi_{k\phi e} = \Delta_k \cdot (c^1/A)/y^1 \cdot (\gamma_{c2\phi} - \gamma_{c2\beta} \cdot \pi_{\beta\phi e1}) - \Delta_k \cdot \dfrac{\theta}{1-\theta} \cdot \pi_{\beta\phi e}$

E. Changes in Lagged Capital and Productivity, k_{t-1} and a_t

Retirees $\qquad \pi_{c2k} = \gamma_{c2k} + \gamma_{c2\beta} \cdot \pi_{\beta k}$ $\qquad\qquad \pi_{c2a} = -\gamma_{c2k} + \gamma_{c2\beta} \cdot \pi_{\beta a}$

Workers $\qquad \pi_{c1k} = \Delta_c \cdot \alpha - \Delta_c \cdot \dfrac{\theta}{1-\theta} \cdot \pi_{\beta k}$ $\qquad \pi_{c1a} = \Delta_c \cdot \alpha - \Delta_c \cdot \dfrac{\theta}{1-\theta} \cdot \pi_{\beta a}$

Investment $\qquad \pi_{kk} = \Delta_k \cdot \alpha - \Delta_k \cdot \dfrac{\theta}{1-\theta} \cdot \pi_{\beta k}$ $\qquad \pi_{ka} = -\Delta_k \cdot \alpha - \Delta_k \cdot \dfrac{\theta}{1-\theta} \cdot \pi_{\beta a}$

Notes: The notation is as in Table 6.1 above. In addition, define

$$\gamma_{c2\beta} = (1 - \delta^*) \cdot \frac{\theta \cdot (1 - \alpha)}{\alpha + \theta \cdot (1 - \alpha)} > 0.$$

Table 6.3   **Alternative Policies in the Numerical Example**

A. Shocks to the Workforce, μ_{1t} and b_{t-1}

	Alternative Systems				
	DB (shock to μ_{1t} or b_{t-1})	DC (shock to μ_{1t} or b_{t-1})	Privatized (shock to μ_{1t} or b_{t-1})	Prefunded (shock to μ_{1t})	Prefunded (shock to b_{t-1})
Policy coefficient	0	1.0	N.A.	0	.5
Effect on:					
Retirees	0.436	0.667	0.667[a]	0.436[b]	0.551[c]
Workers	−0.131	−0.278	−0.278[a]	−0.131[b]	−0.204[c]
Investment	−0.235	−0.500	−0.500	−0.235	−0.368

B. Shocks to the Length of Life, ϕ_t^u and ϕ_{t-1}^e

	Alternative Systems				
	DB (shock to ϕ_t^u or ϕ_{t-1}^e)	DC (shock to ϕ_t^u or ϕ_{t-1}^e)	Privatized (shock to ϕ_t^u or ϕ_{t-1}^e)	Prefunded (shock to ϕ_t^u)	Prefunded (shock to ϕ_{t-1}^e)
Policy coefficient	0	−1.0	N.A.	0	−.5
Effect on:					
Retirees	−0.769	−1.0	−1.0[a]	−0.769[b]	−0.885[c]
Workers	−0.147	0.0	0.0[a]	−0.147[b]	−0.074[c]
Investment	−0.265	0.0	0.0	−0.265	−0.111

Note: The notation is as in tables 6.1–6.2. For defined benefits (DB), defined contributions (DC), and privatized social security, μ_{1t} and b_{t-1} have the same effects as ϕ_t^u and ϕ_{t-1}^e. For the conditionally prefunded system ("prefunded" above), the policy coefficients are generally in the range $\pi_{\beta b1} \in (0, +1)$ and $\pi_{\beta de1} \in (-1, 0)$. For the numerical example, I use +0.5 and −0.5, respectively. N.A. = not applicable.
[a] Equal to the DC case.
[b] Equal to the DB case.
[c] In between.

sure of workers to such shocks, as compared to the DB case. They also magnify the *positive* exposure of retirees. Table 6.2 (panel A) shows that this is true in general, whenever $\pi_{\beta\mu1} > 0$ and $\pi_{\beta b1} > 0$. In addition, $\pi_{\beta b1} > 0$ increases workers' instantaneous negative response to birthrate shocks ($\pi_{kb} < 0$ rises in absolute value; see table 6.2, panel B). By making the capital-labor ratio more volatile, $\pi_{\beta b1} > 0$ also exposes future generations to more risk. These observations reinforce the insights from table 6.1. Large cohorts are already demographically disadvantaged at fixed benefits (DB). Hence, a policy of giving them reduced benefits in order to stabilize tax rates is counterproductive.[27]

27. This verdict may raise questions about the welfare criterion. This is addressed below.

In the case of shocks to the current length of life, a system of defined contributions leaves the old more exposed and allocates less risk to the young than a DB system: in table 6.2 (panel C), if $\pi_{\beta\phi e1} < 0$ and/or $\pi_{\beta\phi u} < 0$, then $\pi_{c1\phi u}$, $\pi_{c1\phi e1}$, $\pi_{k\phi u}$, and $\pi_{k\phi e1}$ are all lower in absolute value, whereas $\pi_{c2\phi u}$ and $\pi_{c2\phi e1}$ are increased. With a DC system, length-of-life risk falls entirely on the old. The policy coefficient $\pi_{\beta\phi e1}$ also influences how period t voters respond to news about changes in the future length of life (ϕ_t^e shocks; see table 6.2, panel D). If workers anticipate reduced future benefits, they save more ($\pi_{\beta\phi e1} < 0$ raises $\pi_{k\phi e}$) and consume less ($\pi_{\beta\phi e1} < 0$ reduces $\pi_{c1\phi e}$).

Table 6.2 provides several additional insights. First, the government can influence the propagation of shocks through the capital-labor ratio (π_{kk}) by making benefits a function of k_{t-1} (setting $\pi_{\beta k} \neq 0$; see panel E). Second, the government can influence the incidence of productivity shocks by varying $\pi_{\beta a}$.[28] Third, note that, for $\pi_{\beta b} = \pi_{\beta\phi e} = 0$, only the workers bear the risk of "bad" news about birthrates and life expectancy (see panels B and D). By setting $\pi_{\beta b}$, $\pi_{\beta\phi e} \neq 0$, the government could spread such risks over young and old. This is not done under any of the policies discussed above.

Overall, table 6.3 provides a comparison of the main policy alternatives. Under DC and private savings systems, all length-of-life risk is carried by the old and none by the young. The DB and prefunded systems shift some of these risks to the young. Under DC and private savings systems, birthrate uncertainty and other shocks to the workforce have a positive effect on the old but a negative effect on the young. This negative comovement of worker and retiree consumption is reduced by the DB and prefunded systems, but, provided that $\theta/(1 - \theta) < \alpha$, it is not eliminated.

6.3 Missing Annuities and Accidental Bequests

This section examines the ramifications of missing annuities and accidental bequests. Without annuities, some shocks to old-age survival lead to accidental bequests (μ_2 shocks). In addition, the existence of accidental bequests affects the propagation of the shocks examined previously.

The macroeconomic dynamics of the log-linearized model without annuities are summarized in table 6.4. Recall that, in the basic model, ϕ shocks reduced retiree consumption while affecting worker consumption only through a change in taxes. In contrast, if savings are not annuitized, fewer unexpected deaths (higher μ_{2t}^u or μ_{2t-1}^e) have a direct negative effect

---

28. Here, $\pi_{\beta a} = 0$ holds for all the main policy alternatives (the DB, DC, and conditionally prefunded systems); i.e., their response to productivity shocks is essentially the same. One could consider policies that respond differently (e.g., a DB system promising fixed real benefits instead of a fixed replacement rate), but productivity risk has ramifications that are beyond the scope of this paper (see Bohn 1998, 1999a). Hence, I focus on policies with $\pi_{\beta a} = 0$ and just note that the government has additional degrees of freedom.

Table 6.4 Macroeconomic Dynamics without Annuities Markets

Effect on:	Elasticity Coefficients	Numerical Example
	A. Shocks to Retiree Survival without Annuities, μ_{2t}^u and μ_{2t-1}^e	
Retirees	$\pi_{c_2\mu_2 u} = \gamma_{c2\beta} \cdot \pi_{\beta\mu_2 e 1}, \quad \pi_{c_2\mu_2 e 1} = \gamma_{c2\beta} \cdot \pi_{\beta\mu_2 e 1},$ where $\gamma_{c2\beta} = (1 - \delta^*) \cdot \dfrac{\theta/\mu_2 \cdot (1-\alpha)}{\alpha + \theta/\mu_2 \cdot (1-\alpha)} > 0$	0
Workers	$\pi_{c_1\mu_2 u} = -\Delta_c \cdot \left[(1-q) \cdot (1 + \pi_{\beta\mu_2 u}) + q \cdot \dfrac{\mu_2}{1-\mu_2} \right] \cdot \dfrac{\theta}{1-\theta}, \quad \pi_{c_1\mu_2 e 1} = -\Delta_c \cdot \left[(1-q) \cdot (1 + \pi_{\beta\mu_2 e 1}) + q \cdot \dfrac{\mu_2}{1-\mu_2} \right] \cdot \dfrac{\theta}{1-\theta}$	−.147
Investment	$\pi_{k_1\mu_2 u} = -\Delta_k \cdot \left[(1-q) \cdot (1 + \pi_{\beta\mu_2 u}) + q \cdot \dfrac{\mu_2}{1-\mu_2} \right] \cdot \dfrac{\theta}{1-\theta}, \quad \pi_{k_1\mu_2 e 1} = -\Delta_k \cdot \left[(1-q) \cdot (1 + \pi_{\beta\mu_2 e 1}) + q \cdot \dfrac{\mu_2}{1-\mu_2} \right] \cdot \dfrac{\theta}{1-\theta}$	−.265
	B. Shocks to Future Retiree Survival without Annuities, μ_{2t}^e	
Retirees	$\mu_{c_2\mu_2 e} = \gamma_{c2\beta} \cdot \pi_{\beta\mu_2 e}$	0
Workers	$\pi_{c_1\mu_2 e} = -[1 - \Delta_c \cdot (c^1/A)/y^1] \cdot (1/\eta - \gamma_{c2\beta} \cdot \pi_{\beta\mu_2 e 1}) - \Delta_c^* \cdot \dfrac{\theta}{1-\theta} \cdot \pi_{\beta\mu_2 e}$	−.125
Investment	$\pi_{k_1\mu_2 e} = \Delta_k \cdot (c^1/A)/y^1 \cdot (1/\eta - \gamma_{c2\beta} \cdot \pi_{\beta\mu_2 e 1}) - \Delta_k^* \cdot \dfrac{\theta}{1-\theta} \cdot \pi_{\beta\mu_2 e}$	.375
	C. Shocks to the Current Workforce, μ_{1t} and b_{t-1}^a	
Retirees	$\pi_{c_2\mu_1} = \gamma_{c2nw} + \gamma_{c2\beta} \cdot \pi_{\beta\mu_1}, \quad \pi_{c2b1} = \gamma_{c2nw} + \gamma_{c2\beta} \cdot \pi_{\beta b1},$ where $\gamma_{c2nw} = (1 - \delta^*) \cdot \left[1 - \alpha - \dfrac{\theta/\mu_2 \cdot (1-\alpha)}{\alpha + \theta/\mu_2 \cdot (1-\alpha)} \right] > 0$	
Workers	$\pi_{c_1\mu_1} = -\Delta_c \cdot \left[(1-q) \cdot \alpha + q \cdot \pi_{Rk} - (1-q) \dfrac{\theta}{1-\theta} \right] - \Delta_c^* \cdot \dfrac{\theta}{1-\theta} \cdot \pi_{\beta\mu_1}$	

$$\pi_{c1b1} = -\Delta_c \cdot \left[(1-q) \cdot \alpha + q \cdot \pi_{Rk} - (1-q) \frac{\theta}{1-\theta} \right] - \Delta_c^* \cdot \frac{\theta}{1-\theta} \cdot \pi_{\beta b1}$$

Investment

$$\pi_{k\mu 1} = -\Delta_k \cdot \left[(1-q) \cdot \alpha + q \cdot \pi_{Rk} - (1-q) \frac{\theta}{1-\theta} \right] - \Delta_k^* \cdot \frac{\theta}{1-\theta} \cdot \pi_{\beta\mu 1},$$

$$\pi_{kb1} = -\Delta_k \cdot \left[(1-q) \cdot \alpha + q \cdot \pi_{Rk} - (1-q) \frac{\theta}{1-\theta} \right] - \Delta_k^* \cdot \frac{\theta}{1-\theta} \cdot \pi_{\beta b1}$$

D. Shocks to the Current Length of Life, ϕ_t^u and ϕ_{t-1}^e [a]

Retirees

$$\pi_{c2\theta u} = -\gamma_{c2b} + \gamma_{c2\beta} \cdot \pi_{\beta\theta u}, \quad \pi_{c2\theta e1} = -\gamma_{c2b} + \gamma_{c2\beta} \cdot \pi_{\beta b1}, \quad \text{where } \gamma_{c2b} = 1 - (1 - (1-\delta^*)) \cdot \frac{\theta/\mu_2 \cdot (1-\alpha)}{\alpha + \theta/\mu_2 \cdot (1-\alpha)} > 0$$

Workers

$$\pi_{c1\theta u} = -\Delta_c^* \cdot \frac{\theta}{1-\theta} \cdot (\pi_{\beta\theta u} + 1), \quad \pi_{c1\theta e1} = -\Delta_c^* \cdot \frac{\theta}{1-\theta} \cdot (\pi_{\beta\theta e1} + 1)$$

Investment

$$\pi_{k\theta u} = -\Delta_k^* \cdot \frac{\theta}{1-\theta} \cdot (\pi_{\beta\theta u} + 1), \quad \pi_{k\theta e1} = -\Delta_k^* \cdot \frac{\theta}{1-\theta} \cdot (\pi_{\beta\theta e1} + 1)$$

E. Shocks to the Current Birthrate, b_t [a]

Retirees

$$\pi_{c2b} = \gamma_{c2\beta} \cdot \pi_{\beta b}$$

Workers

$$\pi_{c1b} = [1 - \Delta_c \cdot (c^1/A)/y^1] \cdot (\gamma_{c2nw} - \pi_{Rk}/\eta + \gamma_\rho/\eta + \gamma_{c2\beta} \cdot \pi_{\beta b1}) - \Delta_c^* \cdot \frac{\theta}{1-\theta} \cdot \pi_{\beta b}$$

Investment

$$\pi_{kb} = -\Delta_k \cdot (c^1/A)/y^1 \cdot (\gamma_{c2nw} - \pi_{Rk}/\eta + \gamma_\rho/\eta + \gamma_{c2\beta} \cdot \pi_{\beta b1}) - \Delta_k^* \cdot \frac{\theta}{1-\theta} \cdot \pi_{\beta b}$$

(continued)

Table 6.4 (continued)

Effect on:	Elasticity Coefficients	Numerical Example
	F. Shocks to the Future Length of Life, ϕ_t^{ea}	
Retirees	$\pi_{c2\phi e} = \gamma_{c2\beta} \cdot \pi_{\beta\phi e}$	
Workers	$\pi_{c1\phi e} = -[1 - \Delta_c \cdot (c^1/A)/y^1] \cdot (\gamma_{c2b} - \gamma_{c2\beta} \cdot \pi_{\beta\phi e1}) - \Delta_c^* \cdot \dfrac{\theta}{1-\theta} \cdot \pi_{\beta\phi e}$	
Investment	$\pi_{k\phi e} = \Delta_k \cdot (c^1/A)/y^1 \cdot (\gamma_{c2b} - \gamma_{c2\beta} \cdot \pi_{\beta\phi e1}) - \Delta_k^* \cdot \dfrac{\theta}{1-\theta} \cdot \pi_{\beta\phi e}$	
	G. Changes in Lagged Capital and Productivity, k_{t-1} and a_t [a]	
Retirees	$\pi_{c2k} = \gamma_{c2k} + \gamma_{c2\beta} \cdot \pi_{\beta k}$, $\quad \pi_{c2a} = -\gamma_{c2k} + \gamma_{c2\beta} \cdot \pi_{\beta a}$	
Workers	$\pi_{c1k} = \Delta_c \cdot [[1-q] \cdot \alpha + q \cdot \pi_{Rk}] - \Delta_c^* \cdot \dfrac{\theta}{1-\theta} \cdot \pi_{\beta k}$, $\quad \pi_{c2a} = -\Delta_c \cdot [[1-q] \cdot \alpha + q \cdot \pi_{Rk}] - \Delta_c^* \cdot \dfrac{\theta}{1-\theta} \cdot \pi_{\beta a}$	
Investment	$\pi_{kk} = \Delta_k \cdot [[1-q] \cdot \alpha + q \cdot \pi_{Rk}] - \Delta_k^* \cdot \dfrac{\theta}{1-\theta} \cdot \pi_{\beta k}$, $\quad \pi_{ka} = -\Delta_k \cdot [[1-q] \cdot \alpha + q \cdot \pi_{Rk}] - \Delta_k^* \cdot \dfrac{\theta}{1-\theta} \cdot \pi_{\beta a}$	

Note: The notation is as in tables 6.1–6.2 above, except for the following symbols:

$q = Q^I/[w \cdot (1-\theta) + Q^I]$ = share of bequests in worker's income;

$\Delta_c^* = \Delta_c \cdot (1-q)$, $\Delta_k^* = \Delta_k \cdot (1-q)$.

[a] As in table 6.2 above, but with modified coefficients if $q \neq 0$ or $\mu_2 \neq 0$.

on the young because of reduced bequests, while the old are affected only through changes in benefits (see panel A). If benefits are held constant, the consumption of the young is further reduced because of higher taxes.

Table 6.4, panel A, also provides numerical values for the limiting case of $q \approx 0$ and a DB social security system. For $q \approx 0$ and DB, survival shocks affect the worker exactly like a length-of-life shock (see table 6.1, panel C, above). The key difference is that retirees are unaffected. Hence, for dealing with μ_2-type shocks, a movement toward defined contributions or privatization looks much more promising than it does for ϕ-type shocks.

Table 6.4, panel B, illustrates how an increase in the expected future probability of survival (μ_2^e) increases workers' incentives to save. Panels C–G show how accidental bequests modify the other policy coefficients as compared to table 6.2 above. The modifications are proportional to the ratio of accidental bequests to bequests plus wage income (q). If this ratio is small, as one might expect in practice, the previous results remain virtually unchanged. For this reason, no new illustrative values are provided.

6.4   Efficient Risk Sharing

If there is scope for risk sharing, what exactly should be done? This section derives a simple efficiency benchmark and explores its policy implications. In general, the set of efficient (ex ante Pareto-optimal) allocations can be obtained by maximizing a welfare function

$$(10) \qquad W = E\left\{ \sum_{t=-1}^{\infty} \Omega_{t-1} \cdot N_{t-1} \cdot U_t \right\}$$

with welfare weights $\Omega_{t-1} > 0$, subject to the feasibility constraints (1)–(4) and given K_0.[29] The efficiency conditions are

$$(11) \qquad \Lambda_t \cdot N_t^W = \Omega_{t-1} \cdot N_{t-1} \cdot \mu_{1t} \cdot \frac{dE_t U_t}{dc_t^1},$$

$$\Lambda_t \cdot N_t^R = \Omega_{t-2} \cdot N_{t-2} \cdot \mu_{1t-1} \cdot \mu_{2t} \cdot \frac{dU_{t-1}}{dc_t^2},$$

$$\Lambda_t = E_t[\Lambda_{t+1} \cdot R_{t+1}^k],$$

29. The definition of efficiency is nontrivial because one might instead consider a welfare function with state-contingent weights. In a model without a childhood period, Peled (1982) has shown that the market allocation without government is Pareto efficient if one interprets generation t individuals born in different states of nature as different individuals and applies state-contingent weights. With a childhood period, the market allocation is inefficient even with state-contingent weights. Moreover, Peled's definition is too weak here because it would rationalize any shift of risk from current to unborn generations as efficient (under some state-contingent welfare weights) and therefore make the policy analysis vacuous. Readers who object on philosophical grounds to the notion of unborn individuals may instead inter-

where Λ_t is the shadow value of the resource constraint (4). Equivalently,

(12a) $$\rho_1 \cdot (c_t^1)^{-\eta} = E_t[R_{t+1}^k \cdot \rho_2 \cdot (c_{t+1}^2)^{-\eta}],$$

(12b) $$\rho_1(b_t) \cdot (c_t^1)^{-\eta} = \frac{\Omega_{t-2}}{\Omega_{t-1}} \cdot \rho_2 \cdot (c_t^2)^{-\eta},$$

define the efficient linkages of consumption over time and across generations. Note that equation (12a) is identical to the individual optimality condition (7a) for generation t's savings with annuities. The fundamentally new equation is (12b). It links period t worker and retiree consumption, and it depends only on population growth and the welfare weights.

For risk-sharing issues, it is again useful to distinguish the economy's perfect-foresight path (obtained by setting all shocks to zero) from the stochastic fluctuation around this path. For the log deviations from the perfect-foresight path, equation (12b) implies

(13) $$\hat{c}_t^1 = \hat{c}_t^2 + \gamma_\rho/\eta \cdot \hat{b}_t.$$

This is a strong restriction on the comovements of worker and retiree consumption: in any efficient allocation, both generations' consumption must respond in equal proportions to *all* unexpected disturbances, except to the extent that parents' consumption needs vary with the number of children (b_t).

The key underlying assumption is CRRA utility, which assigns an equal relative risk aversion to both generations. For utility functions with age-dependent risk aversion, Bohn (1998) has shown that macroeconomic risks would be shared in inverse proportion to the relative risk aversions. The same would be true here, but age-dependent risk aversion would unnecessarily complicate the analysis. Age-dependent risk aversion would not, in any case, overturn the basic point that all risks should be shared across generations.

In addition to sharing risks between living generations, government policy has the ability to reallocate risks between current and future generations by imposing history-dependent policies. This is generally necessary to obtain a first-best allocation, and it typically involves making policies a function of the capital-labor ratio k_{t-1} (see Bohn 1998). For the analysis here, making β_t a function of k_{t-1} would be a distraction. Instead, I focus on the necessary efficiency condition (13) when comparing alternative social security systems. Its key implication for the elasticity coefficients is

---

pret the state-independent weights as an assumption of "distributional neutrality," meaning that we are looking for allocations in which the government does not arbitrarily value individuals born in one state of nature more highly than individuals with equal consumption born in another state.

that, for all shocks, the consumption coefficients for workers and retirees should be equal. The only exceptions are the b_t coefficients to the extent that expenses for children matter.

Applied to the different demographic shocks, the optimality condition (13) yields a set of optimal policy coefficients $\pi^*_{\beta z}$ that are displayed in table 6.5. For shocks to the actual workforce (μ_{1t}, b_{t-1}), the optimal policy coefficients $\pi^*_{\beta\mu1}$ and $\pi^*_{\beta b1}$ are clearly negative for reasonable α and θ values. This is true, not only for $\alpha > \theta/(1 - \theta)$, but even for higher θ values, provided that

$$(14) \qquad \alpha + (\gamma_{c2nw} + \Delta_c \cdot q \cdot \pi_{Rk})/\Delta^*_c > \theta/(1 - \theta).$$

Since the bracketed term is positive, this strengthens the previous observation that large cohorts are worse off than small cohorts even with PAYGO-DB. Intuitively, the bracketed term captures the effect of interest rate movements that favor small cohorts. In the numerical example, $\pi^*_{\beta\mu1}$ $= \pi^*_{\beta b1} = -1.5$ are far below zero. Applied to the current baby-boom/bust situation, this implies that benefits should be increased as the baby-boom

Table 6.5   Optimal Policy Responses to Demographic Shocks

Policy response to changes in the current workforce:

$$\pi^*_{\beta\mu1} = \pi^*_{\beta b1} = -\frac{\gamma_{c2nw} + \Delta_c \cdot q \cdot \pi_{Rk} + \Delta^*_c \cdot [\alpha - \theta/(1 - \theta)]}{\gamma_{c2\beta} + \Delta^*_c \cdot \theta/(1 - \theta)}$$

Policy response to changes in the current birthrate:

$$\pi^*_{\beta b} = \left[1 - \Delta_c \cdot \frac{(c^1/A)}{y^1}\right] \cdot \frac{\gamma_{c2nw} - \pi_{Rk}/\eta + \gamma_{c2\beta} \cdot \pi_{\beta b1}}{\gamma_{c2\beta} + \Delta^*_c \cdot \theta/(1 - \theta)} - \Delta_c \cdot \frac{(c^1/A)}{y^1} \cdot \frac{\gamma_p/\eta}{\gamma_{c2\beta} + \Delta^*_c \cdot \theta/(1 - \theta)}$$

Policy response to changes in the current length of life:

$$\pi^*_{\beta\phi u} = \pi^*_{\beta\phi e1} = \frac{\gamma_{c2\phi} - \Delta^*_c \cdot \theta/(1 - \theta)}{\gamma_{c2\beta} + \Delta^*_c \cdot \theta/(1 - \theta)}$$

Policy response to changes in current retiree survival without annuities:

$$\pi^*_{\beta\mu2u} = \pi^*_{\beta\mu2e1} = -\frac{\Delta_c \cdot [1 - q + q \cdot \mu_2/(1 - \mu_2)] \cdot \theta/(1 - \theta)}{\gamma_{c2\beta} + \Delta^*_c \cdot \theta/(1 - \theta)}$$

Policy response to changes in the future length of life:

$$\pi^*_{\beta\phi e} = -\left[1 - \Delta_c \cdot \frac{(c^1/A)}{y^1}\right] \cdot \frac{\gamma_{c2\phi} - \gamma_{c2\beta} \cdot \pi_{\beta\phi e1}}{\gamma_{c2\beta} + \Delta^*_c \cdot \theta/(1 - \theta)}$$

Policy response to changes in future retiree survival without annuities:

$$\pi^*_{\beta\mu2e} = -\left[1 - \Delta_c \cdot \frac{(c^1/A)}{y^1}\right] \cdot \frac{1/\eta - \gamma_{c2\beta} \cdot \pi_{\beta\mu2e1}}{\gamma_{c2\beta} + \Delta^*_c \cdot \theta/(1 - \theta)}$$

Note: The notation is as in tables 6.1–6.2 and 6.4. The asterisks denote efficient values.

cohort retires. This is contrary to most proposals in the current policy debate.

The optimal response to a current birthrate shock (b_t) is somewhat more complicated. In the formula for $\pi_{\beta b}^*$ in table 6.5, if $\gamma_{c2nw} - \pi_{Rk}/\eta > 0$, the positive income effect of higher future returns on capital exceeds the substitution effect and tends to increase worker consumption. Efficiency would call for this "windfall" to be shared with the old through higher benefits. On the other hand, if $\pi_{\beta b1}^* = \pi_{\beta b1}^* < 0$ takes its optimal negative value, worker income is reduced, which would call for a benefit reduction. The γ_ρ term reflects the cost of children. If workers have higher expenses for more children, a reduction in social security benefits would be efficient. The sum of these effects has an ambiguous sign.

In the numerical example, $\pi_{\beta b}^* = 0.212$ is positive if $\pi_{\beta b1} = 0$ (e.g., with DB), $\pi_{\beta b}^* = 0.441$ is even higher if $\pi_{\beta b1} = 1$ (e.g., with DC), but $\pi_{\beta b}^* = -0.131$ takes a negative value if $\pi_{\beta b1} = \pi_{\beta b1}^* = -1.5$ is set optimally. Intuitively, the lagged policy response $\pi_{\beta b1}$ matters because workers' period t decisions depend on how they expect to be treated by the government as retirees. If a rise in the birthrate signals no change in future benefits (with DB) or increased retirement benefits (with DC), workers expect to be very well off as retirees and increase their current consumption. The optimality condition (13) implies that the good fortune should be shared with current retirees. A reduced birthrate—the current U.S. scenario—would then call for an immediate benefit cut. If future benefits are set optimally, on the other hand, a rise in the birthrate signals a benefit cut, and workers will reduce their consumption. Then the optimal current policy response has the reverse sign.

In any case, efficiency calls for current retirees to share the effect of birthrate shocks. And, unless the baby boomers are confident that future policy makers will follow the advice of this paper (that $\pi_{\beta b1}^* < 0$) rather than the thrust of the current social security debate (moving toward $\pi_{\beta b1} > 0$), they are well advised to reduce current consumption and to save more.

Next, consider length-of-life shocks without effect on accidental bequests (ϕ_t^u, ϕ_{t-1}^e). Recall that, in a DB system, both generations' consumption falls in response to an increase in the length of life. The optimal policy response therefore depends on the relative effect. For reasonably small θ values, the old are more affected than the young (recall table 6.1, panel C, above). Then the benefits to the old should be increased in response to longer life expectancy, that is, $\pi_{\beta \phi u}^* = \pi_{\phi e1}^* > 0$. In the numerical example, $\pi_{\beta \phi u}^* = \pi_{\phi e1}^* = 1.647$ is indeed far above zero.

Without annuities, the results are different. With defined benefits, only the young would bear the cost of survival shocks $(\mu_{2t}^u, \mu_{2t-1}^e)$. A benefit reduction, $\pi_{\beta \mu 2u}^* = \pi_{\mu 2e1}^* < 0$, is therefore efficient. Provided that μ_2 and q are small enough that $\gamma_{c2\beta} > q \cdot \mu_2/(1 - \mu_2) \cdot \theta/(1 - \theta)$, the optimal policy is in the range $-1 < \pi_{\beta \mu 2u}^* = \pi_{\mu 2e1}^* < 0$, and efficiency therefore calls at most for a partial movement to DC. In the numerical example, one finds that $\pi^*_{\beta\mu2u} = \pi^*_{\mu2e1} = -0.389$.

Overall, if one asks the broad question of how social security should respond to lower mortality per se, the right answer is that it depends on the type of shock. If the type is unknown, the large positive π^* coefficient for ϕ shocks in the numerical example as compared to the small negative coefficient for μ_2 shocks suggests that there is no strong case for a benefit reduction.

Finally, for shocks to current life expectancy (ϕ^e_t and μ^e_{2t}), recall that both shocks reduce the consumption of the young without directly affecting the old (see table 6.1, panel D, and table 6.4, panel B). Hence, the optimal policy response is to reduce the benefits to the old, $\pi^*_{\beta\phi e} < 0$ and $\pi^*_{\beta\mu2e} < 0$.[30] Intuitively, increased life expectancy requires resources in the future so that the young need to save more. For the old to share the burden, current social security benefits should be reduced immediately. This conclusion applies regardless of the state of annuity markets.

In the current reform debate, many proposals call for a reduction in benefits as mortality declines, for example, by increasing the retirement age. The analysis here suggests that the efficiency of such benefit cuts depends importantly on their timing. Cuts are efficient if they are imposed quickly (at time t, $\pi^*_{\beta\phi e} < 0$) but not if they are imposed so late that they fall on the longer-lived cohort itself (at time $t + 1$, $\pi^*_{\beta\phi e1} > 0$). None of the systems discussed in the current reform debate is efficient in this sense, nor is the current policy debate moving in the direction of cutting benefits to current retirees.

6.5   Extensions and Empirical Issues

The magnitude of factor-price movements in response to demographic shocks was a key issue in the analysis presented above. Is the model consistent with the empirical evidence? Are there natural extensions of the model that would yield different results? To address these concerns, this section comments on the empirical evidence and on some extensions of the model.

6.5.1   Empirical Evidence

The most direct way to settle questions about the factor-price effects of demographic change would be to refer to empirical evidence—if convincing evidence were available. This is not the case, however. The main prob-

---

30. In the numerical example, one finds $\pi^*_{\beta\phi e} = -0.76$ if $\pi_{\beta\phi e1} = 0$ and $\pi^*_{\beta\phi e} = -1.14$ if $\pi_{\beta\phi e1} = \pi^*_{\beta\phi e1} = 1.647$. Without annuities, $\pi^*_{\beta\mu2e} = -0.057$ if $\pi_{\beta\mu2e1} = 0$ and $\pi^*_{\beta\mu2e} = -0.146$ if $\pi_{\beta\mu2e1} = \pi^*_{\beta\mu2e1} = -0.389$. The $\pi_{\beta\phi e1}$ and $\pi_{\beta\mu2e1}$ coefficients matter because workers take the expected future policy response to any shock to life expectancy into account when they decide about their consumption (as explained in the case of b_t shocks).

lem is that, for generational issues, a single observation takes twenty to thirty years of data. In terms of generational time units, we have only two to three observations for the U.S. economy with social security, perhaps four to five for countries like Germany. Even the idea of retirement—that it is normal for nondisabled adults to stop working just because of their age—is fairly novel. Hence, there are no time-series data of sufficient length and stationarity (without serious structural breaks) to allow credible statistical inferences.[31]

There is, however, some indirect evidence about the effect of demographic changes on wages. First, there is a large literature on cross-country growth that suggests a negative correlation between population growth (or fertility) and per capita income (notably Mankiw, Romer, and Weil 1992; see also Cutler et al. 1990). Assuming near-constant labor shares (Cobb-Douglas production), this suggests a negative correlation between population growth and wages.[32]

Second, there is a labor economics literature examining linkages between demographics and *relative* wages (e.g., Welch 1979; Berger 1985; Easterlin 1987; Murphy and Welch 1992; Macunovich 1998).[33] Easterlin (1987) and Macunovich (1998) focus almost exclusively on demographics and argue that the effects are large. Welch (1979) and Berger (1985) find significant negative effects of cohort size on cohort wages, although they disagree about persistence over a worker's career. Murphy and Welch (1992) argue that demographic variables are only a minor determinant of relative wages, but even they find nontrivial cohort effects.

To be conservative, I focus on Welch (1979) and Murphy and Welch (1992). Welch's (1979) elasticity estimates for the "persistent" effect of cohort size (narrowly defined as a five-year age window) on annual wage income are around -0.20, with some variation across education categories. Murphy and Welch's (1992, 324) simulations imply that a 20 percent increase in the number of young workers reduces their wages by 6–15 percent, suggesting an elasticity of *relative* wages in the range of from -0.30 to -0.75.

For comparison, the overlapping-generations model assumes an elasticity of wages with respect to the *aggregate* workforce of $-\alpha$ or about -0.33, a value well within the range of elasticities given above. Moreover, if capital owners have some ability to substitute labor across narrowly defined age cohorts, the elasticity of wages with respect to the aggregate

31. Poterba (1998) makes similar arguments.
32. There is some debate about the strength of this relation (see Barro and Sala-i-Martin 1995; and Temple 1998). While cross-sectional evidence is attractive to circumvent the lack of multigeneration time series, it also raises new concerns about causality and control variables. Hence, the evidence should be interpreted cautiously.
33. This literature should also be interpreted cautiously. Despite the richness of panel data, the data provide aggregate information about only one to two generations.

workforce should be at least as high as the relative-supply elasticities. Thus, the assumptions of the overlapping-generations model are not inconsistent with the labor economics evidence.

Finally, I should comment on the relation between demographics and the return on capital. The recent review by Poterba (1998) finds little evidence of a systematic relation. Poterba suggests that this may be due to the small number of generational degrees of freedom. Theoretical considerations suggest an additional rationalization: if old capital is a large share of the total return (if $[1 - \delta]/R^k$ is near one), then the elasticity of R^k with respect to the capital-labor ratio is small and may be difficult to detect empirically.[34] Thus, the inability to find an empirical link between demographics and stock returns is not inconsistent with the model.

6.5.2   CES Production

From a theoretical perspective, the magnitude of factor-price movements depends importantly on the elasticity of factor substitution. By assuming Cobb-Douglas technology, the analysis presented above implicitly assumes a unit elasticity. An elasticity of factor substitution above 1.0 will imply smaller factor-price changes than with Cobb-Douglas and, hence, a different allocation of risk. To examine the importance of this issue, this section replaces Cobb-Douglas with a constant elasticity of substitution (CES) production function.

For this section only, let output be produced with a CES technology, $Y_t = [\alpha_\varphi \cdot K_t^{1/(1-\varphi)} + (1 - \alpha_\varphi) \cdot (A_t \cdot N_t^W)^{1/(1-\varphi)}]^{1-\varphi}$, where φ is the elasticity of substitution between capital and labor, and $0 < \alpha_\varphi < 1$. Cobb-Douglas technology is covered as the limiting case $\varphi \to 1$. Leaving all other assumptions unchanged (and setting $\mu_2 = 1$ for simplicity), the economy is still a Markov process with unchanged state variables but with modified dynamics.

Table 6.6 summarizes the consumption and investment dynamics with CES production. The key difference from table 6.2 above is that the elasticities of the wage and the return on capital with respect to movements in the capital-labor ratio are scaled down by a factor φ.[35] In the young generation's response to birthrate shocks, α is replaced by α/φ, and, in π_{Rk}, $(1 - \alpha)/\varphi$ replaces $(1 - \alpha)$, where α is now the steady-state capital share.

The effect of birthrate and other workforce shocks on the fortunes of differently sized cohorts now depends on the relation between α/φ and

---

34. For annual data, Bohn (1999a) suggests $(1 - \delta)/R^k \approx 85$ percent so that $\pi_{Rk} \approx 0.10$. (In the numerical example, the role of δ was ignored for simplicity.) The same argument suggests that the transmission of demographics to the stock market may occur in part through variations in the value of old capital (say, if $1 - \delta$ is stochastic) and not only through the production function. This is an open question left for future research.

35. A variable factor share also complicates the calculation of the old generation's income and alters the propagation of shocks.

Table 6.6 Macroeconomic Dynamics with CES Production

Effect on:	Elasticity Coefficients
	A. Shocks to the Current Workforce, μ_{1t} and b_{t-1}
Retirees	$\pi_{c2\mu1} = \gamma_{c2w} + \gamma_{c2\beta} \cdot \pi_{\beta\mu1}$, $\quad \pi_{c2b1} = \gamma_{c2w} + \gamma_{c2\beta} \cdot \pi_{\beta b1}$
Workers	$\pi_{c1\mu1} = -\Delta_c \cdot \left(\dfrac{\alpha}{\varphi} - \dfrac{\theta}{1-\theta}\right) - \Delta_c \cdot \dfrac{\theta}{1-\theta} \cdot \pi_{\beta\mu1}$, $\quad \pi_{c1b1} = -\Delta_c \cdot \left(\dfrac{\alpha}{\varphi} - \dfrac{\theta}{1-\theta}\right) - \Delta_c \cdot \dfrac{\theta}{1-\theta} \cdot \pi_{\beta b1}$
Investment	$\pi_{k\mu1} = -\Delta_k \cdot \left(\dfrac{\alpha}{\varphi} - \dfrac{\theta}{1-\theta}\right) - \Delta_k \cdot \dfrac{\theta}{1-\theta} \cdot \pi_{\beta\mu1}$, $\quad \pi_{kb1} = -\Delta_k \cdot \left(\dfrac{\alpha}{\varphi} - \dfrac{\theta}{1-\theta}\right) - \Delta_k \cdot \dfrac{\theta}{1-\theta} \cdot \pi_{\beta b1}$
	B. Changes in Lagged Capital and Productivity; k_{t-1} and a_t
Retirees	$\pi_{c2k} = \gamma_{c2k} + \gamma_{c2\beta} \cdot \pi_{\beta k}$, $\quad \pi_{c2a} = -\gamma_{c2k} + \gamma_{c2\beta} \cdot \pi_{\beta a}$
Workers	$\pi_{c1k} = \Delta_c \cdot \alpha/\varphi - \Delta_c \cdot \dfrac{\theta}{1-\theta} \cdot \pi_{\beta k}$, $\quad \pi_{c1a} = -\Delta_c \cdot \alpha/\varphi - \Delta_c \cdot \dfrac{\theta}{1-\theta} \cdot \pi_{\beta a}$
Investment	$\pi_{kk} = \Delta_k \cdot \alpha/\varphi - \Delta_k \cdot \dfrac{\theta}{1-\theta} \cdot \pi_{\beta k}$, $\quad \pi_{ka} = -\Delta_k \cdot \alpha/\varphi - \Delta_k \cdot \dfrac{\theta}{1-\theta} \cdot \pi_{\beta a}$

Note: The notation is as in tables 6.1–6.2, except for the following symbols:

$$\alpha = \frac{\alpha_\varphi \cdot (k/an)^\varphi}{\alpha_\varphi \cdot (k/an)^\varphi + 1 - \alpha_\varphi} = \text{average capital share;}$$

$$\beta^* = \frac{\beta \cdot (w/A)/(1-\delta^*)}{(c^2/A)} = \text{share of old income that is wage indexed;}$$

$$\gamma_{c2k} = (1 - \delta^*) \cdot [\alpha + (1 - \alpha - \beta^*) \cdot (\varphi - 1)/\varphi] + \delta^*;$$

$$\gamma_{c2w} = (1 - \delta^*) \cdot \left[1 - \alpha - (1 - \alpha - \beta^*) \cdot (\varphi - 1)/\varphi - \frac{\theta \cdot (1 - \alpha)}{\alpha + \theta \cdot (1 - \alpha)}\right]; \text{ and}$$

$$\pi_{Rk} = (1 - (1 - \delta)/R^k) \cdot (1 - \alpha)/\varphi.$$

For the effect of shocks not listed here, the formulas in table 6.2 apply with the modified symbols defined here.

$\theta/(1 - \theta)$. Given a defined-benefit social security system, unexpected shocks to the labor force are beneficial to a small cohort if and only if

(15) $\alpha/\varphi > \theta/(1 - \theta)$.

For elasticity values $\varphi < 1$, this inequality is satisfied even more clearly than for Cobb-Douglas. To overturn (15), one would have to argue that the capital-labor elasticity is far above one. In the numerical example with $\theta = 15$ percent and $\alpha = 1/3$, one would need an elasticity above 1.88. The empirical production literature suggests, however, that the elasticity is probably below rather than above one (e.g., Lucas 1969). Hence, it is difficult to question (15) on the basis of production theory.

Outside the model, one might think of international capital and labor movements as factors that could weaken the link between U.S. factor supplies and factor prices. If one interprets $1/\varphi$ more broadly as parameterizing the magnitude of factor-price movements in response to demographic change, increased openness might be interpreted as an increased φ value. Feldstein and Horioka (1980) have documented, however, that international savings-investment linkages have historically been unimportant, justifying a closed-economy analysis.[36]

Thus, concerns that the Cobb-Douglas assumption might overemphasize factor-price movements are probably unwarranted. Based on production-function estimates, Cobb-Douglas might even understate the factor-price movements, which would give small cohorts an even better starting position.

6.5.3   Elastic Labor Supply

Elastic labor supply is another consideration that could change the effect of demographics. The most serious concern is that, if small cohorts supplied more labor, birthrate changes would have a reduced effect on the capital-labor ratio and on factor prices.

A complete model with endogenous labor supply would complicate the analysis too much to fit into this already long paper. Some results can be obtained quite easily, however. Assume DB social security and Cobb-Douglas technology. Then, at any level of per capita labor supply, a large cohort will face a lower after-tax wage than a smaller cohort if and only if the inequality $\alpha > \theta/(1 - \theta)$ is satisfied. Thus, large cohorts face a relatively reduced opportunity set. This shows that labor supply considerations cannot overturn the basic qualitative finding that large cohorts are demographically disadvantaged for $\alpha > \theta/(1 - \theta)$.

Quantitatively, the implications of a variable labor supply depend on a

---

36. Also, openness would presumably matter most if demographic change abroad were orthogonal to that in the United States. But many other countries are undergoing demographic transitions similar to that in the United States.

trade-off between income and substitution effects. The negative income effect of a low wage may induce a large cohort to work more, while the negative substitution effect would encourage taking leisure. If the substitution effect is weak, a variable labor supply might even magnify movements in the effective capital-labor ratio.

6.5.4   Time Aggregation

Factor-price changes and cohort welfare may also be affected by time aggregation. If one used a more elaborate model of the life cycle with multiple working-age periods, large and small cohorts might overlap in the labor force, leading to reduced fluctuations in the labor force and in the retiree-worker ratio. In addition, "middle-aged" workers might supply both capital and labor, which would reduce the welfare effect of factor-price changes.[37] Are such extensions likely to overturn the results obtained here?

A more disaggregate approach would clearly yield different quantitative implications, but it is doubtful that these modifications will overturn any important results. To see why, first consider labor supply. Suppose one started out with, say, cohorts defined by year of birth. Then the significance of being in a small or a large birth cohort depends on the persistence of birthrate shocks and on the substitutability of wages across birth cohorts. If workers of different ages are close substitutes, wage movements are small unless the aggregate labor force varies significantly. And, if shocks are temporary, they would have little effect on the labor force. The baby-boom/bust phenomena suggest, however, that demographic shocks have enough persistence to matter at generational frequencies. And the labor literature (see above) suggests that substitution across cohorts is not perfect.

To sidestep any controversy about relative wage effects, assume for the sake of argument that all workers are perfect substitutes.[38] If small and large cohorts overlap in the labor force, it is true that the magnitude of wage fluctuations would be less than in a crude model that abstracts from such overlap. However, the same overlap would also reduce the fluctuations in the PAYGO tax rate and by the same percentage. Provided that $\alpha > \theta/(1 - \theta)$, changes in the workforce still affect wages more than taxes. Thus, an overlap of large and small cohorts in the workforce is unlikely to affect the *relative* importance of fiscal versus factor-price effects.

Second, consider the issue of middle-aged workers receiving both capital and labor income. This issue is not about the size of factor-price changes but about their welfare effect. Members of a large cohort are less worse off than in the basic model if they receive some of the high capital

---

37. I thank Kevin Murphy, the discussant, for raising this issue. Murphy also raised the issue of retirees receiving labor income, but I doubt that this is quantitatively as significant.
38. Otherwise, even changes in narrowly defined cohorts would have factor-price effects.

incomes generated by their own large cohort size. Note, however, that demographically driven changes in the return to capital were only one of several "transmission mechanisms" in the analysis presented above. Smaller cohorts would be better off than large ones even if the return on capital were held constant. To make large cohorts better off, the demographic effects through the return to capital would have to outweigh the effects through the after-tax wage. Empirically, most of the gross return on aggregate capital on an annual basis is due to the value of old capital (see above). The "within-a-generation" elasticity of R^k with respect to the capital-labor ratio is therefore likely small. In addition, households tend to accumulate financial assets fairly late in their careers (Poterba 1998). Hence, the receipt of capital income by worker households is unlikely to overturn the results from the basic overlapping-generations model.

6.6 Conclusions

The paper examines demographic uncertainty in a neoclassical growth model with overlapping generations. I compare the allocation of risk implied by alternative social security policies to the ex ante efficient allocation. The policy answers depend significantly on how strongly factor prices respond to demographic change. For plausible tax rates and elasticities of factor substitution, small cohorts are actually better off than large cohorts even in a defined-benefit social security system. This is because small cohorts enjoy favorable wage and interest-rate movements. Benefit cuts and/or prefunding in response to an unexpected decline in the birthrate would be inefficient.

The efficient responses to changes in life expectancy depend significantly on the type of change. If individuals know that they will live longer, or if fair annuities are available to diversify the risk of unexpected deaths, a longer life expectancy should trigger an increase in retirement benefits to those who live longer but a benefit reduction to the previous cohort. Reduced benefits to those who expect to live longer are efficient only if increased old-age survival leads to reduced accidental bequests to the next generation.

Overall, the efficiency analysis yields policy conclusions that differ significantly from the proposals in the current reform debate. Notably, the efficient response to a baby boom is to increase the retirement benefits of the baby boomers, even at the cost of tax increases to the baby-bust generation, and the efficient response to news about increased future life expectancy is to cut benefits to current retirees.

With regard to birthrate shocks, I obtain conclusions that differ from the conventional wisdom because my analysis includes endogenous factor-price movements. Factor-price effects are largely ignored in the current policy debate. The Social Security Administration, for example, makes long-run projections of future wages and interest rates by extrapolating past trends. The analysis presented in this paper suggests that the omission of endogenous factor-price movements is seriously misleading under empirically realistic parametric assumptions.

References

Abel, Andrew. 1998. The aggregate effects of including equities in the social security trust fund. University of Pennsylvania. Mimeo.

Altonji, Joseph, Fumio Hayashi, and Laurence Kotlikoff. 1996. Risk sharing between and within families. *Econometrica* 64:261–94.

Barro, Robert, and Xavier Sala-i-Martin. 1995. *Economic growth.* New York: McGraw-Hill.

Berger, Mark. 1985. The effect of cohort size on earnings growth: A reexamination of the evidence. *Journal of Political Economy* 93:561–73.

Bohn, Henning. 1997. Social security reform and financial markets. In *Social security reform: Links to savings, investment, and growth,* ed. Steven Sass and Robert Triest. Boston: Federal Reserve Bank of Boston.

———. 1998. Risk sharing in a stochastic overlapping generations economy. University of California, Santa Barbara. Mimeo.

———. 1999a. Should the social security trust fund hold equities? An intergenerational welfare analysis. *Review of Economic Dynamics* 2:666–97.

———. 1999b. Will social security and medicare remain viable as the U.S. population is aging? *Carnegie-Rochester Conference Series on Public Policy* 50 (June): 1–53.

Congressional Budget Office. 1998. Social security privatization and the annuities market. Washington, D.C.: U.S. Government Printing Office.

Cutler, David, James Poterba, Louise Sheiner, and Lawrence Summers. 1990. An aging society: Opportunity or challenge? *Brookings Papers on Economic Activity,* no. 1:1–56.

Diamond, Peter. 1965. National debt in a neoclassical growth model. *American Economic Review* 55:1126–50.

Easterlin, Richard. 1987. *Birth and fortune: The impact of numbers of personal welfare.* 2d ed. Chicago: University of Chicago Press.

Feldstein, Martin, and Charles Horioka. 1980. Domestic savings and international capital flows. *Economic Journal* 90:314–29.

Lucas, Robert. 1969. Labor-capital substitution in U.S. manufacturing. In *The taxation of income from capital,* ed. Arnold Harberger and Martin Bailey. Washington, D.C.: Brookings.

Macunovich, Diane. 1998. Relative cohort size and inequality in the United States. *American Economic Review* 88:259–64.

Mankiw, Gregory, David Romer, and David Weil. 1992. A contribution to the empirics of economic growth. *Quarterly Journal of Economics* 107:407–37.

Murphy, Kevin, and Finis Welch. 1992. The structure of wages. *Quarterly Journal of Economics* 107:285–326.

Peled, Dan. 1982. Informational diversity over time and the optimality of monetary equilibria. *Journal of Economic Theory* 28:255–74.

Poterba, James. 1998. Population age structure and asset returns: An empirical investigation. NBER Working Paper no. 6774. Cambridge, Mass.: National Bureau of Economic Research.

Shiller, Robert. 1999. Social security and institutions for intergenerational, intra-generational, and international risk sharing. *Carnegie-Rochester Conference Series on Public Policy* 50 (June): 165–204.

Smetters, Kent. 1997. Investing the social security trust fund into equities: Unmasking the large hidden actuarial tax liabilities on future generations. Washington, D.C.: Congressional Budget Office. Mimeo.

Smith, Alasdair. 1982. Intergenerational transfers as social insurance. *Journal of Public Economics* 19:97–106.

Storesletten, Kjetil, Chris Telmer, and Amir Yaron. 1999. The risk-sharing implications of alternative social security arrangements. *Carnegie-Rochester Conference Series on Public Policy* 50 (June): 213–59.

Temple, Jonathan. 1998. The new growth evidence. Oxford University. Mimeo.

Welch, Finis. 1979. Effects of cohort size on earnings: The baby boom babies' financial bust. *Journal of Political Economy* 85:S65–S97.

Comment   Kevin M. Murphy

Henning Bohn's paper makes several important points that sometimes get lost in the debate on the effect of demographic changes on social insurance programs (like the impending retirement of the baby-boom cohorts in the United States). The most important of these points is that it is not the existence of pay-as-you-go social insurance programs that makes demographic changes important or of interest to economists. Demographic changes can have significant effects even without such programs or without government programs of any kind. Neither do the effects of such changes hinge critically on market failures. Changes in demographics, like changes in technology, represent changes in the fundamentals of the economy and as such have real effects on individual outcomes, like the realized levels of wages, interest rates, and consumption. While few would argue with this point, it is also missed or ignored in most analyses.

Bohn also analyzes a somewhat different aspect of risk than that addressed by many others looking at the risk of investment-based social insurance systems. The risk examined by Bohn is not the risk induced by the selection of an investment portfolio (although that may be one way to implement some of the contingent contracting that he advocates in the paper) but the risk induced by the demographic changes themselves. He begins by recognizing that, in a defined-benefit pay-as-you-go system (where benefits for those retired at date t are indexed to wages for workers at date t), small birth cohorts face an added fiscal burden in that they must pay higher social insurance tax rates to finance the benefits of a relatively larger retiree cohort. Such increases in the dependency ratio are

Kevin M. Murphy is the George Pratt Shultz Professor of Economics and Industrial Relations at the Graduate School of Business, University of Chicago, and a research associate of the National Bureau of Economic Research.

the source of much of the doom and gloom over the future of social security in the United States and similar programs in other countries. While Medicare suffers from this as well, other problems (like changes in the consumption of medical care) add to the rising burden there. However, this is not the whole story. While small cohorts are hurt by the social insurance burden, small cohorts may gain for other reasons. Small cohorts may earn higher wages as the labor-capital ratio falls during their working years and relatively high returns on investment as they save for retirement when capital stocks are relatively small owing to a decline in per capita life-cycle savings. Bohn's essential argument is that these other advantages from being in a small birth cohort may more than outweigh the disadvantages induced by a defined-benefit social insurance program.

I should say at this point that Bohn's analysis is significantly broader than I have laid out here. He examines not only fluctuations in birthrates but also fluctuations in technology and changes in both pre- and postretirement life expectancy as well as the effects of alternative annuity market structures. But the essential message is similar: Before we think about how such changes affect our social insurance system, we should examine what broader changes they induce through the market itself. I think that this is indeed an important message.

Bohn presents his analysis using an overlapping-generations model with three generations: children, workers, and retirees. The basic policy role induced in the model is one of ex ante insurance (and to a lesser extent an effort to overcome inefficiencies in the private insurance market). The basic idea is that ex ante contracting between generations can spread the risk of demographic and other shocks and improve expected utility for all generations. Viewed in this way, the social insurance system represents an opportunity for intertemporal risk sharing across generations and is not necessarily a source of additional risk. Our goal, then, he argues, should be to set up a system that counterbalances the risk inherent in the market outcomes. Of course, if private individuals could engage in such trading through trading securities or other assets that embed such risks, then such an undertaking would not be necessary. I think that he should do more on this dimension to convince us that such private mechanisms are not available since that is a key aspect of his analysis.

For now, I continue to work within his framework and assume that neither the dynastic family nor private markets can address these issues. Under these conditions, the essential question is to determine what kind of generation-specific risks are induced by the private market solution. As I mentioned above, Bohn's analysis is based on an extended two-generation overlapping-generations model with the usual model of a working period and a retirement period augmented by a period of childhood, which serves to give the economy advance warning about the size of the coming generation of workers. This formulation serves to generate significant risks. First, the stark separation between workers as the suppliers of labor and the earners of labor income and retirees as holders of capital and earners of capital income makes fluctuations in cohort size translate directly into fluctuations in factor supplies and fluctuations in factor prices translate directly into fluctuations in relative incomes. In a world in which differences in the ownership of capital and labor were less discrete, we would see smaller effects as cohort-size changes would be muted in terms of both how they affect factor supplies and how factor prices feed back on incomes. The incomplete nature of markets inherent in the overlapping-generations structure also limits the ability of private markets to achieve efficient allocations of risk.

To make a long story short, under this structure, the factor-price changes induced by birthrate and other changes more than offset the effects of a social insurance system the size of the U.S. social security and Medicare systems. This means that, from an intertemporal insurance perspective, even with defined benefits small cohorts may still be better off owing to the factor-price effects. Switching to a defined-contribution pay-as-you-go system (where we cut benefits rather than raise taxes as the baby boom retires) would only make the insurance worse. I think that this analysis adds a different perspective than most of us have taken on this issue.

But should we believe it? That to me is a tougher question. First, while I follow Bohn's analysis, I am not sure that such factor-price effects are as large as the model makes out. If we augment the model to have the working-age population supply capital (i.e., we have more than just life-cycle savings) or to allow for outside sources of capital or trade in labor-intensive and capital-intensive goods, then such factor-price effects of cohort size will be reduced. The effects of changing the assumptions can be significant. For example, if over the working life individuals supply 1 unit of labor and 0.5 units of capital and the reverse is true at retirement, then the effects of cohort-size changes are cut by almost 90 percent compared to the case where the young provide 1.5 units of labor and the old provide 1.5 units of capital. This happens since *both* the effects of cohort size on factor supplies and the effects of factor supplies on relative incomes are cut by two-thirds. Hence, it would seem to me that that stark contrast induced by the overlapping-generations structure works to make these effects large. In addition, the overlapping-generations structure limits the ability of private markets to provide such insurance relative to a dynastic family approach or some other framework with effectively longer-lived agents. It need not be that generations are perfectly linked through altruism since I could set up contracts that lead to mutual gains to trade between my descendants and those alive today or the descendants of others with even modest amounts of altruism.

Second, as someone who has looked at the data to try to find the empirical effects of cohort size on wages, I will say that the effects that I have seen are not overwhelming. Whether they are big enough to offset the anticipated social insurance effects is unclear. Indeed, I think that we always tend to underestimate the degree of substitutability that will occur, particularly for such long-run changes. Whether it is through the factor-price equalization of trade, induced technological progress, the effects described above, or other forces, I think that the structure that Bohn lays out is likely to overstate the actual factor-price effects. As a result, I think that we need to examine a wider class of models to see how well this result generalizes to other market and production structures. While Bohn's work provides us with an important data point in this regard, I think that we need to examine things more closely.

Finally, I would like to say that I am not sure that intertemporal insurance is the most important aspect of designing a social insurance system. The taxes used to finance such systems induce significant excess burden, and the benefits structures significantly distort retirement incentives. In my opinion, these effects are likely to be more important than the insurance effects of improved intergenerational insurance. Indeed, the convex nature of the excess burden provides a strong rationale against raising the tax rate in response to having a large retirement-age cohort and toward cutting benefits. It would really help in this regard if the paper provided some estimates of the magnitude of the gains associated with the improvement in insurance that could be compared to the estimates of the deadweight burden from taxation.

Discussion Summary

David Backus noted a caveat in the paper. The capital-labor ratio might behave differently in open economies than in closed economies. In particular, international capital flows could change some of the predictions of the model that are driven by factor-price movements induced by the dynamics of the capital-labor ratio.

Andrew Samwick concurred with Backus's comment.

Stephen Ross noted that the model treats population growth as exogenous. It might be important for analyzing the issues discussed in the paper to acknowledge that population growth is endogenous. Furthermore, he observed that Bohn does not embrace the Ricardian view but instead considered the other extreme, namely, a Rawlsian perspective where one attaches substantial weight to generations to be born in the remote future.

Zvi Bodie stated first that he liked the paper because he believes that it frames the issues in the right way. The actual techniques used are of course debatable. In this context, Bodie noted that, although an abstract neoclassical model looking behind the veil of institutions has many advantages, it is not useful for the study of the optimal institutional mechanism needed for the implementation of the efficient risk-sharing arrangement derived by Bohn. This is nevertheless an important question, studied, for instance, by Martin Feldstein and Andrew Samwick (1998). Finally, Bodie noted that he is not convinced that the current social security system is, or is perceived to be, a true defined-benefit system. It is perhaps better described as a defined-contribution plan.

James Poterba remarked that there is substantial disagreement on the relation between population size, age structure, and factor prices. For instance, larger cohorts may generate more ideas and therefore spur productivity growth more quickly according to some versions of endogenous-growth theory. These issues are very complex and suggest at least that the Easterlin hypothesis has many plausible alternatives. Poterba concluded that Bohn should acknowledge these alternative hypotheses and discuss their implications for the results obtained in the paper.

Directly related to Poterba's comment, *Robert King* noted that it would be interesting to have some—even crude—evidence about the linkages between wages rates and population size. Economic historians have examined this, particularly with respect to immigration flows at various points in time, and have found that the effects are surprisingly small. Some additional discussion that would help one evaluate the magnitude of these effects would be useful.

With respect to the previous comments, *David Cutler* noted that some of the empirical evidence supports the predictions of the model. He further noted that the paper does not consider uncertainty about productivity while at work. In particular, there is no uncertainty about the length of the period during which a young worker is able to work. Integrating this into the model is an important extension. Finally, Cutler remarked that it would be interesting to study which system is best at sharing different types of risks. One may want to consider hybrid systems with different risk-sharing rules, depending on the sort of risk to be insured.

Antonio Rangel noted that the Cobb-Douglas specification for the production function is crucial. In particular, it predicts perfect correlation between wages and interest rates and might therefore be responsible for the similarity between defined-contribution and prefunded (privatized) systems in terms of risk-sharing properties. He also remarked that the paper allows for saving only in the form of physical capital, not in the form of financial assets.

Amir Yaron noted that a defined-contribution system differs from a prefunded system once one considers heterogeneity and liquidity constraints. He also commented that the paper compares steady states and thereby ignores what happens along transition paths. Finally, Yaron wondered what happened to accidental bequests in the model.

Andrew Abel suggested enriching the model by allowing for labor supply elasticity. He argued that an endogenous labor supply is important to consider in a model where the size of the workforce matters so much. First, the fact that retirees do not share in demographic risk would be tempered by this extension. Second, the factor-price movements predicted in the paper would also be smaller when labor is supplied elastically. Finally, labor supply elasticity would endogenize the length of the working life along the lines suggested by Cutler.

Richard Zeckhauser noted that, since the paper is theoretical, its results should not depend on empirical measures. The results should instead be presented in their most general form. With respect to possible empirical exercises to test some of the model's predictions, he cautioned against the use of cross-sectional data: different countries have different social security arrangements, and this might obscure the empirical analysis.

Henning Bohn responded to these comments as follows. First, with respect to the labor supply elasticity, he noted that there would be a substitution and an income effect. It seems that this extension would preserve the main results of the paper, at least for plausible parameter values. In particular, he remarked that the prediction involving the condition on the sign of $\alpha - \theta/(1 - \theta)$ would still obtain. The length of the working life, suggested by Cutler, however, is another issue. This modification of the model could potentially change some of the results. With respect to the comments of Backus and Samwick on the importance of the closed-economy assumption for the factor-price movements derived, Bohn responded that international capital flows would not be sufficiently strong to overturn the results, unless the Feldstein-Horioka puzzle disappears altogether.

Bohn agreed that the Cobb-Douglas assumption was important for the finding that defined-contribution and prefunded systems have identical risk-sharing properties. He added that a paper by Mankiw, Romer, and Weil (1992) shows that the Cobb-Douglas assumption is not rejected by the data. Also, the paper considers an extension to a constant elasticity of substitution production function and shows that, unless the elasticity of factor substitution is above unity, the factor-price movements and other predictions still obtain. Finally, he concluded that an empirical analysis of the link between cohort size and factor-price movements was indeed interesting but beyond the scope of this paper.

References

Feldstein, M., and A. Samwick. 1998. The transition path in privatizing social security. In *Privatizing social security,* ed. M. Feldstein. Chicago: University of Chicago Press.

Mankiw, G., D. Romer, and D. Weil. 1992. A contribution to the empirics of economic growth. *Quarterly Journal of Economics* 107:285–326.

7

The Risk of Social Security Benefit-Rule Changes
Some International Evidence

John McHale

Issues of risk are, understandably, receiving a lot of attention in the debate over the relative merits of investment-based (IB) and pay-as-you-go (PAYGO) social security systems. The risks to retirement income associated with IB systems are well known and at least partly offset the attractiveness of their higher expected returns relative to a PAYGO system.[1] Yet PAYGO systems are not free from risk either. An important source of risk associated with these more traditional social security systems is commonly referred to as *political risk*—defined here to be the risk that benefit rules will be changed through the political process before or during one's retirement, thereby changing the value of retirement benefits. For the United States, evidence that people perceive such a risk comes from opinion surveys that show low confidence in the ability of social security to pay the benefits due under current rules, although those surveyed do expect to receive some benefits (see Reno and Friedland 1997).[2] It is also interesting to note how the reform debate has been framed in terms of "saving social security," especially after President Clinton's 1998 State of the Union address, which had saving the program as its centerpiece. In part, this is an attempt to make use of the risks people perceive in terms of the sustainability of current rules to spur reform.

Under the social security benefit rules for current retirees, the share of state-funded pension expenditures in GDP is set to rise as populations in

John McHale is associate professor of economics at Harvard University.

1. For different perspectives on how risk affects the attractiveness of IB systems, see Geanakoplos, Mitchell, and Zeldes (1998) and Feldstein and Ranguelova (1998).

2. Interestingly, although respondents claimed to have little confidence in social security, they still expressed strong support for the program.

the major industrial economies become older.[3] Population aging is most pronounced for Germany and Italy, where it is projected that there will be one person over sixty-five for every two people of working age by 2030, compared to roughly one for four at present. If current high levels of pension generosity are maintained, old-age cash benefits must grow to account for almost one-quarter of GDP in both countries.[4] In the other G7 countries, where projected aging is not as pronounced and/or current pension benefits are less generous, projected GDP shares are lower, although the increases are still considerable in some cases. These projections of more costly state pension programs have led to concerns about increased labor market distortions (including higher unemployment), inadequate national saving, and declining returns on contributions for future generations of workers. Another possibility, however, is that greater costliness under current rules will lead to changes to those rules and, unless replacement provision is made, inadequate retirement incomes for current workers. Indeed, rule changes that reduce future benefits are not just something that might happen in the future. A number of countries, including Germany and Italy, have already responded by legislating downward adjustments to future benefit generosity.

While reasonably easy to describe, political risk of this kind is hard to quantify. The problem is similar to the problem of estimating credit (or default) risk on fixed-income assets; history is a poor guide to the probabilities and sizes of infrequent discrete adjustments. Nonetheless, given the importance of political risk to economic comparisons of risky retirement-income systems *and* to an understanding of the political economy of reform, it is important to have at least a sense of what these risks are.[5]

This paper takes a small step in assessing political risk. To see what can be learned about the effect on future benefits of the type of benefit reforms that have been pursued in recent years, I examine redefinitions of PAYGO benefit rules in the G7 countries from the mid-1980s through the mid-1990s. Until recent decades, rule changes tended to make systems more

3. Population aging will become pronounced after about 2010 because of the retirement of the post–World War II baby-boom generation and the fall in fertility rates in recent decades. Populations are also aging because of increased longevity.

4. *Generosity* is defined here as the ratio of the average benefit per elderly person to GDP per working-age person. I elaborate on this in sec. 7.1 below.

5. A common measure of the return (or money's worth) on PAYGO contributions is the ratio of the present discounted value of benefits to the present discounted value of contributions (see Geanakoplos, Mitchell, and Zeldes 1998). From the perspective of a worker at a particular point in time, there are a number of factors that make this return uncertain. The worker does not know with certainty his or her subsequent earnings profile, date of retirement, tax rates, length of life, rules for defining benefits, and so on. For this paper, I concentrate on the numerator of this return measure—the present discounted value of the stream of benefits. Moreover, to focus on the effects of changes in benefit rules, I assume fixed expectations for the earnings profile, retirement date, and length of life. The extent of this political risk depends, then, on the effect of various discrete rule changes on the stream of benefits and the probabilities of those changes.

generous rather than less. This was possible because favorable demographics (as baby-boom generations entered the labor force) and the immaturity of earnings-related pension systems made obligations under existing rules easily affordable.[6] Now that rapid population aging is on the horizon and most systems are mature, reform efforts are aimed at curtailing program costs. Recent rule changes have included increases in retirement ages (especially for women), changing the way postretirement benefits are indexed, and increasing the number of years of earnings included in the calculation of the initial benefit.[7] To gauge the effect of these reforms, my approach is to estimate the *change* in the present discounted value of the benefits an "average" household can expect to receive—or gross social security wealth (SSW)—as a result of a reform.

The results from this small sample show that benefit-rule changes that substantially reduce SSW are not unusual responses to projections of sharply rising costs fifteen to thirty years into the future. In some cases, the reforms do reduce the SSW of workers who are already at retirement age, although the sizes of the reductions are typically small. More often, however, the reforms are phased in so that their main burden does not fall on the currently retired or those close to retirement. Young and middle-aged workers appear to be willing to accept large reductions in their gross social security wealth while protecting the currently old. Assuming that the reforms are fully phased in by the time the worker retires, reductions in SSW of between one-quarter and one-third have not been uncommon. For middle-aged workers, this almost certainly means a loss of net social security wealth as well since they are unlikely to benefit to a great extent from resulting lower contribution rates given how the benefit cuts are phased in.[8] One possible explanation for this apparent sacrifice is that these workers see future political risk as related to the size of future contribution rates. By reducing the burden on future generations of workers through legislated future benefit cuts (and/or prefunding through tax increases, as in the United States), it might be that they hope to stem even more draconian cuts later on.

These calculations show that governments have responded to projections of sharp increases in dependency rates by curbing future benefit promises. It is not clear, however, how much of the adjustment to the

6. Small numbers of people were eligible for full pensions, while the contributor pools were large. As a consequence, low tax rates could support quite generous state pensions.

7. In this paper, I concentrate on reforms to the benefits rules of PAYGO systems in the G7 countries. Other major reforms aimed at curbing future tax increases include efforts to prefund future benefit obligations (Canada, Japan, and the United States) and allowing workers to partially opt out of the state system into occupational and personal saving schemes (the United Kingdom).

8. *Net social security wealth* is defined as the difference between the present discounted value of expected benefits and the present discounted value of expected future social security taxes (see Feldstein 1974).

projected demographic trends has already been made and what further adjustments are still to come. A number of factors point to the likelihood of significant further cuts. First, even with the recent reforms, the costs of state pension systems are still projected to rise steeply in most countries. Second, governments have proved willing and able to curb future benefit promises when they threaten to become too costly—which is probably the main message of this paper. And, third, proposals for additional reforms are being formulated and debated in most countries.[9]

The paper is organized as follows. Section 7.1 outlines how demographics and the maturing of benefit systems are creating financial problems in industrial country social security systems and documents that these looming strains have not significantly reduced the generosity of benefits for current beneficiaries. Section 7.2 then describes the mainly forward-looking reforms that have taken place in the 1980s and 1990s and estimates their impact on SSW. In section 7.3, I use a simple political economy model to help think about the puzzle of why self-interested current workers are willing to accept large cuts in their benefits while protecting the currently old. Section 7.4 concludes with some comments on how the response to population aging of cutting PAYGO benefits might affect the adequacy of retirement income in the future and on the possibility of replacing rather than simply reducing retirement income using a mandatory IB system.

7.1 Demographic Trends, Pension Generosity, and Fiscal Strains

It is well known that, under current benefit rules, spending on state pensions as a share of the economy will grow dramatically as populations age (see, e.g., OECD 1997; and Bosworth and Burtless 1998a). This will impose a heavy burden on future workers if they are willing to meet this higher cost, in part because of the expanded distortions brought about by the higher required taxes. If they are not willing to meet this tax burden, future retirees (i.e., current and future workers) are faced with the prospect of having inadequate retirement incomes. One might expect that this prospect would lead to a cut in the generosity of *current* benefits. Such a cut would free up tax revenues to use to prefund future benefits or at least provide a better return on the taxes that are paid (for any given future benefits).

Figure 7.1 shows that there has not been any significant scaling back in the generosity of benefits during the 1980s and 1990s. The figure uses the fact that the cost rate for state pensions (i.e., the state pension expenditure-GDP ratio) can be decomposed into the product of the elderly depen-

---

9. When assessing the overall risk of future benefit-rule changes, we must also keep in mind that, while we are sure that dependency rates will increase sharply over the next thirty years, there is uncertainty about what the exact dependency rates will be.

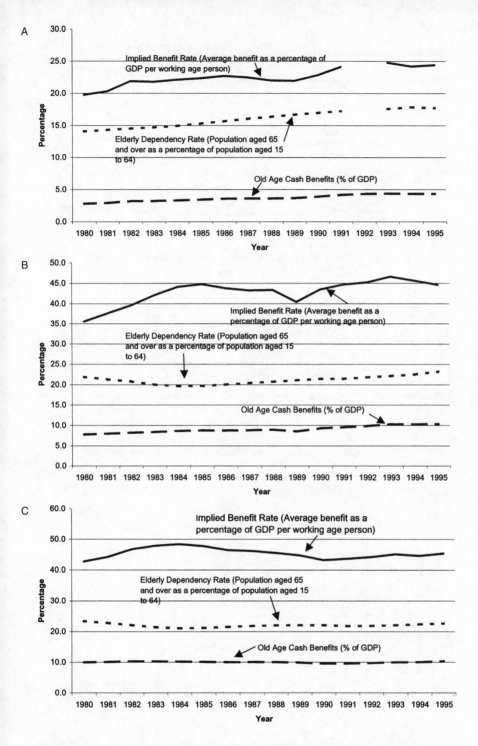

Fig. 7.1   Old-age cash benefits, OECD expenditure (SOCX) and demographic
data: *A*, Canada; *B*, France; *C*, Germany; *D*, Italy; *E*, Japan; *F*, United Kingdom;
G, United States

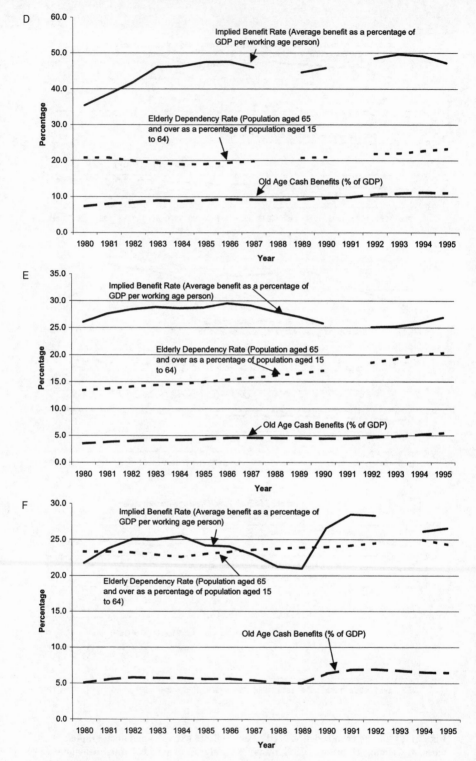

Fig. 7.1   (cont.)

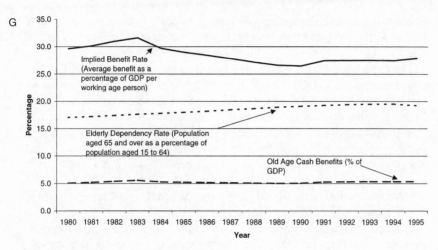

Fig. 7.1   (cont.)

dency rate and the benefit rate. The elderly dependency rate that is used is the ratio of the population age sixty-five or older to the population between age fifteen and age sixty-four. And the *implied* benefit rate is, then, the ratio of the benefit per elderly person to GDP per working-age person:

$$(1) \qquad \frac{\text{expenditure}}{\text{GDP}} = \frac{\text{elderly population}}{\text{working-age population}}$$

$$\times \frac{\text{expenditure/elderly population}}{\text{GDP/working-age population}}$$

$$= \text{dependency rate} \times \text{benefit rate}.$$

Care must be taken in interpreting the benefit rate as a measure of generosity. The denominator in the average benefit-expenditure calculation is the number of elderly (defined as those sixty-five and over), not the number of retirees. Of course, people younger than sixty-five can be retired and receiving benefits, and not all those over sixty-five are retired. This broad generosity measure has the advantage, however, that it captures both the ease of eligibility for benefits (including the ability to access benefits at younger ages) and the average level of benefits paid to those who are actually retired. To see this, note that the broad generosity measure can be decomposed as

$$(2) \quad \text{benefit rate} = \frac{\text{expenditure/elderly population}}{\text{GDP/working-age population}}$$

$$= \frac{\text{retirees}}{\text{elderly population}} \times \frac{\text{expenditure/retirees}}{\text{GDP/working-age population}}.$$

Other things equal, the system will tend to become more generous if there is a trend toward early retirement and/or if the benefits paid to the retired rise relative to income per working-age person.[10]

The expenditure data used in the calculations are from the OECD Social Expenditure (SOCX) database and include all public old-age cash benefits. Survivor benefits are not included for these calculations, although I consider them briefly below. For the United States, to take an example, this comprehensive measure includes retirement benefits paid by the social security and the public employee retirement systems, means-tested benefits paid under supplemental security income (SSI), and benefits paid through a number of smaller programs.[11]

Over this period, the implied generosity of benefits has been in a range of 20–25 percent in Canada, Japan, and the United States, a bit more than this in the United Kingdom, and in the higher range of 35–50 percent in France, Germany, and Italy. The most generous benefits in this sample were recorded in Italy in 1993 at almost 50 percent. The least generous were in Canada in 1980 at just less than 20 percent. Generosity in Canada, France, and Italy has risen over the period (in the latter two quite sharply), has been reasonably stable in Germany and Japan, and has fallen in the United States. Generosity ended up higher in the United Kingdom, following an increase in the implied benefit rate between 1988 and 1991.[12]

The combination of generosity and demographics led the expenditure-GDP ratio to drift upward or remain stable in all countries. The real action, however, is still to come as postwar baby boomers begin to retire. Table 7.1 shows what projected increases in elderly dependency rates

10. Gruber and Wise (1998) document a strong trend toward early retirement in the industrialized economies.

11. These expenditures are only part of the state expenditures that are set to rise as populations age. Another important category of spending that is positively related to the elderly dependency rate is medical care. Kornai and McHale (2000) present time-series and cross-sectional evidence that the total health spending per person is positively related to the elderly dependency rate with an elasticity of between 0.1 and 0.2. They also report regressions that show that the share of total health spending undertaken by the public sector is positively related to the elderly dependency rate. A 1 percentage point increase in the elderly dependency rate is associated with roughly a 3 percentage point increase in the share of total spending undertaken by the public sector, although the size of the coefficient is sensitive to specification.

12. Given that benefit generosity is usually based on a comparison of benefits with wages rather than GDP per working-age person, it is helpful for getting an intuitive sense of the generosity involved to divide the benefit rate by the labor share of GDP. The result can be interpreted as the ratio of the benefit per elderly person to the wage per working-age person. I calculate this labor share as one minus the capital income share as reported in OECD (1998a). For 1995, the labor shares were 0.677 for Canada, 0.589 for France, 0.637 for Germany, 0.577 for Italy, 0.682 for Japan, 0.676 for the United Kingdom, and 0.638 for the United States. The implied benefit rates expressed as a percentage of wage income per working-age person were 36.7 percent for Canada, 75.7 percent for France, 71.3 percent for Germany, 81.8 percent for Italy, 39.4 percent for Japan, 39.3 percent for the United Kingdom, and 43.7 percent for the United States.

Table 7.1   **Total Public Expenditure on Old-Age Cash Benefits Assuming Benefit Rate (average benefit/GDP per working-age person) at 1995 Level— OECD Social Expenditure (SOCX) Database (all public programs)**

	1995	2000	2010	2020	2030
Canada:					
Dependency rate	17.7	18.2	20.4	28.4	39.1
Benefit rate	24.5	24.5	24.5	24.5	24.5
Expenditure-to-GDP ratio	4.3	4.5	5.0	6.9	9.6
France:					
Dependency rate	23.2	23.6	24.6	32.3	39.1
Benefit rate	44.6	44.6	44.6	44.6	44.6
Expenditure-to-GDP ratio	10.4	10.5	11.0	14.4	17.4
Germany:					
Dependency rate	22.7	23.8	30.3	35.4	49.2
Benefit rate	45.4	45.4	45.4	45.4	45.4
Expenditure-to-GDP ratio	10.3	10.8	13.8	16.1	22.3
Italy:					
Dependency rate	23.3	26.5	31.2	37.5	48.3
Benefit rate	47.2	47.2	47.2	47.2	47.2
Expenditure-to-GDP ratio	11.0	12.5	14.7	17.7	22.8
Japan:					
Dependency rate	20.4	24.3	33.0	43.0	44.5
Benefit rate	26.9	26.9	26.9	26.9	26.9
Expenditure-to-GDP ratio	5.5	6.5	8.9	11.6	12.0
United Kingdom:					
Dependency rate	24.3	24.4	25.8	31.2	38.7
Benefit rate	26.6	26.6	26.6	26.6	26.6
Expenditure-to-GDP ratio	6.5	6.5	6.9	8.3	10.3
United States I:[a]					
Dependency rate	19.2	19.0	20.4	27.6	36.8
Benefit rate	27.9	27.9	27.9	27.9	27.9
Expenditure-to-GDP ratio	5.4	5.3	5.7	7.7	10.3
United States II:[b]					
Dependency rate	19.2	18.7	19.1	24.8	31.9
Benefit rate (1995)	27.9	27.9	27.9	27.9	27.9
Expenditure-to-GDP ratio	5.4	5.2	5.3	6.9	8.9

Sources: OECD Social Expenditure (SOCX) database; OECD (1997); and Bosworth and Burtless (1998b).
Note: Expenditure-to-GDP ratio = [(dependency rate)(benefit rate)]/100.
[a] World Bank demographic projections.
[b] SSA demographic projections.

would imply for the cost of old-age benefits *if 1995 benefit rates were maintained.* (Table 7.2 shows how adding in survivor benefits changes these projections.) These mechanically projected trends in this cost rate are quite startling in some cases. At 1995 levels of generosity, old-age benefits account for close to a quarter of GDP in Germany and Italy. In France, given somewhat less pronounced aging, these pensions still account for

Table 7.2   Total Public Expenditure on Old-Age and Survivor Benefits Assuming Benefit Rate (average benefit/GDP per working-age person) at 1995 Level—OECD Social Expenditure (SOCX) Database (all public programs)

	1995	2000	2010	2020	2030
Canada:					
Dependency rate	17.7	18.2	20.4	28.4	39.1
Benefit rate	27.2	27.2	27.2	27.2	27.2
Expenditure-to-GDP ratio	4.8	5.0	5.6	7.7	10.6
France:					
Dependency rate	23.2	23.6	24.6	32.3	39.1
Benefit rate	52.6	52.6	52.6	52.6	52.6
Expenditure-to-GDP ratio	12.2	12.4	12.9	17.0	20.6
Germany:					
Dependency rate	22.7	23.8	30.3	35.4	49.2
Benefit rate	47.9	47.9	47.9	47.9	47.9
Expenditure-to-GDP ratio	10.9	11.4	14.5	17.0	23.6
Italy:					
Dependency rate	23.3	26.5	31.2	37.5	48.3
Benefit rate	58.7	58.7	58.7	58.7	58.7
Expenditure-to-GDP ratio	13.7	15.6	18.3	22.0	28.3
Japan:					
Dependency rate	20.4	24.3	33.0	43.0	44.5
Benefit rate	30.7	30.7	30.7	30.7	30.7
Expenditure-to-GDP ratio	6.3	7.5	10.1	13.2	13.7
United Kingdom:					
Dependency rate	24.3	24.4	25.8	31.2	38.7
Benefit rate	29.9	29.9	29.9	29.9	29.9
Expenditure-to-GDP ratio	7.3	7.3	7.7	9.3	11.6
United States I:[a]					
Dependency rate	19.2	19.0	20.4	27.6	36.8
Benefit rate	32.9	32.9	32.9	32.9	32.9
Expenditure-to-GDP ratio	6.3	6.2	6.7	9.1	12.1
United States II:[b]					
Dependency rate	19.2	18.7	19.1	24.8	31.9
Benefit rate (1995)	32.9	32.9	32.9	32.9	32.9
Expenditure-to-GDP ratio	6.3	6.2	6.3	8.2	10.5

Sources: OECD Social Expenditure (SOCX) database; OECD (1997); and Bosworth and Burtless (1998b).

Note: Expenditure-to-GDP ratio = [(dependency rate)(benefit rate)]/100.

[a] World Bank demographic projections.

[b] SSA demographic projections.

more than 17 percent of GDP. The shares in 2030 are considerably lower in the remaining four countries, primarily because they start with lower shares, although, even for these countries, there is close to a doubling of the share of the economy devoted to state pensions. Japan is an interesting case because the aging of its population leads the other countries but the

Table 7.3   **Pooled OLS Regression for State Pension Expenditure as a Share of GDP, OECD Countries, 1980–95**

Independent Variables	Dependent Variable = Log(Pension Expenditure/GDP)				
	(1)	(2)	(3)	(4)	(5)
Log(elderly dependency rate)	1.64	1.63	1.63	1.64	0.20
	(24.94)	(19.57)	(19.23)	(24.50)	(1.98)
Log(GDP per capita)		0.01	−0.06)		
		(0.08)	(−0.73)		
Log(urbanization rate)			0.11		
			(1.06)		
Log(female share of labor force)			0.22		
			(1.03)		
Time dummies				Yes	
Country dummies					Yes
Constant	−3.10	−3.14	−3.85	−3.16	1.07
Adjusted R^2	0.65	0.64	0.64	0.63	0.96
No. of observations	343	343	343	343	343

Note: t-statistics are given in parentheses.

severity of its problem is still notably less than the large continental European countries by 2030.[13]

These mechanical projections are based on the assumption that the cost rate rises at the same rate as the elderly dependency rate. To get a better sense of how the cost rate has varied with the dependency rate across the OECD over the recent past, I used a simple log-linear OLS regression using the SOCX data for a pooled sample of OECD countries for the period 1980–95. The basic regression equation is

$$(3) \quad \log\left(\frac{\exp}{\text{GDP}}\right)_{it} = \text{Constant} + \beta \log\left(\frac{\text{population} \geq 65}{15 \leq \text{population} \leq 64}\right).$$

The results are reported in table 7.3, and the implied relation between the elderly dependency rate and old-age cash benefits as a share of GDP is shown in figure 7.2. The coefficient on the demographic variable is highly significant in the regressions without country dummies.[14] The addition of other potential determinants of generosity—GDP per capita, the share of the population living in urban areas, and the share of women in the labor force—has little effect on the size or significance of the demographic vari-

13. OECD projections for Japan after 2030 indicate that the share of state pension expenditure continues to rise until 2050, reaching about 16 percent of GDP (OECD 1997). For the other G7 countries, the OECD projections show a leveling off or even a fall in this share after about 2040.

14. With country dummies, the coefficient is significant at the 5 percent level, but the size of the coefficient on the dependency-rate variable is much smaller.

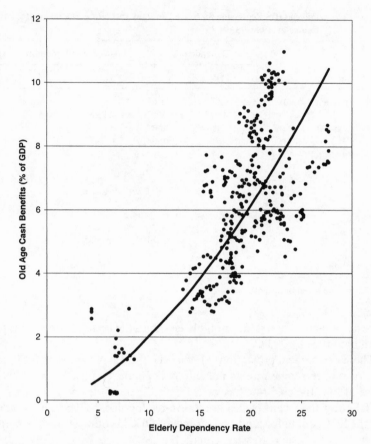

Fig. 7.2   Aging and public pension spending, OECD countries, 1980–95
Note: Regression line: Pension Exp./GDP = 0.045 (Dependency Rate)$^{1.64}$. See regression (1) in table 7.2.

able. The regressions (without country dummies) show that a 10 percent higher elderly dependency rate is associated with a more than 16 percent higher expenditure-GDP ratio. This nonlinear relation might be explained by the increased political influence of the elderly as they grow in numbers—an influence that is surely set to grow. However, given what this relation implies about the future share of total income going to state retirement benefits, it is hard to believe that such a relation can persist. For instance, if this relation were to hold for Italy, the share of old-age cash benefits alone would rise to 36 percent of GDP by 2030! Nonetheless, the regression results do suggest how difficult a task it will be to hold the growth in the expenditure share below the growth in the elderly dependency ratio.

The main focus so far has been on recent trends in state pension spend-

Table 7.4   **OECD Estimates of the Effect of Legislated Reforms—Percentage Change in Expenditure-to-GDP Ratios Relative to 1995 Ratio**

	% Change			
	2000	2010	2020	2030
Canada:				
Assuming constant 1995 benefit rate (from table 7.1)	2.6	14.9	60.0	120.3
OECD estimates given the effect of legislated reforms	−3.8	1.9	32.7	73.1
France:				
Assuming constant 1995 benefit rate (from table 7.1)	1.6	5.9	39.1	68.4
OECD estimates given the effect of legislated reforms	−7.5	−8.5	9.4	27.4
Germany:				
Assuming constant 1995 benefit rate (from table 7.1)	10.9	41.1	64.9	129.2
OECD estimates given the effect of legislated reforms	3.6	6.3	10.8	48.6
Italy:				
Assuming constant 1995 benefit rate (from table 7.1)	13.9	34.1	61.1	107.5
OECD estimates given the effect of legislated reforms	−5.3	−0.8	15.0	52.6
Japan:				
Assuming constant 1995 benefit rate (from table 7.1)	19.2	61.9	110.9	118.3
OECD estimates given the effect of legislated reforms	13.6	45.5	87.9	103.0
United Kingdom:				
Assuming constant 1995 benefit rate (from table 7.1)	0.3	6.1	28.3	59.1
OECD estimates given the effect of legislated reforms	0.0	15.6	13.3	22.2
United States:				
Assuming constant 1995 benefit rate (from table 7.1)	−1.2	6.1	43.5	91.4
OECD estimates given the effect of legislated reforms	2.4	9.8	26.8	61.0

Source: OECD (1997); and author's calculations.

Note: The measure of pension expenditure used in OECD (1997) for their estimates does not exactly match the measure based on all state old-age cash expenditures from the OECD Social Expenditure (SOCX) database used in table 7.1. Thus, the comparison of percentage changes with and without legislated reforms should be seen as indicative only. Both sets of estimates are based on the World Bank demographic projections.

ing and the future implications for this spending if current levels of generosity are maintained. The picture of limited reform hides the anticipated effect of already-legislated changes on future benefits and thereby on future generosity. In the next section, I attempt to estimate the effect of these reforms on social security wealth for certain stylized individuals and households. Before doing so, it is instructive to look at the projected aggregate implications of the legislated future changes. This is done in table 7.4. For each country, the first line shows the percentage change in the expenditure-GDP ratio for various years relative to the level of that ratio in 1995. The second line shows the OECD projections of the percentage change in the ratio *taking into account changes to benefit rules that have already been legislated.* Caution must be used in interpreting this comparison since the definitions of state pensions used do not coincide exactly (see the note to the table). The basic trend is clear, however: already-legislated changes appear to have significantly curbed the future expansion of state pensions as a share of the economy. What are these legislated changes? And what effect do they have on the benefits that people can expect to get when they retire? I provide tenative answers to these questions in the next section.

7.2   Recent Reforms and Their Effect on Social Security Wealth

7.2.1   Assumptions

My goal in this section is to get a sense of the magnitudes of changes to SSW that have resulted from recent reforms. Of course, a given reform will affect different people differently, depending on such factors as gender, age, dependents, place in the earnings distribution, age-earnings profile, and so on.

The approach that I adopt is to look at the effect on some "average" households. Characterizing these individuals requires a number of assumptions and thus should be seen only as suggestive of the effect of the reform on workers around the middle of the earnings distribution. I make six main assumptions:

1. The worker earns the average production wage (as defined by the OECD) at age forty-five.[15]

2. The worker's age-earnings profile is based on that estimated by Mincer (1974; see also Berndt 1991, chap. 5) using cross-sectional U.S. data.[16] Mincer's cross-sectional estimate is combined with assumption 1 and data on real earnings/wage growth from the 1995 IMF *International Financial Statistics* (or the 1995 World Bank *World Tables* for Italy) to produce a stylized age-earnings profile.[17] It is important to have some estimate of the age-earnings profile since different countries use different averaging procedures in assessing relevant lifetime earnings.[18]

3. Expected length of retirement (assuming retirement at the standard

---

15. The OECD (*Tax/Benefit Position of Production Workers*, 1995 or earlier editions) defines an *average production worker* (APW) as an adult full-time production worker in the manufacturing sector whose earnings are equal to the average earnings of such workers (male and female). The values for the wage of an APW are taken from various editions of the OECD publication *The Tax/Benefit Position of Production Workers*.

16. The assumed profiles are based on the following equation: ln earnings = $k + 0.081$ Age $- 00012$ Age^2. To determine the value of k, the earnings of an APW and an age equal to forty-five are substituted into the equation. Given this value of k, the profile is traced out by varying the age.

17. Real earnings growth is based on actual numbers up to 1996. From 1997 on, real earnings are assumed to grow at a rate of 1 percent per year for all countries.

18. The limitations of this assumption are obvious enough. First, age-earnings profiles differ between countries, depending, in part, on such institutional features as union density and deferred-compensation arrangements. Second, age-earnings profiles tend to be steeper for high than for low lifetime earners. Indeed, the hump-shaped profile that I assume tends to be more pronounced for low-income workers.

retirement age) is based on average life expectancy for workers of given ages at the age at the time of the reform and is taken from United Nations (1996) or OECD, (1998b).

4. The household is not entitled to any means-tested retirement benefits. This allows us to concentrate on universal flat-rate benefits and earnings-related benefits. Since I concentrate on workers earning the average production wage, this is probably realistic in most cases. Clearly, my estimates are a poor guide to the effect of reforms on low-income individuals, for whom means-tested benefits are likely to provide a significant portion of their retirement income.

5. The worker retires at the standard retirement age and has sufficient years of contributions to be eligible for full (flat and earnings-related) social security benefits. The worker is not affected by maximum or minimum limits for earnings-related pensions.

6. The real discount rate for discounting future benefits is 3 percent.

With these assumptions, I look at the effect of the reforms on the SSW of single men and women who are forty-five at the time of the reform. For the countries where a non-means-tested dependent spouse allowance is available, I also note the effect on a forty-five-year-old man with a dependent spouse. In addition, I look at the effect of the same reforms on men and women at their respective standard retirement ages, again assuming that these individuals earned the average production wage when aged forty-five.

7.2.2 Stylized Benefit Formulas and Their Use in SSW Calculations

Formulas for calculating retirement benefits differ significantly from country to country. Nonetheless, there are a number of common elements. I focus on three: the standard retirement age (R); the calculation of the benefit at the time of retirement; and the postretirement indexation of benefits. Of these, the calculation of the initial benefit is the least straightforward. Following the approach of OECD (1988), I model the calculation of the initial benefit as the sum of a flat-rate (lump-sum) benefit and an earnings-related component. The benchmark benefit equation at the initial retirement age is

$$(4) \qquad B(R) = B_f + \beta E^a,$$

where $B(R)$ is the benefit at retirement age R, B_f is the flat-rate benefit, β is the replacement rate, and E^a is assessed earnings.[19] E^a is some function

19. The concept of the replacement rate—i.e., the relevant earnings that are to be replaced—being used here is thus country specific. Since most countries under study use earnings over a significant portion of the worker's like in the calculation of assessed earnings, the replacement-rate concept is typically close to the fraction of lifetime earnings that are being replaced. The significant exception is Italy before the 1992 reform, where assessed earnings are based only on the earnings for the five years prior to retirement.

of the annual earnings of the various years of the individual's working life. There are two key elements to this calculation: first, the years that are included and, second, how the earnings are revalued on the basis of average earnings growth. Other things equal, the greater the weight given to peak earning years (roughly the worker's fifties given my assumed age-earnings profile), and the more completely earnings are revalued in line with national earnings growth (assuming that this is positive), the more generous is the benefit formula.

Once the initial benefit is set, I assume that future benefits can be calculated on the basis of a simple indexation rule. The benefit h years into retirement is given by

$$(5) \qquad B(R + h) = B(R) \prod_{t=R+1}^{R+h} [1 + i(t)],$$

where $i(t)$ is the real indexation factor for year t. When benefits are indexed to consumer prices, the benefit will be constant in real terms.[20] When benefits are indexed to nominal wages, the benefit will rise at the rate of real wage growth.[21]

My approach is to calculate gross social security wealth (SSW) for a given benefit formula viewed from a given age, T, during the worker's life. SSW is the present discounted value of implied future benefits, evaluated at the given point in the worker's life. Looked at from this age, SSW is affected by changes in the retirement age, the benefit formula, and the postretirement indexation of benefits (in addition, of course, to the discount rate for future cash flows and the expected years of retirement). This simplified case should give us an idea of the magnitude of wealth changes brought about by changes in the definition of benefit rules.

Letting H be the duration of retirement and d the discount rate, the equation for SSW at age T is

$$(6) \qquad \text{SSW}(T) = \sum_{h=0}^{H} \frac{B(R + h)}{(1 + d)^{R-T+h}}.$$

This formula calculates SSW on the basis of the simplification that the length of remaining life is known with certainty, where that length is set equal to the average remaining life for someone of age T. Of course, a person's remaining life is rarely known with certainty. In the appendix, I discuss how a certain life-span assumption can lead to a biased estimate of SSW when the length of remaining life is uncertain.

---

20. From the vantage point of a given age during the worker's life, the discounted real benefit falls with the length of the individual's retirement.

21. The real discounted benefit will rise (fall) with the length of the retirement if the real wage grows at a faster rate (slower rate) than the discount rate.

7.2.3   Recent Benefit-Formula Reforms in the G7 Countries and Their Effect on SSW

Over the last decade and a half or so, six of the seven major industrialized countries have significantly redefined their retirement-benefit formula. The exception is Canada. Among the six, the reforms that I consider are France (1993), Germany (1992), Italy (1992), Italy (1995), Japan (1994), the United Kingdom (1986), the United Kingdom (1994), and the United States (1983).[22] These reforms range from the relatively major (e.g., Italy [1992, 1995] and the United Kingdom [1994]) to the relatively minor (e.g., Japan [1993] and the United States [1983]).

The stylized benefit formulas prevailing prior to the reforms and used in the calculations are outlined in table 7.5. Table 7.6 then outlines the reforms. It is worth noting once again that I am focusing on only a subset of possible reforms, to wit, changes to the standard retirement age, the initial benefit formula for a worker earning the average wage with a full contribution record, and the postretirement indexation of benefits. For example, the effects of changes in eligibility conditions for a full pension, in the maximum or minimum pension, in the generosity of and eligibility for means-tested benefits, in early retirement benefits and conditions, in accrual rates for later retirements, and so on are not included.[23]

As can be seen from the first column of table 7.4, a number of countries (Germany, Italy, Japan [tier 1 benefits], the United Kingdom, and the United States) have raised their standard retirement age, although typically with a long lead time. There has also been a tendency for a convergence of the standard retirement ages for men and women (Germany, the United Kingdom, and Italy [Dini reforms]). Thus, we will see that women tend to lose more wealth from the reforms than identically situated men.

France, Italy (Amato reforms), and the United Kingdom have also significantly changed the way they assess "average earnings" for their earnings-related pensions. In its 1986 reform, the United Kingdom also reduced its replacement rate from 25 to 20 percent. The Dini reforms in Italy went even further, by moving from an average-earnings-based method for calculating benefits to a contribution-based method.[24] Beyond its effect on SSW, this reform has the potential of reducing labor market distortions by strengthening the link between contributions made and benefits received, thereby making contributions seem less like a tax. This

---

22. Since the mid-1980s, a number of other OECD countries have also reformed their defined-benefit retirement systems. Significant reforms were introduced in Australia (1992), Austria (1985, 1988, 1993), Greece (1990, 1992), Portugal (1993), and Sweden (1994).

23. The benefit streams are calculated before taxes. Since the 1983 U.S. reform included a major change in the tax treatment of benefits, I also estimate the effect on the stream of net of tax benefits for that reform.

24. Sweden is also moving toward such a notional defined-contribution system.

Table 7.5   Stylized Benefit Formulas Prior to Recent Reforms

	Retirement Age (men/women)	Tier 1, Flat-Rate Benefit	Tier 2, Assessed Earnings for Earnings-Related Pension	Tier 2, Replacement Rate[a]	Tier 2, Postretirement Indexation
France (1993)— *regime general*[b]	60/60	No universal flat-rate benefit (a means-tested benefit does exist)	10 highest years, revalued for nominal wage inflation	50%	Gross wage inflation
Germany (1992)	63/60	No universal flat-rate benefit (a means-tested benefit does exist)	Average earnings, revalued for nominal wage inflation	60% (based on 40 years of coverage at 1.5% per year)	Gross wage inflation
Italy (1992)— prior to Amato reforms	60/55	No universal flat-rate benefit (a means-tested benefit does exist)	Last 5 years of earnings; earnings for first 3 years indexed for inflation	Progressive formula; 80% of wage of APW	Gross wage inflation
Italy (1995)— prior to Dini reforms	65/60 (being phased in)	No universal flat-rate benefit (a means-tested benefit does exist)	Lifetime earnings (being phased in)	Progressive formula; 80% of wage of APW	Price inflation
Japan (1994)	60/60 (effective)[c]	National pension program—old-age basic pension: 737, 300 yen ($5,967.62) per year	Average lifetime earnings, revalued for nominal wage inflation	30% (based on 40 years of contributions at 0.75% per year)	Tier 1: price inflation; tier 2: gross wage inflation[d]

Country (year)	Retirement age (M/F)	Benefit	Earnings base	Replacement rate	Indexation
United Kingdom (1986)	65/60	Old-age pension: basic component £1,861.60 ($2,233.92)	Average earnings (between upper and lower limits) of best 20 years, revalued for nominal wage inflation	25%	Price inflation
United Kingdom (1994)	65/60	Old-age pension: basic component £2,185.80 ($4,266.36)	Average earnings (between upper and lower limits)[e] of working life, revalued for nominal wage inflation	20%	Price inflation
United States (1983)	65/65	No universal flat-rate benefit (a means-tested benefit—SSI—does exist)	Average covered earnings of best 35 years, revalued for nominal wage inflation	Progressive formula, 43% at APW based on 1983 bend points	Price inflation

Sources: Disney (1996), Franco and Munzi (1996), Hamann (1997), Leibfritz et al. (1995), OECD (1988), Takayama (1996), SSA, *Social security programs throughout the world* (various editions); Kalisch and Aman (1997); and Roseveare et al. (1996).

[a]Assuming full eligibility for an earnings-related pension.

[b]Most of the population is covered by a two-pillared system comprising the *regime general* and a complementary scheme organized on a socioprofessional basis. Analysis of the French system is complicated by a number of *regime speciaux*, which substitute for the *regime general* for some workers. The 1993 reform was limited to the *regime general* and some related schemes, so I concentrate on that plan here.

[c]The formal retirement age for tier 2 benefits is 65, but workers can retire at 60 without loss of benefits (see Takayama 1996).

[d]Updated every five years rather than annually.

[e]The upper and lower limits are indexed to price inflation.

Table 7.6   Selected Reforms to State Retirement-Income Systems

	Retirement Age	Tier 1, Flat-Rate Benefit	Tier 2, Assessed Earnings for Earnings-Related Pension	Tier 2, Replacement Rate	Tier 2, Postretirement Indexation
France (1993)			Assessment period, 10 → 25 years (phased in by 2008)[a]		Wage indexation → price indexation[b]
Germany (1992)[c]	Men: 63 → 65 years (by 2009); women: 60 → 65 years (by 2018)				Gross wage indexation → net wage indexation
Italy (1992) Amato reforms	Men: 60 → 65 years (over 10 years); women: 55 → 60 years (over 10 years)		Assessment period: 5 → 10 years (over 10 years); lifetime for younger workers; reevaluation of past earnings: inflation plus 1%		Wage indexation → price indexation
Italy (1995) Dini reforms			Lifetime earnings, revalued at inflation plus 1% → contributions over working life, revalued at the growth rate of a 5-year moving average of nominal GDP	New system:[d] for those retiring at 65, benefits are equal to 6.1% of capitalized contributions; smaller coefficients apply to earlier retirements.[e]	
Japan (1994)	60 → 65 years, for tier 1 pensions (by 2014 for men and by 2019 for women)				Gross wage indexation → net wage indexation for tier 2 pensions
United Kingdom (1986)[f]			Assessment period, 20 best years → all working years	25% → 20% (phased in for those reaching retirement age between 1999 and 2009)	

Country				
United Kingdom (1994)	60 → 65 years for women (phased in by 2020)			
United States (1983)[h]	65 → 67 years by 2022 (for workers reaching the early retirement age of 62)	Lower earnings limit (LEL) in year prior to retirement subtracted from revalued earnings → revalued LEL subtracted from revalued earnings[g] (starting in 2000)	Benefits not subject to income tax → benefits subject to income tax in certain circumstances[i]	One-time 6-month delay in the cost-of-living adjustment

Sources: Disney (1996), Franco and Munzi (1996), Hamann (1997), Leibfritz et al. (1995), OECD (1988), Takayama (1996), SSA, *Social security programs throughout the world* (various editions); Kalisch and Aman (1997); and Roseveare et al. (1996).

[a] In addition, the number of years required for a full pension is to be gradually raised from 37½ years to 40 years.

[b] In fact, pensions had been indexed to prices since 1987, with wage indexation being suspended on a yearly basis. The reform institutionalized the new indexation procedure.

[c] Other reforms not included here include more strict rules on early retirement, reduced pension credits for years in higher education, and increases in pensions for low-age workers.

[d] Since employees pay a higher contribution rate than the self-employed, the shift from average-earnings-based benefits to contributions-based benefits means that the reform has a more negative effect on the self-employed. Employees currently face a contribution rate of 32%, as compared to a 15% rate for the self-employed. In fact, the benefits are calculated using "notional" contribution rates of 33% and 20% for employees and the self-employed, respectively. Thus, even though the self-employed take a bigger hit from the change of system, they continue to receive a subsidy (see Hamann 1997).

[e] For those retiring at 60, the coefficient is 5.1%. The earliest allowable retirement age is 57, at which the coefficient drops to 4.7% (Hamann 1997). The stated intention is that these coefficients will be periodically adjusted downward in response to lengthening life expectancy.

[f] Other reforms of the earnings-related pension (SERPS) include a reduction of the survivor's pension from 100% to 50% of the pension that was to be paid to the deceased contributor and an extension of arrangements for contracting out of earnings-related pensions.

[g] The lower earnings limit (LEL) is set equal to the flat-rate basic benefit and is thus adjusted only for price inflation. When real wage growth is positive, this seemingly minor technical adjustment can lead to a substantial benefit cut over time (see Disney 1996).

[h] Other reforms not treated here include increased taxation of benefits, expansion of the program to include new federal employees, and a small payroll-tax increase.

[i] If a taxpayer's combination of adjusted gross income, interest on tax-exempt bonds, and 50% of social security benefits exceeds certain threshold amounts, benefits equal to the lesser of 50% of benefits or 50% of combined income over the threshold amount is subject to income tax. The additional revenue is added to the trust funds. The taxation of benefits was further modified in 1993, when a secondary (higher) threshold was introduced. An amount equal to 85% of combined income over the secondary threshold is now added to the benefits that are subject to income tax. The additional tax revenues are added to the Medicare health insurance trust fund.

reform will have quite different effects on employees than on the self-employed. The reason is that the self-employed faced lower contribution rates under the old system and that the shift to a contribution-based system will therefore hurt them more.

A number of countries have also changed the way they index benefits after retirement. France and Italy have shifted from wage indexation to price indexation, which leads to cumulative benefit cuts over time when real wages are growing. Germany and Japan (for its tier 2 pensions) have changed from gross wage indexation to net wage indexation. Given that contribution rates are expected to grow over time to meet rising benefit costs, this reform is also a form of benefit cut. Tax-rate projections are difficult to make, but, given that payroll-tax rates must rise substantially (even with recent benefit reforms), it is important to allow for the slower growth of net real wages in the calculations. In Germany, the payroll tax is projected to rise from 18.9 percent in 1995 to 27 percent in 2030.[25] If we assume that the gross real wage rises at an average annual compound rate of 1 percent, this implies that the net real wage (assuming that nonpayroll taxes remain constant) rises at a rate of 0.7 percent. For Japan, the contribution rate is projected to rise from 16.5 percent in 1995 to 29.5 percent in 2030.[26] If we again assume 1 percent real wage growth (and constant nonpayroll taxes), this implies that the net real wage rises at the rate of 0.5 percent per year over this period.

Table 7.7 contains the estimates of the changes in the present value of SSW for single men and women who are forty-five at the time of the reform and are earning the average production wage. I assume that all the reforms are fully phased in by the (new) standard retirement age. In most cases, this is accurate, but, in some cases, the lead times are so long that the reforms are still a long way from being fully phased in (e.g., the Italian and U.S. reforms). Given the previously noted differential effect on employees and the self-employed of the second set of Italian reforms, I include separate estimates of the change in SSW for these two types of worker.

The estimated losses in SSW are substantial, although, as noted above, the range is quite large. The largest change is for men after the 1992 Italian reforms (−38 percent).[27] Other big losses occurred for women in the German, Italian, and U.K. reforms. More generally, the effect on SSW tends to be especially large when there is a change in the retirement age and

25. Franco and Munzi (1996), based on estimates made by Germany's Social Advisory Board in 1994.
26. These estimates are taken from Takayama (1996).
27. Male Italian employees retiring at the standard retirement age appear to have gained back some wealth in the 1995 reforms. On the other hand, women and the self-employed—especially the latter—suffered further losses in this second round of reforms. Moreover, Hamann (1997) estimates that male employees retiring before sixty-three are also net losers.

Table 7.7   **Effect of Selected Benefit Reforms on Social Security Wealth (SSW)—Forty-Five-Year-Old Worker Earning the Average Production Wage (assuming reforms are fully phased in by standard retirement age)**

	Average Production Wage (APW)	Prereform SSW as % of APW	Postreform SSW as % of APW	Change in SSW as % of APW	% Change in SSW
France (1993) (francs):					
Men	113,200	543	469	−74	−13.5
Women	113,200	680	576	−104	−15.3
Germany (1992) (deutschemarks):					
Men	49,904	354	328	−26	−7.3
Women[a]	49,904	596	438	−158	−26.2
Italy (1992) (lire):					
Men	28,302,000	841	525	−316	−38
Women	28,302,000	1374	975	−399	−29
Italy (1995) (lire):[b]					
Men (retiring at 65):					
Employee	31,599,600	470	580	+110	+23
Self-employed	31,599,600	470	352	−118	−25
Women (retiring at 60):					
Employee	31,599,600	791	717	−74	−9
Self-employed	31,599,600	791	420	−371	−45
Japan (1994) (yen):[c]					
Men[d]	4,064,645	447	381	−66	−14.8
Women	4,064,645	568	495	−73	−12.4
United Kingdom (1986) (pounds):					
Men[e]	9,118	229	177	−52	−22.8
Women[f]	9,118	469	390	−79	−16.9
United Kingdom (1994) (pounds):					
Men[g]	14,607	201	192	−9	−5
Women	14,607	374	265	−109	−29
United States (1983) (dollars):[h]					
Men[i]	18,357	163	123	−40	−24.6
Women[j]	18,357	250	210	−40	−16.0

[a] The postreform numbers are based on the assumption that the increase in the retirement age is fully phased in by the time the worker retires. Since the increase in the retirement age for women (to 65 from 60) is not due to be fully phased in until 2018, these calculations overstate the effect on a worker who is 45 at the time of the reform.

[b] This reform will affect employees and the self-employed very differently, so the effects on the SSW of these different types of workers are included separately. The reason for the differential effects is that the self-employed pay a much lower contribution rate than do employees. Thus, a shift to contribution-based benefits has a larger negative effect on the implicit wealth of this group.

Postreform calculations are based on a real GDP growth rate of 1.5 percent.

(*continued*)

Table 7.7   (continued)

ᶜThese calculations are made on the assumption that the worker retires at age 60 but after the reform does not receive tier 1 benefits until age 65. If the reform leads retirement to be postponed until age 65, then the benefit losses are larger. Under this assumption, the benefit losses for men and women are 34.9 and 28.7 percent, respectively.

ᵈA married man with a dependent spouse received benefits with a present value equal to 502 percent of the wage of an APW before the reform and equal to 411 percent after the reform (an 18.1 percent reduction in SSW).

ᵉA married man with a dependent spouse received benefits with a present value equal to 288 percent of the wage of an APW before the reform and equal to 236 percent after the reform (an 18.2 percent reduction in SSW).

ᶠThe postreform numbers are based on the assumption that the increase in the retirement age is fully phased in by the time the worker retires. Since the increase in the retirement age for women (to 65 from 60) is not due to be fully phased in until 2020, these calculations overstate the effect on a worker who is 45 at the time of the reform.

ᵍA married man with a dependent spouse received benefits with a present value equal to 267 percent of the wage of an APW before the reform and equal to 258 percent after the reform (a 3 percent reduction in SSW).

ʰThe postreform numbers are based on the assumption that the increase in the retirement age is fully phased in by the time the worker retires. Since the increase in the retirement age to 67 is not due to be fully phased (for a worker reaching the early retirement age of 62) until 2022, these calculations overstate the effect on a worker who is 45 at the time of the reform.

ⁱA married man with a dependent spouse received benefits with a present value equal to 224 percent of the wage of an APW before the reform and equal to 196 percent after the reform (a 20.0 percent reduction in SSW).

If the income of the retiree is high enough that the 50 percent of benefits are now subject to income taxation, then the loss of SSW rises to 30.2 percent.

ʲIf the income of the retiree is high enough that the 50 percent of benefits are now subject to income taxation, then the loss of SSW rises to 22.3 percent.

when there is a shift from wage to price postretirement indexation.[28] Given their longer expected duration of retirement, the effect of the latter reform on women tends to be greater than the effect on identically situated men. In addition, given that the women in some cases had a lower standard retirement age prereform, they have been disproportionately targeted for standard-retirement-age increases in Germany and the United Kingdom.[29] The German reform led to just a −7.3 percent change in SSW for men and a −26.2 percent change for women. The corresponding numbers for the 1994 reform in the United Kingdom are −5 and −29 percent. On the other hand, an equal increase in the retirement age for men and women tends to hurt men proportionately more. The reason is simply that men have shorter life expectancies and that the lost benefits therefore represent a larger fraction of the present discounted value of the prereform benefit stream. For example, the increase in the retirement age that took place as part of the U.S. reform reduces the SSW of men by almost one-quarter

28. Both were part of the Italian reform in 1992.
29. The shift to a contribution-based system with declining coefficients for earlier retirements in the second Italian reform also disproportionately hurts women, given their earlier retirement age under the older system.

while reducing the SSW of women by 16 percent. These estimates are based on average life expectancy for a forty-five-year-old in the United States at the time of the 1983 reform, which was twenty-nine years for men and thirty-four years for women. If retirement takes place at the standard retirement age (sixty-five prior to the reform), these life expectancies imply prereform expected retirements of nine and fourteen years for men and women, respectively. Raising the standard retirement age to sixty-seven and continuing to assume that retirement takes place at the standard retirement age lower the expected retirement by two years for both men and women. Given the relatively short expected retirement for men to begin with, the loss of two years means a large percentage cut in the present discounted value of benefits.

Of course, retirement does not always take place at the standard retirement age. Indeed, Gruber and Wise (1998) document that, in many countries, *most* retirements take place before the standard age, with a large number of people leaving the labor force at the earliest possible date that they can receive benefits. For a number of countries, they also document significant use of disability and unemployment-benefit programs to finance early retirement even when state pension benefits are not available. Given this behavior, it is less clear how raising the standard retirement age affects SSW. For someone who retires before the standard retirement age and continues to retire at the same age after the standard retirement age has risen, we need to know how the increase in the standard retirement age affects the benefits for those taking advantage of early retirement. To take the United States as an example once again, retirement benefits are available as early as age sixty-two. Workers availing themselves of early retirement benefits, however, receive just 80 percent of the annual benefit that they would have received had they waited until age sixty-five. As we have seen, the 1983 reform will eventually increase the standard retirement age to sixty-seven, but a worker will still be allowed to retire at sixty-two with permanently reduced benefits. The benefit penalty for early retirement is now 30 percent rather than 20 percent, however. By itself, this implies a benefit cut (for men and women) of 12.5 percent. For men in particular, this is a smaller cut than the close to 25 percent cut (which was predominantly due to the increase in the standard retirement age) reported in table 7.7. This demonstrates how the results are sensitive to the assumption that we make about retirement behavior, and the reported estimates of the effects of raising standard retirement ages probably reflect the upper bound of the negative effects of such reforms.

The second to last column of table 7.7 also reports the change in SSW as a fraction of the APW. This figure gives us another way of gauging the effect of the reform on the worker. For example, the first number in the column can be interpreted as saying that the 1993 reform of the general regime in France reduced the present discounted value of future benefits (measured in 1993 money units) by an amount equal to 73 percent of the wage of a French APW in 1993. On this measure, the first of the Italian reforms is shown to have been especially severe, reducing SSW (if fully phased in) by more than three times the wage of an APW for both men and women.

Table 7.8 contains estimates of the effect of the reforms on those who retired in the year of the reform at the standard retirement age. With the exception of changes in the form of postretirement indexing, all the reforms in table 7.6 above are phased in and therefore do not affect the initial benefit of the newly retired. For the countries that switched from wage to price indexation—France and Italy—the estimated loss of SSW is between 6 and 11 percent, which is certainly not insignificant. Under the assumptions for tax increases discussed above, the shift from gross wage to net wage indexation—Germany and Japan—leads to cumulative losses of about 2–3 percent.

Although the estimates of wealth changes should be seen as indicative only, the difference between the effects on middle-aged and younger work-

Table 7.8   **Effect of Selected Benefit Reforms on Social Security Wealth (SSW)— Worker at Standard Retirement Age Who Earned the Average Production Wage at Forty-Five**

	% Change in SSW	Reason for Change
France (1993):		Wage indexation → price indexation
Men	−8.5	
Women	−10.0	
Germany (1992):		Gross wage indexation → net wage indexation
Men	−2.1	(assuming gross real wage growth of 1 percent and net real wage growth of 0.7 percent [see text])
Women	−2.8	
Italy (1992):		Wage indexation → price indexation
Men	−3.4	
Women	−11.2	
Italy (1995):		No change, given the long phase-in of reforms
Men	. . .	
Women	. . .	
Japan (1994):		Gross wage indexation → net wage indexation
Men	−2.5	(assuming gross real wage growth of 1 percent and net real wage growth of 0.5 percent [see text])
Women	−3.1	
United Kingdom (1986):		No change, given the long phase-in of reforms
Men	. . .	
Women	. . .	
United Kingdom (1994):		No change, given the long phase-in of reforms
Men	. . .	
Women	. . .	
United States (1993):		6-month cost-of-living adjustment freeze (assuming annual inflation of 3.5%)
Men	−1.7	
Women	−1.7	

ers, on the one hand, and those on the retired and those close to retirement, on the other, is striking. What accounts for this difference in treatment? One reason is almost certainly that those who are still some distance from retirement still have the opportunity to save for retirement and so are in a better position to adjust to the benefit cuts. Yet these adjustments will be painful nonetheless given the magnitude of wealth loss. Putting aside intergenerational altruism, why is it that middle-aged workers are willing to make these adjustments instead of forcing future workers to pay the previously promised benefits? The rhetoric of reform debates suggests that current workers fear that, with rising dependency ratios, overburdened future workers will redefine—or even completely eliminate—PAYGO benefit arrangements. With this in mind, the next section explores a simple model in which self-interested current workers can actually raise their expected benefits by cutting the benefits they promise themselves.

7.3   Repudiation Risk as an Inducement to Early Reform: A Simple Model

The reform case studies produced two main findings about benefit cuts: the currently retired and those close to retirement are usually spared, and middle-aged and younger workers can sometimes face large reductions in their implicit gross SSW. In this section, I briefly explore one explanation for these findings with a simple model. The idea behind the model is that workers bear a fixed cost when they cut the benefits of the old as well as bearing a (nonlinear) cost to paying them benefits. Benefit cuts are avoided unless benefits reach a level that makes it worthwhile to incur the fixed cost. Once benefits are cut, the cuts can be large. If current workers believe that the benefits that they are promising themselves will trigger future reform, then it will be in their interests preemptively to cut their own benefits.

This model relies on the self-interest of current workers to explain why they cut their own future benefits. There are, of course, other reasons to do so, such as a concern for the fairness of the intergenerational distribution (for a discussion of intergenerational accounting, see Kotlikoff [1992]) or a concern for economic efficiency (for an overview of the distortions caused by PAYGO social security, see Feldstein [1996]). The costs to current generations of reducing the unfunded liability of social security are often seen, however, as a major obstacle to reform. Thus, the model suggests how reforms that are considered good on more impartial grounds might still take place even in a world with quite partial individuals.

The model has the following main elements:

1. Current workers promise themselves social security benefits to be paid for by future workers. This is an inherited unfunded liability from the point of view of the future workers.

2. The actual level of benefits is chosen by future workers (say, because they have a majority). This represents political risk from the point of view of current workers. However, future workers face political (or repudiation) costs when they redefine the benefits that the retired had promised themselves, that is, when they repudiate part of the inherited liability. I assume that there is a fixed cost to repudiation and that the cost of repudiation rises linearly with the size of the benefit reduction. We will see that this gives current workers influence over the benefits that they will receive. (I take it that the political costs are sufficiently high to prevent cutting the benefits of the currently retired. Attention is thus on the decision of current workers about what benefits to promise themselves.)

3. The welfare loss to future workers of funding benefits rises nonlinearly with the PAYGO tax that they must pay.

To solve the model, I first determine the optimal choice of benefit reduction by the second generation of workers for a given level of the inherited unfunded liability. There will be some maximum level of benefit that they will choose not to repudiate at all. I show that this level is greater than the level that they would choose if they decide to repudiate. Given that current workers anticipate the responses of future workers (there is no uncertainty in the model), it follows that it is optimal for them to promise themselves benefits at this "maximum" level. If the promised benefits are currently higher than this level, it is in their interest to scale them back.

For simplicity, I assume that there is a single member in the (first) generation of current workers. Each generation lives for two periods, working in the first and retired in the second. The population grows at the rate n so that there are $1 + n$ workers in the second generation. This implies that the dependency ratio, D, in the second period is equal to $1/(1 + n)$.

There is a PAYGO social security system whereby the working generation is taxed and the tax revenue is paid out as a benefit to the retired. For a given actual benefit payment paid to the retired, $B(1)$, a tax of $D \times B(1)$ is levied on each worker to ensure budget balance.

The current worker knows that a future worker will have utility given by

$$(7) \quad u = k - \frac{a}{2}T^2 - D(F - c\Delta B) \quad \text{with repudiation (i.e., } \Delta B < 0),$$

$$u = k - \frac{a}{2}T^2 \quad \text{without repudiation (i.e., } \Delta B = 0),$$

where T is the per worker tax, F is the total fixed cost of repudiation, and ΔB is the change in benefits. Note that the adjustment cost $(F - c\Delta B)$ is multiplied by D $(= 1/[1 + n])$ to put it in per worker terms. Writing the benefit as the sum of the inherited unfunded liability, $B(0)$, and the change in that benefit, the constraint faced by the future worker is

(8) $$T = DB(1) = D[B(0) + \Delta B].$$

Assuming that the future worker does repudiate, I can find what the optimal repudiation will be by substituting the budget-balancing constraint into the utility function and maximizing with respect to ΔB. The optimal change in the benefit is

(9) $$\Delta B = \frac{c}{aD} - B(0)$$

so that the actual benefit paid is

(10) $$B(1) = \frac{c}{aD}.$$

The next step is to find out when the future generation will in fact repudiate. I assume that repudiation will take place if it increases utility (taking into account, of course, the costs of repudiation). The repudiation condition is then

$$\text{repudiate if} \quad k + \frac{1}{2}\frac{c^2}{a} - DF - cDB(0) > k - \frac{a}{2}D^2B(0)^2,$$

where I assume that

$$\frac{1}{2}\frac{c^2}{a} - DF < 0$$

(which implies that future workers have higher utility by not repudiating when the unfunded liability that they face is very low, as can be seen in fig. 7.1 above).

I now turn my attention to the current worker's choice of unfunded liability to place on the future worker. The current worker wants this to be as large as possible and so chooses the largest $B(0)$ that is consistent with no repudiation. This can be found by replacing the inequality in the repudiation constraint with an equality and solving the resulting quadratic for $B(0)$. The roots of this equation are

$$\frac{c}{aD} + \sqrt{\frac{2F}{aD}}$$

and

$$\frac{c}{aD} - \sqrt{\frac{2F}{aD}}.$$

Given that I have assumed that

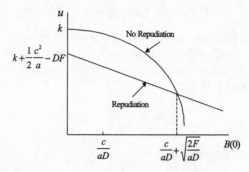

Fig. 7.3   Determination of the maximum future benefit consistent with no repudiation

$$\frac{1}{2}\frac{c^2}{a} - DF < 0,$$

the first root is positive and the second negative. If I rule out negative benefits, then the optimal unfunded liability to place on future workers is

$$(11) \qquad\qquad B(0)^* = B(1)^* = \frac{c}{aD} + \sqrt{\frac{2F}{aD}},$$

That is, the benefit is equal to the repudiation benefit plus a premium that is negatively related to the dependency ratio. The determination of the maximum future benefit consistent with no repudiation is shown graphically in figure 7.3.

The optimal benefit increases with c and F and decreases with a and D. Smaller repudiation costs or more distorting taxes will lower the feasible benefit for a given dependency ratio. Most important, an increase in the future dependency ratio, D, will cause current workers to cut the benefits that they promise themselves.

Figure 7.4 shows how the actual benefits paid, $B(1)$, correspond to the promised benefits, $B(0)$. The two rise together until the repudiation threshold is reached at

$$\frac{c}{aD} + \sqrt{\frac{2F}{aD}}.$$

At that level of the unfunded liability, repudiation occurs, and actual benefits fall to c/aD. This is a rather extreme form of debt "Laffer curve" (as discussed in Krugman [1993, chap. 7]). Debt "forgiveness" in the sense of voluntarily reducing the unfunded liability on the next generation can actually raise the benefits received, making both generations better off. The earlier generation receives higher benefits, and the latter generation avoids the unpleasantness of cutting or redefining benefits for the old.

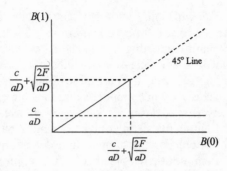

Fig. 7.4   Relation between promised benefit and actual benefit

We can use the PAYGO budget constraint to see how the tax rate changes with the dependency rate:

$$(12) \qquad\qquad T^* = DB(1)^* = \frac{c}{a} + \sqrt{\frac{2FD}{a}}.$$

Given our assumptions, current workers know that future workers will be willing to bear part of the burden of an increase in the dependency ratio with higher tax rates. The marginal willingness of future workers to share the burden, however, decreases with the dependency ratio. In other words, when the dependency ratio (and thus the tax rate) is already high, their willingness to increase the tax rate further in response to an even higher dependency ratio is low.

In conclusion, this simple model produces three main results that are not inconsistent with recent reforms. First, repudiation on retirement-benefit obligations to the currently retired should not take place even when the dependency rate is high (assuming that this high rate was anticipated). Second, benefit promises should be reformed in anticipation of the high dependency ratio to prevent costly repudiations. And, third, an anticipated increase in the dependency rate should lead ultimately to a mix of lower benefits and higher taxes.

7.4   Concluding Comments

This paper has shown that, in response to projections of sharply rising costs of state-provided retirement income, governments have succeeded in legislating significant cuts in future benefits. In most cases, these cuts have not been enough to stabilize the share of GDP being spent by governments on retirement benefits, so it is reasonably safe to predict more benefit cuts if this approach to "saving" social security programs continues to be pursued. Although this paper has focused on attempts to scale back PAYGO programs, I conclude with some comments on the alternatives to this approach to curbing the cost to future taxpayers.

There are two main competing approaches:[30] prefund (using current taxes) future defined-benefit obligations, or substitute privately prefunded defined-contribution (DC) accounts for these obligations (the IB option). What these approaches have in common is that they force current workers to pay for themselves what future workers were to have paid for. This is clear with the prefunding of existing obligations but a bit obscured under the privatization option. For the United States, where privatization has received a lot of attention, there appear to be two approaches to moving to an IB system. The substitution element is clearest in proposals to increase the payroll tax (or use the budget surplus) to fund accounts from which the proceeds would replace an increasing proportion of PAYGO benefits over time (see, e.g., Feldstein and Samwick 1998). The increase in the tax is temporary as the amount needed to fund existing defined-benefit (DB) obligations declines over time as these obligations are replaced by the proceeds from the DC accounts. The alternative approach is to shift some or all payroll taxes into the funding of private DC accounts and to fund remaining PAYGO obligations with a combination of government debt and increases in payroll and nonpayroll taxes (such as a consumption tax).[31] How much of the burden falls on current workers depends on the split between tax increases and debt finance.[32]

What I have stressed so far is how these reforms all place a burden on current workers partly to relieve the burden on future workers. One important difference between the cut-future-benefits and the substitute-current-funding approaches might be their effects on the adequacy of future retirement income. It is possible that current workers will respond to large cuts in the benefits that they are promised by raising their private saving, thereby maintaining their living standards (without having to work longer) in later life. But it seems unwise to rely on this. In the countries where future benefits rules have already been reformed substantially, do younger workers even know how much the benefits that they should be anticipating have fallen? The advantage of prefunding is that an alternative (albeit potentially uncertain) source of retirement income is put in place directly.

This brings me back to where I started and the fact that there is risk in

30. I ignore large-scale cuts in benefits to the currently or soon to be retired as an option.
31. For a proposal of this type, see Kotlikoff and Sachs (1997).
32. If current taxes are not raised at all, then future taxpayers are not being helped. Instead of having to meet unfunded social security obligations, they will have to meet government debt obligations. Thinking in terms of the model of sec. 7.3, however, there might be a difference in the willingness to repudiate on social security obligations and the willingness to repudiate on government debt. Thus, this form of asset swap could still benefit existing workers.

both IB and PAYGO systems. Although there are different ways to characterize the risk, one aspect is the possibility of having inadequate income in retirement. The main finding of this paper is that politically imposed changes in PAYGO benefit rules that have a large effect on the flow of benefits in retirement are not just a possibility—they have already occurred in a number of major economies. And, given that costs are still set to escalate substantially, it is almost certain that more are in store. The decision about partially or fully substituting an IB for a PAYGO system depends, of course, on more than just risk factors (notably, the effects on economic efficiency and inter- and intragenerational distribution). In considering reform options, however, the vulnerability of existing PAYGO defined-benefit rules must be kept in mind.

Appendix

A Note on the Bias Induced by the Certain-Length-of-Life Assumption

How serious a limitation is the assumption of a certain remaining lifetime? In general, the expected SSW of someone with an uncertain remaining lifetime with an expected duration of $R - T + H$ years is *not* the same as the SSW of someone with a certain remaining lifetime of that length. The two are equal under the following restrictive conditions: the real discounted annual benefit is constant over time (this requires that real benefits grow at a rate equal to the real discount rate), and the worker is certain to reach retirement age.

The first assumption implies that SSW is a linear function of the length of retirement. If the worker is certain to reach the retirement age but the discounted real benefit falls over time so that SSW rises at a decreasing rate with the length of retirement, then SSW will be lower under the uncertain-lifetime assumption.[33] In other words, the estimate of SSW based on the certain-remaining-lifetime assumption is biased upward. On the other hand, if the discounted real benefit rises over time (which will be the case if benefits grow at a faster rate than the discount rate), then the estimate is biased downward.

33. The reasoning here is similar to that which shows that expected utility is less than the utility of the expected income for a risk-averse individual. A risk-averse individual has diminishing marginal utility in income. In the case considered here, the individual has diminishing marginal SSW in the number of years of retirement. Given this, and assuming that the individual is certain to reach retirement, then the expected SSW is less than the SSW at expected remaining length of life.

A further complication is added if there is a positive probability of not surviving until retirement age. A simple example of a linear SSW schedule is shown in figure 7A.1. Given the constant discounted real benefit, SSW is higher under the uncertain-lifetime assumption. The worker will live to A_0 with probability p or A_1 with probability $1 - p$, which I assume leads her to expect to live until $R + H$. Note that A_0 is less than R, so there is a positive probability of not reaching retirement age. The expected SSW given the uncertain length of life is SSW^u, which is a probability-weighted average of the zero benefits that are received if the worker does not survive until retirement and the present discounted value of benefits if she survives until A_1. Inspection of the diagram reveals that this level of SSW is greater than the SSW of someone who is certain of dying at age $R + H$ (SSW^c in fig. 7A.1).[34] Thus, the possibility of dying before retirement tends to bias the estimate of social security wealth upward. Our primary concern, however, is with the percentage change in social security wealth that results from a benefit reform rather than with the actual levels of wealth, and there is some reason to hope that the bias is smaller for this calculation. In the case of a linear SSW schedule, for example, a change in the level of the (constant) discounted real benefit level will lead to an equal percentage change in SSW under the certain- and the uncertain-lifetime assumptions.[35]

Summing up, the assumption of the fixed-remaining-length-of-life assumption does introduce a potential bias in estimates of SSW. It is not obvious, however, which way the bias goes. A positive probability of not reaching retirement leads to a downward bias, while the likelihood that

34. It is easy to demonstrate that substituting the expected length of life, $R + H = pA_0 + (1 - p)A_1$ into the equation for the dashed upward-sloping line linking the points $(A_0, 0)$ and $(A_1, SSW[A_1])$ yields a level of SSW equal to SSW^u. Thus, a graphic comparison shows that, with a linear SSW schedule, a positive probability of early death means that expected SSW is greater than the SSW at the expected lifetime. That is, the latter is a downwardly biased estimate of expected SSW. Of course, if the marginal social security wealth is diminishing with the length of the retirement, it is still possible that SSW at the expected lifetime is upwardly biased.

35. Let b be the initial discounted value of the social security benefit for all periods after retirement and b^* be the benefit after reform. For a retirement with a certain length of H, the relative change in SSW is equal to the relative change in the benefit, $(b^* - b)/b$. For an uncertain retirement of length H, and with a positive probability of dying at the preretirement age A_0 some geometry reveals that the relative change in expected SSW wealth is

$$\frac{(b^* - b)\left[\dfrac{(A_1 - R)(R + H - A_0)}{A_1 - A_0}\right]}{b\left[\dfrac{(A_1 - R)(R + H - A_0)}{A_1 - A_0}\right]} = \frac{b^* - b}{b}.$$

Thus, even though making the lifetime uncertain raises the social security wealth for a given benefit level and expected life span, the relative change in wealth that results from a change in the benefit level is, under our special assumptions, the same in each case.

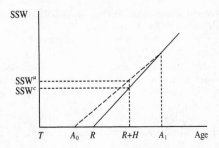

Fig. 7A.1   Expected SSW when there is a chance the worker will not survive until retirement

the real benefit growth rate is less than the discount rate (which is assumed to be 3 percent for the calculations in the paper) leads to an upward bias. Finally, if the benefit growth rate and the discount rate are reasonably close, there is reason to hope that biases in the percentage-*change* calculations that are the focus of the paper are less serious.

References

Berndt, Ernst. 1991. *The practice of econometrics: Classic and contemporary.* Reading, Mass.: Addison-Wesley.
Bosworth, Barry, and Gary Burtless, eds. 1998a. *Aging societies: The global dimension.* Washington, D.C.: Brookings.
———. 1998b. Population aging and economic performance. In *Aging societies: The global dimension,* ed. Barry Bosworth and Gary Burtless. Washington, D.C.: Brookings.
Disney, Richard. 1996. *Can we afford to grow older?* Cambridge, Mass.: MIT Press.
Feldstein, Martin. 1974. Social security, induced retirement, and aggregate capital accumulation. *Journal of Political Economy* 82 (September/October): 905–26.
———. 1996. The missing piece in policy analysis: Social security reform. *American Economic Review* 86, no. 2 (May): 1–14.
Feldstein, Martin, and Elena Ranguelova. 1998. Individual risk and intergenerational risk sharing in an investment-based social security system. Harvard University. Mimeo.
Feldstein, Martin, and Andrew Samwick. 1998. The transition path in privatizing social security. In *Privatizing social security,* ed. Martin Feldstein. Chicago: University of Chicago Press.
Franco, Daniele, and Teresa Munzi. 1996. Public pension expenditure prospects in the European Union: A survey of national projections. *European Economy,* no. 3:1–126.
Geanakoplos, John, Olivia S. Mitchell, and Stephen P. Zeldes. 1998. Social security money's worth. NBER Working Paper no. 6722. Cambridge, Mass.: National Bureau of Economic Research.
Gruber, Jonathan, and David A. Wise. 1998. Introduction and summary. In *Social*

security and retirement around the world, ed. Jonathan Gruber and David A. Wise. Chicago: University of Chicago Press.

Hamann, A. Javier. 1997. The reform of the pension system in Italy. Working Paper no. 97/18. Washington, D.C.: IMF.

IMF. Various issues. *International financial statistics.* Washington, D.C.

Kalisch, David, and Tetsuya Aman. 1997. Retirement income systems: The reform process across OECD countries. Paper delivered at the ILO-OECD Workshop on Pension Reform, Paris, December.

Kornai, Janos, and John McHale. 2000. Is post-Communist health spending unusual? A comparison with established market economies. *Economics of Transition,* forthcoming.

Kotlikoff, Laurence. 1992. *Generational accounting: Knowing who pays, and when, for what we spend.* New York: Free Press.

Kotlikoff, Laurence, and Jeffery Sachs. 1997. It's high time to privatize social security. *Brookings Review* 15, no. 3 (summer): 16–23.

Krugman, Paul. 1993. *Currencies and Crises.* Cambridge, Mass.: MIT Press.

Leibfritz, Willi, Deborah Roseveare, Douglas Fore, and Echard Wurzel. 1995. Aging populations, pension systems, and government budgets: How do they affect saving? Working Paper no. 156. Paris: Economics Department, OECD.

Mincer, Jacob. 1974. *Schooling, experience, and earnings.* New York: Columbia University Press.

OECD. 1988. *Reforming public pensions.* Paris.

———. 1997. *Ageing in OECD countries: A critical policy challenge.* Paris.

———. 1998a. *Economic outlook 64.* Paris, December.

———. 1998b. *OECD health data 98: A comparative analysis of 29 countries.* Paris. CD-ROM.

———. Various editions. *The tax/benefit position of production workers.* Paris.

Reno, Virgina P., and Robert B. Friedland. 1997. Strong support but low confidence. In *Social security in the 21st century,* ed. Eric R. Kingston and James H. Schulz. Oxford: Oxford University Press.

Roseveare, Deborah, Willi Leibfritz, Douglas Fore, and Echard Wurzel. 1996. Ageing populations, pension systems, and government budgets simulations for 20 OECD countries. Working Paper no. 168. Paris: Economics Department, OECD.

Social Security Administration (SSA). Various editions. *Social security programs throughout the world.* Washington, D.C.: Office of International Policy, SSA.

Takayama, Noriyuki. 1996. Possible effects of ageing on the equilibrium of the public pension system in Japan. *European Economy,* no. 3:155–99.

United Nations. 1996. *Demographic yearbook, 1996.* New York.

World Bank. 1995. *World tables.* Washington, D.C.

Comment   David A. Wise

A great deal of attention has been directed to the risk that individuals would face if personal accounts were made part of the social security sys-

David A. Wise is the John F. Stambaugh Professor of Political Economy at the John F. Kennedy School of Government, Harvard University, and director of the Health and Retirement Programs at the National Bureau of Economic Research.

tem. In contrast, little attention has been given to the individual risk associated with government social security programs, perhaps encouraging the presumption that benefits promised under these programs are riskless guarantees. Even reform proposals that purport to assure the future financial solvency of the U.S. social security system by some combination of benefit cuts and tax increases, in part at least to avoid the assumed risk of personal accounts, fail to recognize the demonstration of risk of benefit cuts. The "maintain-benefits" proposal—one of three proposals put forth by the 1994–95 Social Security Advisory Commission—is a good example. The proposal in fact entails substantial cuts in the benefits of future retirees. The important contribution of this paper is to make clear that promised social security benefits are in fact risky "assets."

The calculations showing that recent reform proposals in several countries will substantially reduce the benefits of future retirees in these countries constitute the core of this paper. The benefit reductions are measured by the implied reductions in the present discounted value of social security wealth (SSW). McHale also presents data showing that, while demographic trends are placing increasing pressure on the future financial viability of these social security systems, they have not yet significantly reduced the benefits of current retirees. Finally, McHale gives some thought to why current workers are "willing" to accept large reductions in their future benefits while not insisting on cuts in the benefits of those now in retirement. The evidence makes it clear that benefit reductions for future retirees can be very substantial and thus that substantial risk attaches to benefit "promises." I believe, however, that, while the evidence clearly demonstrates risk, the true risk is substantially greater than the data alone demonstrate, and I believe that McHale would agree with this assessment.

Let me begin by explaining why I believe this to be the case. I assume that *risk* in this case means that realized future benefits may deviate from benefits promised today. If today's promise were guaranteed into the distant future, there would be no risk in the sense of reneging on the promise. Why might the promise be revised? To think about this risk, I find it useful to distinguish between the underlying factors that induce change in the promise, from the magnitude of the change if a change is made. It is this latter change that McHale documents.

Many factors may induce a need to revise the promise. I emphasize a few. One is the error in forecasting future death rates. Many prominent demographers believe that the U.S. Social Security Administration has consistently underestimated the continuing decline in death rates and thus the increase in life expectancy. Realized life expectancy of successive cohorts has consistently been greater than projections. Such errors are one reason for the repeated optimistic assessment of the number of years until the social security trust fund would go broke. In 1983, the projected go-broke year was 2063; the go-broke date was more or less continuously brought nearer, and, by 1997, it had been brought to 2029. Projections of life expectancy are likely to be inaccurate in the future as well. One prominent demographer has told me that his guess is that a baby girl born in the United States today has a life expectancy of one hundred. Whatever the truth may be, there is much uncertainty about it, even among careful analysts of demographic change. Ronald Lee and Shripad Tuljapurkar (1998) have begun to assess the risk associated with demographic uncertainty (fertility and mortality) as well as productivity growth and interest rates. On the basis of their stochastic forecast analysis, they judge that the trust fund could go broke much sooner, or substantially later, than the Social Security Administration projects in either of its three scenarios. Their 95 percent confidence interval includes fund exhaustion in 2014 as well as 2037.

A second factor is incentive effects (or behavioral response). While economists make a living on incentive effects, they are often ignored or unrecognized by many participants in the political decision-making process. In particular, the provisions of the social security systems in many countries place enormous implicit taxes on work after certain ages. Such provisions seem to have been associated with striking declines in the labor force participation of older workers in several of the countries in McHale's analysis. The decline as well as the striking relation between plan provisions and the proportion of older workers in the labor force is documented by Gruber and Wise (1999). Retirement at younger and younger ages exacerbates the financial pressure on social security systems caused by demographic trends.

A third factor is calculation "error." For example, errors in the formula that was to index benefits to inflation in the 1972 U.S. social security legislation (perhaps actually realized before the legislation was implemented) caused enormous "unintended" increases in benefits over a seven-year period before they were corrected. This of course has important implications for the future financial viability of the system. Errors that inflate benefits in one year are likely to mean a reduction in benefits in future years. (As with financial market risk, there is upside as well as downside risk. Those who benefited from the error were lucky; those who later have to pay for it are unlucky.)

A fourth factor is inaction once financial imbalance is recognized. Inaction is likely to increase required adjustments. For example, without individual accounts, social security reform proposals in the United States typically entail benefit reductions of perhaps 25–35 percent if the issue is addressed now. If nothing is done for many years, as some would prefer, the required adjustment would likely be much greater. Indeed, the financial imbalance is much greater in Germany, for example, than in the United States, partly because population aging occurred earlier in Germany than in the United States and no action was taken for some time.

Now, the adjustments needed to balance the system are much greater than those that have been adopted to date (and analyzed by McHale).

McHale has very clearly demonstrated that changes that are made can imply large benefit reductions. I have tried to emphasize that the true risk is likely to be much greater than the reductions in benefits that he calculates. McHale of course recognizes this in saying that further reductions are likely to be in store in many of the countries he analyzes.

Looking at the data in a way somewhat different from the data presented in the McHale paper seems to me to reinforce this judgment. McHale presents data on the "benefit rate" defined by the average benefit per person sixty-five and older relative to GDP per person fifteen to sixty-four. More standard replacement rates—defined by the benefit as a percentage of final earnings—are shown in table 7C.1, together with additional data on plan characteristics (see Gruber and Wise 1999). Countries analyzed by McHale are noted. For a person with median lifetime earnings, the replacement rates at the *early* retirement age range from a high of 91 percent in France and the Netherlands to a low of 20 percent in Canada. The U.S. replacement rate is 41 percent. The replacement rates shown in the table are based on simulations using precise plan provisions in each country prior to proposed reforms. In some cases, these replacement rates differ substantially from those reported by McHale in his table 7.5, and I return to possible reasons for that below. I present the replacement rates here to suggest that to bring the plans in many countries into financial balance would require benefit reductions much greater than those reflected in proposed plan changes reported and analyzed by McHale in tables 7.5–7.8.

To bring the U.S. system into "balance" as indicated by non-individual account reform proposals would require benefit reductions of perhaps 25–35 percent. The U.S. change analyzed by McHale suggests a SSW reduction of about 25 percent for men and 16 percent for women. Surely, the reductions required to bring the German, French, and Italian plans, for example, into financial balance are much greater than the SSW reductions reported in McHale's table 7.7, which are implied by the proposed changes.

Finally, without disparaging the effort and important calculations made by McHale, let me mention several reasons why these calculations may represent only a first step in this kind of analysis, as McHale emphasizes. First, the calculations are based on a "stylized" benefit formula (based on an OECD approach), which may measure the effect of current and proposed plans with substantial error. The difference in the replacement rates reported in table 7C.1 (and based on actual detailed plan provisions) and the rates reported in McHale's table 7.5 may indicate the magnitude of potential differences. Second, McHale's calculations reflect in large part proposed changes in plan normal retirement ages, although he does give

Table 7C.1   Labor Force Participation and Key Plan Features, by Country

Country	Men Not Working Age 55–65 (%)	Men out of Labor Force Age 59 (%)	Early Retirement (ER) Age	Replacement Rate at ER Age (%)	Implicit Tax on Earnings in Next Year (%)	"Tax Force" to Retire, ER Age to 69
Belgium	67	58	"60"	77	82	8.87
France[a]	60	53	60	91	80	7.25
Italy[a]	59	53	"55"	75	81	9.20
Netherlands	58	47	"60"	91	141	8.32
United Kingdom[a]	55	38	60	48	75	3.77
Germany[a]	48	34	60	62	35	3.45
Spain	47	36	60	63	−23	2.49
Canada[a]	45	37	60	20	8	2.37
United States[a]	37	26	62	41	−1	1.57
Sweden	35	26	60	54	28	2.18
Japan[a]	22	13	60	54	47	1.65

Source: Gruber and Wise (1999).

Note: The second to last column in the table measures the implicit tax on earnings if a person works for an additional year following the early retirement age. The last column shows the sum of implicit tax rate from the early retirement age through age 69. Both measures are explained in Gruber and Wise (1999). In some countries, the effective early retirement age is ambiguous. The quotation marks are intended to signal cases where the ambiguity is perhaps the greatest, but the availability of unemployment and disability benefits creates ambiguities in other cases as well. The calculations presented in this table are taken from the individual country papers and pertain to these cases:

Belgium: The social security early retirement age is 60, but employees who are laid off are eligible for large benefits at younger ages. Thus, the accrual, implicit tax, and tax-force measures treat unemployment benefits as early retirement benefits available at 55.

France: Counting social security benefits, available at age 60, but not accounting for guaranteed income benefits for those losing their jobs at age 57 or older.

Italy: Social security benefits for private-sector employees, not counting disability availability.

Netherlands: In addition to public social security benefits, the calculations account for virtually universal employer private pension benefits. The employer plan is assumed to provide for early retirement at age 60. There is no social security early retirement in the Netherlands, but employer early retirement benefits are commonly available at age 60.

United Kingdom: Based on social security benefits only, but counting "incapacity" benefits at 60 as early retirement benefits.

Germany: Counting social security benefits and assuming a person is eligible for "early" disability benefits.

Spain: Based on RGSS (the main social security program).

[a]Countries analyzed by McHale.

some consideration to early retirement. In European countries especially, and even in the United States, only a small fraction of persons work until the normal retirement age, as shown in Gruber and Wise (1999). Much more important in reducing plan costs would be increases in the early retirement age. Third, in many European countries, disability and unemployment insurance programs essentially serve as early retirement programs, which in many cases provide early retirement several years before the nominal social security early retirement age. The provisions of these programs would also have to be changed to bring the overall elderly support programs into balance.

In short, McHale has demonstrated that plan changes can have a large effect on previously "promised" social security benefits. I commend the effort to make such calculations. I believe that the true risk inherent in these programs is in fact much greater than that indicated by the calculation made in the paper.

References

Gruber, Jonathan, and David A. Wise. 1999. Introduction and summary. In *Social security and retirement around the world,* ed. Jonathan Gruber and David Wise. Chicago: University of Chicago Press.
Lee, Ronald, and Shripad Taljapurkar. 1998. Stochastic forecasts for social security. In *Frontiers in the economics of aging,* ed. David A. Wise. Chicago: University of Chicago Press.

Discussion Summary

David Wilcox noted the importance of understanding the reasons for the deterioration of the solvency projections since 1983. Changes in demographic assumptions have actually mirrored the balance and thus are not part of the reason for this evolution. Better explanations implicate initial productivity forecasts that were too optimistic and changes in the methodology used by the actuary, which tended to deteriorate the solvency projections on average. A third reason is that the projections cover only a finite (seventy-five-year) period. Given that the system is projected to be experiencing deep cash-flow deficits in the long term, the incorporation of a new seventy-fifth year into the projection period each year worsens the balance by about 0.08 percent of taxable payroll.

Andrew Samwick stated that he liked the paper very much and wondered what the size of benefit changes has been even outside the current context, that is, throughout the history of the social security system. In particular, he referred to the increases in benefits that occurred during the 1970s in both the United States and the United Kingdom. Incorporating this into the analysis might weaken some of the results in terms of how much current retirees or agents close to retirement are hurt by the more recent downward adjustments of the benefit entitlements.

Zvi Bodie noted that, in order to draw welfare implications from this analysis, one should focus, not on the number of elderly as a fraction of the working-age population, but rather on the number of elderly in need as a fraction of the total population. Bodie expressed the opinion that many elderly choose not to retire as long as they are healthy. Therefore, the proportion of elderly per se is not a relevant concept for public policy issues. Instead, what warrants the attention of policymakers is the fact that one cares about the elderly who are needy and incapable of earning income. The dependency ratios typically analyzed do not reflect this. Bodie concluded that, in his opinion, the crisis was overstated because what underlies the decrease in mortality rates is the fact that the elderly are healthier and are therefore able to work longer.

John Shoven remarked with respect to this comment that numerous lobbies actively seek to lower, not raise, the retirement age.

Henning Bohn liked the paper generally but expressed concern about the measure of government spending used in the empirical part of the paper. First, he noted that the real challenge facing us is medical spending, not cash benefits. If one limits attention to social security cash benefits, then the perspective is definitely too narrow. Second, government cash spending seems to include spending on government-employee pensions. Bohn remarked that this potentially biases the cross-country analysis as countries differ substantially in the size of their public sector. The numbers for cash spending in countries with a large public workforce are therefore inflated artificially, independent of the social burden of the elderly that the country has to support.

James Poterba remarked that the generosity of benefit rules tends to revert to the mean over time, thereby dampening its volatility over longer horizons. In particular, he noted that, in many countries, benefits increased in the 1970s and 1980s (especially when including the programs that David Wise, the discussant, identified as important, e.g., disability), whereas, more recently, some trimming of the sails was seen in the form of benefit reductions. Someone who entered the labor force in 1970 received an unexpected windfall in benefits entitlements in the 1980s and subsequently witnessed reductions in expected benefits in the 1990s. Thus, the risk over a long period could be less than the risk over a shorter horizon.

Martin Feldstein made the following comments. Concerning David Wilcox's question about the reasons for the deterioration over the course of the 1980s and 1990s of the solvency projections, he added that early retirement was a likely cause. He agreed furthermore with Bohn's remark about the importance of Medicare, especially for the future, not so much for the current situation. Finally, he expressed the view that Bodie's opinion on the preference for late rather than early retirement was based on introspection and is most likely not representative of the entire population.

Richard Zeckhauser wondered about the timing of the incentive effects in the context of the diagrams shown by the discussant, David Wise, illustrating the dramatic decline in labor force participation by medium-old people. He asked whether it was not the case that the incentive effects were created before the changes in the generosity of pension benefits. With respect to the dangers of introspection in the context of the preference for early or late retirement, as noted by Feldstein, he referred to popular rhetoric in Europe. The rhetoric claims that the elderly should retire early in order to allow the young to find a job, given the high rates of unemployment.

Zeckhauser furthermore suggested that McHale consider alternative political economy explanations for why the young are willing to accept benefit reforms that are not favorable to them. A first alternative theory, most relevant to the United States, stresses the fact that the elderly are politically much better organized than the young, simply by virtue of being one-issue voters. A second explanation revolves around the (relatively short) horizon of the political decision-making process. Finally, Zeckhauser pointed out that social security closely resembles a contingent claim, where the benefits received are dependent on a particular contingency. This description is more appropriate than the term *risky* social security.

The discussant, *David Wise,* disagreed with Zeckhauser's first comment. Cross-country evidence convincingly shows a tight relation between implicit taxes on working and the proportion of people working between the ages of fifty-five and sixty-five. The incentive effects seem to be quite strong and very relevant for early retirement and the drop in labor force participation.

David Cutler noted that the analysis ignores survivors' benefits. They are nevertheless important.

John McHale agreed with Wilcox's criticism of the use of point distributions and stated that the direction of the bias would be examined. He also noted that the suggestions of Samwick and Poterba to analyze earlier periods of benefit increases would be enlightening. Finally, he remarked that some social security reforms move in the direction mentioned by Zeckhauser. Indeed, both Italy and Germany seem to be evolving toward a system with more explicit contingency-based benefits.

8

Financial Engineering and Social Security Reform

Zvi Bodie

President Clinton this week kicks off what he says will be a
bipartisan effort to reform Social Security as interest groups
line up with conflicting plans to save the national retirement
system. . . . About three dozen groups announced last week
they had joined forces to lobby for privatization, calling
themselves the "Campaign to Save and Strengthen Social
Security." Critics say such a plan is fraught with danger
because benefits would depend on investment know-how and
market swings.
—Donna Smith, reporter for Reuters, Washington, D.C.,
6 December 1998

Suppose that we could introduce into the economic system
any institutions we wish for shifting risks instead of being
confined to those developed historically. . . . We would want
to find a market in which we can insure freely against any
economically relevant event. That is, an individual should be
able to bet, at fixed odds, any amount he wishes on the
occurrence of any event which will affect his welfare in any
way. The odds, or, in a different and more respectable
language, the premium on the insurance, should be
determined, as any other price, so that supply and demand
are equal. Under such a system, productive activity and risk-
bearing can be divorced, each being carried out by the one or
ones best qualified.
—Kenneth Arrow, "Risk, Insurance, and Resource
Allocation," in *Essays in the Theory of Risk Bearing* (1971)

A major concern in the debate about replacing the current U.S. social
security system with a system of self-directed personal investment ac-

Zvi Bodie is professor of finance and economics at the Boston University School of Management.

counts (PIAs) is that ordinary Americans will not be able to cope with the complexities of providing for an adequate income in retirement by investing on their own.[1] The proponents of PIAs point to the benefits of knowing the value of the funds in your own retirement account and having the freedom to make investment choices from an array of options. This investment choice would allow people to select a risk profile consistent with their own preferences and circumstances. But skeptics point out that the greater individual choice in PIAs also poses greater potential risks.

Economists cringe at the suggestion that increasing the choices available to people can make them worse off. If the new set of choices includes the status quo as one alternative, goes the reasoning, then surely one's welfare cannot decrease. This paper attempts to show how to make the economist's reasoning work in the context of PIAs. It seeks to show how government and private-sector financial institutions can offer people a menu of investment choices that are at least as good as the ones they have now. The goal is to allow ordinary people to make informed investment decisions about risk-reward trade-offs and to implement those decisions at the lowest possible cost to themselves and society. Costs are defined to include not only explicit advisory fees or commissions but also the expenditure of one's own leisure time and the time and patience of friends and relatives in deciding how to invest. Social costs include possible market distortions arising from deceptive advertising or from unintended subsidies that may encourage suboptimal risk-taking behavior.

The paper is organized as follows. First, I examine the economic theory of optimal lifetime consumption and portfolio selection to see what guidance it offers for the investment of retirement savings. Then I show how to use financial engineering to produce a menu of investment choices defined by a guaranteed minimum level of benefits plus participation in a reference portfolio of stocks. I then consider the role of the government in implementing a system of private investment accounts. Finally, I critically examine some of the investment advice offered by investment-management firms.

8.1 Life-Cycle Investing and Financial Engineering

The economics literature on household portfolio selection over the life cycle is vast. While many of the scientific issues regarding how people actually make life-cycle investment decisions remain in dispute, much progress has been made in the past forty years in developing *normative* models of how such decisions can be made optimally. Those normative

---

1. In a recent study of the investment behavior of participants in TIAA-CREF, Bodie and Crane (1997) find some cause for "cautious optimism" about the ability of people to make informed choices about asset allocation.

models are today being implemented by a relatively new branch of applied economics called *financial engineering.*

Financial engineering is the practical application of economic theory to the intertemporal allocation of resources and the management of risk. Its principal analytic tools are continuous-time stochastic optimization models and arbitrage-based models of contingent-claims pricing. In this section of the paper, I briefly summarize the development of financial engineering and its application to the investment-management business.

8.1.1   Portfolio Optimization

The application of economic theory to investment management began in 1952 with the Markowitz (1952) mean-variance theory. This theory provided a tractable model for quantifying the risk-return trade-off to be derived from a set of risky assets by identifying the standard deviation of a portfolio's rate of return as its risk and the mean as its reward. The inputs to the Markowitz portfolio-selection process consist of a set of risky assets characterized in terms of their means, standard deviations, and correlations with each other. The outputs are in the form of a menu of risk-return choices arrayed along an "efficient portfolio frontier."

Tobin (1958) added a risk-free asset to the list of inputs and showed how this expanded the efficient frontier and simplified the process of finding the optimal mix. Building on the work of Markowitz and Tobin, Sharpe (1964) and Lintner (1965) investigated the equilibrium structure of asset prices, and their capital asset pricing model (CAPM) became the basis for measuring the risk-adjusted performance of professional portfolio managers.[2] Today, the mean-variance model is at the core of quantitative models for asset allocation and can even be implemented on a personal computer.

In the late 1960s and early 1970s, models of optimal portfolio selection being developed in the academic world became considerably more sophisticated. Merton (1969, 1971, 1975) introduced continuous-time stochastic models into portfolio theory, thereby extending and enriching the static, single-period mean-variance model. He showed that *hedging* can be as important as diversifying in the demand for assets. The desire to hedge against a risk gives rise to a demand for securities that are highly correlated with that risk. For example, a desire to hedge against adverse changes in short-term interest rates induces a demand for long-term bonds. Merton (1973b) also developed the multifactor intertemporal capital asset pricing model (ICAPM) and proved that, in equilibrium, a security's risk premium will reflect not only its beta on the market portfolio but also its betas on commonly shared hedging portfolios.[3]

2. For a more detailed account of these developments, see Bernstein (1992). Markowitz, Sharpe, and Tobin all were awarded Nobel Prizes in economics.
3. For references on dynamic portfolio theory and intertemporal capital asset pricing, see Merton (1992).

The mean-variance approach to quantitative investment management was and is ideally suited to the structure of the mutual fund industry. Mutual funds provide the real-world counterparts to the optimally proportioned portfolios of the theory. Thus, Merton's ICAPM provides a theoretical rationale for investment firms to offer a "family" of optimal hedging portfolios suited to the needs of different clienteles. The firm can put various combinations of its member funds together in proportions that reflect the right mix for customers in various stages of the life cycle. These so-called life-cycle funds are then offered as final products.

8.1.2   Options as Fundamental Building Blocks

The practical role of options and other derivatives is perhaps best understood in the context of the state-preference theory of Arrow (1964) and Debreu (1959). The fundamental building blocks of this theory—known as *Arrow-Debreu securities*—are claims that pay $1.00 contingent on a certain state of the world at a certain date and zero otherwise. The theory developed by Arrow and Debreu provided a general and useful framework for studying many issues in welfare economics and finance; however, until the early 1970s, it was believed that, because pure Arrow-Debreu securities have no real-world counterparts, people would not be able to observe their prices and use them for the allocation of resources and the management of risks.

That view started to change in 1973 with the dramatic discoveries in option-pricing theory by Black and Scholes (1973) and Merton (1973a) and the opening of the Chicago Board Options Exchange.[4] The basic insight underlying these models is that a dynamic portfolio trading strategy in the stock can be found that will replicate the returns from an option on that stock. Hence, to avoid arbitrage opportunities, the option price must always equal the value of this replicating portfolio. The resulting pricing formula has only one input that is not directly observable: the volatility of the return on the stock.

Discovery of the option-pricing model and the technique of dynamic replication was soon followed by its extension to the theory and practice of investment management. Brennan and Schwartz (1976) applied it to the pricing of equity-linked life insurance, and Merton, Scholes, and Gladstein (1978) explored the performance of a portfolio in which 90 percent of the funds were invested in six-month commercial paper and the remainder used to purchase a portfolio of six-month call options on selected individual stocks. This idea was actually put to work with the formation of a new mutual fund, Money Market/Options. Leland (1980) wrote about and implemented a service that he called *portfolio insurance*.[5]

---

4. For the story of how these models were developed, see Scholes (1998) and Merton (1998).

5. Bernstein (1992) has a chapter devoted to these authors' ill-fated venture in portfolio insurance.

Ross (1976), Breeden and Litzenberger (1978), and Banz and Miller (1978) showed that the prices of options could be used to derive the prices of the pure state-time claims envisioned by Arrow and Debreu.[6]

During the 1970s, exchanges were created to trade standardized futures and options contracts on major currencies, on U.S. Treasury bills and bonds, and on stocks. The success of these markets measured in terms of trading volume can be attributed in good part to the increased demand for managing risks in the volatile economic environment of the 1970s. This success in turn strongly affected the speed of adoption of quantitative financial models.

During the 1980s, the user base of financial engineering expanded greatly, becoming global in scope and including commercial and investment banks and institutional investors of all types, especially pension funds. Practitioners in financial institutions actually took on a major role in applied research, including the creation of proprietary databases, the development of new numerical methods for solving partial differential equations, and the implementation of sophisticated estimation techniques for measuring model parameters. By the late 1980s, the computational models used by practitioners in some investment firms became as sophisticated as any found in the academic journals. Indeed, the people developing these applied models were in many cases recruited from university finance departments.

8.1.3   A Continuous-Time Model of Life-Cycle Financial Decisions

In contemporary financial economics, the standard theoretical framework for analyzing life-cycle decisions is Merton's (1969, 1971, 1973a) continuous-time model of optimal consumption and portfolio choice. Merton's model is more general than the older Markowitz model of portfolio choice. The Markowitz model assumes that individuals make decisions "myopically" in a static single-period framework. Merton's model assumes that individuals make choices that maximize their expected utility from the consumption of goods and leisure over their lifetimes and that they are free to change their choices at any time.

There are several distinct time horizons in Merton's model. The *planning horizon* is the total length of time for which one plans. The *time horizon* for the retirement goal would be the balance of one's lifetime. Thus, for a twenty-five-year-old who expects to live to age eighty-five, the retirement planning horizon would be sixty years. As one ages, the planning horizon typically gets shorter and shorter.

The *decision horizon* is the length of time between decisions to revise the portfolio. The length of the decision horizon is controlled by the individual within certain limits. Some people review their portfolios at regular

6. Hakansson (1976) even proposed that financial intermediaries issue a type of Arrow-Debreu security that he dubbed *supershares*.

intervals—once a month (when they pay their bills) or once a year (when they file income-tax forms). People of modest means with most of their wealth invested in bank accounts might review their portfolios very infrequently and at irregular intervals determined by some "triggering" event such as getting married or divorced, having a child, or receiving a bequest. A sudden rise or fall in the price of an asset a person owns might also trigger a review of the portfolio. People with substantial investments in stocks and bonds might review their portfolios every day or even more frequently.

The shortest possible decision horizon is the *trading horizon,* defined as the *minimum* time interval over which investors can revise their portfolios. The length of the trading horizon is not under the control of the individual. Whether the trading horizon is a week, a day, an hour, or a minute is determined by the structure of the markets in the economy (e.g., when the securities exchanges are open or whether organized off-exchange markets exist).

To add more realism to Merton's model, Bodie, Merton, and Samuelson (1992) add a third choice variable—the amount of work people choose to do. In their model, individuals start out with an initial endowment of financial wealth and earning power from labor (their human capital). The market values of both components of wealth—financial and human capital—change continuously and stochastically. The wage rate (the return on human capital) is perfectly positively correlated with the market return on traded assets.[7] Consumption, wealth, and rates of return are all denominated in real terms, that is, in units of the consumption good. At each point of time in the model, individuals determine the amount of their consumption, the proportion of their financial wealth to invest in risky assets (vs. the safe asset), and the fraction of their maximum possible labor income that they will "spend" on leisure so as to maximize their discounted lifetime expected utility.

The model's results indicate that the fraction of an individual's financial wealth optimally invested in equity should "normally" decline with age for two reasons. The first stems from the fact that human capital is usually less risky than equity and that the value of human capital usually declines as a proportion of an individual's total wealth as one ages. For example, in an individual's early years of work, her wealth is often dominated by relatively safe human capital so that a large share of her financial wealth should be in risky assets in order to get sufficient risk in her total wealth.[8]

7. While the assumption of perfect correlation is not entirely realistic, it greatly simplifies the development of the formal model.

8. Other theoretical models support the practical notion that the fraction in equity should normally decline with age. For a review of theoretical models that yield results similar to popular guidelines regarding the age-equity relation, see Samuelson (1994) and Jagganathan and Kocherlakota (1996).

Second, at any given age, the greater the flexibility an individual has to alter her labor supply, the greater the amount she will invest in risky assets. Individuals may be able to offset changes in the value of their financial wealth by changing the amount they work. They may have the opportunity to work longer hours, take on extra jobs, or delay retirement. If younger workers have more opportunity to alter their labor supply than older workers, the share of assets held as risky equity should decline with age.[9]

8.2   Personal Investment Accounts with a Guaranteed Floor

The theory presented in the previous section is silent on the question of what institutions people will use or should use to achieve their optimal lifetime consumption plans. As we know, the mix of government-provided social security, employment-related pension plans, and other private saving in the provision of retirement income varies widely from country to country and even within each country. And it is precisely the question of the optimal institutional mix that is at the center of controversy in the ongoing debate about social security reform in the United States today.

But at least on one point there seems to be a consensus—participation in the reformed social security system should be mandatory, and there should be some minimum guaranteed level of real retirement benefits for everyone who pays into the system. There also seems to be a consensus that, at least for benefits in excess of the guaranteed level, people ought to have some portfolio choice. In the terminology of pension professionals, one can describe such a system as a *floor* plan—a defined-contribution plan with a defined-benefit minimum or floor level. Recently, Brennan and Cao (1996) have shown that, for uninformed investors, such payoff functions may be Pareto efficient. In this section of the paper, I show how to use stock-index options and option prices to produce personal investment accounts with this feature.[10] As is customary, I divide the planning period into two parts: the accumulation phase before retirement and the postretirement phase where the accumulation is paid out as a lifetime annuity.

8.2.1   The Preretirement Phase

Options expand the menu of risk-return choices open to investors. Index options make it possible to combine downside protection with some upside tied to the performance of an underlying index portfolio. Investor interest in this kind of product has grown recently. In 1995, life insurance

9. It should also be noted that the safe asset in the Bodie, Merton, and Samuelson (1992) model is a bond whose interest and principal is denominated in units of the consumption good. Its real-world counterpart would therefore have to be a bond similar to the inflation-protected bonds issued by the U.S. Treasury in 1997.

10. For an earlier version of this idea, see Bodie and Crane (1999).

Table 8.1   **Stock-Index Call-Option Prices**

Years to Maturity	Exercise Price ($)				
	20	40	60	80	100
1	80.98	61.95	42.94	24.59	10.45
2	81.90	63.81	45.82	29.12	16.13
3	82.79	65.58	48.62	33.19	20.92
4	83.63	67.27	51.29	36.88	25.21
9	87.25	74.61	62.57	51.72	42.36
16	91.02	82.21	73.87	66.22	59.31
25	94.28	88.70	83.40	78.44	73.84

Note: These prices were computed using the Black-Scholes formula with $S = \$100$, $r = .05$, and volatility $= .2$.

companies in the United States began to offer five- to seven-year variable annuities that combined a floor with some upside. By 1997, some thirty insurance companies had introduced these products in the United States (e.g., KeyIndex annuities issued by Keyport, a division of Liberty Financial).

Table 8.1 shows prices of call options on a reference portfolio, expressed per $100 share of the portfolio.[11] The prices increase as the number of years to expiration increases and fall as the exercise price rises. For example, the entry $24.59 in the next-to-last column of the first row is the price of a one-year call option on a $100 share of a reference portfolio with an exercise price of 80. The price is $29.12 for an otherwise identical option with a maturity of two years (one row down), and it is $10.45 if the option's exercise price is 100 (one column to the right).

Consider the risk-reward opportunities available to people who divide their wealth between call options and risk-free bonds maturing on the same date that the options expire. These investors are guaranteed a certain minimum rate of return by virtue of the fact that a fraction of their wealth is invested in the risk-free asset, and they cannot lose more than they invest in the options. The reward is the potential additional return that can come if the calls end up "in the money."

The investor's exposure to risk depends on three variables: the exercise price of the calls (X); the fraction of wealth invested in calls (w); and the maturity of the calls (T). A trade-off between reward and risk exists along *each* of these three dimensions of choice. Equation (1) expresses the basic formula that relates the investor's terminal wealth to the value of the refer-

11. Long-term options such as these are called LEAPS, an acronym for long-term equity anticipation securities. Options on the S&P 500 are traded on the Chicago Board Options Exchange under the symbol SPX. They are European-type options, which means that they can be exercised only at their expiration date.

ence portfolio on the option's expiration date and to the three choice variables—X, w, and T:

(1) $$\frac{W_T}{W_0} = (1 - w)e^{rT} + \frac{w}{C(X,T)} \max\left[100\frac{S_T}{S_0} - X,0\right],$$

where W_T is the investor's wealth at time T, r is the risk-free interest rate, $C(X, T)$ is the price of a call with exercise price X expiring at time T, and S_T is the value of the reference portfolio at time T. For ease of interpretation, I make the following transformation from values to annualized continuously compounded rates:

$$R \equiv \frac{1}{T} \ln\left(\frac{W_T}{W_0}\right),$$

where R is the portfolio's rate of return.

Let us examine each of the risk-reward trade-offs one at a time.

Payoff Diagrams

First, consider the trade-off arising from the choice of exercise price. The exercise price determines the threshold value of the market index, that is, the value of the index that must be reached in order for the call option to wind up "in the money" at expiration. The higher this threshold value, the greater the client's exposure to risk. However, since the price of the call falls when X rises, the client's upside participation rate rises along with the increase in risk exposure. Thus, there is a trade-off between risk and reward.

To derive the formula for the payoff function relating R and X, substitute into equation (1) the values $w = .10$, $r = .05$, and $T = 1$ to get

$$\frac{W_1}{W_0} = .9e^{.05} + \frac{.1}{C(X,1)} \max\left[100\frac{S_1}{S_0} - X,0\right].$$

Figures 8.1 and 8.2 illustrate the effect of changing X. Figure 8.1 shows the client's rate of return as a function of the value of the reference portfolio for different exercise prices. The curves all have the kinked shape characteristic of call-option payoff diagrams. In every case, the investment manager invests 90 percent of the client's wealth in the risk-free asset and 10 percent in stock-index calls.[12] The minimum rate of return on the portfolio is therefore the same in all cases: -5.5 percent.

---

12. Note that a call option with an exercise price of zero is equivalent to the stock itself if the stock pays no dividend over the life of the option.

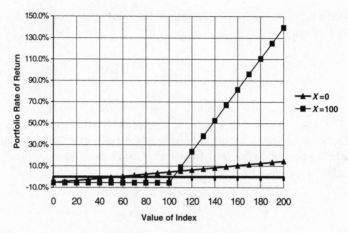

Fig. 8.1   Payoff diagrams with different exercise prices
Note: The portfolio has 90 percent invested in the risk-free asset earning 5 percent and the other 10 percent invested in calls with exercise price X. T = one year, and σ = .2.

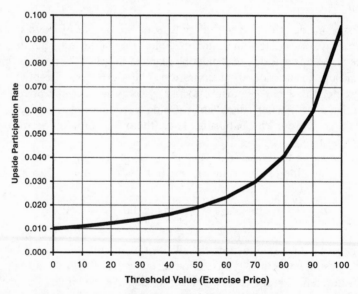

Fig. 8.2   Trade-off between exercise price and participation rate

The higher the exercise price, the steeper the slope to the right of the kink. This slope is the upside participation rate. For example, if X is set at 80, the option price is $24.59, and the upside participation rate is .004. If X is set at the current level of the reference index (X = 100), then the upside participation rate is approximately .010. This trade-off between threshold value (X) and upside participation is shown in figure 8.2.

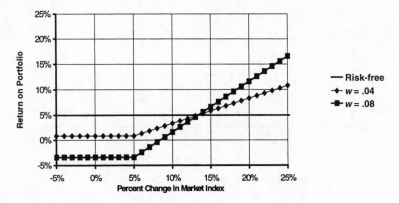

Fig. 8.3   Payoff diagrams with different amounts of wealth at risk
Note: $r = 5$ percent, $T =$ one year, $X = 100e^{.05}$, and $C = 8$. All the payoff functions meet in a common intersection point, whose coordinates are 13.4 and 5 percent.

Risk and Reward in an Options Framework

Now consider what happens if we vary the minimum return (R_{min}) by changing the fraction of wealth at risk (w), holding constant the other two choice variables—X and T. Figure 8.3 shows the portfolio rate of return as a function of the percentage change in the underlying stock index when $r = 5$ percent, $T =$ one year, $X = 100e^{.05}$, and $C = 8$.

Each curve corresponds to a different level of w. The vertical intercept is the minimum rate of return on the portfolio, and the slope of each payoff curve to the right of the kink is the corresponding upside participation rate. The higher the value of w, the lower the minimum return, and the higher the upside participation rate. For all three curves, the kink occurs at the risk-free rate of 5 percent per year because, if the percentage increase in the market index turns out to be less than this, the calls expire worthless. Note that all three payoff curves meet in a common break-even point, where the percentage increase of the market index is 13.4 percent and the portfolio return equals the risk-free interest rate.[13]

The *risk-reward trade-off frontier* shown in figure 8.4 corresponds to $T =$ one year and $X = 100e^{.05}$. The Black-Scholes price of the corresponding call is 8. In figure 8.4, the R_{min} is measured on the horizontal axis, and the upside participation rate is measured on the vertical axis. The slope of this trade-off line is the reward-to-risk ratio.

Effect of the Time Horizon on the Risk-Reward Trade-Off

As discussed in section 8.1.3 above, one can distinguish at least two different meanings of the term *time horizon:* the *planning* horizon and the

---

13. More generally, this intersection point occurs where $S_T/S_0 = e^r(1 + C/100)$.

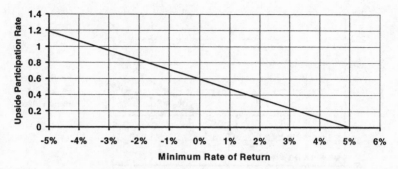

Fig. 8.4   The risk-reward trade-off frontier

decision horizon. The planning horizon is the total length of time for which one plans. The decision horizon is the length of time between decisions to revise the portfolio. The shortest possible decision horizon is the minimum trading interval over which investors can revise their portfolios. In this paper, as in other single-period models of portfolio selection, T refers to the length of the decision horizon, not the length of the planning horizon.

The effect of the length of the time horizon T for an investor who is willing to put 8 percent of his wealth at risk is shown in figure 8.5. Note that, the longer the length of the decision horizon, the worse the trade-off between risk and reward. For instance, the upside participation rate for a one-year period is 100 percent, for four years 50 percent, and for twenty-five years only 20 percent. This occurs because the call price C is an increasing function of T and asymptotically approaches 100 in the limit as T gets larger and larger.

8.2.2   The Postretirement Phase

To this point, I have been discussing the accumulation phase of an investor's life cycle. Now I turn my attention to the postretirement phase of the life cycle, when the appropriate contract is a life annuity. I begin by explaining the way a variable annuity works. An assumed investment rate of return (AIR) is used to convert the total accumulation available at retirement into an annuity with a "notional" benefit payment, B_0. The annuity exceeds (falls short of) this notional value if the cumulative realized rate of return on the underlying reference portfolio exceeds (falls short of) the AIR. Each year, the amount received equals the previous year's benefit times a factor that reflects the actual compared to the assumed investment return:

$$B_t = B_{t-1} \frac{1 + R_t}{1 + \text{AIR}},$$

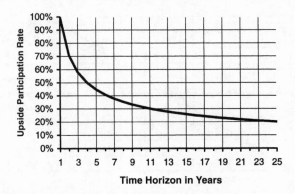

Fig. 8.5 Effect of time horizon on risk-reward trade-off
Note: $w = .08$, $r = 5$ percent, and $X = 100e^{.05}$.

where R_t is the actual real rate of return on the underlying portfolio in year t.

Thus, after t years of retirement, the annual benefit will reflect cumulative investment returns relative to the assumed return in each of the previous years of retirement:

$$B_t = B_t \prod_{i=1}^{t} \left(\frac{1 + R_i}{1 + \text{AIR}} \right).$$

With no loss of generality, we can divide both sides of this equation by the initial notional benefit and call the resulting number *the cumulative return factor:*

$$\frac{B_t}{B_0} = \prod_{i=1}^{t} \left(\frac{1 + R_i}{1 + \text{AIR}} \right) = \frac{\prod_{i=1}^{t}(1 + R_i)}{(1 + \text{AIR})^t}.$$

For simplicity, I use the risk-free real interest rate as the AIR. Assume that enough has been accumulated to qualify for a risk-free annuity of $10,000 per year. Consider three alternative annuity designs: A risk-free real annuity of $10,000 per year for twenty years; a variable annuity with a "notional" benefit payment (B_0) of $10,000; and a variable annuity with a floor and a cap. Figure 8.6 displays the payoff functions for the three alternative annuities as a function of the cumulative return factor. I assume a guaranteed floor equal to $7,000, a risk-free real interest rate of 3.5 percent per year, and an annualized standard deviation of return on the underlying portfolio equal to 15 percent. The question is, What is the value of the cap for the third annuity design?

To address this question, I employ financial engineering. The first step

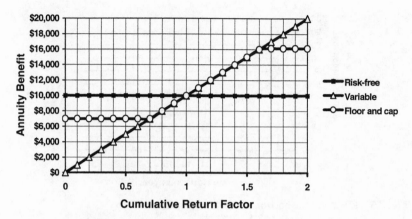

Fig. 8.6   Annuity payoff diagram

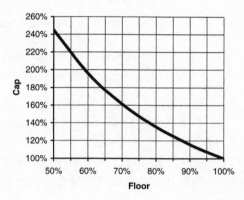

Fig. 8.7   Trade-off between the variable annuity floor and the cap

is to recognize that setting a floor and a cap on the variable benefit payment is equivalent to buying a "collar," that is, buying a European put option with an exercise price of $7,000 and financing it by writing a call with a higher exercise price.[14] Since the annuity consists of a sequence of twenty benefit payments, twenty collars are required, each with a maturity that is one year longer than the previous one. I compute the total price of the twenty puts using the Black-Scholes formula. Since each of the twenty annual payments is capped at the same level, the problem is to find the "exercise price" of the calls that will make their total price equal to the price of the puts.

Figure 8.7 shows the trade-off between the floor and the cap expressed as a percentage of the notional benefit. Thus, with the floor set at 70 per-

14. For a more complete explanation of collars, see Bodie, Kane, and Marcus (1999, 631–32).

cent, the cap must be 161 percent. The higher the floor, the lower the cap. Of course, if the floor is set at 100 percent of the notional benefit, then the cap must also be set at 100 percent.

8.3   The Role of Private-Sector Financial Institutions

How can private-sector financial institutions provide credible guarantees of minimum real rates of return over long periods of time? The simplest organizational structure to perform this function would be that of a mutual fund or an investment trust that buys TIPS (Treasury inflation-protected securities) and index options and distributes a pro rata share to all its shareholders. The index options could be either exchange traded—if the required maturities are actually traded—or synthesized through dynamic replication. With such an organizational form, there can be no risk of default.

Alternatively, the institution could be organized as an insurance company that sells guaranteed investment contracts to its customers and has sufficient investor capital to make its liabilities free of default risk. To minimize the capital required for this purpose, the firm could hedge its liabilities dynamically using index futures contracts. The resulting dynamic hedges would be "model dependent" and therefore less than perfect.[15]

8.4   The Role of Government

In addition to operating what remains of the current social security system and mandating minimum contributions to personal retirement accounts, there are at least two other important roles that have been proposed for the government: to issue inflation-protected bonds for people to invest in and to guarantee a minimum level of retirement benefits from PIAs.

8.4.1   Inflation-Protected Securities

The first of these is critical.[16] The U.S. Treasury started issuing such bonds—TIPS—in January 1997, and policy spokesmen have made it clear that a primary purpose of these securities is to serve as a safe way for people to save for retirement. Their coupons and principal are linked to the CPI. Currently, the longest maturity is thirty years. Qualified financial institutions are allowed to "strip" them to offer customers zero-coupon bonds of any maturity up to thirty years.

15. For an analysis of the methods of making customer-held liabilities free of default risk, see Bodie and Merton (1992).
16. On this point, economists with policy views as diverse as Milton Friedman and James Tobin are in agreement.

In September 1998, the Treasury started selling a new type of inflation-protected savings bond, Series I, which is targeted at lower- and middle-income people. I bonds offer a fixed real rate of interest, which can be extended at the investor's option for up to thirty years. They are tax deferred until cashed in, come in denominations as small as $50, and can be purchased with no commissions. Individuals are limited to buying a maximum of $30,000 worth of them per year.

Merton (1983) has proposed that a superior alternative to indexing retirement annuities to the cost of living is to index them to aggregate per capita consumption. The idea motivating this proposal is that it is *standard-of-living* protection rather than *cost-of-living* protection that is of prime concern to most individuals. With a cost-of-living-linked annuity, the benefit is fixed in real terms regardless of what happens to the standard of living in the economy. Individuals receiving a cost-of-living annuity over a long period of retirement may experience a substantial decline in their *relative* standard of living compared to the rest of the population. According to the proposal, however, pensioners would receive a benefit that changes with per capita consumption, thus maintaining their relative standard of living.

Note that, with indexation to aggregate per capita consumption, there is no need to distinguish between the inflation and the real per capita consumption components of the change. The benefits are simultaneously protected against both. By linking the benefits to per capita consumption rather than the consumer price index, the pension scheme is made more consistent with both finance theory and common sense. One way to describe the per capita consumption annuity proposal is as a defined-contribution plan offering variable-annuity contracts based on an underlying portfolio of bonds that are indexed to aggregate per capita consumption. Merton envisions a major role for the government as a financial innovator in making this type of product possible by issuing consumption-indexed bonds that are free of default risk.

8.4.2   Government Guarantees

Given the existence of default-free TIPs of all maturities, it is hard to see the need for government guarantees of retirement income. Individuals desiring a risk-free retirement income can purchase these bonds or invest in retirement annuities that are collateralized by these bonds. Other methods of guaranteeing retirement income have significant costs (see Bodie and Merton 1992). For example, in the United States, the federal government provides guarantees of corporate defined-benefit pensions through the Pension Benefit Guaranty Corporation.[17] Let us consider some general

17. For an analysis of the Pension Benefit Guaranty Corporation's guarantee program, see Bodie and Merton (1993) or Bodie (1996).

issues that inevitably arise when government serves as the guarantor of such household assets.

In the past, some among both the general public and politicians have mistakenly believed that a loan guarantee costs the government nothing unless there eventually turns out to be a shortfall.[18] However, perhaps owing to the large losses in the deposit insurance funds, such arguments seem to appear less frequently now. Indeed, since 1990, the U.S. government has taken steps in its budget process to account for the cost of the guarantees it issues (see OMB 1993).

Even if it recognizes the cost of its guarantees, the government is not obliged to price them accordingly. There can be political pressure for the government to charge less than the fair market premium for its guarantees or not to charge for them at all. Government guarantees are a politically attractive form of expenditure because they are less "visible" than outright cash outlays or budget allocations. To keep premiums low, the government must require the insured entity to hedge its insured liabilities completely. If the imposition of strict asset restrictions by the government guarantor is also ruled out, then the guarantor is left with no feasible way to perform its guarantee function efficiently.

8.5 Conventional Investment Advice and Economic Theory

There are many sources of advice for investors, including newspaper columns, magazine articles, and web sites on personal investing. In addition, educational materials are provided by mutual fund groups and other providers of financial products. While there are some differences in advice provided by these various sources, a nonexhaustive search indicates that they generally agree on a set of practical guidelines, which can be summarized as follows:

- Investors should have an emergency fund invested in short-term safe assets. This fund should be held outside one's retirement account to avoid the tax and other penalties generally associated with having to withdraw funds prematurely from a retirement account.
- Tax-advantaged assets, such as municipal bonds, should be held outside one's retirement account, and only investors in high tax brackets should invest in them at all.
- Funds saved for retirement should be invested primarily in equities and longer-term fixed-income securities.
- The fraction of assets invested in equities should decline with age. A popular rule of thumb regarding the age-equity relation is that the per-

18. If applied to the private sector, this same mistaken belief would imply that insurance companies do not incur a liability when they issue policies, only when there are actual damage claims.

centage of one's portfolio to invest in equities should be 100 minus one's age. So a person thirty years old should invest 70 percent in equities, and a person aged seventy should invest 30 percent in equities.

• The fraction invested in equities should increase with wealth because a wealthier individual should be able to handle more risk.

This practical advice can be derived from theoretical models similar to the ones presented in section 8.1 above by making suitable assumptions about either the investor's utility function, external borrowing constraints, or the stochastic processes governing security returns.

Nonetheless, there *are* some elements in the reasoning used to support the conventional advice that contradict economic theory. The two I focus on here are the ones that have the most potential to distort policy decisions in all sectors (households, firms, and government agencies): *Stocks are less risky in the long run than in the short run,* and *stocks are a good hedge against inflation in the long run.*

These propositions lead people to think that, the longer their planning horizon, the higher the fraction of their money they should invest in equities. As an example, consider the following "educational" information that appears at the Vanguard Group's web site: "In your early and middle working years, when your investment horizon extends 40 years or more, your primary investment objective should be to accumulate capital for your retirement. At this point in your life, common stocks should be your dominant investment option, for two reasons: Stocks have provided the highest long-term total returns of any major asset class. While stocks also have had the highest volatility level of any asset class, the passage of time has a dampening effect on their short-term fluctuations."

Since the 1960s, Paul Samuelson (1963, 1971, 1989, 1994) has been demonstrating the logical flaw in this reasoning. Using option-pricing theory, I, too, have tried—with little success—to persuade professional investment managers that it is a mistake to think that stocks are less risky in the long run than in the short run (see Bodie 1995).

I think that one reason that so many people still make the mistake is that they (at least implicitly) define *investment risk* as the probability of earning less than some target rate of return. In the practitioner literature, this probability is called *shortfall risk.* It is indeed true that, if the assumed expected rate of return on stocks exceeds the target rate of return, the probability of a shortfall does indeed decline as the time horizon lengthens. But the probability of a shortfall is a flawed measure of risk because it completely ignores how large the potential shortfall might be. A measure of risk should take account of both the probability and the magnitude of the potential shortfall (see Harlow 1991).

The proposition that stocks are a good inflation hedge relies on the fallacious belief that stocks are not risky in the long run. An inflation hedge would allow one to lock in a certain amount of purchasing power at a future date with certainty. As discussed before, the asset with that feature is an inflation-indexed bond maturing on the future date. Stocks do not promise a sure inflation-protected return over any time horizon.

Another reason that people fall into the trap of thinking that stocks are not risky in the long run is that they rely on faulty statistical inference. They are persuaded by the stock market history of the United States and the United Kingdom that, with virtual certainty, stocks will outperform bonds over long periods. There are at least three arguments against drawing such an inference from the historical data. The first is the small number of independent observations of long-period returns; the second is survivorship bias; and the third is that bonds in the past were not protected against inflation.

8.6 Summary and Conclusions

As the world's population ages over the next few decades, governments will shift from pay-as-you-go systems of social security to mandatory self-directed retirement accounts. A major challenge facing the financial services industry is to help people manage the risks of investing for their own retirement. One strategy that is likely to succeed is to provide new contracts for long-term saving that combine the best features of defined-contribution and defined-benefit pension plans.

This paper has attempted to show that financial intermediaries can offer personal investment accounts that "replicate" the best features of defined-benefit pensions. These accounts could offer some choice regarding participation in the "upside" potential of the stock market without jeopardizing the minimum level of benefits mandated by law. It has also attempted to show that the existence of inflation-protected U.S. Treasury bonds makes government guarantees of personal investment accounts unnecessary, that guaranteeing investments in common stocks against the risk of a "shortfall" can be very costly and creates the potential for moral hazard, and that government can play a (perhaps unique) role in enriching the investment opportunity set by issuing securities that are linked to an index of per capita consumption spending.

References

Arrow, Kenneth. 1964. The role of securities in the optimal allocation of risk-bearing. *Review of Economic Studies* 31, no. 2 (April): 91–96.

Banz, R. W., and M. H. Miller. 1978. Prices for state contingent claims: Some estimates and applications. *Journal of Business* 51, no. 4 (October): 653–72.

Bernstein, Peter L. 1992. *Capital ideas.* New York: Free Press.

Black, Fischer, and Myron S. Scholes. 1973. The pricing of options and corporate liabilities. *Journal of Political Economy* 81 (May-June): 637–54.

Bodie, Zvi. 1995. On the risk of stocks in the long run. *Financial Analysts Journal* 51, no. 3 (May/June): 18–22.

———. 1996. What the Pension Benefit Guaranty Corporation can learn from the Federal Savings and Loan Insurance Corporation. *Journal of Financial Services Research* 10, no. 1 (January): 83–100.

Bodie, Zvi, and Dwight B. Crane. 1999. The design and production of new retirement savings products. *Journal of Portfolio Management* 25, no. 2 (winter): 77–82.

Bodie, Zvi, Alex Kane, and Alan B. Marcus. 1999. *Investments.* 4th ed. Burr Ridge, Ill.: Irwin/McGraw-Hill.

Bodie, Zvi, and Robert C. Merton. 1992. On the management of financial guarantees. *Financial Management* 21 (winter): 87–109.

———. 1993. Pension benefit guarantees in the United States: A functional analysis. In *The future of pensions in the United States,* ed. R. Shmitt. Philadelphia: University of Pennsylvania Press.

Bodie, Zvi, R. C. Merton, and W. Samuelson. 1992. Labor supply flexibility and portfolio choice in a life-cycle model. *Journal of Economic Dynamics and Control* 16:427–49.

Breeden, D., and R. Litzenberger. 1978. Prices of state-contingent claims implicit in option prices. *Journal of Business* 51, no. 4 (October): 621–51.

Brennan, Michael J., and H. Cao. 1996. Information, trade, and derivative securities. *Review of Financial Studies* 9:163–208.

Brennan, Michael J., and E. Schwartz. 1976. The pricing of equity-linked life insurance policies with an asset value guarantee. *Journal of Financial Economics* 3 (June): 195–214.

Brown, Stephen J., W. N. Goetzmann, and S. A. Ross. 1995. Survival. *Journal of Finance* 50, no. 3 (July): 853–73.

Debreu, G. 1959. *Theory of value.* New York: Wiley.

Goetzmann, W. N., and P. Jorion. 1999. A century of global stock markets. *Journal of Finance* 54 (June): 953–80.

Hakansson, N. H. 1976. The purchasing power fund: A new kind of financial intermediary. *Financial Analysts Journal* 32, no. 6 (November/December): 2–12.

Harlow, W. V. 1991. Asset allocation in a downside risk framework. *Financial Analysts Journal* (September/October): 28–40.

Jagganathan, R., and N. R. Kocherlakota. 1996. Why should older people invest less in stocks than younger people? *Federal Reserve Bank of Minneapolis Quarterly Review* 20, no. 3 (summer): 11–23.

Leland, Hayne E. 1980. Who should buy portfolio insurance? *Journal of Finance* 35:581–94.

Lintner, John. 1965. The valuation of risk assets and the selection of risky investments in stock portfolios and capital budgets. *Review of Economics and Statistics* 47 (February): 13–37.

Markowitz, Harry. 1952. Portfolio selection. *Journal of Finance* 7 (March): 77–91.

Merton, Robert C. 1969. Lifetime portfolio selection under uncertainty: The continuous-time case. *Review of Economics and Statistics* 51 (August): 247–57. Reprinted in Merton (1992).

———. 1971. Optimum consumption and portfolio rules in a continuous-time model. *Journal of Economic Theory* 3 (December): 373–413. Reprinted in Merton (1992).

———. 1973a. An intertemporal capital asset pricing model. *Econometrica* 41 (September): 867–87. Reprinted in Merton (1992).

————. 1973b. Theory of rational option pricing. *Bell Journal of Economics and Management Science* 4 (spring): 141–83. Reprinted in Merton (1992).

————. 1975. Theory of finance from the perspective of continuous time. *Journal of Financial and Quantitative Analysis* 10 (November): 659–74.

————. 1983. On consumption indexed public pension plans. In *Financial aspects of the United States pension system,* ed. Zvi Bodie and John B. Shoven. Chicago: University of Chicago Press.

————. 1992. *Continuous-time finance.* Rev. ed. Oxford: Blackwell.

————. 1998. Applications of option-pricing theory: Twenty-five years later. *American Economic Review* 88, no. 3 (June): 323–49.

Merton, Robert C., Myron S. Scholes, and M. Gladstein. 1978. The returns and risk of alternative call option portfolio investment strategies. *Journal of Business* 51 (April): 183–242.

Office of Management and Budget (OMB). 1993. Identifying long term obligations and reducing underwriting risks. In *Budget of the US government for 1993,* section 13. Washington, D.C.: U.S. Government Printing Office.

Ross, Stephen A. 1976. Options and efficiency. *Quarterly Journal of Economics* 90 (February): 75–89.

Samuelson, Paul A. 1963. Risk and uncertainty: A fallacy of large numbers. *Scientia* (April-May): 1–6.

————. 1971. The fallacy of maximizing the geometric mean in long sequences of investing or gambling. *Proceedings of the National Academy of Science,* 207–11.

————.1989. The judgement of economic science on rational portfolio management: Timing and long-horizon effects. *Journal of Portfolio Management* (fall): 4–12.

————. 1994. The long-term case for equities and how it can be oversold. *Journal of Portfolio Management* 21, no. 1 (fall): 15–24.

Scholes, Myron S. 1998. Derivatives in a dynamic environment. *American Economic Review* 88, no. 3 (June): 350–70.

Sharpe, William F. 1964. Capital asset prices: A theory of market equilibrium under conditions of risk. *Journal of Finance* 19 (September): 425–42.

Tobin, James. 1958. Liquidity preference as behavior towards risk. *Review of Economic Studies* 25 (February): 68–85.

Comment   Stephen A. Ross

This is a simple paper in the best sense of the term. In a literature that has become ever more complex, this paper takes us back to the basics and grounds the problem of offering investment choices to social security participants in the bedrock of modern financial theory. It begins with a historical introduction that focuses on two central research areas, the continuous-time consumption-portfolio problem and the principle of spanning. The relevance of the continuous-time model of optimal savings and consumption behavior is obvious, but that of spanning may be less

Stephen A. Ross is the Franco Modigliani Professor of Finance and Economics at the Sloan School of Management, Massachusetts Institute of Technology, and a research associate of the National Bureau of Economic Research.

so. It is well known that puts and calls span the space of opportunities. They are like Arrow-Debreu pure contingent claims that offer a dollar in a well-specified state of nature, but they are an interesting alternative in that they embody solutions to financial problems. Calls, for example, allow individuals to circumvent borrowing constraints and achieve a higher degree of leverage while retaining limited liability. More technically, they focus on the outcome of investments, that is, the distribution of returns, rather than on the artificial mathematically defined states in which outcomes occur.

It is useful to follow the pension literature and break the pension problem into the accumulation phase, during which savings takes place, and the payout phase, during which investments are harvested to finance consumption in retirement. Arguing that there seems to be consensus in the policy debate that any reform should leave social security mandatory and should have a minimum guarantee, the paper examines the use of investment accounts with explicit floors on performance during the accumulation phase—a principal guarantee—and participation in a stock index return above the floor. This is equivalent to combining a bond with a call option on the index. It is perplexing and ironic that, while in the United States we are just beginning to examine this as a potential structure for social security, it is a very popular private offering in Europe. (By some estimates, almost half of French bank accounts take this form.)

The form of this contract seems to have been shaped as much by the current debate as by the theory of consumption and portfolio choice over time. In general, having a guaranteed floor is equivalent to assuming that agents have infinite marginal utility below the cutoff level. Above the floor, this form is optimal only if the individual has a particular utility function (lognormal returns would require a constant-relative-risk-aversion utility function with particular parameters). It would be desirable to explore a bit further whether we really are comfortable with this as the appropriate form for preferences, although parsimony does seem to favor a contract with a floor and a linear participation in the index.

Using the standard Black-Scholes formula, the paper computes the value of these accounts for a grid of time horizons and guaranteed benefit floors. (There is a bit of a technical problem since the index pays no dividends and the formula should be adjusted, but this is easily patched.) Formally, if w is the proportion that the account puts into the option component, then the terminal payoff at retirement will be $(1 - w)$ times the amortized amount in the bond account and w times the accumulation in the option, that is,

$$(1 - w)e^{rT} + [w/c(x, T)] \max [100(S_T/S_0) - x, 0],$$

where r is the interest rate, $c(x, T)$ is the value of a call option with maturity T and exercise price x, and $100(S_T/S_0)$ is the ratio of the value of the index at time T to that today at time 0 and where the current index level is taken to be 100. Changing x and T allows us to trace out the sensitivity of this value to the parameters.

While this may seem like a simple exercise in option pricing, it is important to stress that it stands in sharp contrast to the usual methods for evaluating social security reforms. Typically, policy proposals are studied by simulating future investment returns and asking, for example, what level of funding will be required to sustain a given level of benefits with a given probability level. This is a bit like the value-at-risk approach often taken to examine the riskiness of a portfolio or a financial institution, and, while it is sensible, it is also highly dependent on a variety of assumptions about future stock return and, in particular, on the posited size of the equity-risk premium. There is currently a heated debate under way about whether the observed outperformance of the stock market is sustainable for the foreseeable future. The typical simulation methodology stakes policy on a presumption about that issue by drawing future returns from an estimate constructed from the historical record of market returns.

By contrast, the financial market approach advocated by Bodie asks a simpler question: Given the current pricing of financial securities, what is the cost of any particular policy composed of a floor return and an equity "kicker." In effect, this turns the focus of the equity-risk puzzle on its head. The question now becomes, not what the market will do in the future, but, rather, whether the market prices used to compute the value of the options are "correct." If the market is, in some sense, "too high," then that is a consequence of having realized a sequence of unsustainable returns that also, if used to project future returns, will result in an upwardly biased estimate of the risk premium on equities.

Despite this duality, for many questions the financial markets or option-pricing approach is clearly superior. Even if, in some equilibrium sense, we were all to agree that the current level of prices is appropriate, the traditional mode of analysis would still leave open the debate about what is the appropriate assumed future return on stocks. With the option-pricing approach, that rate plays no role in determining the current value of the strategy. In a real sense, the option approach does finesse the equity-risk-premium puzzle. Furthermore, insofar as there is to be a debate about whether the market is too high, any assumed level can be substituted for the current one to produce a different value for the strategy. But the intuitive "gut" check is simpler than that. The financial markets approach produces a clear price for any strategy, that is, the value it would have if one tried to replicate the payoffs with currently priced instruments. Whatever value emerges from that exercise is the price that such a strategy would cost if implemented by the private sector. Any analysis that produces a lower value, then, is tacitly assuming that private-sector pricing is wrong; that is, it is predicated on outguessing the market, and that would seem a rather precarious basis for public policy. (One could argue that the system would be so large that it would actually change pricing itself. While this is difficult to assess, such an effect would probably be marginal at most and is certainly highly conjectural.)

During the accumulation phase, the floor can be set in real terms, and the government issuance of inflation-linked bonds (or per capita consumption-linked bonds) provides a way of achieving a real guarantee. In the payout phase, the government can guarantee the minimum payout level, although Bodie sees little need for this given inflation-protected bonds. Bodie goes on to argue that the private sector could provide this service, given that the government has issued guaranteed linked bonds. Presumably, however, to hedge their liabilities, private institutions would have to rely in part on dynamic replication, and that is subject to model risk, gap-trading risk, and volatility and other parametric risks. For the system to work in an efficient way, there would have to be some form of regulation of these entities as well as private bonding and rating.

Given the economies of scope in such activities, the government would have to play a role—after all, ultimately, it is a government guarantee even if implemented by the private sector. However, given the history of problems with the government regulation of such guaranteed systems, from deposit insurance and savings and loans to guaranteed investment contracts, it would be naive to be sanguine about how well it would work. Equally important, to the extent to which individuals are given investment choices, there will be a demand for financial advice, and no doubt the financial advisory industry would expand dramatically in an effort to satisfy this demand. What is to be the role of government in this process is as yet unresolved. For example, if the government is to be an active purveyor of advice, presumably Bodie would have it side with those who argue that the fraction invested in equities, say, should decrease with age. This is much more obvious to Bodie than to me, particularly given that social security accounts are only a portion of total savings and, also, given the interaction between, for example, wealth and age.

There are, however, some more serious problems with a completely or partially privatized system with its attendant regulatory structure and the inevitable political pressures that will ensue. While I am very sympathetic to the idea of allowing individuals to invest for their retirement and, perhaps, have meaningful choices, I do not think that we can examine policy changes and ignore the political economic implications. Nor is this a matter of idle speculation; there have been significant historical examples from which we can learn.

I think that political pressure will manifest itself in at least two ways. First, if the system is to cost about the same as what we have today, then, inevitably, there must be a nonnegligible chance that a significant percentage of the participants will retire with less savings than they expected. Depending on the form of the system, this may mean that all or a large percentage will have earned only the real rate of return or some fraction of that. In either case, there will be a strong political motivation for the less-advantaged bloc to attempt to achieve through the political mechanism what they did not receive from the market. I have no particular wisdom on what to do about this problem, other than to acknowledge its existence. One thing is clear, however—by both practice and by law, the government seems bound to subgame perfection. That is to say, whatever circumstances it currently faces, the government must myopically seek the optimum. While that might seem desirable, it raises delicate incentive and time-consistency issues. For example, if the government could credibly commit to not aiding those whose investments led them to have less than a minimum amount, individuals might be encouraged to follow policies that kept them away from that floor. Since the government cannot commit not to help individuals in distress, it will always be forced to do so, and it must live with the consequences of individuals who recognize that they have a political "put" for their poor performance and act accordingly.

The only solution to this is to limit individual choices severely, but that raises the second and more subtle issue. When the system is privatized, individuals will be given account statements that detail "their" accumulations. When individuals reach retirement with a given level of accumulation, it may not be politically tenable to continue to deny them the ability to exercise their discretion in the payout phase. This was the experience of the TIAA-CREF system for financing pensions for employees in higher education. In response to individuals who felt that their investment options were too limited in the accumulation phase, TIAA-CREF has greatly expanded the available choices. With this has come the likelihood that the spread of individual performances will be much widened, and that has led to an attendant burden on financial education for participants in the system. In addition, many individuals were no longer content with the requirement that their accumulations be annuitized on retirement.

The first of these responses strongly suggests that, in the face of charges of paternalism, it will be politically difficult to restrain the range of choices open to individuals in the social security system. The second is equally devastating since it implies that it may not be possible to prevent some significant lump-sum distributions on retirement. (Even current tax penalties do not seem an adequate disincentive to prevent this from occurring.) To the extent to which the proceeds are not annuitized, the system no longer owns the ill health of its participants, and risk-averse individuals would have to oversave relative to an insurance system that operated as a tontine and would be subject to the vicissitudes of their own mortality.

Here, form may be as important as substance. Bodie argues that the guaranteed-floor system is usefully partitioned into a guarantee that is equivalent to an indexed bond and a call option on the equity return. This is equivalent (by put-call parity) to a contract that gives the return on an index with a put option at a specified level. In effect, individuals have the option to sell their portfolio back to the issuer—be it a private institution or the government—at a prespecified price. Perhaps, when results are bad, the fact that there is already an action that an individual can force on the government, that is, the put, would ameliorate some of the political pressure even though the numbers are the same. I suspect that this may be so, but, as a financial economist, venturing beyond the value equivalence of the two descriptions is further than I can go with any confidence.

Briefly concluding, then, the financial theoretic approach of Bodie is very appealing on both intellectual and practical grounds. The case is made most strongly for using it to evaluate the costs of proposed social security reforms, but the unresolved political financial issues make the case for the particular reform analyzed and, more generally, for a privatized system less clear.

Discussion Summary

Robert King remarked that, in a previous discussion, Thomas Sargent wondered why certain insurance instruments did not exist and noted that a similar puzzle applies here. About a dozen years ago, Chase Manhattan introduced a security that looked very much like the financial instrument proposed in the Bodie paper: it consisted of an account where the investor earned a particular interest rate and a portion of the market return if the stock market goes up. The accounts-return characteristics were based on Black-Scholes option-pricing principles. When the instrument was finally approved by the U.S. regulatory structure, its subsequent introduction was surprisingly unsuccessful. King noted that this is a major puzzle, which is crucial for the kind of proposal made in the paper. Maybe Chase Manhattan by itself was not able to offer the education that is also called for in the latter part of this paper; maybe there is something more fundamental that could explain the failure. He concluded that, in any event, the paper would benefit from examining that particular market experience in order to understand what actually happened.

John Campbell commented on the last section of the paper, dealing with conventional investment advice. First, Bodie contests Vanguard's statement that stocks appear to be less risky in the long run than in the short run. Campbell stated that the validity of that claim is an empirical issue, not a theoretical or logical one, as suggested in the paper. There is some evidence that the volatility of stocks rises with the horizon more slowly than would be implied by independently and identically distributed (i.i.d.) returns, which could be explained by mean reversion in stock returns. If stocks follow a mean-reverting process, then one can show that, for certain preferences, it is indeed optimal to invest more in stocks on average with a longer horizon. Of course, the mean reversion will also tend to generate market timing: one cannot obtain the positive horizon effect without also having the market timing. The entire topic of stocks for the long run involves quite some detail and subtlety. Campbell expressed the opinion that the treatment of the subject in the paper is too cavalier. The logical points that Samuelson made are "if-then" statements: if returns are i.i.d., and if people have power utility, then the horizon does not matter. But those logical arguments do not settle the practical issue of investing for the long run: that is by and large an empirical matter.

Relatedly, Campbell noted that the treatment of the Canner, Mankiw, and Weil (1997) (henceforth CMW) asset-allocation puzzle in the paper lacks detail. CMW point out that popular investment advice suggests that more conservative investors should have a higher ratio of bonds to stocks. This contrasts with standard mutual fund theorems that prescribe holding risky assets in a given proportion, regardless of risk aversion: more risk-averse people could simply add more cash to the mix and scale back on the mutual fund. As is mentioned in the paper, the explanation for this puzzle given by Brennan and Xia, bringing in intertemporal considerations, goes in the right direction. However, their explanation, ignoring inflation risk, is complete only to the extent that the conventional advice would concern real bonds. This is quite unlikely: the CMW paper was published before inflation-indexed bonds were available, and the investment advice analyzed certainly concerned nominal bonds. Therefore, the issue again becomes empirical: How close are nominal bonds to real bonds? Are they similar enough to justify the conventional advice, or does one need to modify the advice to stress real bonds rather than nominal ones? Campbell and Viceira (in press) report that it all depends. If one thinks that monetary policy will stay fairly stable as in the Greenspan era, then nominal and real bonds are sufficiently similar to rationalize the CMW puzzle using intertemporal considerations, ignoring inflation risk. The advice would be better for real bonds, but it is tolerable for nominal bonds. If, on the other hand, one thinks that there is a risk of going back to inflationary monetary policy, then the conventional advice is not correct and needs modification. Campbell concluded that there is a lot of empirical detail and that he worried that the paper ignores some crucial empirical questions, linking portfolio advice too closely to theoretical considerations.

Mark Warshawsky remarked that TIAA-CREF also considered offering financial products that combined real bonds with call options. They decided, however, that, at least at this stage, it is not feasible to do so because these long-term call options are very expensive. In response, *King* asked why long-term options are necessary. He added that Chase Manhattan's product was based on options with only one-year maturities.

Robert Shiller conjectured that only one- or two-year maturity options are traded, not long-term lifetime options, because most investors buy options for leveraging reasons, rather than to manage their lifetime security risk. An analogous issue is that people have virtually no interest in inflation-indexed bonds. They often complain that real bonds have not performed very well in recent years. Relatedly, an important explanation for the equity-premium puzzle, proposed by Benartzi and Thaler (1995), emphasizes that investors have very short horizons. This theory would be problematic for the ideas in the Bodie paper.

Henning Bohn pointed out that there is a caveat in the discussion of social security reform and financial engineering. Even if long-term call options were publicly traded, an important question to ask is who would be taking the opposite side of these option contracts. It seems important to consider aggregation and general equilibrium issues in this context.

James Poterba noted that Bodie is quite pessimistic about the ability of investors to make sound asset-allocation decisions. He and David Wise (Poterba and Wise 1998) reached a different conclusion in a paper that analyzed the investment decisions within 401(k) plans: except for the poor degree of diversification, the choices with respect to equity exposure did not seem totally anomalous. Poterba also noted that, although indexed bonds invested in a 401(k) or IRA plan earn a known real return, indexed bonds held in taxable accounts do not, both because of the uncertainty about the tax system and because the tax is based on the total cumulated nominal interest. This means that there is uncertainty about what the real after-tax return will be on withdrawal.

Following up on Poterba's first remark, *David Cutler* suggested adding a discussion concerning the tails of the distribution of individual investor choices. For instance, it would be interesting to mention what share of the investor population does not make sound investment decisions.

Martin Feldstein expressed the opinion that the link to social security benefits was missing in the paper. In particular, he gave the example of an individual who has to decide how much to save using these call options to eventually acquire the funds to buy the annuity that figure 8.6 reports. This calculation would be very interesting as it would allow the author to really offer investors finished financial products among which to choose.

Zvi Bodie responded first to Feldstein's question about how much an investor would have to save to achieve some target replacement rate and noted that the answer was straightforward only for investments at the risk-free rate. Any other investment, including call options, would be uncertain. *Feldstein* inquired about the case where the investor buys options to assure a certain probability of meeting the target. *Bodie* replied that, although

Bodie and Crane (1999) considers precisely this, he is concerned about simulations reporting probabilities of achieving or not achieving some target. The problem is related to the disagreement between two papers presented earlier, that by Kent Smetters (chap. 3 in this volume) and that by Feldstein, Ranguelova, and Samwick (chap. 2 in this volume). Bodie argued that the probability of a shortfall is a very misleading measure of risk. It should be contrasted with the cost of insuring against the shortfall, which Bodie believed to be a superior measure: the probability of a shortfall does not consider the weight that one attaches to a shortfall or its severity. Instead, one should concentrate on Arrow-Debreu prices or risk-neutral probabilities, following the insight from option-pricing theory.

With respect to Campbell's remark, Bodie agreed that the treatment in the paper of the proposition that stocks are less risky in the long run than in the short run could be considered too cavalier. He added, however, that his previous work with Robert Merton and William Samuelson (Bodie, Merton, and Samuelson 1992) offers a more detailed and careful analysis of the issue of life-cycle asset allocation and focuses, among other things, on the importance of human capital and labor supply flexibility. The paper is one example of the discussant's remark that the finance literature does not offer clear-cut and unambiguous answers to the question of optimal life-cycle portfolio choice. For instance, it is found that, under certain conditions, it is optimal to increase equity exposure as one ages, whereas, in other circumstances, older investors should hold less risky assets. Bodie concluded that, if anything is cavalier, it is the treatment of the subject by popular investment advisers, stating that, unambiguously and independently of preferences, stocks are less risky in the long run.

In response to King, Bodie noted that it is very rare in the history of the financial industry to find an innovation that has been successful immediately, except perhaps for money market funds, which succeeded from the outset, mainly because of Regulation Q and because of high short-term interest rates in the 1970s. Market conditions matter a lot. Bodie is optimistic about the prospects of the products proposed in the paper in the long run and refers to their success in Europe.

Regarding Shiller's comment that investors are reluctant to buy indexed bonds, Bodie replied that people change their investment behavior sluggishly. He added that part of the problem might be insufficient marketing efforts trying to make indexed bonds known to the general public.

Finally, *David Wise* replied to Shiller's comment, noting that long-term options do exist and are available as over-the-counter products. Moreover, they can be hedged relatively well dynamically using short-term options. Wise concurred with Bodie's discussion of the lack of initial success for many new financial products and gave the example of index funds. He further noted that indexed bonds might not gain popularity in a country like the United States characterized by relatively low and stable inflation.

References

Benartzi, Shlomo, and Richard Thaler. 1995. Myopic loss aversion and the equity premium puzzle. *Quarterly Journal of Economics* 110:73–92.

Bodie, Zvi, and Dwight B. Crane. 1999. The design and production of new retirement savings products. *Journal of Portfolio Management* 25, no. 2 (winter): 77–82.

Bodie, Zvi, R. C. Merton, and W. Samuelson. 1992. Labor supply elasticity and portfolio choice in a life-cycle model. *Journal of Economic Dynamics and Control* 16:427–49.

Campbell, John Y., and Luis M. Viceira. In press. Who should buy long-term bonds? *American Economic Review.*

Canner, Niko, N. Gregory Mankiw, and David N. Weil. 1997. An asset allocation puzzle. *American Economic Review* 87, no. 1:181–91.

Poterba, James M., and David A. Wise. 1998. Individual financial decisions in retirement savings plans and the provision of resources for retirement. In *Privatizing social security,* ed. Martin Feldstein. Chicago: University of Chicago Press.

9

The Role of Real Annuities and Indexed Bonds in an Individual Accounts Retirement Program

Jeffrey R. Brown, Olivia S. Mitchell,
and James M. Poterba

It is better to have a permanent income than to be
fascinating.
—Oscar Wilde, *The Model Millionaire: A Note of Admiration*

The current U.S. social security system provides retirees with a real annuity during their retirement years. After a worker's primary insurance amount has been determined at the date of retirement, the purchasing power of social security benefits remains fixed for the balance of the individual's life. This is accomplished by indexing retirement benefits to annual changes in the consumer price index (CPI). Retirees are therefore insulated from inflation risk, at least as long as their consumption bundle is not too different from the bundle used to compute the CPI.

Several current reform plans propose to supplement, or partially replace, the existing defined-benefit social security system with mandatory individual defined-contribution accounts. These plans are discussed in Gramlich (1996), Mitchell, Myers, and Young (1999), and NASI (1998). In most "individual account" plans, retirees would be required to purchase an annuity with all or part of their accumulated account balances. Yet the existing market for individual annuities in the United States is small, the expected present value of annuity payouts is typically below the

Jeffrey R. Brown is assistant professor of public policy at the Kennedy School of Government, Harvard University, and a faculty research fellow of the National Bureau of Economic Research. Olivia S. Mitchell is the International Foundation of Employee Benefit Plans Professor of Insurance and Risk Management at the Wharton School, University of Pennsylvania, and a research associate of the National Bureau of Economic Research. James M. Poterba is the Mitsui Professor of Economics at the Massachusetts Institute of Technology and director of the Public Economics Program at the National Bureau of Economic Research.

The authors thank Leemore Dafny and especially Amy Finkelstein for outstanding research assistance. They thank Joseph Bellersen, Brett Hammond, Eugene Strum, participants in an NBER preconference, and especially John Campbell and Mark Warshawsky for helpful discussions. The National Science Foundation and the National Institute on Aging (Brown and Poterba), the Pension Research Council at the Wharton School (Mitchell), and the National Bureau of Economic Research provided research support.

purchase price of the annuity, and virtually all annuities currently available offer nominal rather than real payout streams. This has led some to argue that individual account plans would expose retirees to inflation risk that they do not currently face. If individuals purchase nominal annuities with their accumulated funds and the inflation rate is positive during their pay-out period, then the real value of their annuity payouts will decline over time. Even if inflation was *expected* to be positive at the time of the annuity purchase, some individuals may not recognize this, and they may experience an unexpected decline in real payouts. This effect is distinct from the inflation risk that arises from differences between expected and actual inflation rates.

In this paper, we explore four issues concerning real annuities, nominal annuities, and the inflation risks faced by prospective retirees, all of which are relevant to the prospects for individual accounts under social security reform. We begin by describing the annuity market in the United Kingdom. Annuitants in the United Kingdom can select from a wide range of both real and nominal annuity products. The U.K. annuity market demonstrates the feasibility of offering real annuities in the private marketplace. Moreover, the current U.K. annuity market may indicate the direction in which the U.S. annuity market will evolve since indexed bonds promising a fixed real return to investors have been available in the United Kingdom for nearly two decades. The availability of such bonds has made it possible for U.K. insurers to offer real annuity products without bearing inflation risk. Similar bonds have been available in the United States for only two years. Our evaluation of the U.K. annuity market includes an analysis of the relative prices of both real and nominal annuities, and we present estimates of how much a potential annuitant must pay to purchase the inflation insurance provided by a real annuity.

Next, we turn to the annuity market in the United States and investigate the availability of real annuities in this country. In early 1997, the U.S. government introduced Treasury inflation-protection securities (TIPS), and, since then, two products that might be described as *inflation-indexed annuities* have come to market. One, offered by the Irish Life Company of North America (ILONA), promises a constant-purchasing-power stream of benefits. Although this product offers buyers a real stream of annuity payouts, there have been no sales to date. The second, offered by TIAA-CREF, is a variable-payout annuity with payouts linked to returns on the CREF index-linked bond account. We describe the operation of the latter account in some detail and explain why, in practice, the TIAA-CREF variable annuity is not an inflation-indexed annuity. Our analysis of these two products suggests that no commercially significant real annuities are currently available in the U.S. annuity market.

We then consider whether a retiree could use a portfolio of stocks or bonds, in lieu of a portfolio of indexed bonds, to hedge long-term inflation risk. Specifically, we evaluate how much inflation risk annuitants would bear if, instead of purchasing nominal annuities, they purchased variable-payout annuities with payouts linked to various asset portfolios. We assess the potential inflation protection provided by different variable-payout annuities using historical correlation patterns between inflation and nominal returns on stocks, bonds, and bills.

The final portion of the analysis explores the expected-utility consequences of annuitizing retirement resources in alternative ways. A stylized model is used to calculate the expected lifetime utility of a retiree who could purchase a nominal annuity, a real annuity, and a variable-payout equity-linked annuity. In the first and third cases, the retiree would bear some inflation risk. We calibrate this model using available estimates of risk aversion, mortality risks, and the stochastic structure of real returns on corporate stock. Our results suggest that, for plausible values of risk aversion, retirees would not pay very much for the opportunity to purchase a real rather than a nominal annuity. This finding is sensitive, however, to assumptions regarding the stochastic process for inflation. Very high expected inflation rates, or very high levels of inflation variability, can reverse this conclusion.

We also find that a variable-payout annuity with payouts linked to the returns on a portfolio of common stocks is more attractive than a real annuity for consumers with modest risk aversion. This result rests on assumptions about the expected return on stocks relative to riskless assets and hence must be viewed with some caution since there is substantial prospective uncertainty about expected stock returns. The finding nevertheless illustrates the potentially important role of variable-payout annuities as devices for annuitizing assets from individual accounts.

The paper is divided into five sections. Section 9.1 presents our findings on the real and nominal annuity markets in the United Kingdom. Section 9.2 describes two "inflation-linked annuities" offered in the United States. Section 9.3 reports our findings on the correlation between unexpected inflation and real returns on various financial assets and summarizes previous research on this relation. This section also presents evidence on the ex post real payout streams that would have been paid to retirees had they purchased variable-payout annuities at different dates over the last seventy years. Section 9.4 outlines our algorithm for evaluating the utility benefits of access to various types of annuity products. We link this work with the rapidly growing literature on lifetime portfolio allocation in the presence of risky asset returns and uncertain inflation. In a brief concluding section, we sketch directions for future work.

9.1 The Market for Real Annuities in the United Kingdom

We begin our analysis by describing the real annuity market in the United Kingdom since it provides important evidence on both the feasibility of providing real annuities through private insurers and the consumer costs of buying inflation insurance. We then calculate the expected present discounted value of payouts on real and nominal annuities currently available in the United Kingdom.

9.1.1 The Current Structure of the U.K. Annuity Market

Annuities providing a constant real payout stream are widely available in the United Kingdom. This is partly due to the fact that government-issued indexed bonds have been available in the United Kingdom for nearly two decades. Insurance companies holding these bonds can largely hedge the price-level risk that is associated with offering annuity payouts denominated in real rather than in nominal terms. (Payouts on indexed bonds in the United Kingdom adjust to past inflation with a lag, which results in some residual price-level exposure for insurance companies offering real annuities.) Blake (1999) reports that insurers offering nominal annuities typically back them by holding nominal government bonds while those offering real annuities hold indexed bonds.

There are two segments of the individual annuity market in the United Kingdom, defined according to where funds used to purchase the annuity have been accumulated. One market segment involves annuities purchased with tax-qualified retirement funds; the other is focused on annuities purchased outside such plans. Qualified retirement plans in Britain include defined-benefit occupation pension schemes and personal pension plans (PPPs). Most occupation plans are defined-benefit plans, and the annuities that are paid out to their beneficiaries are not purchased in the individual annuity market. PPPs, available since 1988, are retirement-saving plans that are broadly similar to individual retirement accounts in the United States. (Prior to 1988, a similar type of plan was available only to self-employed individuals.) Contributions to PPPs are tax deductible, and income on the assets held in such plans is not taxed until the funds are withdrawn. Budd and Campbell (1998) report that, in the early 1990s, roughly one-quarter of U.K. workers participated in a personal pension plan. These plans are likely to account for most of the purchases of qualified annuities since defined-contribution plans constitute a minority of U.K. occupation pensions.

Those who reach retirement age with assets in a defined-contribution occupation pension, or with assets in a personal pension plan, are legally required to annuitize at least part of their pension accumulation. For this reason, the U.K. market for annuities purchased with funds from qualified pension plans is known as the *compulsory annuity market*. In recent years, there has been some relaxation of the rules requiring annuitization. Currently, a retiree can withdraw up to one-quarter of a personal pension plan accumulation as a lump-sum distribution, and assets can be held in the PPP up to age seventy-five before they must be annuitized.

The U.K. annuity market also includes a second segment, which contains voluntarily purchased annuities. This is known as the "noncompulsory" market. In this second market segment, funds accumulated outside qualified retirement plans are used to purchase annuity products.

The demographic characteristics and mortality prospects of annuity buyers in the compulsory and noncompulsory markets are likely to differ. The set of people who purchase annuities in the voluntary market is likely to have better mortality prospects (i.e., longer life expectancies) than the U.K. population at large. In addition, workers who have PPPs or who are covered by defined-contribution occupation plans are probably not a random subset of the population. They may also have better longevity prospects than those of the population at large. Finkelstein and Poterba (1999) compare the U.K. compulsory and noncompulsory annuity markets and show that payouts as a fraction of premiums are somewhat lower in the noncompulsory market than in the compulsory market. This finding is consistent with the view that adverse selection among annuitants receiving employer pensions is less substantial than adverse selection among people buying individual annuities outside a retirement plan. Our analysis focuses on annuities offered in the "compulsory-annuity" marketplace.

The compulsory annuitization requirement for personal pension plans has created a substantial group of retirement-age individuals in the United Kingdom who must purchase an annuity. To service their needs, annuity brokers exist to help retirees obtain quotes on annuity products. We contacted several of these brokers and requested data on U.K. annuity prices and the terms of annuity contracts. We obtained data from a number of firms. While we have not established precisely how much of the annuity market our sample firms cover, our sample of insurance companies appears to include most of the major annuity providers.

To focus the discussion, we restrict our attention to nominal and inflation-linked single-life annuity products. Here, the term *nominal* is used to refer to values denominated in current pounds (or dollars), while *real* refers to inflation-corrected pounds or dollars. We analyze products offered by nine insurance companies offering retail price index (RPI)-linked single-life annuity policies and fourteen companies offering nominal single-life products. (By comparison, there are nearly one hundred insurance companies offering individual annuity products in the United States, according to A. M. Best's surveys.) We do not consider "graded" nominal annuity policies that offer a rising stream of nominal benefits over the life of the annuitant, with a prespecified nominal escalation rate. Graded annuities provide annuitants with a way of backloading the real value of payouts from their annuities, but they do not insure against inflation fluctuations as real annuities do. We focus our attention on policies that were available in late August 1998, and we consider annuities with a £100,000 purchase price (premium).

Table 9.1 reports mean monthly payouts for both nominal and RPI-

Table 9.1   Summary Statistics on Nominal and Real Annuities Available in the Compulsory Annuity Market in the United Kingdom, 1998

	Average Monthly Payout for a £100,000 Annuity		Coefficient of Variation for Annuity Prices	
Annuity Buyer Characteristics	Nominal	Real	Nominal	Real
Man, 60 years old	666.20	476.35	4.26	6.09
Man, 65 years old	754.80	563.20	3.36	6.29
Man, 70 years old	872.94	679.50	2.88	6.31
Woman, 60 years old	602.99	416.81	5.34	5.02
Woman, 65 years old	666.88	482.70	4.27	4.49
Woman, 70 years old	760.50	575.06	3.65	4.48

Source: Authors' calculations based on data provided by U.K. annuity brokers. Reference date is 21 August 1998. Sample consists of fourteen large insurance companies that provide annuities. Data were provided by Annuity Direct, Ltd. All annuity products analyzed in this table offer a five-year guarantee period.

linked annuities for the firms in our sample. The first two columns show the sample average payout for each type of annuity. They indicate that the first-month payout on a real annuity is between 25 and 30 percent lower than the first-month payout on a nominal annuity. This reduction in initial benefits is sometimes cited as the reason why some consumers shy away from indexed annuities; later in the paper, we discuss a number of other potential explanations for consumer reluctance to purchase real annuities. The data also indicate differences in the ratio of nominal to real annuity payouts across age groups (real annuities are priced more favorably with rising age) and between men and women (real annuities are priced more favorably for men). These presumably reflect mortality-related differences in the expected duration of payouts under different annuity contracts.

We also see substantial variation in the annuity benefits paid by the different insurers, as was previously found for the U.S. annuity market by Mitchell, Poterba, Warshawsky, and Brown (hereafter MPWB) (1999). The third and fourth columns of table 9.1 report the coefficient of variation for monthly annuity payouts in both markets; here, we see that the pricing of indexed annuities varies more than that of nominal annuities. For five of the six "products" defined by the age and gender of the buyer, the coefficient of variation is greater for the real than for the nominal annuity. This may be due to the fact that the effective duration of a real annuity is longer than that of a nominal annuity so that the insurer's cost of providing a real annuity is more sensitive to future developments in mortality patterns. Explaining the observed price dispersion in annuity markets is an important task for future research.

9.1.2   Evaluating the "Money's Worth" of Nominal and Real Annuities

To evaluate the administrative and other costs associated with the individual annuities offered in the U.K. market, we compute the expected present discounted value (EPDV) of payouts for the average nominal and the average index-linked annuity. We compare this EPDV with the premium cost of the annuity to obtain a measure of the "money's worth" of the individual annuity. Warshawsky (1988), Friedman and Warshawsky (1988, 1990), and MPWB (1999) report results of "money's worth" calculations for annuities offered in the United States.

The formula used to calculate the EPDV of a *nominal* annuity with a monthly payout A_n, purchased by an individual of age b, is

$$(1) \qquad V_b(A_n) = \sum_{j=1}^{12 \cdot (115-b)} \frac{A_n \cdot P_j}{\Pi_{k=1}^{j}(1 + i_k)}.$$

We assume that no annuity buyer lives beyond age 115, and we truncate the annuity calculation after $12 \cdot (115 - b)$ months. P_j denotes the probability that an individual of age b years at the time of the annuity purchase survives for at least j months after buying the annuity. The variable i_k denotes the one-month nominal interest rate k months after the annuity purchase.

For a *real* annuity, equation (1) must be modified to recognize that the amount of the payout is time varying in nominal terms but fixed in real terms. The easiest way to handle this is to allow A_r to denote the real monthly payout and to replace the nominal interest rates in the denominator of (1) with corresponding real interest rates. We use r_k to denote the one-month real interest rate k months after the annuity purchase. Such real interest rates can be constructed from the U.K. yield curve for index-linked Treasury securities. The expression that we evaluate to compute the EPDV of a real annuity is

$$(2) \qquad V_b(A_r) = \sum_{j=1}^{12 \cdot (115-b)} \frac{A_r \cdot P_j}{\Pi_{k=1}^{j}(1 + r_k)}.$$

We evaluate (1) and (2) using projected survival probabilities for the U.K. population as a whole. These mortality probabilities are compiled by H.M. Treasury. We use cohort mortality tables for those who reached age sixty, sixty-five, or seventy in 1998. We were not able to obtain mortality tables corresponding to the annuitant population. By using population mortality tables, we are in effect asking what the EPDV of the average annuity would be when viewed from the perspective of an average individual in the population. Of course, the average annuity buyer has a longer life expectancy than the average person in the population. Since a real annuity offers larger payouts near the end of life than a nominal annuity does, using a population rather than an annuitant mortality table overstates the effective cost of purchasing an inflation-indexed annuity relative to a nominal annuity.

Table 9.2 reports EPDV calculations for single-life annuities for men

Table 9.2   **Expected Present Discounted Value of Annuity Payouts for Nominal and Real Annuities Available in the Compulsory Annuity Market, United Kingdom, August 1998**

Characteristics of Annuitant	Nominal Annuity			Inflation-Indexed Annuity		
	Average Payout	Highest Three	Lowest Three	Average Payout	Highest Three	Lowest Three
Male, 60 years old	.921	.953	.873	.867	.916	.808
Male, 65 years old	.908	.936	.868	.854	.898	.797
Male, 70 years old	.889	.917	.853	.836	.881	.783
Female, 60 years old	.928	.966	.861	.876	.924	.832
Female, 65 years old	.907	.942	.857	.857	.892	.812
Female, 70 years old	.886	.920	.841	.836	.869	.790

Source: Authors' calculations as described in the text. Sample consists of fourteen companies with data provided by Annuity Direct, Ltd. See source note to table 9.1 above.

and women of different ages in the compulsory U.K. annuity market. Results for the average annuity payout are given as a simple average across the firms in our sample. We also provide the EPDV using average payouts for the three highest and three lowest annuity payout firms in our sample. The results show that the cost of buying an inflation-protected annuity in the United Kingdom is about 5 percent of the annuity premium. In addition, we find that the EPDV of a nominal annuity contract purchased in conjunction with a qualified retirement-saving plan is 5 percent higher than that for a real annuity. While the EPDV for nominal annuities is approximately 90 percent of the premium cost, the analogous EPDV for real annuities is about 85 percent. This difference in EPDVs might explain Diamond's (1997) claim that most annuitants in the United Kingdom elect nominal rather than real annuities.

Some of the apparent "cost" of inflation protection may arise from adverse selection across various types of annuities. If annuitants who anticipate that they will live much longer than the average annuitant tend to purchase real annuities because their real payout stream is backloaded, then mortality rates for those who buy real annuities may be lower than those for nominal annuity buyers. We do not know whether such mortality differences actually explain the payout differences between nominal and real annuities.

Our estimates of the EPDV of nominal annuity payouts in the United Kingdom are somewhat higher than analogous estimates for nominal annuity products in the United States at roughly the same date. For example, Poterba and Warshawsky (2000) report that the average EPDV on U.S. nominal annuity contracts available to sixty-five-year-old men in 1998 (using the population mortality table) was 84 percent for annuities purchased through qualified retirement-saving plans. The lower U.S. payout may reflect differences in the degree of mortality selection, relative to the population as a whole, in the "qualified" (U.S.) and "compulsory" (U.K.) annuity markets.

Table 9.2 also suggests that there are systematic patterns in the money's-worth values across age groups for both nominal and real annuities in the U.K. market. The EPDV declines as a function of the annuitant's age at the time the annuity is purchased. One possible explanation for this pattern may be that those who retire later tend to have lower mortality rates than those who retire earlier. Age at retirement and age at annuity purchase may be linked more closely in the compulsory annuity market than in the noncompulsory market. We suspect that many compulsory annuity buyers purchase their annuities when they retire, even though current U.K. rules do not require such purchases.

The results shown in table 9.2 indicate that, for a retiree of given age/sex characteristics, there is frequently a 10 percent difference between the average annuity payout from the firms offering the highest payout annuities and those offering the lowest payouts. Such dispersion is consistent with earlier evidence, such as MPWB (1999), suggesting substantial pricing differences in the U.S. market for nominal annuities. This price dispersion raises the question of how potential annuitants choose among the various annuity products. In the U.S. case, MPWB (1999) report little correlation between factors such as the credit rating of the insurance company offering the annuity and the level of the annuity's payout.

In sum, we draw two lessons from the widespread availability of index-linked annuities in the U.K. annuity market. The first is that it is possible for private insurers to develop and offer real annuity products. This is surely easier in a nation with a well-developed market for index-linked bonds. The second lesson is that, on the basis of the current prices of nominal and real annuities, the costs of obtaining inflation insurance are less than 5 percent of the purchase price of a nominal annuity contract.

9.2   Real Annuities in the United States: TIAA-CREF and ILONA

The U.S. individual annuity market differs from that in the United Kingdom in that virtually all annuity products are nominal annuities. Individuals can purchase a variety of products with a graded payout structure so that the nominal value of their payouts (and, for low-enough inflation rates, the real value of payouts) is expected to rise over time. Only two annuity products of which we are aware promise some degree of inflation protection. The first is the "Freedom" CPI-indexed income annuity, offered by the Irish Life Company of North America (ILONA), and the second is the inflation-linked bond account annuity, offered by TIAA-CREF. In this section, we describe how these products work, their current prices and payouts, and the degree to which they provide inflation protection for annuity buyers. We also note that, since Treasury inflation-protection securities (TIPS) were introduced to the U.S. market only recently, additional insurers may offer real annuities as familiarity with these new assets grows. Insurance companies can hedge the inflation risk associated with these price-level-indexed annuity products by purchasing TIPS bonds.

9.2.1   The ILONA Real Annuity

Irish Life PLC, an international insurance firm headquartered in Dublin, offers index-linked annuities in the United States through the Interstate Assurance Company, which is a division of Irish Life of North America. Interstate is a well-regarded company: it had assets of $1.3 billion, and it received a AA rating from Duff and Phelps, an A rating from A. M. Best, and a AA− rating from Standard and Poor's in 1996. The indexed-annuity product from ILONA is the "Freedom CPI-Indexed Income Annuity." The annuity payout rises annually in step with the increase in the prior year's CPI. Annuity benefits from the Freedom CPI-indexed income annuity cannot decline in nominal terms, even if the CPI were to fall from year to year. The minimum purchase requirement for the ILONA annuity product is $10,000, and the maximum purchase is $1 million. The annuity is available to individuals between the ages of sixty-five and eighty-five. There are various payout options, including simple-life annuities, annuities that provide a fixed numbers of years of payouts for certain, and "refund annuities." These annuity products are available both as individual and as joint-and-survivor annuities. Although ILONA offers this real annuity product in the United States, the agent we contacted indicated that thus far no sales of these annuities have been recorded.

Data were obtained on the monthly payouts offered by ILONA's indexed and nominal single-premium immediate annuities for men and women aged sixty-five, seventy, and seventy-five, assuming a premium of $1 million in each case. We also obtained data on joint-and-survivor annuities with 100 percent survivor benefits. Policies purchased in mid-1998 offered a monthly payout on a real annuity at the start of the annuity contract about 30 percent smaller than the payout on a nominal annuity issued to the same individual. Table 9.3 shows that, for men at age sixty-five, the ratio of real to nominal payouts is 69 percent. For women at sixty-five, the ratio is 66 percent, potentially reflecting the longer life expectancy and therefore greater backloading that occurs with a real rather than a nominal annuity for women rather than for men.

To determine the payouts relative to premium cost for these annuities, we calculate the EPDV of annuity payouts for each of the ILONA policies quoted using a procedure similar to that described above. Interest and mortality rates differ somewhat relative to the U.K. calculations. For discount factors in our EPDV calculations, we use the nominal yield curve for zero-coupon U.S. Treasury bonds. We start from the term structure of

Table 9.3   Monthly Annuity Payouts on Single-Premium Annuity Products Offered by ILONA in the U.S. Market, 1998

Annuitant Age and Product	Male, Single-Life Annuity ($)	Female, Single-Life Annuity ($)	Joint-and-Survivor Annuity with Full Survivor Benefits ($)
Age 65, unindexed	7,452	6,720	6,068
Age 65, indexed	5,149	4,432	3,849
Age 70, unindexed	8,520	7,543	6,663
Age 70, indexed	6,262	5,332	4,549
Age 75, unindexed	10,075	8,825	7,594
Age 75, indexed	7,833	6,643	5,552

Note: All payouts correspond to an initial purchase of $1 million. Data were provided by Irish Life of North America (ILONA). For further details, see the text.

yields for zero-coupon Treasury "strips" and work out the pattern of monthly interest rates implied by these yields under the simple-expectations theory of the term structure. Data on the zero-coupon yield curve are published in the *Wall Street Journal,* and we use information from the beginning of June 1998. Because we do not know the precise date at which ILONA offered the annuities that we are pricing, and in the light of the absence of transactions in this annuity market, we select the term structure for the first week of June 1998 as an approximate guide to discount rates in mid-1998. When evaluating the EPDV of the ILONA real annuity, we use the implied short-term real interest rates that can be derived from the term structure of real interest rates on TIPS in early June 1998.

With regard to survival patterns, we have access to two distinct mortality tables for the United States. The first, developed by the Social Security Administration's Office of the Actuary and reported in Bell, Wade, and Goss (1992), applies to the entire population. We update this mortality table to reflect the prospective mortality rates of a sixty-five-year-old (or seventy- or seventy-five-year-old) purchasing an annuity in 1998. For example, in estimating the money's worth of an annuity for a sixty-five-year-old in 1998, we use the projected mortality experience of the 1933 birth cohort. A second set of projected mortality rates corresponds to that relevant to current annuitants. MPWB (1999) develop an algorithm that combines information from the annuity 2000 mortality table (described in Johansen [1996]), the older 1983 individual annuitant mortality table, and the projected rate of mortality improvement implicit in the difference between the Social Security Administration's cohort and period mortality tables for the population. This algorithm generates projected mortality rates for the set of annuitants purchasing annuity contracts in a given year. It is worth noting that the population and annuitant mortality rates differ. For instance, MPWB (1999) report that the 1995 annual mortality rate for annuitants aged sixty-five to seventy-five was roughly half that for the gen-

Table 9.4   Expected Present Discounted Value of Annuity Payouts, Freedom Inflation-Indexed Annuities Offered by ILONA, 1998

	Male Annuitant, Age 65	Male Annuitant, Age 75	Female Annuitant, Age 65	Female Annuitant, Age 75
Calculations using population mortality table:				
Nominal annuity	.864	.830	.889	.887
Real annuity	.702	.720	.708	.762
Calculations using annuitant mortality table:				
Nominal annuity	.987	.984	.966	.967
Real annuity	.822	.872	.782	.841

Note: Each entry shows the expected present discounted value of annuity payouts using the algorithm described in the text. See note to table 9.3 above.

eral population. This mortality differential generates a substantially larger EPDV of annuity payouts with the annuitant rather than the population mortality table.

Table 9.4 reports EPDV calculations for Irish Life real and nominal annuities. (All EPDV calculations use pretax annuity payouts and before-tax interest rates. MPWB [1999] show that pretax and posttax EPDV calculations for U.S. nominal annuities yield similar results.) For nominal annuities valued using the population mortality table, the EPDV of payouts is approximately eighty-five cents per premium dollar for men and eighty-nine cents for women. These values are slightly higher than the average EPDV values based on nominal annuities described in A. M. Best's annuity survey of June 1998, as reported in Poterba and Warshawsky (2000). Using the annuitant mortality table for nominal annuities, the EPDV is larger: approximately ninety-eight cents per premium dollar for men and ninety-seven cents for women.

We next turn to EPDV results for the ILONA real annuity, and we see that the value per dollar of premium is much lower than for the nominal annuity. For instance, a sixty-five-year-old man purchasing a real annuity would expect an EPDV of 70 percent, versus 86 percent for the nominal annuity. At other ages, a similar pattern applies: the money's worth for real annuity products is typically 15–20 percent lower than that for nominal annuities. The fact that inflation protection adds more than 15 percent to the annuity's cost may explain the limited demand for this product in the United States.

9.2.2   Annuities Linked to the CREF Index-Linked Bond Account (ILBA)

In May 1997, the College Equities Retirement Fund (CREF) launched a new investment account that was intended to appeal to those who are saving for retirement as well as to retirees receiving annuity payouts. This product, called the CREF Inflation-Linked Bond Account (ILBA), followed from the federal government's decision to issue TIPS on 29 January 1997. TIAA-CREF (1997a) indicated that its new inflation-linked account was expected to be useful for providing participants with "another investment option that can enhance portfolio diversification and mitigate the long-term impact of inflation on their retirement accumulations and benefits." The fund's goal was described, in TIAA-CREF (1997b), as seeking "a long-term rate of return that outpaces inflation, through a portfolio of inflation-indexed bonds and other securities."

The CREF inflation-linked bond account has grown slowly since its inception. At the end of September 1998, the account had attracted investments of only $131 million, making it the smallest of all the retirement funds offered by TIAA-CREF. To place this amount in context, on the same date the CREF stock fund held $96.9 billion, the TIAA traditional annuity fund held $94.3 billion, and all other TIAA-CREF retirement funds combined held about $25 billion. Most of the funds held in the ILBA are in the accounts of TIAA-CREF active participants rather than retirees, and as such they are still accumulating rather than drawing down assets.

To describe the inflation protection that an annuity linked to the CREF ILBA provides, we need to provide some background on the structure of this account, on the basic structure of variable-annuity products, and on the specific operation of the CREF variable annuity.

The CREF Index-Linked Bond Account

TIAA-CREF (1998b) explains that the ILBA "invests mainly in inflation-indexed bonds issued or guaranteed by the US government, or its agencies and instrumentalities, and in other inflation-indexed securities" with foreign securities capped at 25 percent of the assets. At present, the ILBA holds 98 percent of its assets in U.S. government inflation-linked securities and 2 percent in short-term investments maturing in less than one year. In principle, the fund's asset allocation could become broader in the future, with corporate inflation-indexed securities and those issued by foreign governments potentially being included as well as money market instruments. Expenses total thirty-one basis points annually. This expense ratio is lower than many mutual and pension fund expense levels, but it is as high as other, more actively managed CREF accounts such as the stock account (thirty-one basis points) and the bond market account (twenty-nine basis points) (see www.tiaa-cref.org).

The ILBA has no sales, surrender, or premium charges. Participants may elect this account as one of several investment vehicles into which new retirement contributions may be made and/or into which existing assets from other TIAA-CREF accounts may be transferred. As with other CREF accounts, the participant is limited to one transfer per business day

Table 9.5   Total Return, 1 January 1998–31 December 1998, by
                   TIAA-CREF Account (%)

CREF Accounts		TIAA Accounts	
Inflation-linked bond account	3.48	Traditional annuity	6.71
Growth account	32.89	Real estate account	8.07
Stock account	22.94	Personal annuity stock index	23.84
Equity index account	24.12	account	
Social choice account	18.61		
Global equities account	18.58		
Bond market	8.60		
Money market	5.45		

Source: www.tiaa-cref.org, various pages.

in or out of the account during the accumulation phase. The ILBA may be used as a vehicle for accumulating retirement assets, or it can be used to back the payment stream for a variable-payout annuity. Most of our interest focuses on the second function.

The ILBA account is marked to market daily, meaning that asset values fluctuate and the account could lose money. For example, if real interest rates rose owing to a decline in expected inflation, bond prices could fall. As the fund prospectus (TIAA-CREF 1998a) points out, in such an event, the inflation-linked bond fund's total return would then not actually track inflation every year. This is a key feature of the ILBA, and it means that the account *does not* effectively offer a real payout stream to annuitants who purchase variable-payout annuities tied to the ILBA.

Real interest rate changes are not the only source of variation in ILBA returns. If the principal value of inflation-linked bonds changes in response to inflation shocks, perhaps because investors infer something about the future of real interest rates from inflation news, this would also affect the returns on the ILBA. Similarly, changes in the definition of the CPI might affect the ILBA return. Both these issues also arise with respect to direct investments in Treasury inflation-protection securities (TIPS). The ILBA return for 1998 was 3.48 percent. Table 9.5 illustrates that this made it the lowest-earning fund of all the tax-qualified accounts offered by TIAA-CREF in 1998.

Variable Annuities: General Structure

An annuity with payouts that rise and fall with the value of the CREF ILBA is a special case of a variable-payout annuity. The key distinction between a fixed annuity (including a graded fixed annuity with a prespecified set of changing nominal payouts over time) and a variable annuity is that the payouts on a variable annuity cannot be specified *for certain* at the beginning of the payout period. Rather, a variable annuity is defined by an initial payout amount, which we denote $A(0)$, and an "updating rule" that relates the annuity payout in future periods to the previous payout and the intervening returns on the portfolio that backs the variable annuity.

To determine the initial nominal payout on a single-life variable annuity per dollar of annuity purchase, the insurance company solves an equation like

(3) $$ 1 = \sum_{j=1}^{T} \frac{A(0) \cdot P_j}{(1 + R)^j}, $$

where R is the variable annuity's "assumed interest rate" (AIR) or the "annuity valuation rate" as in Bodie and Pesando (1983). T is the maximum potential life span of the annuitant. This expression would require modification if the annuity guaranteed a fixed number of payments for certain, regardless of the annuitant's longevity, or if there were other specialized features in the annuity contract. This expression ignores expenses and other administrative costs associated with the sales of annuities or the operation of insurance companies.

The annuity-updating rule depends on the return on the assets that back the annuity, which we denote by z_t, according to

(4) $$ A(t + 1) = A(t) \cdot (1 + z_t)/(1 + R). $$

The frequency with which payouts are updated varies across annuity products, and there is no requirement that the payout be updated every time it is paid. One could, for example, have an annuity with monthly payouts but quarterly updating.

In designing a variable annuity, the assumed interest rate (R) is a key parameter. Assuming a high value of R will enable the insurance company to offer a large initial premium, but, for any underlying portfolio, the stream of future payouts will be more likely to decline as the assumed value of R rises. Equation (4) clearly indicates that an individual who purchases a variable annuity will receive payouts that fluctuate with the nominal value of the underlying portfolio.

Specific Provisions of the CREF ILBA-Backed Annuity

When a TIAA-CREF participant terminates employment, he or she can begin receiving retirement benefits. The participant then decides how to manage the payouts from accumulated retirement accounts. This includes deciding whether to annuitize the retirement assets, how much to annuitize, and whether to use an inflation-linked annuity. (Some employers may restrict their retirees' options.) Benefits are payable monthly, although recipients may elect quarterly, semiannual, and annual payouts as an alternative (TIAA-CREF [1998d] provides more detail on these options). In addition, the participant can choose the form and duration of the payout pattern, subject to minimum-distribution rules set by the IRS. If the participant chooses to annuitize part of his or her accumulation, there are a variety of potential annuity structures, including life annuities, ten- and twenty-year certain-payout annuities, and joint-and-survivor as well as single-life products.

Under TIAA-CREF rules, a CREF participant electing an annuity cannot be more than ninety years of age when he or she initially applies for the annuity. TIAA-CREF (1998b) explains that the applicant must select at least one of the annuity accounts initially for the drawdown phase; thereafter, he or she may switch from one annuity account to another as often as once per quarter. There are restrictions on shifting funds from TIAA to CREF: this must take place over a longer horizon. The choice of annuity fund can be altered, but the form of benefit payout cannot be changed once the annuity has been issued.

In order to understand how CREF annuity payments are determined, it is necessary to define the *basic* annuity unit value. This is an amount set each 31 March by dividing an account's total funds in payment status by the actuarial present value of the future annuity benefits to be paid out, assuming a 4 percent nominal interest rate and mortality patterns characteristic of existing CREF annuitants. A unisex version of the mortality table for individual annuitants is used when the applicant first files for an annuity "set back for each complete year elapsed since 1986" (see TIAA-CREF 1998d). The same mortality table is applied to all TIAA-CREF annuity accounts, on the basis of participant mortality experience. Mortality experience is adjusted every quarter.

A newly retired participant seeking to annuitize his retirement sum must have his own accumulation amount translated into an *initial annuity amount* $(A(0))$, determined by dividing his accumulation by the product of an annuity factor and the basic annuity unit value just described. The annuity factor reflects assumed survival probabilities based on the annuitant's age and an effective annual assumed interest rate (AIR) of 4 percent nominal, explained in TIAA-CREF (1998c).

The participant's initial annuity amount is then adjusted over the life of the annuity contract on either a monthly or an annual basis, depending on the participant's election. The adjustment will reflect the actual fund earnings on a "total return" basis, relative to the 4 percent AIR. Actual investment performance is used to update the annuity values as of 1 May for those electing to have their income change annually or monthly for those electing monthly income changes. Because the investment returns on the underlying accounts affect annuity payouts, these TIAA-CREF annuities are variable-payout annuities.

The Extent of Inflation Protection

It is evident that a variable-payout annuity linked to the CREF ILBA does not provide a guaranteed stream of real payouts since it is marked to market daily. Thus, if the price drops, or if the unit value fails to rise with inflation, the participant's unit value would not be constant in real terms. More important, the CREF annuity may fail to keep up with inflation because of the way in which it is designed. When the first-year annuity payout is set, it assumes the 4 percent AIR mentioned above, which is the same rate used for other CREF annuities. In subsequent years, if the unit value of the account were to rise less than 4 percent, payouts would be reduced to reflect this lower valuation. Consider the experience of 1998, when the total return (after expenses) on the ILBA account was 3.48 percent. Since the AIR for the CREF annuity is 4 percent, an annuity in its second- or later-year payout phase would experience a decline in payout of 0.52 percent. Since the price level rose in 1998, it is clear that the annuity payouts are not constant in real terms. A necessary condition for the payouts on this variable annuity not to decline in real terms would be for the real return on the account, that is, on Treasury inflation-protection securities, to exceed 4 percent. At present, it does not.

The precise extent to which payouts on ILBA-backed variable annuities will vary in real terms in the future is an open question. If the prices of inflation-linked bonds are bid up during high-inflation periods and real interest rates decline at such times, this will partly protect the ILBA account value. One relevant comparison for potential annuitants, however, may be between holding a CREF ILBA-backed variable annuity and purchasing TIPS bonds directly. Two considerations are relevant to such a comparison. First, the TIPS bonds offer a more direct form of inflation protection, although they do not provide any risk sharing with respect to mortality risk. Second, there are tax differences between the two investment strategies. TIPS would be taxable if they were not held in a qualified pension account, while the income from bonds held in the CREF ILBA-backed account is not taxed until the proceeds are withdrawn.

The CREF variable-payout annuity linked to the ILBA would be more likely to deliver a future real payout stream if the AIR on this annuity were set equal to the real interest rate on long-term TIPS at the time when the annuity is purchased. In this case, the return on the bond portfolio would typically equal the AIR plus the annual inflation rate, leaving aside some of the risks of holding indexed bonds, such as changes in the way the CPI is constructed. This would provide a mechanism for delivering something closer to a real annuity payout stream. One difficulty with this approach is that it would make it more difficult for annuitants to take advantage of some of the investment flexibility currently provided by CREF. At present, all CREF annuities assume the same AIR, regardless of the assets that back them. This facilitates conversions from one annuity type to another.

To date, there has been very limited demand for CREF's ILBA-backed variable-payout annuities. This lack of demand raises the perennial question of why retirees are not more concerned about inflation protection. One reason often given is "inflation illusion"; that is, people simply do not understand how inflation erodes purchasing power. Another reason may be that inflation-proof assets are new and that investors have not yet learned how to think about such assets. Hammond (personal communication to O. Mitchell, 10 November 1998) notes that inflation-linked bonds in other countries took some time to become popular after they were introduced: "After a flurry of initial interest, inflation bonds in those countries went through a period of quiescence—low liquidity and little interest. Then, with some sort of trigger—renewed inflation or a strong commitment on the part of central government—the market picked up and people began to figure out what the bonds were good for. In the U.K. this process took about ten years." (See Hammond 1999.) The United States today may be in the early stages of this process.

9.2.3   Conclusions about Real Annuities in the United States

Our analysis of the ILONA and TIAA-CREF experience suggests that there is currently no market for genuine real annuities in the United States. While ILONA offers a product that guarantees a real stream of payouts, no one has yet purchased this annuity. This may reflect the fact that the instrument's pricing requires relatively high rates of inflation to generate benefits with EPDVs similar to those of nominal annuities offered by ILONA and other insurers. The inflation-linked bond account offered by CREF has attracted investment funds since it became available in 1997, but the CREF variable annuity with payouts linked to returns on inflation-indexed bonds does not guarantee its buyers a constant real payout stream. Although in practice it may come close to delivering a constant real payout, its performance will depend on the as yet uncertain movements in the prices of Treasury inflation-protection securities (TIPS).

9.3   Asset Returns and Inflation: Another Route to Inflation Insurance

We now shift from our focus on insurance contracts that explicitly provide a constant real income stream for retirees to consider the possibility of using variable-payout annuities linked to assets other than indexed bonds as an alternative means of avoiding inflation risk. Such variable-payout annuities may reduce the effect of inflation in two ways. First, they may offer higher average returns than the assets that are used in pricing real and nominal annuities. These returns may, of course, come at the price of greater payout variability. Second, the prices of the assets that underlie the variable-payout annuities may move in tandem with the price level. In this case, a variable-payout annuity could provide a form of inflation insurance.

To examine these arguments, we begin by summarizing the well-known historical real-return performance of U.S. stocks, bonds, and Treasury-bill investments. We consider an individual who invests $1 in cash or in a portfolio of Treasury bills, long-term bonds, or corporate stock. We calculate the real value of an initial $1 investment after five, ten, twenty, and thirty years. We first perform this calculation in 1926 so that the thirty-year-return interval concludes in 1955. We then repeat the calculation in 1927, 1928, and all subsequent years for which we have enough data to calculate long-term returns. The last year for which we have return information is 1997, so we finish our five-year calculations in 1993, our ten-year calculations in 1988, and so on.

To summarize the results on the real value of each investment, we calculate both the average real value of each investment, averaged across all the years with sufficient data, and the standard deviation of this real return. The results of these calculations appear in table 9.6. The underlying calculations have been done using actual returns on stocks, bills, and bonds over the period 1926–97. For the return after five (thirty) years, there are sixty-six (forty-one) overlapping return intervals. The results presented in table 9.6 show that holding cash worth $1 initially would have a real value of only forty-nine cents after twenty years on average. In contrast, a $1 initial investment in bills or bonds would have increased in real value. For bills, the cumulative real return over twenty years was 1.3 percent, while for bonds it was 16.1 percent.

The last column of table 9.6 shows comparable calculations for corporate stock. Here, the real value of the investment after twenty years would have increased by a factor of 4.5. This implies that an investor who purchased an income stream tied to the total return on the U.S. stock market,

Table 9.6   **Real Value of a One-Dollar Investment after Various Periods, 1926–97 Average**

		Investment Portfolio		
Value after N Years	Cash (no investment return)	Treasury Bills	Treasury Bonds	Corporate Stock
5 years	0.864	1.036	1.128	1.477
	(0.150)	(0.163)	(0.315)	(0.517)
10 years	0.729	1.047	1.233	2.214
	(0.205)	(0.245)	(0.561)	(1.071)
20 years	0.490	1.013	1.161	4.569
	(0.160)	(0.285)	(0.560)	(2.941)
30 years	0.356	1.033	1.112	8.679
	(0.129)	(0.324)	(0.478)	(4.728)

Note: Each entry shows the mean value of a one-dollar initial investment, in real terms, and the standard error (in parentheses) of this value. Calculations are based on authors' computations using actual realizations of inflation, bill, bond, and stock returns over the period 1926–97, as reported in Ibbotson Associates (1998).

such as an equity-linked variable annuity, would have the potential to receive a real income stream that is higher late in retirement than at the beginning of retirement. This stands in stark contrast to the declining real value of the payouts on a fixed nominal annuity contract.

The substantial real return on U.S. equities suggests that one method of obtaining partial long-term protection against inflationary erosion of annuity payouts might be to purchase a portfolio of equities and then to link annuity payouts to equity returns. Such a strategy exposes the annuitant to the substantial intrinsic volatility of the equity market and does not guarantee a fixed real return. The higher average return on equities than on bonds nevertheless reduces the probability of a declining real payout stream from the annuity policy.

In practice, however, variable-annuity policies that offer payouts linked to equity returns do not guarantee real payouts that rise as steeply as table 9.6 suggests. This is because the payouts on a variable annuity depend on the performance of the underlying assets relative to the annuity product's assumed interest rate (AIR) (R in eq. [3]). Therefore, the variable-annuity payout for an equity-linked variable annuity can rise over time only if the equity portfolio returns more than the assumed value of R used in designing the annuity. Bodie and Pesando (1983) assume that R equals the historical average return on the assets that back the annuity in their hypothetical evaluation of variable-payout annuities. In practice, we have found that nominal R values of 3 or 4 percent per year are common, even for equity-linked variable-payout annuities, in the current annuity market. One should note that, if a variable-payout annuity assumed $R = 0$, then the real payouts in table 9.6 would in fact describe the experience of an annuitant since the nominal payout recursion would become $A(t + 1) = A(t) \cdot (1 + z_t)$.

The high average real return on equities implies that an investor holding U.S. stocks over the last seven decades would have experienced a rising real-wealth profile. But, to study whether this is because equities provide a good inflation hedge, we must explore the way U.S. equity returns covary with shocks to the inflation rate. If stocks generate positive returns when the inflation rate rises unexpectedly, then equities operate as an inflation hedge. The fact that U.S. equities have generated substantial positive returns over the period since 1926 does not provide any information on the correlation between inflation and stock returns.

We investigate the historical covariances between real U.S. stock returns, bond returns, bill returns, and unexpected inflation shocks over two sample periods: 1926–97 and 1947–97. If the real return on a particular asset category is not affected by unexpected inflation, then that asset can serve as a valuable inflation hedge. If the real return on the asset declines when inflation rises unexpectedly, however, then that asset does not provide an inflation hedge.

The first step in our analysis involves estimating a time series for "unexpected inflation." We do this by estimating fourth-order autoregessive models relating annual inflation (π_t) to its own lagged values or to its own lagged values as well as those of nominal Treasury-bill rates (i_t). The basic regression specification is either

$$(5a) \quad \pi_t = \rho_0 + \rho_1 \cdot \pi_{t-1} + \rho_2 \cdot \pi_{t-2} + \rho_3 \cdot \pi_{t-3} + \rho_4 \cdot \pi_{t-4}$$
$$+ \phi_1 \cdot i_{t-1} + \phi_2 \cdot i_{t-2} + \phi_3 \cdot i_{t-3} + \phi_4 \cdot i_{t-4} + \varepsilon_{it}$$

or

$$(5b) \quad \pi_t = \rho_0 + \rho_1 \cdot \pi_{t-1} + \rho_2 \cdot \pi_{t-2} + \rho_3 \cdot \pi_{t-3} + \rho_4 \cdot \pi_{t-4} + \varepsilon_{it}.$$

Table 9.7 presents the findings from estimating (5a) and (5b) for the two sample periods. Two broad conclusions emerge from the table. First, there is a great deal of persistence in inflation. The sum of the four coefficients on lagged inflation for the period 1926–97 is .773, while for the period 1947–97 it is .732. There is somewhat greater inflation persistence in the early years of the sample than in the postwar period. We experimented with extending the length of the lag polynomials in (5a) and (5b). While the fourth-order inflation lag in both equations shows a coefficient that is statistically significantly different from zero, higher lagged values were never statistically significant.

Second, the incremental explanatory power of lagged Treasury-bill

Table 9.7   **Estimates of the Inflation Process for the United States, 1930–97**

Explanatory Variable	Lagged Inflation Only, 1930–97	Lagged Inflation and Bills, 1930–97	Lagged Inflation Only, 1947–97	Lagged Inflation and Bills, 1947–97
Constant	.008	.010	.009	.005
	(.005)	(.006)	(.006)	(.006)
Inflation $(t-1)$	.706	.666	.647	.566
	(.113)	(.124)	(.100)	(.106)
Inflation $(t-2)$	−.146	−.086	−.161	−.127
	(.142)	(.148)	(.119)	(.120)
Inflation $(t-3)$	−.223	−.208	−.056	−.066
	(.142)	(.146)	(.118)	(.119)
Inflation $(t-4)$	.436	.447	.302	.280
	(.112)	(.119)	(.099)	(.103)
Bill yield $(t-1)$		.370		.549
		(.340)		(.241)
Bill yield $(t-2)$		−.694		−.677
		(.470)		(.328)
Bill yield $(t-3)$		−.129		.218
		(.483)		(.338)
Bill yield $(t-4)$		.108		.053
		(.338)		(.234)
Adjusted R^2	.507	.500	.544	.571

Source: Authors' calculations using data from Ibbotson Associates (1998).

Table 9.8   Unexpected Inflation and Real Asset Returns, United States,
                   1926–97

Inflation Process	1930–97 Sample			1947–97 Sample		
	Bills	Bonds	Stocks	Bills	Bonds	Stocks
Bills and inflation	−0.827	−1.702	−1.582	−0.580	−3.442	−4.326
	(0.137)	(0.389)	(0.804)	(0.174)	(0.650)	(1.077)
Inflation only	−0.864	−1.672	−1.560	−0.387	−2.515	−4.271
	(0.128)	(0.378)	(0.783)	(0.170)	(0.664)	(0.975)
5-year nonoverlapping	0.191	−1.522	−1.969			
returns, inflation only	(0.437)	(0.657)	(0.670)			

Note: Each entry corresponds to the coefficient λ_i in the regression equation

$$R_{it} = \alpha + \lambda_i \cdot \pi_{u,t} + \varepsilon_{it},$$

where R_{it} denotes the real return on asset i in period t, and $\pi_{u,t}$ denotes the unexpected inflation rate. Estimates are based on authors' analysis of data in Ibbotson Associates (1998), as described in the text.

yields is relatively small after we have controlled for lagged inflation. Bill rates have somewhat greater explanatory power in the postwar period than in the full sample period. Because most of the estimated coefficients on bill rates for both sample periods are statistically insignificant, however, the unexpected inflation series calculated from specifications (5a) and (5b) are likely to yield similar estimates of the correlation between unexpected inflation and asset returns.

We estimate unexpected inflation ($\pi_{u,t}$) by computing the residuals from either (5a) or (5b). These unexpected inflation series incorporate some future information in each case because the coefficients are estimated over the full sample period. We then use these time series as the explanatory variables in regression models in which real stock, bond, or bill returns are the dependent variables:

(6) $R_{it} = \alpha + \lambda_i \cdot \pi_{u,t} + \varepsilon_{it}.$

Table 9.8 shows the coefficient estimates for λ_i from regression models estimated for the two sample periods.

The results provide no evidence to suggest that stocks or bonds have been inflation hedges during the last seventy years. For both these asset categories, a 1 percentage point increase in the rate of unexpected inflation is associated with a decline of more than 1 percent in bond and in stock values. The estimated negative effects are larger, although somewhat less precisely estimated, for the period 1947–97 than for the longer sample. As noted above, the two unexpected inflation series, one corresponding to a lagged-inflation-only predicting equation, the other corresponding to the augmented specification with lagged Treasury-bill returns as well, produce very similar results when they are included on the right-hand side of equation (6).

We also find evidence that unexpected inflation reduces real Treasury-bill returns. The effect on these returns is more muted than that on bond and stock returns, and, for both sample periods, we find that a 1 percentage point increase in unexpected inflation reduces the real return on Treasury bills by less than 1 percentage point. Nevertheless, for both sample periods, we reject the null hypothesis that real Treasury-bill returns are unaffected by inflation surprises.

The finding that unexpected inflation is negatively correlated with real asset returns is broadly consistent with previous research. For example, Barr and Campbell (1996) show that the real interest rate on U.K. indexed bonds appears to covary negatively with inflation. Evans (1998) surveys a number of other empirical papers, using data from several nations and various methodologies, all of which reach similar conclusions. Our findings for equities are consistent with Bodie (1976), who suggested that using equities to hedge inflation risk requires a short position in equities.

One question that some might raise about the results presented in table 9.8 concerns the focus on one-year return horizons. It is possible that the high-frequency correlation between unexpected inflation and asset returns differs from the lower-frequency correlation. Boudoukh and Richardson (1993) present some evidence for both the United States and the United Kingdom suggesting that the nominal return on corporate equities moves together with inflation at long horizons. To explore this issue, we repeated our analysis using real returns and unexpected inflation over five-year intervals. We confined our analysis to the sample period 1926–97 and used an AR(2) model to construct an estimate of unexpected inflation. We focused on nonoverlapping five-year intervals, which provided twelve observations for estimating equation (6). The last row of table 9.8 presents the results. They continue to show a negative correlation between real stock and bond returns and unexpected inflation. The only change relative to the previous findings is that unexpected inflation no longer has a negative effect on real Treasury-bill returns.

Our empirical results therefore suggest that the inflation-hedging properties of equities and long-term bonds are limited. Nevertheless, as Siegel (1998) and others have noted, over long horizons, equities have typically generated very substantial positive real returns. This appears to be the result of a high average real return on equities rather than a positive correlation between equity returns and unexpected inflation. A substantial body of research has tried to explain the high average return on equities in the United States during the last century as a function of the correlation between equity returns and various risk factors. This has proved difficult and has become known as the "equity-premium puzzle."

The weak high-frequency correlation between equity returns and inflation is a challenge to many traditional models of asset pricing since equities represent a claim on real assets that hold their value in real terms. Prior studies have suggested a number of potential explanations for the absence of a positive correlation between inflation and equity returns. Feldstein (1980) focused on the interaction of inflation and corporate tax rules, while Modigliani and Cohn (1979) emphasized inflation illusion among equity investors. We are not aware of any empirical evidence that provides clear guidance for choosing among these explanations.

9.4   Evaluating the Utility Gains from Access to Real Annuities

We have not yet considered how valuable inflation protection might be for a retiree seeking to annuitize his retirement resources. We now address this issue by estimating a potential annuitant's "annuity equivalent wealth" from access to real, nominal, and equity-linked variable-payout annuities. We focus on equity-linked variable annuities because equities have historically earned higher expected returns than other assets and because the findings presented above showed that, while bills offer some inflation protection, their expected return has historically been very small. Bonds offer limited inflation protection and substantially lower average returns, at least historically, than stocks.

The annuity-valuation framework employed is closely related to that developed in Kotlikoff and Spivak (1981) and MPWB (1999). These two studies examine the utility gain that a representative individual receives from access to actuarially fair annuity markets. Brown (1999) provides empirical evidence suggesting that this framework has predictive value for explaining whether individuals plan to annuitize the balance that they accumulate in a defined-contribution plan. In this section, we compare the utility gains associated with access to different types of annuities. Our findings provide some guidance on the value to retirees of real versus nominal annuities.

9.4.1   Analytic Framework for Evaluating Alternative Annuities

Our basic algorithm estimates the utility gains accruing to someone with no annuity who is offered a fixed, nominal annuity on actuarially fair terms, a real annuity on fair terms, and an equity-linked variable annuity. To illustrate our procedure, we explain how we calculate an individual's "annuity equivalent wealth" when this individual is offered access to a fixed nominal annuity. We assume that this individual purchases such an annuity at age sixty-five, which we normalize to be "year 0." This individual receives an annuity payment in each year that he remains alive, and his optimal consumption path will be related to this payout. The annuity payout at age a (A_a) depends on wealth at the beginning of retirement (W_{ret}), potentially on the value of the assets underlying the annuity when the annuitant is age a, and on the annual annuity payout per dollar of premium payment (θ). In the case of a fixed nominal annuity, the nominal value of A_a is independent of age: $A_a = \theta \cdot W_{ret}$. For simplicity, we do not consider the taxes paid on annuity payouts or the taxes on the returns to nonannuity assets. MPWB (1999) find that the relative utilities of different annuity products are not sensitive to the inclusion of tax rules.

To find the actuarially fair ratio of nominal annuity payouts to premium cost, θ, for a sixty-five-year-old male in 1995, we use the Social Security Administration's cohort life table for men born in 1930. We define *actuarial fairness* as equality of the premium cost and the EPDV of annuity payouts. This definition ignores the potentially important role of administrative expenses that are incurred by the insurance company offering the annuity, so it is likely to overstate the payouts that would be available in actual annuity markets. We find θ from the following equation:

$$(7) \qquad 1 = \sum_{j=1}^{50} \frac{\theta \cdot P_j}{[(1 + r)(1 + \pi)]^j}.$$

In this expression, P_j denotes the probability of a sixty-five-year-old retiree remaining alive j years after retirement, r denotes the annual real interest rate, and π is the annual inflation rate. For computational simplicity, we use years rather than months in our annuity valuation and continue to assume that no one survives beyond age 115, so $P_{50} = 0$.

After finding the actuarially fair payout value, we compute the expected discounted value of lifetime utility that would be associated with the consumption stream generated by this nominal annuity. To do this, we assume that individuals have additively separable utility functions of the following form:

$$(8) \qquad U = \sum_{j=1}^{50} P_j \cdot \frac{\left[\left(\dfrac{C_j}{(1 + \pi)^j} \right)^{1-\beta} - 1 \right]}{(1 - \beta) \cdot (1 + \rho)^j}.$$

For this functional form, the parameter β is the individual's coefficient of relative risk aversion. This parameter also determines the degree of intertemporal substitution in consumption. The nominal consumption flow (C_j) is deflated by the price index $(1 + \pi)^j$.

We consider a first case in which our sixty-five-year-old uses all his resources to purchase an annuity contract and a second case in which he purchases an annuity with half his resources. In the second case, we assume that the other half of the individual's resources is invested in a real annuity. This case can be thought of as describing the retiree's choice problem when he has both an individual account balance that can be annuitized and a substantial real retirement annuity like that offered by the current social security system. As explained by Hurd (1987) and MPWB (1999), the marginal value of an increase in annuitization is greater when fewer resources are already annuitized.

We assume that the retiree has wealth at age sixty-five of W_{ret}, and, for illustrative purposes, we focus on the case in which the retiree has no preexisting annuity wealth. We find the optimal consumption path for someone who receives a nominal annuity of θW_{ret} per period. For such an individual, the budget constraint at each age a is given by

$$(9) \qquad W_{a+1} = (W_a + \theta W_{ret} - C_a) \cdot [(1 + r)(1 + \pi)].$$

This specification makes the standard assumption that nominal interest rates rise point for point with inflation even though our previous results call this assumption into question. The retiree with budget constraint (9) also faces an initial condition on wealth after purchasing the annuity: $W_0 = 0$. It is possible that the retiree will save some of the payouts from the annuity contract, and thereby accumulate wealth, in the early years of retirement.

Equation (9) assumes that the investment opportunity set for the retiree consists of a nominal bond that offers a fixed real return r. The utility gains from purchasing an annuity are likely to depend on the set of portfolio options that investors have *outside* their annuity contract. Campbell and Viceira (1998) present some evidence on the optimal structure of portfolios at different points in the life cycle for investors who have access to nominal and real bonds. Extending our framework to allow for more realistic portfolio structure is a natural direction for further work.

We compute the retiree's lifetime expected utility by solving for his optimal consumption path $\{C_a\}$ using stochastic dynamic programming, where the stochastic component of the problem arises from uncertainty regarding date of death. The result is lifetime expected utility as a function of wealth at retirement, $U^* = U^*(W_{ret})$, for the case in which the retiree has access to a nominal annuity contract.

When the retiree does not have access to an annuity market, his problem is to maximize the utility function (8) subject to the budget constraint and initial condition:

$$(10a) \qquad W_{a+1} = (W_a - C_a) \cdot [(1 + r)(1 + \pi)]$$

and

$$(10b) \qquad W_0 = W_{ret}.$$

The optimal consumption path in this case yields a value of lifetime expected utility, again as a function of wealth at retirement, $U^{**} = U^{**}(W_{ret})$, for a retiree with no access to an annuity market.

The *annuity-equivalent wealth* is the amount of wealth that a retiree needs—if he does not have access to an annuity market—to achieve the lifetime utility level that he can attain with access to an annuity market. We assume full annuitization when the annuity market is available. We note in passing that, in some cases, full annuitization does not yield the highest possible level of lifetime expected utility. Hurd (1987, 1989) shows that some individuals can be overannuitized when their optimal consumption path is constrained by the annuity-income flow. This could happen to individuals with high discount rates relative to the interest rate. Nevertheless, our calculations compare full annuitization with no annuitization.

Formally, annuity-equivalent wealth W_{aew} satisfies the equation

$$(11) \qquad\qquad U^{**}(W_{aew}) = U^{*}(W_{ret}).$$

We use a numerical search algorithm to find the value of W_{aew} that satisfies this equation. Since the longevity insurance associated with an annuity makes the individual better off, $W_{aew} > W_{ret}$. The retiree requires more wealth to achieve a given retirement utility level when he does not have access to a nominal annuity market than when he does.

When we report the annuity-equivalent wealth in our results below, we normalize W_{aew} by W_{ret}, and we report W_{aew}/W_{ret}. This makes our calculations directly comparable to those in Kotlikoff and Spivak (1981). Our annuity-equivalent-wealth calculations differ, however, from MPWB's (1999) estimates of the amount of wealth that individuals would be prepared to *give up* in order to invest their remaining wealth in actuarially fair annuities. In MPWB (1999), the central focus is on the divergence between the EPDV of annuity payouts and the purchase price of annuity contracts. Because the EPDV is less than the purchase price, the natural question to ask is what fraction of their wealth individuals would rationally forgo in order to obtain an annuity.

In the present paper, we follow Kotlikoff and Spivak (1981) in asking how much *additional* wealth an individual would need to be as well off without access to an annuity market as with it. Our choice of this approach, rather than the wealth-equivalent approach of MPWB (1999), was largely motivated by computational concerns. In the present setting, we search for W_{aew} in a relatively simple problem, where the only source of uncertainty is mortality risk. Real interest rates are certain in our benchmark case with the budget constraint in (10a). If we used either the nominal or the variable-annuity cases as our benchmark, we would need to search for W_{aew} in a problem that includes both mortality risk and inflation risk. This substantially slowed our numerical solution algorithm.

In simple environments without any preexisting annuities, the annuity-equivalent wealth (AEW) that we report is simply a transformation of the wealth-equivalent (WE) measure in MPWB (1999): WE = 1/AEW. Thus, if we find that a retiree requires 1.5 times as much wealth to achieve a given utility level without access to nominal annuities as with them, we could also interpret this as implying that the retiree would be prepared to give up 33 percent of his wealth (.50/1.5) if he did not have a nominal annuity in order to obtain access to one. When the retiree has some preexisting annuity wealth, however, the relation becomes more complex, and this relation holds approximately but not exactly.

Our analysis of the annuity-equivalent wealth for a nominal annuity generalizes immediately to the case of a real annuity or a variable-payout annuity. For an actuarially fair real annuity, we determine the annual payout per dollar of premium, θ', from the expression

$$(12) \qquad 1 = \sum_{j=1}^{50} \frac{\theta' \cdot P_j}{(1 + r)^j}.$$

This expression is analogous to (7), but the discount factor involves only real interest rates, and the numerator involves only real payouts. As in the discussion above, we find the optimal consumption profile for a consumer who purchases such an annuity, and we then find the annuity-equivalent wealth associated with access to a real annuity.

We also consider the utility consequences of being able to purchase variable-payout annuity products, in particular the case in which annuity payouts are indexed to an underlying portfolio of common stocks. To compute the actuarially fair payout on such variable annuities, we assume that a risk-neutral insurance company offers a variable annuity with an *initial* payout θ'' determined by

$$(13) \qquad 1 = \sum_{j=1}^{50} \frac{\theta'' \cdot P_j}{(1 + R)^j}.$$

In this expression, R is the AIR for the variable-annuity product. The payout in the first period of the annuity purchase is therefore

$$(14) \qquad A_v(0) = \theta'' \cdot W_{ret}.$$

The nominal payout on the variable annuity is determined in subsequent periods by the recursion

$$(15) \qquad A_v(t + 1) = A_v(t) \cdot (1 + z)/(1 + R),$$

where z denotes the nominal return on the equity portfolio.

In considering the equity-linked variable annuity, it is essential to recognize that the initial payout on the annuity policy is increasing in the AIR. The appeal of the equity-linked variable annuity arises from this higher initial payout stream and from the higher average returns earned on the assets invested in the variable annuity.

9.4.2 Calibration of Annuity-Equivalent Wealth

To carry out the annuity-equivalent-wealth calculations described in the previous subsection, we must calibrate the lifetime-utility function, the survival probability distribution, and the distributions for inflation and real returns on the assets that might be held in portfolios backing variable-payout annuities. All results will assume that the utility discount rate ρ is equal to the riskless interest rate r.

Risk Aversion

The parameter β in equation (8) represents the household's degree of risk aversion and its willingness to engage in intertemporal substitution in consumption. This risk-aversion parameter is an important determinant of the gains from annuitization when the real value of annuity payouts in future periods is uncertain because of stochastic asset returns or stochastic inflation.

Most empirical studies that attempt to estimate a value of relative risk aversion from household consumption patterns find values close to unity, which corresponds to log utility. Laibson, Repetto, and Tobacman (1998) summarize this literature. Mehra and Prescott (1985), however, note that much higher levels of risk aversion are required to rationalize the presence of the large premium of corporate equity returns over riskless-bond returns in historical U.S. data. It is difficult to reconcile the empirical evidence of low risk aversion and the existence of the large historical equity premium. Recent work based on survey questions about household tolerance of risk, reported in Barsky et al. (1997), also suggests values higher than unity. In the light of this dispersion of findings, we present calculations using risk-aversion coefficients of 1, 2, 5, and 10. In their related study of the utility gains from annuitization, Baxter and King (chap. 10 in this volume) consider an even wider range of risk-aversion values, ranging from 2 to 25. We are inclined to place the most emphasis on our findings with risk-aversion coefficients between 1 and 5, but we present findings using $\beta = 10$ to provide evidence on the robustness of our findings.

Survival Probabilities

The mortality process that we use in our analysis corresponds to the population mortality table supplied by the Social Security Administration. We use a cohort life table with projected future mortality rates since we are interested in an annuity purchased by someone who is currently of retirement age. We use a 1930 birth cohort table to study a sixty-five-year-old male, so our calculations effectively describe someone who was considering purchasing an annuity in 1995.

The Inflation Process

We use historical data from the period 1926–97 to calibrate the stochastic process for inflation. The average value of inflation over this period is 3.2 percent per year. We assume that the inflation rate in each "year" takes one of six values: -10.2, -1.44, 1.75, 3.82, 9.06, or 18.2 percent. The respective probabilities of these inflation outcomes are assumed to be .01, .19, .3, .3, .19, and .01. These inflation values correspond approximately to the first, tenth, thirty-fifth, sixty-fifth, ninetieth, and ninetieth-ninth percentiles of the annual inflation distribution for the years 1926–97, and they imply an average annual inflation rate of 3.2 percent. We have devoted special attention to the extreme tails of the inflation distribution to make sure that our analysis captures the possibility of a very high inflation period since we might otherwise overstate the value of an annuity that is fixed in nominal terms.

We consider two cases for the inflation process, corresponding to different assumptions about the degree of inflation persistence over time. The first case treats each annual inflation rate as an independent draw from our six-point distribution. This approach to modeling inflation tends to understate the long-run variance of the real value of fixed nominal payments and thus serves as a lower bound on the effect of inflation. Our empirical findings in the last section demonstrate clearly that inflation is a highly persistent process.

In the second case, we incorporate persistence by allowing inflation to follow a stylized AR(1) process. In the first period, inflation is drawn from the same six-point distribution as in the i.i.d. scenario. In later periods, however, there is a probability γ that π_{t+1} will be equal to π_t and a probability $1 - \gamma$ of taking a new draw from the six-point distribution. An attractive feature of this approach is that γ is equal to the AR(1) coefficient in a regression of inflation on its one-period lagged value, and thus γ can be parameterized using historical inflation data. Using U.S. historical data from the period 1926–97, the AR(1) coefficient for inflation is equal to 0.64, and this is the value of γ that we use in modeling a persistent inflation process.

The benefit of avoiding the inflation risk is shown by comparisons between our annuity-equivalent-wealth values when retirees have access to actuarially fair nominal annuity markets and actuarially fair real annuity markets. Our measure is related to, but not equivalent to, Bodie's (1990) analysis of the value of inflation insurance as the cost of purchasing a call option on the consumer price index. His approach generates the cost of *producing* an inflation-indexed income stream, while our approach focuses on the *consumer valuation* of such an income stream.

Risky Asset Returns

Our analysis assumes that investors have access to riskless real returns of 3 percent per year ($r = .03$). While this return is higher than the average return on "riskless" Treasury bills over the period 1926–97, it is lower than the current return on long-term TIPS. We think of TIPS as the riskless asset with respect to retirement saving and therefore use a higher return than the historical real return on Treasury bills. We further assume that inflation raises the nominal return on this riskless asset so that the real return is unaffected by inflation. This is tantamount to assuming that the investor is holding an indexed real bond.

When we consider variable annuity products backed by portfolios of risky securities, we must specify both the mean return associated with these securities and the variability of returns around this mean. Higher mean returns on the portfolios that back variable-payout annuities will make these products more attractive to potential annuitants, while greater risk will reduce their attractiveness.

We consider a variable-payout annuity backed by a broad portfolio of common stocks. Table 9.9 presents historical information on real returns and the standard deviation of real returns for U.S. stocks, bills, and bonds over the period 1926–97. This table is another way of presenting the information in table 9.6 above on real returns over different horizons. We assume throughout that the standard deviation of real returns on equities equals its historical average value of 20.9 percent per year.

In computing the annuity-equivalent wealth for an equity-backed variable annuity, we consider two different assumptions with regard to the mean real return on equities. First, we assume a 6 percent real return (i.e., a 3 percent premium over the indexed-bond return). This assumption about the equity premium is substantially smaller than the historical average differential between stock and bond returns, but it is designed to be conservative. Second, we consider a case with a 9 percent real return on equities, which translates to a 6 percent premium above the real bond.

Table 9.9   **Mean Real Returns and Standard Deviations of Real Returns, 1926–97 (%)**

	1926–97		1947–97	
	Mean Real Return	Standard Deviation	Mean Real Return	Standard Deviation
Treasury bills	0.73	4.17	0.87	2.64
Long-term Treasury bonds	2.57	10.53	2.01	11.13
Equities	9.66	20.46	9.93	16.95

Source: Authors' tabulations using data from Ibbotson Associates (1998).

This is still a smaller equity premium than historical returns suggest, but it yields a real return on equities close to the historical average. The extent to which historical real returns on corporate stock provide guidance on prospective returns is an open issue (for divergent views, see Campbell and Shiller [1998] and Siegel [1998]). In both cases, we assume an AIR on the variable annuity equal to the expected return on the underlying portfolio, following the approach of Bodie and Pesando (1983).

In order to account for the variability in returns, we again use a discrete six-point approximation to capture the distribution of real equity returns. Specifically, we constructed a distribution of the equity excess return over the period 1926–97. By subtracting off the mean excess return and then adding in our assumed 6 or 9 percent mean return, we constructed our distribution of equity returns. This approach allows us to alter our assumption about the mean equity premium over the riskless rate while holding the variance of equity returns at historical levels. We pick points from the first, tenth, thirty-fifth, sixty-fifth, ninetieth, and ninety-ninth percentiles of the distribution and use the probabilities .01, .19, .3, .3, .19, and .01 for these draws. For the case of a 6 percent mean real return, the corresponding points in the return distribution are −.475, −.182, −.036, .156, .306, and .506. For the case of a 9 percent mean real return, the entire distribution of returns is shifted up by .03. Real equity returns are modeled as independent across time. This does not allow for any possible variance compression at long horizons.

9.4.3 Results on the Valuation of Real versus Nominal Annuities

Table 9.10 reports our estimates of the annuity-equivalent wealth for real and nominal annuities. The first three columns report results for the case with no preannuitized wealth, when the potential annuitant places all his wealth in an annuity. Columns 4–6 explore the case in which the potential annuitant already holds half his net worth in a real annuity such as social security. To interpret the results, first consider the case in which the potential annuitant has a logarithmic utility function (CRRA = 1). In this case, the annuity-equivalent wealth is 1.502 for a fixed real annuity. This implies that an individual would be indifferent between having $1 in a real annuity or $1.50 in nonannuitized wealth. Note that the annuity-equivalent wealth for this individual is 1.451 in the case of i.i.d. inflation and 1.424 in the case of persistent inflation. These results suggest that a real annuity is more valuable than a nominal annuity and more so when the inflation process is more persistent.

For a real annuity, the annuity-equivalent wealth is monotonically increasing with the level of risk aversion. When the CRRA coefficient is 10, for example, the annuity-equivalent wealth rises to 2.004, meaning that an individual is indifferent between $2 of nonannuitized wealth and $1 in wealth that can be invested in a real annuity. For fixed nominal annuities

Table 9.10   **Annuity-Equivalent Wealth for Real and Nominal Annuities**

	Individual with No Preexisting Annuity Wealth			Individual with Half of Initial Wealth in Preexisting Real Annuity		
Coefficient of Relative Risk Aversion	Real Annuity	Nominal Annuity: i.i.d. Inflation	Nominal Annuity: Persistent Inflation	Real Annuity	Nominal Annuity: i.i.d. Inflation	Nominal Annuity: Persistent Inflation
1	1.502	1.451	1.424	1.330	1.304	1.286
2	1.650	1.553	1.501	1.441	1.403	1.366
5	1.855	1.616	1.487	1.623	1.515	1.450
10	2.004	1.592	1.346	1.815	1.577	1.451

Source: Authors' calculations. The annuity-equivalent wealth for the nominal annuity is calculated under the assumption that inflation takes one of six possible values, roughly capturing the distribution of inflation outcomes over the period 1926–97. Inflation shocks are independent across periods in the i.i.d. case and follow a stylized AR(1) process in the persistent-inflation case. For further discussion, see the text.

in the presence of uncertain inflation, this monotonic relation between the annuity-equivalent wealth and the level of risk aversion does not hold. This is because there are two effects of risk aversion that work in opposite directions in the case of inflation uncertainty. The first is that higher risk aversion leads one to value an annuitized payout more highly because the annuity eliminates the risk of outliving one's resources. This is the only effect present when examining real annuity products. The second factor, which works in the opposite direction, is that more risk-averse individuals have a greater dislike for the uncertainty introduced into the real annuity stream by stochastic inflation. Increased variability in the real value of the annuity flows reduces utility, and this effect is largest for those with the highest degree of risk aversion.

At low levels of risk aversion, the first effect dominates, and the annuity-equivalent wealth for fixed nominal annuities is rising with risk aversion. For example, moving from CRRA = 1 to CRRA = 2, the annuity-equivalent wealth increases from 1.451 to 1.553 in the i.i.d.-inflation case and from 1.424 to 1.501 in the persistent-inflation case. However, as risk aversion increases further, the second effect becomes stronger, and the annuity-equivalent wealth begins to decrease with risk aversion.

The annuity-equivalent wealth values described above provide information on the amount of incremental wealth that individuals would require to be made as well off as if they had access to annuities, assuming that they have no preexisting annuity coverage. The difference between the annuity-equivalent-wealth values for real and nominal annuities provides information on how valuable a real annuity is relative to a nominal annuity. For example, to achieve a given utility target in a world with i.i.d. inflation, a nominal annuity is worth 5.1 percent of wealth less than a real annuity

(1.502 − 1.451). At higher risk-aversion levels, the differential between real and nominal annuities rises even further. When CRRA = 5 and inflation is i.i.d., the nominal annuity is worth 23.9 percent of wealth less than the real annuity. In the case that is most unfavorable to nominal annuities, that of persistent inflation and a risk-aversion coefficient of 10, access to a real annuity is equivalent to doubling one's initial wealth, while access to a nominal annuity is equivalent to only a one-third increase in wealth.

The results are attenuated when we consider the annuitization decision of an individual who already holds a substantial amount of his wealth in a preexisting real annuity. Such a potential annuitant would require a smaller increment to wealth to achieve the same utility level—without access to a private annuity market—that he could obtain with such access. For example, a consumer with a risk-aversion coefficient of unity would require only a 33 percent increment to his wealth to be made as well off as if he had a real annuity, compared to 50 percent in the case when no wealth was previously annuitized. The presence of a preexisting real annuity offers the potential annuitant some insurance against very low consumption values. This accounts for the diminished value of an additional privately purchased annuity.

When the annuity option is a nominal rather than a real annuity, the effect of having a preexisting real annuity is more complex. When inflation draws are independent across years, the results are similar to those for real annuities: the annuity-equivalent wealth from annuitization declines when there is a preexisting real annuity. When we allow for a persistent-inflation process, however, along with very high values of risk aversion, the results change. For example, when CRRA = 10, the annuity-equivalent wealth is *higher* when the potential annuitant has preannuitized wealth than when he does not. This is because we have assumed that the preexisting annuity is a fixed real annuity, which provides insurance against the annuitant ever experiencing very low values of real income and therefore consumption. Thus, the utility cost of having high and persistent inflation erode the value of a nominal annuity is reduced, and the potential annuitant's willingness to purchase a nominal annuity rises.

9.4.4 Results on the Valuation of Variable Annuities

Table 9.11 reports our findings for the case of equity-linked variable-payout annuities. We assume that the AIR for such annuities corresponds to the average real equity return that is built into our calculations. Once again, we report two panels, corresponding to different degrees of preexisting annuitization. The first column reports results when the average return on equities exceeds that on bonds by 3 percent, so the real return on equities averages 6 percent. For an individual with logarithmic utility in this return environment, an equity-linked variable-payout annuity generates a higher utility level than a real annuity does. In the case of no preex-

Table 9.11   **Annuity-Equivalent Wealth for Equity-Linked Variable-Annuity Products**

Coefficient of Relative Risk Aversion	No Preexisting Annuities		Preexisting Real Annuity Equal to Half of Initial Wealth	
	Real Stock Return 6%	Real Stock Return 9%	Real Stock Return 6%	Real Stock Return 9%
Annuity-Equivalent Wealth				
1	1.623	2.024	1.567	1.953
2	1.499	1.901	1.570	1.957
5	0.921	1.355	1.443	1.789
10	0.331	0.622	1.261	1.563
Annuity-Equivalent Wealth Ratio, Variable Annuity/Real Annuity				
1	1.081	1.348	1.178	1.468
2	0.908	1.152	1.090	1.358
5	0.496	0.730	0.889	1.102
10	0.165	0.310	0.695	0.861

Source: Authors' calculations, as described in the text. The calculations in the bottom panel show the ratio of the annuity-equivalent wealth from the upper panel to the analogous annuity-equivalent wealth from holding a real annuity with an assumed real return of 3 percent. The underlying annuity-equivalent wealth values for the real annuity case are shown in table 9.10, cols. 1 and 4, above. A ratio greater that one indicates that the variable annuity is more valuable than a real annuity. Ratios less than one indicate that the real annuity is more valuable.

isting annuities, the annuity-equivalent wealth for the variable annuity, 1.623, is higher than that for the real annuity in table 9.10 above (1.502). For higher levels of risk aversion, however, a variable annuity with a mean return of 6 percent is worth less than a real annuity. In fact, an individual placing 100 percent of his wealth in a variable annuity can actually be made worse off than he would be if not annuitizing at all when his degree of risk aversion is high enough and the equity distribution is highly uncertain. This is indicated by annuity-equivalent wealth values below unity.

The lower panel of table 9.11 reports the ratio of the annuity-equivalent wealth with an equity-linked variable annuity to that with a real annuity. When these entries are greater than one, a potential annuitant would prefer a variable annuity to a fixed real annuity. When the entry is less than one, the individual would be better off in a real annuity. In the case of log utility, the individual always prefers an equity-linked variable-annuity product. At higher risk-aversion levels, however, the fixed real annuity usually dominates. The same pattern is evident when we allow a higher real return on equities. For three of the eight combinations of risk aversion and real equity returns that we considered, a potential annuitant who was preparing to annuitize all his wealth would prefer the variable to the real annuity. For five of the eight combinations, this outcome also emerges in the case with a preexisting real annuity. Variable annuities are relatively more attractive with preexisting real annuities than without. This is again because the preexisting real annuity provides a minimum consumption floor below which the annuitant will not fall. Therefore, the risk of a very low consumption state resulting from a series of negative equity returns is reduced.

These findings suggest that, for rates of risk aversion commonly cited in the consumption literature, and for plausible rate-of-return assumptions, potential annuitants would often prefer to purchase variable annuities with payouts linked to equity returns rather than real annuities offering constant purchasing power throughout the annuity period. Even when the expected real return on stocks is only 3 percent, the extra return afforded by the variable annuity more than compensates potential annuitants for the inflation risk that they bear. This is particularly evident when the annuitant is already endowed with a real annuity that represents a substantial share of net wealth because, in that case, the risk of very low consumption as a result of adverse variable-annuity returns is mitigated.

Our results on variable annuities are probably sensitive to our restriction of the menu of assets that investors can hold *outside* the variable annuity: we do not allow investments in corporate stock except through the variable-annuity channel. Exploring the robustness of our findings to relaxation of this constraint is an important topic for future work.

9.5   Conclusions and Further Directions

We have provided new evidence on the functioning of existing real annuity markets and on the potential role of nominal, real, and variable-payout annuities in providing income security to retirees. Three conclusions emerge from the analysis.

First, private insurers can and do offer real annuities to potential annuitants. Although at present there is virtually no U.S. market for real annuity products, in the United Kingdom indexed government bonds have been available for nearly two decades, and, there, indexed annuities are widely available. From the standpoint of an annuity purchaser, the cost of purchasing a real rather than a nominal annuity in the United Kingdom is at most 5 percent of the annuity principal.

Second, real returns on a broad-based portfolio of U.S. stocks have historically outpaced inflation by a substantial margin. While extrapolating from historical returns must be done with caution, the past returns suggest that there may be benefits for retirees from investing part of their annuity wealth in a variable-annuity product with returns linked to the returns on corporate stock. Nevertheless, our analysis of the correlation between unexpected inflation and equity returns suggests that the appeal of an equity-linked variable annuity is primarily the result of the equity premium rather than a strong positive correlation between inflation shocks and equity returns. At least at high frequencies, U.S. equities do not appear to offer an inflation hedge.

Third, consumers place a modest value on access to real rather than nominal annuities. We consider our results for retirees with a coefficient of relative risk aversion of two as a "benchmark" case. We find that, if a potential annuitant could not purchase a nominal annuity, he would need roughly 1.5 times as much wealth to achieve the same lifetime utility level that he could obtain with his given wealth and access to a nominal annuity. He would need 1.65 times as much wealth to achieve the utility level that he could obtain if he had access to a real annuity market. These two findings can be combined to suggest that a retiree with access to a real annuity who loses such access would be made worse off by approximately the same amount as he would be if he lost 10 percent of his wealth. Consumers also value access to variable-payout equity-linked annuities, although their demand for such products is quite sensitive to their degree of risk aversion. For moderately risk-averse consumers, with coefficients of relative risk aversion of 2 or less, the annuity-equivalent wealth for an equity-linked variable annuity may be greater than that for a real annuity. This finding obtains even when we assume that the average annual real return on equities is only three hundred basis points higher than the real return on riskless bonds.

These findings bear on two concerns that are raised in connection with social security reform plans that include individual accounts. One is that insurers might not be able to bring to market products providing inflation and longevity protection. Our evidence suggests that this is, in fact, not a concern in the two countries that we have examined. Both have government-issued inflation-indexed bonds that can be used to back private inflation-indexed annuities.

A second concern is that, given a choice, retirees might use their individual account funds to purchase nominal rather than inflation-indexed annuities. This is perceived as a problem to the extent that it exposes retirees to the risk of consumption losses in old age. Our model suggests that the expected utility losses associated with the purchase of a nominal rather than a real annuity are modest. It also implies that consumer demand for inflation-linked annuities in an individual accounts system would be positive, although the extent to which our stylized model describes actual consumer behavior is an open issue. The demand for real annuities is greatest among the most risk-averse consumers. It is also increasing in the degree of persistence of inflation shocks. When inflation is serially independent, the annuity-equivalent wealth for a nominal annuity is higher than when inflation is highly persistent. This is because, conditional on the average inflation rate, the risk of experiencing high and persistent inflation poses a greater threat to real retirement consumption than the risk of a shorter-lived period of high inflation.

The demand for real annuities also tends to be lower for households with a substantial endowment of annuitized wealth. This would include any remaining real defined-benefit promises offered to retirees under a restructured social security system. We estimate that the annuity equivalent wealth of a real annuity is about 5–8 percent less for a consumer holding half his wealth in social security than for one having no real annuity at all. Moore and Mitchell (2000) show that older Americans currently hold close to half their retirement wealth in real social security annuities. This may explain the limited current demand for real annuity products in the United States. If the social security system were changed in a way that reduced the importance of CPI-indexed real annuity payouts, the demand for privately provided annuity products might increase substantially.

Our examination of the interplay between annuity choice, inflation protection, and portfolio risks raises a number of issues that could productively be explored in future work. One pertains to the use of more complex annuity products than the ones considered here. We have not investigated "graded nominal payout products," discussed by Biggs (1969) and King (1995). While graded policies do not offer inflation protection per se, they do provide annuitants with an opportunity to backload their real annuity payouts. Annuity-equivalent wealth values from annuitization in graded policies, relative to that for fixed nominal or real annuities, would be straightforward to calculate in our framework.

A more difficult issue for future research concerns the set of portfolio options available to the individuals considering annuitization and the extent to which such households have access to assets other than riskless bonds. One reason for our result that investors find equity-linked annuities valuable is that our models assume that investors can access the equity market only by using variable annuities. It may be realistic to assume that some low-income and low-net-worth households accumulating retirement resources in an individual accounts system do not hold stock in any other way. For higher net-worth households with greater financial sophistication, this assumption is less appropriate. Extending the current analysis to allow for a richer portfolio structure on the part of potential annuitants is an important direction for further work.

References

Barr, David G., and John Y. Campbell. 1996. Inflation, real interest rates, and the bond market: A study of U.K. nominal and index-linked government bond prices. NBER Working Paper no. 5821. Cambridge, Mass.: National Bureau of Economic Research.
Barsky, Robert B., F. Thomas Juster, Miles S. Kimball, and Matthew D. Shapiro. 1997. Preference parameters and behavioral heterogeneity: An experimental approach in the Health and Retirement Survey. *Quarterly Journal of Economics* 107 (May): 537–80.

Bell, Felicitie, A. Wade, and S. Goss. 1992. Life tables for the United States Social Security Area 1900–2080. Actuarial Study no. 107. Washington, D.C.: Social Security Administration, Office of the Actuary.

Biggs, John H. 1969. Alternatives in variable annuity benefit design. *Transactions of the Society of Actuaries* 21 (November): 495–528.

Blake, David. 1999. Annuity markets: Problem and solutions. Discussion Paper no. PI-9907. Pension Institute, Birkbeck College, London.

Bodie, Zvi. 1976. Common stocks as a hedge against inflation. *Journal of Finance* 31 (May): 459–70.

———. 1990. Inflation insurance. *Journal of Risk and Insurance* 57, no. 4: 634–45.

Bodie, Zvi, and James Pesando. 1983. Retirement annuity design in an inflationary climate. In *Financial aspects of the U.S. pension system,* ed. Zvi Bodie and John Shoven. Chicago: University of Chicago Press.

Boudoukh, Jacob, and Matthew Richardson. 1993. Stock returns and inflation: A long-horizon perspective. *American Economic Review* 83 (December): 1346–55.

Brown, Jeffrey R. 1999. Private pensions, mortality risk, and the decision to annuitize. NBER Working Paper no. 7191. Cambridge, Mass.: National Bureau of Economic Research.

Budd, Alan, and Nigel Campbell. 1998. The roles of the public and private sectors in the U.K. pension system. In *Privatizing social security,* ed. Martin Feldstein. Chicago: University of Chicago Press.

Campbell, John Y., and Robert J. Shiller. 1998. Valuation ratios and the long run stock market outlook. *Journal of Portfolio Management* 24 (winter): 11–26.

Campbell, John Y., and Luis Viceira. 1998. Who should buy long term bonds? NBER Working Paper no. 6801. Cambridge, Mass.: National Bureau of Economic Research.

Diamond, Peter A. 1997. Macroeconomic aspects of social security reform. *Brookings Papers on Economic Activity,* no. 2:1–87.

Evans, Martin D. 1998. Real rates, expected inflation, and inflation risk premia. *Journal of Finance* 53 (February): 187–218.

Feldstein, Martin S. 1980. Inflation, tax rules, and the stock market. *Journal of Monetary Economics* 6 (July): 309–31.

Finkelstein, Amy, and James Poterba. 1999. The market for annuity products in the United Kingdom. NBER Working Paper no. 7168. Cambridge, Mass.: National Bureau of Economic Research.

Friedman, Benjamin, and Mark Warshawsky. 1988. Annuity prices and saving behavior in the United States. In *Pensions in the U.S. economy,* ed. Z. Bodie, J. Shoven, and D. Wise. Chicago: University of Chicago Press.

———. 1990. The cost of annuities: Implications for saving behavior and bequests. *Quarterly Journal of Economics* 105, no. 1 (February): 135–54.

Gramlich, Edward M. 1996. Different approaches for dealing with social security. *Journal of Economic Perspectives* 10 (summer): 55–66.

Hammond, P. Brett. 1999. Using inflation-indexed securities for retirement savings and income: The TIAA-CREF experience. In *Handbook of inflation-indexed bonds,* ed. John Brynjolfsson and Frank J. Fabozzi. New Hope, Pa.: Frank Fabozzi Associates.

Hurd, Michael D. 1987. The marginal value of social security. NBER Working Paper no. 2411. Cambridge, Mass.: National Bureau of Economic Research.

———. 1989. The annuity value of social security. In *The political economy of social security* (Contributions to Economic Analysis, no. 179), ed. B. A. Gustafsson and A. N. Klevmarken. Amsterdam: Elsevier Science.

Ibbotson Associates. 1998. *Stocks, bonds, bills, and inflation: 1998 yearbook.* Chicago.

Johansen, R. 1996. Review of adequacy of 1983 individual annuity mortality table. *Transactions of the Society of Actuaries* 47:101–23.

King, Francis. 1995. *The TIAA graded payment method and the CPI.* TIAA-CREF Research Dialogues, no. 46. New York, December.

Kotlikoff, Laurence J., and Avia Spivak. 1981. The family as an incomplete annuities market. *Journal of Political Economy* 89:372–91.

Laibson, David, Andrea Repetto, and Jeremy Tobacman. 1998. Self control and saving for retirement. *Brookings Papers on Economic Activity,* no. 1:91–196.

Mehra, Rajnish, and Edward Prescott. 1985. The equity premium: A puzzle. *Journal of Monetary Economics* 15:145–61.

Mitchell, Olivia S., Robert Myers, and Howard Young. 1999. *Prospects for social security reform.* Philadelphia: University of Pennsylvania Press.

Mitchell, Olivia S., James M. Poterba, Mark Warshawsky, and Jeffrey R. Brown. 1999. New evidence on the money's worth of individual annuities. *American Economic Review* 89 (December): 1299–1318.

Modigliani, Franco, and Richard Cohn. 1979. Inflation, rational valuation, and the market. *Financial Analysts Journal* 35 (March): 3–23.

Moore, James, and Olivia S. Mitchell. 2000. Projected retirement wealth and saving adequacy. In *Forecasting retirement needs and retirement wealth,* ed. O. S. Mitchell, B. Hammond, and A. Rappaport. Philadelphia: University of Pennsylvania Press.

National Academy of Social Insurance (NASI). 1998. *Evaluating issues in privatizing social security.* Washington, D.C.

Poterba, James M., and Mark Warshawsky. 2000. The costs of annuitizing retirement payouts from individual accounts. In *Administrative aspects of investment-based social security reform,* ed. J. Shoven. Chicago: University of Chicago Press.

Siegel, Jeremy. 1998. *Stocks for the long run.* 2d ed. Burr Ridge, Ill.: Irwin Prof.

TIAA-CREF. 1997a. CREF scheduled to launch inflation-linked bond account on May 1, investment forum. New York, spring.

———. 1997b. Introducing the CREF inflation-linked bond account. New York.

———. 1998a. *Choosing income options.* New York.

———. 1998b. The inflation linked bond account: Supplement of June 1998 to the prospectus of May 1998 for the College Retirement Equities Fund. New York.

———. 1998c. Statement of additional information, May 1998. New York.

———. 1998d. Supplement of June 1998 to the prospectus of May 1998. New York.

Warshawsky, Mark. 1988. Private annuity markets in the United States. *Journal of Risk and Insurance* 55, no. 3 (September): 518–28.

Comment   Mark J. Warshawsky

In this paper, Brown, Mitchell, and Poterba (BMP) collect interesting institutional information and empirical evidence concerning the operation of, and pricing in, nominal and inflation-indexed individual annuity markets in the United Kingdom and the United States. They also present empirical evidence on the historical correlation of inflation and the nominal

Mark J. Warshawsky is director of research at the TIAA-CREF Institute.

The author thanks John Ameriks, who provided assistance, and Brett Hammond and Gene Strum for helpful conversations. Opinions expressed are not necessarily those of TIAA-CREF.

returns on the main U.S. asset classes. Finally, BMP show simulation results of an expected-utility model estimating the relative benefits of different annuity types, including nominal fixed, inflation-indexed, and equity-indexed variable payouts, in two inflation regimes—independently distributed and a persistent process. By presenting in one location different types of information, empirical evidence, and simulation modeling, this paper is extremely useful, I think, to current policy discussions regarding both individual account proposals for social security reform and pension-plan design. The modeling of the inflation environment is quite novel and sophisticated. My comments follow the flow of the paper, touching on most of its parts, but will focus mainly on the broad question of the investor demand for inflation indexation in annuity products.

In the first section of the paper, BMP assemble a data set based on August 1998 quotes from brokers in the United Kingdom for "compulsory" nominal and inflation-indexed individual annuities. They find that the first-month payout for the inflation-indexed annuities is about 30 percent lower than the payout on the nominal annuity. BMP also find that, while there is substantial variation across insurers in the pricing of all annuity types, variation is higher in the indexed market. Finally, when BMP do the now-familiar "money's-worth" calculation, they find that the expected present discounted value (EPDV) of the payouts from nominal annuities is about 5 percent higher than the expected value of payouts from inflation-indexed annuities, 90 percent compared to 85 percent. They also state that these EPDVs are uniformly higher than the EPDVs for nominal individual annuities in the United States—83.5 percent. BMP also note that EPDVs decline with issue age.

In explaining the money's-worth results, BMP cite adverse selection as a possible explanation; that is, those who expect to live longer will prefer inflation-indexed annuities to nominal annuities (which are of shorter duration), and, as people age, they will have better and more specific information about their own mortality prospects. In addition, in the entirely voluntary U.S. market, adverse selection will be a greater factor than in the compulsory U.K. market. This is a nice, coherent story, and it is bolstered because BMP have calculated their mortality probabilities for the U.K. population correctly; that is, they are using a cohort table that includes expected improvements in mortality, as they used in the calculations for the United States. Mortality improvements will affect the EPDVs of inflation-indexed annuities more than those of nominal annuities. BMP state that their interpretation would be confirmed if evidence were found that those who purchase inflation-indexed annuities have longer life expectancies than those who select nominal annuities. It is worth noting, however, from TIAA-CREF mortality experience that TIAA (fixed) annuitants have slightly longer life expectancies than CREF (variable) annuitants, an outcome that runs somewhat counter to the BMP hypothesis.

An alternative or additional explanation for the better pricing of nominal as compared to inflation-indexed annuities in the United Kingdom and of U.K. as compared to U.S. annuities, is that there is simply more volume (i.e., demand) in the U.K. nominal annuity market than in other market segments and that therefore that market is more competitive and efficient. The price-variation evidence is consistent with this latter explanation. It is also possible, despite their somewhat breezy assertion that the availability of such indexed bonds has made it possible for U.K. insurers to offer real annuity products without bearing inflation risk, that U.K. insurers bear greater risks in offering real as opposed to nominal annuities and must charge for these risks. In particular, the insurer of a fixed real annuity must bear the risk of unexpected changes in the real interest rate and must also bear inflation risk for those durations not available in the bond market or not covered by futures, options, and swap contracts. Also, because the investments underlying the real annuity market are more predominantly Treasury than corporate securities, there is an opportunity cost from the loss of the corporate bond risk and tax premium, which in the United States runs at almost one hundred basis points.

In the second part of the paper, BMP turn to the nascent U.S. market for inflation-indexed annuities, represented by one company, Irish Life of North America. They compare the monthly payouts of nominal and inflation-indexed annuities issued by Irish Life in the United States and, similar to their finding in the United Kingdom, discover that the first monthly payout from the inflation-indexed annuity is 30 percent smaller than the payout from the nominal annuity. But, unlike their finding in the United Kingdom, when BMP do the money's-worth calculation for the United States, they find that the EPDV for the Irish Life inflation-indexed annuity is much lower (70 percent) than for its nominal annuity (86.5 percent). I would suppose that these findings, taken together, are explained by a lower (expected) inflation rate in the United States than in the United Kingdom or a higher real interest rate. Of course, as the only issuer of inflation-indexed annuities in the United States (with no reported issues to date), Irish Life's pricing strategy is probably not too influenced by concerns about competition and will not benefit much from economies of scale and scope. In addition, the benefits of financial technology and market development are not yet available in the United States in the inflation-indexed bond arena; there are no swaps, futures, options, or corporate-bond issuers yet.

BMP next explain well the CREF inflation-linked-bond-account (ILBA) variable annuity and cite the unique TIAA graded benefit-payment method. They outline the mechanics of how a variable annuity works in the payout phase and appropriately note the importance of the assumed interest rate (AIR), which for all CREF accounts is 4 percent. In this section of the paper, however, I differ somewhat from BMP's inter-

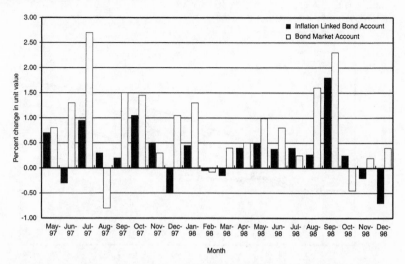

Fig. 9C.1 Month-to-month percent change in unit value for the CREF inflation-linked bond account and the bond account, May 1997–December 1998
Note: May 1997 data are from inception at 1 May 1997.

pretation of the empirical evidence in two areas. It is certainly true that the value of the ILBA is not guaranteed. With the exception of some volatility when the Treasury first issued TIPS and recently, however, the unit value of the ILBA has been quite steady, rising slowly, and is less volatile than the (nominal) CREF bond account. Figure 9C.1 plots the month-to-month change over the period May 1997–December 1998 in the unit values of the inflation-indexed and nominal bond accounts. The nominal bond account shows a higher return but also higher volatility. Also, I would give a somewhat different interpretation of the relative size of the small ILBA compared to the massive CREF stock account. While it is true that, theoretically, when the ILBA was introduced, all CREF participants could have transferred the entire value of their equity accounts to the ILBA, participant behavior is not so volatile. A more appropriate volume comparison is probably to other newly introduced TIAA-CREF variable accounts; that is done in figure 9C.2. There, we see that, while ILBA asset growth has indeed trailed that of other new accounts, its lower return and lack of investor familiarity probably explain most of the divergence.[1]

BMP state that the ILBA variable annuity could improve its ability to deliver an inflation-indexed payout stream by having the AIR reflect the expected real interest rate on TIPS, perhaps with a haircut for conserva-

1. BMP also comment on the relative expense charges among the CREF accounts. It should be noted that a smaller share of the expense charge is devoted to investment expenses; most of the charge is for administrative costs and is equal across all the accounts. Investment expenses are related to the size of the account as well as to the investment strategy used.

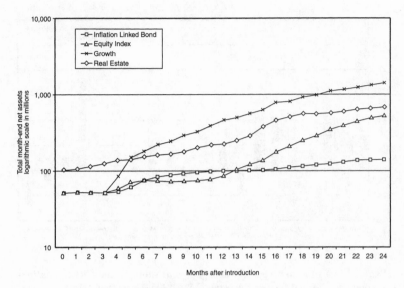

Fig. 9C.2   Net asset growth for new TIAA-CREF accounts

tism; in current conditions, this would suggest an AIR of 3.25 or 3.5 percent. This is a good suggestion *if* the ILBA is viewed in isolation. Except in the rare cases, however, for most older TIAA-CREF participants, it is probably more sensible for a typical annuitant to have a mix of fixed, equity-indexed variable, and inflation-indexed payout streams; for such a mix, a 4 percent AIR overall probably is more logical. Also, states impose various upper and lower limits on the allowable AIR in a variable annuity, and, therefore, practical business considerations for an insurer issuing annuities in all fifty states may dictate restrictions on feasible AIRs. Finally, contrary to the statement in the paper, and as noted above, TIAA and CREF annuity payouts are priced using two different mortality tables.

In the third section of the paper, BMP examine briefly whether the historical performance of bills, bonds, stocks, and inflation would lead one to believe that the correlation of returns and inflation could let equities serve as a replacement for inflation-indexed securities. While BMP caveat their evidence on this score, their findings are largely negative; equities do not offer an inflation hedge. The historically high return of equities seems to be explained by the equity premium rather than by a correlation with inflation.

In the fourth section of the paper, BMP evaluate the utility gains from, that is, the willingness to pay for, access to inflation-indexed annuities, nominal fixed annuities, and equity-indexed variable annuities. They utilize an expected-utility model with an additively separable utility function and mortality, inflation, and real-return uncertainty. The model is calibrated at various levels of risk aversion found in the literature, general population cohort mortality probabilities, and simple uncorrelated six-point distributions of inflation and equity returns related to the historical record (with some adjustments for conservatism and current market conditions). In a major improvement over the version of the paper presented at the conference, BMP also model an inflation process that is persistent from one year to the next. Under these assumptions, BMP find that, at median levels of risk aversion, and with a preexisting real annuity (i.e., social security), the willingness to pay for inflation-indexed annuities is positive but modest.[2] When inflation is a persistent process, however, the (relative) willingness to pay for inflation-indexed annuities is significantly larger, particularly for higher levels of risk aversion. By contrast, they find that, for plausible risk aversion and rate-of-return assumptions, a significant willingness to pay exists for equity-indexed variable annuities compared to inflation-indexed annuities. This result owes to the superior return on equity investments that more than compensates annuitants for the investment risk that they bear. In this latter comparison of annuity types, BMP apparently did not consider the effect of inflation uncertainty, of either the independently distributed or the persistent-process varieties.

There are several real-world complexities that both decrease and increase the importance of inflation risk relative to the original BMP model; on net, I believe, these complexities make inflation risk more significant than that portrayed in the model. Historical inflation, as measured by the CPI, may be overstated; this is certainly the conclusion of the Boskin Commission and seems to be the consensus of the economics profession, and, indeed, recent actions by the Bureau of Labor Statistics (BLS) are tending to lower the reported inflation rate. By contrast, the CPI measures generally used to measure inflation may understate the rate of inflation relevant to the elderly population most likely to purchase life annuities; because of heavier expenditure weights on medical care and housing, the BLS's experimental CPI-E index indicates that, since 1988, the elderly have been exposed to greater inflation than the rest of the population.

Most important, in contrast to their original simple several-point distribution model of the annual inflation rate, and as they now note, in the real world, inflation has been a persistent process. Once inflation gets started, it is hard to contain, and inflation rates tend to ratchet upward. By contrast, once inflation is low, virtuous expectations take hold, and wage and price pressures are held in check. As shown in table 9C.1, simple regression analysis where the dependent variable is the quarterly percentage change in CPI-U over the period 1950 to the present indicates that

2. It would be interesting to reconcile the results of the BMP simulation model with evidence on the inflation-risk premium extant in the bond market (for a model supporting an estimate that the inflation-risk premium in the United States has been forty-one basis points in the past several decades, see Hammond, Fairbanks, and Durham [1999]).

Table 9C.1   **Regression Results on the Persistence of Inflation**

Variable	Coefficient	S.E.	t-Statistic	Prob.
C	1.038227	0.215709	4.813088	0.0000
AR(1)	0.390129	0.071770	5.435854	0.0000
AR(2)	0.134883	0.074733	1.804873	0.0727
AR(3)	0.235019	0.070494	3.333877	0.0010
SAR(4)	0.135348	0.075979	1.781392	0.0764
R^2	0.509494	Mean dependent variable	1.001664	
Adjusted R^2	0.499168	S.D. dependent variable	0.881805	
S.E. of regression	0.624049	Akaike information		
Sum squared residual	73.99306	criterion	1.920131	
Log likelihood	−182.2128	Schwarz criterion	2.004054	
Durbin-Watson statistic	1.971298	F-statistic	49.33878	
		prob(F-statistic)	0.000000	
Inverted AR roots	0.86	0.61	$0.00 − 0.61i$	$−0.00 + 0.61i$
	$−0.24 + 0.47i$	$−0.24 + 0.47i$	$−0.61$	

Note: Author's calculations based on data from the U.S. Bureau of Labor Statistics. Dependent variable = INFLPCT; method = least squares; sample = 1950:1–1998:3; no. of observations = 195.

there is significant autocorrelation in inflation rates; summing the coefficients on lagged terms indicates that the inflation process is, almost, a unit root. Admittedly, the historical period over which this regression is estimated includes some bad experience. Presumably, some lessons were learned, and, therefore, the regression may overstate somewhat the expected persistence of inflation in the future. Nevertheless, I believe that BMP originally leaned too much in the opposite direction, and, therefore, I appreciate the difficult, but ultimately rewarding, work that they recently undertook to model a persistent-inflation process. Temporal persistence effectively increases the risk that inflation represents, particularly to the elderly, whose remaining lifetime is uncertain and whose human capital has effectively been completely depreciated. In fact, it might be interesting to see the effect on their results of a different modeling strategy for inflation; as opposed to an AR(1) process, they could model independently distributed draws of five- or ten-year inflation rates.

Despite its adverse implication for the level of risk being borne, inflation persistence has a somewhat perverse effect on the psychology of the average investor/plan participant and the demand for inflation indexation. When inflation rates are low and heading downward, as in recent years, the demand for inflation indexation will also be low. Thus, cost-of-living adjustments in private defined-benefit pension plans shrink and disappear. Similarly, the inclusion of inflation indexation in investment and annuity products is a hard sell. By contrast, when inflation rates are rising, inflation indexation becomes more popular. Although this is a bit like buying fire insurance after the barn has burned down, pure rationality is not the only influence on human behavior.

BMP end their paper with three conclusions: inflation-indexed annuities can be made available in the private U.S. market, probably at little extra cost; equities, owing to their higher expected return, should have a role in the retirement-income portfolio; and equity-indexed variable annuities offer more to most individuals than inflation-indexed annuities. I agree with all three conclusions, although I believe that the benefits of inflation-indexed annuities of some form are probably a bit higher than those stated by BMP and, paradoxically, that it will be a bit more difficult to offer inflation-indexed annuities in the United States than BMP imply.

In summary, Brown, Mitchell, and Poterba have authored a fascinating and important paper. Their analytic conclusions seem to lead to certain policy recommendations and research agendas. In both social security reform and pension-plan design, the best policy is probably to offer a choice of some combination of nominal fixed, inflation-indexed, and equity-indexed variable annuities. Further research on the appropriate portfolio mix among these forms in the presence of both inflation and investment-return uncertainty would be very helpful.

Reference

Hammond, P. Brett, Andrew C. Fairbanks, and J. Benson Durham. 1999. Understanding the inflation risk premium. In *Handbook of inflation indexed bonds,* ed. John Brynjolfsson and Frank J. Fabozzi. New Hope, Pa.: Frank J. Fabozzi.

Discussion Summary

Andrew Samwick remarked that investors in the model of the paper should be allowed to earn the equity premium outside the annuity. Part of the attractiveness of the variable annuity stems from the high return rather than from the annuity properties. A decomposition would be useful. He further noted that it would be interesting to model the portfolio held outside the annuity as realistically as possible. He suggested using the Survey of Consumer Finances for those purposes. Finally, he argued that incorporating a role for bequests into the analysis would be desirable.

John Campbell followed up on Mark Warshawsky's point about the persistence of the inflation process. He stated that persistence is actually the key to correctly judging inflation risk. In Campbell and Viceira (in press), it was found that, in the postwar period, expected inflation follows a process that has a root near unity. Realized inflation equals of course the expected inflation process combined with noise. From these results, cumulative-price-level uncertainty over a long horizon is vastly greater than would be implied by an independent and identically distributed (i.i.d.) process for inflation. People who have looked at the importance of indexation using short-term models (e.g., Viard 1993) have found trivial benefits because there is simply not enough inflation risk over a single quarter or year. Only when one brings in persistence and calculates the cumulative uncertainty over a decade or so do substantial results obtain.

In addition, *Martin Feldstein* noted that it would be interesting to allow for different regimes for the inflation process, thus distinguishing within the postwar sample the Volcker-Greenspan regime from other less favorable years in a different regime.

Robert Shiller agreed with Campbell's remark and suggested the following rough approximation as an alternative for the Markov modeling strategy in order to capture the persistence of the inflation process. The authors could assume that the inflation rate is 9 percent with probability one in five, not just for one year as is assumed in the paper, but throughout the rest of the retirement. In that case, retirees would value real annuities much more.

Henning Bohn apologized for revisiting the equity-premium puzzle but remarked that an equity-linked account obviously dominates any alternative linked to the bond rate when the equity premium is 3 percent or even 6 percent and the coefficient of relative risk aversion is taken to be only one or two as is reported in table 9.11. *Stephen Zeldes* concurred and noted that this was related to Samwick's earlier remark.

Deborah Lucas suggested taking into account what other income the elderly have already effectively annuitized. Examples are Medicare annuities in the spirit of Hubbard, Skinner, and Zeldes (1995) and home ownership generating a stream of housing services. Given these effective annuitizations, one would expect the elderly to impute low value to the annuitization of retirement income. Lucas concluded that some sensitivity analysis of the results in the paper with respect to these phenomena would be interesting. *Feldstein* added that he considers this issue in an earlier paper (Feldstein 1999).

Stephen Ross agreed with what Campbell and Shiller had noted earlier about the inflation process and remarked that correlations between the rate of inflation and the return on the stock market are low. However, the correlation between estimates of long-run expected inflation and the stock market is more substantial.

David Cutler commented that one might want to consider what happens to consumption needs late in life. For instance, it is conceivable that the use of medical care increases. Such needs could be expected to play a role in the design of the optimal annuity.

In response to the discussion, *Jeffrey Brown* stated first that he and his coauthors agree with the comments concerning the persistence of the inflation process. He added that they did consider experiments along these lines, by drawing inflation shocks only once every five or ten years, rather than annually, so as effectively to introduce some persistence in a simple manner. Unsurprisingly, this intervention made real annuities more valuable than nominal ones. Brown replied that Bohn's question about the combination of realistic equity premia and low levels of risk aversion was important and required more thought. In response to the comment by Warshawsky that the ratios of real to nominal payouts are similar for the U.S. and the U.K. annuities even though the "money's-worth" calculations give different results for the two countries, Brown made two points. First, mortality in the United Kingdom, based on cohort-specific life tables, was more "favorable." Second, and mainly, the real interest rate was substantially lower in the United Kingdom than in the United States.

Poterba noted that Shiller's suggestion to allow for a nonzero probability of high inflation throughout retirement could be thought of as being the opposite polar case of what was done in the paper and had been pursued in Poterba and Warshawsky (1998). With regard to the equity-premium puzzle and the low level of risk aversion, *Brown* stated that calculations for higher coefficients of relative risk aversion would be reported in the final version of the paper. Finally, Brown replied to Ross's comment about the low correlation between equity returns and inflation at high frequency, especially using measured inflation, by referring to work done by Boudoukh and Richardson (1993). He noted that a more elaborate analysis requires modeling the expected inflation process, another interesting extension of this research.

References

Boudoukh, Jacob, and Matthew Richardson. 1993. Stock returns and inflation: A long-horizon perspective. *American Economic Review* 83, no. 5:1346–55.

Campbell, John Y., and Luis M. Viceira. In press. Who should buy long-term bonds? *American Economic Review*.

Feldstein, Martin. 1999. Prefunding Medicare. *American Economic Review* 89, no. 2:222–27.

Hubbard, R. Glenn, Jonathan Skinner, and Stephen P. Zeldes. 1995. Precautionary saving and social insurance. *Journal of Political Economy* 103, no. 2 (April): 360–99.

Poterba, James M., and Mark Warshawsky. 1998. The costs of annuitizing retirement payouts from individual accounts. Working paper. Massachusetts Institute of Technology, Department of Economics.

Viard, Alan D. 1993. The welfare gain from the introduction of indexed bonds. *Journal of Money, Credit, and Banking* 25:612–28.

10

The Role of International Investment in a Privatized Social Security System

Marianne Baxter and Robert G. King

Many proposals to reform the current social security system would permit the investment of retirement funds in risky assets such as equities. Under some proposals, the government would invest in risky assets on the individual's behalf. Under other proposals, these assets would be managed directly by the individual in a "private retirement account" (PRA). In each case, however, the idea is that including risky assets could improve the welfare of social security participants because these assets yield higher returns on average. This paper asks whether there is an important role for international financial assets in a privatized social security system. We find that there are two important reasons to incorporate international investment into reform proposals for social security: diversification benefits and risk-management or hedging benefits. We provide empirical and quantitative work aimed at assessing each of these benefits.

The first reason to invest in international financial assets is that there are well-known benefits from international diversification. A diversified world portfolio yields lower risk for a given expected return than a portfolio of any single nation, even a large nation such as the United States. These diversification benefits are potentially important both for working individuals and for retirees.

The second source of benefits from investing in foreign risky assets—risk-management or hedging benefits—is less frequently discussed. We show that foreign assets may be useful in hedging risk associated with nontraded assets, the most important of which are human capital and

Marianne Baxter is professor of economics at Boston University and a research associate of the National Bureau of Economic Research. Robert G. King is professor of economics at Boston University and a research associate of the National Bureau of Economic Research.

social security. With respect to human capital, the risk derives from uncertainty regarding future labor income. We show that the unexpected movements in labor income are positively correlated with unexpected changes in U.S. aggregate economic activity and are also positively correlated with returns on U.S. risky financial assets. By contrast, unexpected movements in U.S. labor income are less highly correlated with the returns on foreign financial assets. Intuitively, then, a portfolio containing foreign assets will be helpful to U.S. workers in managing the risk of the returns on total wealth, including human wealth.

The second important nontraded asset is the current social security system itself. It appears likely that a reformed social security system will retain elements of the current system, with mandatory "contributions" during one's working life and payouts during the retirement period tied to individual and aggregate labor income histories. As we make clear below, the current social security system contains an important element of aggregate risk that could potentially be managed with foreign assets in a way similar to the hedging of labor income risk described above.

The paper is structured as follows. Section 10.1 provides an overview of social security, focusing on the nature of its cash flows. We show that the current social security claim resembles a flexible-premium deferred variable annuity. Unlike private market annuity products, the rate of return on social security is related to the growth of aggregate labor income rather than being linked to the return on marketable financial assets.

Section 10.2 begins to address the diversification issue by exploring the consequences of allowing individuals to add risky assets to their retirement portfolios. Using data on U.S. and foreign asset returns, we evaluate the extent to which individuals could improve their risk-return trade-off by investing in foreign securities.

Section 10.3 provides evidence on the behavior of labor income, in the aggregate as well as across industries and education groups. We explore whether returns on financial assets are significant explanatory variables for labor income—a necessary condition for financial assets to be useful as hedges for nontraded human capital. We do find significant predictability for many categories of labor income. We also provide an overview of two approaches to computing "returns" on human capital and provide some new evidence on the statistical properties of human capital returns.

Section 10.4 provides a more detailed analysis of the benefits of a reformed social security system that allows retirees to earn returns on the basis of an optimal investment in the stock market during the retirement period. Depending on the extent of risk aversion and some other factors, we find substantial benefits to holding some type of risky asset. Further, there are additional benefits to optimal international portfolio diversification.

Section 10.5 turns to the issue of how retirement funds should be invested during the working years. We use a simple life-cycle model to highlight the issues that are involved, particularly those concerning uncertainty about labor income (human capital returns). We illustrate how optimal portfolio construction depends on the sensitivity of labor income to the returns on financial assets. Our analysis illustrates that the importance of the risk-management motive in the overall demand for particular assets depends critically on whether the variations in income are temporary or permanent. Section 10.6 concludes.

10.1 Social Security: An Overview

Social Security represents a large fraction of the wealth of retirees, as shown in table 10.1. This table describes asset holdings for fifty-one-to sixty-one-year-olds, broken down by income percentiles (data are from the Health and Retirement Survey, as compiled by Gustman et al. [1997] and Gustman and Steinmeier [1998]). For the group as a whole, the value of social security represented 31 percent of other financial assets. Social security value represents a smaller fraction—about 12 percent—of other assets for individuals in the highest and lowest earnings groups. For individuals in the 10–25 percent bracket, social security value is 54 percent of other assets (these individuals have average lifetime earnings of $392,781, or about $13,000 per year, assuming that the individual worked from age twenty-five to age sixty-five).

Social security is also a major source of income for retired persons: the Social Security Administration reports that social security represents 40 percent of all income to the aged population and more than 50 percent of income for two-thirds of "beneficiary units" (couples or nonmarried persons). Social security was the only source of income for 18 percent of the aged population (see SSA 1989, 6).

Under many proposed reforms of social security, an element of the traditional social security system will be kept intact: individuals will be required to make "contributions" to the system, and these contributions will lead to a claim on benefits via a formula similar to the one currently in use. Viewed in finance terms, social security represents a nontraded financial asset—we say that it is nontraded because a worker who has contributed to social security and thus accumulated retirement benefits through the system cannot sell or trade this claim on social security. In this section, we explore the risk and return characteristics of this nontraded financial asset. We begin by reviewing the salient characteristics of the social security claim and then compare this claim to tradable financial assets available in the private market.

Table 10.1   Sources of Wealth at the Retirement Point

	Lifetime Earnings Percentile—All Households									
	0–5	5–10	10–25	25–50	50–75	75–90	90–95	95–100	45–55	All
Social security value	6,230	30,829	61,555	104,097	145,690	167,239	177,754	179,164	128,866	116,455
Other assets:										
Total	57,204	103,225	113,852	243,822	376,769	568,097	772,415	1,431,528	382,344	375,365
House value	24,692	45,612	40,021	60,760	81,026	106,617	134,078	222,910	72,914	78,826
Real estate value	4,793	12,836	15,844	30,293	34,052	54,509	66,207	167,714	37,126	39,227
Business assets	2,799	7,947	7,409	25,665	35,513	41,809	106,917	223,031	36,056	39,724
Financial assets	14,165	15,746	11,634	23,819	35,612	66,931	77,528	202,297	25,972	42,140
IRA assets	3,158	4,012	5,307	9,699	17,188	35,544	53,765	79,254	13,192	19,613
Pension value	1,018	7,002	21,668	70,140	138,436	216,857	289,104	443,382	93,930	124,991
Health insurance value	209	1,109	3,002	6,469	11,315	16,141	13,641	10,860	80,212	8,461
Other	6,370	8,961	8,967	16,977	23,627	29,689	31,175	82,080	22,942	22,383
Ratio of social security to value of other assets	.11	.30	.54	.43	.39	.29	.23	.13	.34	.31
Average lifetime earnings	27,273	144,854	392,781	844,443	1,345,378	1,886,986	2,470,710	5,048,032	1,098,095	1,273,960

Sources: All data are from Gustman et al. (1997) and Gustman and Steinmeier (1998).

10.1.1 Social Security Cash Flows

It will be useful to develop notation for the different types of cash flows embedded in the social security asset. An individual begins his working life at date t, making nominal contributions Z_{t+j} to social security; Z_{t+j} includes employer contributions. These contributions continue until the individual's last period of work, period $t + R$. From retirement at date $t + R + 1$ until the individual's death at date $t + T$, the social security system pays benefits B_{t+R+j} to the individual. We are ignoring survivor benefits and death benefits.

Working Years

A self-employed, covered worker is required to contribute to social security an amount equal to 12.4 percent of earnings up to a cap or ceiling amount denoted CAP_{t+j}. For 1999, the cap is equal to $72,600. Employees' social security contributions, or payments, are 6.2 percent of earnings, and these are matched by an additional 6.2 percent contribution from employers. Thus, the total contribution is

$$Z_{t+j} = 0.124 \cdot \min(W_{t+j}, CAP_{t+j}), \quad j = 1, 2, \ldots, R,$$

where $\min(W_{t+j}, CAP_{t+j})$ is the smaller of wage income and the ceiling amount in period $t + j$.[1]

The Retirement Point and Beyond

When an individual retires at date $t + R$, social security benefits for the retirement period are computed as follows. A worker's earnings during the preretirement years are adjusted to reflect the increase in the general level of wages during the particular working year in which the wages were earned and the retirement date. The idea behind this adjustment, or indexation, is to ensure that a retired worker's benefits reflect the rise in wages that occurred over his working life. This adjustment is carried out through the computation of the individual's "average indexed monthly earnings," or AIME. The AIME is constructed as follows. Let $\overline{W}_{t+j}$ denote the national average wage index for year $t + j$, and let $\overline{W}_{t+R}$ denote the national average wage index for the retirement year, $t + R$.[2] The worker's indexed earnings W_{t+j}^{indexed} are computed as follows:

---

1. The source for this OASDI tax-rate figure is http://www.ssa.gov/OACT/COLA/tax Rates.html. Since the current chapter concentrates on retirement-savings issues, we ignore the hospital insurance (HI) taxes, which are 2.9 percent of a self-employed individual's income and are not subject to a cap.

2. The "national average wage index" computed by social security is actually a measure of average income for covered workers. As such, it is comparable to a measure of average per capita labor income, not an average wage rate.

$$(1) \qquad W^{\text{indexed}}_{t+j} = W_{t+j}\left(\frac{\overline{W}_{t+R}}{\overline{W}_{t+j}}\right), \quad j = 1,2,\ldots,R.$$

The worker's average indexed monthly earnings is then the average over the individual's working life of W^{indexed}_{t+j}:[3]

$$(2) \qquad \text{AIME} = \frac{1}{12}\left[\frac{1}{R+1}\sum_{j=0}^{R}W_{t+j}\left(\frac{\overline{W}_{t+R}}{\overline{W}_{t+j}}\right)\right].$$

The individual's social security benefit, B_{t+R+j}, depends on the individual's AIME. Specifically, the individual's "primary insurance amount," PIA, equals 90 percent of the first $477 of AIME plus 32 percent of AIME over $477 through $2,875 plus 15 percent of AIME over $2,875. The fact that the PIA is a concave function of AIME can be interpreted as implicit taxation, or redistribution, from retirees who had high incomes over their lifetime toward retirees who had lower incomes. Let PIA_{t+R+1} denote the PIA for a worker who retires in period $t + R$ and begins receiving benefits in period $(t + R + 1)$, expressed on an annual basis. In subsequent periods, the PIA will be adjusted for inflation so that nominal benefits are given by

$$B_{t+R+j} = \text{PIA}_{t+R+1}\left(\frac{P_{t+R+1+j}}{P_{t+R+1}}\right), \quad j = 1,2,\ldots,(T - t - R - 1),$$

where $P_{t+R+1+j}$ is the CPI price index.

Social security benefits are best viewed as an annuity flow, an income received by an individual or a household so long as one or more of its members survives. This real annuity is "purchased" through social security contributions during the individual's working life. There are many private market instruments that are similar in general terms, and we turn next to discussing these instruments.

10.1.2   Private Market Assets Similar to Social Security

Under some proposed reforms, social security will be largely or completely privatized. For this reason, it is important to understand what private market financial instruments could be used to replace a government-run social security system. Further, if social security remains as a government-run program but is "modernized" in the sense of offering new products, it is useful to understand the similarities and differences between social security and similar, privately provided products.

In this section, we describe private market annuity products, high-

---

3. The AIME calculation excludes some low-wage years and years of nonemployment—a feature not captured by our formula.

lighting the similarities and differences with the social security annuity. Annuities are technically insurance contracts and are marketed by the major insurance companies. Increasingly, however, annuity products are being offered by insurance company affiliates of the major mutual fund companies, such as Vanguard and Fidelity.

Annuities are typically described by three main attributes:

How Purchased?	Payments Begin?	Rule for Payments?
Single premium	Immediately	Fixed (in nominal terms)
Flexible premium	Deferred	Variable (in nominal terms)

Annuities can be purchased with a single premium (a lump-sum payment at a point in time), or the annuity can be purchased via many payments over time—these are called *flexible premium annuities*. When purchased, the annuity delivery can be immediate (with payments to the individual starting on the day of purchase), or it can be deferred (starting at a later date). Finally, the annuity payouts can be fixed, with the nominal payment fixed over time, or it can be variable. We now describe various annuities in more detail.

Fixed Annuities

A fixed annuity specifies a sequence of known, fixed cash flows that will be received by the annuitant. Generally, the cash flows will continue (once begun) for the lifetime of the annuity owner; alternatively, the time period may be shorter and would be specified in advance of the first distribution. Private annuity markets provide fixed annuities with a variety of survivorship characteristics. Some annuities will provide benefits just for the lifetime of the annuitant; others provide survivor benefits of various kinds (see table 10.2). A "fixed" annuity is not a "real" annuity because the fixed annuity provides a guaranteed stream of fixed, nominal cash payments. Social security, by contrast, indexes the cash payments to the CPI inflation rate.

Variable Annuities

The private annuity market currently provides a broad range of investment options for variable annuities, including money market funds, a variety of bond funds, and several stock funds, including international portfolios. During the accumulation phase, the individual invests in one or more of these funds and is typically allowed to reallocate wealth across the funds with few restrictions.

The "distribution phase" of the annuity begins when the annuitant starts to take distributions, or cash flows, from the annuity. The annuity is called a *deferred annuity* if a period of time elapses between the accumulation and the distribution phases; the annuity is called an *immediate annuity*

Table 10.2   Types of Variable Annuities Offered by Vanguard

Payment Option	Type of Payment	How Long Payments Last
Life annuity	Variable or fixed	For lifetime of annuitant, even if fixed payments exceed the value of the annuity contract.
Joint-and-last survivor annuity	Variable or fixed	For as long as either one of the two annuitants remains alive, even if payments exceed the value of the annuity contract.
Life annuity with period certain	Variable or fixed	For lifetime of annuitant, with choice of at least 120, 180, or 240 months guaranteed. Balance of guaranteed payments goes to beneficiaries if annuitant dies during that period.
Installment or unit refund life annuity	Variable or fixed	For lifetime of annuitant, with guaranteed number of payments based on value of annuity divided by the amount of the first monthly payment. Balance of guaranteed payments goes to beneficiaries if annuitant dies.
Designated-period annuity	Fixed only	For a designated period of between ten and thirty years. Balance of payments goes to beneficiaries if annuitant dies during that period.

Source: The Vanguard Group: http://www.vanguard.com.

if the distribution phase begins immediately after the annuity is purchased.[4]

Owners of variable annuities have many options for how the accumulated assets are paid out. The total accumulated value can be paid out in a single lump sum, or "withdrawals" can be made at irregular intervals. Alternatively, and of the most interest for our purposes, the owner of the variable annuity can choose to annuitize his investment. The decision to annuitize is irreversible. A sample of the choices for annuitization is given in table 10.2, which describes annuitization options available to investors in Vanguard's variable-annuity products. This table shows a wide range of options that vary according to whether the payouts are fixed dollar amounts that vary each period or whether they vary according to the portfolio chosen by the investor. Further, the payout options differ in the length of time that payments are made and the extent to which payments may be transferred to a beneficiary in the event of the annuitant's death.

---

4. Mitchell, Poterba, and Warshawsky (1997, 5) analyze the "money's worth" of single-premium, immediate annuities since it is clear that "the life annuity represents the predominant decumulation method." According to Mitchell, Poterba, and Warshawsky, "Flexible premium payments accounted for $46.6 billion in 1995, compared with $52.5 billion of single premium annuity payments. Single Premium Immediate Annuities, however, accounted for only $6.2 billion of premium payments in 1995, while Single Premium Deferred Annuities accounted for $46.3 billion. The small volume of SPIA purchases suggests that the recent growth of the aggregate annuity market has not resolved the long-standing puzzle, discussed for example in Friedman and Warshawsky (1990), of why individuals do not choose to annuitize their wealth."

10.1.3 Social Security as a Variable Annuity

Using the terminology of the private annuity markets, social security is a flexible-premium, deferred, variable annuity since the "purchases" or contributions to social security vary over time and because the payouts are deferred to the retirement period. Once payouts begin, they are variable in nominal terms owing to CPI indexation. The private annuity from table 10.2 that is closest to the social security annuity is the "joint and last survivor annuity" with fixed payments. This annuity yields fixed payments as long as either of the two annuitants is alive, which is similar to the social security provision to continue to provide benefits to surviving spouses.

Let us take a closer look at the similarities and differences between social security and private annuities. During the accumulation phase, the rate of return on the private annuity is the rate of return on the portfolio that the investor has chosen. Further, the investor in a private annuity may have the right to reallocate invested funds to alternative portfolios without cost. By contrast, the contributor to social security does not choose the investment vehicle for his contributions—social security contributions are ostensibly invested in U.S. Treasury securities. However, the rate of return on the social security "asset" during the accumulation phase is *not* the rate of return on U.S. Treasury securities, as will be discussed more fully in section 10.2 below. There, we argue that the rate of return is related to the rate of change of the U.S. average wage index.

Private annuities and social security also differ during the distribution phase (the retirement period). First, fixed-payment annuities offered by private firms are fixed in nominal terms, while social security payments are indexed to inflation and therefore are fixed in real terms. Second, distributions from private annuities depend proportionately on the value of the annuity investment at the annuitization point. By contrast, the formulas used by the Social Security Administration to compute the AIME and the PIA, combined with rules about the family maximum, mean that distributions from social security are not simple linear functions of the value of contributions. Third, private annuities that have survivor benefits do not condition these benefits on the income or wealth of the survivor. Social security does have conditions of this sort: a surviving spouse who has worked at a high-income job may receive no survivor benefits. This is a redistributive "estate-tax" component built into the current social security system. Finally, private annuities are legal contracts specifying cash flows (or rules for determining cash flows) and cannot be changed.[5] By contrast, social security distributions can be changed by an act of Congress, adding

---

5. The Vanguard variable annuities have "separate-account" status, which means that the assets purchased by the annuitant are not available to the insurance company's creditors in the case of bankruptcy.

an important element of uncertainty for participants in the social security system.

10.2 Evaluating Social Security as a Financial Asset

Many proposals for social security reform allow for individual choice among assets in which to invest retirement funds. Some proposals keep important elements of social security in its current form while allowing additional funds to be invested in assets of the individual's choosing. Other proposals contemplate allowing the social security trust fund to invest in a broader menu of traded financial assets. Our goal in this section is to begin to evaluate the risk-return trade-offs facing investors under the current social security system and also under systems that may be implemented in the future. We pay particular attention to the importance of the diversification benefits provided by including international assets in the investment portfolio.

10.2.1 A First Look at Social Security Risk and Return

This section takes a first look at the risk and return characteristics of social security during the accumulation phase. A worker who contributes $1 to social security will have that $1 "marked up," according to the AIME formula (1), by the rate of change of the social security wage-indexing series for each period between the contribution date and the retirement date. That is, $1 contributed at date t will grow as follows:

(3) $1 at date t grows to

$$\$1 \left(\frac{\overline{W}_{t+1}}{\overline{W}_t} \right) \text{ at date } t + 1,$$

$$\$1 \left(\frac{\overline{W}_{t+1}}{\overline{W}_t} \right) \left(\frac{\overline{W}_{t+2}}{\overline{W}_{t+1}} \right) \text{ at date } t + 2,$$

$$\$1 \left(\frac{\overline{W}_{t+1}}{\overline{W}_t} \right) \left(\frac{\overline{W}_{t+2}}{\overline{W}_{t+1}} \right) \cdots \left(\frac{\overline{W}_{t+R}}{\overline{W}_{t+R-1}} \right) \text{ at retirement date, } t + R.$$

Equation (3) shows that the nominal return during the accumulation phase to $1 "invested" in social security is the growth rate of the wage-indexing series since this is the amount by which the $1 is "marked up" each period up to the retirement date.[6]

---

6. This definition of the return to social security over the accumulation phase ignores elements of risk associated with the possibility of future changes in the rules for "marking up" contributions.

Since many proposals for social security reform call for alternative investment vehicles for social security contributions, it is of interest to compare the risk and return characteristics of investment in the present social security system to some potential, alternative rules governing social security investments. To begin, we studied how closely the growth in the wage-indexing series corresponds to a measure of per capita income growth and per capita GNP growth. The growth rates of these variables, in real terms, are shown in figure 10.1, and summary statistics are given in table 10.3. The wage index and per capita labor income are deflated using the CPI deflator; GNP is deflated using the GNP deflator. The real wage-indexing series grew at only 0.95 percent per year for the period 1951–96, while real per capita income grew at 1.65 percent per year, and per capita real GNP grew at 1.85 percent per year. The wage-indexing series is about as volatile as GNP growth, while per capita labor income is somewhat more volatile. Although per capital real income growth is highly correlated (0.90) with

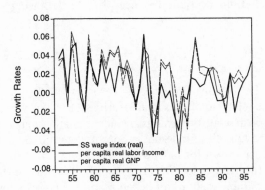

Fig. 10.1   Growth rates of real wage index, per capita labor income, and GNP

Table 10.3   Social Security Wage Index, Labor Income, and GNP, 1951–97

	Social Security Wage Index	Per Capita Labor Income	Per Capita GNP
	Growth Rates		
Mean (% per year)	0.96	1.64	1.85
Standard deviation (% per year)	2.34	2.94	2.39
	Correlations		
Social security wage index	1.00	0.80	0.64
Per capita labor income	0.80	1.00	0.90
Per capita GNP	0.64	0.90	1.00

Note: All variables are expressed in real terms. Wage index and labor income are deflated using the CPI; GNP is deflated using the GNP deflator.

per capita real GNP growth, the growth rate of the wage index has a correlation of only 0.84 with income growth and only 0.64 with GNP growth.[7]

10.2.2   Refining Our Measure of Social Security Risk and Return

In our discussion to this point, we assumed that social security was exactly a *wage-indexed variable annuity* during the accumulation phase, that is, an account in which the individual's contributions bear a return equal to the rate of growth of the aggregate wage index. We found that this made social security a low-risk and low-return asset. Consequently, the typical investor would like to combine other assets with this social security asset as part of a portfolio.

Social security is actually more complicated than this wage-indexed variable annuity. To see how this richer detail could affect the calculations presented above, it is useful to begin by studying the wage-indexed variable annuity a little further. For this purpose, as above, let Z_t be the joint contributions of the employer and the employee. Then we can describe the "wage-indexed fund account balance" by the following accumulation equation,

$$M_t = \frac{\overline{W}_t}{\overline{W}_{t-1}} M_{t-1} + Z_t = (1 + r_t^w) M_{t-1} + Z_t,$$

where the portfolio return is defined by $1 + r_t^w \equiv \overline{W}_t/\overline{W}_{t-1}$. This expression highlights a key element of the social security system that we stressed above: the fact that social security earnings are indexed to the aggregate wage index makes the behavior of this index an important determinant of the return on the social security asset for individuals. The average rate of growth of the index affects the average level of benefits, the variability of this index over time influences the variability of benefits, and the comovement of this index with other assets can be important for portfolio composition.

However, social security is more complicated than this annuity account along several dimensions. First, at retirement, the individual does not receive M_R dollars but rather receives an annuity. This is easily handled since it is straightforward to convert between the market value of the annuity and the market value of the account by using an annuity price. Second, the benefit formula makes the annuity payment depend, not on the individual's contributions, but instead on income history. The social security system's rules imply that accumulated lifetime earnings to date t, denoted LE_t, evolve as

---

7. We were surprised that the wage-indexing series did not bear a closer relation to these measures of aggregate economic activity. To the extent that "macro markets" of the type proposed by Shiller (1993) could allow individuals to hedge aggregate risk, the current social security wage-indexing scheme appears to introduce idiosyncratic risk into the social security asset that could not be hedged with a claim on aggregate GNP.

$$LE_t = \frac{\overline{W}_t}{\overline{W}_{t-1}} LE_{t-1} + W_t.$$

Thus, social security benefits inherit the wage-indexed account's sensitivity to aggregate fluctuations. Further, with a fixed tax rate, there is a simple proportional relation between lifetime earnings and the wage-indexed account balance: the account balance M_t is just the accumulated lifetime earnings LE_t multiplied by the tax rate τ:

$$M_t = \tau \times LE_t.$$

Thus, in a situation where the tax rate is constant, there is a rescaling from the current system's rules to our stylized description of a social security account.

Third, the social security rules make marginal benefits a function of the level of accumulated lifetime earnings. Hence, there is a form of redistribution or insurance built into the system. This distinction can be very important: many studies have shown that social security implicit returns vary widely across individuals (see, e.g., Feldstein and Samwick 1992). But these modifications do not obscure the fact that our social security account balance and individuals' actual benefit payments both vary with the rate of growth of wages.[8] Thus, we study the average social security return and its volatility using our "wage-indexed-annuity" approach in the next sections.

10.2.3 Risk and Return of Traded Financial Assets

Perhaps the most important development of postwar financial economics is the analysis of risk and return of portfolios, as in Markowitz (1959). An important building block for our analysis of the role of international investment in retirement portfolios is therefore the risk-return structure of traded financial assets. The extent to which diversification and risk-management benefits can be obtained by holding foreign assets depends on the correlation between returns on foreign assets and the returns on domestic assets, both traded and nontraded.

We begin by looking at the relation between U.S. and U.K. equity returns over the period 1918–96, as reported in table 10.4. The returns are annual and are expressed in real, local currency units, deflated using consumer price indices.[9] Over this period, U.K. returns had higher real returns and higher volatility compared with the United States. The correlation between equity returns in the United States and the United Kingdom was 0.52.

If the end of the Bretton-Woods system and the recent increase in open-

---

8. To determine the evolution of an individual's benefit payments through time, it may be necessary to scale the average return by a factor determined by the shape of the benefit function.

9. Data are from Campbell (1999).

Table 10.4   U.S. and U.K. Equity Returns, 1918–96

	U.S. Equity Return	U.K. Equity Return
Mean (% per year)	9.41	10.54
Standard deviation (% per year)	20.41	26.16
	Correlations	
U.S. equity return	1.00	0.52
U.K. equity return	0.52	1.00

Sources: Data are from various sources, as described by Campbell (1999).

Note: All returns are computed from real, local currency units, deflated using the consumer price index (United Kingdom) and the Gustman-Steinmeier consumption deflator (United States).

ness of financial markets means that the structure of asset returns has changed, it may be useful to focus on a shorter, more recent time period. Table 10.5 gives information on equity and bond returns for a variety of portfolios, using quarterly data from 1970:1–1998:1. Returns are real, U.S. dollar returns, deflated using the GNP deflator. The equity returns are total returns, as reported by Morgan Stanley Capital International. The bond returns are total returns on long-term government securities, published by the IMF. The "Europe" bond portfolio is an equally weighted portfolio of the United Kingdom, France, Italy, Germany, and Switzerland. The "Asia" bond portfolio is an equally weighted portfolio of Japan and Australia. The broad impression from table 10.5 is that equity and bond returns were positively correlated across countries during this period. In particular, the correlation of U.S. equity returns with other equity returns is reasonably high: 0.67 in the case of the United States–Europe and 0.43 in the case of the United States–the Far East. The correlation of U.S. equity returns with bond returns is lower, suggesting a potentially important role for U.S. and foreign bonds in a diversified portfolio.

To give an idea of the extent of the benefits from diversification among traded assets, figure 10.2 shows the "efficient frontier" for combinations of U.S. and foreign assets. The inner (dashed) line is the frontier for U.S. assets only—combinations of U.S. equities and U.S. bonds. The points with a star inside a circle are U.S. assets (bonds and equities); the open circles are foreign assets. The outer (solid) line is the frontier for U.S. and foreign assets combined. This graph indicates that diversifying internationally could be beneficial in terms of improving the risk-return trade-off for a U.S. investor.

10.2.4 Expanding the Menu of Social Security Assets

This section investigates the benefits of broadening the menu of assets that investors may use for their retirement savings, either as part of add-on PRAs of the type proposed by Feldstein and Samwick (1997) or as part of a "modernized" social security scheme run by the government.

Table 10.5   **Social Security and Traded Financial Assets (annual data, 1970–97)**

	Social Security	Equities			Long-Term Government Bonds		
		United States	Europe	Far East	United States	Europe	Asia
		A. Returns and Standard Deviations					
Mean return							
(% per year)	0.24	8.43	9.12	11.20	5.04	5.90	5.91
Standard deviation							
(% per year)	2.16	16.17	18.80	29.68	11.84	13.21	14.74
		B. Correlation with Other Assets					
Social security	1.00	0.33	0.23	0.40	0.18	0.19	0.29
Equities:							
United States	0.33	1.00	0.68	0.27	0.58	0.21	0.16
Europe	0.23	0.68	1.00	0.48	0.42	0.58	0.43
Far East	0.40	0.27	0.48	1.00	0.13	0.34	0.60
Bonds:							
United States	0.18	0.58	0.42	0.13	1.00	0.42	0.23
Europe	0.19	0.21	0.58	0.34	0.42	1.00	0.75
Asia	0.29	0.16	0.43	0.60	0.23	0.75	1.00

Source: Equity returns are total returns as reported by Morgan Stanley Capital International. Bond returns are total returns on long-term government bonds as reported by the IMF.

Note: The social security return is the growth rate of the wage-indexing series, deflated using the CPI. All other returns are in real U.S. dollars, deflated using the GNP deflator.

In this section, we will be focusing only on the diversification benefits obtained through a broader menu of assets; the potential for risk-management benefits will be considered later.

Figure 10.3 shows the risk-return trade-off that can be achieved by combining the traditional social security "asset" described earlier with other traded financial assets. This figure should be interpreted as describing the risk-return trade-off facing a worker in the accumulation phase (i.e., still saving for retirement). The statistics used to compute this trade-off are given in table 10.5.[10] Social security is the asset in the lower-left-hand corner of the figure, with an average return of 0.24 percent per year and a standard deviation of 2.16 percent. As before, the dashed line represents the trade-off for investors who confine their portfolios to U.S. assets: in this case, social security plus U.S. bonds and equities. The solid line represents the trade-off for investors who invest in combinations of social security, U.S. assets, and foreign assets.

How useful are international assets to a retirement investor, through the diversification channel stressed here? The answer depends critically on several factors: the tolerance of the investor for the higher levels of risk entailed in international investments; the risk-return profile of the inves-

10. We experimented with using a longer time period, 1951–96, with only two traded securities: U.S. and U.K. equity returns (these are the only returns that we have for this longer time period). The results were qualitatively very similar to those reported in the text.

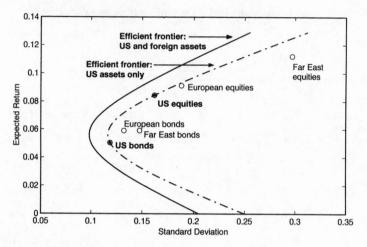

Fig. 10.2   Portfolios of traded assets

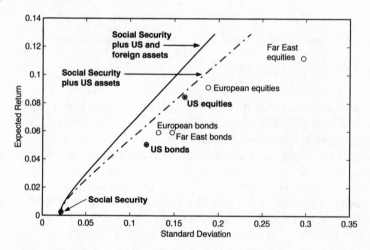

Fig. 10.3   Portfolios combining social security with other assets

tor's current portfolio; and the constraints on the investor that are due to the rules of particular retirement schemes.

Consider, for example, an investor who is invested 100 percent in the current social security system. Now imagine that this individual can undertake a small amount of investment in financial assets of his or her choice, either through PRAs or through some other scheme. How much does it matter whether this investor makes use of (or has access to) international investments? To be more concrete, suppose that the investor wants to earn an expected return of 3.00 percent per year rather than 0.25 percent per year (the return from investing 100 percent in the current

Table 10.6   **Portfolios Combining Social Security with Other Assets**

	100% Social Security	3% Return, U.S. Assets Only	3% Return with International Assets	8% Return, U.S. Assets	8% Return with International Assets
Portfolio share (%) in:					
Social security	100	58.8	58.5	−12.8	−12.0
U.S. equities	...	23.0	17.9	69.1	54.9
European equities	...	...	−4.2	...	−16.4
Far East equities	...	...	3.0	...	12.0
U.S. bonds	...	18.1	5.6	43.7	9.7
European bonds	...	...	17.9	...	38.9
Asian bonds	...	...	1.2	...	2.9
Expected return (% per year)	0.24	3.00	3.00	8.00	8.00
Portfolio S.D. (% per year)	2.16	5.80	5.10	14.71	12.27
"Reward-to-risk" ratio: $E(R)/\sigma$	0.12	0.52	0.59	0.54	0.65

social security scheme). If the investor confines himself to social security plus U.S. assets, the portfolio shares necessary to achieve this return are as follows: 58.8 percent in social security, 23.1 percent in U.S. equities, and 18.1 percent in U.S. bonds (for more detail, see table 10.6). The standard deviation of this portfolio is 5.8 percent per year. Adding international investments reduces the standard deviation of the portfolio only slightly, to 5.1 percent per year (the portfolio fractions are as follows: social security, 58.8 percent; U.S. equities, 17.9 percent; European equities, −0.4 percent; Far Eastern equities, 0.3 percent; U.S. bonds, 0.6 percent; European bonds, 17.9 percent; and Asian bonds, 1.2 percent).

When the individual's starting point is being fully invested in the current social security scheme and the investor is contemplating only "small" increases in the risk and return of his portfolio, there are large gains to including stocks or long-term bonds in the portfolio. This situation would apply to investors who are very risk averse or are effectively risk averse because of their position in their life cycle or income level. It would also apply to investors who are constrained by the rules of a modified social security scheme that permitted only small fractions of one's investment portfolio to be invested in assets of the individual's choice. The marginal gains to international diversification are small, however, compared with investing all the risky component of one's portfolio in domestic assets.

The benefits to international diversification are more noticeable when the circumstances or preferences permit individuals to take on higher levels of risk in their retirement portfolios. For example, table 10.6 shows that a portfolio with an expected return of 10 percent has a standard deviation of 14.71 percent when only U.S. assets are considered as opposed to 12.27 percent when international assets are part of the portfolio.[11]

10.3 Human Capital as a Nontraded Asset

Human capital is the single most important asset for most individuals. Since labor income represents about two-thirds of GNP, human capital represents roughly two-thirds of aggregate national wealth. There will be variations across individuals: young people who have had little opportunity to save and who have most of their working lives ahead of them will have a higher fraction of total wealth in the form of human capital; retirees will have a relatively small ratio of human capital to total wealth.

Table 10.7 gives an idea of the importance of human capital relative net worth for different types of individuals.[12] We computed the value of human capital by assuming a real growth rate of 2 percent per year for labor income over the individual's remaining working life and discounted future labor income at the real rate r. If human capital is viewed as riskless or as having only idiosyncratic risk, then it would be appropriate to use the risk-free interest rate, say, $r = 0.02$, to discount future labor income. If, alternatively, human capital is about as risky as risky financial assets, then it would be more appropriate to use a discount such as $r = 0.08$, approximately the average long-run return on equity. No matter which method is used to discount future labor income, table 10.7 shows that human capital is the most important single asset held by nonretired individuals. It is especially important for low-income and young individuals. Even for individuals who are near retirement, those in the fifty-five-to sixty-five-year age bracket, human capital is still the largest component of wealth.

Human capital is a risky asset because of uncertainty in labor income, which represents the flow of "dividends" from this asset. Part of the volatility of an individual's labor income may be common across all individuals, which can be characterized as "aggregate" risk. The remaining component of income volatility is individual-specific, "idiosyncratic" risk. This section looks at the characteristics of labor income volatility and the re-

---

11. Portfolio shares in the U.S.-only portfolio are as follows: -12.8 percent in social security (or, nearly equivalently, borrowing Treasury bills); 69.1 percent in U.S. equities; and 43.7 percent in U.S. bonds. Portfolio shares in the international portfolio are -12 percent social security, 54.8 percent U.S. equities, -16.4 percent European equities, 12.0 percent Far Eastern equities, 9.7 percent U.S. bonds, 48.9 percent European bonds, and 2.3 percent Asian bonds.

12. Friend and Blume (1975) also treat human capital as a nontraded, risky asset and use data from an earlier Survey of Consumer Finances to compute an estimate of human capital as a fraction of net worth.

Table 10.7   **Human Capital and Net Worth**

	Future Years of Work	Median 1995 Income	Median 1995 Net Worth	1995 Income/ Net Worth	Human Capital/ Net Worth: $r = 0.02$; $g = 0.02$	Human Capital/ Net Worth: $r = 0.08$; $g = 0.02$
Income group:						
Less than $10,000	23	5,000	4,800	1.0	23.5	12.7
$10,000–$24,999	23	17,500	30,000	0.6	13.2	7.1
$25,000–$49,999	23	37,500	54,900	0.7	15.4	8.3
$50,000–$99,999	23	75,000	121,100	0.6	14.0	7.5
$100,000 and more	23	200,000	485,900	0.4	9.3	5.0
Age of head:						
Under 35	37	26,700	11,400	2.3	85.0	34.3
35–44	25	39,100	48,500	0.8	19.8	10.2
45–54	15	41,100	90,500	0.5	6.7	4.4
55–65	5	36,000	110,800	0.3	1.6	1.3
65–74	1	19,500	104,100	0.2	0.2	0.2
75 and more	0	17,300	95,100	0.2	0.0	0.0
Education of head:						
No high school diploma	23	15,700	26,300	0.6	13.5	7.3
High school diploma	23	26,700	50,000	0.5	12.0	6.5
Some college	23	29,800	43,200	0.7	15.6	8.4
College degree	23	46,300	104,100	0.4	10.0	5.4
Race or ethnicity of head:						
White non-Hispanic	23	48,600	73,900	0.7	14.8	8.0
Nonwhite or Hispanic	23	29,500	16,500	1.8	40.3	21.8
Current work status of head:						
Professional, managerial	23	72,700	89,300	0.8	18.4	9.9
Technical, sales, clerical	23	46,200	43,300	1.1	24.1	13.0
Precision production	23	43,800	43,500	1.0	22.7	12.3
Machine operators and laborers	23	35,600	37,300	1.0	21.5	11.6
Service occupations	23	27,200	15,800	1.7	38.8	21.0
Self-employed	23	79,000	152,900	0.5	11.7	6.3
Retired	0	27,300	81,600	0.3	0.0	0.0
Other not working	23	19,900	4,500	4.4	99.7	53.9

(continued)

Table 10.7   (continued)

Source: All data are from the 1995 Survey of Consumer Finances, as summarized in Kennickell, Starr-McCluer, and Sunden (1997).

Note: Number of years of remaining working life generally assumed to be 23 (midpoint of working from age 20 to age 65). In the case of age groups, the number of years for an individual at the midpoint of the age group is used.

Median income for the "income-group" breakdown is the midpoint of the range, except for the highest group (more than $100,000), for which we have arbitrarily used the figure $200,000 as the median.

To calculate the ratio of the value of human capital to net worth, we capitalized current income over the individual's remaining working life assuming that real income rises at the rate g and using a real discount rate of r. This calculation assumes that current income consists of wage income only, which may not be a good assumption for higher-income individuals. However, this error will bias upward the human capital/net worth ratio for individuals with high net worth and thus high levels of nonwage income, thus reducing the disparity between high- and low-wage groups.

turns to human capital. Because human capital is a nontraded asset, it is necessary to compute synthetic returns on this asset by combining observable data on labor income and other variables with an asset-pricing model. This section reviews prior studies that have used alternative methods for computing these synthetic returns and provides some new results. Next, we investigate how the nontradability of human capital affects portfolio composition. Intuitively, traded financial assets with returns that are highly correlated with human capital returns can be used to hedge human capital risk. We evaluate the extent to which domestic as opposed to international assets may be useful as hedging tools.

10.3.1   Labor Income Volatility

As an initial measure of the risk associated with human capital, we can look at the volatility of labor income and its relation to the business cycle. If labor income followed a simple random walk, then the return to human capital is simply the growth rate of labor income. The data do not support the random-walk model for human capital, but we begin by looking at the raw volatility of labor income growth.

Aggregate Labor Income

We begin by looking at a measure of aggregate labor income.[13] As we saw in figure 10.1 above, the growth rates of real GNP and real labor income move together quite closely. In prior work, Baxter and Jermann (1997) studied data from the United States and three other OECD countries and found that one cannot reject the hypothesis that aggregate labor income is cointegrated with GNP with a cointegrating vector of $[1-1]$ (implying that labor's share is stationary). Because aggregate labor income

---

13. Our measure of aggregate labor income is computed as the sum of compensation of employees (Citibase code GCOMP) and proprietor's income (GPROJ), deflated using the GNP deflator (GD).

moves so closely with aggregate GNP, a claim to aggregate labor income in the United States is almost the same thing as a claim on aggregate GNP. Although the "macro markets" proposed by Shiller (1993) do not (yet) exist, it is useful to note that a market in GNP could provide a useful hedging vehicle for the risk associated with aggregate labor income.

Labor Income at the Industry Level

This section looks at the properties of labor income at the industry level. We are interested in learning how the volatility of labor income and its relation to the business cycle differ across industries. We gathered data on unemployment rates, u_{jt}, hourly wage rates, w_{jt}, and hours worked per employed person, h_{jt}, for nine manufacturing industries indexed by $j = 1$, $2, \ldots, 9$. We wanted a measure of the earnings that would be received in an industry in a particular period, taking into account the possibility of being unemployed. Thus, we computed a measure of the "unemployment-corrected" total earnings in industry j as follows:

$$\text{earnings}_{jt} = (1 - u_{jt})w_{jt}h_{jt}.$$

Table 10.8 shows how the mean growth rate of real earnings and its volatility differ across industries; the growth rate of real GNP is included for comparison.[14] Panel A shows that there is a great deal of cross-industry variability in the behavior of unemployment-corrected labor income growth. In each of these manufacturing industries, the mean growth rate of wages is lower than the mean growth rate of GNP. Only two industries—services and wholesale trade—had wage growth that was less volatile than GNP growth. Most industries had wage growth that was substantially more volatile than GNP growth—more than twice as volatile for construction and mining.

To get an idea of the cyclic sensitivity of wages in these industries, we ran a regression of wage growth on GNP growth and have reported the coefficient on GNP growth together with the R^2 of this regression.[15] The "beta" coefficient gives an idea of the cyclic sensitivity of wage growth to GNP growth; we intend the terminology to suggest an individual stock's "beta" with respect to a market index. If there were a market claim on GNP, this beta would help determine the loading on GNP in the hedge portfolio for that category of labor income. The R^2 of the regression indicates how much of the volatility of wage growth in a particular industry

---

14. We have used the GNP deflator for wages instead of the CPI because we are interested in comparing the behavior of real earnings with real GNP. Conceptual problems with the CPI deflator, combined with the fact that the ratio of the CPI to the GNP deflator exhibits a significant upward trend over our sample, with at least one significant "jump" around 1980, led us to use the same deflator for all variables.

15. For most industries, adding further lags of GNP growth did not increase the adjusted R^2 of the regression.

Table 10.8   Volatility of Labor Income Growth across Industries (quarterly data, 1964:2–1993:4)

	GNP	Construction	FIRE	Manufacturing Durables	Manufacturing Nondurables	Mining	Retail Trade	Services	Transportation & Utilities	Wholesale Trade
				A. Mean Growth Rates and Standard Deviations						
Mean growth rate (% per quarter)	0.74	0.06	0.12	0.12	0.14	0.11	−0.21	0.16	0.08	0.03
Standard deviation (% per quarter)	0.97	2.31	1.00	1.97	1.24	2.41	1.23	0.89	1.26	0.87
Beta on GNP growth	1.00	0.95	0.30	1.19	0.62	0.88	0.60	0.22	0.53	0.52
R^2 of regression on GNP growth	1.00	0.15	0.09	0.33	0.23	0.12	0.21	0.06	0.16	0.30
				B. Correlation across Industries						
GNP	1.00	0.41	0.29	0.59	0.48	0.36	0.47	0.24	0.41	0.56
Construction	0.41	1.00	0.20	0.42	0.38	0.25	0.21	0.30	0.32	0.39
FIRE	0.29	0.20	1.00	0.24	0.30	0.18	0.27	0.52	0.11	0.50
Manufacturing: Durables	0.59	0.42	0.24	1.00	0.68	0.24	0.30	0.24	0.55	0.51
Manufacturing: Nondurables	0.48	0.38	0.30	0.68	1.00	0.17	0.37	0.35	0.49	0.52
Mining	0.36	0.25	0.18	0.24	0.17	1.00	0.29	0.16	0.15	0.22
Retail trade	0.47	0.21	0.27	0.30	0.37	0.29	1.00	0.37	0.33	0.61
Services	0.24	0.30	0.52	0.24	0.35	0.16	0.37	1.00	0.20	0.50
Transportation & utilities	0.41	0.32	0.11	0.55	0.49	0.15	0.33	0.20	1.00	0.24
Wholesale trade	0.56	0.39	0.50	0.51	0.52	0.22	0.61	0.50	0.24	1.00

Note: All data are in real U.S. dollars, deflated using the GNP deflator.

represents "aggregate risk," where we take *aggregate risk* to mean the risk associated with aggregate movements in GNP or changes in aggregate wages, which we have seen are nearly the same thing.

Table 10.8 shows that the manufacturing industries differ widely in their sensitivity to GNP changes, with estimated betas ranging from a low of 0.22 for services to coefficients close to 1.0 for construction, durables manufacturing, and mining. The R^2's for these regressions are rather low, indicating that most of the volatility in labor income growth in these industries is idiosyncratic. An implication is that human capital risk for workers in these industries would not be hedged very well with a claim on GNP.

Labor Income by Education Group

It is likely that the risk-return characteristics of human capital differ across income groups. Campbell, Cocco, Gomes, and Maenhout (chap. 11 in this volume) have constructed information on income by education group that will allow us to investigate this hypothesis. They specify a model of income for individual i at date t of the form[16]

$$\log Y_{it} = f(t, Z_{it}) + v_{it} + \varepsilon_{it},$$

where $f(t, Z_{it})$ depends on age and other individual characteristics Z_{it}, v_{it} follows a random walk with innovation u_{it}, and ε_{it} is a temporary shock. Letting $\hat{f}(t, Z_{it})$ denote the fitted value of $f(t, Z_{it})$, Campbell et al. define

$$\log Y_{it}^* = \log Y_{it} - \hat{f}(t, Z_{it}),$$

which effectively purges income of fluctuations due to age or other identifiable demographic characteristics.

Campbell et al. generously provided annual data from 1971 to 1992 on the average value of Y_{jt}^* for individuals within education group j. There are three such groups: never finished high school; finished high school; and additional education beyond the high school level. Table 10.9 shows the standard deviation of the growth rates of the $Y_{it}^* (\Delta Y_{it}^*)$ and their sensitivity to GNP growth. The standard deviation of ΔY_{it}^* for the group that never finished high school (group 1) is nearly twice the standard deviation of GNP growth, whereas the highest education group has ΔY_{it}^* about as volatile as GNP growth. In terms of correlations, ΔY_{it}^* is highly correlated with GNP growth for the lowest education group, with a correlation of 0.83; for the middle education group, the correlation is 0.71, but it is only 0.33 for the group with the highest education level. The last line in the table shows the beta in a regression on GNP growth similar to the one run for the industry groups above, together with the R^2's for these regressions.

---

16. The following uses the notation of Campbell et al., not the notation of the present paper.

Table 10.9   Volatility of Labor Income Growth across Education Groups (annual
                     data, 1971–96)

	Less Than High School	Finished High School	More Than High School
	A. Mean Growth Rates and Standard Deviations		
Mean growth rate (% per year)[a]	−0.06	0.03	0.02
Standard deviation (% per year)	5.23	3.22	2.58
Beta on GNP growth	1.63	0.86	0.32
R^2 of regression on GNP growth	0.68	0.50	0.11
	B. Correlation across Education Groups		
Less than high school	1.00	0.63	0.20
Finished high school	0.63	1.00	0.60
More than high school	0.20	0.60	1.00

[a] Mean growth rate computed from labor income growth purged of age and other demographic effects.

The lowest education group has a large value of beta at 1.63, while the highest education group has a beta of only 0.32. Further, the R^2 is 0.68 for the lowest education group but only 0.11 for the group with the most education. These results suggest that there are important differences across education groups in the extent of aggregate as opposed to idiosyncratic risk in labor income and thus the extent to which claims on aggregate output could be used to hedge this risk. Specifically, the lowest education group seems to be the most exposed to aggregate risk, while the highest education group seems to be the least exposed.

10.3.2   Hedging Human Capital Risk

This section explores issues associated with hedging human capital risk. While we have documented that labor income is volatile, implying that human capital is risky, it remains to be seen whether existing financial assets could be useful in hedging this risk. Financial assets will be useful as hedges against human capital risk if they have significant predictive power for current and future labor income growth. This subsection explores whether such predictive power can be found in the data.[17]

Our results on the predictability of labor income growth using financial asset returns are summarized in table 10.10. We consider a variety of measures of labor income and several different possibilities for traded financial assets. In panel A, we consider aggregate, per capita labor income as our measure of the flow of "dividends" from human capital; the traded finan-

17. Davis and Willen (1998) also address the question of the benefits of using financial assets to hedge human capital.

Table 10.10   **Labor Income, Social Security, and Equity Returns**
$$\Delta \log y_t = c + \beta \Delta \log y_{t-1} + \Gamma_{US}(L)r_t^{US} + \Gamma_{UK}(L)r_t^{UK} + \varepsilon_t$$

	β (S.E.)	U.S. Equities	U.K. Equities	Far East Equities	R^2, Regression with $\Delta \log y_{t-1}$ Only	R^2, Regression with Equity Returns
		Sum of Coefficients in $\Gamma(L)$ (*p*-value for *F*-test that sum is zero)				
A. Results for Aggregate Labor Income per Capita and Social Security (annual data, 1951–97)[a]						
Aggregate real labor income (per capita)	.489 (.113)	.06 (.07)	.06 (.00)		.080	.477
Social security (rate of growth of aggregate wage index	.315 (.131)	.06 (.07)	.03 (.12)		.078	.430
B. Results for Aggregate Labor Income (quarterly data, 1969:4–1998:1)[b]						
Aggregate real labor income	.445 (.087)	.05 (.07)	.03 (.97)	.03 (.01)	.326	.541
C. Results for Nine Manufacturing Industries (quarterly data, 1969:4–1998:1)[c]						
Construction	.060 (.098)	.13 (.08)	−.06 (.38)	.06 (.09)	.006	.166
FIRE	.064 (.115)	.01 (.85)	.00 (.31)	.02 (.31)	.006	.111
Manufacturing: durables	.170 (.098)	.14 (.02)	−.05 (.41)	.06 (.45)	.081	.309
Manufacturing: nondurables	.104 (.098)	.13 (.00)	−.02 (.60)	.03 (.12)	.042	.34
Mining	−.092 (.099)	.03 (.67)	.03 (.69)	.03 (.45)	.023	.129
Retail trade	−.104 (.101)	.10 (.02)	−.00 (.94)	.01 (.56)	.000	.211
Services	.053 (.108)	.04 (.13)	−.01 (.77)	.02 (.19)	.000	.182
Transportation & utilities	−.010 (.101)	.07 (.07)	−.01 (.78)	.02 (.36)	.002	.217
Wholesale trade	.169 (.100)	.06 (.03)	−.00 (.89)	.01 (.37)	.038	.207
D. Results for Different Educational Groups (annual data, 1971–96)[d]						
Less than high school	−.276 (.285)	.00 (.99)	.12 (.60)	.01 (.91)	.186	.290
Finished high school	.323 (.339)	.12 (.25)	−.08 (.50)	.05 (.36)	.076	.342
More than high school	−.027 (.274)	.02 (.74)	.07 (.42)	.01 (.90)	.013	.439

[a]Polynomials $\Gamma(L)$ contain lags 0 and 1.
[b]Polynomials $\Gamma(L)$ contain lags 0–4.
[c]Polynomials $\Gamma(L)$ contain lags 0–3.
[d]Polynomials $\Gamma(L)$ contain lags 0 and 1.

cial assets that we consider are U.S. and U.K. equities. Our data are annual, covering the period 1951–98. We ran a regression of the form

$$\Delta \log y_t = c + \beta \Delta \log y_{t-1} + \Gamma_{US}(L)r_t^{US} + \Gamma_{UK}(L)r_t^{UK} + \varepsilon_t,$$

where we included lags 0 and 1 in the polynomials $\Gamma_{US}(L)$ and $\Gamma_{UK}(L)$. We found that U.S. and U.K. equities each had significant predictive power for aggregate, per capita labor income growth. This suggests an important role for both U.S. and U.K. equities in hedging human capital risk, where the measure of human capital is aggregate labor income. For an individual, this result could be interpreted as implying that U.S. and U.K. equities could be useful in hedging the *aggregate* component of his human capital risk.

The last row of panel A runs a similar regression for the "social security asset"—the rate of growth of the wage-indexing series. Here, we find that U.S. equities but not U.K. equities are useful predictors for the growth rate of the wage-indexing series.

Panel B of table 10.10 looks at the predictability of aggregate labor income (not per capita) when the traded assets include U.S. equities, European equities, and Far East equities. The sample is quarterly, 1969:4–1998:1. Again, we find an important role for U.S. equities in hedging aggregate human capital risk. European equities are not significant predictors of aggregate labor income growth, but Far East equities are strongly significant. At least over this time period, then, U.S. and Far East (mainly Japanese) equities would have provided useful hedges for aggregate human capital.

Panel C of table 10.10 looks at the predictability of labor income growth in nine industries, using the same quarterly data set for financial variables. We find that the U.S. equity return is a significant predictor of labor income growth in six of the nine industries, while European and Far East equities are never significant. The strongest results are for those industries known for their cyclic sensitivity: construction and the manufacturing industries. Our results imply that U.S. equities could provide a useful hedge for human capital risk in several industries.

Finally, panel D looks at the predictability of labor income growth for the education groups described above. We find no equity return that is a significant predictor of labor income growth, although including the equity returns in the regressions does increase the fit of the regressions substantially.

Overall, our findings suggest that returns on financial assets, notably U.S. equities, are significant predictors of labor income growth. These results suggest an important role for U.S. equities in hedging the risk of nontraded human capital. Specifically, an individual whose labor income growth is positively correlated with U.S. equity returns would hedge by holding a reduced fraction of his portfolio of traded financial assets in the form of U.S. equities. As a consequence, the individual's holdings of foreign assets or risk-free assets would necessarily be increased.

10.3.3 Computing Human Capital Returns: Literature Review

Since human capital is a nontraded asset, measuring human capital returns requires an asset-pricing model that links observable cash flows from human capital to returns on this asset. This section summarizes alternative approaches that have been used in the literature.

The Approach of Campbell

Campbell (1996) constructs a multifactor model of asset returns in which risky human capital plays an important role. By assuming that the conditional expected return on human capital is equal to the conditional expected return on financial wealth, Campbell derives the following expression for the return on human capital:

$$(4) \quad r_{y,t+1} - E_t r_{y,t+1} = (E_{t+1} - E_t)\sum_{j=0}^{\infty} \rho^j \Delta y_{t+1+j} - (E_{t+1} - E_t)\sum_{j=0}^{\infty} \rho^j r_{a,t+1+j},$$

where $r_{y,t+1}$ is the return on human capital, Δy_{t+1+j} is the growth rate of labor income, $r_{a,t+1+j}$ is the return on financial assets, and ρ is a discount factor. Thus, human capital returns are high when there are upward revisions in expected future labor income growth but low when expected future returns on financial assets are high because the given stream of labor income is discounted at a higher rate. Campbell finds that there is important predictability of future labor income growth using current and lagged labor income growth and that, in monthly data at least, financial market variables also help predict labor income growth. Campbell also finds that most of the variability in the return on human capital is accounted for by the variance of the "discount rate news" term, $(E_{t+1} - E_t) \sum_{j=0}^{\infty} \rho^j r_{a,t+1+j}$. Specifically, the variance of the human capital return in monthly data is reported as 20.8 (percent per month), while the variance of the labor income news is only 1.256. Thus, the correlation between human capital returns and returns on financial assets is necessarily quite high: 0.94 for the monthly data and 0.54 for the annual data.[18]

The Approach of Baxter and Jermann

Baxter and Jermann (1997) use a somewhat different approach, working with a version of (4) in which expected returns on financial assets are

---

18. In earlier work, Fama and Schwert (1977) study human capital returns in a version of (4) that assumed that labor income growth could not be forecast and where there was assumed to be no variation in expected future discount rates. These alternative assumptions explain why Fama and Schwert found little relation between human capital returns and returns on financial assets.

constant. The starting point for the Baxter-Jermann work is the observation that labor's share of GNP appears to be stationary so that labor income and capital income are cointegrated. They specify a vector error correction model (VECM) for labor income growth and capital income growth as follows:

(5)
$$\Delta d_{L,t+1} = \delta_L + \beta_L(L)\Delta d_{Lt} + \gamma_L(L)\Delta d_{Kt}$$
$$+ \alpha_L(d_{Lt} - d_{Kt}) + \varepsilon_{L,t+1},$$

(6)
$$\Delta d_{K,t+1} = \delta_K + \beta_K(L)\Delta d_{Lt} + \gamma_K(L)\Delta d_{Kt}$$
$$+ \alpha_K(d_{Lt} - d_{Kt}) + \varepsilon_{K,t+1},$$

where d_{Lt} denotes the log of labor income, d_{Kt} denotes the log of capital income, $\Delta d_{L,t+1} \equiv d_{L,t+1} - d_{Lt}$, $\Delta d_{K,t+1} \equiv d_{K,t+1} - d_{Kt}$, and $\beta_L(L)$, $\beta_K(L)$, $\gamma_L(L)$, and $\gamma_K(L)$ are polynomials in the lag operator, L. Returns to labor and capital were then computed as follows:

(7)
$$r^L_{t,t+1} - E(r^L_{t,t+1}) = (E_{t+1} - E_t)\left(\sum_{j=0}^{\infty} \rho^j \Delta d_{L,t+1+j}\right),$$

(8)
$$r^K_{t,t+1} - E(r^K_{t,t+1}) = (E_{t+1} - E_t)\left(\sum_{j=0}^{\infty} \rho^j \Delta d_{K,t+1+j}\right).$$

Because labor and capital income share a common stochastic trend, and because returns on an asset are dominated by revisions in the expected trend component, labor and capital returns were found to be very highly correlated, with the correlation exceeding 0.92 for the United States, Japan, and Germany and a correlation of 0.78 for the United Kingdom. If the return on physical capital is best proxied by the return on the unlevered stock market, as argued by Black (1987), then these results suggest a high correlation between human capital returns and returns on the domestic stock market.

Returns on Human Capital: Some New Evidence

This section uses a version of the approach of Shiller (1993) and Baxter and Jermann (1997) to compute U.S. aggregate human capital returns where the "dividend" flow is aggregate U.S. labor income. This approach is distinct from Campbell's because it assumes that the discount rate is constant. Thus, all variation in returns is due to changes in expected future dividend flows.

We want to explore how useful domestic and foreign assets may be in hedging human capital risk. Intuitively, traded financial assets are useful as hedges for human capital risk if they have returns that are highly correlated with human capital returns. Further, traded financial assets are important determinants of the returns on human capital to the extent that returns on financial assets help predict future growth in labor income. Thus, we estimated a process for income of the form

$$(9) \qquad \Delta \log y_t = c + \Gamma_Y(L)\Delta \log y_{t-1} + \Gamma_{US}(L)r_t^{US}$$
$$+ \Gamma_{\text{foreign}}(L)r_t^{\text{foreign}} + \varepsilon_t$$

and computed returns on human capital using the formula

$$(10) \qquad r_{t,t+1}^Y - E(r_{t,t+1}^Y) = (E_{t+1} - E_t)\left(\sum_{j=0}^{\infty} \rho^j \Delta y_{t+1+j}\right).$$

Table 10.11 contains information on the return characteristics of various measures of labor income. The structure of table 10.11 parallels that of table 10.10 above in terms of the measure of labor income considered and the menu of financial assets. In each case, we report results for several choices of lag length in the polynomials $\Gamma_j(L)$ since the choice of lag length significantly affects our results in some cases.

Panel A has results for per capita labor income. The standard deviation of the returns on this measure of human capital is about .04 (4 percent per year)—about one-third as volatile as U.S. equities. Our results indicate that human capital returns are strongly correlated with U.S. equity returns and with U.K. equity returns as well; there is some evidence that the correlation with the U.S. equity return is stronger. The results for the social security asset are similar, except that the social security returns are uniformly more correlated with U.S. equity returns than with U.K. returns.

Panel B contains results for quarterly aggregate labor income and three equity portfolios. We find that this measure of aggregate human capital returns is positively correlated with U.S. equity returns as well as being positively correlated with European and Far East equity returns. There is no clear evidence on which financial asset is most highly correlated with human capital; the results are sensitive to the lag length in the VAR for labor income growth.

Panel C contains results for human capital by industry. In general, human capital returns at the industry are positively correlated with U.S. and foreign equities. The results are quite sensitive to lag length, however, and it is difficult to draw clear conclusions from this table. It appears that those industries that we identified earlier as "cyclically sensitive"—construction and the manufacturing of durables and nondurables—are the industries with the highest correlation with U.S. equity returns. However, we also estimate high correlation between human capital returns and U.S. equity returns in the wholesale and retail trade industries. Finally, panel D contains results for the three education groups. The results here are quite sensitive to lag length, and the correlations are in some cases negative. Our

Table 10.11   **Human Capital Returns**

	No. of Lags in VAR	S.D. of Human Capital Return	Correlation between Human Capital Return and Equity Return		
			U.S. Equities	U.K. Equities	Far East Equities

A. Results for Aggregate Labor Income per Capita and Social Security (annual data, 1951–97)

	No. of Lags in VAR	S.D. of Human Capital Return	U.S. Equities	U.K. Equities	Far East Equities
Aggregate real labor income	1	.0434	.68	.71	
(per capita)	2	.0369	.55	.50	
	3	.0359	.71	.45	
	4	.0254	.54	.34	
Social security (rate of growth	1	.0309	.65	.64	
of aggregate wage index)	2	.0267	.63	.50	
	3	.0343	.75	.64	
	4	.0318	.61	.57	

B. Results for Aggregate Labor Income (quarterly data, 1969:4–1998:1)

	No. of Lags in VAR	S.D. of Human Capital Return	U.S. Equities	U.K. Equities	Far East Equities
Aggregate real labor income	1	.0157	.12	.23	.33
	2	.0158	.38	.52	.50
	3	.0181	.49	.52	.54
	4	.0162	.60	.56	.63

C. Results for Nine Manufacturing Industries (quarterly data, 1969:4–1998:1)

	No. of Lags in VAR	S.D. of Human Capital Return	U.S. Equities	U.K. Equities	Far East Equities
Construction	1	.0304	.18	.13	.25
	2	.0215	.23	.26	.39
	3	.0255	.52	.34	.49
	4	.0354	.64	.36	.53
FIRE	1	.0126	.42	.40	.38
	2	.0109	.37	.46	.41
	3	.0136	.32	.33	.37
	4	.0158	.42	.33	.30
Manufacturing: durables	1	.0287	.25	.24	.28
	2	.0252	.46	.39	.49
	3	.0281	.60	.39	.51
	4	.0248	.56	.37	.47
Manufacturing: nondurables	1	.0181	.45	.42	.38
	2	.0164	.62	.50	.47
	3	.0187	.72	.52	.51
	4	.0178	.69	.55	.49
Mining	1	.0213	.11	.19	.20
	2	.0216	.12	.17	.30
	3	.0215	.29	.27	.36
	4	.0212	.36	.25	.42
Retail trade	1	.0118	.38	.46	.43
	2	.0168	.58	.49	.44
	3	.0171	.63	.45	.41
	4	.0213	.63	.41	.43
Services	1	.0120	.21	.30	.31
	2	.0103	.35	.42	.45
	3	.0112	.59	.48	.57
	4	.0207	.57	.34	.37
Transportation & utilities	1	.0156	.18	.19	.20
	2	.0150	.37	.33	.40
	3	.0174	.49	.33	.38
	4	.0227	.43	.32	.18
Wholesale trade	1	.0124	.39	.36	.38
	2	.0134	.47	.38	.40
	3	.0149	.56	.39	.42
	4	.0172	.56	.32	.39

Table 10.11   (continued)

	No. of Lags in VAR	S.D. of Human Capital Return	Correlation between Human Capital Return and Equity Return		
			U.S. Equities	U.K. Equities	Far East Equities
D. Results for Different Education Groups (annual data, 1971–96)					
Less than high school	1	.0424	.22	.33	.30
	2	.0458	−.17	−.14	−.04
High school	1	.0429	.43	.35	.43
	2	.0267	.16	.25	.28
More than high school	1	.0293	.50	.61	.41
	2	.0236	.56	.35	.54

interpretation is that the very short sample period (twenty-four years, annual data) is insufficient to estimate (9) with any precision.

10.4 Quantifying the Benefits of Social Security Reform to Retirees

Under social security, individuals receive a certain real annuity with spousal survival rights. By contrast, in the private variable-annuities market, individuals can receive annuity payments that depend on the returns on risky portfolios. Thus, one direction for social security reform is to expand the menu of annuities available to social security participants during the retirement period. For example, individuals might choose a certain real annuity, as under the current plan, or they might choose a risky portfolio whose return depended on the domestic or international stock markets. Further, they might choose some of each.

In this section, we provide a detailed analysis of the benefits to social security reform that would accrue to retirees if they were free to choose the nature of the annuity payment that they would receive, with a specific focus on the benefits from investment in international risky assets. We work with a basic model designed to highlight the issues. We also discuss the implications of extending the model in various directions. The discussion focuses on a household that is at retirement age, which we view as exogenously determined and denote as R as above, and that can live until a maximum age T. We use a utility-based model because we are interested in learning about the determinants of the demand for risky assets as a fraction of wealth, the fraction of this demand that is for international assets, the likelihood that short-sales constraints bind, and the cost of restrictions on the composition of the portfolio.

10.4.1 Preferences

We assume that households have time-separable preferences and that momentary utility is

$$u(c_t, \underline{c}_t) = \frac{1}{1 - \sigma}[(c_t - \underline{c}_t)^{1-\sigma}].$$

According to this expression, individuals derive utility from the deviation of the level of consumption, c_t, from a mandated level of consumption, $\underline{c}_t$. We have written utility in this form for several reasons. First, it allows for a "subsistence" level of consumption, $\underline{c}_t$, the importance of which is frequently discussed in public policy discussions of social security and other transfer programs. Second, the inclusion of $\underline{c}_t$ may be viewed as representing "habitual" levels of consumption that are built up over the prior work years (in this latter interpretation, we might wish to include additional terms in the utility function to represent the utility benefits from these levels). In either case, the parameter σ governs risk aversion (higher values of σ correspond to higher relative risk aversion) and intertemporal substitution (higher values of σ correspond to a lower elasticity of intertemporal substitution).

We consider a group of individuals who are at the retirement point, age R, at calendar date t. We assume that individuals have a subjective discount factor β. Further, individuals have a probability π_j of living for j periods after retirement, and they discount future utility flows accordingly. Thus, at the retirement point, expected utility is

$$E_t\left\{\sum_{j=0}^{T-R} \pi_j \beta^j u(c_{t+j}, \underline{c}_{t+j})\right\}.$$

10.4.2 Retirement Portfolios with a Certain Lifetime

The initial focus of our discussion is on optimal portfolio construction when the life span, denoted by T, is known with certainty. Each period, the individual begins with a level of wealth, a, and must choose how much to save. The individual must also decide how to allocate his portfolio: we call the fractions allocated into different assets x_b, x_d, x_i, with the subscript indicating the short-term bond (b), the domestic risky asset (d), or the international risky asset (i). With a certain lifetime, the individual maximizes expected utility over the retirement period:

(11)
$$E_t\left\{\sum_{j=0}^{T-R} \beta^j u(c_{t+j}, \underline{c}_{t+j})\right\}.$$

Letting b_t denote social security benefits, asset evolution can be described with the following three equations:

(12) $a_{t+1} = [x_{bt}(1 + r_{b,t+1}) + x_{dt}(1 + r_{d,t+1}) + x_{it}(1 + r_{i,t+1})]f_t,$

(13) $1 = [x_{bt} + x_{dt} + x_{it}],$

(14) $c_t + f_t = a_t + b_t.$

Equation (12) states that the future wealth level is determined by saving, f_t, and portfolio shares and portfolio returns, through the term $[x_{bt}(1 + r_{b,t+1}) + x_{dt}(1 + r_{d,t+1}) + x_{it}(1 + r_{i,t+1})]$. Equation (13) defines the restriction on the portfolio shares, and equation (14) is the constraint on consumption and accumulation. The individual holds a portfolio with the return

$$1 + \tilde{r}_{t+1} = [x_{bt}(1 + r_{b,t+1}) + x_{dt}(1 + r_{d,t+1}) + x_{it}(1 + r_{i,t+1})].$$

Equivalently, this portfolio return is $1 + \tilde{r}_{t+1} = [(1 + r_{b,t+1}) + x_{dt}(r_{d,t+1} - r_{b,t+1}) + x_{it}(r_{i,t+1} - r_{b,t+1})]$ when we impose the requirement (13) that the portfolio shares sum to one.

Basic Results from Financial Economics

This portfolio problem has been much studied in finance (see, e.g., Levhari and Srinvasan 1969; Samuelson 1969; and Hakansson 1970) under the assumption that there are no social security payments and no subsistence-consumption levels. We begin by summarizing the key results of this literature. One is that the marginal propensity to consume out of wealth depends on the length of the remaining lifetime and the distribution of returns but not on the level of wealth. Another result is that the portfolio shares x are independent of the level of wealth *and* the length of the lifetime. We draw on these ideas in our discussion below and in our computation of the welfare benefits to individuals.

In general, these key results derive from studying the mathematical conditions that describe the household's optimal consumption-investment decisions. Optimal saving over time requires that

$$Du(c_t) = E_t\{(1 + \tilde{r}_{t+1})Du(c_{t+1})\},$$

that is, that the marginal cost of forgoing consumption today is equated to the expected benefit of more wealth and consumption in the future. In addition, the household requires

$$E_t\{(r_{d,t+1} - r_{b,t+1})Du(c_{t+1})\} = 0,$$

$$E_t\{(r_{i,t+1} - r_{b,t+1})Du(c_{t+1})\} = 0.$$

That is, the retiree investor needs to make sure that the benefits from investing in particular risky assets are worth the opportunity cost of investing in the risk-free bond.

The Value Functions

In a dynamic programming analysis of the optimal consumption and investment decision, the value functions play a key role. These functions express the utility that an individual of a particular age $(R + 1, R + 2, \ldots)$ receives if consumption and investment are undertaken optimally.

To write these compactly, we let γ_t denote the household's age at date t. Then the value function for this household, with asset holdings a_t, is given by

$$V(a_t,\gamma_t) = \max_{c_t,x_t}\{u(c_t) + \beta E_t V(a_{t+1},\gamma_{t+1})\},$$

where the maximization is undertaken subject to the constraints (12)–(14). One can show that the value functions for this retirement problem take the form

$$v(a,\gamma) = (1 - \sigma)^{-1}q(\gamma)^{1-\sigma}a^{1-\sigma},$$

where $q(\gamma)$ embeds information on the portfolio return earned by individuals.[19]

Nontraded Risk-Free Assets or Subsistence Consumption

One standard extension of this basic model has been to treat the individual as having a known endowment of a nontraded asset. In our context, this could be known transfer payments that the individual expects to receive (e.g., social security benefits). This nontraded stream of income that will be received with certainty is equivalent to a (positive) endowment of bonds. In this circumstance, the bond quantities chosen in the analysis presented above must be corrected for the endowment of the bond-like nontraded asset. A nonstochastic subsistence level can be analyzed in much the same manner, except that there is a negative endowment of

19. The algebra is as follows. First, use the optimal saving condition to show that there is a marginal propensity to consume out of wealth, $\mu(\gamma)$, which satisfies

$$\mu(\gamma)^{-\sigma} = \beta E(1 + \tilde{r})^{1-\sigma}\mu(\gamma')^{-\sigma}[1 - \mu(\gamma)]^{-\sigma},$$

where $\mu(\gamma')$ is the marginal propensity to consume of an individual one period older. Second, conjecture

$$v(a,\gamma) = q(\gamma)^{1-\sigma}\left\{\frac{1}{1 - \sigma}a^{1-\sigma}\right\}$$

so that the value recursion, together with the optimal consumption decision $c(a, \gamma) = \mu(\gamma)a$, implies

$$v(a,\gamma) = \left\{\frac{1}{1 - \sigma}[\mu(\gamma)a]^{1-\sigma}\right\} + \beta E v(a',\gamma')$$

$$= \left\{\frac{1}{1 - \sigma}[\mu(\gamma)a]^{1-\sigma}\right\} + \beta q(\gamma')^{1-\sigma}E\left\{\frac{1}{1 - \sigma}(a')^{1-\sigma}\right\}$$

$$= \left\{\frac{1}{1 - \sigma}[\mu(\gamma)a]^{1-\sigma}\right\} + \beta q(\gamma')^{1-\sigma}E\{((1 + \tilde{r})(1 - \mu(\gamma))a)^{1-\sigma}\}.$$

Then, the conjecture is correct is the following coefficient recursion is satisfied:

$$q(\gamma)^{1-\sigma} = [\mu(\gamma)^{1-\sigma} + (1 - \mu(\gamma))^{1-\sigma}E\{\beta(1 + \tilde{r})^{1-\sigma}q(\gamma')^{1-\sigma}\}.$$

bonds from this source: the individual is required to be able to finance subsistence consumption before anything else (otherwise, he faces infinitely negative utility).

Taking both these features together, and calling the nontraded asset's income stream $\underline{b}$, the analysis presented above would then apply (at the retirement date) to a modified wealth measure,

$$\hat{a}_t = \left[a_t + \sum_{j=0}^{T-R} \left(\frac{1}{1 + r_b} \right)^j (\underline{b}_{t+j} - \underline{c}_{t+j}) \right].$$

That is, the individual's modified wealth measure $\hat{a}_t$ includes measured financial wealth plus the present value of the nontraded asset's income stream less the present value of the mandated consumption level. This modified wealth measure would be allocated into risky assets and bonds proportionately as described previously so that the individual's net demand for bonds at date t would be

$$\sum_{j=0}^{T-R} \left(\frac{1}{1 + r_b} \right)^j (\underline{c}_{t+j} - \underline{b}_{t+j}) + x_b \hat{a}_t.$$

Thus, there would be the proportional demand for bonds discussed earlier, $x_b \hat{a}_t$, plus some additional bond purchases necessary to cover the excess of required (subsistence) consumption over the income from the nontraded asset. Endowing individuals with a claim to social security payments is equivalent to endowing them with a bond. This would therefore reduce individuals' demand for other bonds, leading to a redistribution of private portfolios away from bonds and toward other risky assets that pay higher rates of return.

10.4.3   Results for Specific Portfolio Opportunities

What retirement portfolios would individuals choose if their investment opportunities were described by the recent risk and return characteristics of traded financial assets? In this section, we use the analytic framework that we just discussed to determine how individuals would structure their retirement portfolios given their degree of risk aversion, σ, and some specific domestic and foreign portfolios.

We use the U.S. stock market as the domestic asset and consider four different definitions of the international portfolio (returns on U.K. stocks, returns on a world portfolio composed of 50 percent European and 50 percent Far East stocks, and then the European and Far East stocks in isolation). Our results are summarized in table 10.12: this table shows how portfolio choice depends on risk aversion and on the specific foreign portfolio under consideration.

Table 10.12 Composition of Retirement Portfolios

	Fraction of Portfolio in Risky Assets				Fraction of Risky Assets in U.S. Assets			
σ	U.S.-U.K., 1918–95 (1)	U.S.-Non-U.S., 1970–97 (2)	U.S.-Europe, 1970–97 (3)	U.S.-Far East, 1970–97 (4)	U.S.-U.K., 1918–95 (1)	U.S.-Non-U.S., 1970–97 (2)	U.S.-Europe, 1970–97 (3)	U.S.-Far East, 1970–97 (4)
2	1.11	1.58	1.48	1.55	0.66	0.59	0.61	0.76
3	0.74	1.07	1.00	1.05	0.66	0.60	0.61	0.76
4	0.56	0.80	0.75	0.79	0.66	0.60	0.61	0.76
5	0.44	0.64	0.60	0.63	0.66	0.60	0.61	0.76
10	0.22	0.32	0.30	0.31	0.66	0.60	0.61	0.77
15	0.15	0.21	0.20	0.21	0.66	0.60	0.61	0.77
20	0.11	0.16	0.15	0.16	0.66	0.60	0.61	0.77
25	0.09	0.13	0.12	0.13	0.66	0.60	0.61	0.77

Note: Portfolio allocations were determined for four different statistical processes for returns, estimated from the data as indicated in the column headings. These statistics are as follows (the risk-free rate is 0.02): (1) U.S.-U.K., 1918–95: $E[R(US)] = 0.0941$; $E[R(UK)] = 0.0941$; $\sigma(US) = 0.1054$; $\sigma(UK) = 0.2041$; corr(US, UK) = 0.52; (2) U.S.-Non-U.S., 1970–97: $E[R(US)] = 0.0843$; $E[R(Non)] = 0.1016$; $\sigma(US) = 0.1617$; $\sigma(Non) = 0.2106$; corr(US, Non-US) = 0.50; non-U.S. portfolio is 50 percent Europe, 50 percent Far East; (3) U.S.-Europe, 1970–97: $E[R(US)] = 0.0843$; $E[R(Eur)] = 0.0912$; $\sigma(US) = 0.1617$; $\sigma(Eur) = 0.1880$; corr(US, Eur) = 0.68; (4) U.S.-Far East, 1970–97: $E[R(US)] = 0.0843$; $E[R(Far East)] = 0.1120$; $\sigma(US) = 0.1617$; $\sigma(UK) = 0.2968$; corr(US, Far East) = 0.27.

The extent of risk aversion has a major effect on the extent to which individuals invest in stocks. When risk aversion is low, with $\sigma = 2$, individuals want to hold about 150 percent of their retirement portfolio in the form of risky domestic and foreign assets; they would have to borrow at the risk-free rate in order to accomplish this. As the degree of risk aversion rises, the share of the retirement portfolio invested in risky assets falls: when $\sigma = 5$, the share of risky assets is about 60 percent, falling to about 20 percent for $\sigma = 15$.

The share of risky assets in the retirement portfolio is not very sensitive to the choice of the international portfolio. The share of the risky portfolio invested in U.S. assets is between 66 and 77 percent, depending on the particular international portfolio under consideration. Our results indicate that the U.S. share in total risky assets is quite insensitive to the level of risk aversion.[20]

Overall, these results indicate that retired individuals will generally prefer to hold a retirement portfolio that is risky, in contrast to the riskless real benefit stream that comes from the current social security system. That is, they would prefer to have a portfolio including a mix of domestic and international assets along with some safe assets.

Welfare Gains from Including Equities during Retirement

The prior subsection showed that there was an important role for risky assets in individuals' retirement portfolios, for all but extremely risk-averse individuals. The current social security system is set up so that the portfolio held by a retired person is essentially a real, risk-free bond. It is natural to ask how much better off individuals would be if their retirement portfolios instead contained risky assets. Of course, the answer will depend on the length of the retirement horizon and the individual's degree of risk aversion.

To answer this question, we proceed as follows. Let a^b denote the asset holdings of a retired person who invests all his assets in the risk-free bond. An individual of age γ with assets a^b invested only in bonds has value function

$$v(a^b, \gamma) = (1 - \sigma)^{-1} q^b(\gamma)^{1-\sigma}(a^b)^{1-\sigma}.$$

Now consider an individual who invests in equities and bonds to maximize expected retirement-period utility. Let a^e denote this individual's wealth; at age γ, the value function of this individual is then

$$v(a^e, \gamma) = (1 - \sigma)^{-1} q^e(\gamma)^{1-\sigma}(a^e)^{1-\sigma}.$$

---

20. This result is related to the standard result of the Markowitz model augmented with a risk-free asset: all investors hold the same risky portfolio, but investors with different levels of risk aversion hold different mixes of the risky and risk-free assets.

We set the value functions implied by the two portfolio strategies equal to each other, $v(a^b, \gamma) = v(a^e, \gamma)$, and then ask what wealth levels a^b and a^e are implied by this equality. It is intuitive that higher wealth levels will be needed to deliver a specific level of retirement-period utility (as summarized by the value function) when the individual is constrained to hold only the risk-free bond. Specifically, $v^b = v^e$ implies $a^b q^b = a^e q^e$. Allowing an individual to move from a bond-only portfolio to his optimal bond/stock portfolio is equivalent to giving the individual an increase in wealth, in percentage terms, equal to $100 \times [(q^e/q^b) - 1]$.

Table 10.13 reports the welfare gains from allowing individuals to move from a bond-only portfolio to the optimal portfolio, as measured by the effective increase in individual wealth. We display the effective increase in wealth for various levels of risk aversion, various lengths of the retirement period, and four different specifications of the available risky assets. The greatest gain in welfare from allowing risky investment naturally occurs for investors with low risk aversion and long retirement periods. For this group, the increase in effective wealth from allowing risky investment ranges from 55 to 75 percent. However, we find that there are notable increases in effective wealth even for investors with higher risk aversion or

Table 10.13   Welfare Gains from Risky Investment during Retirement

	Duration of Retirement Period				Duration of Retirement Period			
σ	5	10	15	25	5	10	15	25
	Foreign Asset Is U.K. Equities, 1918–95				Foreign Asset Is Non-U.S. Equities, 1970–97			
2	8.48	19.53	31.02	55.00	11.36	26.51	42.62	77.18
3	5.58	12.64	19.78	34.10	7.48	17.09	26.93	47.02
4	4.15	9.34	14.52	24.74	5.56	12.60	19.69	33.85
5	3.30	7.41	11.47	19.42	4.43	9.98	15.52	26.45
10	1.63	3.64	5.60	9.37	2.19	4.89	7.54	12.65
15	1.09	2.41	3.70	6.17	1.46	3.24	4.98	8.31
20	0.81	1.80	2.77	4.60	1.09	2.42	3.71	6.19
20	0.65	1.44	2.21	3.67	0.87	1.93	2.96	4.93
	Foreign Asset Is European Equities, 1970–97				Foreign Asset Is Far East Equities, 1970–97			
2	9.95	23.08	36.88	66.11	11.09	25.85	41.51	75.03
3	6.55	14.92	23.44	40.67	7.30	16.68	26.27	45.82
4	4.88	11.02	17.18	29.41	5.44	12.31	19.22	33.02
5	3.89	8.74	13.56	23.04	4.33	9.75	15.15	25.82
10	1.92	4.29	6.61	11.07	2.14	4.78	7.36	12.36
15	1.28	2.84	4.37	7.29	1.42	3.16	4.86	8.12
20	0.96	2.13	3.26	5.43	1.06	2.37	3.63	6.05
25	0.76	1.70	2.60	4.33	0.85	1.89	2.90	4.82

shorter horizons. The increase in effective wealth drops below 5 percent only when the retirement horizon is less than ten years or when risk aversion exceeds $\sigma = 10$. An increase in retirement wealth between 5 and 75 percent would certainly be considered economically important by most households. We therefore conclude that there are sizable benefits to including risky assets in the retirement portfolios of most individuals.[21]

Welfare Costs of Portfolio Restrictions

Many proposals for social security reform call for investors to have the opportunity to invest in risky assets. These proposals differ, however, in their recommendations concerning the menu of risky assets available to individuals. The Feldstein and Samwick (1997) proposal, for example, calls for individuals to invest in a diversified portfolio of U.S. assets. The Kotlikoff and Sachs (1998) proposal, on the other hand, calls for retirement funds to be invested in a diversified world portfolio. This subsection investigates the welfare implications of restricting investors to holding only U.S. assets in the risky part of their retirement portfolio. We also rule out short sales of all assets, including the risk-free bond.

Table 10.14 shows how these restrictions affect the welfare of the retired investor. We begin by noting that the "no-short-sales" constraint does not bind except for the least risk-averse investors ($\sigma = 2$). Panel A shows that the fraction of the portfolio invested in risky securities falls when investors are constrained to hold only U.S. securities: the $\sigma = 3$ investor reduces his risky holdings from 105 to 93 percent of his assets; the $\sigma = 10$ investor reduces risky holdings from 31 to 28 percent of assets.

The reduction in welfare from the portfolio restrictions is shown in table 10.14, panel B. The good news from this table is that allowing individuals to invest only in U.S. equities (as well as bonds) would deliver substantial welfare gains to retired individuals, relative to a situation in which retirees are required to hold just a risk-free bond. The bad news is that restricting the portfolio to only U.S. assets means that individuals receive only about 80 percent of the welfare increase that could be gained by permitting international diversification. These results reinforce the impression from figure 10.3 above, which showed great improvements in the risk-return trade-off from combining traditional social security with U.S. bonds and equities. It was unclear from that figure how important adding international investments might be in terms of generating increased welfare; this analysis suggests that the marginal contribution to individual welfare from international investment could be quite important to a retired individual.

21. Remember that these welfare gains apply only to allowing a specified asset pool to be invested in risky assets at the retirement point. This computation does not consider the potential for risky investment during the working years to deliver a larger value for the individual's assets at the retirement point.

Table 10.14   **Effect of Portfolio Constraints on Welfare of Retirees**

A. Effects on Portfolio Shares

σ	Unconstrained		Constrained
	Fraction of Portfolio in Risky Asset	U.S. as Fraction of Risky Assets	Fraction of Portfolio in U.S. Risky Assets
2	1.55	0.76	1.00
3	1.05	0.76	0.93
4	0.79	0.76	0.70
5	0.63	0.76	0.56
10	0.31	0.77	0.28
15	0.21	0.77	0.19
20	0.16	0.77	0.13
25	0.13	0.77	0.11

B. Effect of Portfolio Constraints on Welfare

Risk Aversion, σ	Constrained?		Constr./ Unconstr.	Constrained?		Constr./ Unconstr.
	No	Yes		No	Yes	
	5 Years			10 Years		
2	11.09	8.21	0.74	25.85	18.88	0.73
3	7.30	5.89	0.81	16.68	13.37	0.80
4	5.44	4.39	0.81	12.31	9.89	0.80
5	4.33	3.49	0.81	9.75	7.84	0.80
10	2.14	1.73	0.81	4.78	3.86	0.81
15	1.42	1.15	0.81	3.16	2.56	0.81
20	1.06	0.86	0.81	2.37	1.91	0.81
25	0.85	0.69	0.81	1.89	1.53	0.81
	15 Years			25 Years		
2	41.51	29.95	0.72	75.03	53.00	0.71
3	26.27	20.95	0.80	45.82	36.19	0.79
4	19.22	15.38	0.80	33.02	26.25	0.79
5	15.15	12.16	0.80	25.82	20.60	0.80
10	7.36	5.93	0.81	12.36	9.93	0.80
15	4.86	3.92	0.81	8.12	6.54	0.81
20	3.63	2.93	0.81	6.05	4.88	0.81
25	2.90	2.34	0.81	4.82	3.89	0.81

Note: Foreign portfolio is Far East equity portfolio.

Effects of Social Security Reform on Various Wealth Groups

In section 10.1 above, we noted that social security represented varying fractions of financial wealth for different income classes of workers at the retirement point. Retirement wealth was mostly social security and housing for the poorest Americans, while it was a much smaller fraction for more affluent citizens.

The benefits discussed above accrued to a household moving from an initial position in which all wealth is invested in safe assets to a new position in which the individual holds an optimal retirement portfolio, abstracting from any consideration of subsistence consumption. We can use our modifications of the basic consumption-investment problem, which introduced social security benefits and subsistence consumption, to determine the implications for various wealth groups of broadening the menu of retirement assets.

Rich Retirees. There may be little benefit to rich retirees of introducing the possibility of risky investment during retirement since these retirees have substantial non-social security, nonhousing wealth. Therefore, when they are endowed with a benefit by the social security system during retirement, they will simply hold fewer riskless assets in their portfolios. In fact, they might well not exercise the new right to reallocate their social security wealth away from its existing form since they had already reallocated other parts of their portfolio.

In terms of the analysis presented above, the demand for risky assets on the part of rich retirees would be

$$(x_d + x_i)\left[a_t + \sum_{j=0}^{T-R}\left(\frac{1}{1 + r_b}\right)^j \underline{b}_{t+j}\right];$$

that is, it would be proportional to financial wealth plus the present value of social security payments. Higher social security benefits would raise the demand for risky assets. The demand for riskless bonds would be a little more complicated:

$$(1 - x_d - x_i)\left[a_t + \sum_{j=0}^{T-R}\left(\frac{1}{1 + r_b}\right)^j \underline{b}_{t+j}\right] - \sum_{j=0}^{T-R}\left(\frac{1}{1 + r_b}\right)^j \underline{b}_{t+j}.$$

This demand would be a fraction of total wealth, including financial assets and social security payments, but one would then net out the quantity of riskless assets that the social security claim implicitly represents. Higher social security payments would reduce the demands for riskless assets since the demand can be rewritten as

$$(1 - x_d - x_i)q_t - (x_d + x_i)\left[\sum_{j=0}^{T-R}\left(\frac{1}{1 + r_b}\right)^j \underline{b}_{t+j}\right].$$

Further, if the government allowed (or required) these individuals to have a risky social security claim, then they would reduce risky assets in private retirement accounts so that their net portfolio shares were x_d and x_i.

Poor Retirees. Now consider a poor retiree whose income consists only of social security distributions and who has little or no financial wealth apart from the claim on the social security system. If this individual has a subsistence consumption level that is a large fraction of social security wealth, then he too would not reallocate much of a privatized social security account toward risky assets. That is, if this individual has a small level of our modified wealth measure,

$$\hat{a}_t = \left[a_t + \sum_{j=0}^{T-R}\left(\frac{1}{1 + r_b}\right)^j (\underline{b}_{t+j} - \underline{c}_{t+j})\right],$$

then he would have little demand for risky assets. Yet a poor retiree without substantial subsistence consumption requirements—one with a low level of financial wealth, for whom social security payments are the main basis for retirement consumption—would get the larger welfare gains from investing in risky assets, as discussed above.

10.4.4   Optimal Portfolios with an Uncertain Lifetime

We now turn to investigating a situation in which individuals have uncertain lifetimes. We assume that individuals can purchase annuities from a competitive, zero-cost insurance company. There are two effects of this modification, relative to our prior analysis of the certain-lifetime case. First, in the presence of less than certain survival, individuals effectively discount the future more heavily and wish to tilt their consumption profiles toward the present. Second, in the presence of less than certain survival, insurance companies price the longer-term components of annuities more cheaply, thus encouraging individuals to substitute toward the future. When annuities are priced in an actuarially fair manner, as we will assume, then these two substitution responses offset each other. Individuals can then simply purchase a higher level of consumption in all periods in which they are alive. The portfolio shares of risky assets—held by the insurance company in response to the preferences of households—are unaffected by uncertain lifetimes.

We assume that there are insurance companies that offer annuities with returns linked to the returns on risky assets. Suppose that a competitive, zero-cost insurance company faces a population of individuals with actuarial survival probabilities π_j (i.e., π_j denotes the probability that an individual is alive at age j). Then the insurance company could offer certain, real annuities (backed by bonds) to retirement-age individuals. In particular, the insurance company would offer annuities that took the following general form to an individual retiring at date t, considering the allocation of retirement wealth at $t + 1$ so as to support consumption in the $T - R$ periods $t + 1, t + 2, \ldots, t + T - R$. The insurance company will provide the individual with a specified pattern of consumption beginning at $t + 1$ (conditional on survival) and lasting for the remainder of his retirement life. In return, the individual or his estate would turn over

$$\sum_{j=1}^{T-R} \pi_j \left(\frac{1}{1 + r_b} \right)^{j-1} c_{t+j}$$

units of bonds to the insurance company at date $t + 1$. That is, the price of the annuity increases with the survival probabilities and the level of real payments but falls with the real interest rate.

The top panel of figure 10.4 shows the U.S. survival probabilities, conditional on attaining sixty-five years of age, based on the general population. The expected remaining lifetime for such an individual is about 17.5 years. We use these survival probabilities in all our computations below, although it would be interesting to explore how certain computations would

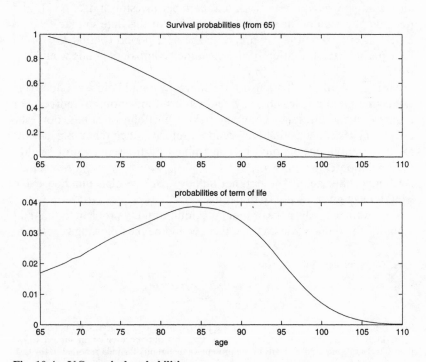

Fig. 10.4   U.S. survival probabilities

Table 10.15   Annuity Factors for U.S. General Population

	Real Interest Rate				
	.00	.01	.02	.03	.04
Annuity growth rate:					
.00	17.48	15.77	14.33	13.09	12.04
.01	19.49	17.48	15.79	14.35	13.13
.02	21.85	19.47	17.48	15.80	14.38
.03	24.62	21.80	19.45	17.48	15.82
.04	27.90	24.53	21.75	19.42	17.48

differ for subgroups of the population that have alternative survival probabilities. Table 10.15 presents annuity factors under actuarial fair insurance and at various real interest rates.[22] This table shows that a real interest rate of 2 percent and the U.S. survival probabilities imply that the price of an annuity paying a level real stream is \$14.33 per dollar of annuity payment. The table also reports prices of real annuities that grow at various rates.

To help us think about more complicated annuities that the insurance company might offer, it is useful first to think about the insurance company's balance sheet under the assumption that such riskless annuities are "backed" by insurance-company investments in the safe bond. The insurance company would begin with b dollars per investor at date $t + 1$, and it would pay each of the surviving investors c at this date so that it would have $b_{t+2} = (1 + r_b)(b_{t+1} - \pi_1 c_{t+1})$ in the next period (period $t + 2$). In later periods, the evolution of the insurance company's bonds would satisfy $b_{t+j+1} = (1 + r_b)(b_{t+j} - \pi_j c_{t+j})$.[23]

More generally, such an insurance company could hold any underlying assets and make any feasible payment pattern to its group of retirees. For example, if the insurance company held a portfolio of bonds, domestic assets, and risky assets that bore random return $\tilde{r}$, then the disbursements to the annuityholders would be constrained by the sequence of wealth-accumulation constraints $a_{t+j+1} = (1 + \tilde{r}_{t+j+1})(a_{t+j} - \pi_j c_{t+j})$. We can accordingly think about the optimal annuity package that our household would select given its utility function.

If we were to analyze the optimal portfolio/annuity problem for an individual with an uncertain lifetime, there would be the following generaliza-

22. The elements in this table are

$$\sum_{j=1}^{T-R} \pi_j \left(\frac{1 + \gamma}{1 + r_b} \right)^{j-1}$$

for various real growth rates and real interest rates, using the U.S. survival probabilities.

23. Imposing $c_{t+j} = (1 + \gamma^{j-1})c_{t+1}$, and solving this difference equation subject to the terminal condition $b_{T+1} = 0$, leads to the present-value annuity formula reported in the text.

tions of the standard consumption-investment portfolio problem: the marginal propensity to consume out of wealth depends on the extent of the individual's uncertainty about his or her horizon, but the portfolio shares are exactly those that are relevant in the model with a certain horizon. Further, we would find a value function that incorporates the uncertainty that individuals have about their lifetimes, which takes the general form of that in the standard problem, that is, $v(a) = (1/1 - \sigma)[qa]^{1-\sigma}$, with the q now depending on survival probabilities as well as the distribution of portfolio returns, time preference, and risk aversion. Hence, there are two general lessons that we describe in the next two subsections.

The Optimal Retirement Account Is a Variable Annuity

The optimal package of retirement benefits is a variable annuity where the return is linked to the returns on risky investments. This retirement annuity combines portfolio management with the sharing of life risks. Individuals earn higher average returns on this account, relative to the current "flat" annuity provided by social security, because the insurance company holds some risky assets in its portfolio. ·Yet, since the insurance company can pool the risks of uncertain lifetime for individuals, as with fixed-payment annuities, it can provide each individual with a higher level of consumption than would be the case if the individual had to hold the risky assets directly and guard against the risks of uncertain lifetime by himself.

Benefits from Including Risky Assets in the Retirement Annuity

With annuitization of retirement wealth, the effects of portfolio composition can be explored in the same manner that we used in the analysis of certain lifetimes presented above. These results are reported in table 10.16.

There are important benefits to holding a variable annuity for all but

Table 10.16   **Effects of Portfolio Constraints with Uncertain Lifetime**

| | Expected Retirement = 17.5 Years | | |
| | Constrained? | | Constr./ |
Risk Aversion, σ	No	Yes	Unconstr.
2	61.08	43.80	.72
3	37.94	30.20	.80
4	27.59	22.07	.80
5	21.70	17.41	.80
10	10.52	8.48	.81
15	6.95	5.61	.81
20	5.19	4.19	.81
25	4.14	3.34	.81

the most risk-averse investors. There are also additional benefits to international diversification. Since the life table used in constructing figure 10.4 implies that the expected lifetime is about 17.5 years, the results in table 10.16 are intermediate to those shown in table 10.14 above for certain retirement periods of fifteen and twenty-five years.

For example, when the individual has a risk-aversion coefficient of $\sigma = 5$, then allowing the retirement portfolio's returns to depend on risky assets would produce a utility gain that is equivalent to an increase in wealth of 21.7 percent. Most of this gain could be achieved from investing in either domestic stocks or international stocks alone. However, moving from a portfolio of domestic stocks to a fully diversified portfolio yields an increase in the wealth equivalent from 17.4 to 21.7 percent. As before, larger gains would accrue to less risk-averse retirees and smaller ones to retirees who were more risk averse.

10.5   Life-Cycle Portfolio Choice and Nontraded Assets

This section sketches a life-cycle model of portfolio choice that we use to discuss the importance of international investment during the accumulation phase of a privatized social security system. There are two main lessons that we draw from the analysis. First, nontraded assets such as human capital and social security can affect the demands for traded financial assets. Second, the hedging demand for traded financial assets depends importantly on the persistence of income shocks and the degree to which these shocks are correlated with the returns on traded financial assets.

10.5.1   A Model of Life-Cycle Saving

An individual living in this economy is economically active from an initial working date, at which time his age is $\gamma = 0$, until his death at age $\gamma = T$. A worker who is young ($\gamma = 0$) in period t will maximize the expected value of discounted lifetime utility from consumption:

$$E_t \sum_{\gamma=0}^{T} \beta^\gamma u_\gamma(c_{t+\gamma}).$$

Note that the period utility function u_γ may depend on the individual's age.

Each worker has labor income received as an endowment during the working years, denoted by $y_{0,t}, y_{1,t+1}, \ldots, y_{R,t+R}$, where R is the retirement date. A typical worker has a "hump-shaped" path of lifetime income, with income rising during the early working years and then declining as the worker nears retirement. While lifetime income is expected to have this profile, a typical worker faces considerable uncertainty about the exact levels of future income.

We model the social security system as follows. There is a social security account in which an individual's contributions $z_{\gamma t} = \tau_{\gamma t} y_{\gamma t}$ accumulate according to

$$m_{\gamma t} = (1 + r_t^w)m_{\gamma-1,t-1} + z_{\gamma t},$$

where r_t^w is the (net) growth rate of the wage-indexing series used by social security to mark up individuals' past contributions.[24] Benefits, denoted by g, are an increasing function of accumulated contributions:

$$g(m_{Rt}), \quad g' > 0.$$

As before, there are three marketable financial assets: a short-term real bond, a home-country equity portfolio, and a foreign (rest-of-the-world) equity portfolio, with returns r_{bt}, r_{dt}, and r_{it}, respectively.

Individuals' decisions regarding consumption, saving, and portfolio choice will depend on their age as well their level of wealth, their history of social security contributions and expected future benefits, and the expected returns on traded financial assets. In the equations presented below, we suppress the age subscript attached to each choice variable.

Individual decisions will satisfy the following equations:

(15) $$a_{t+1} = [x_{bt}(1 + r_{b,t+1}) + x_{dt}(1 + r_{d,t+1}) + x_{it}(1 + r_{i,t+1})]f_t,$$

(16) $$1 = [x_{bt} + x_{dt} + x_{it}],$$

(17) $$c_t + f_t = a_t + y_t + g_t - z_t.$$

As before, the first of these three equations describes the evolution of portfolio wealth over time, and the second equation simply states that portfolio shares in the three traded financial assets add to one.[25] Equation (17) says that the individual has financial assets a and income net of taxes $y + g - z$, which can be allocated between the purchase of new financial assets f and current consumption c. The individual also has a retirement account with balance m. Individual income and asset returns are functions of an exogenous state vector δ that evolves as a Markov process. There is nothing about the individual's decision problem that makes it depend directly on time, although it does depend on age. Thus, we may rewrite the individual's problem in dynamic programming form as follows:

---

24. In this section, all lowercase variables refer to variables measured in real terms, i.e., in goods units. Otherwise, the variable definitions are the same as in sec. 10.2 above.

25. Equation (17) differs from its sec. 10.4 counterpart, eq. (14), only in that labor income y_t and social security taxes z_t and benefits g_t enter on the right-hand side of the last expression as additional variables that affect wealth. A typical individual either will be working and paying taxes z_t or will be retired and receiving benefits g_t.

(18) $v(a + y + g - z,m,\gamma,\delta)$

$$= \max_{c,f,x_d,x_i,x_b} \{u(c,\gamma) + E[v(a' + y' + g' - z',m',\gamma',\delta')]|\delta\},$$

subject to the equality constraints given above. This expression uses the conventional dynamic programming "prime" notation to refer to next period's asset positions, incomes, returns, and states. There may also be inequality constraints, reflecting prohibitions on the short selling of assets and borrowing against future income ($x_b \geq 0$, $x_i \geq 0$, $x_d \geq 0$, $f \geq 0$).

In general, it is difficult to solve this type of dynamic program, even numerically. First, there is a large range for accumulated assets over the life cycle: the evidence in table 10.1 above indicates that the median retiring household had retirement assets that were roughly 40 percent of lifetime income or about sixteen times average annual income, assuming a forty-year working life. Second, there are many periods of life: for each period, the optimal choices must be calculated as well as the associated value function. Third, many variables may be important for forecasting individual income profiles. Fourth, and finally, there are several reasonable constraints that one would like to place on individuals' choices, such as short-sales constraints on assets and constraints preventing borrowing against future income. Each of these considerations substantially increases the complexity of the computational problem.[26]

For the purpose of the present paper, we proceed as follows. First, we review results from the prior literature that are relevant to the current problem, and then we discuss the general form of the optimal decision regarding portfolio choice when there is uncertainty regarding future labor income and asset returns. Second, we present results on optimal portfolio choice in a situation in which marketable financial assets can be used to perfectly hedge the risk associated with labor income uncertainty.

10.5.2   Life-Cycle Portfolio Choice under Uncertainty

Early contributions to the social security literature studied a model of life-cycle consumption and saving without uncertainty (see, e.g., Samuelson 1958). A chief finding from that literature was that social security depresses private saving by taking away income during the work years and returning it as social security benefits during the retirement period. Life-cycle models with income uncertainty will inherit this property, but they additionally focus attention on the effects of social security on portfolio allocation.

---

26. In applied dynamic programming terms, the economic considerations discussed in the text mean that there is a large state space over which the value function and optimal policies must be constructed, that there are many periods of life over which the value function and optimal policies must be constructed, that there are a number of "exogenous state variables" relevant to the problem, and that there are corners on the decision problem. Each of these considerations increases the complexity of the numerical dynamic programming problem.

The dynamic programming problem for an age γ worker was given in equation (18) above. The first-order condition for efficient choice of the portfolio share invested in domestic risky assets, x_d, under the assumption that an increase in x_d will be offset by a corresponding decrease in the share devoted to bonds, x_b, is given by the following:

(19) $$E\{Du(c')f(r_d' - r_b')\} = 0.$$

A similar expression describes optimal choice of the international risky asset:

(20) $$E\{Du(c')f(r_i' - r_b')\} = 0.$$

To highlight the economic issues that determine optimal portfolio choice, we rewrite equations (19) and (20) as follows:

(21) $$f\{E[Du(c')]E(r_d' - r_b') + \text{cov}[Du(c'),(r_d' - r_b')]\} = 0,$$

(22) $$f\{E[Du(c')]E(r_i' - r_b') + \text{cov}[Du(c'),(r_i' - r_b')]\} = 0,$$

where future consumption is given by

(23) $$c' = (1 + \tilde{r}')f + g' + y' - z' - f'.$$

Equations (21) and (22) highlight the two key influences on asset demand in this life-cycle setting. The first term in each equation involves the expected (excess) return on the risky assets: the higher the expected return on the asset, the more desirable it becomes as part of a portfolio. The second term in each equation involves the covariation of future consumption with the return on the particular risky asset. An asset is more desirable if it has a high return in states of nature in which the marginal utility of consumption is high. Abstracting from variations in marginal utility due to age dependence of the period utility function, this amounts to saying that an asset is valuable when high payoffs coincide with periods in which consumption would otherwise be low.

Let us consider a specific situation suggested by the empirical work of the prior section. Consider a working individual for whom the rate of growth of wages is positively correlated with current and past domestic equity returns but is uncorrelated with current and past returns on foreign assets. For this individual, the positive covariance between domestic risky assets and consumption means that domestic risky assets are less desirable than foreign risky assets yielding the same expected return. If all individuals experienced the same covariation of labor income growth with domestic and international assets, in equilibrium the expected return on domestic risky assets would have to be higher than the expected return on international assets. If individuals differ in the extent to which labor income growth is correlated with domestic assets, then our model suggests that individuals with a higher correlation will hold smaller shares of domestic assets in their overall portfolio of risky assets.

The presence of social security as a nontraded asset also has implications for the structure of the portfolio of marketable assets. In particular, our preceding empirical analysis suggested that the growth of the wage index—which is approximately the return on the social security account—is positively correlated with domestic assets but not particularly correlated with international assets. Accordingly, individuals would tend to substitute away from domestic risky assets and toward safe assets and international risky assets because of risky social security returns.

10.5.3   Portfolio Choice in the Perfect Spanning Case

The preceding section showed that there is the potential for an important hedging motive that will work to reduce holdings of domestic marketable assets if the returns on these assets are correlated with the returns on nontraded assets such as human capital or social security.

In addition to this general point, there is an important additional issue that we discuss in this section, which relates to nontraded human capital. We show that the hedging effects are most important if income is subject to permanent changes and if these permanent changes are correlated with the returns on marketable assets. In this subsection, we describe a model that is designed to highlight this distinction, studying asset accumulation and portfolio choice under the assumption that labor income is exactly related to (perfectly spanned by) the returns on traded financial assets.

Transitory Income Risks

Suppose that age γ labor income is linearly related to the returns on traded financial assets as follows:

$$(24) \qquad y_{\gamma t} = \bar{y}_\gamma [l_{b\gamma}(1 + r_{bt}) + l_{d\gamma}(1 + r_{dt}) + l_{i\gamma}(1 + r_{it})],$$

where $\bar{y}_\gamma$ is a constant "benchmark" level of age γ income, $l_{b\gamma}$ denotes the sensitivity of age γ labor income to the return on the risk-free bond, $l_{d\gamma}$ denotes the sensitivity of labor income to the returns on domestic risky assets, and $l_{i\gamma}$ denotes the sensitivity of labor income to foreign risky assets.

So long as the returns on the three financial assets are serially independent random variables, labor income risk is transitory in equation (24). This model of transitory income risks implies a particular hedging strategy. At date $t - 1$, the household can construct a perfect hedge for future labor income by selling $l_{b\gamma}\bar{y}_\gamma$ units of bonds, selling $l_{d\gamma}\bar{y}_\gamma$ units of domestic risky assets, and selling $l_{i\gamma}\bar{y}_\gamma$ units of international risky assets. The revenue generated by constructing the hedge is

$$[l_{b\gamma} + l_{d\gamma} + l_{i\gamma}]\bar{y}_\gamma,$$

which can also be interpreted as the date $t - 1$ value of $y_{\gamma t}$. By engaging in security transactions that hedge the labor income risks *perfectly,* the household has essentially converted its risky labor income into a certain labor income stream. Thus, it is appropriate to value human wealth using the risk-free interest rate so that an age γ household facing a constant, risk-free interest rate r_b would have human wealth, or human capital, equal to[27]

(25)
$$h_{\gamma t} = \sum_{j=\gamma}^{R} \left(\frac{1}{1 + r_b} \right)^{j-\gamma-1} ([l_{bj} + l_{dj} + l_{ij}]\bar{y}_j).$$

Each worker can hedge the risk of labor income fluctuations by appropriately structuring the financial asset portfolio, working one period ahead to offset the next period's income shocks. The precise details of the portfolio construction depend on the extent to which labor income looks like a bond (as reflected in a large l_{bj}), or like a domestic risky asset (l_{dj}), or like an international risky asset (l_{ij}).

Having hedged future labor income, the worker then chooses his optimal (age-dependent) portfolio. To simplify matters, we assume that the household's total demand for risky assets at each age is a constant fraction of the sum of its financial and human wealth (a fraction ρ of total wealth). This would in fact be the optimal policy if there were constant relative-risk-aversion utility as in section 10.3 above. Then a household with financial assets $a_{\gamma t}$ and human capital $h_{\gamma t}$ will have demand for risky assets equal to $\rho(a_{\gamma t} + h_{\gamma t})$ and demand for riskless assets equal to $(1 - \rho)(a_{\gamma t} + h_{\gamma t})$. Suppose further that the demand for risky assets is split between domestic assets and foreign assets, with shares φ and $(1 - \varphi)$, respectively. Then, combining the hedging and diversification motives, the net demand for domestic assets is

(26)
$$\varphi\rho(a_{\gamma t} + h_{\gamma t}) - l_{d\gamma}\bar{y}_\gamma,$$

and the net demand for international assets is

(27)
$$(1 - \varphi)\rho(a_{\gamma t} + h_{\gamma t}) - l_{i\gamma}\bar{y}_\gamma.$$

These expressions illustrate several aspects of the demand for assets in the presence of nontraded labor income when there is complete spanning. First, the net demands for domestic and international risky assets are simply the direct demand for risky assets (terms such as $\varphi\rho[a_{\gamma t} + h_{\gamma t}]$) less

---

27. This calculation assumes that the household first hedges its labor income during the period prior to its entry into the workforce (which would be $\gamma = -1$ in our notation) and in all subsequent periods. The discount factor applied to future age j labor income is $(1/1 + r_b)^{j-\gamma-1}$ because we are taking present values of the hedged cash flows, which arise at age $j - \gamma - 1$.

the hedging demand (terms such as $l_{d\gamma}\bar{y}_\gamma$). Second, when income disturbances are temporary, it is likely that the direct demand for risky assets will dominate the hedging demand since human capital is much larger than current income for most ages, as shown in table 10.7 above. That is, $h_{\gamma t} > y_{\gamma t}$. Third, the "loadings" $l_{d\gamma}$ and $l_{i\gamma}$ determine the sign of the hedging demand. If domestic labor income moved one for one with domestic security returns, then $l_{d\gamma} = 1$, with $l_{i\gamma} = l_{d\gamma} = 0$. In this case, explored previously by Baxter and Jermann (1997), there is a large reduction in the demand for domestic assets owing to hedging demand. The empirical analysis summarized in table 10.10 above showed a more modest level of $l_{d\gamma}$, although it still suggested $l_{d\gamma} > 0$, and a likely level of $l_{i\gamma} \approx 0$.

Permanent Income Risks

We now turn to an alternative model of labor income dynamics in which there are permanent shocks to the level of an individual's income. Specifically, we assume that

(28) $$y_{\gamma t} = \bar{y}_{\gamma t},$$

(29) $$\bar{y}_{\gamma t} = \bar{y}_{\gamma-1,t-1}[l_{b\gamma}(1 + r_b) + l_{d\gamma}(1 + r_{dt}) + l_{i\gamma}(1 + r_{it})].$$

Our own empirical evidence, as shown in table 10.10, as well as evidence provided by Campbell et al. (chap. 11 in this volume), suggests that this is a better model of the linkages between security returns and income flows than the transitory-shock model of the preceding section.[28] At the same time, this model is simplistic because it omits correlation between lagged security returns and current income flows, but it will serve to make our main point.

Since income at date t is a linear combination of security returns, it can be completely hedged at $t - 1$: the individual needs to sell only $\bar{y}_{\gamma-1,t-1}l_{b\gamma}$ units of bonds, $\bar{y}_{\gamma-1,t-1}l_{d\gamma}$ units of domestic stocks, and $\bar{y}_{\gamma-1,t-1}l_{i\gamma}$ units of international stocks to accomplish this objective. Taken together, these transactions produce a date $t - 1$ value of $y_{\gamma t}$ equal to

$$\bar{y}_{\gamma-1,t-1}[l_{b\gamma} + l_{d\gamma} + l_{i\gamma}].$$

Note that this expression looks much like the previous one for the model with transitory shocks, except that $\bar{y}_{\gamma-1,t-1}$ replaces $\bar{y}_\gamma$ as the "base" level of income for period t.

But, while this transaction completely hedges date t labor income, it is only a start on hedging human capital risk. That is, when there is a shock

---

28. Table 10.10 provides evidence in favor of this specification because domestic stock returns are significantly related to the growth rate of labor income. If the temporary-shock model of labor income growth were correct, there could be no significant relation between stock returns and income growth.

to $\bar{y}_t$, there are implications for incomes that will be received at $t + 1$, $t + 2, \ldots$ as well as at t. A dynamic hedging plan is necessary, one that takes into account these consequences for future cash flows. Typically, this plan requires a much greater volume of hedging transactions in domestic and international stocks than in the transitory-income case that we studied above.

To determine the nature of this plan, let us begin by defining human wealth for an individual at date t and age γ implicitly according to the recursive formula

$$h_{\gamma t} = [y_{\gamma t}] + \frac{1}{1 + r_b}[h_{\gamma+1,t+1}].$$

That is, the "hedged" value of human capital is equal to the hedged value of date t income plus the hedged value of human capital next period. We find it convenient to denote these hedged values with a shorthand notation so that $[y_{\gamma t}]$ is read as "the market value at date $t - 1$ of a portfolio of securities that exactly replicates the stochastic income stream $y_{\gamma t}$." We discount future human capital at a constant riskless rate because of the perfect spanning assumption.

To determine how the value of human capital is linked together at different dates and the hedging transactions on which it is based, think first about the retirement-age individual who just has $h_{Rt} = [y_{Rt}]$ and no value of his future human capital to worry about. Previously, we have determined that his income has date $t - 1$ value equal to $\bar{y}_{r-1,t-1}(l_{bR} + l_{dR} + l_{iR})$. Thus, the date t value of his human wealth is

$$h_{Rt} = [y_{Rt}] = \bar{y}_{R-1,t-1}(l_{bR} + l_{dR} + l_{iR})(1 + r_b).$$

Now let us look at the human wealth of an individual who is age $R - 1$: his human wealth is the sum of the value of current income and future human wealth:

$$h_{R-1,t} = [y_{R-1,t}] + \frac{1}{1 + r_b}[h_{R,t+1}]$$

$$= [y_{R-1,t}] + \frac{1}{1 + r_b}[\bar{y}_{R-1,t}(l_{bR} + l_{dR} + l_{iR})(1 + r_b)].$$

The second line of this expression indicates that future human wealth is proportional to $\bar{y}_{R-1,t}$ since this variable scales all future income flows. Further, since (28) makes current income also equal to $\bar{y}_{R-1,t}$, we can write the value of human capital as

$$h_{R-1,t} = [\bar{y}_{R-1,t}](1 + \bar{l}_R)$$

by defining the composite parameter $\bar{l}_R = (l_{bR} + l_{dR} + l_{iR})$. The key point is that the time-varying "base level" of future income flows can itself be hedged with the three financial assets: it is simply necessary to make larger rearrangements than previously in recognition of changing levels of $\bar{y}$. In particular, each unit of $\bar{y}_{R-1,t}$ has a hedged value of

$$[\bar{y}_{R-1,t}] = \bar{y}_{R-2,t-1}(l_{b,R-1} + l_{d,R-1} + l_{i,R-1})(1 + r_b) = \bar{y}_{R-2,t-1}\bar{l}_{R-1}.$$

But, since there are $(1 + \bar{l}_R)$ of these units, the total value is

$$[\bar{y}_{R-1,t}] = [\bar{y}_{R-1,t}](1 + \bar{l}_R) = \bar{y}_{R-2,t-1}\bar{l}_{R-1}(1 + r_b)(1 + \bar{l}_R).$$

Thus, the value of human capital again depends proportionately on current income, and it also depends on the sensitivity of future income flows to security returns.

Proceeding in the same way, the value of human capital at any age is given by

$$h_{\gamma t} = \bar{y}_{\gamma-1,t-1}(1 + r_b)L_\gamma,$$

with the composite expression L_γ obeying the recursion $L_\gamma = \bar{l}_\gamma(1 + L_{\gamma+1})$.

Overall, with income subject to permanent fluctuations, there is now a very different scale of hedging transactions for the individual: the hedging demand is now proportional to human capital rather than proportional to current income. The demand for domestic assets contains two components as above: the investment demand, which is proportional to total wealth and can be written as $\varphi\rho(a_{\gamma t} + h_{\gamma t})$, and the hedging demand against stochastic changes in $\bar{y}_{\gamma-1,t-1}$, which is proportional to human capital. This hedging demand takes the form $l_{d,\gamma-1}h_{\gamma t}$ since it is the sensitivity of $\bar{y}_{\gamma-1,t+1}$ to domestic returns that motivates the hedging demand: the larger is $l_{d,\gamma-1}$, the larger is the hedging demand. The overall demand for domestic assets is

(30) $$\varphi\rho(a_{\gamma t} + h_{\gamma t}) - l_{d,\gamma-1}h_{\gamma t}.$$

Similarly, the overall demand for international assets is

(31) $$(1 - \varphi)\rho(a_{\gamma t} + h_{\gamma t}) - l_{i,\gamma-1}h_{\gamma t}.$$

When income shocks are permanent, the market demands for domestic and international risky assets involve a risk-management, or hedging, component that is proportional to human capital rather than proportional to labor income, as in the temporary case (see [26] and [27] above).

Some Examples

Table 10.17 provides some examples that highlight the importance of permanent versus temporary income shocks for individuals with varying

Table 10.17   Portfolio Composition for Various Groups

Case and Individual	Risky Asset Share in Overall Portfolio ρ	Share of Risky Portfolio in Domestic Assets φ	Human Capital/ Net Worth h/a	Income/ Net Worth y/a	Loading on Domestic Assets l(d)	Loading on Int'l Assets l(i)	Portfolio Shares Absent Hedging Motive (%) x(d)	x(i)	Temporary Income Shocks: Domestic and Int'l Portfolio Shares as % of Total Wealth x(d)	x(i)	Permanent Income Shocks: Domestic and Int'l Portfolio Shares as % of Total Wealth x(d)	x(i)
Benchmark cases:												
1 Young worker, age <35	0.75	0.50	60.00	2.30	0.10	0.00	38	38	37	38	28	38
2 Worker aged 35–44	0.75	0.50	15.00	0.65	0.10	0.00	38	38	37	38	28	38
3 Worker aged 55–65	0.75	0.50	1.40	0.30	0.10	0.00	38	38	36	38	32	38
4 Retired worker	0.75	0.50	0.01	0.20	0.10	0.00	38	38	36	38	37	38
5 Income <$10,000	0.75	0.50	18.00	1.00	0.10	0.00	38	38	37	38	28	38
6 Income $50K–$100K	0.75	0.50	7.15	0.60	0.10	0.00	38	38	37	38	29	38
Sensitivity analysis												
7 Young worker, age <35	0.75	0.50	60.00	2.30	**0.20**	0.00	38	38	37	38	18	38
8 Young worker; age <35	**1.00**	0.50	60.00	2.30	**0.20**	0.00	50	50	49	50	30	50
9 Young worker, age <35	**1.00**	0.50	60.00	2.30	**0.30**	0.00	50	50	49	50	20	50
10 Young worker; age <35	**1.00**	0.50	60.00	2.30	**0.40**	0.00	50	50	48	50	11	50
11 Worker aged 55–65	**0.25**	0.50	1.40	0.30	0.10	0.00	13	13	11	13	7	13
12 Worker aged 55–65	**0.25**	0.50	1.40	0.30	**0.20**	0.00	13	13	10	13	1	13
13 Worker aged 55–65	**0.25**	0.50	1.40	0.30	**0.40**	0.00	13	13	8	13	−11	13
14 Income <$10,000	**0.05**	0.50	18.00	1.00	0.10	0.00	3	3	2	3	−7	3
15 Income <$10,000	**0.05**	0.50	18.00	1.00	**0.30**	0.00	3	3	1	3	−26	3
16 Income, $50K–$100K	**1.00**	0.50	7.15	0.60	0.10	0.00	50	50	49	50	41	50
17 Income, $50K–$100K	**1.00**	0.50	7.15	0.60	**0.30**	0.00	50	50	48	50	24	50
18 Baxter-Jermann	**1.00**	0.50	2.00	0.20	1.00	0.00	50	50	43	50	−17	50

Note: Boldface indicates deviations from corresponding benchmark case.

human capital-wealth ratios. The table also shows how variation in the target-portfolio shares devoted to alternative assets and variation in the asset "loadings" $l_{d,\gamma-1}$ and $l_{i,\gamma-1}$ affect overall portfolio composition:

	Transitory Shocks	Permanent Shocks
Domestic share	$\rho\varphi - \dfrac{l_d(y/a)}{1 + (h/a)}$	$\rho\varphi - \dfrac{l_d(h/a)}{1 + (h/a)}$
International share	$\rho\varphi - \dfrac{l_i(y/a)}{1 + (h/a)}$	$\rho\varphi - \dfrac{l_i(h/a)}{1 + (h/a)}$

To study the influence of human capital, we must specify the ratio of human capital to financial wealth, the ratio of current income to financial wealth, and the factor loadings. The first entry in table 10.17 is for a young worker under age thirty-five. From table 10.7 above, we find that a typical human capital-wealth ratio for this worker would be about 60, while the income-wealth ratio is 2.3. From table 10.10 above, we find that a typical loading on domestic assets might be about $l_{d,\gamma-1} = .10$, while the loading on international assets is approximately $l_{i,\gamma-1} = 0$. We assume that this individual wishes to hold a share of risky assets $\rho = 0.75$ and a share of international risky assets $\varphi = 0.50$. Then, if there were no human capital, individuals would demand domestic and foreign risky assets in amounts each equal to $(0.75)(0.50) = 0.375$, or approximately 38 percent of their wealth—this is shown in columns 9 and 10 of table 10.17.

When we consider the hedging motive for holding risky assets, we find that there is a smaller market demand for domestic risky assets since individuals already hold a substantial amount of these through their labor income streams. When income shocks are temporary, the individual reduces his holdings of domestic assets slightly, from 38 percent of wealth to 37 percent. When income shocks are permanent, however, there is a much greater reduction in holdings of domestic assets, from 38 percent of wealth to 28 percent.

Cases 2–6 in table 10.17 present results for individuals of various ages and income levels, where the human capital/net worth and income/net worth figures are taken from table 10.7. The desired portfolio shares ρ and φ are the same as in case 1, as are the assumed loadings l_d and l_i. Despite the variation across these cases in the levels of human capital, income, and net worth, the overall effect on portfolios is quite similar for all workers except those near retirement. For workers close to or in retirement, the distinction between permanent and temporary shocks is of little importance.

The lower part of table 10.17 presents a sensitivity analysis, varying the desired portfolio shares and the loading on domestic assets in ways that seem empirically reasonable. These results show that the hedging effect that reduces holdings of domestic assets is most likely to lead to negative desired holdings of domestic assets when the desired share of risky assets in the overall portfolio, ρ, is low and when the loading on domestic assets, l_d, is high. In these cases, labor income is itself a risky asset that is highly correlated with domestic traded assets, so achieving a low-risk overall portfolio involves establishing a short position in traded domestic assets and using the proceeds to invest in risk-free bonds.

While the models studied in this section are very stark, they show how substantially the optimal allocation of financial wealth can differ from the actual nature of risky-asset positions when there is a very important nontraded asset. We expect that the force of hedging mechanisms would carry over into more realistic settings with constraints on the saving and investment behavior of households and additional idiosyncratic or aggregate sources of risk that would make it impossible to exactly hedge labor income with marketable financial assets.

Borrowing and Short-Sales Constraints

There are two types of constraints that are likely to be important for young workers: borrowing constraints and short-sales constraints. First, as stressed by Campbell et al. (chap. 11 in this volume), it may well be the case that young workers efficiently have very low levels of saving, possibly even negative saving, given their forecasts of future income growth. If it is impossible to borrow against future human capital, then individuals may maintain essentially zero financial assets for a dozen working years or more. A key implication for social security reform is that these individuals would benefit from having their "contributions" deferred until later in life.

Second, we have seen that households with low ratios of financial assets to human capital may wish to establish negative positions in domestic risky assets. Short-sales constraints would preclude them from holding negative quantities of domestic risky assets, and borrowing constraints would preclude them from investing more than their current financial wealth in international risky assets if their preferences would otherwise induce them to do so. As a result, if "forced saving" must take place through the social security system, then it would be beneficial to working participants to have a substantial share of its investment be in the form of international risky assets.

10.6 Conclusion

Plans for social security reform that incorporate public or private investment in risky assets will necessarily face the consideration of the question with which we began this chapter: Should there be investment in international risky assets?

We identified two reasons for public and private investment in international risky assets. The first is diversification benefits: by holding a portfolio that includes international risky assets, it is possible to have a less volatile portfolio return for any expected return that a public or private investor seeks to earn. The second is a risk-management benefit. If domestic labor income is more highly dependent on domestic risky-asset returns than it is on international risky-asset returns, then it is desirable for public and private investors to increase the relative importance of international investments.

We provided quantitative evidence on the potential value to risk-averse retirees of changing the certain real annuity in the social security system to an annuity whose payments would be based on international and domestic risky assets, similar to some products presently provided by the private financial system through insurance companies and purchased by sophisticated investors. These benefits depend on the extent of risk aversion, on the importance of fixed components of consumption, and on the share in retirement assets that social security payments represent. But they can be considerable, equal to a 20 percent increase in the level of retirement wealth or more, and the diversification benefit from investing in international risky assets is responsible for one-quarter of this increase.

We also showed, by example, that international risky assets could potentially play an important portfolio role during the accumulation phase of retirement saving, the prime working years. To earn high portfolio returns, it is desirable to invest in risky assets. But domestic assets have the drawback that their returns are low when labor income is low, which induces individuals to shift toward risk-free assets and international risky assets. The extent of this risk-management, or hedging, effect on portfolio composition depends on the statistical relation between human capital returns, domestic risky-asset returns, and international risky-asset returns. Our chapter accordingly provided a discussion of alternative methods of measuring human capital returns—the changes in the present value of labor incomes—and econometric evidence about the correlation between these returns and those on market financial assets. The pattern of results was consistent with there being important risk-management benefits to holding international assets since human capital returns are more highly correlated with domestic returns than with international returns.

References

Baxter, Marianne, and Urban J. Jermann. 1997. The international diversification puzzle is worse than you think. *American Economic Review* 87, no. 1 (March): 170–80.

Black, Fischer. 1987. *Business cycles and equilibrium.* New York: Basil Blackwell.

Campbell, John Y. 1996. Understanding risk and return. *Journal of Political Economy* 104, no. 2 (April): 298–345.

———. 1999. Asset prices, consumption, and the business cycle. In *Handbook of Macroeconomics,* ed. J. B. Taylor and M. Woodford. Amsterdam: Elsevier Science.

Davis, Steven, and Paul Willen. 1998. Using financial assets to hedge labor income risks: Estimating the benefits. University of Chicago, December. Typescript.

Fama, Eugene, and William Schwert. 1977. Human capital and capital market equilibrium. *Journal of Financial Economics* 4, no. 1 (January): 95–125.

Feldstein, Martin, and Andrew Samwick. 1992. Social security rules and marginal tax rates. *National Tax Journal* 45, no. 1 (March): 1–22.

———. 1997. The economics of prefunding social security and medicare benefits. In *NBER Macroeconomics Annual,* ed. B. Bernanke and J. Rotemberg. Cambridge, Mass.: MIT Press.

Friedman, Benjamin, and Mark Warshawsky. 1990. The cost of annuities: Implications for saving behavior and bequests. *Quarterly Journal of Economics* 105, no. 1 (February): 135–54.

Friend, Irwin, and Marshall E. Blume. 1975. The demand for risky assets. *American Economic Review* 65, no. 5 (December): 900–922.

Gustman, Alan, Olivia Mitchell, Andrew Samwick, and Thomas Steinmeier. 1997. Pension and social security wealth in the Health and Retirement Study. NBER Working Paper no. 5912. Cambridge, Mass.: National Bureau of Economic Research, February.

Gustman, Alan, and Thomas Steinmeier. 1998. Effects of pensions on savings: Analysis with data from the Health and Retirement Study. NBER Working Paper no. 6681. Cambridge, Mass.: National Bureau of Economic Research, August.

Hakansson, Nils H. 1970. Optimal investment and consumption strategies under risk for a class of utility functions. *Econometrica* 38, no. 5 (September): 587–607.

Kennickell, Arthur, Martha Starr-McCluer, and Annika Sunden. 1997. Family finances in the U.S.: Recent evidence from the Survey of Consumer Finances. *Federal Reserve Bulletin* (January).

Kotlikoff, Laurence J., and Jeffrey Sachs. 1998. The personal security system: A framework for reforming social security. *Federal Reserve Bank of St. Louis Review* 80, no. 2 (March–April): 11–13.

Levhari, David, and T. N. Srinvasan. 1969. Optimal savings under uncertainty. *Review of Economic Studies* 36, no. 1 (April): 153–63.

Markowitz, Harry. 1959. *Portfolio selection: Efficient diversification of investments.* New York: Wiley.

Mitchell, Olivia, James Poterba, and Mark Warshawsky. 1997. New evidence on the money's worth of individual annuities. NBER Working Paper no. 6002. Cambridge, Mass.: National Bureau of Economic Research, April.

Samuelson, P. A. 1958. An exact consumption-loan model of interest with or without the social contrivance of money. *Journal of Political Economy* 66, no. 6 (December): 467–82.

———. 1969. Lifetime portfolio selection by dynamic stochastic programming. *Review of Economics and Statistics* 51, no. 3 (August): 239–46.

Shiller, Robert J. 1993. *Macro markets: Creating institutions for managing society's largest economic risks.* Oxford: Clarendon.

Social Security Administration (SSA). Office of Research and Statistics. 1989. *Facts and figures about social security, 1988.* Washington, D.C.: U.S. Government Printing Office.

Comment   David Backus

It is a pleasure to discuss this paper, which touches on some classic issues in finance and introduces some new ones as well. I would like to discuss some of these issues on their own, then turn to specific points made in the paper.

International Diversification

Baxter and King follow a long and distinguished tradition in touting the benefits of international diversification. The theoretical argument is straightforward: adding international assets expands the investment-opportunity set, which cannot hurt. The question in practice is how large the benefits are. Since Zvi Bodie is a founding member of this group, let me quote Bodie, Kane, and Marcus (1996, 833–34) on the subject: "There is a marked reduction in risk for a portfolio that includes foreign as well as US stocks, so rational investors should invest across borders. Adding international to national investments enhances the power of portfolio diversification. Indeed, the figure indicates that the risk of an internationally diversified portfolio can be reduced to less than one half the level of a diversified US portfolio." With this kind of background, I cannot resist the temptation to argue the opposite.

Let me offer three contrarian counterarguments against the tide of sentiment in favor of international diversification, some of which are mentioned in the Bodie, Kane, and Marcus book.

Counterargument 1: The Gains Are Small. Especially for investments in the developed world (most of the available supply of marketable assets), the returns are so closely related to those in the United States that the gains from diversification are small. Consider this table adapted from Vanguard's web site:

Portfolio	Mean Return (%)	S.D. of Return (%)
100% domestic	16.6	14.2
80% domestic, 20% foreign	16.4	13.8
50% domestic, 50% foreign	16.1	14.3

(These numbers are based on annual returns between 1977 and 1997 for broad-based indexes for the United States and the developed world.) I interpret the last column as saying that the gains are small. Baxter and King's figure 10.2 is similar, in my view, in suggesting that the gains are

David Backus is professor of economics and international business at the Stern School of Business, New York University, and a research associate of the National Bureau of Economic Research.

relatively modest. (The substantially larger gains cited by Bodie, Kane, and Marcus are based on portfolios of individual stocks, for which there is some question—for me, anyway—about the precision of the estimated correlations and the structure of the portfolios.)

Counterargument 2: Returns on Foreign Assets Are Erratic. We all know that disasters happen, and they seem to happen more often in other countries. This is especially true for emerging markets, where the correlations are small (hence a greater possibility of diversification) but the likelihood of disaster is large. I think of this as reflected in higher moments of asset returns (skewness and kurtosis, say) or possibly in return distributions in which such moments do not exist (the α-stable class, e.g.). Either way, it is easy to imagine that disasters might reduce one's appetite for foreign investment. The key issue here is how extreme outcomes for returns on individual assets affect the distribution of returns on portfolios. Research on the subject is limited, but Longin and Solnik (1998) argue persuasively that international equity returns are more highly correlated in crashes than in general, suggesting that international diversification provides limited protection against them.

Counterargument 3: Institutional Frictions Are Greater Abroad. My colleague Ingo Walter told me a story some years ago that has stuck with me. Ingo is a pretty sophisticated investor, and he wanted to buy some Deutsche Bank stock. Deutsche Bank is hardly an obscure stock, but he estimates that the transaction costs totaled about 2.5 percent, an enormous amount by U.S. standards. Nor are local investors immune, either in Germany or elsewhere. In Walter (1998), he reports that average management fees in Chile's private pension system have been over 3 percent, even though most of the assets are domestic. Things may improve with time, but transaction costs are clearly higher outside the United States, even for developed countries. (Bodie, Kane, and Marcus [1996] have a nice summary of the developed world in table 26.4.)

A number of other "frictions" might be added to the list. For foreign investments, I would mention transparency, including accounting and disclosure standards (cf. Daimler's German and American financial statements); custody and ownership (custody fraud is a popular line of work in India and Russia); taxation (withholding tax on dividends paid to foreign investors in Canada and on capital gains in Malaysia); and traditional robbery of foreigners (Canada's forced purchase of PetroFina in the early 1980s). These frictions are potentially large, and the examples should make it clear that they are not limited to emerging markets.

In short, I would say that the days of complete and open global financial markets are still ahead of us. As of now, it is an open question how much international diversification one should recommend to a typical U.S. investor. That has not stopped me from making international investments, but it makes me hesitant to tell my parents to do the same.

Social Security and Capital Markets

Although they are not developed in the paper, there are several possible links between pension reform, including changes in social security programs, and the development of capital markets in general. These links are potentially more important, in a welfare sense, than the direct effect on the returns available to individuals on their retirement savings and, for that reason, are worth at least a quick mention.

The first link is between pensions and capital markets. Pension reform is invariably followed closely by changes in the structure of capital markets, typically with larger amounts of money available for investments in private equity. The United States is a striking example. Probably the biggest single factor affecting the growth of the U.S. mutual fund industry over the last fifty years has been ERISA, and much of this growth has come in equity funds. The gradual shift from defined-benefit to defined-contribution plans has created a source of funds for U.S. capital markets that issuers have been quick to tap. In the Netherlands and Chile, partial privatization of pensions led to rapid growth in the pool of marketable assets. Both countries experienced substantial increases in the ratio of market capitalization to GDP. We might expect similar developments in other countries as they change their social security systems in response to the fiscal problems facing them in the next century.

A second link is through saving. Chile remains something of a mystery, but it is clear that the privatization of social security was followed by a dramatic increase in the savings rate. One possibility is that greater efficiency in the financial system reduced the wedge between returns paid by borrowers and those received by investors.

A third link is political. I think that it is plausible that more widespread ownership of firms will change the political calculus, leading voters to demand rules with greater transparency and responsiveness to creditors. I still wonder how much of the U.S. financial system is dictated by efficiency and how much by the unusual preferences and traditions of Americans, but it is tempting to speculate that world markets will look more like those of the United States in a decade.

I think that all this matters, primarily because of the connection between capital market development with aggregate economic performance. This view is not held by everyone, but I find the work of King and Levine (1993) and Sylla (1999) (among many others) persuasive on the subject.

Baxter and King

Baxter and King extend our understanding of pensions and international diversification in several directions. One contribution is their analysis of returns on retirement assets. In stark contrast to what one might find on Vanguard's web site or in a finance textbook, they show that over 40 percent of a typical person's assets consist of claims on the social security system. Since the returns on these claims are correlated with those on domestic assets, the benefits of international diversification in the rest of the portfolio are correspondingly larger. Another contribution is their analysis of human capital. Here, too, they show that the presence of an additional asset has substantial quantitative implications for investments in other assets. Since returns on human capital are correlated with those on equity (both are sensitive to the business cycle), international diversification is useful in hedging them. In short, the presence of social security and human capital has a substantial effect on the optimal choice of financial investments, including investments abroad.

Personally, I think that a system in which individuals invest more of their retirement assets is probably a good thing: good for them and good for the economy as a whole. Done in moderation, international diversification doubtless is a good thing, too. This paper is an ambitious attempt to quantify both and should raise the level of discussion for years to come.

References

Bodie, Zvi, Alex Kane, and Alan Marcus. 1996. *Investments.* 3d ed. Chicago: Irwin.

King, Robert, and Ross Levine. 1993. Finance, entrepreneurship, and growth: Theory and evidence. *Journal of Monetary Economics* 32:513–42.

Longin, Francois, and Bruno Solnik. 1998. Correlation structure of international equity markets during extremely volatile periods. ESSEC and HEC. Typescript.

Sylla, Richard. 1999. Emerging markets in history: The United States, Japan, and Argentina. In *Global competition and integration,* ed. R. Sato, R. Ramachandran, and K. Mino. Boston: Kluwer.

Walter, Ingo. 1998. The global asset management industry: Competitive structure and performance. Stern School of Business, New York University. Typescript.

Discussion Summary

James Poterba followed up on a remark by the discussant, David Backus, about the importance of transaction costs. He suggested implementing this empirically by looking, for instance, at the transaction costs charged by Vanguard for their international equity index fund and incorporating these into the construction of the mean-variance frontier. He also commented on the interplay between issues studied in the paper and annuitization. He referred to his work with Jeffrey Brown and Olivia Mitchell (chap. 9 in this volume), which finds that variable or equity-linked annuities are very attractive given the historical equity premium. Of course, one might question how relevant the (very generous) historical equity premium is for studying possible strategies to modify social security in the future.

Zvi Bodie noted that the NBER held its first conference on the financial aspects of the U.S. pension system in 1981. He urged everyone to read a paper presented at that occasion by Robert Merton (see Merton 1985) as it provides insights into some fundamental issues that are particularly relevant for this paper. In particular, Merton shows how social security allows agents to transfer human capital from the beginning of life to later on, when agents have insufficient human capital. Social security can thus be viewed as a way of completing markets, given that human capital is a nontradable asset. Related to this, Bodie remarked that the paper by Baxter and King identifies risk with the standard deviation of the dollar return. He argued that this technical definition has no normative content. What economists would prefer as a numeraire for measuring risk is the variability of lifetime consumption. In terms of this more appropriate definition of risk, social security may very well be a powerful way of reducing risk.

John Shoven commented on the stylized introduction to social security in the paper. The authors mention a 15.3 percent tax for social security, not noticing, however, that Medicare, disability, and other programs receive a substantial fraction out of this. Correcting for this, the tax rate for social security itself is in the neighborhood of 10 percent. Furthermore, he commented on table 10.5, which reports a 2.4 percent mean return on social security and a 2.16 percent standard deviation. He noted that these numbers are based entirely on mean real wage growth and as such do not recognize that benefits are paid out as annuities. This ignores any effects on both the mean and the standard deviation of possible longevity improvements of changes in the retirement age or in the taxation of benefits.

Henning Bohn made two comments. First, he too criticized the computation of the return on social security. He argued that the current system clearly includes a tax on past liabilities. A measure of the return on social security therefore must consider what people get from a lifetime perspective. Moreover, the authors should distinguish between the marginal and the average return, as these would not be expected to coincide. The reason is that the current social security tax can be thought of as being partly a tax and partly forced savings. Therefore, if one considers changing marginally our investment in it, then presumably the tax is given or sunk, while on the margin one would obtain a return that may be quite different from the average return.

Second, Bohn wondered why Baxter and King focus on annual data and classify long-term government bonds as risky securities. For someone interested in achieving a constant consumption stream, a thirty-year indexed bond is probably a very safe asset. Similarly, most of the volatility in human capital is due to variations in the rate of return at which the income stream from wages is being discounted. This might be misleading from the perspective of someone seeking to obtain a constant consumption stream: both the present value of financing a given consumption stream and the price of a long-term bond (or the value of human capital) will change in response to fluctuations in the real interest rate. This individual is therefore not affected by interest-rate risk as the effects simply cancel out.

Stephen Zeldes remarked that figure 10.3 mixes two effects: the gain from international diversification and another gain that really derives from ignoring the unfunded liability inherent in the current social security system. The latter should not be included.

Antonio Rangel concurred and added that the policy experiment takes a dollar from the social security contributions and invests it. But, when doing so, one should acknowledge the tax increase necessary for the unfunded liabilities.

Stephen Ross noted that the moments of the returns on international investments are measured very imprecisely. Estimation risk should therefore be acknowledged in this context. Second, he remarked that the presentation of the theory of diversification could be misleading. An investor does not stand to gain when his investment-opportunity set is expanded by adding an asset with a zero alpha and an orthogonal error term with respect to the other assets. Ross argued that foreign assets are likely to satisfy these conditions. Therefore, international diversification is attractive only to the extent that it yields hedging benefits. Finally, he noted that, to put everything in the right perspective, one should realize that the market capitalization of General Electric is larger than the market capitalization of all emerging markets. Emerging markets are therefore negligible in size.

Martin Feldstein asked the authors to clarify the source of what the paper presents as the riskiness of social security. He also raised the point that the paper studies the gains of international diversification in the context of a fully developed social security system and suggested examining the potential gains during the accumulation phase as well. Finally, with respect to Poterba's remark about transaction costs, Feldstein referred to an interesting paper by Geert Bekaert and Michael Urias (1996) studying emerging markets that indicates that the efficiency gain of investing in such stocks is outweighed if the investment must be done through a country closed-end fund.

Richard Zeckhauser argued that, while emerging markets are likely to be of little importance for the American population, the reverse is definitely not true. Many emerging markets are subject to severe restrictions and regulations. Allowing investors in these countries to invest abroad, and especially in well-developed capital markets, would lead to substantial welfare gains. Second, he noted that Medicare is an important part of transfers to the elderly. To the extent that the elderly face risks associated with increases in the cost of medical services, one might want to consider investing in pharmaceutical companies in an effort to hedge these risks.

David Wilcox remarked that the interpretation of the equity-premium puzzle and the plausibility of the assumed degree of risk aversion (σ) are crucial for the paper. In order to generate the portfolio behavior observed in the data (e.g., the Survey of Consumer Finances), one must assume absurd values for the coefficient of risk aversion. If Baxter and King were to use such parameter values in their analysis, the gains from diversification would likely be significantly smaller. Wilcox also pointed out that aggregate wage indexation is useful as a mechanism to make the elderly share in aggregate productivity risk and thereby reduces the risk-sharing burden on the rest of society.

In response to these comments, *Robert King* first clarified the methodology used to obtain the rate of return on social security. He explained how social security can be viewed in a simplified way as a wage-indexed variable annuity. King acknowledged that this simplification misses some subtleties (e.g., concerning the benefit function) but did not expect these significantly to affect the results in terms of the variability of the return as the implicit holding-period return on AIME (average indexed monthly earnings) was being calculated correctly. He added that the final version of the paper would include a section refining this measure of the risk and return on social security and discussing some of the subtleties involved.

King further stated that he agreed with Bodie's comment on the importance of risky human capital. He noted in addition that the paper uses the concept of risk in a number of different ways. The final section of the paper conducts the welfare analysis along the lines suggested by Bodie, that is, using the "normative" measure of risk.

Finally, he expressed the opinion that Ross raised an intriguing point about the uncertainty in mean returns on domestic and especially international portfolios. King proposed putting confidence intervals around the results obtained in the welfare analysis in order to take this into account.

Marianne Baxter responded to the comments of Zeldes and Rangel by noting that the analysis implicitly assumes the existence of a lump-sum tax in order to bear the unfunded liability. With respect to Wilcox's concern about a realistic value for the coefficient of relative risk aversion (σ) in the light of the equity-premium puzzle, she noted that the data of TIAA-CREF can be rationalized using moderate parameter values, that is, σ smaller than 20. *Wilcox* responded that many people consider 2 or 3 to be a reasonable value for σ. *Baxter* concluded that such values are virtually impossible to reconcile with the observation that half the population holds no securities at all.

References

Bekaert, Geert, and Michael S. Urias. 1996. Diversification, integration, and emerging market closed-end funds. *Journal of Finance* 51 (July): 835–69.

Merton, Robert C. 1985. Insurance aspects of pensions: Comment. In *Pensions, labor, and individual choice,* ed. David A. Wise. Chicago: University of Chicago Press.

11

Investing Retirement Wealth
A Life-Cycle Model

John Y. Campbell, João F. Cocco, Francisco J. Gomes,
and Pascal J. Maenhout

During the past few decades, American households have begun to display increasing financial sophistication and awareness of rates of return on alternative investments. At the same time, the implicit rate of return on contributions to the social security system has declined as the system has matured, and this rate of return is projected to decline further in the twenty-first century in response to unfavorable demographic trends (Geanakoplos, Mitchell, and Zeldes 1999). Not surprisingly, politicians and the public have become interested in the possibility of moving to a privatized system in which retirement contributions earn market-based rates of return.

Unfortunately, it is not straightforward to compare alternative retirement systems. Three important issues affect the comparison and invalidate simple rate-of-return calculations. First, the return on the current system is low in part because of the overhang of unfunded liabilities. Past generations have received a gift that must be paid off before the economy can enjoy the steady-state benefits of any new system. Second, capital income taxation puts a wedge between pretax and after-tax rates of return. Welfare calculations should take account of the tax revenue generated by capi-

John Y. Campbell is the Otto Eckstein Professor of Applied Economics at Harvard University and a research associate of the National Bureau of Economic Research. João F. Cocco is assistant professor of finance at London Business School. Francisco J. Gomes and Pascal J. Maenhout are graduate students in economics at Harvard University.

Campbell gratefully acknowledges the financial support of the National Science Foundation, Cocco of the Banco de Portugal, Cocco and Gomes of Fundacão para a Ciencia e Tecnologia, Portugal, and Maenhout of the Fund for Scientific Research Flanders. The authors are grateful for the helpful comments of David Cutler, David Weil, Amir Yaron, and other conference participants.

tal accumulation (in some systems, this tax revenue is forgiven, and private retirement accounts earn higher pretax rates of return). Third, returns on alternative financial assets can differ if these assets have different risk characteristics. A valid comparison of rates of return must adjust for risk.

This paper focuses on the last issue, the evaluation of alternative investments with different risk characteristics. From the point of view of households, the current social security system represents a defined-benefit pension plan in which income realizations through life are tied to annuity payments in retirement. This is similar to a system in which households are forced to accumulate a riskless asset in a retirement-savings account.

Some commentators have recently argued that households would be better off if their retirement savings were invested in risky assets such as equities that have a higher average return. This could be achieved within the present system if the social security trust funds were invested in equities; alternatively, within a privatized system, household retirement accounts could include equity investments.

If a household can borrow to invest in equities, however, then the accumulation of riskless assets within a social security account need not restrict the household's overall portfolio. The household can undo riskless social security accumulation by borrowing outside the retirement account; the household's overall portfolio can be made just as risky as if the retirement account itself were invested in equities. Thus, any claimed benefits for a change in the social security system must depend on the presence of portfolio constraints that prevent this sort of asset transformation.

Two different sorts of constraints are potentially relevant. First, a household may be unable to borrow at the riskless interest rate to finance equity investments (Constantinides, Donaldson, and Mehra 1998). Second, a household may face fixed costs of equity market participation; if these fixed costs exceed the benefit of participation, the household may hold no equities (Abel 1998). These constraints may affect different households differently. The first constraint is particularly likely to bind on a household whose unconstrained optimal equity position is particularly large, while the second constraint is particularly likely to bind on a poor household with little total wealth. These different sorts of households may be differentially affected by a social security reform that alters portfolio constraints.

Clear understanding of these issues requires a well-developed normative theory of optimal portfolio choice over the life cycle. Until very recently, however, theoretical work on this subject lagged far behind the familiar theory of single-period optimal portfolio choice. Samuelson (1969) and Merton (1969, 1971) showed that there are conditions under which long-lived investors choose the same portfolios as single-period investors so that the investment horizon is irrelevant; unfortunately, these conditions are highly restrictive in that they include power utility, returns on safe and risky investments that are independently and identically distributed (i.i.d.) over time, and, most disturbing of all, the absence of labor income.

In the last few years, economists have returned to this topic and have begun to explore long-run portfolio choice when these restrictions are relaxed. Ross (1999) shows how horizon effects can emerge from more general models of preferences. Brennan and Xia (1998), Campbell and Viceira (in press), and Wachter (1998b) consider changes over time in the riskless real interest rate, while Balduzzi and Lynch (1999), Barberis (2000), Brandt (1999), Campbell and Viceira (1999), Kim and Omberg (1996), Samuelson (1991), and Wachter (1998a) consider changes over time in the equity premium, and Brennan, Schwartz, and Lagnado (1997) and Liu (1998) allow a more complex pattern of variation in both the real interest rate and the equity premium. The effect of labor income on portfolio choice has been explored by Bertaut and Haliassos (1997), Bodie, Merton, and Samuelson (1991), Cocco, Gomes, and Maenhout (CGM) (1998), Gakidis (1997), Heaton and Lucas (1997), Storesletten, Telmer, and Yaron (1998), and Viceira (in press), among others.

In this paper, we concentrate on the effect of labor income. The theoretical literature on this subject can be loosely summarized as follows. A household with labor income has an implicit holding of a nontradable asset, human capital, that represents a claim to the stream of future labor income. This nontradable asset can "crowd out" explicit asset holdings. If labor income is literally riskless, then riskless asset holdings are strongly crowded out, and the household will tilt its portfolio strongly toward risky assets (Bodie, Merton, and Samuelson 1991). If the household is constrained from borrowing to finance risky investments, the solution may be a corner at which the portfolio is 100 percent risky assets. If labor income is risky but uncorrelated with risky financial assets, then riskless asset holdings are still crowded out, but less strongly; the portfolio tilt toward risky assets is reduced (Viceira, in press). If labor income is positively correlated with risky financial assets, then risky assets can actually be crowded out, tilting the portfolio toward safe financial assets.

Under the assumption that income shocks are uncorrelated or only weakly correlated with stock returns, these results suggest that households that expect high future labor income—discounted at some appropriate rate and measured relative to financial wealth—should have the strongest desire to hold stocks. In a life-cycle model with a realistic age profile of income, the discounted value of expected future income increases relative to financial wealth in the very early part of adulthood but peaks fairly early and then declines as workers approach retirement. This suggests that fairly young (but not the very youngest) households are the most likely to be affected by borrowing constraints that limit their equity positions. While empirical evidence on household portfolio allocation is fragmentary, a few recent empirical papers have found that, over the life cycle, household portfolios have hump-shaped equity positions and U-shaped positions in safe assets, consistent with the message of the theoretical literature (Bertaut and Haliassos 1997; Heaton and Lucas 2000; Poterba and Samwick 1997).

A complicating factor is that many households, particularly younger and poorer ones, appear to hold no equities at all. This is inconsistent with simple frictionless models of optimal portfolio choice but may be explained if there is a fixed cost of participating in equity markets. Such a fixed cost would deter young households from buying equities, but, later in the life cycle, these households might find it worthwhile to begin participating if their wealth levels are high enough to justify paying the cost.

In this paper, we explore the quantitative importance of these effects by solving a calibrated life-cycle model of consumption and portfolio choice with labor income uncertainty. The model is set in partial equilibrium and takes as given the stochastic properties of income and asset returns. We closely follow CGM (1998) but augment their model to allow us to explore alternative retirement-savings systems and fixed costs of equity market participation.

We also ask whether heterogeneity across households is likely to have a large effect on optimal investment patterns. This issue is important for the debate over social security privatization. A privatized system can allow greater individual choice over the investment of retirement wealth, but opponents argue that some individuals may fail to invest optimally and that privatization may increase administrative costs. Whatever the merits of these arguments, it is important to understand the potential gains from individual choice in the absence of administrative costs and optimization failures. To explore this issue, we compare the labor income risk of individuals working in different sectors of the economy and study the sensitivity of optimal choices to differences in the rate of time preference and the coefficient of relative risk aversion.

The organization of the paper is as follows. Section 11.1 lays out our life-cycle model and calibrates the parameters. Section 11.2 presents benchmark results in graphic form. Section 11.3 explores heterogeneity across households. Section 11.4 conducts a welfare analysis, and section 11.5 concludes.

11.1 A Life-Cycle Model of Portfolio Choice

11.1.1 Model Specification

Time Parameters and Preferences

We let t denote adult age. The investor is adult for a maximum of T periods, of which he works the first K. For simplicity, K is assumed to be exogenous and deterministic. We allow for uncertain life span in the manner of Hubbard, Skinner, and Zeldes (1994). Let p_t denote the probability that the investor is alive at date $t + 1$, conditional on being alive at date t. Then investor i's preferences are described by the time-separable power utility function

$$(1) \qquad E_1 \sum_{t=1}^{T} \delta^{t-1} \left(\prod_{j=0}^{t-1} p_j \right) \frac{C_{it}^{1-\gamma}}{1 - \gamma},$$

where C_{it} is the level of date t consumption, $\gamma > 0$ is the coefficient of relative risk aversion, and $\delta < 1$ is the discount factor. We assume that the individual derives no utility from leaving a bequest.

The Labor Income Process

Investor i's age t labor income, Y_{it}, is exogenously given by

$$(2) \qquad \log(Y_{it}) = f(t, Z_{it}) + v_{it} + \varepsilon_{it} \quad \text{for } t \le K,$$

where $f(t, Z_{it})$ is a deterministic function of age and other individual characteristics Z_{it}, ε_{it} is an idiosyncratic temporary shock distributed as $N(0, \sigma_\varepsilon^2)$, and v_{it} is given by

$$(3) \qquad v_{it} = v_{i,t-1} + u_{it},$$

where u_{it} is distributed as $N(0, \sigma_u^2)$ and is uncorrelated with ε_{it}. Thus, log income is the sum of a deterministic component that can be calibrated to capture the hump shape of earnings over the life cycle and two random components, one permanent and one transitory. We assume that the temporary shock ε_{it} is uncorrelated across households, but we decompose the permanent shock u_{it} into an aggregate component ξ_t and an idiosyncratic component ω_{it}, uncorrelated across households:

$$(4) \qquad u_{it} = \xi_t + \omega_{it}.$$

This decomposition implies that the random component of aggregate labor income follows a random walk, an assumption made by Fama and Schwert (1977) and Jagannathan and Wang (1996). While macroeconomists such as Campbell (1996), Campbell and Mankiw (1989), and Pischke (1995) have found empirical evidence for short-term persistence in aggregate quarterly labor income growth, the simplification to a random walk should have little effect on optimal consumption and portfolio choice over the life cycle.

Financial Assets

We assume that there are two assets in which the agent can invest: a riskless asset with gross real return $\bar{R}_f$, which we call *Treasury bills,* and a risky asset with gross real return R_t, which we call *stocks*. The excess return on the risky asset, $R_{t+1} - \overline{R}_f$, is given by

$$(5) \qquad\qquad R_{t+1} - \overline{R}_f = \mu + \eta_{t+1},$$

where η_{t+1}, the period $t + 1$ innovation to excess returns, is assumed to be i.i.d. over time and distributed as $N(0, \sigma_\eta^2)$. We allow innovations to excess returns to be correlated with innovations to the aggregate component of permanent labor income, and we write the correlation coefficient as $\rho_{\xi\eta}$. We also allow for fixed costs of equity market participation: to have access to the stock market, the investor must pay a one-time monetary fixed cost equal to F.

Retirement and Liquid Wealth

We model a system of mandatory saving for retirement in the following simple way. During working life, the individual must save a fraction, θ, of current labor income as retirement wealth. Under this assumption, disposable labor income, Y_{it}^d, is given by

$$(6) \qquad\qquad Y_{it}^d = (1 - \theta)Y_{it} \quad \text{for } t \le K.$$

The amount θY_{it} is added to retirement wealth, denoted by W_{it}^R. During working life, retirement wealth is illiquid; the individual cannot consume it or borrow against it. At age K, retirement wealth is rolled into a riskless annuity so that the individual receives in each of the retirement years the annuity value corresponding to W_{iK}^R. This assumption of riskless annuitization affects the portfolio choices of older investors. An interesting extension of our work would be to allow investors to choose between riskless and variable annuities.

We consider several alternative systems governing the investment of retirement wealth during working life. In the first system, the individual is forced to hold retirement wealth in riskless assets. This implies that $W_{it}^R = B_{it}^R$, where B_{it}^R is the dollar amount of retirement wealth that investor i has in riskless assets. In alternative systems, retirement wealth is partially or fully invested in risky assets, but the allocation remains constant over time and is not controlled by the investor. We interpret this as the Social Security Administration managing the individual's retirement account. For this reason, the fixed cost of investing in stocks applies only to investments outside the retirement account.

Investors also have liquid wealth outside their retirement accounts. We denote liquid wealth of investor i at date t by W_{it}^L and liquid holdings of bills and stocks by B_{it}^L and S_{it}^L, respectively. We assume that the investor faces the following borrowing and short-sales constraints:

$$(7) \qquad\qquad B_{it}^L \ge 0,$$

(8) $$S_{it}^L \geq 0.$$

The borrowing constraint (7) ensures that the investor's allocation to bills in both the liquid and the retirement accounts is nonnegative at all dates. It prevents the investor from borrowing against future labor income or retirement wealth. The short-sales constraint (8) ensures that the investor's allocation to equities is nonnegative at all dates.

The Household's Optimization Problem

In each period of a household's working life ($t \leq K$), the timing of events is as follows. The investor starts the period with liquid wealth W_{it}^L and retirement wealth W_{it}^R. Then labor income Y_{it} is realized. Following Deaton (1991), we denote *cash on hand* in period t by

(9) $$X_{it} = W_{it}^L + (1 - \theta)Y_{it}.$$

The investor must decide how much to consume, C_{it}, whether to pay the fixed cost of entering the stock market (if he has not done so before), and how to allocate the remaining cash on hand between stocks and bills. We denote the proportion of liquid wealth invested in stocks by α_{it}^L. The proportion of retirement wealth invested in stocks, α_{it}^R, is given exogenously by the retirement system and does not vary over time, so $\alpha_{it}^R = \alpha_i^R$ for all t. We consider different values for α_i^R.

Next-period liquid wealth and retirement wealth are then given by

(10) $$W_{i,t+1}^L = R_{p,i,t+1}^L[W_{it}^L + (1 - \theta)Y_{it} - C_{it} - (f_{it} - f_{i,t-1})F],$$

(11) $$W_{i,t+1}^R = R_{p,i,t+1}^R[W_{it}^R + \theta_t Y_{it}],$$

where f_{it} is a binary variable that equals zero until the investor pays the fixed cost of entering the stock market and equals one thereafter, and $R_{p,i,t+1}^j$ is the return on the portfolio held from period t to period $t + 1$:

(12) $$R_{p,i,t+1}^j \equiv \alpha_{it}^j R_{t+1} + (1 - \alpha_{it}^j)\overline{R}_f, \quad j = L,R.$$

Here, α_{it}^L is freely chosen when $f_{it} = 1$ and equals zero when $f_{it} = 0$.

After retirement ($t > K$), the problem takes the same form except that retirement wealth no longer accumulates. Instead, it is annuitized and provides riskless income $A(W_{iK}^R)$. After-tax labor income $(1 - \theta)Y_{it}$ in (9) and (10) is replaced by $A(W_{iK}^R)$.

The problem that the investor faces is to maximize (1) subject to the working-life and retirement versions of (2)–(12) plus the constraints that consumption must be nonnegative at all dates. The control variables of the problem are $\{C_t, \alpha_{it}^L, f_{it}\}_{t=1}^T$. The state variables are $\{t, X_{it}, W_{it}^R, v_{it}, f_{i,t-1}\}_{t=1}^T$. The problem is to solve for the policy rules as a function of the state variables, that is, $C_{it}(X_{it}, W_{it}^R, v_{it}, f_{i,t-1})$, $\alpha_{it}^L(X_{it}, W_{it}^R, v_{it}, f_{i,t-1})$, and $f_{it}(X_{it}, W_{it}^R, v_{it}, f_{i,t-1})$.

Numerical Solution

This problem cannot be solved analytically. We derive the policy functions numerically by discretizing the state space and the variables over which the choices are made and by using Gaussian quadrature to approximate the distributions of the innovations to the labor income process and risky asset returns (Tauchen and Hussey 1991). The problem is then solved by using backward induction. In period T, the investor consumes all his wealth, and the value function coincides with the instantaneous utility. In every period t prior to T, and for each admissible combination of the state variables, we compute the value associated with each level of consumption, decision to pay the fixed cost of entering the stock market, and share of liquid wealth invested in stocks. This value is equal to current utility plus the expected discounted continuation value. To compute this continuation value for points that do not lie on the grid, we use cubic spline interpolation. The combinations of the choice variables ruled out by the constraints of the problem are given a very large (negative) utility such that they are never optimal. We optimize over the different choices using grid search.

When the fixed cost of equity market participation F is equal to zero, we simplify the solution by exploiting the scale independence of the maximization problem and rewriting all variables as ratios to the permanent component of labor income.

11.1.2   Calibration

Time Parameters and Preferences

Adult age starts at age twenty for households without a college degree and at age twenty-two for households with a college degree. The age of retirement is set to sixty-five for all households. The investor dies with probability one at age one hundred. Prior to this age, we use the mortality tables of the National Center for Health Statistics to parameterize the conditional survival probabilities, p_j for $j = 1, \ldots, T$. We set the discount factor δ to 0.96 and the coefficient of relative risk aversion γ to 5. In variations of the benchmark case, we also consider investors who are extremely impatient with $\delta = 0.80$, comparatively risk tolerant with $\gamma = 2$, and extremely risk averse with $\gamma = 10$.

The Labor Income Process

To estimate the labor income process, we follow CGM (1998). Here, we briefly describe the data and estimation method.

We use the family questionnaire of the Panel Study on Income Dynamics (PSID) to estimate equations (2) and (3), which give labor income as a function of age and other characteristics. Families that are part of the

Survey of Economic Opportunities subsample are dropped to obtain a random sample. Only households with a male head are used as the age profile of income may differ across male- and female-headed households and relatively few observations are available for female-headed households. Retirees, nonrespondents, students, homemakers, and household heads younger than twenty (twenty-two for college-educated households) or older than sixty-five are also eliminated from the sample.

Like CGM (1998) and Storesletten, Telmer, and Yaron (1998, 1999), we take a broad definition of labor income so as implicitly to allow for insurance mechanisms—other than asset accumulation—that households use to protect themselves against pure labor income risk. Such insurance mechanisms include welfare programs that effectively set a lower bound on the support of nonasset income, endogenous variation in the labor supply of both male and female household members, financial help from relatives and friends, and so on. Thus, we define *labor income* as total reported labor income plus unemployment compensation, workers' compensation, social security, supplemental social security, other welfare, child support, and total transfers (mainly help from relatives), all this for both head of household and, if present, his spouse. Observations that still report zero for this broad income category are dropped. Labor income defined this way is deflated using the consumer price index, with 1992 as the base year. The sample starts in 1970, so a household appears at most twenty-four times in the sample. Households with fewer observations are retained in the panel.

The estimation controls for family-specific fixed effects. To control for education, the sample is split into three groups: households without high school education, a second group with high school education but without a college degree, and, finally, college graduates. This sample split is intended to accommodate the well-established finding that age profiles differ in shape across education groups (Attanasio 1995; Hubbard, Skinner, and Zeldes 1994). For each education group, the function $f(t, Z_{it})$ is assumed to be additively separable in t and Z_{it}. The vector Z_{it} of personal characteristics, other than age and the fixed household effect, includes marital status and household composition. Household composition equals the additional number of family members in the household besides the head and, if present, his spouse.

Ideally, one should also control for occupation. Using PSID data, this is problematic because, from the 1975 wave onward, the majority of the unemployed report no occupation and are categorized together with people who are not in the labor force. But modeling unemployment as a switch in occupation is inappropriate as the possibility of unemployment through layoff is one of the main sources of labor income risk. We explore this in greater detail in section 11.3 below.

To obtain age profiles suitable for the simulation model of life-cycle

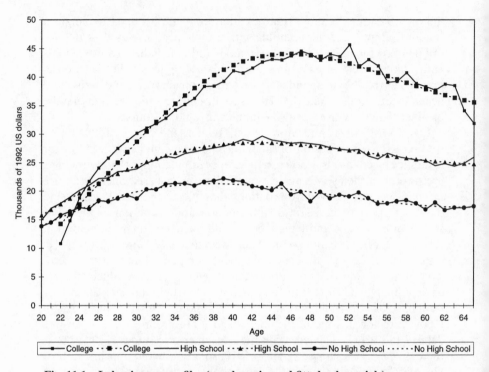

Fig. 11.1   Labor income profiles (age dummies and fitted polynomials)
Note: The solid line gives the underlying age dummies, the dotted line a third-order polynomial fitted to these age dummies.

portfolio choice, we fit a third-order polynomial to the age dummies estimated from the PSID. The resulting income profiles are similar to those used in Attanasio (1995), Carroll and Summers (1991), and Gourinchas and Parker (1996). They are plotted in figure 11.1, along with the underlying age dummies for each of the three education groups.

To estimate the variances of permanent and temporary shocks to labor income, we follow Carroll and Samwick (1997). Defining Y_{it}^* as

(13) $$\log(Y_{it}^*) \equiv \log(Y_{it}) - \hat{f}(t, Z_{it}),$$

then

(14) $$\text{var}\,[\log(Y_{i,t+d}^*) - \log(Y_{it}^*)] = d\sigma_u^2 + 2\sigma_\varepsilon^2.$$

We estimate σ_u^2 and σ_ε^2 by running an OLS regression of $\text{var}[\log(Y_{i,t+d}^*) - \log(Y_{it}^*)]$ on d and a constant term. We find that groups with less education tend to have more variable transitory income shocks but less variable permanent shocks than groups with more education. Table 11.1 reports these variances.

Table 11.1   **Baseline Parameters**

Description	Parameter Value
Retirement age (K)	65
Discount factor (δ)	.96
Risk aversion (γ)	5
Variance of transitory shocks (σ_ε^2):	
No high school	.1056
High school	.0738
College	.0584
Variance of permanent shocks (σ_u^2):	
No high school	.0105
High school	.0106
College	.0169
Sensitivity to stock returns (β):	
No high school	.0956
High school	.0627
College	.0733
Correlation with stock returns ($\rho_{\xi\eta}$):	
No high school	.3280
High school	.3709
College	.5155
Riskless rate ($\overline{R}_F - 1$)	.02
Mean excess return on stocks (μ)	.04
Standard stock return (σ_η)	.157
Fixed cost (F)	0 or 10,000
Social security tax rate (θ)	.10

We use a similar procedure to estimate the correlation between labor income shocks and stock returns, $\rho_{\xi\eta}$. The change in $\log(Y_{it}^*)$ can be written as

$$(15) \qquad \Delta \log(Y_{it}^*) = \xi_t + \omega_{it} + \varepsilon_{it} - \varepsilon_{i,t-1}.$$

Averaging across individuals gives

$$(16) \qquad \overline{\Delta\log(Y_{it}^*)} = \xi_t.$$

The correlation coefficient is then easily computed from the OLS regression of $\overline{\Delta\log(Y_{it}^*)}$ on demeaned excess returns:

$$(17) \qquad \overline{\Delta \log(Y_{it}^*)} = \beta(R_{t+1} - \overline{R}_f - \mu) + \psi_t.$$

As an empirical measure for the excess return on our stylized risky asset, we use CRSP (Center for Research in Securities Prices) data on the New York Stock Exchange value-weighted stock return relative to the Treasury-bill rate. For all education groups, the regression coefficients are strikingly low and insignificant. To allow for potential lags in the realization of labor income, we repeat the exercise with the excess stock return lagged one year. The relation becomes much stronger: the regression coefficient now varies from 0.06 to 0.10 and the correlation coefficient from 0.32 to 0.52, as reported in table 11.1. Interestingly, the correlation of labor income with the stock market is larger and more significant for households with higher education.[1]

In our portfolio-choice model, allowing for lags in the relation between innovations in stock returns and permanent shocks to labor income unfortunately requires an additional state variable. We therefore assume that the correlation is contemporaneous. The model requires the variances of both ξ_t, the aggregate permanent labor income shock that is correlated with stock market risk, and ω_{it}, the idiosyncratic permanent shock to labor income. The first variance is obtained immediately as the variance of $\overline{\Delta\log(Y_{it}^*)}$. Subtracting this variance from the total variance of u_{it} gives then the variance of ω_{it}.

Other Parameters

The riskless real interest rate is assumed to be constant at 2 percent. We set the equity premium μ equal to 4 percent. This is well below the long-run historical average but represents a reasonable compromise between that average and lower forward-looking estimates based on the observation that stock prices have tended to increase in recent years relative to corporate earnings (Blanchard 1993; Campbell and Shiller 1998). We set the standard deviation of innovations to the risky asset σ_η to 0.157. Recall that the classic formula for the risky-asset portfolio share, under power utility with i.i.d. returns and no labor income, is $\mu/\gamma\sigma_\eta^2$. With these parameters, the implied risky asset share would be about one-third at the benchmark risk aversion of 5; we find higher optimal shares in our model only because of the presence of labor income. We set the fixed cost of equity market participation to zero in the benchmark case, but we go on to consider a $10,000 fixed cost.

The proportion of labor income θ that is added to retirement wealth is equal to 10 percent of current labor income when retirement wealth accumulates at the riskless rate. This value implies an average replacement ratio at age sixty-five of 60 percent. When retirement wealth is also invested in stocks, we either fix θ at the same 10 percent value or adjust it so as to maintain the replacement ratio at 60 percent. We will show that the value of θ has a very important effect on our results. Table 11.1 summarizes the parameters used in the baseline case.

---

1. We also examined the relation of labor income shocks with lagged returns on long-term government bonds. These results are reported in sec. 11.3 below.

11.2   Benchmark Results: A Graphic Summary

The first comparison that we consider is between a system with riskless retirement accumulation ($\alpha^R = 0$) and one in which at each age half of retirement wealth is invested in stocks ($\alpha^R = .5$). In the latter system, we reduce the social security tax rate from 10 to 6 percent so that, on average, the replacement ratio is the same in both systems and equal to 0.6. At retirement, the account is annuitized at the riskless interest rate so that, on average, and given survival probabilities, the system has zero balance.

To study the behavior of the variables in the model, we calculate cross-sectional averages across ten thousand households receiving different draws of income and asset returns and plot them against age. Figure 11.2 plots labor income net of social security contributions, consumption, liquid wealth, and retirement wealth for households with a high school degree (the life-cycle patterns for other education groups are similar). Figure 11.2*A* illustrates the system in which retirement wealth is fully invested in the riskless asset, and figure 11.2*B* illustrates the system in which retirement wealth is partially invested in stocks.

In both systems, the average consumer is borrowing constrained early in life. Consumption tracks net income very closely, and little savings accumulate outside the retirement account until after age forty. These limited savings early in life are driven by the precautionary savings motive; thus, like Gourinchas and Parker (1996), we find that younger consumers are buffer-stock savers rather than life-cycle savers in the classic sense. Consumption rises with income early in life because of borrowing constraints and falls later as increased mortality drives up the effective rate of time preference; thus, consumption profiles are hump shaped over life, as found in the literature on life-cycle consumption behavior.[2]

Investment of some retirement wealth in stocks has an income effect. Because the average return on stocks is higher than the average return on bills, and because younger consumers have neither the desire nor the liquid wealth to offset a shift of retirement wealth into stocks, the shift increases average lifetime resources. Since we reduce the social security tax rate to keep the average replacement ratio constant across systems, the investment of retirement wealth in stocks frees up resources in the working years. These additional resources are consumed early in life since, at this stage, households are borrowing constrained.

Of course, the investment of retirement wealth in stocks has a cost: it imposes additional risk on households. In midlife, households react by increasing their precautionary saving, accumulating more liquid wealth, and consuming less relative to income. After retirement, the additional

---

2. We could generate a more pronounced hump shape in consumption if we added age-specific preference shocks to the model.

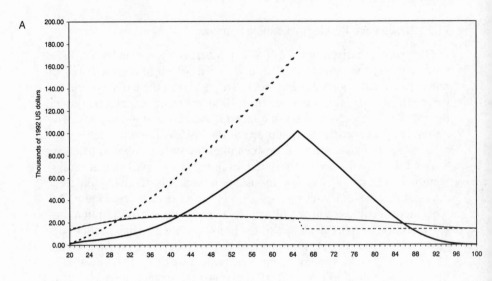

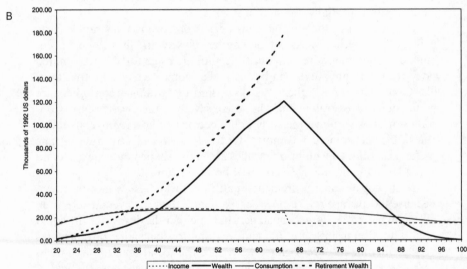

Fig. 11.2   Consumption, income, wealth, and annuity: *A*, Retirement wealth fully invested in the safe asset; *B*, Retirement wealth invested 50/50 in risky/safe asset

wealth is run down since, at this stage, retirement wealth is rolled into a riskless annuity. These patterns show up in the paths of consumption relative to income in figure 11.2.

Figure 11.3 plots liquid wealth and liquid holdings of equities and bills over the life cycle. In each retirement system, the borrowing constraint binds for young households; they would like to take more equity risk but

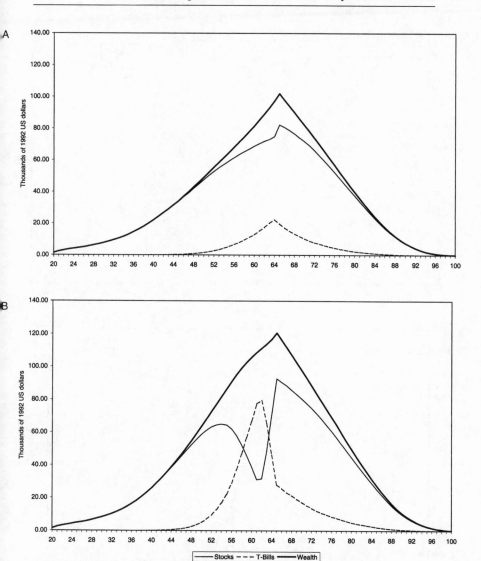

Fig. 11.3 **Wealth, stocks, and Treasury bills:** *A*, **Retirement wealth fully invested in the safe asset;** *B*, **Retirement wealth invested 50/50 in risky/safe asset**

are unable to do so. For approximately the first twenty years of life, they hold 100 percent of their portfolios in the form of equity. Households in midlife hold bills, but these holdings decrease again after retirement.

Figure 11.4 plots the portfolio share of stocks in liquid wealth. The crucial variables for portfolio composition are liquid wealth, retirement wealth, and future labor income. In the model, although future labor

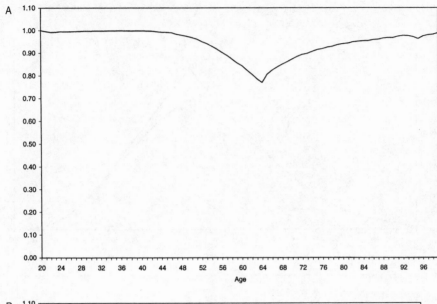

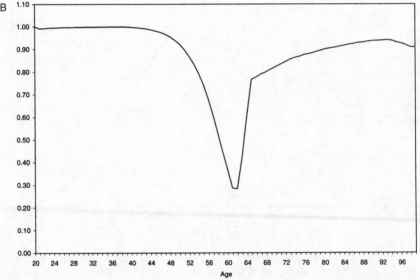

Fig. 11.4   Liquid portfolio share invested in stocks: *A*, Retirement wealth fully invested in the safe asset; *B*, Retirement wealth invested 50/50 in risky/safe asset

income is risky, it can be thought of as implicit holdings of a riskless asset. Innovations to labor income are positively correlated with innovations to stock returns, but this correlation is not sufficiently large for future labor income to resemble more closely stocks than bills. Since early in life the implicit holdings of the riskless asset in the form of future labor income are large, the investor wishes to invest what little liquid wealth he has fully into stocks. From age forty on, liquid wealth increases relative to future labor income and retirement wealth so that implicit holdings of the riskless asset become less important. This induces a shift in the composition of liquid wealth toward bills. After retirement, liquid wealth is run down more rapidly than the implicit annuitized holdings of the riskless asset. As this happens, the implicit holdings of the riskless asset become relatively more important, inducing a shift in portfolio composition back toward stocks.

These considerations explain the life-cycle patterns in both figure 11.4*A* and figure 11.4*B*. There are, however, important differences in magnitudes between the two figures. In figure 11.4*B*, the midlife decrease in the share invested in stocks is much more dramatic. Since the investor already holds risky assets in the retirement account, he wishes to hold a safer liquid portfolio.

Another way to understand these results is to compare the patterns of current utility of consumption over the life cycle. Figure 11.5*A* shows the ratio of average current utility for households in the 50/50 system to the average current utility of households in the 100/0 system. We see that most of the gain from investing retirement wealth in stocks occurs early in life. The source of this gain is the higher levels of consumption that a lower social security contribution allows. Return risk in the retirement account allows some households to end up poorer so that, after age fifty-five, current utility is on average higher in the 100/0 system.

Return risk also increases the dispersion of utility. The standard deviations of current utility across households with different income and return realizations are higher in the 50/50 system than in the 100/0 system. Figure 11.5*B* reports the ratio of these standard deviations in the two systems. These ex post differences raise important practical issues for designers of retirement systems because they may create an incentive to bail out cohorts negatively affected by lower stock-return realizations.

Of course, a proper welfare analysis requires the discounting of current utility over the life cycle. We defer such an analysis to section 11.4 below.

One limitation of the results reported so far is that they counterfactually predict 100 percent stock market participation among younger investors. However, we can modify this prediction, with little effect on other aspects of the model, by adding a fixed cost of stock market participation. Figure 11.6 reports results with a $10,000 fixed cost. The fraction of households that have paid the fixed cost and the average share of assets invested in

A

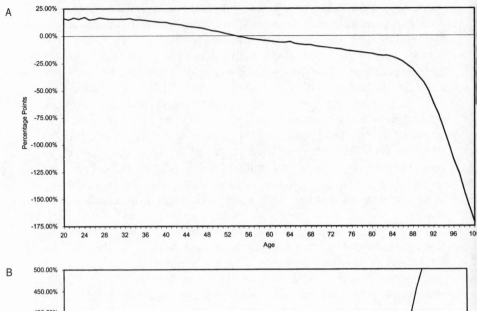

B

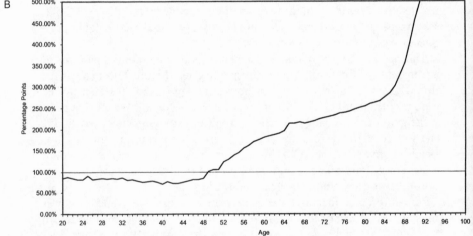

Fig. 11.5   *A*, Utility gain; *B*, Utility dispersion (ratio of standard deviations)

stocks are plotted for each retirement system. Early in life, the two series move almost perfectly together, showing that young investors are either entirely in or entirely out of the market; later in life, all investors have paid the fixed cost, and the model behaves much as it did in the absence of the cost.

11.3   Heterogeneity

In the previous section, we studied a representative household with a high school education but no college degree. Results are similar for repre-

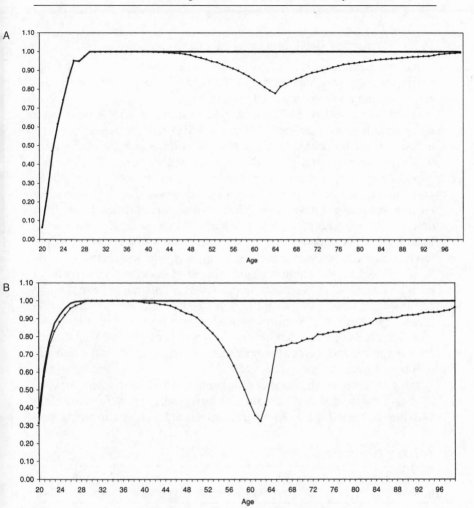

Fig. 11.6   Liquid portfolio share invested in stocks and participation rate: *A,* **Retirement wealth fully invested in the safe asset and fixed cost of entering in the stock market;** *B,* **Retirement wealth invested 50/50 in risky/safe asset and fixed cost of entering the stock market**

sentative households in the other two education groups. However, households may differ along other dimensions. For example, labor income processes may differ for households that work in different industries and for self-employed households. Also, some households may be more impatient or risk averse than others, as found by Barsky et al. (1997). These differences across households may have important effects on optimal investment strategies. In this section, we consider this issue.

11.3.1   Measuring Heterogeneity in Labor Income

We first consider variation in the stochastic structure of the labor income process across industries and then study differences between self-
employed and non-self-employed households.

We use the two-digit SIC classification to split households into twelve
different industries. Starting in 1972, the PSID reports both the current
industry of the household head if currently working and the last industry
if currently unemployed. This is the information that we use. Three caveats
apply, however. First, we ignore the industry of the spouse. This might be
problematic because the spouse's labor income is added to the head's labor
income, yet it might have quite different risk characteristics. Second, on
average, 16 percent of our respondents switch industries each year.
Business-cycle considerations (like the anticipation of a recession) might
force people out of cyclic sectors and into less volatile industries. As we
do not model the switching decision, our estimates of the sensitivities of
labor income shocks to financial market risks for different industries might
be biased. However, we did not find any significant effects when we re-
gressed the number of industry switchers onto innovations in business-
cycle indicators. Third, there is a timing issue because the labor income
reported in the PSID is for the previous calendar year while the industry
concerns the current job.

Table 11.2 reports the number of household-year observations for each
of the thirty-six different education-industry cells. There is tremendous
variation across industries, with particularly small numbers in mining, per-

Table 11.2   Cell Sizes

Industry	No High School	High School	College	Total
Agriculture	765	1,165	381	2,311
Mining	119	360	98	577
Manufacturing	3,116	7,319	2,430	12,865
Construction	1,414	2,938	494	4,846
Transportation, communications	828	3,172	701	4,701
Trade	1,072	4,661	1,445	7,178
Finance, real estate, insurance	109	995	965	2,069
Business services	439	1,437	548	2,424
Personal services	159	358	108	625
Recreation	39	236	110	385
Professional services	356	1,738	3,883	5,977
Public administration	339	2,357	1,097	3,793
Self-employed	1,115	3,562	2,242	6,919
Non-self-employed	7,640	23,174	10,018	40,832
Total	8,755	26,736	12,260	47,751

sonal services, and recreation. These industries are omitted from tables 11.3–11.5 below. As a further cutoff, we drop cells in which any PSID wave contains fewer than twenty observations; these cells are left blank in tables 11.3–11.5. We do, however, include observations in these small cells when estimating column and row totals, that is, when reporting the results for a given industry across all education levels or for a given education group across all industries.

We reestimate age profiles of labor income for the shorter PSID sample beginning in 1972 and including industry dummies in the vector Z_{it} of personal characteristics. That is, we allow industry to influence only the level and not the shape of the age profile for a household with a given amount of education. We then estimate the stochastic model of labor income separately for each education-industry cell.[3]

Table 11.3 reports the total variance of income, and its decomposition into permanent and transitory components, for each different education-industry cell. Agriculture has by far the highest variance of labor income shocks. Other industries subject to significant labor income shocks are construction and business services. The variance decomposition indicates that labor income shocks for construction workers without a high school degree are entirely temporary. At the other extreme, permanent income shocks are especially important for college graduates in public administration. As a general pattern, the relative importance of permanent shocks seems to increase with education attainment. This was already documented for the column totals but seems robust within individual industries.

The bottom of table 11.3 splits the sample in a different way, by distinguishing self-employed from non-self-employed households. (We included both types of households in the industry analysis since there are too few self-employed households to allow an industry decomposition.) Income variability is dramatically larger for self-employed households. Income shocks are entirely temporary for the self-employed without a high school degree but are disproportionately permanent for the self-employed in the two higher education groups.

Table 11.4 considers heterogeneity in the sensitivity of different households' income shocks to lagged stock returns. Table 11.5 repeats the exercise replacing lagged stock returns with lagged returns on long-term government bonds. Unfortunately, the small cell sizes mean that the results are often statistically insignificant for individual industries, but there are many interesting patterns. Stock market risk seems especially relevant for people in manufacturing, construction, and public administration. Interest-rate risk shows up for agriculture, professional services, and finance, real

---

3. We also report results aggregating across industries and education groups. Note that these differ slightly from the results reported in sec. 11.2 above because, here, our sample starts in 1972 and we include industry dummies in the estimation of age profiles for labor income.

Table 11.3   Variance Decomposition

	No High School		High School		College		All	
Industry	Total	Permanent/ Total	Total	Permanent/ Total	Total	Permanent/ Total	Total	Permanent/ Total
Agriculture	…	…	.3094	.1350	…	…	.3166	.0786
Manufacturing	.0579	.0973	.0506	.0912	.0469	.2483	.0529	.1315
Construction	.1097	.0000	.1030	.1394	…	…	.1080	.1451
Transportation, communications	.1119	.3058	.0553	.0833	.0721	.2586	.0672	.1616
Trade	.0997	.1707	.0890	.1254	.0826	.2382	.0895	.1591
Finance, real estate, insurance	…	…	.0930	.1264	…	…	.0906	.1471
Business services	…	…	.1275	.1820	.0732	.1953	.1188	.1789
Professional services	…	…	.0702	.1180	.0361	.2594	.0773	.1478
Public administration	…	…	.0470	.1657	…	…	.0450	.1882
Self-employed	.3695	.0000	.2199	.2192	.1985	.1909	.2302	.1634
Non-self-employed	.0655	.0762	.0535	.0969	.0418	.1768	.0545	.1124
All	.1057	.0683	.0829	.1306	.0744	.2390	.0868	.1413

Note: All positive variances are significantly different from zero at the 0.1 percent level. Two variances estimated to be negative have been set to zero.

Table 11.4   Regression of Permanent Aggregate Shock on Lagged Excess Stock Returns

Industry	No High School		High School		College		All	
	β	ρ	β	ρ	β	ρ	β	ρ
Agriculture	⋯	⋯	.3333	.3507	⋯	⋯	.1754	.2218
Manufacturing	.1025*	.3381	.0750	.2786	.0577	.2057	.0829*	.3524
Construction	.3197**	.6577	.0770	.2423	⋯	⋯	.1333**	.5527
Transportation, communications	−.1778	.2983	.0488	.3234	−.0440	.1095	.0294	.1879
Trade	.1163	.2128	−.0050	.0245	−.0093	.0224	.0075	.0283
Finance, real estate, insurance	⋯	⋯	.0360	.0693	⋯	⋯	.0461	.1281
Business services	⋯	⋯	−.0156	.0265	.0622	.3457	.0804	.1949
Professional services	⋯	⋯	.0320	.0860	.2195**	.5094	.0479	.2644
Public administration	⋯	⋯	.0634	.2302	⋯	⋯	.1072**	.4237
Self-employed	.0916	.0964	.0753	.1652	.1869*	.4164	.1119	.3159
Non-self-employed	.1022*	.3970	.0681*	.4148	.0462	.2998	.0710**	.4638
All	.0937	.3170	.0689*	.3785	.0721**	.4943	.0762**	.4562

*Significant at the 10 percent level.
**Significant at the 5 percent level.

Table 11.5   Regression of Permanent Aggregate Shock on Lagged Excess Bond Returns

Industry	No High School		High School		College		All	
	β	ρ	β	ρ	β	ρ	β	ρ
Agriculture	...	...	.5750**	.4244	...	...	.5735**	.5083
Manufacturing	.2020**	.4674	.0750	.2786	.1050	.2627	.1221*	.3637
Construction	.1371	.1977	.1788*	.3961	...	...	.1378*	.4005
Transportation, communications	−.1723	.2027	.0632	.2943	.0012	.0022	.0485	.2177
Trade	.1822	.2324	.0835	.2608	.1995	.3283	.0754	.1980
Finance, real estate, insurance	...	...	.1562	.2074	...	...	.1936*	.3779
Business services	...	...	−.2202	.2638	...	...	−.0941	.1600
Professional services	...	...	.0199	.0374	.1319**	.5138	.1174**	.4540
Public administration	...	...	.1539*	.3926	.1230	.2000	.1329*	.3685
Self-employed	.3653	.2693	.1912	.2941	.1391	.2173	.2124**	.4204
Non-self-employed	.1223	.3330	.1021**	.4361	.1290**	.5874	.1152**	.5279
All	.1511*	.3586	.1168**	.4501	.1316**	.6326	.1300**	.5457

*Significant at the 10 percent level.
**Significant at the 5 percent level.

estate, and insurance in addition to the stock market-sensitive sectors. Among college graduates, the self-employed are especially exposed to stock market risk, while interest-rate risk is far more important for the non-self-employed. This finding supports the conclusion of Heaton and Lucas (2000) that privately owned business risk is an especially important substitute for stock market risk in the portfolios of many wealthy households.

11.3.2   Effects of Heterogeneity on Portfolio Choice

In this section, we illustrate the effects of investor heterogeneity on optimal consumption and portfolio choice. First, we consider heterogeneity of preferences, calculating optimal behavior for highly risk-averse investors with $\gamma = 10$ and impatient investors with $\delta = 0.8$. Second, we consider differences in labor income risk of the sort illustrated in section 11.3.1 above. To highlight these differences, we simulate the behavior of households whose income is particularly risky and highly correlated with asset returns: self-employed college graduates.

Table 11.6 shows average consumption and liquid wealth (in thousands of dollars) and the share of liquid wealth invested in stocks for different age groups. This is a more compact way for us to summarize the informa-

Table 11.6   **Life-Cycle Profiles**

Age	Baseline Case			$\gamma = 10$		$\delta = 0.8$		Self-Employed	
	0/100	50/50[a]	50/50	0/100	50/50	0/100	50/50	0/100	50/50
				Consumption					
20–35	20.22	20.26	21.07	20.13	20.88	20.53	20.61	25.09	26.10
36–50	25.48	26.11	26.15	25.12	24.86	26.50	26.47	38.39	38.28
51–65	24.61	26.06	25.46	24.23	24.54	23.94	23.78	35.23	35.35
66–80	22.43	26.64	24.19	22.65	24.46	15.95	15.73	32.67	34.02
81–100	16.98	25.61	18.27	19.04	20.60	14.27	14.27	27.26	28.70
				Wealth					
20–35	5.94	5.77	6.39	8.20	7.92	3.39	2.73	12.84	13.75
36–50	29.34	23.17	35.87	39.28	50.57	7.25	5.64	65.75	81.99
51–65	75.77	40.34	96.26	100.16	126.78	10.23	7.83	173.70	195.02
66–80	77.28	26.06	92.81	105.50	128.71	5.71	4.71	159.76	169.73
81–100	13.60	4.15	18.40	30.85	39.94	0.11	0.11	46.75	52.00
				Liquid portfolio share in stocks					
20–35	1.00	0.93	1.00	0.97	0.97	0.99	0.99	0.57	0.53
36–50	0.99	1.00	0.98	0.95	0.72	1.00	1.00	0.91	0.68
51–65	0.88	0.81	0.61	0.61	0.08	1.00	0.90	0.57	0.14
66–80	0.90	0.96	0.85	0.57	0.49	1.00	1.00	0.54	0.51
81–100	0.92	0.58	0.90	0.68	0.57	1.00	1.00	0.61	0.53
				Tax rates (%)					
	10.00	10.00	6.00	10.00	6.00	10.00	6.00	10.50	6.75

[a]Refers to the scenario where the tax rate is held constant at the same level as in the 0/100 case, implying a higher average replacement ratio.

tion presented graphically in figures 11.2–11.4 above. The first three columns of table 11.6 use the baseline parameters and consider retirement systems with $\alpha^R = 0$, $\alpha^R = 0.5$ and the same 10 percent tax rate as with $\alpha^R = 0$, and $\alpha^R = 0.5$ and a lower 6 percent tax rate that maintains the same average replacement ratio as with $\alpha^R = 0$.

The next two columns of table 11.6 present results for a higher risk-aversion coefficient of 10 rather than 5. Since the tax rates do not depend on γ, they are the same as in the baseline case. To understand the results for higher γ, it is important to remember that, with isoelastic preferences, this parameter measures both risk aversion and prudence (Kimball 1990). Greater prudence increases precautionary savings and explains why highly risk-averse investors consume less, and save more, until age sixty-five. After this age, the precautionary savings motive is reduced since there is no labor income risk and retirement wealth is converted into a riskless annuity. Thus, highly risk-averse investors consume more after retirement.

Table 11.6 also shows that, as one would expect, highly risk-averse investors have a lower portfolio share in stocks. One interesting pattern that is not visible in the table is that, very early in life, these investors' equity portfolio share is increasing with age. This pattern does not show up for investors with $\gamma = 5$ because, in early life, these investors are constrained by their inability to borrow to finance equity investments. The reason for this increasing pattern is explained in CGM (1998). In the presence of an increasing labor income profile, the annuity value of future labor income, equivalent to implicit holdings of the riskless asset, increases with age at first as peak earnings years move closer in time. Investors respond to this increase by shifting liquid wealth toward risky financial assets. Later on, the annuity value of future labor income starts to decrease as peak earnings are realized and retirement approaches; investors respond by shifting out of stocks in middle age.

The next two columns of table 11.6 show optimal consumption, wealth, and portfolio allocation for impatient households with $\delta = 0.8$. These households consume more early in life (roughly up to age fifty) and less later. They accumulate almost no wealth, never holding more than about $10,000 in liquid assets. What little wealth they do accumulate they hold in stocks; their exposure to the stock market is so small that they are extremely tolerant of equity risk.

The last two columns of table 11.6 report results for self-employed college-educated households. The preference parameters are the same as in the baseline case, but the results are quite different from the first three columns of table 11.6, which apply to households with only a high school education. The tax rate in the 50/50 system is set to 6.75 percent to maintain the average replacement ratio for self-employed college-educated households. Looking at the share of liquid wealth invested in stocks, there are two distinctive features: the share invested in risky financial assets is much lower, and it exhibits a clear hump shape. The higher variance of labor income shocks and the large positive correlation between the latter and innovations to stock returns crowd out investment in risky financial assets. This effect is particularly strong early in life, when the investor has accumulated little liquid wealth.

11.4 Welfare Analysis

We have presented detailed results describing the effects of alternative retirement systems on consumption, wealth accumulation, and portfolio choice. We now turn to the welfare implications of these systems.

We evaluate each system by discounting current utilities back from the end to the beginning of adult life (twenty, or twenty-two for college-educated households). We renormalize discounted utility into consumption-equivalent units so that a 5 percent increase represents the increase in utility that would be produced by a 5 percent increase in consumption at every date. We calculate the expectation of discounted lifetime utility at age twenty across all realizations of income and risky-asset returns; in order to measure the variability of outcomes, we also calculate the standard deviation of discounted lifetime utility across these realizations. Finally, we assess welfare effects on retired households by repeating the same exercise discounting back only to age sixty-five.

The top panel of table 11.7 reports results for the benchmark case of a household with risk aversion $\gamma = 5$ and a high school education. In the top row, all retirement wealth is invested in the riskless asset; in the second row, half of retirement wealth is invested in stocks, but the tax rate is held constant at 10 percent; in the third row, half of retirement wealth is invested in stocks, and the tax rate is lowered to 6 percent to maintain the average replacement ratio at 60 percent; and, in the fourth row, all retirement wealth is invested in stocks, and the tax rate is lowered to 3.75 percent to maintain the average replacement ratio. The third and fourth columns give the mean and standard deviation of discounted lifetime utility in consumption-equivalent units (thousands of dollars of consumption) at age twenty, the fifth and sixth columns report the same moments at age sixty-five, and the remaining columns report the percentage changes in these moments relative to the benchmark case of riskless retirement wealth.

The table shows that a shift from a riskless retirement system to one that is 50 percent invested in stocks, with a lower payroll-tax rate, increases the welfare of the typical twenty-year-old household by 3.7 percent. Most of the welfare gain is due to the reduction in the tax rate; the household gains only 0.5 percent if the payroll-tax rate is held constant. The standard deviation of lifetime utilities across households with different income and asset-return realizations also increases modestly, by 3.4 percent if the payroll-tax rate is reduced and 2.9 percent if it is held constant.

Table 11.7   Welfare Analysis

	Tax Rate (%)	Welfare Age 20		Welfare Age 65		Gain Age 20 (%)		Gain Age 65 (%)	
		Mean	S.D.	Mean	S.D.	Mean	S.D.	Mean	S.D.
Baseline:									
0/100	10.00	18.67	1.75	22.69	3.42				
50/50[a]	10.00	18.76	1.80	27.30	7.41	0.48	2.86	20.32	116.67
50/50	6.00	19.36	1.81	24.46	6.22	3.70	3.43	7.80	81.87
100/0	3.50	19.59	1.96	24.92	9.77	4.93	12.00	9.83	185.67
$\gamma = 10$:									
0/100	10.00	16.08	2.17	22.53	2.54				
50/50[a]	10.00	16.05	2.19	27.54	6.62	-0.18	0.95	22.22	160.81
50/50	6.00	16.78	2.26	24.42	5.68	4.35	4.15	8.39	123.62
$\gamma = 2$:									
0/100	10.00	20.71	1.17	22.03	3.27				
50/50[a]	10.00	21.18	1.30	29.86	8.57	2.31	11.15	35.57	161.92
50/50	6.00	21.50	1.33	23.11	6.25	3.83	13.79	4.91	90.94
		Welfare Age 22				Gain Age 22			
College-educated self-employed:									
0/100	10.50	17.64	2.90	31.20	5.09				
50/50[a]	10.50	17.63	2.89	37.96	10.13	-0.07	-0.36	21.66	99.11
50/50	6.75	18.31	2.95	32.83	7.79	3.80	1.72	5.22	53.05

[a]Refers to the scenario where the tax rate is held constant at the same level as in the 0/100 case, implying a higher average replacement ratio.

Households also prefer the risky retirement system at age sixty-five; their discounted utility is on average 7.8 percent higher if the payroll-tax rate is reduced and 20.3 percent higher if it is held constant (for then they have accumulated greater wealth over their working life and at age sixty-five are able to enjoy the benefits). A further shift in the retirement system to 100 percent equity investment, with a payroll-tax rate that is lower again, produces even larger utility gains but also considerably greater variability of outcomes.

The next panel of table 11.7 considers a highly risk-averse household with $\gamma = 10$. This household is not usually constrained in its equity holdings under the riskless retirement system, and it actually loses slightly if the retirement system is shifted into equities without any reduction in the payroll-tax rate. But, if the payroll-tax rate is reduced, the highly risk-averse household actually gains more than the benchmark household, 4.4 percent rather than 3.7 percent. The reason is that, under power utility, higher risk aversion implies a lower elasticity of intertemporal substitution—that is, a stronger desire to smooth consumption intertemporally—and the higher disposable income associated with a lower tax rate allows the household to smooth consumption more effectively over the life cycle.

The next panel of table 11.7 considers a comparatively risk-tolerant household with $\gamma = 2$. The results here are the mirror image of those for the highly risk-averse household. The risk-tolerant household gains more than the benchmark household if the payroll-tax rate is fixed (for it is particularly anxious to relax constraints on its equity holdings) but gains less if the payroll-tax rate is reduced (since improved opportunities to smooth consumption over the life cycle are less important for this household).

The last panel of table 11.7 reports results for a household headed by a self-employed college graduate. This household has risky labor income that is unusually correlated with the stock market, so its desired stockholdings are smaller than those of the benchmark household; it actually loses slightly from the investment of retirement wealth in equities with a fixed tax rate. On the other hand, this household also has a particularly pronounced hump shape in labor income, so it is particularly anxious to smooth consumption over the life cycle. The household gains 3.8 percent from a risky retirement system with a lower payroll-tax rate, comparable to the results for the benchmark household.

All the results in table 11.7 can be criticized on the grounds that they are derived from a model in which there is no role for a social security system. Since households save and invest their liquid wealth optimally, the mandatory saving and rigid asset allocation of the retirement system can only reduce their welfare. In this setting, any reform that effectively reduces the scale of social security will increase welfare.

As a partial response to this concern, in table 11.8 we report a "paternalistic" welfare analysis in which the government uses different utility parameters than those of the household itself. In the first panel, the household is impatient, with $\delta = 0.8$; left to its own devices, it will do very little saving for retirement, as illustrated in table 11.6 above. The government, however, discounts utility using $\delta = 0.96$, as in our benchmark case. Here, there is a modest welfare gain of 2.0 percent from a shift of retirement wealth toward equities with a fixed tax rate but a small welfare loss of −0.6 percent if the payroll-tax rate is reduced. The reason, of course, is that, from the government's point of view, people make poor use of their tax cuts, spending them early in life and failing to save enough for retirement.

The second panel of table 11.8 reports results when the household is highly risk averse, with $\gamma = 10$, but the government is risk tolerant, with $\gamma = 2$. In this case, a shift of retirement wealth toward equities forces households to take on more risk, which improves their welfare from the government's point of view. Welfare rises by 1.7 and 2.4 percent, respectively, in the cases with fixed and reduced payroll-tax rates.

All the results that we have reported so far assume that the riskless real interest rate is fixed at 2 percent and the equity premium at 4 percent. As

Table 11.8   Paternalistic Welfare Analysis

	Tax Rate (%)	Welfare Age 20		Welfare Age 65		Gain Age 20 (%)		Gain Age 65 (%)	
		Mean	S.D.	Mean	S.D.	Mean	S.D.	Mean	S.D.
δ too low:									
0/100	10.00	18.13	1.64	17.26	1.31				
50/50[a]	10.00	18.50	1.77	25.33	8.05	2.04	7.93	46.76	514.50
50/50	6.00	18.03	1.62	17.03	1.20	−0.55	−1.22	−1.33	−8.40
γ too high:									
0/100	10.00	20.67	1.09	20.26	2.75				
50/50[a]	10.00	21.02	1.22	30.59	7.34	1.69	12.12	50.96	166.82
50/50	6.00	21.17	1.21	27.39	6.24	2.42	11.01	35.19	126.91

[a]Refers to the scenario where the tax rate is held constant at the same level as in the 0/100 case, implying a higher average replacement ratio.

a final exercise, in table 11.9 we consider variations in these parameters. This is a valuable check on the robustness of our basic results; it also enables us to consider what might happen to welfare if the investment of retirement wealth in risky assets reduced the equilibrium equity premium.

The top panel of table 11.9 repeats the first three rows of table 11.7 for the benchmark case. The second and third panels consider two alternative scenarios in which the equity premium is 1 percentage point lower at 3 percent. In the first alternative, the equity premium falls, but the riskless interest rate is unchanged, so the expected equity return falls by 1 percentage point. This is a scenario envisaged by critics of social security investment in equities who worry that such a reform would drive up stock prices and drive down expected stock returns. In the second alternative, the equity premium falls, but the riskless interest rate rises by 1 percentage point, leaving the expected equity return unchanged. This scenario is predicted by general equilibrium models in which the return to risky capital is fixed by technology, such as Cox, Ingersoll, and Ross (1985) or Abel (chap. 5 in this volume).

Within each of the alternative scenarios, the welfare gains produced by risky investment of retirement wealth are similar to but slightly smaller than those in the benchmark case. In rows 6, 8, 11, and 13, table 11.9 compares welfare in the alternative scenarios with risky investment of retirement wealth to welfare in the benchmark case with riskless investment of retirement wealth. This is a crude way to capture the possibility that risky investment of retirement wealth might lower the equity premium. It turns out that the results are critically dependent on the way in which the equity premium falls. If it falls through lower stock returns, as in the first alternative, then welfare gains are reduced from 3.7 to 2.8 percent. If it falls through a higher riskless rate, as in the second alternative, then welfare gains are actually increased to 5.0 percent.

Table 11.9   **Welfare Analysis with Alternative Mean Asset Returns**

	Tax Rate (%)	Welfare Age 20		Welfare Age 65		Gain Age 20 (%)		Gain Age 65 (%)	
		Mean	S.D.	Mean	S.D.	Mean	S.D.	Mean	S.D.
Baseline case ($\mu = 4\%$, $\overline{R}_F = 1.02$):									
0/100	10.00	18.67	1.75	22.69	3.42				
50/50[a]	10.00	18.76	1.80	27.30	7.41	0.48	2.86	20.32	116.67
50/50	6.00	19.36	1.81	24.46	6.22	3.70	3.43	7.80	81.87
Alternative 1 ($\mu = 3\%$, $\overline{R}_F = 1.02$):									
0/100	10.00	18.57	1.70	22.15	3.53				
50/50[a]	10.00	18.63	1.78	25.13	6.64	0.33	4.43	13.48	87.89
[b]						−0.22	1.73	10.75	94.05
50/50	7.25	19.20	1.82	25.49	6.74	3.38	6.69	15.11	90.74
[b]						2.82	3.93	12.35	97.00
Alternative 2 ($\mu = 3\%$, $\overline{R}_F = 1.03$):									
0/100	7.00	19.30	1.79	24.20	4.16				
50/50[a]	7.00	19.32	1.84	26.76	6.88	0.12	2.81	10.60	65.38
[b]						3.50	5.16	17.96	101.16
50/50	4.75	19.61	1.83	25.07	6.11	1.61	2.23	3.60	46.88
[b]						5.03	4.57	10.49	78.65

[a] Refers to the scenario where the tax rate is held constant at the same level as in the 0/100 case, implying a higher average replacement ratio.
[b] Computes the welfare gain relative to the baseline case, i.e., under the initial assumption for asset returns of $\mu = 4\%$ and $\overline{R}_F = 1.02$.

11.5 Conclusion

Decisions about the quantity and form of retirement saving are among the most important that a typical household takes in the course of a lifetime. Despite the importance of the issue, until very recently financial economists have had little quantitative understanding of the factors that should affect this decision. This gap in our knowledge has made it hard to give sound advice to policy makers considering reforms in retirement systems.

In this paper, we have built a partial equilibrium life-cycle model that can be used to explore the properties of alternative systems. In our benchmark case, we find a welfare gain equivalent to 3.7 percent of consumption from the investment of half of retirement wealth into equities, accompanied by a reduction in the social security tax rate to maintain the same average replacement rate of income in retirement. The main channel through which these gains are realized is that a lower social security tax rate helps households smooth their consumption over the life cycle. The gains from equity investment of retirement wealth are smaller, about 0.5

percent of consumption, when the social security tax rate is held constant at its initial level. Interestingly, in our model, particularly risk-averse households are particularly keen to smooth consumption and thus experience even larger gains from reduced tax rates made possible by equity returns on retirement wealth. This is true despite the fact that risk-averse households are less enthusiastic equity investors.

While these results are encouraging for proponents of equity investment by the social security system, we note two caveats. First, lower security tax rates reduce welfare by 0.6 percent of consumption in a model in which investors are extremely impatient, with a low time-discount factor of 0.8, but the government judges their welfare using a higher time-discount factor of 0.96. This calculation is a crude way to capture factors that might lead to inadequate private saving and justify a mandatory retirement-saving system. In this model, however, there is a substantial gain of 2.0 percent from social security equity investment with fixed tax rates. These findings suggest that the appropriate adjustment of tax rates will depend on detailed assumptions about the behavior of households but that, under a wide range of assumptions, there are welfare gains to be had by investing some retirement wealth into equities.

Second, a system with partial investment of retirement wealth in the equity market has greater variability of outcomes across cohorts. Particularly negative outcomes for some cohorts might provoke pressure for political bailouts, and the anticipation of bailouts might change the consumption behavior modeled here. This is an important issue for research on social security reform.

Using data from the PSID, we study heterogeneity in labor income processes across households. We find that some households—particularly self-employed college graduates—are exposed to much greater volatility in their labor income than are typical households. The labor income of these households also tends to be more highly correlated with returns on stocks and long-term bonds. This heterogeneity affects optimal investment strategies and may help justify social security reform that includes an element of personal choice.

We also consider the possibility that the investment of retirement wealth in equities might reduce the equity premium. We do not build a general equilibrium model to study this issue, but we do compare results under alternative assumptions about the equity premium. We find that it matters greatly whether the equity premium falls through a decline in the expected return on stocks or through a rise in the riskless interest rate. In the former case, the welfare gains from investing retirement wealth in equities are reduced, while, in the latter case, they are actually greater than in our benchmark model.

In evaluating our results, it is important to be aware of several respects in which our model is oversimplified. First, we consider only self-financing retirement systems in which there is no net payment from any household to any other. Thus, we ignore the redistributive features of the present social security system, and we have nothing to say about the overhang of liabilities to previous generations implied by the present system. Second, we assume that asset returns are independently and identically distributed. Thus, we ignore the variation in real interest rates and equity premia that is the subject of much recent research. Third, we abstract from the existence of owner-occupied housing. This is an important omission since housing is the main component of wealth for many people. Cocco (1998) takes a first step toward the realistic incorporation of housing into a life-cycle model. Fourth, we assume that labor income shocks have constant variances. Some researchers have argued that the variance of idiosyncratic shocks to labor income is higher when the economy is weak and risky-asset returns are low; this can have important effects on the demand for risky assets, as shown by Mankiw (1986), Constantinides and Duffie (1996), and Storesletten, Telmer, and Yaron (1998). Finally, we assume that labor income and the retirement age are exogenous to the household. Bodie, Merton, and Samuelson (1991) point out that households with flexible labor supply can afford to hold riskier portfolios because they can adjust to negative asset returns both by changing their consumption and by changing their labor supply. An important task for future research is to incorporate these and other realistic complications into the basic life-cycle model of portfolio choice.

References

Abel, Andrew B. 1998. The aggregate effects of including equities in the social security trust fund. Wharton School, University of Pennsylvania. Typescript.

Attanasio, Orazio. 1995. The intertemporal allocation of consumption: Theory and evidence. *Carnegie-Rochester Conference Series on Public Policy* 42:39–89.

Balduzzi, Perluigi, and Anthony Lynch. 1999. Transaction costs and predictability: Some utility cost calculations. *Journal of Financial Economics* 52: 47–78.

Barberis, Nicholas C. 2000. How big are hedging demands? Evidence from long-horizon asset allocation. *Journal of Finance* 55 (February): 225–64.

Barsky, Robert B., F. Thomas Juster, Miles S. Kimball, and Matthew D. Shapiro. 1997. Preference parameters and behavioral heterogeneity: An experimental approach in the Health and Retirement Study. *Quarterly Journal of Economics* 112:537–79.

Bertaut, Carol C., and Michael Haliassos. 1997. Precautionary portfolio behavior from a life-cycle perspective. *Journal of Economic Dynamics and Control* 21: 1511–42.

Blanchard, Olivier J. 1993. Movements in the equity premium. *Brookings Papers on Economic Activity*, no. 2:75–118.

Bodie, Zvi, Robert C. Merton, and William Samuelson. 1991. Labor supply flexibility and portfolio choice in a life cycle model. *Journal of Economic Dynamics and Control* 16:427–49.

Brandt, Michael W. 1999. Estimating portfolio and consumption choice: A conditional Euler equations approach. *Journal of Finance* 54 (October): 1609–45.

Brennan, Michael J., Eduardo S. Schwartz, and Ronald Lagnado. 1997. Strategic asset allocation. *Journal of Economic Dynamics and Control* 21:1377–1403.

Brennan, Michael J., and Y. Xia. 1998. Resolution of a financial puzzle. Anderson Graduate School of Management, University of California, Los Angeles. Typescript.

Campbell, John Y. 1996. Understanding risk and return. *Journal of Political Economy* 104:298–345.

Campbell, John Y., and N. Gregory Mankiw. 1989. Consumption, income, and interest rates: Reinterpreting the time series evidence. In *NBER Macroeconomics Annual,* ed. Olivier Blanchard and Stanley Fischer, 185–216. Cambridge, Mass.: MIT Press.

Campbell, John Y., and Robert J. Shiller. 1998. Valuation ratios and the long-run stock market outlook. *Journal of Portfolio Management* 24:11–26.

Campbell, John Y., and Luis M. Viceira. 1999. Consumption and portfolio decisions when expected returns are time varying. *Quarterly Journal of Economics* 114:433–95.

———. In press. Who should buy long-term bonds? *American Economic Review.*

Carroll, Christopher D., and Andrew A. Samwick. 1997. The nature of precautionary wealth. *Journal of Monetary Economics* 40 (September): 41–71.

Carroll, Christopher D., and Lawrence H. Summers. 1991. Consumption growth parallels income growth: Some new evidence. In *National savings and economic performance,* ed. B. D. Bernheim and John B. Shoven. Chicago: University of Chicago Press.

Cocco, João F. 1998. Owner-occupied housing, permanent income, and portfolio choice. Harvard University. Typescript.

Cocco, João F., Francisco J. Gomes, and Pascal J. Maenhout. 1998. Consumption and portfolio choice over the life-cycle. Harvard University. Typescript.

Constantinides, George M., John B. Donaldson, and Rajnish Mehra. 1998. Junior can't borrow: A new perspective on the equity premium puzzle. NBER Working Paper no. 6617. Cambridge, Mass.: National Bureau of Economic Research.

Constantinides, George M., and Darrell Duffie. 1996. Asset pricing with heterogeneous consumers. *Journal of Political Economy* 104:219–40.

Cox, John, Jonathan E. Ingersoll Jr., and Stephen A. Ross. 1985. A theory of the term structure of interest rates. *Econometrica* 53:385–408.

Deaton, Angus S. 1991. Savings and liquidity constraints. *Econometrica* 59: 1221–48.

Fama, Eugene F., and G. William Schwert. 1977. Human capital and capital market equilibrium. *Journal of Financial Economics* 5:115–46.

Gakidis, Harry. 1997. Earnings uncertainty and life-cycle portfolio choice. Massachusetts Institute of Technology. Typescript.

Geanakoplos, John, Olivia S. Mitchell, and Stephen P. Zeldes. 1999. Social security money's worth. In *Prospects for social security reform,* ed. Olivia S. Mitchell, Robert J. Myers, and Howard Young. Philadelphia: University of Pennsylvania Press.

Gourinchas, Pierre-Olivier, and Jonathan Parker. 1996. Consumption over the life cycle. Massachusetts Institute of Technology. Typescript.

Heaton, John, and Deborah J. Lucas. 1997. Market frictions, saving behavior, and portfolio choice. *Macroeconomic Dynamics* 1:76–101.

———. 2000. Portfolio choice and asset prices: The importance of entrepreneurial risk. *Journal of Finance* 55:1163–98.

Hubbard, Glenn, Jonathan S. Skinner, and Stephen Zeldes. 1994. The importance of precautionary motives for explaining individual and aggregate saving. *Carnegie-Rochester Conference Series on Public Policy* 40:59–125.

Jagannathan, Ravi, and Zhenyu Wang. 1996. The conditional CAPM and the cross section of expected returns. *Journal of Finance* 51:3–53.

Kim, Tong Suk, and Edward Omberg. 1996. Dynamic nonmyopic portfolio behavior. *Review of Financial Studies* 9:141–61.

Kimball, Miles. 1990. Precautionary saving in the small and in the large. *Econometrica* 58:53–73.

Liu, Jun. 1998. Portfolio selection in stochastic environments. Stanford University. Typescript.

Mankiw, N. Gregory. 1986. The equity premium and the concentration of aggregate shocks. *Journal of Financial Economics* 17:211–19.

Merton, Robert C. 1969. Lifetime portfolio selection under uncertainty: The continuous time case. *Review of Economics and Statistics* 51:247–57.

———. 1971. Optimum consumption and portfolio rules in a continuous-time model. *Journal of Economic Theory* 3:373–413.

Pischke, Jörn-Steffen. 1995. Individual income, incomplete information, and aggregate consumption. *Econometrica* 63:805–40.

Poterba, James M., and Andrew A. Samwick. 1997. Household portfolio allocation over the life cycle. NBER Working Paper no. 6185. Cambridge, Mass.: National Bureau of Economic Research.

Ross, Stephen A. 1999. Samuelson's fallacy of large numbers revisited. Massachusetts Institute of Technology. Typescript.

Samuelson, Paul A. 1969. Lifetime portfolio selection by dynamic stochastic programming. *Review of Economics and Statistics* 51:239–46.

———. 1991. Long-run risk tolerance when equity returns are mean regressing: Pseudoparadoxes and vindication of a "Businessman's Risk." In *Money, macroeconomics, and economic policy: Essays in honor of James Tobin,* ed. William C. Brainard, William D. Nordhaus, and Harold W. Watts. Cambridge, Mass.: MIT Press.

Storesletten, Kjetil, Chris I. Telmer, and Amir Yaron. 1998. Asset pricing with idiosyncratic risk and overlapping generations. Carnegie-Mellon University. Typescript.

———. 1999. The risk sharing implications of alternative social security arrangements. *Carnegie-Rochester Conference Series on Public Policy* 50:213–59.

Tauchen, George, and R. Hussey. 1991. Quadrature-based methods for obtaining approximate solutions to nonlinear asset pricing models. *Econometrica* 59: 371–96.

Viceira, Luis M. In press. Optimal portfolio choice for long-horizon investors with nontradable income. *Journal of Finance.*

Wachter, Jessica. 1998a. Portfolio and consumption decisions under mean-reverting returns: An exact solution for complete markets. Harvard University. Typescript.

———. 1998b. Risk aversion and allocation to long-term bonds. Harvard University. Typescript.

Comment   Amir Yaron

The goal of "Investing Retirement Wealth: A Life-Cycle Model" by John Y. Campbell, João F. Cocco, Francisco J. Gomes, and Pascal J. Maenhout is to analyze quantitatively the effects that different mandatory *retirement* plans have on savings, portfolio choice, and welfare. Campbell et al.'s analysis concentrates on retirement accounts that are based on a defined-contribution system. They ask what the ramifications are of investing at least part of the retirement account in equity, relative to investing it completely in risk-free bonds. Their analysis is motivated by the recent evidence on the projected decline in implicit rates of return on investments in social security and notable plans to alleviate these problems by privatizing components of social security or by investing part of the social security trust fund in equities (see Advisory Council on Social Security 1996). Both plans rely on the historically higher rates of return that stocks have yielded over Treasury bills—the "equity premium."

It should be clear that, absent any frictions, changes in the investment profile of a defined-contribution retirement account will be completely neutralized by agents' adjustments to the portfolio of their private savings. In the light of this, Campbell et al. go to great lengths to specify a rich labor supply process and various borrowing and stock market participation constraints. It is the interaction among these factors that governs the quantitative changes in optimal portfolio allocations and hence any changes in savings and welfare.

My analysis of the paper starts by summarizing Campbell et al.'s main findings. I then proceed to analyze, within a two-period model, the effects that borrowing constraints and fixed costs of entering into the stock market have on portfolio allocations—and point toward the factors that I believe yield the results that the authors obtain. The last part discusses some outstanding issues regarding their analysis.

Campbell et al.'s main results can be summarized as follows: (1) When fixed costs are *not* present, they find that most young agents hold 100 percent stocks. (2) Once fixed costs are introduced, most agents participate in the stock market by the age of thirty. (3) The responses of portfolio allocations are qualitatively similar to the case when there are no fixed costs. They find substantial welfare gains, on the order of 3.7–4.9 percent of annual consumption, when half of retirement savings is invested in equity and taxes are adjusted to equate replacement ratios at retirement. (4) Most of the welfare gains are due to the income effect and influence mainly the young. (5) They find evidence for significant differences in income processes across occupations and industrial sectors—a feature that alters agents' portfolio choice.

Amir Yaron is assistant professor of finance at the Wharton School, University of Pennsylvania, and a faculty research fellow of the National Bureau of Economic Research.

Portfolio Choice

There are three factors that play a key role in Campbell et al.'s framework. The first two are borrowing constraints and fixed costs preventing agents from participating in the stock market. The third factor is the labor income profile that agents face. I find it useful to start by analyzing the implications of the borrowing and fixed-cost constraints within a simplified two-period life-cycle model. To do this, it is instructive to think of an environment where an agent maximizes expected utility over two periods by choosing the first-period rate of savings, κ, out of disposable wealth, $W - T$, and the proportion of savings invested in equity, α^L. The proportion of the retirement account that is invested in equity, α^R, is not under the agent's control. The retirement account is financed by the tax collected in the first period, T. Formally, agents face the following problem:

$$\max_{\{\kappa, \alpha^L\}} \quad U(c_1) + \beta EU(c_2) \quad \text{subject to:}$$

$$c_1 = (1 - \kappa)(W - T),$$

$$c_2 = \kappa(W - T)R_p^L + TR_p^R,$$

$$R_p^i = \alpha^i R + (1 - \alpha^i)R_f, \quad i = L, R,$$

$$0 \le \alpha^i \le 1, \quad i = L, R,$$

$$0 \le \kappa \le 1.$$

The issues with which Campbell et al. are concerned can now be cast in terms of this framework. They ask in a more realistic life-cycle setup, How do κ and α^L change with age? How do κ and α^L respond to an increase in α^R?

Campbell et al.'s setup is geared toward getting realistic age profiles for κ and α^L in the base case when the retirement accounts are fully invested in risk-free bonds. Table 11C.1 summarizes the changes in first-period consumption, $\Delta\kappa(W - T)$, and the share invested in equity in the liquid investment account, α^L, in response to an increase in the equity share of the retirement account—namely, $\Delta\alpha^R > 0$.

The first entry in table 11C.1, the northwestern quadrant, when there are no borrowing constraints and no fixed costs is the complete frictionless

Table 11C.1   **Response to $\Delta\alpha^R > 0$ ($\Delta T = 0$, Δ savings $= -\Delta C = \Delta\kappa[W - T]$)**

	No Fixed Costs	Binding Fixed Costs
No borrowing constraints	$\Delta C = 0$ $\Delta\alpha^L < 0$	$\Delta C > 0$ $\Delta\alpha^L = 0$
Binding borrowing constraints	$\Delta C > 0$ $\Delta\alpha^L = 0$	$\Delta C = 0$ $\Delta\alpha^L = 0$

environment mentioned earlier. In this situation, agents undo the government's increased investment in equity in the retirement account. Hence, the amount invested in equity in the private liquid account must decline to ensure that the overall investment in risky equity out of total wealth is unchanged. Consequently, there are no changes in consumption and savings.

The southeastern block in table 11C.1 describes the situation in which agents both are constrained from borrowing and are facing binding fixed costs preventing entry into the stock market. In this case, a one-dollar switch into equity in the retirement account increases second-period income by $E(R) - R_f$—the "equity premium." Agents then desire to borrow and invest in stocks even more. However, as long as the stock market participation costs and borrowing constraints are still binding, agents are constrained at zero bond- and stockholdings in the liquid savings account ($B^L = S^L = 0$). As a consequence, agents cannot change their first-period consumption or savings.

The northeastern block of table 11C.1 describes the situation in which agents are not constrained from borrowing but are facing fixed costs that prevent them from entering the stock market. Again, agents benefit from the "equity premium," namely, for each dollar invested in the retirement account, they now receive an extra $E(R) - R_f$ dollars in the second period. The fact that agents are constrained from investing in the stock market implies that, had this constraint not existed, they would save more by investing part of first-period wealth in equity. Agents do not choose to increase their bondholdings (and hence save more) because they were already at their constrained optimum before the change in the retirement portfolio. Therefore, the best that agents can do is to smooth consumption by increasing consumption in the first period. Hence, savings are reduced.

Finally, the southwestern block of the table describes the case where there are no fixed costs but the borrowing constraints are binding. In this case, once retirement accounts are invested in equity, agents can potentially reduce their increased second-period income by divesting away from equity. The fact that the borrowing constraint is binding implies that agents still prefer to buy more stocks but are constrained from doing so by the borrowing constraint. In the light of the increased income in the second period, and in order to smooth consumption, agents choose to increase consumption during the first period and continue to allocate 100 percent of their private savings to stocks.

The analysis presented above indicates that an increase in the share invested in equity in the retirement portfolio (i.e., a rise in α^R) should lead to a *reduction* in overall savings and a *reduction* in the share invested in equity in the private liquid accounts. This is true as long as there is some mass of agents who are completely unconstrained (the northwestern quadrant) and some others who are facing binding borrowing constraints but no fixed costs or binding fixed costs without binding borrowing costs (the southwestern and northeastern quadrants, respectively). Campbell et al. obtain, however, a significant increase in overall savings (see their fig. 11.2 or fig. 11C.1 below) and relatively small changes in the share invested in equity in the liquid savings accounts. The key reason that Campbell et al. find an increase in savings, as opposed to what the simple model presented above suggests, is the stage in the life cycle in which the increased "equity-premium" income is received. In the analysis presented above, the benefits from investing in equity accrue during the second period—the retirement stage. On the other hand, Campbell et al. choose to fix the level of retirement benefits across the different investment experiments. With an increased equity share in the retirement accounts, lower taxes need to be levied in order to reach the level of retirement benefits available before. In the notation used above, this implies a smaller T—that is, Campbell et al. deliver the benefits during the first period. Receiving the benefits in the first period of life allows for a few effects. First, some agents may now be able to enter the stock market, whereas before they were constrained from doing so. Second, because agents now have relatively more income in the first period, they will save more during the first period in order to smooth consumption. This is the main channel that leads to the increase in savings that Campbell et al. find.

Another factor affecting Campbell et al.'s analysis that is absent in the simple two-period model presented above is the fact that labor income is stochastic and has a deterministic hump-shape component. As can be seen in figures 11.2 and 11.3, consumption tracks income very closely in the very early stages of life. The increased income, discussed above, translates almost entirely into an increase in consumption in those highly constrained early stages of life and only later to a rise in savings. The increase in utility shows up in terms of larger consumption during these first years of the life cycle. In summary, welfare, savings, and portfolio choice are quite sensitive to whether the benefits from the "equity premium" are given in the form of increased benefits at retirement or in the form of lower taxes during the working years. Abel (chap. 5 in this volume) makes similar arguments for explaining the different results that he gets concerning capital accumulations when he analyzes a defined-benefit and a defined-contribution system.

It would be interesting to get a quantitative feel for how much the welfare gains Campbell et al. report really depend on the variation in life-cycle labor income processes relative to the alleviation of the borrowing constraint. In figure 11C.1, I plot the combined investment in risky equity both in the liquid and in the retirement account relative to total wealth in both accounts. Namely, I plot $\alpha \equiv (S^L + S^R)/(W^R + W^L)$. Two key features emerge from this figure. First, in both cases, α, the fraction invested in equity as a fraction of total wealth, tends not to move as much over the

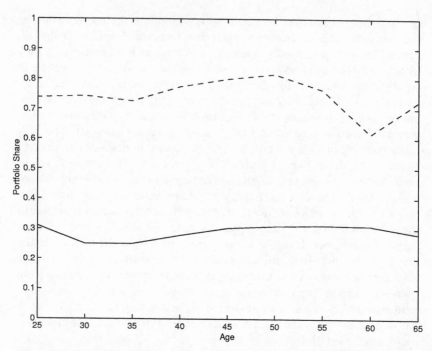

Fig. 11C.1   Portfolio share of stocks out of total wealth: $\alpha = (S^L + S^R)/(W^R + W^L)$

Note: α is based on figs. 11.2 and 11.3 in Campbell et al. and on linearly extrapolating income in between five years. The dotted line shows share out of just financial wealth, and the solid line shows total wealth.

life cycle as α^L (see Campbell et al.'s fig. 11.4). This is of course partly due to the fact that the denominator is now much larger as it includes both retirement and liquid wealth and to the fact that α^L offsets to some degree some of the changes in α^R. The second key observation is that α shifts up in almost parallel fashion once retirement accounts are invested in equity. As mentioned earlier, since agents like to be at 100 percent stocks or very close to it, investing in equity through the retirement account alleviates this constraint and allows agents to get closer to their unconstrained desired portfolio position. It seems that relaxing the borrowing constraint is the dominating factor for the welfare gains that Campbell et al. find while the specific variations in the labor income process are of secondary importance.

Welfare Gains—Other Factors

The welfare gains that Campbell et al. find are large. In the light of this, it is important to consider what factors might alter these welfare gains. Campbell et al. analyze a defined-contribution system. In a defined-benefit system, as in the current social security system, there are important nonlinearities in the benefits formula. First, there is cap for contributions to social security. This implies that wealthy agents are not as negatively affected by having retirement accounts being invested in bonds since their mandatory retirement account is a relatively small portion of their overall retirement plans. Second, social security currently provides a minimum level of benefits. For the very poor, having such a floor level of benefits may be more attractive than the gain from investing their very low level of wealth in equities. Both these factors make me think that, had the authors analyzed a system that is closer to the current one, the welfare gains would be much smaller.

A second important factor that may affect welfare gains, which Campbell et al. acknowledge is absent from their framework, is an account of the transition or debt that would be required in moving from the current system to the one that they in fact analyze. Storesletten, Telmer, and Yaron (1999) show that accounting for the debt that would need to be raised in order to keep up promises to the old is crucial in evaluating welfare gains across alternative social security plans. They show that accounting for the debt burden to the old can cut the welfare gains in half.

Finally, much of the discussion on restructuring social security deals with whether to invest the trust fund in equity or to allow a component of social security to be privatized in a similar fashion to the defined-contribution framework analyzed by Campbell et al. One benefit of the current social security system is its implicit longevity insurance through the annuity provisions that it provides. A crucial aspect of Campbell et al.'s analysis is the fact that, even when the system becomes more privatized, these actuarially fair annuities will be available. There is a long literature documenting how private retirement annuities are far from being fairly priced (see Friedman and Warshawsky 1990). If uninsurable labor income is an important component of overall income, as is the case in Campbell et al.'s analysis, the availability of annuities will crucially affect agents' savings. Storesletten, Telmer, and Yaron (1999) show that, in a general equilibrium framework, the availability of annuities is quantitatively important in comparing alternatives to social security. Hence, a fully privatized defined-contribution system, in which agents need to acquire retirement annuities privately, will not provide as much mortality insurance as the current system as long as private annuity markets are still not completely actuarially fair.

In summary, Campbell et al. provide a rich framework for evaluating the welfare benefits of increasing the equity share of investments in a defined-contribution retirement system. Their analysis provides interesting information about the channels and magnitude by which welfare is increased. A natural next step would be to account for some of the issues mentioned above and reevaluate their results in a general equilibrium framework.

References

Advisory Council on Social Security. 1996. *Report of the 1994–1996 Advisory Council on Social Security.* Vols. 1 and 2. Washington, D.C.

Friedman, B., and M. Warshawsky. 1990. The cost of annuities: Implications for saving behavior and bequests. *Quarterly Journal of Economics* 105:135–54.

Storesletten, K., C. I. Telmer, and A. Yaron. 1999. The risk sharing implications of alternative social security arrangements. *Carnegie-Rochester Conference Series on Public Policy* 50:213–60.

Discussion Summary

James Poterba noted that the young participate very quickly in equity markets in this model. He conjectured that including housing in the analysis would probably eliminate this counterfactual prediction by effectively shortening the horizon of the young. He suggested examining this nontrivial extension of an already quite involved model in another paper. In such an extended model, a tax cut resulting from social security reform will allow young agents to accumulate wealth faster toward a downpayment. This would be an additional source of welfare gains.

Antonio Rangel remarked that, although the model does not assign an explicit role to the government, it could be used to answer an intriguing question, namely, What is the value of relaxing constraints? Rangel envisioned an analysis of the value of being able to buy some of the labor income of the next cohort, both in environments with and in those without constraints, with a subsequent comparison.

Robert Shiller remarked that the authors are probably overestimating the amount of heterogeneity in the PSID data set, for a number of reasons. First, the data are self-reported and therefore likely subject to measurement error. Second, a lot of income changes are essentially job changes, deliberately chosen by agents, rather than exogenous shocks hitting them. For instance, people might move to another city with a higher cost of living and therefore change jobs. Similarly, they might work overtime temporarily because of liquidity constraints due to the purchase of a house or drop out of the labor force for family reasons. Shiller concluded that, while the model does not include these changes in the information sets of agents, in fact they often are important.

Andrew Samwick wondered what could be the reason for the low degree of stock market participation observed among the young as opposed to the high demand for stocks predicted by the model. A first—but minor—reason could be that young households are not the natural tax clientele simply by having low income. Samwick conjectured that a more important reason might be impatience. Impatient consumers would accumulate only a small buffer stock early in life, as opposed to what is found in the model assuming a relatively low discount rate.

Henning Bohn commented on the idea of making the payroll tax age dependent. Although this seems natural to consider in a model with liquidity constraints early in life, it might be less so in the context of the current system with redistributional components for strategic reasons. What makes the current system viable, according to a vast literature, is that the very young taxpayers making contributions constitute only a small minority. In addition, older taxpayers already have substantial resources sunk into the system by the time they become the median-age voter and have a vested interest in preserving the system. Lowering payroll taxes for the young could erode the support for the current system.

Robert King wanted to follow up on Bohn, but from a different perspective. An interesting result of the paper is that individuals are quite likely to be constrained during the first ten years of the life cycle. Baxter and King (chap. 10 in this volume) did similar simulations in the absence of any asset-allocation choice and obtained the same results, independent of preferences or of the annuity structure. They conducted a welfare analysis very much like the one Campbell et al. report and also obtained considerable welfare gains associated with relaxing those constraints. King concluded that this may well be one of the central insights of this paper and of this project. Practically, it would suggest that the U.S. system should be changed to allow individuals to postpone paying contributions until later in life, rather than to start contributing in the earliest, liquidity-constrained years.

Martin Feldstein remarked in response that anything that lowers the tax rate in equilibrium will have that effect and reduce the burden on the young. *Amir Yaron* concurred but noted that changing the timing of the contributions in an age-dependent way, as suggested by King, would be a more direct approach.

First, with respect to including housing into the analysis, *John Campbell* agreed that this would be an important extension of the model. He noted that one of the authors, João Cocco, has done work on this (see Cocco 1999). The effects of housing on portfolio choice are not straightforward and are more complex than would be anticipated. For one thing, it might actually increase risk taking by the young, and hence the demand for stocks, as owner-occupied housing, providing consumption services, might act as a consumption floor. *Francisco Gomes* also referred in this context to empirical work by Heaton and Lucas (1997) on the relation between mortgages and portfolio composition.

With respect to Samwick's comment that the high demand for stocks by the young might be due to the low discount rate assumed, *Campbell* remarked that the results are quite robust to changes in this parameter. Previous work considered a rate of time preference of 0.10 and obtained similar results. *Pascal Maenhout* noted that Gakidis (1997) assumes an extreme discount rate of 0.40 in order to match the data in a calibration exercise using the method of simulated moments.

Regarding the discussion of the optimality of age-dependent tax rates, *Gomes* agreed that this was an important prediction of the model. Allowing the young to consume more leads to substantial welfare gains.

Finally, *Campbell* agreed with Shiller on the issue of overstating the amount of heterogeneity but noted that many other papers in a large literature follow a similar procedure and are thus subject to the same criticism.

References

Cocco, João F. 1999. Owner-occupied housing, permanent income, and portfolio choice. Harvard University. Typescript.

Gakidis, Harry. 1997. Earnings uncertainty and life-cycle portfolio choice. Massachusetts Institute of Technology. Typescript.

Heaton, John, and Deborah J. Lucas. 1997. Portfolio choice and asset prices: The importance of entrepreneurial risk. Northwestern University. Typescript.

Contributors

Andrew B. Abel
Department of Finance
The Wharton School
University of Pennsylvania
2315 Steinberg-Dietrich Hall
3620 Locust Walk
Philadelphia, PA 19104-6367

David Backus
Stern School of Business
New York University
44 West 4th Street
New York, NY 10012-1126

Marianne Baxter
Department of Economics
Boston University
270 Bay State Road
Boston, MA 02215

Zvi Bodie
Boston University School of
    Management
595 Commonwealth Avenue
Boston, MA 02215

Henning Bohn
Department of Economics
University of California
Santa Barbara, CA 93106

Jeffrey R. Brown
John F. Kennedy School of
    Government
Harvard University
79 John F. Kennedy Street
Cambridge, MA 02138

John Y. Campbell
Department of Economics
Littauer Center 213
Harvard University
Cambridge, MA 02138

João F. Cocco
Finance Department
London Business School
Regent's Park
London NW1 45A
England

Martin Feldstein
National Bureau of Economics
    Research
1050 Massachusetts Avenue
Cambridge, MA 02138

Francisco J. Gomes
Department of Economics
Littauer Center
Harvard University
Cambridge, MA 02138

Robert G. King
Department of Economics
Boston University
270 Bay State Road
Boston, MA 02215

Deborah Lucas
Department of Finance
J. L. Kellogg Graduate School of
    Management
Northwestern University
2001 Sheridan Road
Evanston, IL 60208

Thomas E. MaCurdy
Department of Economics
Stanford University
Stanford, CA 94305-6072

Pascal J. Maenhout
Department of Economics
Littauer Center
Harvard University
Cambridge, MA 02138

John McHale
Department of Economics
Littauer Center 230
Harvard University
Cambridge, MA 02138

Olivia S. Mitchell
Department of Insurance & Risk
    Management
The Wharton School
University of Pennsylvania
3641 Locust Walk, 307 CPC
Philadelphia, PA 19104-6218

Kevin M. Murphy
Graduate School of Business
The University of Chicago
1101 East 58th Street
Chicago, IL 60637

James M. Poterba
Department of Economics, E52-350
Massachusetts Institute of Technology
50 Memorial Drive
Cambridge, MA 02142-1347

Antonio Rangel
Department of Economics
Stanford University
Stanford, CA 94305

Elena Ranguelova
Department of Economics
Littauer Center
Harvard University
Cambridge, MA 02138

Stephen A. Ross
Massachusetts Institute of Technology
Sloan School of Management
50 Memorial Drive, E52-450
Cambridge, MA 02142-1347

Andrew Samwick
Department of Economics
6106 Rockefeller Hall
Dartmouth College
Hanover, NH 03755-3514

Thomas J. Sargent
Hoover Institution
HHMB-Room 243
Stanford University
Stanford, CA 94305-6010

Robert J. Shiller
Cowles Foundation for Research in
    Economics
Yale University
Box 208281
30 Hillhouse Avenue, Room 23a
New Haven, CT 06520-8281

John B. Shoven
National Bureau of Economic
    Research
30 Alta Road
Stanford, CA 94305-8715

Kent Smetters
Department of Insurance & Risk
    Management
University of Pennsylvania
3641 Locust Walk, CPC-302
Philadelphia, PA 19104-6218

Mark J. Warshawsky
TIAA-CREF Institute
730 Third Avenue, 24th Floor
New York, NY 10017-3206

David W. Wilcox
U.S. Department of the Treasury
1500 Pennsylvania Avenue, NW
Room 3454
Washington, DC 20220

David A. Wise
John F. Kennedy School of
    Government
Harvard University
79 John F. Kennedy Street
Cambridge, MA 02138

Amir Yaron
The Wharton School
2256 Steinberg-Dietrich Hall
University of Pennsylvania
Philadelphia, PA 19104-6367

Richard Zeckhauser
John F. Kennedy School of
    Government
Harvard University
79 John F. Kennedy Street
Cambridge, MA 02138

Stephen P. Zeldes
Graduate School of Business
Columbia University
3022 Broadway, Uris 605B
New York, NY 10027-6902

Author Index

Aaron, Henry J., 14–16, 30
Abel, Andrew B., 185, 197, 201, 207, 440, 468
Advisory Council on Social Security, 474
Altonji, Joseph, 208
Aman, Tetsuya, 264–65t, 266–67t
Arrow, Kenneth, 291, 294
Attanasio, Orazio, 447, 448
Auerbach, Alan, 148

Balduzzi, Perluigi, 441
Banz, R. W., 295
Barberis, Nicholas C., 441
Barr, David G., 343
Barreto, Flavio, 97
Barro, Robert J., 157, 234n32
Barsky, Robert B., 349, 457
Baxter, Marianne, 127n5, 390, 397, 398, 422
Behrman, Jere R., 144–45
Bekaert, Geert, 435
Bell, Felicitie, 331
Benartzi, Shlomo, 318
Berger, Mark, 234
Berndt, Ernst, 260
Bernstein, Peter L., 293, 294n5
Bertaut, Carol C., 441, 442
Biggs, John H., 358
Black, Fischer, 95, 100, 294, 398
Blake, David, 324
Blanchard, Olivier, 83n1, 154n2, 450
Blume, Marshall, 388n12

Board of Trustees of the Social Security System, 43, 44
Bodie, Zvi, 93n5, 94nn6, 7, 292n1, 296, 297nn9, 10, 305n15, 306, 308, 319, 335, 340, 343, 350, 352, 430, 431, 441, 471
Bohn, Henning, 96n8, 117, 159, 186, 203, 206, 207, 209n10, 210n12, 211, 214, 215nn19, 20, 225n28, 230, 235n34
Boskin, Michael, 45
Bosworth, Barry, 250
Boudoukh, Jacob, 343, 369
Brandt, Michael W., 441
Breeden, D., 295
Brennan, Michael J., 294, 297, 441
Brown, Jeffrey, 326–27, 329, 331–32, 344, 345, 347, 348
Budd, Alan, 324
Burtless, Gary, 250

Campbell, John Y., 28, 93n4, 346, 352, 367, 383n9, 384t, 393, 397, 441, 443, 450
Campbell, Nigel, 324
Canner, Niko, 317
Cao, H., 297
Carroll, Christopher D., 448
Cass, David, 83n1, 127n5
Clinton, Bill, 14, 247, 291
Cocco, J. F., 441, 442, 446, 447, 464, 471, 481
Cohn, Richard, 344
Congressional Budget Office (CBO), 212

Levine, Ross, 432
Liebman, J., 4
Lintner, John, 293
Litzenberger, R., 295
Liu, Jun, 441
Lo, Andrew W., 28
Longin, Francois, 431
Lucas, Deborah, 441, 442, 463, 481
Lucas, Robert, 117, 120n2, 141, 237
Lynch, Anthony, 441

MacKinlay, A. Craig, 28
Macunovich, Diane, 234
MaCurdy, Thomas E., 13, 40
Maenhout, Pascal J., 441, 442, 446, 447, 464
Mankiw, N. Gregory, 234, 246, 317, 443, 471
Manuelli, R., 117, 129
Marcus, Alan J., 94n6, 430, 431
Markowitz, Harry, 293, 383
McHale, John, 43n1, 212, 254n11
Mehra, Rajnish, 35, 73, 93n2, 110, 179, 181, 349, 440
Merton, Robert, 94n6, 95, 96n8, 293, 294, 295, 296, 297n9, 305n15, 306, 319, 434, 440, 441, 471
Miller, M. H., 295
Mincer, Jacob, 260
Mitchell, Olivia, 33, 38, 89, 97, 198, 247n1, 248n5, 321, 326–27, 329, 331–32, 344, 345, 347, 348, 358, 378n4, 439
Modigliani, Franco, 344
Moore, James, 358
Muench, T., 117, 120n2, 141, 142
Munzi, Teresa, 264–65t, 266–67t, 268n25
Murphy, Kevin, 234
Myers, Robert, 321

National Academy of Social Insurance (NASI), 321

Office of Management and Budget (OMB), 307
Omberg, Edward, 441
Organization for Economic Cooperation and Development (OECD), 250, 254n12, 257n13, 261, 264–65t, 266–67t

Parker, Jonathan, 448, 451
Peled, D., 117, 120n2, 121, 129, 141, 229n29

Pesando, James, 335, 340, 352
Phelan, Christopher, 148
Pischke, Jörn-Steffen, 443
Poterba, James, 28, 45, 50, 62–63, 134, 234n31, 235, 239, 318, 325, 326–27, 328, 329, 331–32, 344, 345, 347, 348, 369, 378n4, 442
Prescott, Edward C., 35, 73, 93n2, 179, 181, 349

Rangel, Antonio, 138n9
Ranguelova, Elena, 41, 58n20, 63, 69n28, 72n29, 73n32, 88, 94, 247n1
Reischauer, Robert D., 14–16, 30
Reno, Virginia P., 247
Repetto, Andrea, 349
Richardson, Matthew, 343, 369
Romer, David, 234, 246
Rosenzweig, Mark R., 144–45
Roseveare, Deborah, 264–65t, 266–67t
Ross, Stephen A., 95, 295, 441, 468

Sachs, Jeffrey, 278n31, 409
Sala-i-Martin, Xavier, 157, 234n32
Samuelson, Paul, 1, 83, 92, 128, 142, 296n8, 308, 403, 418, 440, 441
Samuelson, William, 296, 297n9, 319, 441, 471
Samwick, Andrew, 23–24, 41, 43, 52n14, 55n17, 92n1, 94, 97, 100, 245, 278, 383, 384, 409, 448
Schieber, Sylvester J., 14–15
Scholes, Myron, 95, 100, 294
Schwartz, E., 294, 441
Schwert, William, 397n18, 443
Sharpe, William, 293
Shavell, Steven, 147–48
Shell, K., 127n5
Shiller, Robert J., 30, 93nn3, 4, 207, 352, 382n7, 391, 398, 450
Shipman, William, 92n1, 94
Shoven, John B., 4, 13, 14–15, 40
Siegel, Jeremy J., 28, 35, 89, 343, 352
Skinner, Jonathan, 368, 443, 447
Smeeding, Timothy, 147
Smetters, Kent, 91, 94, 95, 98n10, 99, 101, 102, 207
Smith, Alasdair, 117, 205n5
Smith, Donna, 291
Social Security Administration (SSA), 373
Solnik, Bruno, 431
Spivak, Avia, 344, 347

Subject Index

Advisory Council on Social Security: maintain-benefits reform proposal, 6, 14–16, 283

AIME. *See* Average indexed monthly earnings (AIME)

Assumed interest rate (AIR): for CREF ILBA-backed annuity, 336–37, 362–63; for variable annuities, 335, 340; initial annuity payout given, 348

Annuities: annuity-equivalent wealth (AEW), 347–52; compared to social security annuity, 376–77; fixed, 37; framework for evaluating alternative, 344–49; high return on variable, 367; missing markets for, 225–29; optimal retirement account as variable, 415; in privatized system, 9; risky assets in, 415–16; Social Security as variable, 379–80; types and payouts of variable, 377–78; utility gains from access to real, 344–56; valuation of real versus nominal, 352–54; valuation of variable, 354–56

Annuity market, United Kingdom, 322–29; annuity brokers, 325; compulsory and voluntary parts of, 324–25; nominal and real products offered in, 325–29, 362

Annuity market, United States, 322; CPI-indexed income annuity, 329–32; infla-

tion-linked bond account annuity, 329, 332–38; variable annuities, 334–35

APW. *See* Average production worker (APW)

Arbitrage: with privatization of social security, 97, 108–9

Arrow-Debreu securities, 294

Average indexed monthly earnings (AIME): computed by Social Security Administration, 379, 380; of individual, 375–76; individual social security benefit depends on, 376

Average production worker (APW): change in SSW as percent of, 271–72; defined, 260n15

Benefit formulas: reforms in G7 countries and effect on SSW, 263–73; in SSW calculations, 261–62

Bequests, accidental, 225–29

Bonds: annuities linked to CREF index-linked bond account (ILBA), 332–38; risk and annual real returns on government, 33–35, 37–39; riskiness of zero-coupon and long-term, 37–39. *See also* Treasury Inflation-Protected Securities (TIPS)

Bonds, indexed: in U.K. annuity market, 322, 324; in U.S. annuity market, 322

Capital-asset pricing model (CAPM), 293; intertemporal (Merton), 293–94